The
Humanities

LIBRARY SCIENCE TEXT SERIES

Audiovisual Technology Primer. By Albert J. Casciero and Raymond G. Roney.

The Collection Program in Elementary and Middle Schools: Concepts, Practices, and Information Sources. By Phyllis J. Van Orden.

The Collection Program in High Schools: Concepts, Practices, and Information Sources. By Phyllis J. Van Orden.

Developing Library and Information Center Collections. 2d ed. By G. Edward Evans.

The Humanities: A Selective Guide to Information Sources. 3d ed. By Ron Blazek and Elizabeth Aversa

Immroth's Guide to the Library of Congress Classification. 3d ed. By Lois Mai Chan.

Introduction to Cataloging and Classification. By Bohdan S. Wynar. 7th edition by Arlene G. Taylor.

Introduction to Library Automation. By James Rice.

Introduction to Library Science: Basic Elements of Library Service. By Jesse H. Shera.

Introduction to Library Services for Library Technicians. By Barbara E. Chernik.

Introduction to Public Services for Library Technicians. 4th ed. By Marty Bloomberg.

Introduction to Technical Services for Library Technicians. 5th ed. By Marty Bloomberg and G. Edward Evans.

Introduction to United States Public Documents. 3d ed. By Joe Morehead.

The Library in Society. By A. Robert Rogers and Kathryn McChesney.

Library Instruction for Librarians. By Anne F. Roberts.

Library Management. 3d ed. By Robert D. Stueart and Barbara B. Moran.

Micrographics. 2d ed. By William Saffady.

Online Reference and Information Retrieval. 2d ed. By Roger C. Palmer.

Problems in Library Management. By A. J. Anderson.

The School Librarian as Educator. 2d ed. By Lillian Biermann Wehmeyer.

The School Library Media Center. 4th ed. By Emanuel T. Prostano and Joyce S. Prostano.

Science and Engineering Literature: A Guide to Reference Sources. 3d ed. By H. Robert Malinowsky and Jeanne M. Richardson.

The Humanities

A Selective Guide to Information Sources

THIRD EDITION

Ron Blazek

Professor
Florida State University

and

Elizabeth Aversa

Assistant Professor
University of Maryland, College Park

1988

Libraries Unlimited, Inc.
Englewood, Colorado

LIBRARIES UNLIMITED, INC.
P.O. Box 6633
Englewood, CO 80155-6633

Library of Congress Cataloging-in-Publication Data

Blazek, Ron.
    The humanities : a selective guide to information sources / Ron
Blazek, and Elizabeth Aversa. -- 3rd ed.
    xvii, 382 p. 17x25 cm. -- (Library science text series)
    ISBN 0-87287-558-X; ISBN 0-87287-594-6 (pbk.)
    1. Bibliography--Bibliography--Humanities. 2. Humanities--
Bibliography. 3. Reference books--Humanities--Bibliography.
4. Humanities--Information services--Directories. I. Aversa,
Elizabeth Smith. II. Title. III. Series.
Z6265.B53 1988
[AZ221]
016.0160013--dc19   87-33907
                                         CIP

CONTENTS

PREFACE TO THE THIRD EDITION

Librarians, scholars, and teachers of literature and reference sources in the humanities have depended upon A. Robert Rogers's *The Humanities: A Selective Guide to Information Sources* since its first edition in 1974. The untimely death of Dr. Rogers in 1985 has left a gap among the tools of reference librarianship and bibliography. Rogers's second edition, which was well received in 1979, remains a widely used, though now dated, text. The objective of the present edition is to fill the gap with a work which is useful to teachers and students in schools of library and information science, reference librarians, collection development officers in libraries, humanities scholars, and others who have information needs in the broad discipline.

This third edition, based on the 1979 edition, grew out of concerns of the authors, both of whom teach advanced level reference courses in graduate library schools, for an updated guide to humanities information resources. At the same time, Rogers's second edition was used in both authors' courses, one at Florida State University and the other then at Drexel University, and it was agreed that Rogers's format should be retained in the new edition. Permission to incorporate still useful segments of the text from the "Access" chapters of the second edition was obtained from Mrs. A. Robert Rogers through Libraries Unlimited, Inc. The format of this volume, then, is similar to the second edition and the present authors divided the task with Professor Blazek assuming responsibility for revision and updating of the "Sources" chapters and Professor Aversa, the "Access" chapters.

"ACCESS" CHAPTERS

The odd-numbered chapters (1-11) relate to accessing information. A "working definition" of each discipline has been added as a brief section preceding the "major division of the field" segments in each of these chapters. These sections will serve as aids to students with limited backgrounds in the fields described.

A section on "use and user studies" has also been added to each "Access" chapter. The objective of these sections is to direct the reader to relevant use and user studies for the specific disciplines of the humanities.

The topic of "computers in the humanities," while deserving a separate chapter in the first two editions of the guide, is now important enough for each field that a section has been added to each of these chapters. As with the "use and user studies" sections, the reader is referred to further readings and reviews on this important topic.

Additionally, online databases appropriate to the humanities are covered in sections of the "Access" chapters. The coverage here is limited to those databases available through DIALOG Information Services, Inc., BRS Information Technologies, and H. W. Wilson's WILSONLINE as of January 1987. The reader will do well to check the various information services' catalogs for new resources and updated years of coverage for the files. (Entries in the "Sources" chapters also include notations of online availability of individual databases so the user of this guide has two ways to find appropriate online sources.)

This change in the format from previous editions reflects the present and growing importance of online technology to the fields of the humanities.

"SOURCES" CHAPTERS

The even-numbered chapters (2-12) cover individual sources of information or the reference tools themselves. Prior to his death, Dr. Rogers had begun the arduous process of revision by contacting bibliographic specialists in the various disciplines as he had done earlier in preparing the second edition. He had asked these experts to furnish ratings of the titles in their field included in the second edition. These ratings were based on a four-point scale ranging from (NR), not recommended to (V), vital. At the time of his death, all but one of the experts had replied.

The present co-author wrote to each of the experts, thanked them for their contribution, and secured the evaluation from the individual who had not yet responded. These specialists are identified in the acknowledgments section. It was clear after examining all the reports that the number of vital and recommended items when combined with the many new publications and other important ones that had been omitted previously would produce an unwieldy total for a publication of this type.

It was felt that a work which is to serve as a textbook for prospective librarians and at the same time assist both librarians and scholars as a literature guide should be compact but also provide annotations in depth. Therefore, in line with the need to narrow down the total number of entries, titles of periodicals were eliminated unless they had reference value. In such cases they were placed in appropriate sections on current awareness or serial bibliography. Instead of a separate category on periodicals, there is a systematic attempt to identify guides to serial publications in each discipline. "Sources" chapters, therefore, contain reference tools only, with computerized databases integrated with books. When any of the print items are available online, the database is noted and described. Several databases which do not appear in print format are also treated within their appropriate reference category (index, bibliography, etc.). Online availability is indicated by an asterisk in both the numbered entries and the indexes.

All chapters identifying the principal information sources have been completely reworked and all annotations for tools previously included have been updated, revised, and expanded. Every numbered entry is described in enough detail to provide adequate comprehension of the scope and coverage of the tool covered. In most cases, additional details concerning audience, arrangement, special features, authority, and even history of the work are furnished. Annotations range from 100 to 235 words, with an average of about 135 words each. Unlike previous editions, there are numerous cross-references linking the entries.

The entire job of writing the annotations was completed in a five-month period from January to June 1987 while the co-author was on sabbatical leave from his position at Florida State University. The job of selection, identification, and location of materials and reviews had begun a year earlier and was continued throughout the writing phase. Emphasis has been given to the need to identify new titles and new editions, and the project was conducted with the assistance of a cadre of interested and energetic young people, some of whom were paid and some of whom earned college credits. These individuals are also identified in the acknowledgments section.

Titles were added during the editing phase through October 1987, and forthcoming editions have been identified. In regard to recency of material, the relatively compressed writing period (although a brutal nightmare for the writer) was advantageous in terms of producing the latest works. The criteria for selection involved a possible trio of considerations which included the previously explained (1) acknowledgment of value by experts, and/or (2) favorable reviews, and/or (3) familiarity of the author through his experience as instructor of humanities reference for the past sixteen years.

The final product represents a literature guide of 973 major entries as compared to a total of 1,200 in the second edition. In truth, it represents a decrease of only 61 reference sources from the 1,034 that appeared in the earlier work, once the periodical segments were deleted. The 973 tools are useful or important items for which information is presented in depth and is up-to-date at time of writing. In many cases, additional titles are identified within the body of the annotated entry. This is done cautiously and only in such cases where lack of mention might be regarded as an oversight and reflects the existence of related reference works.

Proportions of the total number of major entries within the "Sources" chapters remain approximately the same as in the second edition with slight increases in four of the six major divisions and a slight decline in Visual Arts and in Performing Arts.

REFERENCE SOURCES

	Second edition		Third edition	
	#	%	#	%
General	13	1.3	17	1.7
Philosophy	38	3.7	56	5.8
Religion	136	13.2	138	14.2
Visual Arts	229	22.1	209	21.5
Performing Arts	352	34.0	294	30.2
Language and Literature	266	25.7	259	26.6
	1,034	99.9	973	100.0

Although the bibliographic style of the entries in certain respects resembles that used by Rogers in the second edition, arrangement of entries in the present work is alphabetical by title within the categories. Names of both authors and editors are placed in the same field position following the edition statement regardless of Library of Congress designation of their status. This should alleviate certain frustrations in determining whether the title or its editor belong in the main-entry position. It resolves all difficulties in determining why certain individuals are accorded author status while others who do the same type of work are identified as editors or compilers. In any case, the indexes are to be employed to provide access when either a name or title is known. Places of publication are included as part of the imprint, and series are identified contrary to the earlier practice of omitting them.

USEFUL SOURCES OF INFORMATION

In the course of preparation of this edition, standard reference works have been of considerable help. Among the most valuable for preparation of the "Access" chapters were *Encyclopedia of Associations; Research Centers Directory; Encyclopaedia Britannica: Macropaedia*, 15th edition; the several volumes of the *Annual Review of Information Science and Technology* and the *Proceedings, International Conferences on Computers and the Humanities. DIALOG's Database Catalog*, the *BRS Brief System Guide*, and the *WILSONLINE Tutorial* provided information for the "Online Resources" section of the chapters. Previous editions of Rogers provided the format, some text, and guidance to the important issues to cover.

For the "Sources" chapters, the new technology was indispensable in identifying and verifying both old and new material. OCLC was a constant in the lives of the co-author and his bibliographic assistants. DIALOG Information Services, especially File 137, *Book Review Index*, was used daily. Also important was the print version of *Book Review Digest* (since WILSONLINE was unavailable). Especially fruitful in producing useful reviews was *American Reference Books Annual*, Eugene Sheehy's *Guide to Reference Books* (10th edition), and such review journals as *Choice, Booklist, Library Journal,* and *Reference Books Bulletin.*

ACKNOWLEDGMENTS

Obviously, a work of this kind cannot be completed without the help of others. The co-authors take this opportunity to express their deep appreciation to the experts who took the time to respond to the initial request of Dr. Rogers for evaluation of titles in the second edition and later assured Professor Blazek of their continued interest in the project. They are Dr. Hans E. Bynagle, Chief Librarian, Whitworth College, Spokane, Washington (philosophy); Dr. Edwin S. Gleaves, Chair, Department of Library and Information Science, George Peabody College/Vanderbilt University, Nashville, Tennessee (language and literature); Dr. Betty Jo Irvine, Fine Arts Librarian, Indiana University, Bloomington (art); Michael A. Keller, Head of the Music Library, University of California, Berkeley (music); Patricia Lowry, Head, Philosophy, Religion, and Education Department, Akron-Summit County Public Library, Akron, Ohio (religion); Dale Manning, English Bibliographer/Reference Librarian, Vanderbilt University (language and literature); and Edmund F. SantaVicca, Humanities Reference Bibliographer, Cleveland State University, Cleveland, Ohio (performing arts). During the writing period, advice and counsel was generously given by Dale Hudson, Music Librarian, Florida State University.

Thanks are owed to Karen Desaulniers, Librarian of the School of Library and Information Studies at Florida State University and to the reference staff of Santa Fe Junior College in Gainesville, Florida, June Littler, Mary McCarty, Karen Moore, and Jean Thomas. Much of the work of writing the annotations was accomplished there during the co-author's frequent visits and their many kindnesses made these visits productive and even enjoyable. Mr. William Wilson, Librarian of the College of Library and Information Services (CLIS) Library at the University of Maryland, Mr. William Pitt, and the staff of that library provided invaluable help in locating references for the "Accessing Information" chapters. Mrs. Cathy Wilt, at Drexel University, provided help in the use of databases by the co-author in the school's Resource Center.

Also deserving of recognition are the students of Florida State University School of Library and Information Studies who participated in the identification of titles and location of reviews. Special mention should go to doctoral candidates Theresa Griffin Maggio and Dania Bilal. Ms. Maggio served as chief bibliographic assistant and word-processing person during the critical writing period, while Ms. Bilal served in various capacities from bibliographer to word-processing person through the entire period of the creation and development of this work. Contributing to this effort were the following master's degree students: Beth Gurd, Hal Hubener, Janet Lawrence, Frank Marotti, Lisa Spillers, and Chester Wright. Also participating in the bibliographic work were the co-author's two sons, David Blazek and Daniel Blazek. Ms. Peggy Page of the school's secretarial staff provided occasional clerical assistance. Without all of these people, the effort would have taken far longer, and may never have been completed.

LIST OF ABBREVIATIONS
AND SYMBOLS

Ann.	annual
Ann. cum.	annual cumulations
Aufl.	Auflage (edition)
Bi.	bimonthly
Bienn.	biennial
Bienn. cum.	biennial cumulations
Col.	columns
Comp.	compiled
Comps.	compilers
Corr.	corrected
Enl.	enlarged
Exp.	expanded
Irreg.	irregular
Mo.	monthly
Q.	quarterly
Quin. cum.	quinquennial cumulations
Rev.	revised
Semiann.	semiannual
Supp.	supplement(s)
Trans.	translated
Wk.	weekly
*	available online

1 INTRODUCTION TO THE HUMANITIES

The Commission on the Humanities, in their 1980 report *The Humanities in American Life*, suggest that "fields alone do not define the humanities" and that "the essence of the humanities is a spirit or attitude toward humanity."[1] While this is surely true, and many writers support this view of the large discipline, it is necessary for the librarian to have a filing system for knowledge and a guide to that filing system if 5,000 years of knowledge in the humanities are to be accessible to modern scholars. The labels on our filing system, then, are the fields which we call the humanities.

So which disciplines constitute the humanities? In classical and early Christian times, the scope of this field seemed very broad. Literature constituted the core, but virtually every discipline relating to the mind of man was, at one time or another, considered part of the humanities. In the Renaissance period, the term *humanities* was used in opposition to the term *divinity* and seemed to embrace any area of study outside the field of religion. In the nineteenth century, the term was used to include those disciplines that could not be considered part of the natural sciences. By the twentieth century, the fields of study that dealt with social, rather than natural, phenomena had emerged, along with "scientific" methods of investigation in the several social sciences. The humanities remain, then, those fields which are "dedicated to the disciplined development of verbal, perceptual, and imaginative skills needed to understand experience."[2] The fields of study which we include in this guide to the information sources in humanities are philosophy, religion, the visual arts, the performing arts, and language and literature.

The reader may ask, "What about history?" Although many consider history as a central humanities field, research methods in history and indications of the similarities between information use in history and in the social sciences lead us to place history closer to the social sciences for the purpose of constructing a source guide.

The student wishing to explore the nature and scope of the humanities has access to many resources. For an excellent general overview, the articles "The Humanities" and "The History of Humanistic Scholarship" in the *Encyclopaedia Britannica: Macropaedia* (15th edition, revised 1985, v.20, pp. 722-35) may be consulted. Volumes of the *Princeton Studies: Humanistic Scholarship in America*

(Princeton, 1963-) and *One Great Society* by Howard Mumford Jones (Harcourt, 1959) provide reflective treatment of the humanities. The reader may also find useful the "Future of the Humanities" (*Daedalus* 98 [Summer 1969]: 605-869). "The Humanities: Imagination and Action" (*Teachers College Record* 82 [Winter 1980]: 165-316) contains essays on the future of humanistic studies, the relationships between academic disciplines, and the humanities curriculum. Teaching of the humanities is also the focus of Walter Kaufmann's *The Future of the Humanities* (Crowell, 1977), while thorough consideration of the place of the humanities in schools, higher education, and the community is addressed in the previously cited report, *The Humanities in American Life* (University of California Press, 1980). Librarians will be particularly interested in the chapters in this report entitled "Cultural Institutions," "Problems of Support," and "Sources of Support" for the humanities.

Coverage of funding and sources of support for work in the humanities may also be found in *A Casebook of Grant Proposals in the Humanities*, edited by William E. Coleman and others (Neal-Schuman, 1982), Virginia White's *Grants for the Arts* (Plenum, 1980), and Coleman's *Grants in the Humanities: A Scholar's Guide to Funding Sources*, 2nd edition (Neal-Schuman, 1984). Librarians will find information about funding for humanities projects in libraries by contacting Humanities Projects in Libraries, Division of General Programs, National Endowment for the Humanities (Room 420, 1100 Pennsylvania Avenue, N.W., Washington, DC 20506) for the latest "Guidelines and Application Instructions."

The important issues of publishing and reviewing in the humanities are discussed in "Book Reviewing Practices of Journals in the Humanities" by J. Budd (*Scholarly Publishing* 13 [1982]: 363-71), H. S. Bailey's "The Economics of Publishing in the Humanities" (*Scholarly Publishing* 8 [1977]: 223-31), and "The Politics of Reviewing and the Ethics of Translating and Editing," in Walter Kaufmann's *The Future of the Humanities* (Crowell, 1977). Terence Moore's article "Academic Publishing and Literary Criticism" (*MLN* 99 [December 1984]: 1162-66) discusses scholarly monograph publishing.

NATURE OF SCHOLARSHIP IN THE HUMANITIES

The remainder of this introductory chapter is devoted to the nature of scholarship in the humanities and the types of literature available to the librarian seeking to meet user requests for information, inspiration, and enlightenment.

At the outset, it should be remarked that humanistic research is differentiated most sharply from research in the natural sciences by the constant intrusion of questions of value. To the scientist *qua* scientist, such considerations are, indeed, intrusions. They interfere with and damage the quality of research concerned with objective, empirically verifiable data and with experimental results that can be replicated by other researchers. "Informed judgment" might play a part in deciding what experiments to conduct, but "refined sensibility" would have no impact on the outcome. Yet these are the "bread of life" for the humanistic scholar, whether dealing with a poem, a piece of music, a painting, a religious doctrine, or a philosophical theory. Thus, humanistic scholarship has traditionally been intimately intertwined with considerations of value.

One consequence of this connection between scholarship and value systems is the peculiarly personal and individualistic nature of humanistic research.

Unlike colleagues in the natural sciences or even, to a lesser degree, in the social sciences, the humanist finds research to be such an intimately personal matter that it is more difficult than in other disciplines to function effectively as a member of a team. The results of team effort are more likely to be compromise and mediocrity than productive division of labor. Collaborative efforts are, of course, possible. But they require special planning and are not nearly as "normal" as in the natural sciences.

A further result of this state of affairs is the general lack of ability on the part of the humanistic scholar to delegate bibliographic searching to others. The interconnections within the researcher's mind are so subtle and complex that it is necessary to examine personally the index entry or abstract to identify an item of potential relevance, and the original book or article to determine its actual relevance. The problem is, of course, compounded by the lack of standardized and controlled vocabularies of the sort that have become increasingly common in the pure and applied sciences. Yet the humanistic scholar needs help in the form of access to a wide variety of finding aids.

Part of the problem faced by the humanistic scholar also relates to the nature of "knowledge" in the humanities. It is not likely to consist of hard, identifiable facts such as formulas in chemistry, or population and income statistics from census data. Facts there are, aplenty, but their sum total is considerably less than what the humanist is looking for. To know the number of times that Shakespeare used the word *mince* in *Hamlet* is to tell us very little of importance about *Hamlet*. Yet the patient accumulation and analysis of factual data (often with the aid of the computer) can lay the foundation for knowledge of a higher order.

Closely related to the nature of "knowledge" is the question of "progress." In the natural sciences, knowledge tends to be "progressive." Each significant experiment either confirms, modifies, or overturns some piece of existing "knowledge." This is true whether the item in question is a new virus that has been detected through more sophisticated laboratory equipment or a far-ranging perception of relationships, such as the replacement of Newtonian physics with Einsteinian. In the humanities, no such "progress" is observable. Sophocles's *Antigone*, the Bhagavad-Gita, Michelangelo's *Pietà*, or Mozart's *The Magic Flute* are not superseded as was the "phlogiston" theory in chemistry. Perception of beauty, insight into the human condition, and artistic creativity are not cumulative, though patterns of influence can be traced. Indeed, there is often a tendency for a work of artistic genius to be followed by a host of inferior imitations—not by new works that refine and improve it!

The factors noted in the preceding paragraphs have their impact on patterns of use of library materials. For the humanist and the social scientist, the library is the heart of the research enterprise. For the natural scientist, the laboratory is at the center, with the library in a supporting role. In this respect, the position of the creative artist (as distinct from the researcher) in the humanities may more nearly resemble that of the scientist—as anyone who has witnessed "dialogue" between a sculptor and an art historian can testify!

The centrality of the library for the humanistic researcher is still accompanied by the centrality of the monograph as distinct from the periodical article. Although there have been fewer user studies in the humanities than in other fields, the pattern of preference for books and pamphlets continues to emerge—in sharp contrast to the preference of the natural scientist for journal articles, reprints, and preprints.

Another characteristic reported in such few user studies as we have is the greater spread of individual titles used by researchers in the humanities. Whereas a relatively small number of journals contain a high proportion of the frequently cited articles in fields like chemistry and mathematics, the same high degree of concentration in journal or monographic titles has not been observed in the humanities. This is not to deny that critical studies tend to cluster around certain landmark works, but the spread of titles in which the criticisms appear is greater and the concentration much less intense.

A third use pattern that distinguishes humanistic from scientific researchers is a much greater time spread in materials. Whereas publications of the last five years are crucial to scientific research, with usage dropping off rapidly after that, the humanist is likely to be equally interested in publications of twenty, forty, or fifty years ago. Indeed, if one considers the "classics" in each field (as distinct from modern editions or reproductions), the range of interest may readily extend to items 2,000 or 3,000 years old.

A fourth distinguishing use pattern which has been identified is that humanists appear to have a greater need to browse their research materials than do scientists or social scientists. Although little systematic evidence has been collected to support this use pattern, experiential accounts strongly suggest this practice. It should be noted that additional work is required to substantiate these claims and to determine if the browsing is based upon the information needs of humanists or if their browsing is the result of a less systematically organized literature than one finds in the harder disciplines of the natural and social sciences.

Finally, something must be said about publication and citation practices in the arts and humanities. When the Institute for Scientific Information introduced its *Arts and Humanities Citation Index* in 1978, Eugene Garfield, in the announcement, pointed out that inconsistent citation practices, citations to unpublished manuscripts and catalogs, and references to original sources embedded in texts but without explicit citation are but three problems which had to be considered in developing the index. For further discussion of these problems, see Garfield's "Will ISI's *Arts and Humanities Citation Index* Revolutionize Scholarship?" in *Essays of an Information Scientist, Volume 3, 1977-1978* (ISI Press, 1980, pp. 204-8).

User studies which will clarify the generalizations about humanists' scholarly practices and information seeking behaviors are not numerous. However, the number of these studies has increased and some are quite comprehensive. An excellent starting point for the reader is Sue Stone's "Humanities Scholars: Information Needs and Uses" (*Journal of Documentation* 38 [December 1982]: 292-313), which reviews information needs and use studies of humanities scholars in university settings from 1970 onward. Over 150 references are cited in Stone's paper, supporting her discussions of definitions of the humanities, scholars and their work, secondary services, computers and the humanities, the role of the library in the humanities, comparisons of the humanities with other disciplines, and the future of the humanities. More recent, and more limited in scope, is "Humanities Collection Management—An Impressionistic/Realistic/Optimistic Appraisal of the State of the Art," by Anna H. Perrault (*Collection Management* 5 [Fall/Winter 1983]: 1-23). An older review, "User Studies in the Humanities: A Survey and a Proposal" by Lois Bebout, Donald Davis, Jr., and Donald Oehlerts (*RQ* 15 [Fall 1975]: 40-44) provides background from earlier use studies and a brief table which compares information seeking behaviors of scientists and social scientists, and hypotheses about humanists' information search habits. Like the

Stone article, the bibliography of this article is also comprehensive, including early master's theses.

Two very different approaches to studying use and users in the humanities find similar results in terms of age of documents used, scatter of materials, and document types. "An Analysis of Humanists' Requests Received by an Information Service for the Humanities" by Aida Mendez (*Journal of Information Science* 9 [1984]: 97-105) is based on bibliographic searches and document requests, while Eugene Garfield's "Is Information Retrieval in the Arts and Humanities Inherently Different from That in Science?" (*Library Quarterly* 50 [1980]: 40-57) looks at citation data from the *Arts and Humanities Citation Index* and develops conclusions and new hypotheses from citation as a form of use.

Additional studies of information needs and use in humanities include The University of Sheffield's Centre for Research on User Studies's *User Studies: An Introductory Guide and Select Bibliography*, edited by Geoffrey Ford (Sheffield, 1977) and *Information Needs in the Humanities: Two Postal Surveys* by Cynthia Corkill and Margaret Mann (Sheffield, 1978). Finally, Karl J. Weintraub's "The Humanistic Scholar and the Library" (*Library Quarterly* 50 [1980]: 22-39) characterizes humanities scholarship as it relates to various developments in librarianship.

MATERIALS AND ACCESS
IN THE HUMANITIES

The working scholar in a humanistic discipline tends to perceive the materials with which to work as falling into three broad categories: 1) original texts or artifacts, 2) critical literature, and 3) literature designed for specific groups or purposes. Each of these categories requires further elaboration.

The heart of all humanistic study is the original creative work, whether this is an epic poem, a piece of sculpture, a symphony, a devotional psalm, or a discourse on the nature of the good life. Without the outpourings of creative genius and the lesser efforts at creativity, there would be no enduring contribution to the illumination of the human condition—and nothing for humanistic scholars to analyze and interpret.

The second major category, utterly dependent upon the first, is critical literature. Normally, this takes the form of analysis, interpretation, or commentary on a particular creative work, on a group of creative works, or on the output of a given historical period. It may also include efforts to develop general theories of criticism and even histories of critical theories.

The literature designed for specific groups or purposes may be further subdivided into popularizations, access tools, and professional literature. Popularizations have been common in the field of religion for centuries. In other disciplines, their advent is more recent. The rise of the art museum movement in the nineteenth century, for example, and the twentieth-century addition of an educational role to the curatorial function have created demand for inexpensive books with reproductions of acknowledged masterpieces and simple commentary. Books on music appreciation now reach wide audiences. Ironically, philosophy and literature, once scarcely in need of popularization, became increasingly narrow and technical in the early years of the twentieth century, necessitating special efforts to bridge the gap. A good popularization should simplify without distortion or misinformation.

Access tools cover most of the items commonly thought of by reference librarians: bibliographies, indexes, abstracts, encyclopedias, dictionaries, handbooks, atlases, etc. The exponential growth of knowledge in the twentieth century has been in no small measure dependent on the increasing availability and sophistication of these access tools.

The professional literature is designed by practitioners within each discipline for their mutual enlightenment and the advancement of knowledge. Typically, it is created through the efforts of one or more major professional societies at the national level in each country and a host of specialized, regional, or local groups. Journals, indexes, and abstracts are the most typical outputs, although conference proceedings and current awareness (tables of contents) services are also common.

Bibliographic organization has been the subject of numerous conferences and publications since the late 1940s. Among the important works related directly to the humanities are two older works still useful today: "The Humanities: Characteristics of the Literature, Problems of Use, and Bibliographic Organization in the Field," by Karl H. Kraeling, in Jesse H. Shera and Margaret Egans, eds., *Bibliographic Organization* (University of Chicago Press, 1951, pp. 109-26) and Conrad H. Rawski's "Bibliographic Organization in the Humanities" (*Wilson Library Bulletin* 40 [April 1966]: 738-50). The topic of bibliographic organization is also discussed by John Phillip Immroth in "Information Needs for the Humanities," in *Information Science: Search for Identity* (Dekker, 1974, pp. 249-62) and in "Humanities and Its Literature," in the *Encyclopedia of Library and Information Science* (Dekker, 1974, v.11, pp. 71-83).

Three British publications concerning humanities information also deserve attention. Sue Stone has edited the report entitled *Humanities Information Research: Proceedings of a Seminar, 1980* (CRUS Occasional Paper 4, British Library & Development Department Report 5588 [Sheffield, England, University of Sheffield, 1980]). *Recent Initiatives in Communication in Humanities*, edited by M. Katzen and S. Howley (London, British Library, 1984), and D. B. Smith, ed., *Information Problems in the Humanities: Report on the British Library Seminar* (London, British Library, 1976) also discuss the issue of information and research needs of humanists.

Issues in classification and indexing for humanities are covered by D. W. Langridge in his *Classification and Indexing in the Humanities* (Butterworths, 1976). Particularly useful are the chapters entitled "The Construction of Special Classification Schemes in the Humanities" and "Indexing in the Humanities" (pp. 95-116 and 117-34). Other authors' works, cited in the discipline specific chapters of this guide, cover bibliographic organization in the different fields of the humanities.

Library resources in the humanities have been reviewed in "Humanities Libraries and Collections" by Thomas D. Gillies in *Encyclopedia of Library and Information Science* (Dekker, 1974, v.11, pp. 64-71). *The Landscape of Literatures: Use of Subject Collections in a University Library*, by Paul Metz (American Library Association, 1983) will also prove useful. The CRL (Center for Research Libraries) *Handbook* (latest edition) is an additional source of information on library resources, as are directories of special library collections produced and distributed by local and regional library associations.

Public library resources in the humanities are the focus of Herbert Goldhor and Linda Smith's *A Study of Public Library Book Collections in the Humanities* (ERIC, 1980, 51p., ED 179 189) and Goldhor's "U.S. Public Library Adult Non-fiction Book Collections in the Humanities" (*Collection Management* 3 [Spring 1979]: 31-43). *The Role of the Humanities in the Public Library*, edited by Robert N. Broadus (American Library Association, 1980) will also be of interest to the librarian.

Access to primary material in the humanities is discussed by B. O. Aboyade in "Access to Primary Source Materials in the Humanities" (*International Library Review* 8 [June 1976]: 309-16). Access to serials is addressed in a citation study, "Periodical Use in a University Music Library," by R. Griscom (*Serials Librarian* 7 [Spring 1983]: 35-52). Librarians Kathryn B. Wilson and Joanne D. Eustis discuss the influence of the collection on humanities scholarship in "The Impact of User Frustration on Humanities Research" (*College and Research Libraries* 42 [July 1981]: 361-65).

The student of librarianship will still find much useful information in *The Humanities and the Library*, by Lester Asheim (American Library Association, 1957). Despite the age of this work, the marriage of classification, cataloging, and subject content continues to be a fruitful approach.

Thomas P. Slavens's *Retrieval of Information in the Humanities and the Social Sciences: Problems as Aids to Learning* (Dekker, 1981) provides practice queries for students of reference and resource work. The test questions in Slavens's *Information Sources in the Humanities* (Campus Publishers, 1968) remain useful, also.

Several reference works provide starting points in the search for humanities resources. Eugene P. Sheehy's *Guide to Reference Books* (10th edition, American Library Association, 1986) devotes over 300 pages to the humanities. Excellent annotations for selected major reference works are found in *Reference Books in the Social Sciences and Humanities*, by Rolland E. Stevens and Donald G. Davis, Jr. (4th edition, Stipes, 1977). A. J. Walford's *Guide to Reference Material* (4th edition, Library Association, 1980-1986) also gives extensive attention to the humanities. For the librarian or user of smaller library collections, *Reference Sources for Small and Medium-sized Libraries* (4th edition, American Library Association, 1984) devotes one-third of its coverage to humanities materials and is particularly good for frequently used sources in the applied and popular arts.

American Reference Books Annual (Libraries Unlimited, 1970-) provides comprehensive coverage and reviews of new reference books. The arrangement of this source, and its extensive coverage of the humanities (approximately one-fourth of the reviews annually are humanities related) make this a particularly useful adjunct to standard guides.

COMPUTERS IN THE HUMANITIES

The impact of the computer on humanities scholarship cannot be understated. The student needs only to consider the number of papers cited in two reviews of humanities applications in the *Annual Review of Information Science and Technology* (*ARIST*). In 1972 Joseph Raben and R. L. Widmann produced the first *ARIST* review of information systems applications in the humanities,

"Information Systems Applications in the Humanities" (*ARIST*, v.7, ASIS, 1972, pp. 439-69). By 1981 an extensive update was needed ("Information Systems and Services in the Humanities," edited by Joseph Raben and Sarah K. Burton, *ARIST*, v.16, ASIS, 1981, pp. 247-66), and the update included reports of regularly scheduled conferences, both national and international, on computers in the humanities and on the formation of the Association for Computers and the Humanities (ACH).

A volume which has been called a "primer on computer literacy" for the humanities is the proceedings of the *Sixth International Conference on Computers and the Humanities*, edited by Sarah K. Burton and Douglas D. Short (Computer Science Press, 1983). Over 100 papers comprise this volume, and they range from general articles to summaries of very specific applications of computers to research and teaching in the humanities. The student who wishes to follow the historical development of computer applications in the field might compare the coverage of the Burton and Short volume with an earlier work edited by Edmund A. Bowles, *Computers in Humanistic Research* (Prentice-Hall, 1967).

Another work which discusses the use of computers in humanities is Susan Hockey's *A Guide to Computer Applications in the Humanities* (Johns Hopkins University Press, 1980). This work is primarily concerned with applications to literary- and language-related research, though the generalist will be interested in chapter 9, "Indexing, Cataloguing and Information Retrieval" (pp. 189-219), which covers "the various ways in which the computer can be used to manipulate information which is structured in some way."

For the reader interested in how humanists acquire computer knowledge, an article by Joseph Rudman entitled "Computer Courses for Humanists—A Survey" (*Computers and the Humanities* 12 [1978]: 253-59) will provide a perspective.

Finally, the journal *Computers and the Humanities* should not be overlooked as a source of information.

Aside from computer applications in humanities research, a second area of computer use has become increasingly important in reference work. This is the use of computerized databases of bibliographic, full text, directory, and numeric information. Although there are presently fewer online databases for the humanities than for the social and physical sciences, the number has increased and will continue to be a valuable source for the researcher and the humanist whose interest areas are interdisciplinary.

A useful directory of database sources is *Computer Readable Data Bases: A Directory and Data Sourcebook*, edited by Martha Williams and others (Knowledge Industry, 198-). All subject areas are covered, and periodic updates keep the source current. Cuadra Associates produces *Directory of Online Databases* (Cuadra, 198-) which is issued quarterly with updates. The American Society for Information Science has published *Database Directory 1984-1985* (Knowledge Industry, 1984), which includes many databases in the humanities disciplines. Major search systems or commercial vendors of databases issue periodic directories or catalogs of databases offered through their systems: DIALOG Information Services, Inc. (3460 Hillview Ave., Palo Alto, CA 94304), the H. W. Wilson Company (950 University Ave., Bronx, NY 10452), and BRS Information Technologies (1200 Rte. 7, Latham, NY 12110) all include humanities databases among their offerings. It should be noted that many of the indexes covered in this guide are available online commercially, and are so designated in the individual chapters. The most important of the online sources are also mentioned in the text of the "Accessing Information" chapters.

A new online offering, since 1984, is provided by the H. W. Wilson Company. WILSONLINE is the online system for searching the H. W. Wilson indexes. *Humanities Index* is now included in the WILSONLINE system, as is the more general *Readers' Guide to Periodical Literature*. Both cover the humanities generally. Other WILSONLINE databases are discussed in the discipline-specific chapters of this guide.

Many information databases are currently being processed for digital storage on CD-ROM disks, which have 1,000 times the storage capacity of a regular floppy disk.

The reader who wishes to learn more about the issues surrounding online access in the humanities will want to consult Anne Liebold's "Bibliographic Data Bases in the Humanities: A Performance Study," in *Sixth International Conference on Computers and the Humanities*, edited by Sarah K. Burton and Douglas D. Short (Computer Science Press, 1983, pp. 368-82). Eileen M. Mackesy's "A Perspective on Secondary Access Services in the Humanities" (*Journal of the American Society for Information Science* 33 [May 1982]: 146-51) presents an historical and recent picture of the state of secondary services and online access, while "On-line Searching and the Humanities: Relevance, Resistance and Marketing Strategies," by Scott Stebelman, in *National Online Meeting: Proceedings of the Second National Online Meeting, March 24-26, 1981* (Learned Information, 1981, pp. 443-53) discusses issues specific to online searching in the humanities. *Data Bases in the Humanities and Social Sciences*, edited by Robert F. Allen (Paradigm, 1985) offers additional readings on educational, bibliographic, and data files. History and languages are particularly well covered among the papers which were presented at an international conference on databases in humanities and social sciences. A 1980 volume, edited by Joseph Raben and Gregory A. Marks and carrying the same title (North-Holland, 1980), provides readings from an earlier conference.

The journals *Online, Database*, and *Online Review* offer the online humanist up-to-date information on online services, databases, and issues.

Finally, "A Study of Humanities Faculty Library Information Seeking Behavior" by Elaine Broadbent (*Cataloging and Classification Quarterly* 6 [Spring 1986]: 23-37) addresses needs of faculty as they relate to designing an online library catalog system in a university library, and David Crawford's "Meeting Scholarly Information Needs in an Automated Environment: A Humanist's Perspective" (*College and Research Libraries* 47 [November 1986]: 569-74) calls for communication among developers of database products.

NOTES

[1]Commission on the Humanities, *The Humanities in American Life* (Berkeley, Calif.: University of California Press, 1980).

[2]Ibid.

2 SOURCES OF GENERAL IMPORTANCE TO THE HUMANITIES

BIBLIOGRAPHIC GUIDES

Reference Books

1. **American Reference Books Annual.** 1970- . Ann. Bohdan S. Wynar, ed. Littleton, Colo., Libraries Unlimited.

This is the most complete and detailed source of information regarding reference books published in this country in a single year; the 1987 volume contains nearly 1,800 entries. Reviews are thorough and average about 200-225 words in length, although there are variations depending upon the individual reviewer or the tool being reviewed. The work is divided into four major areas, one of which is the humanities, which accounts for about 30 percent of the total coverage in twelve chapters ("Decorative Arts," "Music," "Fine Arts," etc.). Access is easily provided through a detailed table of contents and excellent indexes covering author/title and subject. Quinquennial indexes are available for 1970-1974, 1975-1979, and 1980-1984 to facilitate searching.

2. **Guide to Reference Books.** 10th ed. Eugene P. Sheehy. Chicago, American Library Association, 1986. 1560p.

The new edition of this massive source contains annotations of 14,000 reference books appearing through the end of 1984. Similar to the previous editions, it is divided into five major sections: "General Reference," "Humanities," "Social Sciences," "History and Area Studies," and "Pure and Applied Sciences." Predictably, reference works in the humanities represent approximately one-third of the total number of entries. Although the coverage is international in scope, there is a known emphasis on both American publications and the English language in general. Arrangement is by subject and type of tool, employing a unique alphanumeric system now familiar to its audience. Annotations tend to be brief and descriptive, and the volume is updated through biennial supplements often criticized for their lack of promptness. It remains the most important reference literature guide for the majority of American librarians due to its comprehensive nature. Its excellent detailed index expedites the search for titles as well as names of individuals responsible for them.

3. **Walford's Guide to Reference Material.** 4th ed. A. J. Walford. London, Library Association, 1980-1986. 3v.

The British counterpart to Sheehy (see entry 2), Walford is another standard source of information and remains a close second to its American rival among academic reference librarians in the United States. Considered by some to be more balanced in coverage, with better annotations in some respects, there is a predictable bias toward British and European sources. The two guides complement each other and generally are found side by side. Walford's fourth edition follows an established pattern of publication in three volumes issued at different times, science and technology being covered first in 1980. Volume 2, *Social and Historical Sciences, Philosophy and Religion* (1982) and volume 3, *Generalities, Languages, the Arts and Literature* (1986) each provide a strong focus for humanities reference. Arrangement of entries in all volumes is by Universal Decimal Classification and access is provided through author/title indexes in each volume and a subject index to the entire set in volume 3.

The entire set is currently undergoing extensive revision, and the fifth edition of volume 3 is earmarked for publication in 1990. New editions of other volumes will be released on an irregular basis.

Periodicals

4. **Magazines for Libraries.** 5th ed. Bill Katz and Linda Sternberg Katz, eds. New York, R. R. Bowker, 1986. 1057p.

Like its previous editions, the fifth edition of *Magazines for Libraries* seeks to identify and describe the best and most useful magazines for the average primary or secondary school, public, academic or special library. Over 100 consultants in different subject areas selected and annotated some 6,500 titles from among over 65,000 possibilities. As in the previous editions, entries are organized by subject and coded according to the appropriate audience. This is an extensive revision with review, modification, or deletion of all entries as well as addition of new titles. About 75 percent of the titles have been returned from the previous edition and 25 percent represent new titles. Humanities areas are well served from the standpoint of reference and collection management through the inclusion of such subject headings as art, music, dance, etc. Titles of indexing and abstracting services covering each magazine follow the full bibliographical description. The annotations show purpose, scope, and audience, with some evaluation provided. Each subject section begins with a short introduction and a recommended list of core periodicals essential for a basic collection.

*5. **Ulrich's International Periodicals Directory: A Classified Guide to Current Periodicals, Foreign and Domestic.** 1932- . Ann. New York, R. R. Bowker.

In its twenty-sixth edition (1987-1988), the leading guide to world periodical publications covers nearly 70,000 periodicals in 534 subject categories. Entries are arranged alphabetically by subject and include title, frequency, publisher, country of publication, and Dewey Decimal Classification number. Additional information such as ISSN, year of inception, circulation, subscription price, etc., is included when known. The new edition adds 4,700 new titles and updates 45,000 entries from the previous issue. Limited to publications which appear more often than once a year on a regular basis, Ulrich's has set the standard in the field. Its complementary work, *Irregular Serials and Annuals: An International Directory* (R. R. Bowker, 1967-), in its thirteenth edition (1987-1988), provides similar coverage of 37,000 serials, annuals, proceedings, and other publications issued irregularly or less frequently than twice a year. Over 2,000 titles have been newly added and 28,000 entries have been updated since the previous edition. Updating for both directories takes place on a quarterly basis through *Bowker International Serials Database Update* (1985-) which continues *Ulrich's Quarterly* (1977-1984). The entire family is available online through BRS and DIALOG. The database (same name as entry) is updated every six weeks with approximately 5,000 new or revised records, and as of mid-1987 contains about 135,000 serials. Also available is Ulrich's Plus, providing similar coverage on quarterly updated compact disks.

Computerized Databases

*6. **Data Base Directory.** 1984- . Semiann. White Plains, N.Y., Knowledge Industry Publications.

For the year 1986/1987 there is a summer 1987 supplement which updates the Winter 1986 issue. Beginning in 1988, the directory will become an annual publication. The monthly supplemental newsletter *DataBase Alert* will continue as before. The purpose of this directory is to identify and describe machine-readable databases available for public access in North America. These include databases of all types (full-text, alphanumeric, bibliographic, referral, etc.). With the third edition in 1986, there is coverage of approximately 2,400 different databases employing about 2,900 different files. Provided in each entry are names of producers and vendors, time coverage, file size, types of records and documents, language, and pricing information. An interesting feature is the index of database alternative names, making it possible to link files with certain popular names in lieu of cross-references. *Data Base Directory Service/Knowledge Industry Publications Database* is available online through BRS, and offers a full-text retrieval system for annotations in the directory and its supplement. With both a monthly newsletter and online access, this provides an unbeatable combination in retrieving current information.

*7. **Directory of Online Databases.** Fall 1979- . Q. Santa Monica, Calif., Cuadra Associates.

Now in its eighth volume (January 1987), the directory has kept pace with the rapid growth in the industry and offers information on 3,369 databases and distinctly named files within 2,823 database families. Entries are arranged alphabetically and include the name, type, producer, online service, conditions, language, coverage, time span, and frequency of updating as well as content. In addition to subject and producer indexes, there is a gateway index identifying the different databases served by the various gateway systems, although gateway linkages are no longer included in the entries themselves. A telecommunications index is an additional feature. Annual subscriptions include two complete directory issues (January and July) and two updates (April and October). *Cuadra Directory of Databases* is available online through West Publishing Company as a WESTLAW database. This provides quick access to the file. However, it is updated only twice a year.

Library Collections

*8. **Subject Collections: A Guide to Special Book Collections and Subject Emphasis as Reported by University, College, Public, and Special Libraries and Museums in the United States and Canada.** 6th ed. Rev. and enl. Lee Ash, et al., eds. New York, R. R. Bowker, 1985. 2v.

The sixth edition of *Subject Collections* provides access to the special collections of over 11,000 libraries and museums in the United States and Canada. As was true of the previous edition, "virtually all libraries included in this book are listed in the *American Library Directory*" (R. R. Bowker, 1923-). Libraries are listed under an alphabetical subject arrangement. The entries for museums have increased. The editors continue to urge museums to report their holdings more explicitly, as they "are often unique ... and should be part of the corpus of research materials available." The result of this continuing effort to collect more and better information is a work that has become a standard purchase for most libraries. One should use the *Library of Congress Subject Headings* list in order to make full use of available entries. Reviewed as an extremely laudable and much-needed work.

9. **Subject Collections in European Libraries.** 2nd ed. Richard Lewanski, comp. New York, R. R. Bowker, 1978. 495p.

Intended as a companion volume to Lee Ash's *Subject Collections* (see entry 8), this work contains 12,000 entries identifying subject collections abroad. It is arranged by subject, using the Dewey Decimal Classification, and the information is based on a questionnaire mailed to some 10,000 libraries selected from national and local library directories and other sources. According to the preface, only about 25 percent of the libraries answered the questionnaire; consequently, most of the information included in this volume is based on secondary sources. Each entry includes the name of the institution, address, director (when given), year established, special items, size of collections, and restrictions in use, if any. This new edition occasionally includes hours of service, availability of photocopying facilities, and types of catalogs or periodicals published by a given institution. The volume concludes with a subject index, which serves as a kind of alphabetical key to the classification scheme. Although criticized for certain technical deficiencies and inaccuracies in identifying collections, due to the magnitude of the effort it should be considered a successful tool and certainly worthy of inclusion.

10. **Subject Directory of Special Libraries and Information Centers.** 10th ed. Brigitte T. Darnay, et al., eds. Detroit, Gale, 1987. 5v.

Intended as a companion to the tenth edition of the *Directory of Special Libraries and Information Centers* (Gale, 1987), this extensive publication covers some 18,000 special libraries and information centers in the United States and Canada. It is the classified arrangement that continues to make this work so useful to scholars and researchers and earns it a major entry in this guide. Volume 4 contains sections on area/ethnic, art, geography/map, history, humanities, music, religion and theology, social science, theater, and urban/regional planning. Within each subject designation, U.S. libraries are listed first, followed by Canadian libraries. A typical entry includes the official name, sponsor, organization, address, director, other professional personnel, collection size, description of subjects, policy, and publications. In addition to a subject index, each volume contains an alternative name index which provides cross-references from variant names for libraries.

INDEXES, ABSTRACTS, AND SERIAL BIBLIOGRAPHIES

11. **American Humanities Index.** 1975- . Q. Ann. cum. Troy, N.Y., Whitston.

Designed for the scholar and serious student, this work provides access to creative, critical, and scholarly serials in the arts and humanities. Supposedly, these are not indexed elsewhere or indexed in services not universally available. There would appear to be little duplication with the *Humanities Index* (see entry 16). The Fall 1986 issue covers 261 journals, many of which would be considered little magazines. Some are devoted to the work of a single author or subject. Individual poems are listed under "Poems" and individual stories under "Stories" as well as under the authors' names. Although a number of the entries are, indeed, found in other indexes not considered uncommon, the work does perform a needed service for identifying those titles not otherwise covered.

*12.   **Arts and Humanities Citation Index.** 1978- . 3/yr. Ann. cum. Philadelphia, Institute for Scientific Information.

Since it began as the third of the three major citation indexes from ISI, this work has established itself as a leading resource for scholars and students. Issued in three parts, January/April, May/August, and finally an annual cumulation of six volumes, it offers unparalleled coverage of journals. (The 1986 issue indexed approximately 1,300 journals fully and another 5,600 partially.) Reviews of books and performances are found easily, but novices should read carefully the explanation of the various indexes—*Source, Permuterm Subject, Citation,* and *Corporate*—in order to exploit the work to its fullest degree. When these are understood properly, the searcher can move in either direction, beginning with an author listing of indexed journal articles in the *Source Index* or finding the references in the bibliographies or footnotes of those articles in the *Citation Index.* Keywords from the titles can be used to locate the articles in the subject index.

*Arts and Humanities Search is available online through BRS and its auxiliary services. This contains a file of 600,000 citations from 1,300 journals in the various fields of the humanities and social sciences dating from 1980 to the present. The student should not hesitate to use the *Social Sciences Citation Index* (ISI) as well, for there are many items of historical and cultural interest relevant to humanities study. Also, *Social Scisearch is available through both BRS and DIALOG and has over 1,000,000 citations, some of which (philosophy, history, archaeology, etc.) are of interest to the humanist.

13.   **British Humanities Index.** 1962- . Q. Ann. cum. London, Library Association.

Published under its present title since 1962, this index supersedes, in part, the *Subject Index to Periodicals* (London, Library Association, 1915-1961). The January/March 1987 issue lists 325 British and Commonwealth periodicals in the humanities and social sciences which are indexed quarterly by subject, with annual cumulations that include author indexes. There is relatively little overlap with *Humanities Index* (see entry 16), more with *Arts and Humanities Citation Index* (see entry 12), though the latter is much more comprehensive and very different in purpose. The subjects covered are surprisingly varied, and "Humanities" in the title is misleading if construed in a strict and narrow sense. One of the areas treated in-depth, for example, is economics; thus such subject headings as "Marketing," "Advertising," "Product Development," "Stock Exchange," and "Steel Industry" are found, with many others from the social sciences. These seem to go well, however, with the more representative humanities designations ("Theatre," "Protestantism," "Music," "Art," etc.) when the librarian comprehends the nature of the tool.

14.   **Current Contents: Arts and Humanities.** 1979- . Wk. Philadelphia, Institute for Scientific Information.

Having completed its eighth volume in 1986, this weekly current awareness service provides tables of contents from over 1,300 journals in art and architecture, performing arts, literature, language and linguistics, history, philosophy, and religion on an international basis. Each issue of each journal is covered as often as it is published and there are over 100 journal titles each week. A section on current book contents, in which a few recent multiauthored books are highlighted, appears infrequently. There is a title word index listing the keywords in the titles of every article and book indexed in each issue. There are also an author index which lists professional addresses and a directory of publishers. A pattern has been established for the inclusion of a triannual cumulative index (fifth, twenty-first, and thirty-eighth issues). It should be remembered that this is one of seven different publications in the series, and others may be useful, especially *Current Contents: Social and Behavioral Sciences* (Institute for Scientific Information, 1974-). This covers about the same number of journals and includes titles in linguistics. Of great importance to researchers is the availability of all articles indexed through a document delivery service from ISI. This can be accessed by mail, telephone, or online through BRS, DIALOG, and SDC.

*15. Dissertation Abstracts International. 1938- . Mo. Ann. cum. Ann Arbor, Mich., University Microfilms International.

The major source of information on doctoral dissertations worldwide, this service appears in two major segments, A, "The Humanities and Social Sciences," and B, "The Sciences and Engineering." The former is divided into five major sections covering communications, education, language and literature, philosophy and religion, and the social sciences. Since 1976 (v.37), section C, "European Abstracts," has been available and is published quarterly. Entries are arranged by broad subject categories with the authors choosing the category which best describes the general content. The abstracts are prepared by the authors and run from 300-350 words in length. In most cases, it is possible to order the dissertation from University Microfilms. Although each issue contains both a keyword title index and an author index, it is recommended that one consult *Comprehensive Dissertation Index* to expedite the search. *Dissertation Abstracts Online, available through BRS and its component services and DIALOG, provides quick access to dissertations from 1861 to date. Full abstracts are provided and updating occurs with the same frequency as the publisher's various offerings (monthly for *DAI*, quarterly for *Masters Abstracts*, etc.). Each year the file increases on the average by 30,000 dissertations and 2,500 master's theses.

*16. Humanities Index. 1975- . Q. Ann. cum. New York, H. W. Wilson.

The leading cumulative index to English-language periodicals in the humanities, this work has been published in its present form since 1974, when *Social Sciences and Humanities Index* (1965-1974) was separated into two publications. Since that time both *Humanities Index* and *Social Sciences Index* have gained an excellent reputation among the other Wilson indexes. *Humanities Index* lists over 300 periodicals from all areas of the humanities and in some cases, the social sciences. The same can be said of *Social Sciences Index*, which has its share of titles which might be found useful to the humanities specialist or student. Both should be employed regularly in searching the literature. Both indexes are available online also through WILSONLINE. *Humanities Index database was reported to have a file of 72,000 records as of June 1986, having begun in February 1984. *Social Sciences Index database had 91,000 records at the same time with the same period of coverage. Both are updated twice a week and will add about 36,000 records a year. Both indexes are available on the new CD-ROM search system, WILSONDISC, which will be updated on a semiannual basis.

17. Index to Social Sciences & Humanities Proceedings. 1979- . Q. Ann. cum. Philadelphia, Institute for Scientific Information.

Developed in the same format as the earlier publication in the sciences, ISI has provided an access tool for papers presented at conferences, seminars, symposia, colloquia, conventions and workshops, and published as proceedings. Humanities coverage includes art, architecture, classics, dance, film, television, folklore, theater, etc. The entries provide current awareness for the specialist, particularly important since innovations often are introduced when experts convene. For each entry, full bibliographic information is given for the publication, including the publisher and ordering information. This is followed by a list of individual papers with names and addresses of authors. Indexes give access to each main entry by title, authors and editors, category, sponsor, meeting location, and the organizational affiliation of each cited author. Although currency is indicated in the preface, users should be aware that proceedings are often published long after the event. The proceeding publications selected for the work are considered by the publisher to be the most significant, in which the majority of the material is printed for the first time.

CHAPTER

3 ACCESSING INFORMATION IN PHILOSOPHY

WORKING DEFINITION OF PHILOSOPHY

Although the term *philosophy* is derived from two Greek words usually translated as "love of wisdom," there is reason to believe that the original usage was somewhat broader, connoting free play of the intellect over a wide range of human problems and even including such qualities as curiosity, shrewdness, and practicality. A gradual narrowing of meaning began in antiquity and has proceeded in stages until modern times. Socrates differentiated his activity from that of the sophists by stressing the raising of questions for clarification in the course of discussion, as distinct from giving answers or teaching techniques for winning arguments. This emphasis on critical examination of issues remained central to philosophic method in the succeeding centuries. Encyclopedic concepts of philosophy were finally shattered by the rise of modern science in the seventeenth century. First the natural sciences emerged as separate disciplines; later the social and behavioral sciences effected their separation from philosophy. The combination of philosophy and psychology which characterizes some reference tools produced around the turn of the twentieth century is evidence of the late departure of psychology and the other behavioral and social sciences from the broad field of philosophy.

Stripped of the natural and social sciences, what remains now as philosophy? First, there are questions about the nature of ultimate reality. Then there is the matter of knowledge as a whole as well as the interrelationships of the specialized branches of it. There are questions of methodology and presuppositions of the individual disciplines. (The phrase "philosophy of ..." is often assigned to this type of endeavor.) Finally, there are normative issues for which there are no scientifically verifiable answers.

It may be said, then, that philosophy is the discipline which is concerned with basic principles of reality, methods of investigation and study, and the logical structures, systems and interrelationships among all fields of knowledge. For additional definitions of philosophy, and discussions of the problems of defining the field, the reader should see Alan R. Lacy's *A Dictionary of Philosophy* (Routledge, 1976) and Anthony Flew's *A Dictionary of Philosophy* (St. Martin's, 1979).

17

MAJOR DIVISIONS OF THE FIELD

Philosophy today is customarily divided into five areas: metaphysics, epistemology, logic, ethics, and aesthetics. Metaphysics may be further subdivided into ontology and cosmology. Ontology is concerned with the nature of ultimate reality, or sometimes referred to as "being." It includes consideration of whether reality has one basic component (monism), two (dualism), or many (pluralism). Monistic philosophies discuss whether reality is ultimately mental or spiritual (idealism), or physical (materialism). Dualistic philosophies commonly regard both matter and mind as irreducible ultimate components. Cosmology is concerned with questions about origins and processes. The nature of causality has been a frequent topic for debate. Although a few have argued for pure chance, more philosophers have emphasized either antecedent causes (i.e., preceding events that cause the event under consideration to happen) or final causes (ends or purposes that exert an influence on the outcome of events). Many of the former persuasion are convinced that there is no room for either chance or freedom in the chain of causality. These determinists are called mechanists if they also believe that reality is ultimately physical. Philosophers who emphasize final causes are known as teleologists.

Epistemology is concerned with the scope and limits of human knowledge. What can we know? With what degree of certainty? Rationalists stress the role of human reason. Empiricists emphasize the importance of data derived from experience. It is generally agreed that there are two types of knowledge: *a priori*, which is knowable without reference to experience and which alone possesses theoretical certainty (e.g., the principles of logic and mathematics); and *a posteriori*, which is derived from experience and possesses only approximate certainty (e.g., the findings of the sciences).

Logic deals with the principles of correct reasoning or valid inference. It differs from psychology in that it does not describe how people actually think but prescribes certain canons to be followed if they would think correctly. Deductive logic (sometimes known as Aristotelian or traditional logic) arose in antiquity and is concerned with the process by which correct conclusions can be drawn from sets of anxioms known or believed to be true. Its most familiar form is the syllogism, which consists of three parts: a major premise, a minor premise, and a conclusion:

> All men are mortal.
> Socrates is a man.
> Therefore, Socrates is mortal.

Inductive logic is a result of the development of modern scientific methods. It deals with the canons of valid inference, but is concerned with probabilities rather than certainties and frequently involves the use of statistics. It is, in a sense, the opposite of deductive logic (which proceeds from the general to the particular) in that it attempts to reach valid generalizations from an enumeration of particulars.

In ethics, the questions relate to matters of conduct. Can certain actions be considered morally right or wrong? If so, on what basis? Should the interests of the self have priority (egoism)? Or the interests of others (altruism)? Or is there some greater good (*summum bonum*) to which both should be subordinate? Ethical theories may be classified by the manner in which criteria for right actions are discovered or by the nature of the highest good. In the first group, authoritarians stress submission to the will of God or some other external authority. Rationalists stress the free activity of the mind in examining all aspects of a question. Intuitionists stress the importance of obedience to conscience. Emotive theorists stress feeling as the proper ground for ethical decision making. In the second classification, hedonists regard pleasure as the highest good. Eudaemonists pursue happiness. Perfectionists seek the ideal fulfillment of human life. Kantians stress purity of motive and universalizability of individual ethical decisions.

The nature of beauty is the subject matter of aesthetics. The concerns of the philosopher may be differentiated from those of the psychologist and those of the critic. The psychologist concentrates on human reactions to aesthetic objects. The critic focuses on individual works of art or on general principles of criticism, usually within the confines of a particular discipline. The philosopher is broadly concerned with beauty per se, whether in art or nature. Does beauty inhere in the beautiful object? Are there objective criteria by which it may be determined? Or is beauty a subjective experience, with no universally valid norms? Classical theories tend to stress objectivity. Romantic theories emphasize individualism and subjectivity.

The student desiring a concise introduction to philosophy should read "Philosophy," by C. I. Lewis in the *Encyclopedia Americana* (1978 edition, v.21, pp. 769-77) or the G. S. Davis article "Philosophy," in *Academic American Encyclopedia* (1987 ed., v.15, pp. 240-47). Still useful is John Passmore's "Philosophy," in *The Encyclopedia of Philosophy* (Macmillan, 1967, v.6, pp. 216-26). Passmore's "Philosophy, Historiography of," in the *Encyclopedia of Philosophy* (v.6, pp. 226-30) and S. N. Hampshire's "Philosophy, History of," in *Encyclopedia Americana* (v.21, pp. 777-82) provide historical perspectives.

Several articles are of particular importance to the librarian. Volume 6 of *The Encyclopedia of Philosophy* contains three articles by William Gerber: "Philosophical Bibliographies," "Philosophical Dictionaries and Encyclopedias," and "Philosophical Journals." The article on philosophy in Lester Asheim's *The Humanities and the Library* (American Library Association, 1956, pp. 61-99) is also valuable, as is the later volume *Research Guide in Philosophy*, by Martin A. Bertman (General Learning, 1974). Bertman's list of journals in philosophy is annotated and updates earlier listings.

Many introductions and histories of philosophy are extremely technical and therefore forbidding to the layperson. An exception is Bertrand Russell's *A History of Western Philosophy* (Simon & Schuster, 1945), which remains useful despite its age. Martin Bertman's *Research Guide in Philosophy* includes another easy-to-read history, as does the ever-popular *Story of Philosophy*, by Will Durant (Simon & Schuster, 1926).

USE AND USERS OF
PHILOSOPHY INFORMATION

A thorough search of the literature of use and user studies reveals that little research has been done on literature use by philosophers. However, there is evidence that the literature of the field is widely used and that certain authors, both ancient and current, are well cited. A listing of the 100 most cited authors from the *1977-1978 Arts and Humanities Citation Index* (ISI Press, 1978) includes Plato and Aristotle (with 1,233 and 1,361 citations respectively) as well as Karl Popper, Paul Ricoeur, and John Rawls (all contemporary writers with more than 150 citations each in 1977-1978). Indeed, the most cited of all the authors listed was Karl Marx, whose work received over 1,600 citations in the 1977-1978 issue of *AHCI*. Half of those citations were in philosophy journals, according to Engene Garfield, whose article is the source of these data.[1]

The types of materials in philosophy reveal that laypersons, general students, and technical scholars are the main users of information in philosophy. Henry J. Koren, in his *Research in Philosophy—A Bibliographical Introduction to Philosophy and a Few Suggestions for Dissertations* (Duquesne University Press, 1966), suggests that philosophical books may be divided into "popularizing works, text books, and strictly scholarly works," and that approaches taken in these books vary from the historical to the problematic and methodic, to the "ism" approach which covers a system or trend of thought.

MAJOR CLASSIFICATION SCHEMES

Utilization of shelf arrangement as a tool for philosophic information retrieval must be considered secondary to other approaches, but some knowledge of the major library classification schemes will be advantageous. In order of approximate frequency of use, these are: the Dewey Decimal Classification (DDC) and Library of Congress Classification (LC).

From the standpoint of user needs, there are three principal approaches to the arrangement of philosophic writings: 1) By individual philosophers. This approach is particularly helpful for those who wish to study either the total thought system of a philosopher or a particular work. It is doubly helpful if secondary works (commentaries, criticism, etc.) are also shelved with the primary sources. 2) By specialized branches of the discipline (metaphysics, epistemology, logic, ethics, aesthetics). 3) By interrelationships and influences (periods, schools of thought, language and nationality groupings, etc.). Most classification systems attempt to achieve some balance among these differing (and somewhat conflicting) approaches.

First devised by Melvil Dewey in 1876, the Decimal Classification (DDC) has been frequently updated and expanded. The section on philosophy (100-199) is the least successful; the latest edition (19th), by its inclusion of psychology, still reflects a late-nineteenth-century view of the world. It is frequently criticized for its separation of philosophical viewpoints from the sections on ancient, medieval, and modern philosophy, and for its failure to include a section on aesthetics (which DDC places with the arts in the 700s). Nevertheless, it is the most commonly used library classification system. Examples illustrating the major divisions and selected subdivisions are shown in figure 3.1.

100	PHILOSOPHY AND RELATED DISCIPLINES	162	Deducation
		165	Fallacies and sources of error
101	Theory of philosophy	166	Syllogisms
103	Dictionaries of philosophy	167	Hypotheses
105	Serials on philosophy	168	Argument and persuasion
106	Organizations of philosophy	169	Analogy
107	Study and teaching of philosophy		
109	Historical treatment of philosophy	170	ETHICS
		171	Systems and doctrines
110	METAPHYSICS	172	Political ethics
111	Ontology	173	Ethics of family relationships
113	Cosmology	174	Economic, professional and occupational ethics
114	Space		
115	Time	175	Ethics of recreation and leisure
116	Evolution	176	Ethics of sex and reproduction
117	Structure	177	Ethics of social relations
118	Force and energy	178	Ethics of consumption
119	Number and quantity	179	Other ethical norms
120	EPISTEMOLOGY, CAUSATION HUMANKIND	180	ANCIENT, MEDIEVAL, ORIENTAL PHILOSOPHY
121	Epistemology	181	Oriental
122	Causation	182	Pre-Socratic Greek
123	Determinism and indeterminism	183	Sophistic, Socratic and related Greek
		184	Platonic
130	PARANORMAL PHENOMENA AND ARTS	185	Aristotelian
		186	Skeptic and Neoplatonic
		187	Epicurean
140	SPECIFIC PHILOSOPHICAL VIEWPOINTS	188	Stoic
		189	Medieval Western
141	Idealism and related systems and		
142	Critical philosophy	190	MODERN WESTERN PHILOSOPHY
143	Intuitionism and Bergsonism		
144	Humanism and related systems	191	United States and Canada
145	Sensationalism and ideology	192	British Isles
146	Naturalism and related systems	193	Germany and Austria
147	Pantheism and related systems	194	France
148	Liberalism and other systems	195	Italy
149	Other systems and doctrines	196	Spain and Portugal
		197	Russia and Finland
150	PSYCHOLOGY	198	Scandinavia
		199	Other countries
160	LOGIC		
161	Induction		

Fig. 3.1. Examples of DDC subject divisions in philosophy and related disciplines.

The Library of Congress (LC) schedule for philosophy was first published in 1910 and revised in 1979. LC includes psychology, but otherwise is generally superior to DDC. Subclass B is designed to keep the works of individual philosophers together and to place philosophers in relation to periods, countries, and schools of thought. The general pattern for individual philosophers is 1) collected works, 2) separate works, 3) biography and criticism. LC also has sections for the major divisions of the field (including aesthetics). The principal divisions are shown in figure 3.2.

```
B    PHILOSOPHY (GENERAL)
         Serials, Collections, etc.
         History and systems
BC   LOGIC
BD   SPECULATIVE PHILOSOPHY
         General philosophical works
         Metaphysics
         Epistemology
         Methodology
         Ontology
         Cosmology
BF   PSYCHOLOGY
         Parapsychology
         Occult sciences
BH   AESTHETICS
BJ   ETHICS
         Social usages, Etiquette
```

Fig. 3.2. Principal LC divisions of "Philosophy."

Although some special philosophy classifications have been developed, their use appears to have been confined to the arrangement of certain bibliographies.

SUBJECT HEADINGS FREQUENTLY USED

Searching library catalogs (whether in card, book, or computer form) continues to play an important role in the retrieval of philosophical information. Although many subject indexes in recent years have been constructed on the basis of keywords from document titles, or from text, most library subject catalogs use a controlled or standardized vocabulary embodied in a list of subject headings. Such lists usually include guidance on choice of main headings, methods of subdividing major topics, and cross-references to lead the user to the headings chosen or to related topics.

The overwhelming majority of large American libraries today follow the *Subject Headings Used in the Dictionary Catalogs of the Library of Congress* (10th edition, Library of Congress, 1986) or its machine-readable counterpart. These headings enable the reader looking for a specific topic in philosophy to go directly to that heading. The disadvantage is that philosophic topics are scattered throughout an entire alphabetic sequence. This is true whether the library uses a "dictionary" catalog (in which the entries for authors, titles, and subjects are interfiled in one alphabetic sequence) or a "divided" catalog (in which the subject portion is separate from the author-title section).

This chapter includes some information that will not be repeated in later chapters on "Accessing Information." Examples of subject headings are provided in figure 3.3, reproduced from the tenth edition of *Subject Headings Used in the Dictionary Catalogs of the Library of Congress*. These examples are followed by a discussion of basic principles based largely on David Judson Haykin's *Subject Headings: A Practical Guide* (Government Printing Office, 1951) and the second edition of *Library of Congress Subject Headings: Principles and Application*, by Lois M. Chan (Libraries Unlimited, 1986). Haykin, as chief of the Subject Cataloging Division of the Library of Congress, helped to shape the system he describes.

Philosophers *(Indirect)*
  sa Alchemists
     Ethicists
     Logicians
     Philosopher-kings
  x Philosophy – Biography
  – Relationship with women

GEOGRAPHIC SUBDIVISIONS

  – Greece
  sa Seven wise men of Greece
Philosophers, Ancient *(B108-708)*
Philosophers, Islamic
  See Philosophers, Muslim
Philosophers, Jewish *(Indirect)*
  x Jewish philosophers
Philosophers, Medieval *(B720-785)*
Philosophers, Modern
  x Modern philosophers
Philosophers, Muslim
  x Islamic philosophers
     Muslim philosophers
     Philosophers, Islamic
Philosophers' egg
  See Alchemy
Philosophers in art
Philosophers' stone
  See Alchemy
Philosophical analysis
  See Analysis (Philosophy)
Philosophical anthropology *(BD450)*
  sa Fallibility
     Femininity (Philosophy)
     Humanism
     Man – Animal nature
     Man (Theology)
     Mind and body
     Persons
  x Anthropology, Philosophical
     Man (Philosophy)
  xx Civilization – Philosophy
     Humanism
     Life
     Man
     Ontology
     Persons
Philosophical grammar
  See Grammar, Comparative and
     general
Philosophical literature
  xx Philosophy – History
Philosophical recreations *(GV1507.P43)*
  x Recreations, Philosophical
  xx Amusements
     Games

Philosophical theology *(BT40)*
  x Theology, Philosophical
  xx Christianity – Philosophy
     Natural theology
     Philosophy
     Philosophy and religion
     Religion – Philosophy
     Theology, Doctrinal
Philosophy *(Indirect)* *(B-BJ)*
  sa Absurd (Philosophy)
     Accidents (Philosophy)
     Act (Philosophy)
     Aesthetics
     Agent (Philosophy)
     Alienation (Philosophy)
     Analysis (Philosophy)
     Atomism
     Attribute (Philosophy)
     Authenticity (Philosophy)
     Axioms
     Banality (Philosophy)
     Becoming (Philosophy)
     Belief and doubt
     Body, Human (Philosophy)
     Causation
     Chain of being (Philosophy)
     Children and philosophy
     Christianity – Philosophy
     Communism and philosophy
     Comparison (Philosophy)
     Compensation (Philosophy)
     Complexity (Philosophy)
     Comprehension (Theory of
       knowledge)
     Consciousness
     Consequentialism (Ethics)
     Constitution (Philosophy)
     Construction (Philosophy)
     Constructivism (Philosophy)
     Contradiction
     Convention (Philosophy)
     Cosmology
     Creation
     Criticism (Philosophy)
     Cycles
     Cynicism
     Depth (Philosophy)
     Description (Philosophy)
     Determinism (Philosophy)
     Difference (Philosophy)
     Disposition (Philosophy)
     Distinction (Philosophy)
     Dualism
     Egosim
     Ends and means

Philosophy *(Indirect) (B-BJ)*
  (Continued)
      Engagement (Philosophy)
      Entity (Philosophy)
      Epiphanism
      Essence (Philosophy)
      Ethics
      Ethnophilosophy
      Events (Philosophy)
      Evidence
      Exact (Philosophy)
      Experience
      Explanation (Philosophy)
      Expression (Philosophy)
      Extension (Philosophy)
      Face (Philosophy)
      Facts (Philosophy)
      Fate and fatalism
      Femininity (Philosophy)
      Finalism (Philosophy)
      Finite, The
      Formalization (Philosophy)
      Four elements (Philosophy)
      Free will and determinism
      Gnosticism
      Goal (Philosophy)
      God
      Good and evil
      Habit (Philosophy)
      Harmony (Philosophy)
      Hedonism
      Heuristic
      Humanism
      Hylozoism
      Idea (Philosophy)
      Idealism
      Ideals (Philosophy)
      Ideology
      Illusion (Philosophy)
      Imagination (Philosophy)
      Immaterialism (Philosophy)
      Immortality (Philosophy)
      Individuation
      Ineffable, The
      Infallibility (Philosophy)
      Innate ideas (Philosophy)
      Instinct (Philosophy)
      Instrumentalism (Philosophy)
      Intentionality (Philosophy)
      Interaction (Philosophy)
      Interest (Philosophy)
      Interpretation (Philosophy)
      Intuition
      Irrationalism (Philosophy)
      Isolation (Philosophy)
      Justice (Philosophy)
      Knowledge, Theory of
      Law (Philosophy)
      Logic

Many (Philosophy)
Materialism
Mean (Philosophy)
Meaning (Philosophy)
Meaninglessness (Philosophy)
Mechanism (Philosophy)
Metaphysics
Mind and body
Monadology
Monism
Mysticism
Naturalism
Negation of negation (Dialectical
  materialism)
Negativity (Philosophy)
Neoplatonism
New, The
Nihilism (Philosophy)
Nominalism
Nonexistent objects (Philosophy)
Norm (Philosophy)
Object (Philosophy)
One (The One in philosophy)
Ontologism
Ontology
Operationalism
Opinion (Philosophy)
Opposition, Theory of
Optimism
Order (Philosophy)
Organism (Philosophy)
Panpsychism
Pantheism
Parapsychology and philosophy
Participation
Peace (Philosophy)
Perception
Perception (Philosophy)
Performative (Philosophy)
Personalism
Perspective (Philosophy)
Pessimism
Phenomenalism
Philosophical theology
Platonists
Play (Philosophy)
Pluralism
Polarity (Philosophy)
Positivism
Possibility
Power (Philosophy)
Practice (Philosophy)
Pragmatism
Presentation (Philosophy)
Principle (Philosophy)
Process philosophy
Psychoanalysis and philosophy
Psychology
Purity (Philosophy)
Quality (Philosophy)

Quantity (Philosophy)
Rationalism
Reaction (Philosophy)
Realism
Reality
Reductionism
Reference (Philosophy)
Reflection (Philosophy)
Relation (Philosophy)
Relevance (Philosophy)
Renunciation (Philosophy)
Repetition (Philosophy)
Representation (Philosophy)
Right and left (Philosophy)
Scholasticism
Secret (Philosophy)
Self (Philosophy)
Sense (Philosophy)
Separation (Philosophy)
Silence (Philosophy)
Simplicity (Philosophy)
Situation (Philosophy)
Skepticism
Soul
Space and time
Specialism (Philosophy)
Spiritualism (Philosophy)
Spontaneity (Philosophy)
Strategy (Philosophy)
Structuralism
Style (Philosophy)
Subject (Philosophy)
Sufficient reason
Teleology
Theism
Theory (Philosophy)
Thomists
Thought and thinking
Topic (Philosophy)
Tradition (Philosophy)
Transcendence (Philosophy)
Transcendentalism
Triads (Philosophy)
Truth
Universals (Philosophy)
Utilitarianism
War (Philosophy)
Whole and parts (Philosophy)
Will
Wonder (Philosophy)
subdivision Philosophy *under*
  subjects, e.g. Art — Philosophy
 x Mental philosophy
xx Cosmology
  Ontology
— Biography
See Philosophers
— History *(B69-4695)*
 sa Philosophical literature

— Introductions *(BD10-28)*
— Library resources
 sa Philosophy libraries
— Methodology
See Methodology
Philosophy, African *(B5300-5320)*
 x African philosophy
Philosophy, Afro-American
See Afro-American philosophy
Philosophy, American *(B851-945)*
 sa Afro-American philosophy
  Mercersburg theology
— 18th century
— 19th century
— 20th century *(B934-945)*
Philosophy, American, [Arab, Chinese, etc.]
— 20th century
Philosophy, Analytical
See Analysis (Philosophy)
Philosophy, Ancient *(B108-708)*
  Here are entered works dealing with
    ancient philosophy in general and
    with Greek and Roman philosophy
    in particular.
 sa Ataraxia
  Atomism
  Cosmology, Ancient
  Cynics (Greek philosophy)
  Diaeresis (Philosophy)
  Eleatics
  Gnosticism
  Manichaeism
  Megarians (Greek philosophy)
  Neoplatonism
  Peripatetics
  Platonists
  Pythagoras and Pythagorean school
  Science, Ancient
  Skeptics (Greek philosophy)
  Sophists (Greek philosophy)
  Stoics
 x Ancient philosophy
  Greek philosophy
  Philosophy, Greek
  Philosophy, Roman
  Roman philosophy
— Oriental influences
xx Civilization, Oriental
— Phoenician influences *(B180)*
xx Phoenicia — Civilization
Philosophy, Arab *(Medieval, B740-753)*
 sa Philosophy, Islamic
 x Arabic philosophy
  Philosophy, Arabic
Philosophy, Arabic
See Philosophy, Arab
  Philosophy, Islamic
Philosophy, Argentine *(B1030-1034)*
 x Argentine philosophy

Philosophy, Asian
  See Philosophy, Oriental
Philosophy, Australian *(B5700-5704)*
  x Australian philosophy
Philosophy, Australian aboriginal
  x Australian aboriginal philosophy
Philosophy, Austrian *(B2521-3396)*
  x Austrian philosophy
  xx Philosophy, German
  —19th century
  —20th century
Philosophy, Azerbaijani
  x Azerbaijani philosophy
Philosophy, Babylonian *(B145-148)*
  sa Cosmology, Babylonian
  x Babylonian philosophy
Philosophy, Baganda *(DT433.242)*
  x Baganda philosophy
Philosophy, Basque
  x Basque philosophy
Philosophy, Bonpo
  sa Bonpo logic
  x Bonpo philosophy
Philosophy, Brazilian *(B1040-1044)*
  x Brazilian philosophy
Philosophy, British
  sa Philosophy, English
  x British philosophy
  xx Philosophy, English
    Philosophy, Modern
  —18th century *(B1301)*
Philosophy, Buddhist *(B162)*
  sa Abhidharma
    Anātman
    Atman
    Buddhism—Doctrines
    Buddhism and philosophy
    Buddhist logic
    Cosmogony, Buddhist
    Cosmology, Buddhist
    Knowledge, Theory of (Buddhism)
    Mādhyamika (Buddhism)
    Man (Buddhism)
    Matter (Buddhism)
    No-mind (Buddhism)
    Philosophy, Indic
    Pratyaya
    Sunyata
    Time (Buddhism)
    Truth (Buddhism)
    Vijñaptimātratā
    Yogācāra (Buddhism)
  x Buddhist philosophy
  xx Philosophy, Hindu
    Philosophy, Indic
  —Introductions
Philosophy, Bulgarian
  x Bulgarian philosophy

Philosophy, Byelorussian
  x Byelorussian philosophy
    Philosophy, White Russian
Philosophy, Canadian
  x Canadian philosophy
Philosophy, Chinese
  sa Ch'eng
    Ch'i (Chinese philosophy)
    Legalism (Chinese philosophy)
    Moism
    Neo-Confucianism
    Philosophy, Confucian
    Philosophy, Taoist
    Tao
    Yin-yang
  x Chinese philosophy
  —To 221 B.C. *(B126)*
  —221 B.C.-960 A.D. *(B126)*
  —960-1644 *(B126)*
  —1644-1912 *(B5230-5234)*
  —19th century
  —20th century
Philosophy, Comparative *(B799)*
  sa Ethics, Comparative
  x Comparative philosophy
  xx East and West
    Philosophy, Oriental
Philosophy, Confucian *(Indirect)*
    (B127.C65)
  sa Confucianists
    Jen
    Li
  x Confucian philosophy
  xx Confucianism
    Philosophy, Chinese
Philosophy, Croatian *(B4841-4845)*
  x Croatian philosophy
  xx Philosophy, Yugoslav
Philosophy, Cuban *(B1028)*
  x Cuban philosophy
Philosophy, Czech
  —19th century
  —20th century
Philosophy, Doctor of
  See Doctor of philosophy degree
Philosophy, Dogon (African people)
    (DT551.42)
  x Dogon (African people) philosophy
Philosophy, Dutch
  x Dutch philosophy
Philosophy, East Indian
  See Philosophy, Indic
Philosophy, Ecuadorian *(B1055-1059)*
  x Ecuadorian philosophy
Philosophy, English
  sa Philosophy, British
  xx Philosophy, British
    Philosophy, Modern
  —13th century

    —16th century *(B776.E5)*
    —17th century *(B1131-1299)*
    —18th century *(B1300-1559)*
    —19th century *(B1573-1612)*
    —20th century *(B1614-1674)*
    sa Bloomsburg group
Philosophy, Fataleka (Solomon Islands
    people) *(DU850)*
    x Fataleka (Solomon Islands people)
      philosophy
Philosophy, French
    sa Libertines (French philosophers)
    xx Philosophy, Modern
    —16th century
    —17th century *(B1815-1818)*
    —18th century *(B1911-1925)*
    —19th century *(B2185-8)*
    —20th century *(B2421-4)*
Philosophy, German
    sa Philosophy, Austrian
    xx Philosophy, Modern
    —18th century
    —19th century
    —20th century *(B3181)*
    —Green influences
    xx Greece—Civilization
Philosophy, Greek
    See Philosophy, Ancient
Philosophy, Gurma (African people)
    x Gurma (African people) philosophy
    xx Ethnophilosophy—Burkina Faso
Philosophy, Hindu
    sa Advaita
      Anātman
      Atman
      Mosmogony, Hindu
      Cosmology, Hindu
      Dharma
      Dvaita (Vedanta)
      Hindu logic
      Knowledge, Theory of (Hinduism)
      Lokàyata
      Maya (Hinduism)
      Mimamsa
      Nyaya
      Philosophy, Buddhist
      Philosophy, Indic
      Vaiśeṣika
      Yoga
    xx Philosophy, Indic
Philosophy, Igbo (African people)
    (DT515.45.I33)
    x Igbo (African people) philosophy
Philosophy, Indic *(B130-133)*
    sa Abankàra
      Avidyà
      Classification—Books—
        Philosophy Indic
      Jiva
      Krama

      Mokṣa
      Philosophy, Buddhist
      Philosophy, Hindu
      Śuddhàdvaita
      Upamàna
    x Indic philosophy
      Philosophy, East Indian
    xx Philosophy, Buddhist
      Philosophy, Hindu
    —Modern period, 1600-
    —20th century
Philosophy, Indonesian *(B5210-5214)*
    x Indonesian philosophy
Philosophy, Islamic *(Indirect)* *(B163;*
      Medieval, B740-753)
    sa Cosmology, Islamic
      Islam and philosophy
      Islam and reason
      Islamic ethics
      Knowledge, Theory of (Islam)
      Values (Islam)
    x Arabic philosophy
      Islamic philosophy
      Muslim philosophy
      Philosophy, Arabic
      Philosophy, Muslim
    xx Philosophy, Arab
    —Greek [etc.] influences
Philosophy, Israeli *(B5055-5059)*
    sa Philosophy, Jewish
    x Israeli philosophy
    xx Philosophy, Jewish
Philosophy, Italian
    —17th century
    —18th century
    —19th century
    —20th century
Philosophy, Jaina *(B162.5)*
    sa Cosmology, Jaina
      Jaina logic
      Knowledge, Theory of (Jainism)
    x Jaina philosophy
Philosophy, Japanese
    sa Kokugaku
      Mitogaku
      Yōmeigaku
    —To 1600
    —19th century
    —20th century
Philosophy, Jewish *(Indirect)*
    sa Cosmology, Jewish
      Hasidism—Philosophy
      Judaism and philosophy
      Philosophy, Israeli
    x Jewish philosophy
      Jews—Philosophy
    xx Bible—Philosophy
      Philosophy, Israeli

Philosophy, Kgaga (African people)
   (DT764.K42)
   x   Kgaga (African people) philosophy
   xx Ethnophilosophy
Philosophy, Korean
   sa Sirhak school
   x   Korean philosophy
Philosophy, Latin American   *(B1001-1008)*
   x   Latin American philosophy
Philosophy, Latvian
   x   Latvian philosophy
Philosophy, Lithuanian
   x   Lithuanian philosophy
Philosophy, Malagasy   *(B5460-5464)*
   x   Malagasy philosophy
Philosophy, Marxist   *(Indirect)*   *(B809.8)*
   sa Dialectical materialism
   x   Marxian philosophy
         Marxist philosophy
   xx Communism and philosophy
Philosophy, Mechanistic
   See Mechanism (Philosophy)
Philosophy, Medieval   *(B720-785)*
   sa Cosmology, Medieval
         Scholasticism
         Summists
         Thomists
   x   Medieval philosophy
   xx Scholasticism
   — Islamic influences
   xx Civilization, Islamic
Philosophy, Mexican   *(B1015-1019)*
   x   Mexican philosophy
Philosophy, Minangkabau (Indonesian
   people)
   x   Minanghabau (Indonesian people)
         philosophy
   xx Ethnophilosophy — Indonesia
Philosophy, Modern   *(B790-4695)*
   sa Evolution
         Existential phenomenology
         Existentialism
         Humanism — 20th century
         Humanism, Religious
         Neo-Scholasticism
         Phenomenology
         Philosophy, British
         Positivism
         Pragmatism
         Semantics (Philosophy)
         Transcendentalism
         Philosophy, English; Philosophy,
            French; Philosophy, German;
            and similar headings
   x   Modern philosophy
   — 16th century
   See Philosophy, Renaissance
   — 17th century   *(B801)*
   — 18th century   *(B802)*
   sa Enlightenment
   — 19th century   *(B803)*

— 20th century   *(B804)*
Philosophy, Moral
   See Ethics
Philosophy, Muslim
   See Philosophy, Islamic
Philosophy, Natural
   See Physics
Philosophy, Ordinary-language
   See Ordinary-language philosophy
Philosophy, Oriental   *(Ancient, B121-162.7;*
         Modern, B5000-5020)
   sa Philosophy, Comparative
   x   Asian philosophy
         Oriental philosophy
         Philosophy, Asian
Philosophy, Pakistani
   x   Pakistani philosophy
Philosophy, Patristic
   See Fathers of the church
Philosophy, Polish
   17th century
   — 19th century
   — 20th century
Philosophy, Portuguese   *(B4591-4598)*
   x   Portuguese philosophy
   — 20th century
Philosophy, Primitive
   See Ethnophilosophy
Philosophy, Renaissance   *(B770-785)*
   x   Philosophy, Modern — 16th century
         Renaissance philosophy
Philosophy, Roman
   See Philosophy, Ancient
Philosophy, Romanian
   x   Romanian philosophy
Philosophy, Russian
   x   Russian philosophy
   — 19th century
   — 20th century   *(B4231)*
Philosophy, Scottish
   x   Scottish philosophy
Philosophy, Shinto   *(B162.6)*
   sa Cosmogony, Shinto
         Cosmology, Shinto
   x   Shinto philosophy
Philosophy, Sikh
   sa Sikh ethics
   x   Sikh philosophy
   xx Sikhism
Philosophy, Slovak
   x   Slovak philosophy
Philosophy, Southeast Asian
   x   Southeast Asian philosophy
Philosophy, Spanish
   x   Spanish philosophy
   — 19th century
   — 20th century
Philosophy, Swedish
   x   Swedish philosophy

Philosophy, Taoist *(B163)*
   x Taoist philosophy
  xx Philosophy, Chinese
Philosophy, Tibetan
   x Tibetan philosophy
Philosophy, Ukrainian *(B4751-4755)*
   x Ukrainian philosophy
Philosophy, Venezuelan *(B1080-1084)*
   x Venezuelan philosophy
  —20th century
Philosophy, White Russian
  See Philosophy, Byelorussian
Philosophy, Yoruba
   x Yoruba philosophy
Philosophy, Yugoslav
  sa Philosophy, Croatian
Philosophy, Zulu
   x Zulu philosophy
Philosophy and astronomy
  See Astronomy—Philosophy
Philosophy and Islam
  See Islam and philosophy
Philosophy and Judaism
  See Judaism and philosophy
Philosophy and religion
  sa Buddhism and philosophy
    Catholic Church and philosophy
    Christianity—Philosophy
    Faith and reason
    Islam and philosophy
    Judiasm and philosophy
    Philosophical theology
    Religion—Philosophy
   x Christianity and philosophy
    Religion and philosophy
  xx Religion—Philosophy
 Note under Faith and reason
Philosophy and science *(Indirect)(B67)*
  sa Science—Philosophy
  xx Science
Philosophy and social sciences *(B63)*
  xx Social sciences

Philosophy and the Catholic Church
  See Catholic Church and philosophy
Philosophy and the Koran
  See Koran and philosophy
Philosophy in literature *(PN49)*
  sa Existentialism in literature
Philosophy libraries *(Indirect)*
   x Libraries, Philosophy
  xx Humanities libraries
    Libraries, Special
    Philosophy—Library resources
Philosophy of history
  See History—Philosophy
Philosophy of international law
  See International law—Philosophy
Philosophy of language
  See Languages—Philosophy
Philosophy of law
  See Law—Philosophy
Philosophy of literature
  See Literature—Philosophy
Philosophy of medicine
  See Medicine—Philosophy
Philosophy of nature *(BD581)*
  sa Cosmology
    Natural theology
    Nature—Religious aspects
    Nature (Aesthetics)
    Uniformity of nature
   x Nature—Philosophy
    Nature, Philosophy of
  xx Cosmology
    Natural theology
Philosophy of psychiatry
  See Psychiatry—Philosophy
Philosophy of rhetoric
  See Rhetoric—Philosophy
Philosophy of teaching
  See Education—Philosophy

Fig. 3.3. Library of Congress subject headings in philosophy.

To use these headings as a guide in the formulation of a search strategy, it is helpful to understand the basic forms subject headings may take:

1. **Simple nouns as headings.** This form is the most direct, immediate, and uncomplicated. If adequate to the task, it is normally preferred. The most obvious example, in this context, is "Philosophy."

2. **Adjectival headings.** These may be in natural or inverted form. An example of the natural form would be "Philosophical anthropology"; an example of the inverted form would be "Philosophy, American." The choice is determined by the need to emphasize those search words of

greatest importance to the intended user. In the first example, the word *philosophical* is more significant to the philosophy student than the word *anthropology*. In the second example, the word *American* would be of significance to the person seeking information on American philosophy, but the natural order would bury the topic among dozens (perhaps hundreds) of other entries beginning with *American*. Since the prime topic is philosophy, with American philosophy as one variety, the inverted form is chosen.

3. **Phrase headings.** These usually consist of nouns connected by a preposition. An example would be "Philosophy in literature." Sometimes, it is necessary to invert the natural word order to emphasize a key search term. There is no ready example from the philosophy list, but an example from another field would be "Plants, Protection of." Another type of phrase heading is the so-called "compound heading," which is made up of two or more coordinate elements connected by "and." An example from the list would be "Philosophy and religion."

It frequently happens that the approaches described above do not result in headings that are sufficiently specific. In such cases, further division of the topic will be required. The techniques most frequently used for division are as follows:

1. **By form.** This plan of division is not based on the content of a work but on its manner of arrangement or the purpose it is intended to serve. Examples would include:

> Philosophy — Bibliography
> Philosophy — Dictionaries
> Philosophy — Directories
> Philosophy — Outlines, Syllabi, etc.
> Philosophy — Study and teaching.

2. **By political or geographic area.** Formerly, there were two principal methods of local division: direct and indirect. If the direct method was used, the name of a specific place occurred immediately after the dash, indicating a division of the main heading. If the indirect approach was chosen, the name of a country or larger unit was inserted between the main heading and the specific place. Places likely to be familiar to American users were entered directly. Places less likely to be familiar will be entered indirectly. The lack of clear criteria for differentiation and the advent of machine-readable cataloging records produced pressure for greater uniformity. Since 1975, the Library of Congress has moved to the indirect method of subdivision with a few minor exceptions. Philosophy is not the best subject to choose for examples, since the need for geographic subdivision in philosophy is largely achieved in another way — namely, by use of the inverted form of adjectival headings, such as "Philosophy, English," or "Philosophy, French."

3. **By period.** This represents a departure from the customary alphabetical approach in that headings for generally accepted historical periods are arranged *chronologically*. In philosophy, this technique is used to subdivide under the different countries. Thus, we find that "Philosophy, French—17th century" precedes "Philosophy, French—18th century" although an alphabetical arrangement would have reversed that order. It should be noted, however, that very broad periods for philosophy as a whole are filed in *alphabetical* sequence. Thus, "Philosophy, Ancient" precedes "Philosophy, Arab," and "Philosophy, Medieval" follows "Philosophy, Jewish."

It should also be noted that any formal list of subject headings will not include one very large category of subject entries—individual names as subjects. These may be personal (e.g., "James, William") or corporate (e.g., "American Philosophical Association"). In the case of very prominent or prolific writers, the entries may be further subdivided—e.g., "Dewey, John—Addresses, essays, lectures."

A subject heading system must make provision for the user who may choose as his initial search term a word or phrase other than the one used in the system. Usually this will be a synonym for the term chosen. The necessary connections are provided by means of *see* references, which direct the reader from headings not used to those that are used. In the list of LC subject headings provided in figure 3.3, the chosen terms are given in boldface type and other terms in lighter type. The cross-reference "Philosophy—Biography. *See* Philosophers" is given in light type. The heading "Philosophers" appears in boldface type. Under this heading in boldface type is the following entry in light type: "*x* Philosophy—Biography." The symbol "*x*" is used to indicate that a *see* reference has been made from "Philosophy—Biography" to "Philosophers."

A subject heading system also provides the user with access to other headings that might lead to relevant information. This is done by means of *see also* references. These may direct the user to other topics of equal breadth and scope, or they may direct him to more specific subjects. A good example of the latter type is the list of more than seventy-five specific *see also* references under "Philosophy." (The symbol "*sa*" preceding this list indicates that these are *see also* references.) It is customary to enumerate all of these specific headings, which will be found elsewhere in the catalog. Sometimes, a more generalized kind of *see also* reference is given after the full enumeration of specific *see also* references. An example of this type of heading from the philosophy list occurs under "Philosophy, Modern." After an enumeration of twelve specific *see also* references, this general *see also* reference is given: "Philosophy, English [French, German, etc.]."

The symbol "*xx*" is used to indicate the reverse pattern of *see also* references and is sometimes defined as *see also from*. Thus, under "Philosophy," there occurs "*xx* Cosmology." This means that there will be a cross-reference "Cosmology. *See also* Philosophy" in the catalog.

To remove doubt or confusion about what may or may not be covered by certain subject headings, scope notes are provided. These are relatively infrequent, usually noting limitations and sometimes referring to other entries. An example from the 1986 list may be found under "Philosophy, Ancient."

Comparison of the list reproduced in figure 3.3 with the subject catalog of a medium-sized or larger library will make it apparent that many more headings are used in practice than are enumerated in the list. Most of these headings are formed in accordance with the principles already discussed and can readily be anticipated by the searcher who understands these principles. Checking the *Library of Congress Catalogs: Subject Catalog* will reveal examples. It should be noted, however, that new terms are constantly coming into use and older terms are being revised or deleted. Even in a relatively stable field like philosophy half a dozen to a dozen changes will typically be reported in each new supplement to *Subject Headings Used in the Dictionary Catalogs of the Library of Congress.* One such change was the cancellation of the heading "Philosophy, Mohammedan" and the substitution of the more modern "Philosophy, Islamic."

Ease and precision in philosophic information retrieval will be greatly facilitated by understanding the filing system used in a particular library. The dictionary catalog or the subject portion of a divided catalog will normally follow an alphabetical arrangement, but a chronological arrangement is used wherever a division by date seems more logical than a strictly alphabetical sequence.

Alphabetical arrangements usually follow one of two patterns. The first is the "letter-by-letter" method used in many reference tools, including several indexes and encyclopedias. With this method, all the words in the heading are treated as parts of one unit. Filing proceeds strictly on the basis of the order of the letters in the unit as a whole, regardless of whether they are in separate short words or in a single long word. Thus, "Newark" would precede "New York." Libraries have not favored this method because it tends to scatter closely related topics. Instead, most libraries have adopted the "word by word" or "nothing before something" approach, in which each word is treated as a separate unit for filing purposes. Using this method, "New York" would precede "Newark" in the catalog. Within this general framework of "word by word" filing, the Library of Congress has developed the following sequence for subject headings:

1. Main heading alone

2. Main heading plus time subdivisions (if applicable) — indicated by dashes

3. Main heading plus form and subject subdivisions (interfiled alphabetically) — indicated by dashes

4. Main heading plus geographic subdivisions (if applicable) — also indicated by dashes

5. Inversions, indicated by commas

6. Phrases

As noted above, a chronological arrangement is used whenever a division by date seems more logical than a strictly alphabetical sequence. In philosophy, the practice is not altogether consistent. Broad periods, with definitely assignable names, are filed in alphabetical sequence with other inverted headings (e.g., "Philosophy, Ancient," "Philosophy, Medieval," and "Philosophy, Modern").

But the last-named is then subdivided chronologically (e.g., "Philosophy, Modern — 16th century," "Philosophy, Modern — 17th century," etc.). Period subdivisions are also used under the headings for philosophy in different countries (e.g., "Philosophy, French — 20th century").

COMPUTERS IN PHILOSOPHY

Discussion of the use of computers in philosophy is notably absent in the several reviews of computer applications in the arts and humanities. Raben and Burton, in "Information Systems and Services in the Arts and Humanities" (*ARIST*, v.16, 1981, pp. 247-66) list specific works on applications in literature and language, history, theater, musicology, and visual arts. Philosophy is not mentioned in this or in J. Raben and R. L. Widmann's "Information Systems Applications in the Humanities" (*ARIST*, v.7, 1972, pp. 439-69). The chapter "The Computer and the Humanities," in the second edition of this guide does not mention philosophy as a field of computer applications, either.

The lack of reports of computer applications to research in philosophy was obvious enough to evoke William Plank's "Metaphysical Implications in Computer-assisted Research in the Humanities: Where Are the Philosophers?" in *Sixth International Conference on Computers and the Humanities*, edited by Sarah K. Burton and Douglas D. Short (Computer Science Press, 1983, pp. 521-24).

Concordances and word indexes, which are the primary application of computers to literature, do hold promise for the analysis of philosophical works as well. The multivolume work which has been years in development and which covers the works of St. Thomas Aquinas, *Index Thomisticus*, is the subject of "The Annals of Humanities Computing: The Index Thomisticus" (*Computers and the Humanities* 14 [October 1980]: 83-90).

Computerized database searching has been introduced in philosophy with the availability of PHILOSOPHER'S INDEX (1940-present). Produced by the Philosophy Documentation Center at Bowling Green University, the database corresponds to the print index of the same title and is available through DIALOG. A Robert Rogers's article "A Comparison of Manual and Online Searches in the Preparation of Philosophy Pathfinders" (*Journal of Education for Library and Information Science* 26 [Summer 1985]: 54-55) suggests that online searching has not replaced manual searching in the field.

MAJOR SOCIETIES, INFORMATION CENTERS, AND SPECIAL COLLECTIONS IN PHILOSOPHY

It has become a truism to say that the competent reference librarian will employ information sources beyond the collections of one library. The role of bibliographies, indexes, and union catalogs (both online and printed) is already familiar and need not be elaborated here. What may be helpful, however, is some discussion of supplementary information sources. In philosophy, these may be grouped into three categories: philosophical societies, information centers, and special collections. In the following paragraphs, no attempt at completeness is made; rather, a sampling of major sources is offered, together with suggestions about where additional information may be found.

UNESCO has supported international philosophical activities in a variety of ways. In 1946, it recognized the International Council of Scientific Unions (The Hague) as a coordinating body. One of its branches is the International Union of the History and Philosophy of Science (Paris), which in turn has national committees in over two dozen countries and which maintains affiliations with both national and international organizations. Another organization which was recognized by UNESCO is the International Council for Philosophy and Humanistic Studies (1 Rue Miollers, F75732, Paris, France). This council is composed of many international nongovernmental organizations, such as the International Union of Academies (Brussels) and the International Federation of Societies of Philosophy (Brussels). The latter, comprising nearly 100 philosophical societies in more than thirty-five countries, sponsors international congresses every five years. UNESCO provides grants for the activities of some of these groups and for certain philosophical documentation centers.

Further details concerning international philosophical societies and leading groups outside North America may be found in the latest edition of the *International Directory of Philosophy and Philosophers* (Philosophy Documentation Center, Bowling Green, Ohio). Current information concerning philosophical congresses can be found in the "Chroniques" section of the *Revue philosophique de Louvain.*

The most comprehensive philosophical society in the United States is the American Philosophical Association, founded in 1900 to promote not only the exchange of ideas among philosophers but also creative and scholarly activity in philosophy. Membership is restricted to those qualified to teach philosophy at the college or university level, and national and regional groups elect officers and sponsor annual conferences. The Association publishes the *APA Bulletin, Proceedings and Addresses of the American Philosophical Society*, and *Jobs in Philosophy*, as well as several newsletters. The reader may learn more by writing to the Association (University of Delaware, Newark, DE 19716).

Phi Sigma Tau was founded in 1931 to promote ties between philosophy students and departments of philosophy. It publishes *Dialogue* and its *Newsletter* (Department of Philosophy, Marquette University, Milwaukee, WI 53233).

Another major organization is the American Catholic Philosophical Association, founded in 1926, with a membership of over 1,600. Its publications include *The New Scholasticism* and its *Proceedings* (The American Catholic Philosophical Association, The Catholic University of America, Washington, DC 20064).

There are also many specialized societies. Sometimes the interest centers about a particular philosopher (e.g., the International Hegel Association); sometimes, it is focused on a particular topic (like phenomenology or existential philosophy). Finally, state, local, and regional groups also exist. Details may be found on the specialized groups in the "Societies" section of the latest *Directory of American Philosophers.*

Information centers both in the United States and abroad are working in publication, indexing, and retrieval of information in philosophy. The Philosophy Documentation Center (Bowling Green State University, Bowling Green, OH 43404) exists to collect, store, and disseminate bibliographic data in philosophy. The Center publishes *The Philosopher's Index*, an index with abstracts, which is available in print and online.

The Philosophy Information Center (Philosophy Institute, University of Düsseldorf, Düsseldorf, West Germany) cooperates in the production of *The Philosopher's Index* by providing subject headings and abstracts of articles published in all German journals. The Center also makes use of a Siemens computer to produce its own series of bibliographies and indexes, such as *Gesamtregister zur Zeitschrift für Philosophische Forschung 1-21 (1946-1967)* and *Gesamtregister der Kant-Studien* (v.1, 1897-1925; v.2, 1926-1969).

Le Centre Nationale de la Recherche Scientifique, through its Centre de Documentation, Sciences Humaines (54, Boulevard Raspall, Paris VIe, France), lists or abstracts periodical articles in its *Bulletin signalétique—Section philosophie*, a quarterly publication with annual cumulative indexes. The director of this center also supervises the Cercle Internationale de Recherches Philosophiques par Ordinateur (CIRPHO), a new organization to promote philosophical research which arose out of the Montreal Congress (1971) of the Congrès des Sociétés de Philosophie de Langue Française.

Over twenty-five national centers participate in the work of L'Institut International de Philosophie (8, Rue Jean Calvin, F75005, Paris, France), which publishes a quarterly bulletin entitled *Bibliographie de la philosophie* with the aid of a grant from UNESCO and which cooperates with L'Institut Supérieure de Philosophie de l'Université Catholique de Louvain in publication of *Répertoire bibliographique de la philosophie*, which is also subsidized by UNESCO.

Although not concerned solely with philosophy, the Institute of East European Studies (University of Fribourg, Switzerland) is a major source of information on Marxist philosophy.

Another major source of such information is Zentralstelle für die philosophischen Information und Dokumentation (GRD-108 Berlin, Taubenstrasse 19/23), which tries to cover all Marxist philosophical literature in *Bibliographie Philosophie* (1967-).

More detailed coverage of philosophical research and publication projects (especially those making use of computers) is contained in "L'informatique au service de la philosophie; réalisations et projects," by Christian Wenin (*Revue philosophique de Louvain* 6 [May 1972]: 177-211).

Special collections in philosophy may attempt to cover the discipline as a whole, some period in the history of philosophy, some special topic, or the works of an individual philosopher:

- The House Library of Philosophy at the University of Southern California contains more than 40,000 volumes and covers virtually every period from medieval manuscripts to the latest contemporary publications. A catalog of this collection was published in 1968 by G. K. Hall.

- The Professor Don C. Allen Collection at the University of California, San Diego, concentrates on the Renaissance period.

- The General Library of the University of Michigan has a large collection dealing with Arabic philosophy.

- The Weston College Library (Massachusetts) attempts to be comprehensive in Catholic philosophy, while the Dominican College Library (Washington, DC) specializes in Thomist works and attempts to collect all works by Dominican authors.

- The Van Pelt Library of the University of Pennsylvania has a collection of nearly 3,000 manuscripts dating from the fifteenth to the nineteenth centuries and dealing mainly with Hindu philosophy, religion, and grammar.

- The Special Collections Department of the Columbia University Libraries and the Jewish Institute of Religion Library of Hebrew Union College (Cincinnati) have distinguished Spinoza collections.

- In 1968, McMaster University Library (Hamilton, ONT, Canada) acquired the papers of Bertrand Russell—more than 250,000 items. Information is disseminated in *Russell: The Journal of the Bertrand Russell Archives.*

NOTES

[1]Eugene Garfield, "Is Information Retrieval in the Arts and Humanities Inherently Different from That in Science ...?" *Library Quarterly* 50 (1980): 40-57.

4 PRINCIPAL INFORMATION SOURCES IN PHILOSOPHY

BIBLIOGRAPHIC GUIDES

General

18. The Philosopher's Guide to Sources, Research Tools, Professional Life, and Related Fields. Richard T. De George. Lawrence, Kans., Regents Press of Kansas, 1980. 261p.

A successor to De George's 1971 publication, the new guide has been reworked and expanded into a more comprehensive offering. In addition to the coverage of philosophy, there are two additional sections, one on general research tools in the related fields of religion, humanities, and fine arts, the other on mathematics, etc. Of course, the major emphasis is on philosophy tools: bibliographies, indexes, dictionaries, encyclopedias, standard histories, etc. These are treated in section 1. This section is divided into general works; sources for the history of philosophy with subdivisions by both period and individual philosopher; and branches, movements, and geographic regions of systematic philosophy. There are chapters on the serial literature and professional societies as well. Although the work must be considered an important contribution to the bibliography of philosophy, it does not provide annotations for all entries. Some of the existing annotations are relatively meager and have little value in determining the value of the item.

19. Philosophy: A Guide to the Reference Literature. Hans E. Bynagle. Littleton, Colo., Libraries Unlimited, 1986. 170p.

The emphasis here is on English-language works, and although it is less comprehensive than De George's work (see entry 18), Bynagle has made an important contribution. Especially useful is the emphasis given to description and evaluation of the reference literature. Lengthy annotations make it possible for the user to make an assessment of the content or utility of every item. Over 400 reference tools published up to mid-1985 are included, with separate entries. Separate chapters are given to both general and specialized sources in some cases, with bibliographies receiving especially careful attention through coverage in five chapters. There is a chapter on core journals and one on professional associations which should be helpful to the individual in locating additional information regarding topics or movements. Standard histories are not included. The guide represents an important source of information regarding reference material in the field due to its recency and scope.

20. **Philosophy: Its Nature, Methods and Basic Sources.** Sebastian A. Matczak. New York, Learned Publication, 1975. 280p.

Similar to De George's work (see entry 18) in terms of comprehensiveness with a liberal number of general as well as philosophical resources, and to Bynagle's work (see entry 19) with its emphasis on English-language resources, Matczak's book is intended to make the student aware of the basic tools for research and of the problems of philosophy when taken as a whole. Divided into five parts beginning with a section of brief exposition on the nature of philosophy, the coverage proceeds to general and specific bibliographies which include individual philosopher subdivisions. Part 3 covers the basic encyclopedias, dictionaries, and biographical sources. Part 4 enumerates the periodical literature, with its guides. The fifth segment identifies societies, academies, and associations as well as libraries. There is an index of names as well as a selective bibliography. Annotations are minimal.

21. **Research Guide in Philosophy.** Martin A. Bertman. Morristown, N.J., General Learning, 1974. 252p.

Developed for the undergraduate, this work has served a useful purpose since its appearance over a decade ago. With the passage of time, its utility diminishes with respect to the specifics regarding the evaluations of individual titles, many of which have been superseded. Important still, however, is the general treatment of research strategies. Such expositions as those on note taking, philosophical problems, documentation, and the use of a college library still may serve to alleviate some of the stress in adjusting to college life. Listings complete with symbols representing ratings for reference works, sources for study of the history of philosophy, and fields of philosophy are provided as well. A glossary of terms is also included.

22. **Research Guide to Philosophy.** Terrence N. Tice and Thomas P. Slavens. Chicago, American Library Association, 1983. 608p. (Sources of Information in the Humanities, No. 3).

This unique work is a guide from two professors at the University of Michigan. Tice is a philosopher and has contributed the major portion of the volume, consisting of thirty bibliographical essays under two categorical headings, "The History of Philosophy" and "Areas of Philosophy." The former includes thirteen chapters covering ancient to modern philosophy, with special emphasis on the nineteenth and twentieth centuries. Each chapter begins with a description of general trends with excellent bibliographies, followed by coverage of major philosophers with bibliographies.

The "areas" segment contains seventeen chapters developed along the same plan and covering both core and peripheral studies (epistemology and logic as well as philosophy of various disciplines). The essays are lucid and well developed and cover the monographic literature up to 1982, identifying over 4,000 publications. An author-title index is provided. The final section, by Slavens, a professor of library science (and general editor of the series) is a selective listing, with good annotations, of some fifty major reference books.

Periodicals

23. **Periodica Philosophica: Eine Internationale Bibliografie Philosophischer Zeitschriften von den Anfängen bis zur Gegenwart.** Wolfram Hogrebe, et al. Düsseldorf, West Germany, Philosophia Verlag, 1972. 728col.

A comprehensive international listing of 5,000 journals of philosophy from all periods, this remains a useful source of information for purposes of identification. Periodicals are listed by title and entries provide country and place of publication, publisher, frequency, dates of publication, and first issue numbers. Final issue numbers are provided in cases where the periodical is defunct. Special field of interest is denoted as well. Philosophy as a field of study is interpreted broadly, and many titles, such as those in general humanistic studies and psychology, represent a peripheral or migratory association with the field. Changes of title are recorded and access is provided through both a classified index and a country index.

24. **Philosophy Journals and Serials: An Analytical Guide.** Douglas H. Rubens, comp. Westport, Conn., Greenwood Press, 1987. 147p.

A thorough and well-designed guide to 335 journals and serials in the English language, this work should be of use to those who are seeking information regarding possible purchase or submission of manuscripts. Entries provide full annotations regarding publishers, prices, circulation, acceptance rates, target audiences, and coverage in abstracting and indexing services. There is commentary regarding the journal's point of view and some indication of strengths and weaknesses. Special features are also pointed out. An examination of the journals covered reveals a wide range of subject matter from the traditional studies of metaphysics to such specialties as learning and behavior and even psychic phenomena. Arrangement is alphabetical by title and access is provided through subject and geographical indexes.

BIBLIOGRAPHIES AND CATALOGS

General

25. **Bibliographia philosophica, 1934-1945.** G. A. de Brie. Bruxelles, Belgium, Editiones Spectrum, 1950-1954. 2v.

Long a standard in the field of philosophy bibliography, the passage of time continues to diminish the overall importance of this work's coverage, since it deals with a very brief, specific time period. The major purpose was to fill the gap in bibliographic control after the war because of the suspension of publication of one of the leading serial bibliographies, *Bibliographie de la philosophie* (see entry 43). The first volume covers the history of philosophy and is arranged chronologically, while the second volume employs a classified arrangement similar to the *Répertoire bibliographique de la philosophie* (see entry 49) in identifying publications dealing with philosophical doctrine. With the avowed purpose of listing all literature (books, reviews, and articles) in the major Western languages for the twelve-year period, the volumes provide access to over 48,000 entries through a name index.

26. **Bibliography of Philosophical Bibliographies.** Herbert Guerry, ed. Westport, Conn., Greenwood Press, 1977. 332p.

Divided into two parts, covering alphabetically both individual philosophers and subjects, this work lists over 2,300 philosophical bibliographies published during the period 1450 to 1974. It is international in scope, although the discussion of the work in the second edition of this guide (see pp. 33-34) rightly pointed out some of the problems in finding "Confucianism" since there is no cross-reference to "Chinese Philosophy." In most cases, the bibliographies were either published separately or in the journal literature with only a few major works that appeared as appendices to monographs or as parts of larger bibliographies. Most entries are not annotated and those annotations that exist generally are limited to an enumeration of the number of items. Due to its comprehensive nature and the relative scarcity of this type of work in the field, it must be considered an important publication. A name index refers to entry numbers.

27. **Bibliography of Philosophy, Psychology, and Cognate Subjects.** Benjamin Rand. New York, Macmillan, 1905; repr., New York, Peter Smith, 1949. 2v.

One of the landmark bibliographies in the field, this work was published as volume 3 of James Mark Baldwin's *Dictionary of Philosophy and Psychology*. It attempts to provide comprehensive coverage of the major books and periodical articles up to the time of its publication at the turn of the century. It was published in two parts, sometimes referred to as volumes, although this may confuse the fact that the work itself was considered a single volume of a larger publication. The first volume or part covers bibliography and the history of philosophy and includes individual philosophers listed alphabetically. The second part treats the topics of systematic philosophy, logic, aesthetics, ethics, etc., subdivided by both form and subject. Although criticized for omissions in coverage of philosophy of certain disciplines, the importance of this work is understood and it remains an important source of bibliographic information, especially for materials of the nineteenth century.

28. **Dissertations in Philosophy Accepted at American Universities, 1861-1975.** Thomas C. Bechtle and Mary F. Riley. New York, Garland, 1978. 537p.

An extensive author listing of over 7,500 dissertations accepted at 120 universities in the United States and Canada, this work is generally limited to those degrees earned in a department of philosophy and does not embrace the many peripheral efforts. There were cases, however, which were exceptions due to their major focus on philosophical concepts. There is a notable effort to include materials not represented in other bibliographical aids, especially the early dissertations prior to 1912. Entries contain author and title, university, date, and the *Dissertation Abstracts* (see entry 15) number when available. There is a fairly detailed subject index which employs both broad and specific terminology, but still has been criticized for certain omissions.

29. **Grundriss der Geschichte der Philosophie.** Friedrich Ueberweg. 11.-12. Aufl. Berlin, Mittler, 1923-1928; repr., Basel, Switzerland, Schwabe, 1951-1957, 1960- ; Darmstadt, West Germany, Wissenschaftliche Buchgesellschaft, 1967- . 5v.

An important history of philosophy, this work has received even more attention through the years for its rich bibliographic coverage. For this reason, it is considered a necessary tool for philosophical study and has often appeared in the bibliographic sections of literature guides (as it does here). The eleventh and twelfth editions were especially important in this regard and several reprintings have taken place over the years. The coverage represents ancient to modern philosophy. Bibliographies include both primary and secondary sources, both periodical and monographic, up to about 1920. It should be noted that the English translation of this work was completed in the nineteenth century from the fourth edition, and lacks the bibliographies. A new edition has begun to appear as *Völlig Neubearbite Ausgabe* (Basel, Switzerland, Schwabe, 1983- , in progress).

30. **Handbuch der Geschichte der Philosophie.** Wilhelm Totok. Frankfurt, West Germany, Klosterman, 1964 (v.1); 1974 (v.2); 1980 (v.3); 1982 (v.4, pt.1). (In progress).

Developed as a supplementary bibliography to the Ueberweg work (see entry 29), this work covers the literature of philosophy from 1920 to the time of publication of each of the volumes. It is a work of great magnitude and judged to be thorough in its coverage of the history of philosophy, beginning with ancient philosophy in volume 1. At present, the first part of volume 4, covering the seventeenth century, has been completed. It is international in its coverage of books. Bynagle warns of its forbidding nature through extensive use of abbreviations and its presentation of bibliographic listings in paragraph form. Nevertheless, it must be regarded as an extraordinary vehicle for bibliographic control, especially for writings in the Western languages. Author and subject indexes conclude each volume.

31. **The History of Ideas: A Bibliographical Introduction.** Jeremy L. Tobey. Santa Barbara, Calif., ABC-Clio, 1975-1977. 2v.

These two volumes present a series of well-developed and thoughtful bibliographic essays of importance to both the student and the specialist. Volume 1 covers classical antiquity and volume 2 embraces medieval and early modern Europe. Considered to be a useful resource in its treatment of "important research and reference tools and scholarly works on the history of ideas and its related fields," much of the coverage in both volumes is devoted to philosophy and aesthetics. The philosopher will find much of value also in the treatment given science and religion. There appears to be an emphasis on English-language resources identified in the bibliographic essays, and Tobey's ideas are expressed clearly. These are welcome since they give evidence of his depth of understanding of the issues and serve to clarify certain alternatives for the reader. There are an index of periodicals and an author-title index.

32. **A History of the Bibliography of Philosophy.** Michael Jasenas. New York, Georg Olms, 1973. 188p.

Informative essays describe bibliographies of philosophy published in Western languages between 1592 and 1960. Concentrating on bibliographies that cover the whole of philosophy, the content is divided into five major chapter headings or phases of bibliographic growth ("Renaissance," "Modern," "German Aukflärung," "Post-Kantian," and "Twentieth Century"). The essays are useful not only in describing the bibliographies themselves, but in providing insight into the historical influences regarding their production and development. In describing these influences, attention is given to major figures. Appendix 1 arranges the bibliographies both chronologically and alphabetically, thus providing a handy bibliography of bibliographies listing. A second such listing covers bibliographies not described in the text. Appendix 2 is a short-title list of major philosophical works. Concludes with a name index.

33. **Manuel de bibliographie philosophique.** Gilbert Varet. Paris, Presses Universitaires de France, 1956. 2v.

Another of the standard works in the field, this is a selective bibliography of approximately 20,000 books and articles published primarily from 1914 to 1934. This emphasis on World War I and the postwar era complements the coverage of de Brie's *Bibliographia philosophica* (see entry 25), completed just two years earlier. Volume 1 treats the subject historically, beginning with Oriental philosophy and moving forward to the present. There are subdivisions by period and by individual. Works in all languages are included. For prolific authors, the most important editions are mentioned. Volume 2 is concerned with the development of systematic thinking. One section covers philosophy of art, religion, and history; another, philosophy of the sciences; and a third, political philosophy, educational psychology, etc. There are many brief annotations. A general index of names is given at the end of volume 1.

34. **Philosophy and Psychology.** Harvard University Library. Cambridge, Mass., Harvard University Press, 1973. 2v. (Widener Library Shelflist, 42-43).

This is a listing of the materials in philosophy contained in the Widener Library of Harvard University. Nearly 59,000 items are documented, representing books, periodicals, and pamphlets concerned with the various branches of philosophy (metaphysics, cosmology, ontology, epistemology, logic, and aesthetics), as well as psychology proper. Divided into four parts, the work contains a classification schedule, a shelflist arrangement of all entries by call number, a chronological listing of date of publication of those same entries, and an author and title listing. The first three segments are contained in volume 1, while volume 2 is made up exclusively of the list of authors and titles. Although its utility diminishes with time, the work is still important because of the extensive collection of materials represented in this excellent research library.

35. **Sarva-Darsana-Sangraha: A Bibliographical Guide to the Global History of Philosophy.** John C. Plott and Paul D. Mays. Leiden, Netherlands, Brill, 1969. 305p.

Although this work is becoming dated, it remains the only annotated bibliography which includes a wide range of Eastern philosophies. Certain strategic errors are noted by Bynagle in his annotated bibliography (see entry 19) in fulfilling its purpose to promote the "globalization" of the history of philosophy through integration of Western and Eastern contributions. One such error is the usage of period labels such as "classical" or "medieval" to categorize Eastern as well as Western thought. In any case, the attempt to provide a remedy for the traditional omission of Eastern philosophy and philosophers in bibliographic control devices is worthwhile. Designed for the use of students at both the undergraduate and graduate levels, the guide represents a classified, annotated bibliography in which items of special importance are marked with asterisks. The appendices contain a syllabus outline of global history of philosophy as well as a synchronological chart to the study. A name index is provided.

36. **World Philosophy: Essay Reviews of 225 Major Works.** Frank N. Magill, ed.; Ian P. McGreal, assoc. ed. Englewood Cliffs, N.J., Salem Press, 1982. 5v.

This is an expansion of Magill's earlier *Masterpieces of World Philosophy in Summary Form* (Salem Press, 1961), in which 200 philosophical classics were summarized in a manner similar to other works by Magill. The new set retains the summaries or essay reviews of the earliest edition and adds twenty-five more, but with a new feature considered by the editors to be its major purpose: the inclusion of a section on pertinent literature which provides for each essay-review at least two critical commentaries. These critical studies are as detailed as the essay-reviews (600-1,000 words) and are significant features designed to make a useful work even more so. Following the critical commentaries are annotated lists of relevant secondary sources for additional reading. Since these listings contain only English-language materials, their utility for serious students is somewhat limited, but the work itself is meant to appeal to a wider audience than that offered by scholars. For laypersons and undergraduates, it is a most welcome effort.

Philosophy Books 1982-1986 Thomas May, ed
Bowling Green, OH   1991

Burr World Philosophy: A Contemporary
Bibliography

Specialized by Topic or Region*

37. **Bioethics: A Guide to Information Sources.** Doris Mueller Goldstein. Detroit, Gale, 1982. 366p.

The field of bioethics has become extremely active and important in the discipline of philosophy, so much so that a guide to the literature will have real value. The most important feature is an annotated bibliography of about 1,000 important documents based on the collection of the Bioethics Library at the Kennedy Institute where Goldstein is library director. This segment is part 3 of the guide and is organized under such topics as abortion, behavior control, and death and dying. Organizations, programs, and special collections are enumerated in part 1, while the second part considers general sources (periodicals, bibliographies, encyclopedias, etc.). Authors, titles, and subjects are combined in a single index for quick access.

38. **Death: A Bibliographical Guide.** Albert J. Miller and Michael James Acri. Metuchen, N.J., Scarecrow, 1977. 420p.

An example of a highly specialized topical bibliography taken from the field of bioethics is this annotated work by Miller and Acri. There are over 3,800 entries embracing a variety of forms (periodical articles, books, essays, miscellaneous works, and audiovisual materials). Death is treated from many angles and the literature represents such fields as medicine, law, psychology, sociology, and theology as well as philosophy. The work has been criticized by reviewers for certain omissions (a common failure of bibliographies in general) but also for inaccurate citations. Nevertheless, it must be commended for its attempt to provide such detailed coverage of the topic. English-language titles are emphasized and access is provided through subject as well as author and title indexes.

39. **Encyclopedia of Indian Philosophies: Bibliography.** Karl H. Potter. Rev. ed. Princeton, N.J., Princeton University Press, 1983. 1023p.

This is a revised and much expanded version of the 1970 publication originally published as the initial volume of *The Encyclopedia of Indian Philosophies* (Delhi, Banarsidass, 1970-). The earlier edition listed over 9,200 sources in an attempt to present the concepts of Indian philosophy and the contents of Indian philosophical texts to a wider public. The bibliography was the initial volume of the projected encyclopedia and helped establish its scope. The encyclopedia is still in progress and only two other volumes have been published. Meanwhile the revised edition of the bibliography has added over 4,000 items incorporating the supplementary lists published in the *Journal of Indian Philosophy* (Dordrecht, Holland, D. Reidel, 1970-), as well as new material. Three of the four main sections deal with Sanskrit texts, authorship, and dates, while section 4 presents secondary literature in Western languages. Several indexes (name, title, subject) provide access.

40. **Guide to Chinese Philosophy.** Charles Wei-Hsün Fu and Wing-tsit Chan. Boston, G. K. Hall, 1978. 262p.

This is an annotated bibliography mainly of English-language sources that would be useful to the student or nonspecialist. Naturally, the serious scholar would be interested in the original language texts rather than most of the material presented here. The guide is divided into sixteen sections, beginning with "History of Chinese Philosophy," which

---

*Numerous bibliographies are available on individual philosophers. These can be identified through the bibliographic guides.

Business Ethics and Responsibility. Bick.

covers the various schools in sequence from pre-Confucian to Marxism. Topics such as ethics and human nature are treated in the next twelve chapters, while the final three chapters concern analytical sources, comparative philosophy, and significant texts. There is an author and title index. Prepared as part of the Asian Philosophies and Religions Project of the Council for Intercultural Studies and Programs, this work supercedes Chan's *An Outline and an Annotated Bibliography of Chinese Philosophy* (Yale University Press, 1969).

41. **Marxist Philosophy: A Bibliographical Guide.** John Lachs. Chapel Hill, N.C., University of North Carolina Press, 1967. 166p.

A good example of a bibliography specialized to a philosophical school or movement, Lachs's work is still considered an excellent resource tool, since it has not been superseded. This is a scholarly effort with comprehensive coverage of both books and periodical articles in thirty-eight chapters. Full bibliographic description is given but no annotations are provided. Many texts translated from the Russian are included in the total of over 1,500 publications, primarily in English but with French and German items as well. Most chapters represent some aspect of Marxist-Leninist thought and all begin with a brief critical essay. There are chapters on journals of importance as well as reference works and bibliographies, and an author index. Soviet books and articles in philosophy are found in *Bibliographie der sowjetischen philosophie/Bibliography of Soviet Philosophy* (Dordrecht, Holland, D. Reidel, 1959-1968, 7v.). Writings on the subject of Soviet philosophy are represented in the bibliographies reported in *Studies in Soviet Thought* (Dordrecht, Holland, D. Reidel, 1961- , 8/yr.).

INDEXES, ABSTRACTS, AND
SERIAL BIBLIOGRAPHIES

42. **Bibliografia filosofica italiana.** 1949- . Ann. Firenze, Italy, Olschki. Publisher varies.

This is an annual bibliography of writings by Italian philosophers. There is a classified arrangement employing both historical periods and branches of philosophy. Originally published in Milan by Marzorati, since 1980 it has been produced in Florence by Olschki, it covers both periodical articles and monographs. There is a name index. The work is sponsored by the Centro di Studi Filosofici Christiani di Gallarate, which is responsible for the editing. Two retrospective bibliographies have since been published and should be used for a complete search, *Bibliografia filosofica italiana, 1850-1900* (Rome, ABETE, 1969) and *Filosofica italiana dal 1900 al 1950* (Rome, Ed. Delfino, 1950-1956. 4v.). These cover books and periodical articles arranged under philosophers' names, and are sponsored by the Instituto di Studi Filosofici with the collaboration of the Centro di Studi. Volume 4 of the latter work represents an annotated list of Italian philosophical journals, 1900-1955, and has been published separately.

43. **Bibliographie de la philosophie.** 1937-1958. Paris, Vrin.

A now defunct serial bibliography published under the auspices of the Institut International de Philosophie, this work provides listings without annotations of philosophical books and articles. A polylingual quarterly publication, it covered philosophy in an exhaustive manner, identifying both well-known and obscure publications. During the postwar period, it reviewed over 700 journals for relevant articles. It was suspended during the war years (mid-1939-1945), creating the need for the later publication of de Brie's

Bibliographia philosophica (see entry 25). Two major divisions of each issue were an alphabetical author listing and a systematic subject index. The latter included a chronological/geographical section; an index of philosophers who were the subjects of books and articles in the first part; and an index of concepts and terms, with books and periodical articles identified under each term. Coverage of periodical articles was dropped in a change of editorial policy. (See also entry 44.)

44. **Bibliographie de la philosophie/Bibliography of Philosophy.** 1954- . Q. Paris, Vrin.
    A dual-language title accompanied the change in editorial policy of this work (see entry 43). Published under the sponsorship of several international organizations including the Institut Internationale de Philosophie and the International Federation of Philosophical Societies, it receives aid from UNESCO and the French National Centre for Scientific Research. Now published as an abstract journal for books only, the abstracts appear in the language of the original work if in English, French, German, Italian, or Spanish. Abstracts of books written in other languages are provided either in English or French. There is a classified arrangement under ten broad divisions of philosophy. Indexes appear only in the final issue of each volume, in which access is provided through authors, titles, and keywords. An "Index of Names" is also given which gathers all publishers, translators, and individuals mentioned in titles and in abstracts.

*45. **Bibliography of Bioethics.** 1975- . Ann. Detroit, Gale. (Publisher varies).
    Presently sponsored by the Kennedy Institute of Ethics at Georgetown University, this annual bibliography has taken on added importance in the past few years owing to the publicity given questions of medical ethics and malpractice insurance rates. Abstracts have started to appear since the ninth volume (1983), but are limited to articles appearing in a few selected key journals in the field. The coverage includes a variety of forms—books, articles, audiovisual materials, court decisions, bills, and even unpublished documents— as it seeks to include everything in the English language on the topic. Three broad categories are employed—health care ethics, research ethics, and public policy guidelines. There are both author and title indexes as well as the major access vehicle, the subject index. Additional features are a thesaurus and a listing of bibliographic sources. Corresponding to this work is the computerized database *BIOETHICSLINE (Kennedy Institute of Ethics) which provides cumulative coverage online of the entire file from the beginning to the present. Presently not available through any commercial vendor, access is possible through searching of MEDLARS files. Direct searches are available to authorized individuals and organizations such as selected academic, medical, and special libraries.

*46. **Bulletin signalétique 519: Philosophie.** 1947- . Q. Ann. cum. Paris, Centre National de la Recherche Scientifique. ⇒ FRANCIS Bulletin signalétique
    Having undergone several name changes, the work continues to provide quarterly coverage of philosophy periodical literature from all over the world. It started out as *Bulletin analytique: Philosophie* (1947-1955), then became *Bulletin signalétique*, with a variety of subtitles until 1970, when the present title was adopted. It employs a classified arrangement to embrace articles from over 4,000 periodicals. Brief abstracts are given in French regardless of the language of the original article. Book reviews are cited and abstracts given, although books are not listed routinely. Separate author and subject indexes appear in each issue as does an index of journals covered. All three indexes cumulate annually. There is a corresponding database which is available through EasyNet gateway system. *FRANCIS: Philosophie (Centre de Documentation) is part of the ongoing indexing and abstracting program of the French Centre National de la Recherche Scientifique. Coverage of philosophy is available from 1972 to the present.

*47. The Philosopher's Index: An International Index to Philosophical Periodicals and Books. 1967- . Q. Ann. cum. Bowling Green, Ohio, Philosophy Documentation Center, Bowling Green State University.

Today considered the most important source for philosophers in the Anglo-American tradition, this work provides abstracts in English for articles from all major philosophy journals in English, French, German, Spanish, and Italian, with selective inclusion from journals in other languages. Originally limited to articles from British and American periodicals, the scope expanded as it matured, and books were added in 1980. Book material is limited to that in the English language only but includes monographs, translations, bibliographies, biographies, textbooks, dissertations, dictionaries, and anthologies. There are both subject and author listings for all entries, with the abstracts appearing in the author section. There is a separate index for book reviews. A corresponding database, *PHILOSOPHER'S INDEX, is updated on a quarterly basis and includes abstracts from the retrospective publications (see entry 48) as well. Book reviews are not included online. The service is available through DIALOG and EasyNet gateway system. There is an aid to the database written by Richard H. Lineback, entitled *The Philosopher's Index Thesaurus* (Philosophy Documentation Center, 1979) which should prove of some use to searchers.

*48. The Philosopher's Index: A Retrospective Index to U.S. Publications from 1940. Bowling Green, Ohio, Philosophy Documentation Center, Bowling Green State University, 1978. 3v.

Developed to expand the coverage of the ongoing current index which began in 1967, this retrospective effort covers the journal literature from 1940 to 1966 and books published from 1940 to 1976. (Books were not picked up in the current series until 1980, so a small gap still exists.) Total coverage is of some 15,000 articles and 6,000 books. Developed in the style of the current index (see entry 47), the first two volumes represent the subject index, while volume 3 contains the author listing with abstracts. A complementary work edited by Richard H. Lineback, **The Philosopher's Index: A Retrospective Index to Non-U.S. English Language Publications from 1940* (Philosophy Documentation Center, 1980, 3v.) follows a similar format and arrangement. It includes approximately 12,000 articles from some seventy periodicals published between 1940 and 1966, and some 5,000 books published between 1940 and 1978. Entries from both retrospective publications are available online.

49. Répertoire bibliographique de la philosophie. 1949- . Q. Louvain, Belgium, Institut Supérieur de Philosophie.

With the increasing work of the Philosophy Documentation Center (see entries 47 and 48) and the fuller development of the indexing and abstracting programs of the French Centre National de la Recherche Scientifique (see entry 46), the impact of the *Répertoire* has diminished. However, it must still be considered an important tool for bibliographic work in the field, since it covers a number of journals and books not found elsewhere. Books and periodical articles are covered in a single classified arrangement, with an attempt to provide an exhaustive bibliography of current writings in Catalan, Dutch, English, French, German, Italian, Latin, Portuguese, and Spanish. Writings in other languages may be included, but not with the same fidelity. No indexes appear until the November issue, which contains book reviews and a cumulated name index for authors, translators, reviewers, and philosophers mentioned in the titles of cited works. From 1934 to 1948, its predecessor appeared as an appendix to *Revue néo-scholastique de philosophie.* From 1939, it also appeared under the title *Bibliographische Repertorium* as a supplement of the Dutch *Tijdschrift voor Philosophie*. As such, it continued even during World War II, when *Revue néo-scholastique* was suspended. Since 1949, it has been an independent supplement to *Revue philosophique de Louvain*.

DICTIONARIES, ENCYCLOPEDIAS, AND HANDBOOKS

General

50. **A Dictionary of Philosophy.** 2nd ed. Anthony Flew, editorial consultant and Jennifer Speake, ed. New York, St. Martin's Press, 1984. 351p.
Considered by several reviewers to be the best dictionary in the field, it provides concise treatment of the subject. Good lucid definitions for the most part are easily understood by the layperson, although some articles tend to be more technical. Flew is a well-known British philosopher, now retired from the University of Reading, and it is unclear to what degree he took part in this revision. His name, however, establishes authority for the work, and Rogers found precious little change from the earlier edition in his *ARBA* 1985 review. The dictionary does include biographical articles on philosophers, which are brief but serve to identify the individuals cited. There is some coverage of Oriental philosophy, but the emphasis is definitely Anglo-American, with coverage of European subject matter second in importance.

51. **Dictionary of Philosophy.** Ivan Timofeevich Frolov, ed. New York, International Publishing, 1985. 464p.
This is an English translation of a standard Soviet dictionary and represents philosophy from the perspective of Marxism-Leninism. Non-Western philosophy and ancient philosophy are treated objectively, but modern thought and the various exponents are described in relation to the development of communism. Thus the definitions and identifications are sprinkled with a variety of labels such as "bourgeois." It is interesting to note that Stalin is not mentioned in the present edition, which reflects the present position of the Soviet state. The work is valuable, however, for its inclusion of many Russian philosophers who are unfamiliar to those with a Western orientation, and therefore should be regarded as a worthwhile addition to the collection.

52. **A Dictionary of Philosophy.** 2nd ed. Alan Robert Lacey. London, Routledge & Kegan Paul, 1986. 266p.
Designed for the layperson or student, this dictionary does an excellent job in describing the problems and questions of the discipline through its brief but informative definitions. The emphasis is on Anglo-American philosophy, particularly that which concerns epistemological or logical topics. It covers all periods, branches, and schools of ancient, medieval, and modern philosophy in Western thought, but unfortunately no coverage is given to Eastern philosophy. There are a number of entries for individual philosophers. It is regarded as being especially strong in bibliographies, some of which are extensive for a work of this size. These are provided for many of the entries and are extremely useful for the intended audience in suggesting related works. There are numerous cross-references as well.

53. **Dictionary of the History of Ideas: Studies of Selected Pivotal Ideas.** Philip P. Wiener, ed.-in-chief. New York, Scribner's, 1973-1974. 4v. plus index.

Considered to be a significant contribution to the reference literature of philosophy and related fields, this encyclopedic work contains over 300 lengthy articles, all signed, on a wide array of subjects in intellectual history. Distinguished scholars from various disciplines have served as contributors in order to "establish some sense of unity of human thought and its cultural manifestation in a world of ever-increasing specialization and alienation." Not restricted to philosophical material in its interdisciplinary, multicultural coverage, the work offers a rich body of information for philosophical inquiry. Broadly, the areas of coverage embrace the sciences and the external order of nature; anthropology, psychology, religion, and philosophy and human nature; literature and the arts; attitudes toward the historical sciences; economic, legal, and political institutions and ideologies; religious and philosophical ideas; and mathematics and logic. Bibliographies are included and the articles are arranged alphabetically. A separate index volume provides access.

54. **Enciclopedia filosofica.** 2nd ed. Sansoni, 1968-1969. 6v.

Prior to publication of *The Encyclopedia of Philosophy* (see entry 55), the earlier edition of this work in four volumes was the most comprehensive tool of its kind. Always considered to be a scholarly encyclopedia, it contains signed articles and good bibliographies. Arrangement is dictionary style with individuals, places, ideas, schools, movements, and other topical material in one alphabet. There is an emphasis on Continental European philosophy, the coverage of Italian thought and thinkers being especially strong, although the work is respected for its international coverage. Eastern philosophy is treated, but as one might expect, much less fully than Western thought. The volumes are arranged in columns rather than pages, and volume 6 has three major indexes (theoretical concepts, historical development, and terms and personal names for which entries do not appear but which received references in the text).

55. **The Encyclopedia of Philosophy.** Paul Edwards, ed.-in-chief. New York, Macmillan, 1967. 8v.; repr., 1972, 8v. in 4.

The compilers of this monumental set tried to cover the whole of philosophy (Eastern and Western) and its points of contact with other disciplines. The encyclopedia contains nearly 1,500 articles, some the length of small books and most with copious bibliographies. There are excellent articles on philosophical movements, major ideas, the philosophy of various subject fields, the history of philosophy in different countries, and biographies of major philosophers. Coverage of ancient, medieval, and early modern philosophers is generally good. Coverage of contemporary philosophers is better for Western Europe, North America, and India than for the Soviet bloc and the People's Republic of China. There are good articles on philosophical bibliographies, dictionaries, encyclopedias, and journals. The editor has tried to minimize editorial bias, but leans toward the Anglo-American tradition. Articles are long. The integrated approach has been preferred to a series of short articles. Smaller topics can be located by means of a detailed index in volume 8. More than 1,500 philosophers from all over the world contributed, and 150 scholars from the United States, Great Britain, and Europe served on the editorial board. This is likely to remain the definitive encyclopedia of philosophy for many years to come.

56. **Handbook of World Philosophy: Contemporary Developments since 1945.** John R. Burr, ed. Westport, Conn., Greenwood Press, 1980. 641p.

A collection of twenty-eight essays grouped by six regions (Western Europe, Australia, and Israel; Eastern Europe; the Americas; Africa and the Republic of South Africa; Islamic countries; and Asia), this work provides an international survey of philosophical directions, tendencies, and cross-currents since 1945. The essays describe the thoughts, work, and activities up to about 1977. Within the regions, there are many

Talking Philosophy: A Word Book - philosophical thesaurus. Sparks, A. W.

subdivisions by country and each essay/article is accompanied by a substantial bibliography. The work has been criticized for a certain unevenness of coverage; for example, "France receives twice as much space as any other country." This is a worthwhile tool since much of the coverage by country is not duplicated elsewhere, not even in the multivolume encyclopedias. There are both subject and name indexes, as well as a directory of philosophical associations and a list of congresses and meetings in the appendices.

57. **Historisches Wörterbuch der Philosophie.** Joachim Ritter, ed. Basel, Switzerland, Schwabe, 1971- . (In progress).

Over 700 scholars have contributed to this revision of Rudolf Eisler's *Wörterbuch der Philosophischen Begriffe* (Berlin, Mittler, 1910). Some subjects covered in the earlier work (e.g., psychology) have been dropped and new materials added. Other topics are revised and updated. The articles, ranging in length from a few sentences to several pages, treat the historical development of philosophical terms and concepts in a very scholarly manner. Documentation is abundant and up-to-date. An index and list of abbreviations is to be included in each volume. "It should be noted that articles on individual philosophers are not within the scope of this dictionary, although schools of thought based on the teachings of a single man are discussed (*College & Research Libraries* 33 [January 1972]: 42). At present there are five volumes completed (through Mn); volume 5 was published in 1980. Work has slowed perceptibly since Ritter's death in the mid 1970s.

58. **Vocabulaire technique et critique de la philosophie.** 15th ed. André Lalande, ed. Paris, Presses Universitaires de France, 1985. 1323p.

This is an old standard in the field, the first complete edition having been published in 1926. It has been consistent and predictable in its revisions and retains a position of importance as a reference tool. Prior to the first complete edition it appeared in twenty-one segments published in the *Bulletin de la Société Française de Philosophie* between 1902 and 1923. Definitions are good; additional coverage is given to examples of use by philosophers, along with etymologies and bibliographic notes. German, English, and Italian equivalents are provided as well. The emphasis is on clarification of terms and ideas; therefore there are no biographical entries.

Specialized by Topic or Region

59. **The Concise Encyclopedia of Western Philosophy and Philosophers.** 2nd ed. James O. Urmson, ed. London, Hutchinson, 1975. 319p.

Long a popular reference tool, this work was written for the intelligent layperson or nonspecialist. About fifty distinguished contributors participated in the effort, and Urmson has succeeded in putting together a useful source of information on Western philosophers and their contributions. In addition to the biographies, there is coverage of trends and, of course, definitions of terms. Articles are brief to moderate in length and favor the contributions and individuals associated with Anglo-American thought. (Indeed, the list of contributors shows a similar orientation.) Little attention is given to the highly technical problems, and philosophers who have not been translated into the English language have been deemphasized. No bibliographies are provided, which limits the volume's use to identification purposes. Portraits are given for the philosophers.

60. **Dictionary of Asian Philosophies.** St. Elmo Nauman, Jr. New York, Philosophical Library, 1978. 372p.

This work should provide a corrective to the bias toward Western philosophy found in most tools and in most library reference collections. "Asian philosophies" is interpreted to include the thinkers of the Middle East as well as the Far East, and the work covers philosophers, schools, texts, terms, and concepts. Entries vary considerably in length from one sentence to monographic proportions. A number of omissions have been pointed out by Bynagle in his annotated bibliography (see entry 19), such as the lack of a survey article on Islamic philosophy, even though such articles exist for Indian philosophy and for Jewish philosophy. One would have to agree with the judgment that the work is not as useful as it could be. It is also true, however, that there is no other one-volume work which is focused on Eastern philosophy in this manner.

61.   **Dictionary of Logic as Applied in the Study of Language: Concepts/Methods/ Theories.** Witold Marciszewski, ed. The Hague, Martinus Nijhoff, 1981. 436p.

International in coverage, the nature of this work is explained in the introduction. The phrase in the title "as applied to the study of language" is important for an understanding of its scope. Articles are lengthy, signed by the authors, and have both citations and bibliographies. There is a general bibliography at the end, as well as an index of symbols. Brief definitions of specific topics and references to the articles in which more extended discussion occurs will be found in the "Subject Index and Glossary." The general bibliography is international in scope, with a strong emphasis on mathematical logic. Individual articles make heavy use of mathematical formulae. Since there are precious few dictionaries devoted to logic, and none previously in English, this represents a useful source of information.

62.   **Dictionary of Marxist Thought.** Tom Bottomore, ed. Cambridge, Mass., Harvard University Press, 1983. 587p.

Considered to be an excellent and valuable work, this is a product of Anglo-American scholarship which examines the essence of contemporary Marxist thought in such areas as aesthetics, ethics, and theory of knowledge. It goes beyond Marxist philosophy in its analysis of the concepts involved. Excellent treatment is given such elements as alienation and dialectics. Philosophical schools and movements within Marxism are treated and individual philosophers are identified and discussed. Although criticized for uneven quality in the array of topics and subjects presented, it must be considered a valuable source for a non-Soviet perspective of Marxist thought. Due to the timeliness of the topic and the nature of the ongoing debates regarding Marxism, it is important to have a work of this type in the English language.

63.   **Encyclopedia of Bioethics.** Warren T. Reich, ed.-in-chief. New York, Free Press, 1978. 4v.

This is a comprehensive work on the important field of bioethics, treating the ethical and social issues of life sciences, medicine, health care, and the health professions. Philosophical perspectives are provided, among others, since the work is interdisciplinary in nature. Elements are included which embrace the study of history, theology, science, law, and the social sciences. For the philosopher, there is value not only in the specialized area of bioethics but in the excellent coverage given general ethical theory under "Ethics." The twelve articles in this segment can be used to supplement and update the coverage in *The Encyclopedia of Philosophy* (see entry 55). Entries are arranged alphabetically from "Abortion" to "Women and biomedicine," and in many cases are composed of several writings from different authors. There is an attempt to avoid technical language and to achieve a universal perspective, since fifteen countries are represented by the 285

Blackwell Companions to Philosophy Series

Encyclopedia of Ethics, Becker

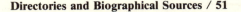

contributors. The work has a comprehensive index and cross-references are supplied. It would be useful to have a "supplement" to this work in order to see more recent views on the topics.

64. **Greek Philosophical Terms: A Historical Lexicon.** Francis Edward Peters. New York, New York University Press, 1967. 234p.

Designed for the intermediate student rather than the beginner or the specialist, this is a useful specialized dictionary for the study of Greek philosophers. Entries are arranged alphabetically in the main section according to English transliteration of the Greek terms, facilitating access and making the volume a convenient vehicle. It attempts to provide a source of study for those who wish to trace the development of philosophical language from its origins in the life of the Greek people. There is an emphasis (predictably) on terms taken from Plato and Aristotle, but both the early Greeks and the later schools are covered. An English-Greek index expedites the search considerably when trying to determine the Greek influences on an English term. Liberal cross-references to passages from Greek philosophy are used to aid in study.

DIRECTORIES AND
BIOGRAPHICAL SOURCES

65. **Directory of American Philosophers, 1986-87.** 13th ed. Archie J. Bahm, ed. Bowling Green, Ohio, Philosophy Documentation Center, Bowling Green State University, 1986. 414p.

The most recent edition of this biennial work basically continues the familiar format of the previous publications. The main part is composed of a directory of American college and university departments of philosophy arranged alphabetically by state, then by name. There is a listing of faculty members for each entry, along with the address and telephone number of the department. Canadian colleges and universities receive similar treatment in a separate listing and are arranged alphabetically by province, then name. Additional information is provided in separate sections on assistantships, societies, institutes, publishers, and journals in the field. Separate indexes provide ready access through names of philosophers (primarily the faculty members), institutions, publishers, journals, centers and institutes, and societies. The final section provides statistics on size of philosophy departments, number of philosophers, etc. A complementary source is *International Directory of Philosophy and Philosophers* (see entry 66).

66. **International Directory of Philosophy and Philosophers, 1986-89.** 6th ed. Ramona Cormier and Richard H. Lineback, eds. Bowling Green, Ohio, Philosophy Documentation Center, Bowling Green State University, 1986. 299p.

A companion and supplementary work to *Directory of American Philosophers* (see entry 65), this publication excludes the United States and Canada. A pattern has emerged in which a new edition appears every four years, an improvement over its earlier irregular frequency (1st ed., 1966; 2nd ed., 1972). Like its companion work, the format remains largely unchanged. Part 1 covers international organizations of philosophy, while part 2 remains the major contribution, listing college and university philosophy departments alphabetically by country or region and providing listings of faculty members. New entries in this edition include the Central African Republic, the People's Republic of China, Gabon, Panama, Qatar, and Togo. Part 3 contains the indexes, which permit access by name of philosopher, university, center, society, journal, or publisher.

67. **Philosophen-Lexikon: Handwörterbuch der Philosophie nach Personen.** Werner Ziegenfuss. Berlin, de Gruyter, 1949/1950. 2v.

A standard biographical dictionary in the field, this work covers philosophers of all countries from all periods of time. There is an emphasis on nineteenth- and twentieth-century individuals. For each entry, there are a biographical sketch, a critical and analytical commentary of the person's contribution or impact, a listing of the major publications (*Schriften*), and an index-listing of works (both monographs and articles) that evaluate his or her contributions (*Literature*). Known for its extensive bibliographies which in many cases make up the bulk of the entries, this work has stood the test of time. Despite a definite bias toward German philosophers (Kant gets thirty-four pages to Plato's ten), it must still be regarded as a useful source of information.

68. **Thinkers of the Twentieth Century: A Biographical, Bibliographical and Critical Dictionary.** Elizabeth Devine, et al., eds. Detroit, Gale, 1984. 643p.

An excellent biographical dictionary of recent years is this representation of 430 individuals who have been labeled "thinkers." About 100 of these are philosophers in the strict sense (Sartre, Buber, Wittgenstein, etc.), but many others were known for their philosophical impact (Gandhi, Durkheim, C. S. Lewis, etc.). Most of the thinkers were writers whose contributions influenced our times. There is a biographical sketch for each individual, accompanied by a listing of his or her books. Also, a list of biographies and a list of critical studies are included. An excellent feature is the interpretive essay of approximately 2,000 words, written by an informed contributor, which analyzes the individual's life and influence. The lack of a subject index is the main drawback to an otherwise extraordinary resource tool.

HISTORIES

69. **A History of Greek Philosophy.** William Keith Chambers Guthrie. Cambridge, Mass., Cambridge University Press, 1962-1981. 6v.

Since the appearance of the first volume in 1962, this work has been extolled by scholars for its erudition, technical accuracy, and insight, while at the same time remaining lucid and readable. Beginning with the pre-Socratics of early vintage in volume 1, it progresses to the later pre-Socratics in volume 2, and to the fifth century in volume 3. Plato is covered in his earlier period in volume 4, and his later period in volume 5. The final volume is devoted to Aristotle. The six volumes comprise a monumental contribution to the study of classical philosophy, even though Guthrie died before fulfilling his intention to provide a complete link to neo-Platonism. Each volume is thoroughly documented with references, and provides a strong bibliography and an index.

70. **The History of Philosophy.** Émile Bréhier. Trans. by Joseph Thomas and Wade Baskin. Chicago, University of Chicago Press, 1963-1969. 7v.

Originally published in France during the period 1926-1932, this work went through eight editions before it was translated into English. Through the years it has become a standard history, known for its clarity and comprehensive nature. The bibliographies for each chapter are selective and considered of high quality. Volume 1 covers the Hellenic Age; volume 2, the Hellenistic Age and Roman Age; volume 3, the Middle Ages and the Renaissance; volume 4, the seventeenth century; volume 5, the eighteenth century; volume 6, the nineteenth century, period of systems, 1800-1850; and volume 7, contemporary philosophy since 1850. The translation, mainly the work of Baskin, is highly readable and informative, and its presence will be appreciated in any philosophy collection.

71. **A History of Philosophy.** Frederick Charles Copleston. New York, Image Books, 1985. 9v. in 3.

Written from the standpoint of a scholastic philosopher (Father Copleston was a Jesuit priest and Professor of the History of Philosophy at Heythrop College, Oxford), this work has become a standard history of philosophy in the English language. Beginning with ancient times (Greece and Rome) the coverage progresses through the various schools of Western philosophy — Neoplatonism, Scholasticism, Rationalism, Empiricism, Romanticism, and Utilitarianism — using representative philosophers as labels for each of the volumes (e.g., volume 2, *Augustine to Scotus*). The ninth volume is the most recent and covers French philosophy through Existentialism and Sartre. Each volume was published with a good bibliography and index. The present edition employs a compact format which combines three volumes in one for the entire set.

72. **A History of Western Philosophy.** Bertrand Russell. New York, Simon & Schuster, 1945. 895p.

Originally developed as a series of lectures for presentation at the Barnes Foundation in Pennsylvania, the purpose of this work is to portray the philosophy of the West as an "integral part of social and political life." That Russell achieved this purpose was a point of question among reviewers at the time. Criticized for a superficial treatment of both history and philosophy and a highly opinionated style which gives short shrift to thinkers whose positions he found politically disagreeable, Russell's work is still regarded as one of the important popularizations. There is an emphasis on social, economic, and political conditions which reflect the author's progressive leanings. Coverage is given to all major philosophers and many minor ones. One of the most interesting works in the field from the standpoint of style.

73. **The Library of Living Philosophers.** Paul A. Schilpp, ed. Evanston, Ill., Northwestern University, 1939-1949 (vols. 1-7); Open Court, 1952- (v. 8-). (In progress).

Considered a major series in contemporary philosophy, each volume is devoted to a biobibliographical study of a single philosopher. The format of the series has remained constant, and one can generally expect the following sequence of information: a philosophical autobiography which emphasizes the philosophical position of the individual; a series of critical, expository essays on the philosopher by well-known scholars; and a reply by the philosopher. Bibliographies are provided. A slight departure occurred in the case of Sartre (v.16, 1981) whose failing eyesight did not permit him to read and respond to the essays. The format has worked well through the years in facilitating a discussion and airing of viewpoints of prominent philosophers. By early 1987, eighteen volumes had been completed, the most recent one being on W. V. Quine (1986). A second edition has appeared for Jaspers in 1981, and one for John Dewey in 1982. Reportedly, a study on von Wright is in the works.

Women Philosophers: The Biocritical Sourcebook

Durant. A Story of Philosophy

5 ACCESSING INFORMATION IN RELIGION

WORKING DEFINITION OF RELIGION

The word *religion* is thought to derive from the Latin *religare*, which means "to bind," thus offering an explanation of the general use of the term as a set of beliefs to which the follower is devoted or bound.

More broadly stated, the study of religion includes both the beliefs and behaviors that, according to John F. Wilson and Thomas P. Slavens, "express as a system the basic shape or texture of the culture or subculture under observation."[1] Lester Asheim suggested a more familiar definition: religion being "the study of man's beliefs and practices in relation to God, gods, or the supernatural."[2] Religion influences other disciplines of the humanities and social sciences as well. Every student will be able to identify religious influences and themes in art, music, literature, history, anthropology, law, sociology, and psychology.

There are several approaches to the study of religion: the historical approach, the social science approach, and the study of the spiritual/phenomenological aspects. A discussion of these approaches is found in John Macquarrie's article, "Religion," in *Academic American Encyclopedia* (1987 ed., v.16, pp. 137-41). The articles "Religion, Philosophy of," (v.26, pp. 538-47) and "Religion, The Study and Classification of," (v.26, pp. 548-69) in *Encyclopaedia Britannica: Macropaedia* (15th edition, revised 1985) offer perspectives on approaches to the study of religion.

MAJOR DIVISIONS OF THE FIELD

Religions are commonly classified as being predominantly sacramental, prophetic, or mystical. Sacramental religions place great emphasis on the observance of ritual and on the sacredness of certain objects. Eastern Orthodoxy and Roman Catholicism are familiar examples. Prophetic religions emphasize communication of the Divine Will in verbal form, often with a strong moralistic emphasis. Islam and Protestantism reflect this approach. Mystical religions stress direct encounter with God and view words, rituals, and sacred objects as auxiliary aids at best, or hindrances at worst, to that full communion which is seen as the ultimate goal of all religious striving. Certain branches of Hinduism and Buddhism are examples of this type.

The literature generated by the religions of the world may be conveniently analyzed under the following headings: 1) personal religion, 2) theology, 3) philosophy of religion, and 4) science of religion.

Personal religion is the primary and most direct source of religious writing. It is intimately related to the experiences of the individual and reflections about their significance. A major class of documents in this category would be the sacred scriptures of the world's great religions. Closely related to the sacred writings are those documents of explication and interpretation commonly known as commentaries. Finally, there is a much larger body of literature that does not have the same authoritative standing as the sacred scriptures and their commentaries. Works in this category may be devotional, autobiographical, or biographical. In this group also would be included a large number of popularizations.

Theology is an attempt to express in intellectually coherent form the principal doctrines of a religion. It is the product of reflection upon the primary sources of religion. It differs from philosophy in that the basic truth of the religious position is accepted, and attention is given to its systematic and thoughtful exposition. The field has many subdivisions. Within the Christian tradition, systematic (or topic-oriented) theology and biblical theology have been especially important, but there is also a substantial body of literature on moral, ascetic, mystical, symbolic, pastoral, philosophical, liturgical, and natural theology as well.

The philosophy of religion is an attempt to relate the religious experience to other spheres of experience. It differs from theology in that it makes fewer assumptions about the truth of a religious position, at least in the beginning. It differs from philosophy in its selection of religion as the area for speculative investigation. Perhaps it could best be described as a bridge between philosophy and theology.

The science of religion has also generated a substantial body of literature. Here, emphasis is placed on a comparative and historical approach, with no presuppositions about (and possibly no interest in) the truth or falsity of the religions being examined. Whereas the locus of interest in the first three categories is usually one of the world's living religions, this is not usually the case in the scientific study of religion, where a purely objective approach to the description and comparison of religious phenomena represents the ideal.

The student wishing to read about religion and its subfields will find helpful *Religion: A Humanistic Field*, by Clyde A. Holbrook (Prentice-Hall, 1963), *Religion*, edited by Paul Ramsey (Prentice-Hall, 1965), and *Religion in America*, by Winthrop S. Hudson (4th edition, Scribner's, 1987). (The first two titles are now out-of-print.) *The Study of Religion in Colleges and Universities*, edited by Paul Ramsey and John F. Wilson (Princeton University Press, 1970) is also useful, particularly for the academic librarian, student of religion, or teacher. For those interested in less than book length introductions, the chapter "Religion" in Asheim's *The Humanities and the Library* (American Library Association, 1956, pp. 1-60) is still excellent.

John F. Wilson and Thomas P. Slavens's *Research Guide to Religious Studies* (American Library Association, 1982) is another guide to the field. The first part consists of a survey of the literature of the field and the second part is a guide to the important literature and reference sources. The annotations are somewhat marginal and only titles published after 1977 are included. Another guide, this one featuring a more conservative viewpoint, is Cyril J. Barber's

Introduction to Theological Research (Moody Press, 1982).* This guide is intended for the beginning Bible student, and reflects Barber's background as an evangelical bibliographer. It includes sections on how to use a library.

The librarian may turn to numerous articles on religious material. Although older, Charles Harvey Arnold's bibliographical essay "Philosophy and Religion" (*Library Trends* 15 [January 1967]: 459-77) is still useful. "The Classification of Philosophy, Religion and the Occult," in D. W. Langridge's *Classification and Indexing in the Humanities* (Butterworths, 1976, pp. 59-77) will also be of interest. *Church and Synagogue Libraries*, edited by John F. Harvey (Scarecrow, 1980) addresses church and synagogue librarianship, while Joyce L. White's "Church and Synagogue Libraries: Resources for the Public Library" (*Library Journal* 109 [15 October 1984]: 1894-96] offers the public library perspective. G. Stein's "Collecting Freethought and Atheist Books" (*AB Bookman's Weekly* 77 [20 January 1986]: 205-6) and "Christian Books" (*Library Acquisitions* 9 [1985]: 297-98) stress acquisitions. College and university librarians will find P. Schlueter's "Building a Basic Collection in Religion and Literature: A Suggested Collection for Academic Libraries" (*Choice* 12 [February 1976]: 1533-36 +) helpful for selecting the basics; for the last decade, some updating will be required. A report of a study, entitled "Searching the Scriptures: A Citation Study in the Literature of Biblical Studies: Report and Commentary," by Maurine L. Gleason and James F. Deffenbaugh (*Collection Management* 6 [Fall/Winter 1984]: 107-17), suggests an approach to be used with other collection development tools. Parish libraries are addressed in "Current Concerns ..." (*Catholic Library World* 55 [May/June 1984]: 428-29), and in other issues of the same journal. Searching *Library Literature* for recent updates on religious literature and libraries will keep the librarian current.

USE AND USERS OF INFORMATION IN RELIGION

A search of the literature of librarianship reveals a distinct lack of user and use studies specifically devoted to the area of religion. It may be posited that this is the result of the many types of materials available and the multiple viewpoints and audiences addressed by religious materials. Users of historical studies, for instance, are unlikely to be users of the devotional and inspirational literatures; indeed, few library collections will include historical, devotional, informative, and the wide range of doctrinal-interpretive works. The difficulty of investigating uses of the literature through citation studies, a method useful in other fields of the humanities, is compounded by the fact that many uses do not result in publication and that there are probably many references made to scriptural works which are not formally cited. Uses of the literatures of subfields of religion and of particular collections can be studied via the citation method, and Gleason and Deffenbaugh (*Collection Management* 6 [Fall/Winter 1984]: 107-17) call for such studies in their paper "Searching the Scriptures ..."

Derek J. de Solla Price, in his "Citation Measures of Hard Science, Soft Science, Technology and Non-Science," in *Communication among Scientists and Engineers*, edited by C. E. Nelson and D. K. Pollock (Heath, 1970, pp. 3-22)

---

*This title and its comments were suggested by Peter Silvestro; his contribution is appreciated.

includes two religious journals among the humanities journals sampled for the age of references cited ("Price's Index"). Among the seventeen humanities journals, *Anglican Theological Review* and *Journal of American Academy of Religion* cited more references (twenty-four and twenty-five per article, respectively) and cited more current references (20 percent and 38 percent within the last five years) than the other journals indexed. While limited in scope as far as religious journals are concerned, the Price work suggests a method for further citation studies in religion. John W. Heussman's doctoral dissertation, "The Literature Cited in Theological Journals and Its Relation to Seminary Library Circulation" (University of Illinois, 1970) provides a broader view of the use of theological journals in a specific setting.

It is evident that the readership of religious material is large: Asheim reported that religion is among the largest subject areas in contemporary publishing.[3] Use and user studies, focusing on particular types of materials or individual collections, are needed in support of publishing and librarianship.

COMPUTERS IN RELIGION

The application of computer technology in the field of religion has largely addressed the problem of concordance and word index construction. Father Roberto Busa's concordance to the works of Thomas Aquinas, discussed in the chapter "Accessing Information in Philosophy," was the earliest attempt, and probably the most time-consuming since the project began in the 1940s and neared completion by the mid-1970s. Susan Hockey, in *A Guide to Computer Applications in the Humanities* (Johns Hopkins University Press, 1980, p. 15) refers to a similar early application in the form of a word index to the Gothic Bible published in 1976. D. M. Burton has written extensively on the topic of concordancing in *Computers and the Humanities* (various issues).

It appears that while the primary use of computers in religion is presently concordancing, the computer is also being used in information retrieval in the field. *Religion Index*, produced by the American Theological Library Association, is available online through DIALOG (File 190) and BRS (RELI). Updated biannually, RELIGION INDEX in its online format enables the user to access abstracts and bibliographic data on the journal literature, book reviews, and multiauthor works in religion. Nonbibliographic databases in religion include CHURCHNEWS INTERNATIONAL and UNITED METHODIST INFORMATION.

Finally, as with other collections, computerized cataloging and publishing touches religious collections. "The Mt. Angel Abbey Rare Book and Manuscript Project Revisited: A Case Study in Automated Cataloguing and Publishing" by Lawrence J. McCrank and Jay Elvove in *Sixth International Conference on Computers and the Humanities* (Computer Science Press, 1983, pp. 415-30) describes one such project in detail.

MAJOR RELIGIOUS ORGANIZATIONS, INFORMATION CENTERS, AND SPECIAL COLLECTIONS

Religious organizations are major sources of information. These may be denominational, ecumenical, or academic. The number of denominational organizations (especially in the United States) is immense. Certain useful generalizations can be made about the larger religious groups. Generally, they maintain national offices and have extensive publishing programs. Much of their publishing is designed to serve the needs of local congregations for devotional and educational materials; but a number of denominations maintain research staffs at the national level, and nearly all of them gather such basic statistics as size of church membership and Sunday school attendance. Most also issue a variety of directories as well as reports of national, regional, or state conferences and other activities. Most support theological seminaries, and some have parochial schools and colleges as well. Many maintain collections of historical and other materials pertaining to the denomination. Some are active in promoting church libraries among their local congregations. Although the Lutherans, Southern Baptists, and United Methodists have such organizations, the Catholic Library Association (461 West Lancaster Ave., Haverford, PA 19041) probably has the widest range of activities, including publication of *Catholic Library World* and *Catholic Periodical and Literature Index.*

Ecumenical cooperation is exemplified by the work of the National Council of Churches of Christ in the U.S.A. (475 Riverside Dr., New York, NY 10115), which includes publication of the *Yearbook of American and Canadian Churches,* and by the activities of the Church and Synagogue Library Association (P.O. Box 1130, Bryn Mawr, PA 19010), which publishes *Church and Synagogue Libraries.*

The oldest of the academic organizations in this country is the Association for the Sociology of Religion (Sociology Department, Washington and Jefferson College, Washington, PA 15301), which was founded prior to World War II and which publishes a quarterly journal entitled *Sociological Analysis.* The largest of the academic groups is the Society for the Scientific Study of Religion (Box 68A, University of Connecticut, Storrs, CT 06268), which publishes the *Journal for the Scientific Study of Religion.* At the same address is the smaller and more recent Religious Research Association, which publishes *Review of Religious Research.* The role of special congresses should not be overlooked.

In response to a need for greater coordination of research and improved dissemination of religious information, an organization known as the Association for the Development of Religious Information Systems (ADRIS) came into existence. They published the *International Directory of Religious Information Systems* in 1971, and continue to publish the quarterly *ADRIS Newsletter* (Marquette University Department of Social and Cultural Sciences, 526 N. 14th St., Milwaukee, WI 53233). In Europe, the source of coordination is the International Federation of Institutes for Social and Socio-Religious Research (Louvain, Belgium).

Only a few of the major information centers can be mentioned. The Office of Research, Evaluation and Planning of the National Council of Churches is noteworthy for its extensive research efforts and its computerized inventory of more than 2,000 documents in the H. Paul Douglass Collection of research reports. The American Theological Library Association (St. Meinrad School of Theology, Archabbey Library, St. Meinrad, IN 47577) publishes *Religion Index One* and *Religion Index Two*, monographs, bibliographies, and a newsletter. A major Catholic research effort is conducted by the Center for Applied Research in the Apostolate (3700 Oakview Terrace, Washington, DC 20017). The Centre Protestant d'Etudes et de Documentation (8, Villa du Parc Montsouris, Paris 14e, France) publishes a bulletin and cooperates closely with a similar research center in Strasbourg. IDOC/North America (145 E. 49th St., New York, NY 10017) is part of an international religious documentation network that operates in over thirty countries.

The number of special collections in the field of religion is immense. The best starting point for a search is under "Religion" in *Subject Collections*, by Lee Ash (6th edition, R. R. Bowker, 1985). Related headings cited by Ash and the names of individual religions (e.g., "Buddha and Buddhism"), denominations (e.g., "Baptists") and religious leaders (e.g., "Wesley, John") will prove fruitful for more specialized inquiries. G. K. Hall & Co. have published catalogs of some of the more outstanding collections, such as the American Jewish Archives (Cincinnati), the Klau Library of Hebrew Union College — Jewish Institute of Religion (Cincinnati), the Pontifical Institute of Medieval Studies (Toronto), Union Theological Seminary (New York), Dr. Williams' Library (London), and Institut des Études Augustiniennes (Paris).

Thomas P. Slavens's *Theological Libraries at Oxford* (Saur, 1984) will also be of interest to the student of special collections and religious libraries.

NOTES

[1]John F. Wilson and Thomas P. Slavens, *Research Guide to Religious Studies* (Chicago: American Library Association, 1982), p. 4.

[2]Lester Asheim, *The Humanities and the Library* (Chicago: American Library Association, 1956), p. 2.

[3]Ibid., p. 5.

6 PRINCIPAL INFORMATION SOURCES IN RELIGION, MYTHOLOGY, AND FOLKLORE

BIBLIOGRAPHIC GUIDES AND INTRODUCTORY WORKS

General

74. **Church and State in America: A Bibliographical Guide. The Colonial and Early National Periods.** John F. Wilson, ed. New York, Greenwood Press, 1986. 436p.

This is a collection of eleven bibliographical essays prepared by young scholars in the field. Following each essay is a bibliography of recent writings (the past twenty-five years), although some of the very important older studies are also included. Wilson provides an exposition of the work in the introduction, in which he describes his preference for the listing of references which are broadly based rather than narrow in scope and are critical rather than prescriptive in tone. This work is a product of the Project on the Church-State Issue in American Culture at Princeton University, where Wilson occupies an endowed chair. It represents an important attempt to enumerate those books and articles of comparative and historical nature that examine the early relationships between religious and political interests in our country. There is an author-subject index.

75. **Library Research Guide to Religion and Theology: Illustrated Search Strategy and Sources.** 2nd ed. rev. James R. Kennedy, Jr. Ann Arbor, Mich., Pierian, 1984. 59p. (Library Research Guides Series, No. 1).

Since the appearance of the first edition in 1974, this compact little volume has become recognized as an important aid to students in conducting their library research. As the reference librarian at Earlham College (noted for its heavy involvement in bibliographic instruction), Kennedy has produced literature guides which are useful and informative. In this most recent edition of the work on religion, he has continued his coverage of the aspects which have proved to be of interest, such as the choice and refinement of term paper topics. His "Library Knowledge Test" is still featured in order to help the user determine his or her ability. Most important of course is the information provided on the various tools and resources (bibliographic sources, commentaries, dictionaries, etc.) as well as databases which have come into the field. Sample questions are provided and a title index is included.

76. **A Reader's Guide to the Great Religions.** Rev. ed. Charles J. Adams, ed. New York, Free Press, 1977. 512p.

Considered one of the most useful guides and one of the most authoritative works in the field, this collection of thirteen bibliographical essays covers the history and traditions of the world's major religions. Each chapter is written by a specialist and includes a brief introduction followed by authoritative evaluation of many of the cited works. Topical coverage is given to primitive religion, the ancient world, Mexico, Central and South America, Hinduism, Buddhism, Sikhs, Jainas, China, Japan, Judaism, Christianity, and Islam. The appendix contains an essay entitled "The History of the History of Religions." The work represents a substantial enlargement of the earlier edition and must be considered a leading tool in the field. There are both author and subject indexes.

77. **Reference Works for Theological Research: An Annotated Selective Bibliographical Guide.** 2nd ed. Robert J. Kepple. Lanham, Md., University Press of America, 1981. 283p.

Developed originally as a textbook for students of his course on theological research methods, the author's second edition represents an enlargement and expansion of the earlier offering. In the first section of this enlightening aid, works are grouped by type and coverage is given to general reference works, and to specialized encyclopedias, handbooks, directories, bibliographies, etc., as well as government publications and aids in writing and publishing. The second section presents a topical approach and covers reference literature for research on subjects such as practical theology and worship and liturgy. The scope is limited for the most part to the Christian religion, with only brief coverage of Catholic materials because they are covered by McCabe's *Critical Guide to Catholic Reference Books* (see entry 92). Nevertheless, it is extremely useful for the number of reference items listed. There is an author and title index. Supplements have appeared in 1982, 1983, and 1986, with a new edition in the offing.

78. **Religions of the World.** Niels C. Nielsen, et al. New York, St. Martin's Press, 1983. 688p.

Another of the excellent resources to the religions of the world is this eight-part handbook. Each part is compiled by an eminent scholar in the field. Designed for students as an introductory tool, it should prove to be a useful resource for those with an advanced interest as well. The first of the eight sections explores the basic questions and concepts which all religions share and also treats the important extinct religions of the past (Middle East, Greece, and Rome). The remaining parts are given to the major living religions; Hinduism; Buddhism; Chinese and Japanese religions; Jainism; Zoroastrianism, and Sikhism; Judaism; Christianity; and Islam. There are many illustrations and the work provides a balanced treatment of the various faiths. Bibliographical notes for each chapter as well as an annotated bibliography are included at the end.

79. **Research Guide to Religious Studies.** John F. Wilson and Thomas P. Slavens. Chicago, American Library Association, 1982. 192p. (Sources of Information in the Humanities, no. 1).

The first in a series of study guides to various disciplines within the humanities in which Slavens serves as general editor and co-author with a noted authority in the field, the intent is to help librarians, students, and other interested persons to use the resources. Wilson, a noted scholar and professor of religious studies at Princeton University, contributed the major part of the work, part 1, "Introduction to Religious Scholarship." His contribution is a group of bibliographic essays in which the field is surveyed and the important sources identified. The second part, by Slavens, a professor of library science at the University of Michigan, is a fifty-page annotated listing of important reference sources.

The annotations are detailed although the listings are somewhat dated. More breadth is found in Kepple (see entry 77), who provides more tools but less information about each one. The guide is useful for the intended audience, and the essays serve to enlighten the reader about the state of the literature.

80. **Theological and Religious Reference Materials.** G. E. Gorman and Lyn Gorman. New York, Greenwood Press, 1984-1986. 3v. (In progress, projected 4v.). (Bibliographies and Indexes in Religious Studies).

The objective of this series of guides is to introduce students to the complete range of reference sources likely to be encountered in a program of religious studies. At present, three of the projected four volumes have been published, which when completed will approximate the generally accepted divisions of theology. Volume 1 represents general theology; volume 2 establishes coverage of doctrine; and volume 3 embraces practical theology. The final volume, still in progress, will deal with comparative theology, and will also cover non-Christian religions. Each volume is meant to be used separately and provides several thousand annotated entries on the subject matter, along with excellent introductory material regarding the nature of the topic. Each volume is indexed separately by author, title, and broad subject.

Periodicals

81. **A Guide to Indexed Periodicals in Religion.** John J. Regazzi and Theodore C. Hines. Metuchen, N.J., Scarecrow, 1975. 314p.

One of the well-known guides in the field, this work provides coverage of some 2,700 periodical titles indexed or abstracted by seventeen different services. The services are limited to those which specialize in religion and do not include those general indexes which may cover religion as part of a broader scheme. The indexes are listed initially together with their abbreviations. This is followed by an alphabetical listing of all periodical titles and an indication of which services cover them. There is an inverted title list by keywords from the titles with similar information given, and finally, a listing by services of the periodicals they include. Still regarded as a useful tool although the passage of time decreases its efficiency and value.

82. **Religious Bibliographies in Serial Literature: A Guide.** Michael J. Walsh, comp. Association of British Theological and Philosophical Libraries. Westport, Conn., Greenwood Press, 1981. 216p.

A useful and practical listing, this particular work targets the serial literature in terms of its ability to provide bibliographic coverage. There is a listing of 178 titles most of which are indexes or journals with regular or major bibliographic sections or segments. The descriptions are detailed and provide awareness of content, and analysis of completeness, availability, and general utility. Arrangement is also described. Scope is broad and includes most serials in the Western languages, and certain peripheral titles although they may not deal primarily with religion. There are subject and title indexes to provide ready access. Although the work exhibits a slight bias toward European serials, it represents an important contribution to the literature.

83. **Religious Periodicals Directory.** Graham Cornish, ed. Santa Barbara, Calif., ABC-Clio, 1986. 330p. (Clio Periodicals Directories).

Religion is interpreted in a broad manner for purposes of inclusion in this directory, and it embraces periodical titles from a variety of related fields (history, anthropology, art, literature, etc.). The scope is international and includes periodicals from a range of denominations and sects. Periodicals are arranged alphabetically under one of six geographic regions: Canada and the United States; Latin America; Europe; Africa; the Middle East; and Asia and the Pacific Region. Countries are listed alphabetically within the regions, and entries include title, publisher, language, frequency, and years of publication. Coverage by indexing and abstracting services is also indicated. There are both title and subject-geographic indexes. Over 1,700 periodicals are covered.

84. **Religious Periodicals of the United States: Academic and Scholarly Journals.** Charles H. Lippy, ed. Westport, Conn., Greenwood Press, 1986. 607p. (Historical Guides to the World's Periodicals and Newspapers).

This is a highly selective but useful guide for those who would seek to identify scholarly and academically oriented journals in the field of religion and religious studies. It is the only guide of its type to provide a complete focus on journals published in this country. It is likely to be the only one to treat the topic in such detail. Slightly more than 100 journals are covered. Each entry is described in terms of its subject matter, publishing history, and extraordinary features. Indexing services are identified. Information regarding title changes, volumes, publication, circulation, and editors are included. Appendices provide material of interest such as a chronology of the periodicals covered and a listing of denomination. A comprehensive index by titles and authors concludes the work.

BIBLIOGRAPHIES AND CATALOGS

General

85. **A Bibliography of Bibliographies in Religion.** John Graves Barrow. Ann Arbor, Mich., Edwards, 1955; repr. 1969. 489p.

A standard work, although old, this volume represents an important attempt to identify all separately published bibliographies in religion. Based on the author's doctoral dissertation at Yale in 1930, it is arranged by broad subject, then by dates of publication. The emphasis is on Christianity, but it does include a section on non-Christian religions along with church history, the Bible, and the Reformation. There is also a section on important individuals. Bibliographies date from the fifteenth century and each one has been inspected by the author. Each entry provides title, publishing information, size, pagination, library location where found, and brief annotation. There is a name index to provide access.

86. **A Critical Bibliography of Religion in America.** Nelson R. Burr. Princeton, N.J., Princeton University Press, 1961. 2v.

Although getting on in years, this work remains important in the field because it provides an excellent bibliographic commentary on the history of religion in the United States. Published as volume 4 (in two volumes) of *Religion in American Life* by James Ward Smith and A. Leland Jamison, the bibliography is often listed separately and is the most important contribution of the set. The bibliography is comprehensive and provides the best coverage of the topic to date, with the inclusion of both primary and secondary sources. It begins with a general introductory section on bibliographic guides, followed by sections covering the evolutionary development of American religion, religion and society, religion in the arts and literature, and intellectual history and theology. Christianity receives the most emphasis, reflecting its prominent position in this country, but other religions are not overlooked. Author and title indexes provide access. Coverage is continued through *American Religion and Philosophy: A Guide to Information Sources* by Ernest Robert Sandeen and Frederick Hale (Gale, 1978). This is a general survey of recent secondary and key primary sources which have appeared subsequent to Burr.

87. **Psychology and Theology in Western Thought, 1672-1965: A Historical and Annotated Bibliography.** Hendrika Vande Kempe and H. Newton Maloney. Millwood, N.Y., Kraus, 1984. 367p. (Bibliographies in the History of Psychology and Psychiatry).

A strong bibliographic coverage of less accessible sources over a period of 300 years makes this an excellent resource for both the student and the scholar. This work describes itself as complementary to other major bibliographies, and it is limited to those publications reflecting the Western or Judeo-Christian perspective. It represents a successful attempt to provide a historical bibliography on the relationship between psychology and theology. There are over 1,000 entries identifying book-length publications (monographs and pamphlets, but not periodical articles) arranged chronologically under various categories. Annotations describe the relevance of the work. The work is well indexed and access is possible through name, institution, title, and subject. A supplementary effort is *Psychology of Religion: A Guide to Information Sources*, by Donald Capps, et al. (Gale, 1976); this is a classified, partially annotated bibliography of 5,000 books and articles published after 1950, with special emphasis on the years 1960-1974.

88. **Religious Books, 1876-1982.** New York, R. R. Bowker, 1983. 4v.

This massive bibliography of 130,000 entries provides a listing of more than 100 years of religious titles published and distributed in this country. Organized by LC subject heading, this tool draws on the database of the *American Book Publishing Record*, which contains all U.S. monographs from the *National Union Catalog* and MARC tapes in addition to those cataloged by Bowker. Aside from the core religious subjects (Bible, church history, denominations, etc.), it includes peripheral topics such as astrology, magic, and psychology. The first three volumes employ a subject approach through LC subject headings, while volume 4 provides author and title access. The work has been criticized for errors in certain subject headings, inclusion of questionable peripheral subject areas, and the inclusion of only first authors in the author index.

Christian

89. **Alphabetical Arrangement of Main Entries from the Shelf List.** Union Theological Seminary. Library. Boston, G. K. Hall, 1960; repr. 1965. 10v.

The Union Theological Seminary is known to have one of the outstanding collections of religious literature in the country. Although the content of the collection is not limited to works of the Christian faith, its denominational tie and its clear emphasis on those works which provide insight into the history, influence, doctrine, and philosophical character of Christianity justify its inclusion in this section. One of the most useful multivolume sets of the holdings of this library is the shelflist rearranged by main entry, which provides ready access by author and in some cases by title. Subject access is possible through use of another ten-volume set, *The Shelf List of the Union Theological Seminary Library in New York City, In Classification Order* (G. K. Hall, 1960). The *Alphabetical Arrangement* omits holdings from the McAlpin Collection of British History and Theology because there is a separate publication of the catalog of this special collection.

90. **Bibliography of Published Articles on American Presbyterianism, 1901-1980.** Harold M. Parker, Jr. Westport, Conn., Greenwood Press, 1985. 261p. (Bibliographies and Indexes in Religious Studies, No. 4).

Students and scholars of American Protestantism will find this recent work to be of great value in revealing the development of Presbyterianism in this country through a variety of published articles. The work includes but does not limit itself to national and regional secular reviews of a historical nature. Church reviews are also used, but house organs of churches are excluded. The author has compiled an excellent bibliography of nearly 3,000 articles, some of which would most assuredly be overlooked due to their nondescriptive or misleading titles or their surprising presence in certain journals. Entries are arranged by author, and indexed by topic. Library locations are indicated since much of the material will be difficult to obtain.

91. **A Bibliography of the Catholic Church, Representing Holdings of American Libraries Reported to the National Union Catalog in the Library of Congress.** London, Mansell, 1970. 572p.

Taken from volumes 99-100 of the *National Union Catalog, Pre-1956 Imprints*, this work includes 16,000 main and added entries with organizational and form headings used for the Catholic Church. Although out-of-print at present, it has lasting value for those libraries who have purchased it, and it represents a handy and convenient access tool for publications of administrative, legislative, and judicial organs of the Church. There is an extremely large listing of the official liturgical literature, with about 10,000 entries listed under the category "Liturgy and Ritual." Included here are hundreds of different editions of the Roman Missal, Books of Hours, and various manuals. It remains an excellent example of specialized bibliography by denomination. (See also listings in Sheehy [entry 2] under separate denominations.)

92. **Critical Guide to Catholic Reference Books.** 2nd ed. James Patrick McCabe. Littleton, Colo., Libraries Unlimited, 1980. 282p. (Research Studies in Library Science, No. 2).

The first edition of this book appeared in 1971, and was considered a meritorious effort in its task of evaluating 900 reference works that dealt with Catholic subjects or provided a Catholic perspective. The new edition has been updated and expanded to over 1,100 entries. It retains its basic format of five major chapters dealing with general reference works, theology, the humanities, the social sciences, and history. The main emphasis is on English-language titles, although foreign-language works are identified if well known, comprehensive in coverage, and scholarly, or if there is no English-language equivalent. Annotations are well developed and access is provided through a comprehensive author, title, and subject index.

93. **The Howard University Bibliography of African and Afro-American Religious Studies, with Locations in American Libraries.** Ethel L. Williams and Clifton F. Brown. Wilmington, Del., Scholarly Resources, 1977. 525p.

A revision and expansion of an earlier work by the same authors, this is a classified bibliography of 13,000 books, periodical articles, and parts of books. They are identified by library location, and include both primary and secondary sources from over 230 libraries and archives. Works are arranged alphabetically by author under one of the following categories: "African Heritage," "Christianity and Slavery in the New World," "The Black Man and His Religious Life in the Americas," "Civil Rights Movement," and the "Contemporary Religious Scene." Although it might be misleading to place this tool under the category of "Christian" bibliography, the majority of the publications represent that perspective. Annotations are provided in some cases to clarify ambiguous titles. Indexed by author.

Non-Christian

94. **Bibliography of New Religious Movements in Primal Societies.** Harold W. Turner. Boston, G. K. Hall, 1977-1978. 2v. (In progress).

Planned as a series of four volumes, only volume 1, *Black Africa* and volume 2, *North America*, have appeared to date. Still to come are volumes on Latin America and the Caribbean, and on Asia (including Oceania). The focus of the total effort is to represent those religious movements "which arise in the interaction of a primal society with another society where there is great disparity of power or sophistication." The volume *Black Africa* was designed to correct, supplement, and update *A Comprehensive Bibliography of Modern African Religious Movements*, by Turner and Robert Cameron Mitchell (Northwestern University Press, 1966; repr., University Microfilms, 1985). Approximately 1,900 entries are given, with brief annotations. The second volume on North America emphasizes the United States, with subdivisions of Indian tribes, cults, etc., with smaller sections for Canada and northern Mexico, and some information on Greenland. Both volumes provide indexes of authors and sources.

95. **Guide to Buddhist Religion.** Frank E. Reynolds, et al. Boston, G. K. Hall, 1981. 415p. (The Asian Philosophies and Religions Resource Guides).

One of the initial publications in a projected seven-part series to provide basic resources for the study of Asian religions and philosophies, the guide provides an annotated listing of 4,000 items. Categories which are used in all volumes are general history, religious thought, sacred texts, popular practices, art, religious involvement in social life and politics, ritual and practice, etc. There is particular attention paid to the inclusion of appropriate articles from research journals. It has been noted that there is no annotated listing of journals used in this particular guide. There is an emphasis on English-language materials, and access is provided through author-title and subject indexes. (See also entries 96 and 97.)

96. **Guide to Hindu Religion.** David J. Dell, et al. Boston, G. K. Hall, 1981. 461p. (The Asian Philosophies and Religions Resource Guides).

An annotated bibliography of 2,000 items, this work follows the procedure and pattern for the series (see entries 95 and 97). There is an excellent breadth in terms of coverage, with consideration given to art and anthropology. Annotations are well developed and descriptive of the topic under which the entry appears. Singled out for special praise by reviewers is this guide's section on bibliographies and research aids. An attractive special feature for this work is its annotated listing of journals. An unfortunate circumstance is the author's oversight in providing adequate access. There is neither a subject nor a title index but only an author approach. Happily, this inadequacy is not shared by other volumes in the series. Still, the work is extremely important for what it does.

97. **Guide to Islam.** David Ede, et al. Boston, G. K. Hall, 1983. 261p. (The Asian Philosophies and Religions Resource Guides).

Following the pattern of other volumes in the series (see entries 95 and 96), this guide is intended to provide the English-language reader with a sufficient choice of significant publications in order to learn about Islam as a religion and a civilization. Intended for the student at both graduate and undergraduate levels, the guide provides an annotated bibliography of nearly 3,000 items, mostly English-language books and articles. Most were published prior to 1977, a drawback for those expecting more recent coverage. As is true of all guides in the series, any of the publications listed may be obtained through the Institute for the Advanced Study of World Religions in xerography or microformat when not available elsewhere. It is reported that a supplement is being prepared to update the coverage. Like others in the series, this is a useful and welcome effort.

98. **2000 Books and More: An Annotated and Selected Bibliography of Jewish History and Thought.** Jonathan Kaplan, ed. Jerusalem, Magnes Press, Hebrew University, 1983. 483p.

This annotated bibliography of books on Jewish history and thought proposes to furnish students, teachers, and librarians with a basic list of sources of major importance in the study of the topic. International in scope, it includes works in Hebrew, English, German, Spanish, Portuguese, and French. It has proved to be a useful tool both in book selection and in Jewish studies. Major divisions are historical periods, subdivided into smaller time segments or topics. There is also a listing of publications by Jewish communities. Cross-references are employed to link editions published in different languages. Annotations are brief. The introduction is in both English and Hebrew, as is a name index.

INDEXES, ABSTRACTS, AND
SERIAL BIBLIOGRAPHIES

*99. **Bulletin signalétique 527: Sciences religieuses.** Vol. 24, 1970- . Q. Paris, Centre National de la Recherche Scientifique.

This important abstracting journal is part of the massive indexing effort of the Centre National. The Centre began indexing periodical literature of the sciences in 1940, then added humanities coverage in 1947. Philosophy and religion were covered together in *Bulletin analytique: Philosophie* (vols. 1-9); *Bulletin signalétique: Philosophie. Science humaines* (vols. 10-14); *Sciences humaines: Philosophie* (vols. 15-22); and *Philosophie, sciences religieuses* (v.23). They were separated in 1970, with each discipline retaining the volume number in its new journal title. Now many disciplines have been added, including journals in the social sciences. All are covered by separate indexes bearing a number and subtitle. Thousands of international journals are covered on a quarterly basis in the humanities and social sciences and monthly in the sciences. The information is stored in a computerized database identified by a collective acronym *FRANCIS. This particular index is available online through *FRANCIS; Histoire des sciences et des techniques which (as of January 1987) contains about 65,000 citations, half of them with abstracts, dating from 1972. It adds about 1,000 records per quarter and is available through Questel.

100. **Catholic Periodical and Literature Index.** Vol. 14, 1967/1968- . Bi. Bienn. cum. Haversford, Pa., Catholic Library Association.

The leading current index of the Catholic faith, this work was created from a combination of two earlier efforts. *Guide to Catholic Literature, 1888-1940* (Romig, 1940) provided an author-subject-title approach in identifying books and booklets pertinent to the Catholic faith or by Catholic authors. This was continued as an annual publication with four-year cumulations until 1967. *Catholic Periodical Index* (Catholic Library Association) indexed periodicals in the English language from 1939 to 1967 on a quarterly basis, with coverage back to 1930. The present work covers both books and articles. It provides annotations and an author-title-subject approach to about 25,000 adult books either by Catholics or on subjects of interest to Catholics, published during each calendar year. It regularly indexes some 135 periodicals, primarily in the English language. Articles are indexed by author and subject.

101. **Index to Jewish Periodicals.** 1963- . Semiann. Cleveland Heights, Ohio, The Index.
   Beginning as a publication of the College of Jewish Studies in Shaker Heights, Ohio, this small index has held its own through the years. It generally indexes forty to forty-five periodicals relating to the Jewish faith or regarding Jewish life. It is considered an excellent source of information in identifying the thoughts and writings especially of American Jewry. All periodicals are in the English language, and book reviews are indexed. The material is indexed by author and subject and represents a wide range of interests and scholarship. Both popular and scholarly journals are included. The work is numbered as a quarterly, with each of the two issues receiving two numbers (1-2, July-December, and 3-4, January-June).

102. **The Quarterly Index Islamicus.** 1977- . Q. 5-year cum. London, Mansell.
   This index provides a good coverage of books, articles, and essays on Islamic subjects. Over 1,300 periodicals are examined as well as anthologies and festschriften. There has been an increased coverage of social science issues in the past few years. This serial grew out of an earlier monographic publication, *Index Islamicus, 1906-1955*, by J. D. Pearson (London, University. School of Oriental Studies. Library, 1958). This provided a catalog of some 26,000 articles in many languages on Islamic subjects. After issuing four supplements (1956-1960, 1961-1965, 1966-1970, and 1971-1975) in which 33,000 additional articles were identified, Pearson began his editorship of the *Quarterly*. The fifth supplement (1976-1980) is in two volumes with both monographs and articles receiving separate treatment. It cumulates the contents of the first five volumes or twenty issues of the *Quarterly*.

*103. **Religion Index One: Periodicals.** 1949/1953- . Semiann. Bienn. cum. Chicago, American Theological Library Association.
   Beginning in 1953 with indexing from 1949, the *Index to Religious Periodical Literature* established itself as the leading current index representing the Protestant viewpoint. With the title change in 1977, this tradition has continued and the present work has expanded its coverage to embrace over 300 titles in Western languages. Book reviews are listed separately, as always. While primarily concentrating on Protestantism, the index has traditionally demonstrated an ecumenical outlook and still selectively includes several Jewish and Catholic periodicals. It is indexed by subject and author, with a separate index for book reviews. *Religion Index Two: Multi-Author Works* (1976-) first appeared in 1978 and represents an index of composite works (compilations, anthologies, festschriften, proceedings, etc.) published during the year covered. The entire file of this very important family dating back to 1949 is available through DIALOG and BRS. The *ATLA RELIGION DATABASE is updated each month and adds 30,000 records per year (250,000 as of October 1985).

104. **Religious and Inspirational Books and Serials in Print 1987.** Bienn. New York, R. R. Bowker, 1987. 1700p.

Although convention generally treats this as a monograph in style of entry, it is a biennial publication originally entitled *Religious Books and Serials in Print* and has appeared since 1978. A useful reference tool, it brings together in handy and convenient form a massive amount of bibliographic information. Although available elsewhere, this material would require the expenditure of time and energy to retrieve. The work provides listings of 60,000 books and 3,700 serials from 3,000 different publishers. It is developed from several of the Bowker databases, *Books in Print*, and *Forthcoming Books*. Each entry is arranged under an LC subject heading, while a liberal use of cross-references serves to make the necessary links. Also included are a subject area directory and a "Sacred Works Index." The "Sacred Works Index" lists available editions of the Bible and other sacred writings. Books are indexed by author, title, and subject, while serials are located through title and subject. Publishers are listed in the manner of other Bowker works.

105. **Religious and Theological Abstracts.** 1958- . Q. Myerstown, Pa., Religious and Theological Abstracts, Inc.

Highly regarded as a nonsectarian abstracting service which covers 150 journals on an international basis. Abstracts are in English and average about 100 words in length. Journals represent a wide range of interests and beliefs and include representative titles of Christian, Jewish, and Muslim origins. There are five major categories or topical divisions: biblical, theological, historical, practical, and sociological. Each section is further subdivided, with numbers being given to each entry. Subject, author, and scripture indexes appear on an annual basis in the final issue of each volume. A list of abstractors accompanies each issue and abstracts are generally signed with initials.

106. **Science of Religion: Abstracts and Index of Recent Articles.** Vol. 5, 1980- . Q. Amsterdam, Free University, and Leeds, England, University of Leeds.

This provides a continuation of an earlier bibliography which enjoyed an excellent reputation in the field. *International Bibliography of the History of Religions* (Leiden, Netherlands, Brill, 1952/1954-1979) was published under the auspices of the International Council for Philosophy and Humanistic Studies by the International Association for the History of Religions and received UNESCO support. An annual publication it listed books, articles, and reviews for the year covered on the history of the various religions of the world. International in coverage, listings appeared in the language of the original document in a classified arrangement. An author index was provided. The present work retains the same sponsorship, with volumes 1-4 appearing under the title *Science of Religion Bulletin*. It covers approximately 250 journals representing all religions and time periods. Each issue is indexed by author and subject, both of which cumulate in the final issue of each volume.

DICTIONARIES, ENCYCLOPEDIAS, AND HANDBOOKS

General

107. **Abingdon Dictionary of Living Religions.** Keith Crim, et al. Nashville, Tenn., Abingdon, 1981. 830p.

Developed as a guide to the historical background as well as the belief systems and rites of religions that are still being practiced, this volume provides coverage of relevant issues and topics in an alphabetical arrangement. There are approximately 1,600 signed articles of varying length, with the religions receiving extensive coverage of anywhere from twelve to fifteen pages each. Many of the entries are biographical in nature and cover personalities associated with the religions. There is a fair amount of illustrative material: colored plates, maps (both in color and black-and-white), photographs, figures, and diagrams. Designed to be less technical than *A Dictionary of Comparative Religion* (see entry 108), this useful work includes cross-references and bibliographies.

108. **A Dictionary of Comparative Religion.** S. G. F. Brandon. New York, Scribner's, 1970. 704p.

Considered a standard in the field, this work of British scholarship covers the beliefs, rituals, important personalities, schools, councils, and sacred books of the various religions of the world. Articles are brief, signed by the contributor, and generally have bibliographies. There is a certain degree of complexity associated with the comprehension of some of the articles, not true of *Abingdon Dictionary of Living Religions* (see entry 107). Unlike *Abingdon*, however, this work includes religions not extant and provides a strong focus on intellectual history in its efforts "to treat the various religions proportionately to their significance in the history of human culture." Coverage of the Eastern religions is very strong and sectional editors describe Buddhism, Hinduism, Islam, China, and the Far East. There are no illustrations. The work has a synoptic index which groups all relevant entries under the name of the religion, as well as a general index of names and subjects. For optimal reference service, both Brandon and *Abingdon* should be used.

109. **Eerdmans' Handbook to the World's Religions.** R. Pierce Beaver, et al., consulting eds. Grand Rapids, Mich., Eerdmans, 1982. 448p.

Another fine product from this reputable publishing house is this handbook which treats the world's religions. History, scriptures, worship, and customs are described in an easy-to-use and convenient fashion. Generally brief in coverage, there is great breadth in the scope of this effort which includes religions both living and dead. Some 300 photographs, 100 in color, add to the attractiveness and appeal of this volume. Development of religion is handled through descriptions of the nature of religious study, personalities and places of major importance, and origins and history. Unlike Brandon (see entry 108), in this volume Christianity is given separate treatment, while ancient religions account for about one-third of the text. The "Rapid Fact-finder" is a glossary of terms and personalities. Subject access is provided through a general index.

110. **Encyclopaedia of Religion and Ethics.** A. J. Hastings, et al., eds. New York, Scribner's, 1910-1927; repr., 1961. 13v.

Through the years, this work has been recognized as an outstanding example of scholarship and erudition. It remains the most comprehensive religious encyclopedia in the English language and has never been superseded or equalled in its treatment. Although old, it is not outdated, and provides long, scholarly articles on belief systems, customs, various religions, and national characters of religious movements in various countries of the world. Most impressive are the comprehensive articles on various social topics relating to ethical or religious matters, and the depth provided for exposition of various abstractions such as happiness. Anthropology, mythology, folklore, biology, psychology, and economics are among the elements considered in this expansive work. Articles range from brief (personalities get only a few lines of identification) to monographic in length. The final volume has an analytical index, an index to foreign words, an index to scripture passages, and an index to authors of articles. Although the work is of liberal, Protestant authorship, there is little sectarian bias.

111. **The Encyclopedia of American Religions.** 2nd ed. J. Gordon Melton. Detroit, Gale, 1987. 899p.

Although the first edition received mixed reviews at the time of publication, the title has achieved a position of some prominence with reference librarians. The new edition covers 1,350 religious bodies in a manner similar to the first edition. There is a categorical arrangement which embraces seventeen religious families in twenty-two chapter headings. Such traditional groups as Lutheran, Reformed Presbyterian, Pietist-Methodist, and Eastern and Western Liturgical, etc., are treated along with more modern systems like the Communal, Metaphysical, Psychic, and New Age families. Information is provided on the various bodies (history, development, organizational aspects) as well as bibliography and bibliographic notes. Provides much more depth of coverage than Frank Spencer Mead's *Handbook of Denominations in the United States*, eighth edition, revised by Samuel S. Hill (Abingdon, 1985).

112. **The Facts on File Dictionary of Religions.** John R. Hinnells, ed. New York, Facts on File, 1984. 550p.

One of the more recent contributions is this dictionary from a noted scholar and authority, in which an attempt has been made to provide an exposition of all religions of the world in relatively compact format. It has succeeded as a reference tool of convenience and covers the various aspects associated with religious bodies. Good coverage is given to the current religions and their mystical counterparts, representing such movements as astrology, magic, and the occult. Technical terms, leading figures, and deities are covered in a lucid and learned manner. Bibliographies are given for the study of religion in general and for each of the major religions of the world. A synoptic index relates terms of relevance to a particular religion, and several illustrations and maps are provided.

113. **A Handbook of Living Religions.** John R. Hinnells, ed. New York, Viking Penguin, 1984. 528p.

A clear and lucid coverage of the living religions of the world, this work provides much more depth than does the *Abingdon Dictionary of Living Religions* (see entry 107). The handbook provides a detailed survey of the religions of our time in regard to their practices, tenets, rites, customs, teachings, and traditions. Christianity and Judaism are covered, as are Hinduism, Islam, Zoroastrianism, Sikhism, Bahaism, etc. Written by many contributors, the general pattern of coverage for each religion includes several segments beginning with an introduction (primary sources) and progressing to historical development, critical assumptions, main teachings, practices, traditions, and twentieth-century development. Concluding each chapter is a brief bibliography of each religion. There are a general index and a general bibliography at the end of the work.

114. **The New Westminster Dictionary of Liturgy and Worship.** J. G. Davies, ed. Philadelphia, Westminster, 1986. 544p.

Published in both Great Britain and the United States, this excellent reference tool first appeared in 1972. The new edition represents a revision and slight expansion of the earlier publication, with about sixty new entries as well as modification of existing ones. It has been described by reviewers as having a greater spirit of ecumenicism which provides an attitude more receptive to ethnic pluralism and greater participation by the laity in church ritual. Treatment of women is timely, with articles on ordination of women, the Feminist

Liturgical Movement, and women and worship. Emphasis is on conceptual awareness rather than definitions of precise terms, and it is quite possible that a person unfamiliar with terminology may not come away with a precise meaning. Articles vary in length and cover both Christian and non-Christian religions. The tool provides a necessary ingredient to the religion collection.

Christian

115. **Christian Symbols Ancient and Modern: A Handbook for Students.** Heather Child and Dorothy Colles. New York, Scribner's, 1971. 270p.

One of the standard tools in iconography is this highly regarded exposition of the use of Christian symbols in the conduct or services of the Church. There are numerous illustrations, including line drawings and photographs accompanying descriptive passages, which makes the work a useful item to a variety of readers. Artists and craftsmen may well be enlightened in their search for thematic material in producing their own work, while students will be informed of the rich heritage of visual symbolism found in the Christian religion. Symbols included are those found in the decorative or applied arts of carving, embroidery, stained glass, etc. The work is divided into categories of representation, with chapters on the cross, the trinity, images of Christ, the Virgin Mary, the Holy Spirit, angels, etc. There are an index and a brief bibliography.

116. **Dictionary of Christian Lore and Legend.** J. C. J. Metford. New York, Thames and Hudson, 1983. 272p.

This work succeeds in its purpose to provide a guide to the major elements of the Christian tradition as represented in the arts, music, and literature. There are over 1,700, generally brief definitions, covering architectural features of church buildings as centers of worship, the liturgy, symbols and symbolism, biblical characters, saints, and tales of the Christian religion. "Lore" is interpreted to be knowledge relating to Christian culture, while "legend" represents narrative which should be read regardless of belief in its veracity. Developed as a resource for the nonspecialist, the work is written in a clear, readable style, and provides numerous illustrations in black-and-white. There are cross-references but no bibliographies.

117. **A Dictionary of Hymnology Setting Forth the Origin and History of Christian Hymns of All Ages and Nations.** John Julian. New York, Scribner's, 1907; repr., Grand Rapids, Mich., Kregel, 1985. 2v.

The years have continued to add to the reputation of this work, which is still the standard in the field for information on the history of Christian hymns in the Western languages. First appearing in 1892, it has gone through several printings, including an initial revision to correct some typographical errors in 1907. Coverage is universal in terms of time and place, but there is an emphasis on hymns of English-speaking countries. To use the work to best advantage one should become familiar with the composition. The first part is the dictionary, with separate entries on history, biography, and topical matters. This is followed by a cross-reference index to first lines, then an index of authors, translators, etc., followed by two appendices providing additions and corrections to articles in the dictionary. The last two segments are another supplement and indexes to the appendices and supplement. Another helpful work is Katharine Smith Diehl's *Hymns and Tunes: An Index* (Scarecrow, 1966) which indexes tunes from seventy-eight hymnals.

118. **Dictionary of Theology.** 2nd ed., new rev. ed. Karl Rahner and Herbert Vorgrimler. New York, Crossroad, 1985.

The original edition of this work was intended for the German educated layperson interested in Catholic dogmatic theology, and the English translation in 1965 was heralded as a success. The new edition has been thoroughly revised on the basis of subsequent revisions of the German edition. The dictionary represents an excellent effort by two Roman Catholic theologians to provide a handy and useful exposition of Catholic theology, and represents a wide array of nonbiblical subject matter. Considered a modern work for the modern Catholic, its related areas of coverage include philosophy, psychology, and sociology. The entries are relatively short but show variation depending on the term being defined. There are numerous cross-references, and no bibliographies. A worthwhile effort for purposes of brief identification of all elements related to Catholic theology.

A recent work is Millard J. Erickson's *Concise Dictionary of Christian Theology* (Baker Book, 1986). This is a compact but informative dictionary describing terms, individuals, and issues, with some coverage of related areas of philosophy and church history.

119. **Dictionnaire d'archéologie chrétienne et de liturgie.** Fernand Cabrol and Henri Leclerq. Paris, Letouzey, 1907-1953. 15v.

Another standard in the field, this excellent and profound treatment of Christian liturgy and archaeology is without peer. Originally published as the third multivolume set in a series of sets collectively entitled *Encyclopédie des sciences ecclesiastiques* (Paris, Letouzey, 1907-), it remains the most important and unique work of the series. There are excellent articles, all signed with good bibliographies on all aspects of liturgy and archaeology of the early Christian religion to the time of Charlemagne. Coverage includes monuments, iconography, epigraphy, designs, diagrams, rites and ceremonies, numismatics, and symbols. Latin terms are defined as well. No other compendium of antiquities rivals this work for depth of coverage.

120. **The Encyclopedia of Religion.** Mircea Eliade, ed.-in-chief. New York, Macmillan, 1986. 15v.

Eliade's comprehensive encyclopedia provides broad essays on religious traditions, individuals, and themes. Its coverage is worldwide and up-to-date. Emphasis is on detailed examination of individual traditions and comparative study of religions with each other. Articles provide an overview of the topic, details on particular aspects of the topic, and some bibliography (although this is not complete). Biographical and narrow topics occasionally receive briefer treatment. The work is aimed at the student or nonspecialist, but the great amount of information provided makes it valuable to the serious scholar as well. Unfortunately the index volume has not yet been published (it is expected out in 1987).

121. **An Encyclopedia of Religion.** Virgilius Ture Anselm Ferm. New York, Philosophical Library, 1945. 844p.

Like an old friend, this volume retains a place in the minds of reference librarians and on the shelves of reference collections. It represents a broad coverage of all religions even though it is written from a Protestant point of view. Entries are generally brief and cover a variety of topics: terms are defined; feast names are identified; persons, movements, and institutions are explained. One is surprised at the breadth of coverage of this one-volume work which is international in scope. It is particularly good in the coverage of Oriental religion, and identifies various denominations, theologies, and personalities associated with all faiths. Bibliographies are included. It is easy to use (dictionary arrangement) and highly informative, making it a perennial favorite. One should consult Sheehy (see entry 2) or the bibliographic guides for dictionaries and encyclopedias on the specific denominations of the Protestant faith.

122. **Encyclopedia of Theology: The Concise Sacramentum Mundi.** Karl Rahner, ed. New York, Seabury, 1975; repr., New York, Crossroad, 1982. 1841p.

With publication of the six-volume *Sacramentum Mundi: An Encyclopedia of Theology*, also edited by Rahner and others in the period 1968-1970, the Roman Catholic faith received an eminent work of scholarship which reflected the perspective subsequent to Vatican II. Extremely technical in parts, it was not meant for the layperson but rather the scholar, specialist, or serious student. Topical material embraced a wide range of subjects. Five years later, this concise edition, which was meant to appeal to the interested layperson, appeared. The emphasis was on ideas and movements, as it was in the original, and many of the articles were taken from the larger work and others of its kind. Coverage includes theological topics and current issues of importance. The language is clear and non-technical, and references to source materials are provided within the text.

123. **Lexikon für Theologie und Kirche.** Michael Buchberger, et al. Freiberg, Switzerland, Herder, 1957-1965. 10v.

One of the outstanding multivolume sets of Roman Catholic scholarship, this work is recognized for its extensive coverage of theology and issues surrounding the Church. All articles are signed and are arranged alphabetically. There is an emphasis on European, especially German scholarship. Articles are monographic in length when treating topics of major importance; other topics receive correspondingly less emphasis and are relatively brief. Coverage includes various religions, practices, observances and rites. Bibliographical citations are given, and personalities are included. The final volume is an index. A three-volume supplement which features documents and commentary regarding the Second Vatican Council, appeared in the period 1966-1968. The supplement follows a classified arrangement.

124. **New Catholic Encyclopedia.** New York, McGraw-Hill, 1967-1979; repr., Palatine, Ill., Publishers Guild, 1981. 17v.

Prepared under the supervision of an editorial staff from the Catholic University of America, this represents a completely new work rather than a revision of *The Catholic Encyclopedia* (1907-1922, 17v.). The older work continues to be used because of its excellent in-depth coverage of topics in medieval literature, history, philosophy, art, etc., as well as matters of Catholic doctrine. *New Catholic Encyclopedia* represents a timely and clearly written exposition from the perspective of the Catholic faith in the twentieth century. There are approximately 17,000 articles, all signed, on the Catholic Church in the world today, with an emphasis on the United States and the English-speaking world. Biographies are limited to deceased people. Bibliographies are given for most articles. Volume 15 is an index, volume 16 is a supplement covering developments from 1964 to 1974, and volume 17 includes supplementary coverage of change in the Church. Both supplementary volumes reflect a certain freedom of thought in the articles on abortion, contraception, women as priests, etc., which are handled in an objective and impartial manner. A newer work which serves to supplement the encyclopedia is *The Catholic Fact Book* by John Deedy (Thomas More, 1986). It contains much information on Church history, basic tenets, personalities, events, and documents as well as definitions of terminology. Smaller libraries may use it as an alternative to the more costly encyclopedia.

125. **Oxford Dictionary of the Christian Church.** 2nd ed. F. L. Cross and E. A. Livingstone. New York, Oxford University Press, 1974. 1518p.

Together with Ferm (see entry 121), this work is a comprehensive, one-volume compendium on religious subject matter. There are over 6,000 entries from nearly 250 contributors. It is especially useful for biographies, definitions, theologies, and heresies. Doctrines, movements, church bodies, events, and holidays are included. Bibliographies are routinely provided for most articles. Articles are not signed. Intended for the intelligent layperson, this work provides balanced coverage, and special attention has been given to the councils and policies which have undergone change. The Eastern Church is given more detailed treatment in this edition than was true of the earlier work.

126. **Die Religion in Geschichte und Gegenwart. Handwörterbuch für Theologie und Religionswissenschaft.** Tübingen, West Germany, Mohr, 1957-1965; repr., 1986. 7v.

One of the outstanding multivolume sets written from the Protestant point of view, this work has earned a reputation for excellence in scholarship. Known and identified simply as *RGG*, it features signed articles and bibliographies of considerable length. It includes biographical sketches of living as well as dead persons and is an important contribution by German Protestant scholarship. Biographical notes on the over 3,000 contributors are found in volume 7, the "Registerband." There is an extensive subject index. Another work of in-depth scholarship is *Theologische Realenzyklopädie* (de Gruyter, 1976-), which is projected to fill thirty volumes. So far thirteen volumes have been completed, and the work contains long signed articles of a profound nature, complete with bibliographies. It is less concerned with a strictly Protestant point of view than an earlier work on the subject which served as the basis for the *Schaff-Herzog Encyclopedia* (see entry 127).

127. **Schaff-Herzog Encyclopedia. The New Schaff-Herzog Encyclopedia of Religious Knowledge.** New York, Funk and Wagnalls, 1908-1912; repr., Grand Rapids, Mich., Baker, 1949-1950. 13v.

Based on the third edition of the monumental German work by J. J. Herzog, *Realencyklopädie für Protestantische Theologie und Kirche* (Leipzig, Germany, Hinricks, 1869-1913), this remains one of the most important works from a Protestant perspective in the English language. It provides excellent, in-depth coverage on a variety of topics, including other religions and religious leaders of all affiliations. Much of the material from the German work has been revised and abridged to make it a more readable but no less authoritative effort. Designed to present information on biblical, historical, doctrinal, and practical theology, it presents information on sects, denominations, churches, organizations, missions, doctrines, and religious controversies. A supplement, entitled *Twentieth Century Encyclopedia of Religious Knowledge* (Baker, 1955. 2v.), attempted to bring the basic set up-to-date with biographical sketches, articles on subjects of more recent interest, and revision of outdated entries.

128. **The Westminster Dictionary of Christian Ethics.** James F. Childress and John Macquarrie, eds. Philadelphia, Westminster, 1986. 678p.

In this extensive revision of Macquarrie's *Dictionary of Christian Ethics* (Westminster, 1967), only about 40 percent of the entries were retained, and these were updated if necessary. Contributors from different parts of the English-speaking world, representing the various elements within the Judeo-Christian tradition, have provided a modern approach in examining the relevant issues of contemporary society. Not limited to theologians, this work presents the perspectives of philosophers, lawyers, and physicians in analyzing developments in science, health care, medicine, etc. Such sensitive bioethical subjects as abortion, euthanasia, and human experimentation are considered. Traditional concepts are covered, as are biblical ethics. There are no entries for individual thinkers; rather a thematic approach is taken in which individuals are described. A name index provides access within this context. Like its predecessor, this work should become a standard source.

129. **The Westminster Dictionary of Christian Theology.** Alan Richardson and John Bowden, eds. Philadelphia, Westminster, 1983. 614p.

Although based on Richardson's earlier work (Westminster, 1969; repr., London, S. C. M., 1972), which was recognized as the standard for Protestant theology, Bowden has produced an important new tool. Some 175 contributors from Europe and the United States, representing Protestant, Anglican, Catholic, and Orthodox traditions, provide an emphasis on theological thought in a historical context. There are nearly 600 signed articles, with bibliographies covering theology in a variety of settings: biblical, patristic, medieval, reformation, and modern. Biographical sketches have been eliminated in the same manner as in the other Westminster publication, *The Westminster Dictionary of Christian Ethics* (see entry 128). More important is the lack of bibliographic coverage for about one-fourth of the entries, which may be regarded as a deficiency of serious proportions.

130. **World Christian Encyclopedia: A Comparative Study of Churches and Religions in the Modern World, AD 1900-2000.** David D. Barnett, ed. New York, Oxford University Prress, 1982. 1010p.

Based on an extensive survey and twelve years in the making, this work represents a major accomplishment in providing a detailed exposition of the entire realm of Christianity. Covering nearly 21,000 different denominations representing the beliefs of nearly 9,000 different groupings of people speaking over 7,000 languages, it is far and away the most comprehensive statistical reference work on churches and missions. Many non-Christian religions are covered as well. The volume is divided into fourteen major segments, beginning with a status report on Christianity in the twentieth century, followed by a chronology, methodology of the survey, a cultural classification of peoples, etc. Of major importance is the seventh part, which presents the survey (arranged country by country), providing demographic and cultural information as well as narratives of the non-Christian religions and analyses of Christian history and current status. The remaining sections include statistics, a dictionary, a bibliography, an atlas, directories of individuals and organizations, and a set of indexes.

Non-Christian

131. **Dictionary of Non-Christian Religions.** 2nd ed. Geoffrey Parrinder. Amersham Bucks, England, Hulton, 1981. 320p.

A slight revision, but not an expansion, of the author's earlier edition in 1971, this remains an important and useful work for its rather unique general coverage of non-Christian faiths. The belief systems, practices, gods, heroes, cults, and observances of non-Christian religions are covered. There is an emphasis on the systems of Hinduism, Buddhism, and Islam since they represent the largest non-Christian faiths, but other parts of the world are not neglected. Post-biblical Judaism, the Americas, Australasia, and Africa are covered in ample fashion. Entries are generally brief but informative, and include cross-references when necessary. There are numerous illustrations, both photographs and drawings. Entries lack bibliographies but a general reading list is supplied at the end. Also included are lists of dynasties from different regions.

132. **Encyclopaedia Judaica.** New York, Macmillan, 1972. 16v.

A comprehensive and authoritative treatment of all aspects of Jewish life is provided in approximately 25,000 articles, most of which are signed by a panel of some 1,800 international contributors and 300 editors. Most entries conclude with bibliographies which stress English-language materials. An interesting point worth noting is the placement of the index in volume 1 in order to assure its use to exploit the resource to its fullest degree. Biographical sketches are included and represent universal coverage of both living and deceased people. A yearbook series was begun the year following publication of the encyclopedia, but its frequency varies. An important publication in 1982 was the *Encyclopaedia Judaica Decennial Book, 1973-1982* (Jerusalem, Encyclopaedia Judaica) which covers the ten-year period 1972-1981 and includes updates, revisions, etc., complete with cross-references to the major work. *The Jewish Encyclopedia* (Funk and Wagnalls, 1901-1906, 12v.) still remains a useful tool in interpreting the customs, tradition, and practices of Jewish life to a Christian audience.

133. **Encyclopaedia of Islam.** New ed. H. A. R. Gibb, et al., eds. Leiden, Netherlands, Brill, 1954- ; London, Luzac, 1954-1983. (In progress).

The original 1913 edition of this work served as a dictionary of the geography, ethnography, and biography of the Islamic peoples and was regarded as a scholarly and authoritative publication. Revision began in 1954 and has proceeded slowly but steadily since that time, with the publication of separate fascicles which later become parts of bound volumes. The new work when completed will have succeeded in providing a more current exposition of the Islamic tradition with greater attention given to history, geography, and culture. Arrangement is alphabetical but includes terms from the Arabic which in translation may not be as familiar as English expressions. Cross-references are provided in many cases. Articles vary in length from a paragraph to several pages depending upon the topic. An index is available to the first three volumes, and another is planned upon completion of volume 6 (now in progress). *Shorter Encyclopaedia of Islam*, edited by Gibb and J. H. Kramers (Leiden, Netherlands, Brill, 1953) is a one-volume abridgement of the earlier edition which contains only those articles dealing with law and religion.

134. **Encyclopedic Handbook of Cults in America.** J. Gordon Melton. New York, Garland, 1986. 278p.

A timely and informative handbook of alternative religions, this includes material as recent as late 1985. Melton, long an authority on religion in American life and founder of the Institute for the Study of American Religion, has put together an objective compendium of information. Especially useful is the opening descriptive essay defining cults and their opponents in the United States. Coverage is given to twenty-eight different groups, ranging from the more established Rosicrucians to the more recent and publicized Unification Church. Each group is described in terms of leading figures, belief systems, organizational structure, and controversies. Bibliographies are provided. A name index and a detailed table of contents facilitate access.

135. **Harper's Dictionary of Hinduism: Its Mythology, Folklore, Philosophy, Literature, and History.** Margaret Stutley and James Stutley. San Francisco, Harper & Row, 1977. 416p.

Harris. Contemporary Religions: A World Guide

Critically acclaimed at the time of its publication as the major dictionary of Hinduism, this work was a product of twenty years of research. It represents an excellent blend of scholarship and readability and fulfills its mission to meet the requirements of both the student and the general reader. There are 2,500 entries, most of which are fairly brief, although some are quite long. The coverage is of classical Hinduism from its beginnings well before the dawn of Christianity to the fifteenth century. Entries include rites, practices, concepts, myths, places, and events of importance. There are references to library texts and sources are frequently identified. There is a fifteen-page bibliography. The interested party should consult Sheehy (see entry 2) or the bibliographic guides in the field for sources of information on particular religions such as Buddhism, Shintoism, Zoroastrianism, etc.

DIRECTORIES AND ANNUALS

136. **American Jewish Yearbook.** 1899- . Ann. Philadelphia, Jewish Publishing Society.
    Designed to review events of the year relating to Jewish affairs in the United States and other countries of the world. Feature articles appear at the beginning of the work, followed by signed articles on a variety of subjects regarding developments in the American Jewish community. These are treated in some detail, followed by briefer treatment of conditions in other countries. Included also are directories of various organizations in the United States and Canada, biographies, necrologies, and bibliographies. Among these resource items is a useful listing of Jewish periodicals, and a summary Jewish calendar. Volume 83 (1983) has an index of feature articles from 1951-1982. Each volume is approached through a detailed name and subject index.

137. **A Directory of Religious Bodies in the United States.** J. Gordon Melton. New York, Garland, 1977. 305p.
    From the time of its publication, this directory earned the respect of librarians and users for its excellent brief coverage of nearly 1,300 religious bodies in this country. Arrangement is alphabetical by name of the body in the first part of the work and information is provided regarding location and publications. The second part provides a classified arrangement in which denominations and sects are organized under broader categories such as Baptist Family, Lutheran Family, and non-Christian groups. This codification scheme appears to be successful and well conceived. There is a bibliography or reading list of materials relating to American religious groups at the end. More detailed directory information for large churches will be found in the *Yearbook of American and Canadian Churches* (see entry 140).

138. **Directory of Religious Organizations in the United States.** 2nd ed. Falls Church, Va., McGrath, 1982. 518p.
    A classified listing of over 1,600 religious and lay organizations in the field of religion, this is an update of a work published five years earlier. Its reception has been good in libraries and the information is presented in a handy and useful manner. All organizations listed are regarded as having a religious purpose. Representative organizations are departments of national churches, professional associations and societies, volunteer groups of various types, government agencies, businesses, and fraternal societies. Information given includes religious affiliation, address and location, officers, purpose, activities, founding date, publications, and membership. Information is supplied by the organization. Many of these organizations are not easily found elsewhere; therefore, the work represents a desirable addition to the collection.

√ Directory of Departments and Programs of Religious Studies in N. America

139. **Official Catholic Directory.** 1886- . Ann. New York, P. J. Kenedy.

Although there have been some variations in title through the years, this directory has been a predictable commodity and represents a standard reference tool. Developed with the purpose of providing up-to-date, accurate information on a yearly basis, it serves an important function in disseminating the reports of statistical and institutional information as provided by diocesan authorities. Coverage includes the organization, clergy, missions, schools, churches, and religious orders of the Catholic Church in the United States and other countries. Arrangement is by hierarchical order of the Church under countries and subdivisions of countries. Dioceses are listed by states and detailed information is provided regarding names of individuals serving in various positions. Traditionally, the index has appeared at the beginning of the volume.

140. **Yearbook of American and Canadian Churches.** 1916- . Ann. Nashville, Tenn., Abingdon.

Although its title, publisher, and frequency of appearance have varied in the past, this work has assumed an important position as a reporting tool for statistics and developments of major religious bodies in the United States and Canada. Originally limited to Protestant religious bodies, it has changed character through time and now covers the organizations and activities of all faiths. Consisting of three major sections plus an index, greatest coverage is in the second segment, "Directories," which is classified by categories. Separate listings are given for American and Canadian groups, but each entry provides a brief historical overview, listing of officers, organizational information, and a list of periodicals. The first part provides "a calendar with a four-year projection of major religious dates for all faiths," and the third section presents statistics regarding financial conditions and membership. The index groups denominations under generic headings such as "Baptist Bodies."

BIOGRAPHICAL SOURCES

141. **Biographical Dictionary of American Cult and Sect Leaders.** J. Gordon Melton. New York, Garland, 1986. 354p.

Melton has had a great deal of success in reading the desires of the marketplace, and this most recent work should be a welcome addition to the well-rounded reference collection. Focusing on what has come to be called alternative religions, he has provided a comprehensive coverage of 213 founders and major leaders of American cults and sects. Coverage is limited to deceased personalities. A sect is considered to be a group in protest of the mainstream church, and a cult is defined as a more radical new spiritual option. Some of the groups have become mainstream, such as the Mormon church. The biographies are well written and informative, from 300 to 500 words in length, and include bibliographies by and about the personality. Appendices provide classification of the personalities by tradition, birthplace, and religious influences. A good general index is given.

142. **Dictionary of American Catholic Biography.** John J. Delaney. Garden City, N.Y., Doubleday, 1984. 621p.

In this volume, an attempt has been made to provide factual information regarding the lives and activities of Catholics who have been influential in this country. The work covers about 1,500 individuals, all of whom are deceased, but whose dates range from the colonial period to the present. In addition to theologians, the entries include a distinguished listing of performers, artists, athletes, and politicians. Such people as Bing Crosby, Arturo Toscanini, Babe Ruth, and John F. Kennedy are included as well as those of more controversial nature such as Joseph McCarthy. Each entry covers birth information, education, activities, achievements, and date and place of death. This appears to be a useful source for its stated purpose. For coverage on an international basis see the earlier work *Dictionary of Catholic Biography*, by Delaney and James Edward Tobin (Doubleday, 1961) which covers nearly 15,000 individuals from earliest times to the present.

143. **Dictionary of American Religious Biography.** Henry Warner Bowden. Westport, Conn., Greenwood Press, 1977. 572p.

A retrospective biographical dictionary which is limited to religious figures who died before 1 July 1976. Detailed treatment is given to 425 religious leaders who represent a wide range of denominations and belief systems. Included are such diverse figures as Increase Mather and Martin Luther King, Jr. Each entry begins with a brief career overview and personal and educational data. Following this is a detailed narrative sketch which includes both expository and evaluative commentary. A special attempt has been made to include women and minorities as well as dissidents from mainstream activity. Bibliographies which provide references by and about the biographee are included with each entry. There is a name and subject index.

144. **Lives of the Saints.** Alban Butler, Herbert Thurston, and Donald Attwater, eds. New York, P. J. Kenedy, 1956; repr., Westminster, Md., Christian Classics, 1981. 4v.

In this revision and abridgement of Thurston's earlier twelve-volume edition (1926-1938), much of the original material has been included without change. Some brief treatments were deleted and some biographies of recently canonized saints have been added. The homilies have been omitted. The purpose of the work is to present information on the principal saints familiar to English-speaking Catholics. The saints are listed by months and days, which requires in many cases the use of the index to locate the entry. A good biography of the individual's life is followed by a listing of sources. Each volume is indexed, and a general name index for the set appears in volume 4.

145. **The Oxford Dictionary of Popes.** J. N. D. Kelly. New York, Oxford University Press, 1986. 347p.

A recent biographical dictionary which covers all 264 popes who followed Peter, this work should meet with a welcome reception. Entries for each pope are arranged chronologically and cover family, social and educational background, life prior to becoming the head of the Church, and career activities while shouldering the responsibility of office. In general, the biographies are considered to be impartial and informative, although at times gossip and innuendo find their way into the descriptions. There is an appendix on "Pope Joan" which explores the myth of a female pope. Each entry provides a bibliography of source materials for both his life and official acts. An excellent detailed index provides easy access.

146. **The Oxford Dictionary of Saints.** 2nd ed. David Hugh Farmer. New York, Oxford University Press, 1987. 512p.

An informative biographical dictionary which covers the lives of the saints of Great Britain. Over 1,000 saints are treated; some were native to the country, others were considered important by the British, and still others died in England. This work provides entries for all the saints recorded in English place names, in the calendar of the Book of Common Prayer, the Sarum rite, and the Calendar of the Roman Catholic church. It also includes coverage of the leading saints of Ireland, Scotland, and Wales. Arrangement is alphabetical by Christian names for those who lived prior to the sixteenth century and by surname for those who followed. There are selective bibliographies which provide references to official sources. An index of places associated with particular saints is also included.

147. **Who's Who in American Jewry.** 1980 ed. Los Angeles, Calif., Standard Who's Who, 1980.

A useful and informative publication providing coverage of over 6,000 notable Jewish men and women in the United States and Canada, this work is recognized for its comprehensive treatment of both individuals and institutions. The first part includes the biographical coverage of those who have achieved distinction in a particular field or area of human endeavor as well as those who hold positions of leadership either in the Jewish community or on the national scene. The second segment incorporates the *Directory of American Jewish Institutions*, which provides information regarding over 9,000 Jewish institutions. This is arranged by state.

148. **Who's Who in Religion, 1985.** 3rd ed. Chicago, Marquis, 1985. 439p.

Beginning with what looked to be a yearly or possibly biennial publication with the first two editions published between 1975 and 1977, the work has undergone a hiatus which happily has ended with the publication of the third edition in 1985. The earlier editions covered individuals in a much more extensive fashion (16,000 in the first edition and 18,000 in the second edition) while the new issue limits itself to around 7,000 religious and lay leaders, church officials, clergy, and educators. These people have achieved a position of prominence in the United States, and selections for inclusion were aided by a special advisory board of Marquis. Biographies provide information on occupation, family, creative works, activities, memberships, etc. The work covers all denominations and represents a valuable resource tool. For sources of biographical information specialized to particular Protestant and other denominations, check bibliographic guides and Sheehy (see entry 2).

HISTORIES AND ATLASES

149. **The Cambridge History of Judaism.** W. D. Davies and Louis Finkelstein, eds. New York, Cambridge University, 1984- . (In progress).

Projected for completion in four volumes, this work presents a scholarly history of the Jews from the destruction of the temple in 586 B.C. to the period of the closure of the Mishnah in 250 A.D. It embraces not only the developments in Israel but in Babylonia and Egypt as well. Volume 1 (the only issue thus far) presents an introduction in its coverage of the geography of Palestine and the Levant and is termed the "Persian Period." This consists of a series of sixteen essays, erudite but readable, related to the development of Jewish culture in this period. New data are utilized in the inquiry, which represents a work of ecumenical proportions since the contributors are of various backgrounds and national origins. As is true of other Cambridge efforts, the bibliographies are full and of value to those who would research further. There are an index and chronological tables.

150. **Christian Spirituality: Origins to the Twelfth Century.** Bernard McGinn and John Meyerdorff, eds. New York, Crossroad, 1985. 502p. (World Spirituality: An Encyclopedic History of the Religious Quest, v. 16).

Although this is numbered volume 16 in a projected twenty-five-volume set, it is the first to reach the marketplace. (The plan is to complete the set in five years through the publication of five volumes per year.) Spirituality is generally defined as "that inner dimension of the person called by certain traditions, the spirit," and the appearance of the first volume indicates the magnitude of the entire effort once completed. Attempting to respond to an increased consciousness on the part of the world's citizenry and increasing intercourse between Eastern and Western religions, the multivolume history will have no equal in this field of endeavor. The volume is composed of a series of essays, each of which can be used alone or in context with others. The contributors and the editorial board are distinguished scholars of ecumenical character who have generated an outstanding narrative on early church spirituality in a variety of contexts (iconography, art, literature, Monasticism, etc.). An index is provided at the end.

151. **Eerdmans' Handbook to Christianity in America**. Mark Noll, et al. Grand Rapids, Mich., Eerdmans, 1983. 507p.

The work is divided into four sections, chronologically sequenced: "God and the Colonies," "Christianity and Democracy," "The Era of Crisis," and "Christianity in the Secular Age." It provides an exposition of the entire Christian experience in a historical context beginning with the early Puritans and bringing the reader to the modern evangelicals. There are numerous graphs, charts, and diagrams illustrating the points made in the text. The work is both interesting and useful in its interpretation of the Christian experience in this country. For purposes of enlightenment, quotations help the reader comprehend the thoughts of those being studied. There is a detailed table of contents, but no index.

152. **Handbook of Church History**. Hubert Jedin and John Dolan, eds. New York, Herder and Herder, 1965-1981. 10v.

Translated from Jedin's *Handbuch der Kirchengeschichte* (3rd edition, New York, Herder, 1962-1979; 7v. in 10), this represents a major contribution to church history from a Roman Catholic viewpoint. The purpose is to examine both the Church's external career in the world and its inner life. Major events and personalities are described and explained with respect to their impact on or relationship to such elements as church doctrine, liturgy, dogma, organization, and literature. Beginning with volume 1, "From the Apostolic Community to Constantine," by Karl Baus, the sequence of events is presented in scholarly fashion. Each volume is a work of separate authorship, with three written by Roger Aubert. The final volume treats the church in the modern age and provides an appropriate capstone to an erudite, well-conceived effort. A related set is *A History of Christianity*, by Kenneth S. Latourette (Harper & Row, 1975, 2v.).

153. **Historical Atlas of Religion in America.** Rev. ed. Edwin S. Gaustad. New York, Harper & Row, 1976. 189p.

Originally published in 1962, this more recent edition substitutes maps of counties for those of states. (State maps were considered by the publishers to be inconsequential.) This atlas attempts to show the expansion and development of religion in the United States from colonial times in the mid-seventeenth century to 1970. The emphasis is on Christianity, but other faiths are examined as well. The maps are integrated with descriptive narrative and charts and tables to provide insight into the type of development which took place within church groups and denominations. One is able to compare the development of Christian influence in terms of numerical distributions. There are separate indexes for authors and titles, places, and religious bodies as well as names and subjects.

154. **Historical Atlas of the Religions of the World.** Isma'il Ragi Faruqi. New York, Macmillan, 1974. 346p.

Developed by the editor with an international team of scholars, this work provides not only excellent and authoritative historical maps, but scholarly narratives on the histories of religion. These are integrated with the graphic material, which in addition to maps, includes photographs, tables, and charts describing the links of religion to cultural and geographic locations. Past religions are covered first, contemporary ethnic and universal religions next, and finally, specific areas and religions. There is an appendix of chronologies of the various religions treated, with the current religions being subdivided by the particular denominations which comprise them. There is a detailed table of contents, and subject and name indexes provide access.

155. **The Macmillan Atlas History of Christianity.** Franklin Hamlin Littell. New York, Macmillan, 1976. 176p.

Arranged by historical periods, this work illustrates the development of Christianity through graphic representation of its encounters and in some cases its disputes with other ideologies and belief systems. Developed with a Protestant perspective, it provides chronological coverage of the emergence and growth of Christianity in considering such topics as the Jewish matrix, the Carolinginian Empire, and the age of Colonialism. There are nearly 200 maps and over 100 separate illustrations linked to the textual description, providing a useful framework for comprehension of the material presented. There is some variation in size and detail among the maps but, in general, they are quite adequate. Access is provided through a general index.

156. **Profiles in Belief: The Religious Bodies of the United States and Canada.** Arthur Carl Piepkorn. New York, Harper & Row, 1977- . (In progress).

Work has slowed perceptibly in this excellent effort, which was projected to be a seven-volume set. The first four volumes (in three) were completed by 1979 in short order, but since then there has been no further publication. An extremely comprehensive directory with a good coverage of the historical background of the various religious bodies in the United States, the urgency of completion has been lessened considerably with the appearance of other works listed in both the "Directories and Annuals" and the "Dictionaries, Encyclopedias, and Handbooks" segments of this chapter. Nevertheless, it represents an important contribution in the volumes completed, which deal with various aspects of the Catholic faith (volume 1), Protestanism (volume 2), and Pentecostalism (volumes 3 and 4). Each contains articles which include history, beliefs, statistics, and practices, as well as addresses.

THE BIBLE

The books of the Old Testament were written in Hebrew at various times between 1200 and 100 B.C. Final decisions as to which ones should be included in the Jewish canon (list of divinely inspired books) appear to have been made around 100 A.D. A notable translation into Greek, known as the *Septuagint*, was made in the third and second centuries B.C. It included some books not officially accepted as part of the Jewish canon. The books of the New Testament were written in Greek, mainly in the last half of the first century A.D. By the end of the second century, the contents of today's New Testament were fairly clear. The first complete list of the twenty-seven books accepted today appeared in the *Easter*

Letter of Athanasius in 367 A.D. A major translation of the Bible into Latin (known as the *Vulgate*) was completed by Jerome in 404 A.D. Articles in general encyclopedias give further details. The most detailed description of Bible origin and development is found in *The Cambridge History of the Bible* (see entry 194). A chapter on Bibles and related texts, in volume 4, in *The Best in the Literature of Philosophy of World Religions*, of *The Reader's Adviser* (13th edition, R. R. Bowker, 1986-1987, 6v.) describes various versions and editions. Only a few of the major English-language versions are listed here, and they are given in chronological order of initial publication.

Versions and Editions

157. King James or Authorized Version (1611).

Because of the majestic beauty of its language, this version is still a favorite among Protestants. Numerous editions are in print. The most frequently used of all Protestant Bibles, a recent version (1982) has introduced modern language "where necessary."

158. Douay Bible (1582-1610, rev. by Challoner in 1749-1750).

Translated from the *Vulgate*, this version has been for Roman Catholics what the *King James* has been for Protestants. Differs from Protestant versions inasmuch as the Apocryphal books are accepted as canonical and integrated in the text.

159. American Standard Version or *American Revised Version* (1901).

Published shortly after the *English Revised Version* (1885), it has been widely used by American Protestants. A revision first appeared in 1971 as the *New American Standard Bible* from World Publishing Company. Other publishers followed suit.

160. The Holy Scriptures. Jewish Publication Society, 1908.

Various editions of the Old Testament Bible have appeared in English since this work was published. The most recently completed revision is a three-volume edition of a new translation of the *Holy Scriptures According to the Masoretic Text* done over a twenty-year period, 1962-1982. It includes volume 1, *The Torah*, volume 2, *The Prophets*, and volume 3, *The Writings*.

161. Revised Standard Version. Nashville, Tenn., Nelson, 1952.

This revision into modern English by a group of American scholars from many denominations attempts to follow the style of the *King James Version*. There is both a Protestant edition and a Catholic edition with the Apocrypha.

162. The Jerusalem Bible. Garden City, N.Y., Doubleday, 1966.

Preceded by a French edition (1956) prepared by the Dominicans at L'Ecole Biblique in Jerusalem, the English version is a direct translation from the original languages, with references to the French edition. It won the Thomas More Association Medal for "the most distinguished contribution to Catholic literature in 1966." A new edition appeared in 1985, entitled *The New Jerusalem Bible*.

163. The New English Bible. New York, Oxford University Press, 1971.

The result of more than twenty years of work by a group of scholars to translate the Bible into clear, modern English, this one differs from the *Revised Standard Version* in that no effort was made to follow the style of the *King James Version*. Representatives from the various Protestant churches of the British Isles combined to provide a more faithful rendering of the available texts.

164. **The New American Bible.** New York, P. J. Kenedy, 1971.
Sponsored by the Bishops' Committee of the Confraternity of Christian Doctrine, this is a thoroughly modern translation for American Catholics, including the deuterocanonical books. It includes textual notes on Old Testament readings and an encyclopedic dictionary of biblical and general Catholic information.

Other modern Bibles include the *Living Bible: Holman Illustrated Edition*, by Kenneth N. Taylor (Holman, 1973) and the *New Testament in Modern English*, by J. B. Philips (rev. ed., Macmillan, 1973).

Bibliographies, Indexes, and Abstracts

165. **International Zeitschriftenschau für Bibelwissenschaft und Grenzgebiete/International Review of Biblical Studies.** 1951/1952- . Ann. Tübingen, West Germany, Verlag Katholisches Bibelwerk.
An annual publication which provides abstracts of Bible studies which appear as periodical articles, monographic works, or essays in collections. Titles of the studies appear in the language of the original document, although most abstracts are in German. Entries are arranged by classification of the subject covered; access is facilitated by an index of authors. Another international bibliography of foreign extraction is *Elenchus Bibliographicus Biblicus* (Rome, Biblical Institute, 1968- , v.49-), which has appeared as a separate publication since 1968. Prior to that time, it appeared as part of the journal *Biblica*. This Italian publication provides extensive listings of biblical scholarship, also on an annual basis, and has author and subject indexes.

166. **Multi-Purpose Tools for Bible Study.** 3rd ed. Frederick W. Danker. St. Louis, Mo., Concordia, 1970. 295p.
Although this work is getting on in years and is showing signs of obsolescence, it is still the best literature guide to the study of the Bible. It provides excellent coverage of standard reference tools which, of course, should be supplemented with a more recent bibliographic aid. Designed primarily for the serious student or researcher rather than the layperson, it provides chapters on such tools as concordances, Hebrew and Greek grammars and lexicons, and Bible dictionaries and commentaries. In addition to chapters that list and describe these aids, there are additional chapters that facilitate their use. A more recent work which might be used to update the material is *The Bible Study Resource Guide*, by Joseph D. Allison (Nelson, 1982). This is designed for the layperson and provides the explanations of the Bible versions and the reference tools that relate to them.

167. **New Testament Abstracts: A Record of Current Periodical Literature.** 1956- . 3/yr. Cambridge, Mass., Weston School of Theology.
Now in its thirty-first year, this is the oldest continuing abstract service on Bible studies in the English language. The abstracts cover the literature on the Bible which has appeared in a variety of Western languages from periodicals of varied extraction. Catholic, Protestant, and Jewish periodicals all contribute the source material. Each volume contains indexes of scripture texts, authors, book reviews, and book notices published in the third issue. All abstracts appear in English regardless of the language of the original

publication. The work is divided into two segments, periodicals and books, covering Gospels, Acts, Epistles, Revelation, biblical theology, and the world of the New Testament. Some 350 journals are selectively abstracted.

168. **Old Testament Abstracts.** 1978- . 3/yr. Washington, D.C., Catholic Biblical Association of America.

Developed on the model of *New Testament Abstracts* (see entry 167) in terms of its thrice-yearly frequency and its style of coverage, this newer work has also made a significant contribution in an area not previously covered by an abstracting service. Each year approximately 350 journals from various denominations and geographic regions provide the source material for nearly 1,000 abstracts in English. These articles cover all aspects of Old Testament study (Pentateuch, the historical books, the writings, etc.). Like the earlier service, this one also provides a separate listing of book reviews, and indexes of authors and scripture texts. In addition, there is an index of words in ancient languages such as Hebrew.

169. **The Word of God: A Guide to English Versions of the Bible.** Lloyd R. Bailey, ed. Atlanta, Ga., John Knox, 1982. 228p.

A well-conceived and informative literature guide to nine different English-language versions of the Bible, this work presents the essays of distinguished authors who were given the task of evaluating the Bible in terms of the criteria they deem important. They were asked to consider the original manuscripts, interpretations provided by translators, and English usage. The Bibles selected were the *Revised Standard Version, New English Bible, New Jewish Version, New American Standard Bible, Jerusalem Bible, Today's English Version, Living Bible, New American Bible,* and *New International Version.* The appendices include a commentary about the *King James Version* as well as a summary comparison by Bailey. There is an index to scripture references.

Concordances and Quotations

170. **Analytical Concordance to the Bible.** 22nd American ed., rev. by W. B. Stevenson. Robert Young. New York, Funk and Wagnalls, 1955; repr., Grand Rapids, Mich., Eerdmans, 1973. 1090p.

The subtitle reads: "About 311,000 references, subdivided under the Hebrew and Greek originals, with the literal meaning and pronunciation of each." Names of people and places are included. There are supplements in this edition which have appeared for the first time: "Recent Discoveries in Bible Lands," by W. F. Albright, and "The Canon of Scripture," by R. K. Harrison and E. F. Harrison. The main text consists of the word listings (nouns, adjectives, verbs, and adverbs) in alphabetical order. These are identified with scriptural passages as well as definitions and indications of original forms in Greek, Hebrew and Aramaic when necessary. The analytical coverage of words in the ancient languages has given this work a reputation for comprehensiveness and has established it as a landmark effort. Based on the *King James Version.*

171. **An Analytical Concordance to the Revised Standard Version of the New Testament.** Clinton Morrison. Philadelphia, Westminster, 1979. 770p.

In what appears to be an attempt to emulate the work of Young (see entry 170), Morrison has apparently been successful in establishing the first modern analytical Bible concordance. Whether it achieves the same recognition and ultimately the same status as did Young with his work on the *King James Version*, is secondary to the fact that a work such as this was needed. The *Revised Standard Version* is considered to be a more authoritative translation than was *King James*, and its analysis of the English and original Greek wording makes it an important vehicle for both students and scholars. The concordance is divided into two parts, the concordance itself and an index-lexicon. The concordance provides for each English word references to Scripture as well as definitions, Greek phraseology, and English transliterations. The index-lexicon identifies the transliterated Greek words with the English words used in the Bible, thus serving as an index to the concordance.

172. **Complete Concordance to the Bible (Douay Version).** Newton Wayland Thompson and Raymond Stock. St. Louis, Mo., Herder, 1945. 1914p.

The Douay version is the old edition (still revered by many) which has occupied a prominent place in the rites of Catholics through the years. A parallel can be drawn to the *King James Version* in its remarkable longevity and appeal in the light of many subsequest discoveries, revisions, and new translations. Therefore this concordance retains an important position in libraries that serve the needs of Catholic patrons. First published in 1942, the concordance was revised and expanded only three years later with the addition of many words and references. Citations to passages with excerpts from them are found after each listed word. Provides a good coverage of words in the Bible except for those of very common, nondistinctive character.

173. **Cruden's Complete Concordance to the Old and New Testament.** Grand Rapids, Mich., Zondervan, 1976. 783p.

The most famous of the concordances, it was first published in 1737 and has achieved a classic position among reference books of this type. It has been revised, reedited, and published under a variety of imprints since that time. A paperback edition was published in 1976. It presents about 250,000 English words from the *King James Version* in alphabetical order. Not nearly as complete as some of its successors in coverage of the canon, it remains useful for its treatment of the Apocrypha. The work is divided into three sections: common words, proper names, and apocryphal words. It provides definitions for proper names and for common words with obscure meanings. Some of the modern reprints omit the Apocrypha section, which greatly affects its value as a reference tool.

174. **The Home Book of Bible Quotations.** Burton Egbert Stevenson. New York, Harper & Row, 1949; repr., 1977. 645p.

As part of the familiar Home Book series, this work has been a popular tool for libraries over the years. A quotation handbook based on the *King James Version* with some references to variations in the *Revised Version*, quotations are arranged alphabetically by subject or keywords. There is a concordance-type index to facilitate access. Coverage includes the Apocrypha of both the Old and New Testaments. The subjects are listed in the table of contents, while the index identifies the wording of the scriptures with references given to the subjects. Subjects may be persons, places, emotions, acts, concepts, etc. Exact references are given to Bible passages. A more recent quotation handbook based on the same version is *Biblical Quotations*, edited by Jennifer Speake (Facts on File, 1983). The arrangement employed is by books of the Bible with an index of keywords and subjects or thematic headings.

175. **Modern Concordance to the New Testament.** Michael Darton, ed. Garden City, N.Y., Doubleday, 1976. 786p.

Based on an earlier French work, this provides a thematic approach to the New Testament geared to its representation in several modern English versions. An alphabetical arrangement of major themes is subdivided by classified groupings of more specific, thematic elements. The ultimate purpose is to provide a guide to the Greek text which serves as the basis for the modern Bible translations, thus the organization of the themes is based upon the Greek scripts. Headings are in English with Greek equivalents provided. There are indexes of both English and Greek words. These will be used especially to locate a particular passage or verse when only a word is known.

176. **Nelson's Complete Concordance of the New American Bible.** Stephen J. Hartdegan, gen. ed. Nashville, Tenn., Nelson, 1977. 1274p.

The Nelson Company has been active in the last decade in developing new concordances with the aid of the computer. This work on the *New American Bible* (a relatively recent translation by Catholic scholars), presents 300,000 entries grouped under 18,000 key terms. These major terms are arranged alphabetically and are subdivided by entries which are listed in order of their occurrence in the Bible. Keywords are set off in boldface capitals to facilitate their use. Frequency of appearance is indicated for keywords as well. References are provided for exact locations in the Bible. A list of omitted words representing nonsignificant descriptors is given in the preface.

177. **Strong's Exhaustive Concordance of the Bible with Key-word Comparison.** Rev. ed. James Strong. Nashville, Tenn., Abingdon, 1980.

This is a reprint of one of the classic concordances, originally published in 1894. Strong's work is regarded as the most complete in terms of its coverage of every word of the *King James Version* (including article adjectives and other nondistinctive types). These are listed alphabetically in two places with the important words in the main text and the forty-seven common words in the appendix. In addition, there is a comparative treatment given to the *Revised Version* which includes the American variations, and shows the differences in wording. There are brief dictionaries of the original Hebrew and Greek terms with references to the English words. The apocryphal books are not covered. *The New Strong's Exhaustive Concordance of the Bible* (Nelson, 1984) is one of the modern computer-generated concordances which has produced a pleasant, new format. This involves changes in sequence of information presented in the entries, simplified instructions, and the addition of some helpful new features.

Dictionaries, Encyclopedias, and Handbooks

178. **Dictionary of Proper Names and Places in the Bible.** O. Odelaine and R. Séguineau. Garden City, N.Y., Doubleday, 1981. 479p.

Translated from the French and adapted by Matthew J. O'Connell, this has proved to be a useful dictionary of proper names identified in the *Jerusalem Bible*. Although the majority of these words can be found in other Bible dictionaries, it is unique in its coverage of this modern version. Coverage is provided of words in both the Old and New Testaments and entries include the English form of the name, transliteration of the Hebrew or Greek form as originally used, frequency of occurrence in the Bible, definition and etymology, as well as an indication of its importance. There is an introductory essay explaining the purpose of the work and the importance of biblical names. There are name listings and chronological tables. A word of caution: indexing may not be complete for each word, and it may appear more frequently than the number of references provided.

179. **Encyclopedia of Biblical Theology: The Complete Sacramentum Verbi.** 3rd ed. Johannes B. Bauer. New York, Crossroad, 1981. 1141p.

This work was translated from the German language and represents the combined efforts of biblical experts from West Germany, Austria, France, and Switzerland. It is a highpoint of erudition and consistency for Roman Catholic scholarship and covers important words, their changes of meaning, and significance. Articles are cogent, well written, and provide an analysis of the reasoning behind Catholic theological beliefs. Although of scholarly quality, the tool can be used by the laity. Entries range from a few paragraphs to several pages in length, depending upon the importance or significance of the topic. Articles are signed and provide bibliographies of both English- and foreign-language sources. There are indexes of biblical passages and of Hebrew and Greek words, among others.

180. **The Illustrated Bible Dictionary.** Wheaton, Ill., Tyndale, 1980. 3v.

A complete revision and expansion of the popular *New Bible Dictionary* (Tyndale, 1962; rev., 1965), this work has been prepared by a distinguished group of editors. Contributions from 165 scholars from the United States, Great Britain, Australia, and other countries make this a work of international significance for English-speaking people. Articles cover the *Revised Standard Version* in terms of its books, people, major words, and doctrines. Coverage also is given to background information on the history, geography, customs, and culture of Israel and surrounding countries. There are more than 1,600 photographs, some of which are in color, maps, charts, diagrams, and tables. Bibliographies are provided as well. The work is impressive in depth, quality, and physical format and should be considered on the same level as the *Interpreter's Dictionary of the Bible* (see entry 182).

181. **The International Standard Bible Encyclopedia.** Rev. ed. Geoffrey W. Bromiley, gen. ed. Grand Rapids, Mich., Eerdmans, 1979- . (In progress).

Since its original edition in 1915, and revision in 1930, this work has been regarded as a standard for library purchase and a classic in the field. The new edition is projected as a five-volume set, and all indications are that it will assume a similar position of importance. Volume 3 was completed in 1986, just slightly behind schedule, bringing the coverage from A to P. Designed for teachers, students, pastors, and interested laypersons, it covers all persons and places mentioned in the *Revised Standard Version* along with references to similar words in the *King James Version*, the *American Standard Version*, and the *New English Bible*. Entries include pronunciation, etymology, and evolution of meaning through both the Old Testament and New Testament. There are numerous illustrations, some in color. Also covered are terms relating to theology. Cross-references are supplied. Volume 4 is projected for publication in 1988, and volume 5, in 1989.

182. **The Interpreter's Dictionary of the Bible: An Illustrated Encyclopedia.** New York, Abingdon, 1962. 4v. supp., 1976.

Considered the leading scholarly encyclopedic dictionary, it covers both the *King James Version* and the *Revised Standard Version*. Its full subtitle indicates its purpose in "identifying and explaining all proper names and significant terms and subjects in the Holy Scriptures, including the Apocrypha, with attention to archaeological discoveries and research into the life and faith of ancient times." It is a work of modern scholarship which includes references to the Dead Sea Scrolls and other recently investigated ancient manuscripts. Developed for the use of preachers, scholars, students, teachers, and general readers, it has met the needs of this diverse grouping in an extraordinary manner. Each important article receives a bibliography, and the work provides maps and illustrations, some of which are in color. An indispensable source, it proves to be an excellent companion to *The Interpreter's Bible* (see entry 190). The fifth volume or supplement represented a departure from the past in adding new articles of ecumenical nature as well as updating material needing revision.

183. **Nelson's Bible Encyclopedia for the Family: A Comprehensive Guide to the World of the Bible.** Nashville, Tenn., Nelson, 1982. 288p.

One of the several publications which in the recent past has established the family, especially the young people, as the target audience. The format is attractive and tends to appeal to a variety of age levels. Coverage is given to the complete world of the Bible in twenty chapters, beginning with "The Bible's Story," and then leading into its contents, translation, archaeology, the home, family, clothes, geography, etc. Chapters are subdivided by nations or geographic regions. The articles are written in simple, easy-to-understand language in a clear manner, and are well illustrated in colorful fashion. Charts and drawings (some of comic book variety) are provided. The work was developed through the efforts of the Scripture Union, an interdenominational, international organization.

184. **The New International Dictionary of Biblical Archaeology.** Edward M. Blaiklock and R. K. Harrison, eds. Grand Rapids, Mich., Zondervan, 1983. 485p.

Considered to be an outstanding, comprehensive scholarly dictionary which covers all aspects of biblical archaeology. Entries are provided for personal names, place names, deities, texts, languages, animals, architecture, archaeological techniques, furniture, etc. There are more than 800 articles from twenty contributors from all over the world. Articles are signed and include bibliographies and cross-references. They vary in length from a few columns to a dozen pages or more. There are more than 200 photographs, including a sixteen-page section in full color. Maps are incorporated, although possibly not as frequently as needed. Emphasis is on providing facts of interest to a wide audience; theological interpretation is left to the reader.

185. **The New Unger's Bible Handbook.** Rev. and updated. Merrill F. Unger. Chicago, Moody, 1984. 720p.

Since 1966, this work has held a respected position among reference tools. It has had a conservative orientation based on the evangelical tradition. The new edition continues in the same vein, and it will have appeal for the layperson. Attractive in format, the descriptions provided are brief and to-the-point with little identification of scholarly source material. There are numerous illustrations, including photographs, drawings, maps, charts, diagrams, and colorful chronologies. The books of the Bible are explained in regard to their place in canonical literature, authorship, and themes. Brief background articles cover related aspects of Bible study such as history and archaeology. An earlier work intended for the same audience is *Abingdon Bible Handbook* by Edward P. Blair (Abingdon, 1975). Blair is a conservative but presents an impartial summary of both liberal and conservative views.

186. **Theological Dictionary of the New Testament.** Gerhard Kittel and Gerhard Friedrich, eds. Grand Rapids, Mich., Eerdmans, 1985. 1356p.

This is an abridgement of the author's monumental ten-volume work of the same name (Eerdmans, 1964-1976), translated from the German by Geoffrey W. Bromiley, who also was responsible for this shorter version. The earlier, major work brought contributions from many specialists. It defined in great length the Christian meanings of 2,300

Greek terms, some articles reaching monographic proportions. Known as "Kittel," it is regarded as an indispensable aid for scholarship. The new "Kittel" retains the same number of entries as does the original, but shortens them in drastic fashion. Entries still cover history, variant meanings, and connotations, but the emphasis is on biblical usage with far less attention given to original context. Designed to appeal to a wide range of users, from beginning students to scholars and specialists in need of a convenient information source who do not mind the deletion of bibliographical references.

187. **Theological Dictionary of the Old Testament.** Johannes G. Botterweck and Helmer Ringgren. Grand Rapids, Mich., Eerdmans, 1974- . (In progress).

Projected as a twelve-volume set, this is a translation of a German work also in progress. The English translation by John T. Willis is progressing at a rate which closely matches its initial production in German. Considered to be an extremely valuable resource for students and scholars, it provides lengthy, technical articles on important words, tracing the etymology in ancient languages. Definitions are given, as are expositions of semantic relations and the word's social, cultural, and historical context. There is a liberal provision of footnotes and bibliographies, and students will appreciate the discussions of the theological importance of the words. Articles are signed by contributors who are noted scholars. It should be considered as a companion to the full set of Kittel's *Theological Dictionary of the New Testament* (see entry 186).

Commentaries

188. **Encyclopedia of Biblical Interpretations: A Millenial Anthology.** Manaham M. Kasher. New York, American Biblical Encyclopedia Society, 1953- . (In progress).

This is a translation by Rabbi Harry Freedman of an extensive thirty-five-volume set which is being shortened somewhat in the process of translation. About half of the original edition has been covered in the nine volumes produced thus far. It presents a collection of Jewish interpretations of and commentaries on the Bible from the time of Moses to the Talmudic-Midrashic period. Each verse of the Bible is covered and the sources are identified. Included among the commentary are both exegetical works and parables, with careful documentation of the sources both modern and ancient. Bibliographies and indexes are included in each volume.

189. **The Jerome Biblical Commentary.** Raymond E. Brown, et al. Englewood Cliffs, N.J., Prentice-Hall, 1968. 2v. in 1.

This continues to be recognized as an important work. It provides a brief but informative commentary by Roman Catholic scholars from American universities on the various parts of the Bible. There are eighty articles on the individual books of the Bible, the Pentateuch, Wisdom Literature, criticism of both the Old and New Testaments, biblical geography, Pauline and Johannine theology, etc. Bibliographies are also provided. The perspective in which the work was undertaken reflects the ecumenicism developed through the Second Vatican Council, and the book emerged as a product of the increased emphasis on the part of the Roman Catholic Church on biblical scholarship. There may be some narrowness in its limitation to American contributors only, but it does provide an indication of the heart and mind of that sector.

190. **The Interpreter's Bible.** New York, Abingdon-Cokesbury, 1951-1957. 12v.

An outstanding work in every way, the subtitle states "The Holy Scriptures in the *King James* and *Revised Standard* versions, with general articles and introduction, exegesis, and exposition for each book of the Bible." A product of the combined energies of some of the best minds in the area of biblical scholarship, most of the large Protestant denominations were represented among the consulting editors. Some 125 contributors were involved, and today it is among the most important English-language works. Treating the texts of both the *King James* and *Revised Standard* versions, each passage is submitted to analysis and receives both exegesis and exposition. (The former provides awareness of the setting and the meanings of words in the phrases, while the latter provides the present-day meanings of the passages.) The work also provides introductory material, maps, and topical articles. Developed for the general reader as well as the specialist, this is an indispensable tool for Bible study.

191. **Interpreter's Concise Commentary.** Nashville, Tenn., Abingdon, 1983. 8v.

This is a revision of *The Interpreter's One-Volume Commentary on the Bible*, edited by Charles Laymon (Abingdon, 1971), and similarly is based on the *Revised Standard Version*. It has been divided into eight paperback volumes, each of which deals with a different aspect or issue. The volumes cover *The Pentateuch, Old Testament History, Wisdom Literature and Poetry, The Major Prophets, The Minor Prophets and the Apocrypha, The Gospels, Acts and Paul's Letters,* and *Revelation and the General Epistles.* The contributors represent a wide range of scholars and different parts of the world. Commentary is generally lucid, with information given regarding historical, literary, and linguistic study of the Bible. Each volume has an introduction, bibliographies, and maps. In general, the set represents a good purchase at a reasonable price.

192. **Peake's Commentary on the Bible.** Rev. ed. Matthew Black and H. H. Rowley, eds. New York, Nelson, 1962; repr., 1985. 1126p.

Another standard work based on the *Revised Standard Version*, the original edition appeared in 1919 with a supplement in 1936. The present edition was completely revised and updated by a team of illustrious British and American Bible scholars. They have signed their articles and list their credentials. The revision was undertaken due to the discovery of ancient manuscripts requiring the development of new versions of the Bible and new interpretations of a number of the passages. There are articles on a variety of general subjects and topical matters as well as the analyses of the Bible passages. The work concludes with a general index, set of maps, and geographical dictionary.

Histories and Atlases

193. **Atlas of the Bible.** Luc H. Grollenberg. J. M. H. Reid and H. H. Rowley, trs. and eds. New York, Nelson, 1956. 165p.

This known standard in the field, originally a Dutch publication, is a scholarly work which traces the historical development of the Bible from its beginning in the time of Abraham to the time of Christ. There are approximately thirty-five maps, carefully developed and well presented in color. Historical development is portrayed in graphic fashion in over 400 black-and-white photographs. These are integrated with an excellent and thorough textual narrative which provides an enlightening summary of biblical history, geography, and archaeology. At the end, there is a detailed gazetteer-type index which identifies individuals, geographical features, and peoples who were deemed to be significant in history.

More recent but less familiar titles include *Atlas of the Bible* (Nelson, 1985) and the *Reader's Digest Atlas of the Bible* (Random House, 1981).

194.   **Cambridge History of the Bible.** Cambridge, England, Cambridge University Press, 1963-1970. 3v.

An important standard in the field, this is an authoritative and scholarly record of the development of the Bible. The volumes appeared at different times, with number 1 being the last to appear. Volume 1 covers the period from the beginning to Jerome and provides exposition of both the Old Testament and the New Testament and the Bible in the early Church. Volume 2 covers the Western world to the time of the Reformation, providing descriptions of book production and Bible illustration in early times. Volume 3, the first published, treats the most recent period, from the Reformation to the present day. Each volume has a table of contents, bibliography, an index of biblical references, and a detailed, general index. There is no comprehensive index to the entire set.

195.   **The Macmillan Bible Atlas.** Rev. ed. Jochanan Aharoni and Michael Avi-Yonah. New York, Macmillan, 1977. 184p.

Considered a work of sound scholarship and skillful cartography, this atlas contains a large number of maps (264). On close inspection, one fails to find much difference between this revision and the earlier edition of 1968. Number of pages, maps, and size remain the same. Most of the revision centers on maps of the city of Jerusalem. The atlas covers the period from 3000 B.C. to 200 A.D. and graphically depicts social and political events pertaining to the influence of religious, political, economic, and military events during the periods of the Old and New Testaments. It uses the *Revised Standard Version* for its quotations and place names. Although criticized for certain weaknesses in physical format, its scholarship and fruitful yield are acknowledged by all.

196.   **New Bible Atlas.** J. J. Bimson, et al., eds. Wheaton, Ill., Tyndale, 1985. 128p.

A recent effort which has made an impact on the field, this atlas was developed out of the same research activity which created *The Illustrated Bible Dictionary* (see entry 180). A product of British scholarship, it provides some eighty maps, which compares favorably with other biblical atlases except for *The Macmillan Bible Atlas* (see entry 195). Most of the maps are in color and illustrate a variety of events in biblical history. Cartographically, it is as good as or better than other current atlases, and it is superior to *Macmillan* in clarity and visual interest. Topography, geological features, vegetation, climate, and trade routes are depicted. There are numerous photographs and ample expository narrative providing summaries of biblical history. In general it is a far more attractive publication than most of the older atlases and should be welcomed by both laypersons and serious students.

197.   **Oxford Bible Atlas.** 3rd ed. Herbert G. May. New York, Oxford University Press, 1984. 144p.

As part of the new breed of recently produced Bible atlases, much attention has gone into the physical appearance of this volume. It is a well-illustrated, attractive effort which has emphasized the recent findings in biblical scholarship and archaeological study. Beginning with an introduction which describes the climate and geographic features of the area around Palestine, the story of the Israelites is graphically presented through maps and illustrative material from the time of Saul in 1025 B.C. to the fall of Jerusalem in 70 A.D. Both topographical and historical maps are used to enlighten the reader about the context in which biblical history was made. There is not as much textual narrative as is found in other atlases.

MYTHOLOGY AND FOLKLORE

Bibliographies, Indexes, Abstracts, Etc.

198. **A Bibliography of North American Folklore and Folksong.** 2nd ed. rev. Charles Haywood. New York, Dover, 1961; repr., New York, Peter Smith. 2v.

Since its original edition in 1951, this work has achieved an enviable reputation as a comprehensive, classified bibliography which covers printed music and recordings as well as books. The more recent edition was a corrected revision of the initial effort, and added an index of composers, arrangers, and performers to the author and subject index. Title entries for individual songs are included. There are some descriptive and evaluative annotations. Volume 1 covers the American people north of Mexico, including Canada, and volume 2, the American Indians north of Mexico, including the Eskimos. Another work of importance is Katherine Smith Diehl's *Religions, Mythologies, Folklores: An Annotated Bibliography* (Scarecrow, 1962), which includes nearly 2,500 numbered items in a classified arrangement with an author and title index. *American Folklore: A Bibliography, 1950-1974* by Cathleen C. and John T. Flanagan (Scarecrow, 1977) provides brief annotations.

199. **Folklife Sourcebook: A Directory of Folklife Resources in the United States and Canada.** Peter T. Bartis and Barbara C. Fertig. Washington, D.C., Library of Congress, 1986. 152p. (Publications of the American Folklife Center, no. 14).

This is the most recent effort at control of resources in the field of American folklore. It represents a directory of organizations which house materials, offer programming, or publish resource material on folklife. These include federal agencies, state folk cultural programs, societies and other organizations, institutions, and foundations. Serial publications are listed. All receive treatment in separate sections of the work, with the Archives of Folklore, Folklife, and Ethnomusicology being described in section 6. Entries provide address, initial year, telephone number, regulations regarding access and services, research facilities, collection size and format with special collections noted, and publications. Arrangement is alphabetical by state or city. There are additional listings of educational programs in universities, recording companies, and other helpful directories.

200. **Index to Fairy Tales, 1949-1972: Including Folklore, Legends and Myths in Collections.** Norma Olin Ireland. Westwood, Mass., F. W. Faxon, 1973. 741p. Supp. 1973-1977, 1979, 259p. (Reprinted by Scarecrow, 1985).

Compiled as a continuation of Mary Huse Eastman's *Index to Fairy Tales, Myths and Legends* (F. W. Faxon, 1926, supps., 1937, 1952), this work indexes over 400 anthologies under titles and subjects. Collections of fairy tales, folklore, legends, and myths from all over the world are included in the coverage. Authors are identified only if their names appear in the titles, but the subject indexing is detailed, facilitating access. Since this volume presents itself as the third supplement to Eastman, its own supplement, which covers the period 1973-1977, is also considered the fourth supplement to Eastman. An additional 130 collections are indexed, most of which were published during this time period.

201. **Jewish Folklore: An Annotated Bibliography.** Eli Yassif. New York, Garland, 1986. 341p. (Garland Folklore Bibliographies, v. 10).

This is an annotated bibliography of international proportions on 100 years of contributions to the study of Jewish folklore. Textbooks and anthologies of folklore are not included. Annotations are both descriptive and evaluative and provide detailed information of the important and representative studies. The period covered ranges from 1872 to 1980 and represents over 1,300 numbered entries. The bibliography is arranged alphabetically by author and is selective in the entries that were chosen for inclusion. Areas of study excluded are East European Jewish culture and Judeo-Spanish folklore. A general index is provided for access which covers themes, motifs, names, and approaches. The compiler is a professor at Ben-Gurion University in Israel and is a recognized authority in the field of Hebrew literature.

Dictionaries, Encyclopedias, and Handbooks

202.   **Brewer's Dictionary of Phrase and Fable.** Centenary ed. Ivor H. Evans, ed. New York, Harper & Row, 1981. 1213p.

Since its appearance in 1870, Ebenezer Brewer's work has undergone frequent revision and has come to be regarded as a standard in the field. Arranged alphabetically are allusions, heroes of mythology and fiction, popular colloquial and proverbial phrases, titles, and linguistic oddities of various sorts. Because of its eclectic character and expansive scope, it is considered a work of value both for general reference and for purposes of entertainment relating to the interest or curiosity of the user. The centenary edition seeks "to return more closely to Dr. Brewer's original conception" and has deleted many entries of nondistinctive words which would be found in the general dictionary. More contemporary phrases have been added. Libraries should not discard the old edition but use both of them for reference.

203.   **Bulfinch's Mythology: The Age of Fable; The Age of Chivalry; Legends of Charlemagne.** Thomas Bulfinch. New York, Crowell, 1970. 957p.

Bulfinch was a nineteenth-century accountant who spent much of his leisure in the pursuit of classical studies, which he had begun earlier in life as a student at Harvard. By convention, his three books on mythology and legend have become part of a one-volume trilogy. This edition retains the original text, but is enlarged and enhanced through additional material and a thorough revision of the index. The result is an excellent and informative dictionary-index which provides definitions and identifications of some length of all the proper nouns covered in the text, with references to the pages of the tales in which they are found. Hundreds of tales are related, beginning with Prometheus and continuing through the period of Charlemagne. These are translated or collected from a variety of sources, making this an unusually convenient resource for study of folklore and legend. Another standard in the field, *The Golden Bough*, by Sir James George Frazer, provides an interpretation of the growth and development of mystical belief systems and their relationship to customs and institutions. The original two-volume edition (1890) was later expanded to twelve volumes and has appeared in the form of one-volume abridgements. It is an outstanding piece of classical scholarship, with copious notes and references to source material.

204.   **A Dictionary of British Folk-Tales in the English Language.** Katharine M. Briggs. Bloomington, Ind., Indiana University Press, 1970-1971. 4v.

This extensive collection of the folk narratives and folk legends of Britain, either represented in the original form or summarized, is compiled from various printed and manuscript sources found in the F. J. Norton Collection in London. Recognized as one of the leading authorities on British folktales, Briggs has provided a distinction between folk narrative (folk-fiction for purpose of entertainment) and folk legend (once believed to be true). Part A is devoted to folk narratives (fables, fairy tales, jocular tales, novelle, and nursery tales) in keeping with the standard Aarne-Thompson classification scheme. Part B covers the folk legends such as fairies, ghosts, or giants. Within each category, the entries appear alphabetically by title (creating some difficulties in the cases of those which have elusive titles). There are approximately 850 entries in part A and over 1,200 in part B. Each part contains a bibliography, a classified index, and an index of titles.

205. **Dictionary of Classical Mythology: Symbols, Attributes, and Associations.** Robert E. Bell. Santa Barbara, Calif., ABC-Clio, 1982. 390p.

Considered an important contribution for a number of reasons, one of which is the topical arrangement given to the entries. Classical mythology is interpreted to be that of Greece and Rome, with references to other ancient belief systems (Assyrian, Egyptian, Etruscan, and Phoenician) when they relate to Greco-Roman topics. Subject entries are diverse and represent a good share of minor points and features such as "wine." There are numerous cross-references with citations to source material. The volume makes an excellent tool for authors in finding classical allusions. A list of surnames and a guide to persona appears at the end of the book. Although out-of-print librarians will continue to use *Crowell's Handbook of Classical Mythology*, by Edward Tripp (Crowell, 1970), which presents an alphabetical arrangement of characters and events with descriptions ranging from brief to extensive in length. Other related sources include *The Concise Dictionary of Greek & Roman Mythology* (Harper & Row, 1986) and *The Dictionary of Classical Mythology* (Basil Blackwell, 1986).

206. **A Dictionary of World Mythology.** Rev. and exp. ed. Arthur Cotterell. Oxford, Oxford University Press, 1986. 314p.

A revision and expansion of the 1980 edition, this work continues to be an important and useful source of information for the reference librarian. Unlike many of the other efforts in this category, this one provides excellent coverage of the more exotic and difficult to locate geographic locales. Although Europe is also covered, the major contribution is the inclusion of Asia, the Americas, Africa, and Oceania since this material is more unique and less duplicated in other sources. Sections are divided along geographic lines and each section is given an introductory overview of the historical development of myth and religion in that area. Under each section, entries are arranged alphabetically and include deities, place names, and terms. An index and maps have been added to the new edition. Also included are a bibliography and illustrations.

207. **An Encyclopedia of Fairies: Hobgoblins, Brownies, Bogies and Other Supernatural Creatures.** Katharine M. Briggs. New York, Pantheon, 1976. 481p.

A standard in the field, this work provides an alphabetical arrangement of entries dealing with the realm of the supernatural. These include individual creatures, descriptive articles regarding various phenomena, and identifications of related elements. Illustrations in the form of twenty-one black-and-white plates are included. These may well have been improved had they been in color. The coverage is of the world of the supernatural as represented in the tradition of Great Britain over the past 1,000 years. Descriptions are brief but informative for the most part, with citations to sources and cross-references. Pronunciations are included where needed. The bibliography at the end is followed by an index of types and motifs based on Stith Thompson's *Motif Index of Folk Literature* (Indiana University Press, 1955-1958, 6v.). The Thompson work provides a scheme of classification of the narrative elements in folktales, ballads, myths, fables, romances, etc. Volume 6 is an index.

208. Funk and Wagnall's Standard Dictionary of Folklore, Mythology, and Legend. Maria Leach, ed.; Jerome Fried, assoc. ed. New York, Funk and Wagnalls, 1973. 1236p.

Originally published as a two-volume work in 1949-1950, this has become the basic tool for reference in the field. The present effort is a reprint of that original edition. It has been repackaged into one volume with the addition of a key to the 2,405 countries, regions, cultures, areas, people, tribes, and ethnic groups described in the text. Entries are arranged alphabetically. Coverage is comprehensive and includes lengthy, signed survey articles of an authoritative nature on individual regions and major topics, complete with bibliographies, as well as concise articles on beliefs, customs, gods, heroes, songs, tales, dances, motifs, proverbs, games, etc. The dictionary is known for its richness of material.

209. The Illustrated Who's Who in Mythology. Michael Senior. New York, Macmillan, 1985. 223p.

This is an attractive, well-written, easy-to-understand dictionary of mythological figures from all over the world. Represented are Greek, Egyptian, Hindu, Indian, Chinese, Mayan, Hebrew, Scandinavian, Japanese, Russian, and other cultures. Entries are arranged alphabetically, beginning with Abraham, and number over 1,200 in all. The real utility of the work is in its breadth of coverage, since material on many of these cultures is not easily found in other works of ready reference. As its title implies, illustrations are a major feature, and black-and-white photographs appear on almost every page. There is also a sixteen-page section of fine color plates. Entries are generally brief in terms of description of the characters, with those from the more literate traditions receiving more space. Sources are given at the end of many entries. The seven-page introduction provides an excellent explanation of what constitutes mythology. The work concludes with a four-page index of themes.

210. Man, Myth and Magic: The Illustrated Encyclopedia of Mythology, Religion, and the Unknown. New ed. Richard Cavendish, ed.-in-chief. Compiled and edited by Yvonne Deutsch. New York, Marshall Cavendish, 1983. 12v. (Ref. ed., 1985).

Originally published in Great Britain in weekly installments, the first edition of this work appeared in 1970 in twenty-four volumes and was criticized for presenting certain material that was not needed or irrelevant. This edition has eliminated those segments. Coverage embraces a wide variety of topical matter, alphabetically arranged from volume 1 to volume 11. The twelfth volume is an index which refers to main articles and to topics. There is a bibliography with classified subject guides. Cross-references are used throughout. Illustrations are plentiful and appear on almost every page; some are in color. Coverage is given to such topics as alchemy, sorcery, witchcraft, etc., with long survey articles on the religions of the world. Among the many contributors who have provided signed articles are some of the very distinguished scholars of our time. This should prove to be a useful source of information.

211. Mythical and Fabulous Creatures: A Sourcebook and Research Guide. Malcolm South, ed. Westport, Conn., Greenwood Press, 1987. 393p.

This is an important new work which provides detailed studies by South and seventeen colleagues on twenty different creatures. Part I of the work is divided into four segments, beginning with "Birds and Beasts" (unicorn, dragon, phoenix, roc, griffin, chimera, and basilisk). The coverage continues with "Human Animal Composites" (manticora, mermaids, sirens, harpies, gorgon medusa, sphinx, minotaur, satyr, and centaur). "Creatures of the Darkness" covers vampires and werewolves, and the work concludes with "Giants and Fairies." The essays provide in-depth information on each creature and cover its origin as well as its treatment in literature, film, and art from ancient to modern times. A useful bibliography is furnished at the end of each essay. Part II contains a bibliography of general works on the subject as well as on individual creatures that do not fit into the four categories established in part I.

This is considered a top-notch reference book for both students and interested laypersons. Another new title is *Encyclopedia of Things That Never Were: Creatures, Places, and People,* by Michael Page and Robert Ingpen (Viking Penguin, 1987). This should prove to be a useful work for identification of fictional and fantastic characters. Over 400 entries from over 100 different source titles of witchcraft, mythology, astrology, and classic adventure fiction are furnished. Entries are ample and range from 150 to 2,000 words in length. The work is well illustrated in color.

7 ACCESSING INFORMATION IN THE VISUAL ARTS*

WORKING DEFINITION OF THE VISUAL ARTS

The term *art* is derived from the Latin word *ars*, which means skill or ability. At the time of the Italian Renaissance, the craft guilds were known as "arti," and the word "arte" denoted craftsmanship, skill, mastery of form, or inventiveness. The phrase "visual arts" serves to differentiate a group of arts that are nonverbal in character and that communicate by means of symbols and the juxtaposition of formal elements. This communication takes place through the creation of emotional moods and through expansion of the range of aesthetic experience. "Beauty," as such, is not an integral part of art, but more a matter of subjective judgment. Nevertheless, certain concepts of harmony, balance, and contrast have become a part of our way of thinking about art as a result of Greek speculation about the nature of beauty. "Style" normally refers to the whole body of work produced at a given time in history; however, there may be regional and national styles as well as one basic style for a period. In modern times, attention has even been given to the "styles" of individual artists. "Iconography" is the use of symbols by artists to express universal ideas; the Gothic style of architecture, for example, symbolized man's reaching out toward God.

MAJOR DIVISIONS OF THE FIELD

The visual arts may be divided into four main groups: 1) pictorial arts, 2) plastic arts, 3) building arts, and 4) minor arts.

The pictorial arts employ flat, two-dimensional, surfaces. The term is most frequently applied to painting, but it can also include drawing, graphic arts, photography (including motion pictures), and mosaics. Painting may be done with oil, tempera, water color, or other media. Drawing is usually with pencil, pen and ink, wash, crayon, pastel, or charcoal. The graphic arts are produced

---

*Betty Jo Irvine made suggestions regarding the revision of this chapter; her comments are appreciated by the editors.

by the printing process, with three basic methods employed: 1) intaglio, in which the design is hollowed out of a flat surface (as in engravings and etchings) and the ink is gathered in the hollows for transmission to the paper; 2) cameo, or relief, in which the design is on a raised surface (as in woodcuts, mezzotint, aquatint, or drypoint) and only the raised surface is inked; and 3) planographic, in which a completely flat surface is used and the design created by using substances that will either attract or repel ink. This process is often known as lithography because the flat surface was frequently made of stone. The pictorial arts employ one or more of three basic forms: 1) murals, in which the pictures are on the walls of buildings, either painted directly on the walls or painted on canvases and permanently attached to the walls; 2) panels, which are generally painted on canvas or wood and are sometimes known as easel paintings; and 3) pages, which may be illuminated manuscripts or produced as a result of the printing process. The basic problems with which the pictorial artist must cope include surface, design, movement, space, and form. These are commonly solved by use of line, color, values (light and dark), and perspective.

In the plastic arts (of which sculpture is the outstanding example), ideas are expressed by means of three-dimensional objects. The materials used include stone, metal, wood, clay, plaster, or synthetics (such as plastic). The techniques used—which are determined by the materials—might include carving, casting, modeling, or welding. The finished product may be free-standing or bas-relief (part of a wall or surface). In sculpture, the human figure has traditionally provided the most common subject matter, although the twentieth century has seen increased use of abstractions.

In the building arts (architecture), spaces are enclosed in such a way as to meet certain practical needs (as in homes, factories, schools, or office buildings) and to make some kind of symbolic statement of basic values. These values may be utilitarian and the symbolic statement very pedestrian, or they may be related to the highest aspirations of the human spirit. Factories and gasoline stations are frequently examples of the former, and Gothic cathedrals are often cited as examples of the latter. Architects design buildings of three basic types: 1) trabeated, in which a lintel (or beam) is supported by two posts; 2) arcuated, in which arches are created capable of supporting rounded vaults and domes; and 3) cantilevered, in which only one post is required to support a lintel. The materials used in construction will determine which type is used. Wood is useful for trabeated construction, but brick and stone can be better adapted to the requirements of arcuated construction. Large-scale cantilevered construction became possible only with the advent of structural steel and reinforced concrete.

The minor arts are a special group, often classified on the basis of materials used: ceramics, glass, metals, textiles, ivory, precious gems, woods, reeds, synthetics, etc. Ordinarily, they follow the same styles as the major art forms. The end products may be useful everyday objects such as coins, baskets, utensils, furniture, clothing, weapons, and harness; or they may be ornamental items such as jewelry, stained-glass windows, and much interior decoration.

A good general history and information on how to locate articles on more specific topics is the article "Art," by Eugene Johnson in *Encyclopedia Americana* (1981 edition, v.2, pp. 382-89). The article entitled "Arts, Classification of the" in *Encyclopaedia Britannica: Macropaedia* (15th edition, revised 1985, v.14, pp. 98-102) and related articles are at a slightly more advanced level, but they are still intended for the general reader. More technical and detailed information may be found in "Art," by Giulio Carlo Argan, in *Encyclopedia of World Art* (McGraw Hill, 1959, v.1, pp. 764-810) and its supplement (v.16, 1983), and "Esthetics," by Ugo Spirito, in the same encyclopedia (v.5, pp. 28-75). Articles on numerous other art-related topics will be found in this encyclopedia. E. Louis Lucas, a noted authority on art bibliography, wrote the article "Art Literature" for the *Encyclopedia of Library and Information Science* (Dekker, 1968-1983, v.1, pp. 621-26).

Some students may wish to pursue the topic further. Most of the encyclopedia articles include bibliographies. An excellent introduction to the area of art history is "The Field of Art History," in *Research Guide to the History of Western Art*, by W. Eugene Kleinbauer and Thomas P. Slavens (American Library Association, 1982). Rudolf Arnheim's *Art and Visual Perception* (rev. edition, University of California Press, 1974) deals with the psychology of art. Joseph A. Krause adopts a comparative approach in *The Nature of Art* (Prentice-Hall, 1969), which is designed for the layperson rather than the art specialist. *How to Look at Art* (Watts, 1966) and *Understanding the Arts* (rev. edition, Holt, 1963), both by Bernard S. Myers, take an art appreciation approach and are still used.

ART LIBRARIANSHIP

Unlike philosophy and religion, where the conventional techniques of librarianship will generally cover most situations, the visual arts pose several distinct problems for librarians. As a result, a specialized branch of the discipline has developed over the years. Lester Asheim's chapter "Art," in *The Humanities and the Library* (pp. 100-50) is still an excellent starting point for the student interested in everything from art research to the care of paintings and slides.

Another excellent work is *Guide to Basic Information Sources in the Visual Arts*, by Gerd Muehsam (Jeffrey Norton; ABC-Clio, 1978). In chapter 2, "How to Research a Work of Art," the author deals with several of the distinctive types of publications: *catalogues raisonnés*, *oeuvre* catalogs, museum publications, exhibition catalogs, and the *corpus*. The *catalogue raisonné* is defined and described as follows:

> a systematic, descriptive, and critical listing or catalog of all known, or documented, authentic works by a particular artist — or of all his known works in one medium. Each entry aims at providing all ascertainable data on the work in question: (1) title, date, and signature if any, as well as size and medium; (2) present location or owner and provenance (previous recorded owners and history of the work); (3) description, comments, analysis, or literary documentation; (4) bibliographical references to books and periodicals; (5) listings of exhibitions and reproductions. Usually there is also an illustration. The entries are numbered consecutively. These catalog numbers are often referred to in the scholarly literature about the artist and permanently identify a particular work.[1]

The *oeuvre* catalog is similar but may omit bibliographical documentation and provenance. Museum catalogs are defined as catalogs of a museum's permanent collection. Exhibition catalogs, on the other hand, may include works from many museums and private owners, brought together for a particular exhibition. They are first-rate sources of information, but bibliographical control was extremely difficult before the appearance of the *Worldwide Art Catalogue Bulletin* (1963/1964-). The *corpus* attempts to do for an entire category of art what the *catalogue raisonné* does for an individual artist. Because of their scope, international collaboration on these is often necessary.

Art libraries and their collections are well covered in the literature. A basic source of information is Wolfgang Freitag's "Art Libraries and Collections," in *Encyclopedia of Library and Information Science* (v.1, pp. 571-621). William B. Walker's "Art Libraries: International and Interdisciplinary," presented first at the 1977 IFLA Conference and then published in *Art Libraries Journal* (3 [Spring 1978]: 9-20) and reprinted in *Special Libraries* (69 [December 1978]: 475-81), is still of interest. Judith A. Hoffberg and Stanley W. Hess have prepared for the Art Libraries Society of North America (ARLIS/NA) the *Directory of Art Libraries and Visual Resource Collections in North America* (distr., ABC-Clio, 1978). The annual *ALA Yearbook* covers developments and activities in its regular entry "Art Libraries."

Art librarianship is given an historical treatment in Sarah Scott Gibson's "The Past as Prologue: The Evolution of Art Librarianship" in *Drexel Library Quarterly* (19 [Summer 1983]: 3-17). The field of art librarianship as a whole is covered in Phillip Pacey's *Art Library Manual* (R. R. Bowker, 1977). Various aspects of art librarianship are discussed in "Music and Fine Arts in the General Library," edited by Guy A. Marco and Wolfgang Freitag (*Library Trends* 23 [January 1975]: 321-546). ARLIS/NA has published *Standards for Staffing Art Libraries* (1977).

Reference work is discussed in Muehsam's *Guide to Information Sources in the Visual Arts* and in such articles as D. Toyne's "Requests at the Falmouth School of Art" (*ARLIS Newsletter*, no. 24 [September 1975]: 7-9) and Christine Whittington's "Architectural History: A Core Collection" (*Reference Services Review* 15 [Summer 1987]: 37-45). Lois Jones's *Art Research Methods and Resources: A Guide to Finding Art Information* (Kendall/Hunt, 1978) as well as the section "Reference Works" in *Research Guide to the History of Western Art*, by Kleinbauer and Slavens will help the reference librarian to assist patrons in finding materials in the art collection. Of special interest to the reference librarian is Alex Ross's "State of the Art Sources: Visual Arts Encyclopedias" (*Reference Services Review* 11 [Winter 1983]: 55-58). One of the most recent sources is *Art Libraries and Information Services: Development, Organization, and Management*, by Lois Swan Jones and Sarah Scott Gibson (Academic Press, 1986).

Classification of materials in the arts has been covered in *Organising the Arts*, by Peter F. Broxis (Archon, 1968) and in "Library Classification Systems and the Visual Arts," edited by David J. Patten (ARLIS/NA, 1978). The topic of indexing is discussed in "Contextual Indexing and Faceted Taxonomic Access System," by Robin Mutrux and James D. Anderson (*Drexel Library Quarterly* 19 [Summer 1983]: 91-109) and in "Subject Indexing in the Visual Arts," by T. C. Fawcett (*Art Libraries Journal* 4 [Spring 1979]: 5-17).

Selection, acquisitions, and collection development issues are the subjects of numerous papers in the literature. A good place to start is "Art," in *Selecting Materials for Libraries*, by R. N. Broadus (2nd edition, H. W. Wilson, 1981, pp. 339-51). Wanda V. Dole's "Austerity and the Arts: Collection Development in the

1980's" (*Drexel Library Quarterly* 19 [Summer 1983]: 28-37) and Peggy Ann Kuznerz's "Collection Evaluation Techniques in the Academic Art Library" in the same issue (pp. 38-51) both address these topics. Papers presented on acquisitions topics at the 1982 ARLIS/NA Conference are published in *Library Acquisitions* (7 [1983]: 3-20).

Finally, the particular problems of dealing with exhibition catalogues are addressed in Beth Houghton's "Acquisition of Exhibition Catalogues," in *Art Libraries Journal* (9 [Autumn/Winter 1984]: 67-78).

Three articles in *Drexel Library Quarterly* (19 [Summer 1983]) pertain to special types of art materials: Helene E. Roberts writes on visual documentation, Catherine Stover on museum archives, and Janet Dalberto on collecting artists' books.

Picture files have received substantial attention, particularly from the Special Libraries Association. Renata Shaw's *Picture Searching: Tools and Techniques* (Special Libraries Association, 1973) is one of a series of bibliographies issued by SLA. Ann Novotny and Rosemary Eakins's *Picture Sources 3* (Special Libraries Association, 1975) covers collections of prints and photographs in the United States and Canada. *The Picture Reference File*, by Harold H. Hart (Hart, 1976-1977) and *The Picture Researcher's Handbook*, by Hilary Evans, Mary Evans, and Andra Nelki (Scribner's, 1975) are guides to picture sources.

Slide collections are covered with great thoroughness in *Slide Libraries: A Guide to Academic Institutions and Museums*, second edition, by Betty Jo Irvine (Libraries Unlimited, 1979). The use of slides is discussed in Juan R. Freudenthal's "The Slide as a Communication Tool: A State of the Art Survey," (*School Media Quarterly* 2 [Winter 1974]: 109-15). The Eastman Kodak Company has issued a pamphlet, "How to Teach with Slides," and the Visual Resources Association sponsored the latest revision of the standard reference work, *Slide Buyers' Guide*, edited by Norine D. Cashman and Mark M. Braunstein (5th edition, Libraries Unlimited, 1985).

USE AND USERS OF VISUAL ARTS INFORMATION

Users of visual art information and libraries can be categorized as art professionals (art historians, artists, art educators, critics, curators, architects); students of the visual arts who are enrolled in art schools, colleges and universities, and secondary schools; and the interested public (museum goers, collectors, and others for whom art is a hobby or avocation). The article "Art Libraries and Collections" in the *Encyclopedia of Library and Information Science* (v.1, pp. 571-621) by Wolfgang Freitag, covers the myriad needs of visual arts information users.

Interest in use and users of art information is not a new phenomenon: an early article on use of art materials was "The Use of Art Books," by Katherine Patten (*Bulletin of the American Library Association* 1 [July 1907]: 183). More recent works on the topic include Phillip Pacey's "How Art Students Use Libraries—If They Do" (*Art Libraries Journal* 7 [Spring 1982]: 33-38) and Deirdre Corcoran Stam's "How Art Historians Look for Information," in *Art Documentation* (3 [Winter 1984]: 117-19).

COMPUTERS IN THE VISUAL ARTS

The literature of computer applications in the visual arts is large and continues to expand rapidly. The computer is used in the arts in a wide variety of ways, from computer-assisted design in architecture to computer graphics and computerized information retrieval in art museums. Several reviews offer overviews of developments in computer applications in the visual arts: "Information Systems and Services in the Arts and Humanities," by Joseph Raben and Sarah K. Burton in *Annual Review of Information Science and Technology* (ASIS, 1981) covers visual arts information systems (v.16, pp. 254-56), while the chapter by Cynthia McLaughlin "The Computer and the Humanities," in the second edition of this guide, discusses art and architecture from 1960 to 1978 (pp. 270-73). Jasia Reichardt's *The Computer in Art* (Van Nostrand, 1971) describes additional applications in the visual arts, and Karen Markey's *Subject Access to Visual Resources Collections: A Model for Computer Construction of Thematic Catalogs* (Greenwood Press, 1986) discusses subject analysis of still visual material and proposes a methodology for providing subject access to visual resources. Markey's "Visual Arts Resources and Computers" in *Annual Review of Information Science and Technology* (ASIS, 1984) provides an excellent review (v.19, pp. 271-309).

An information service specifically on automated projects in the history of art and related visual art fields was created in 1986 to gather and disseminate information on computer projects in support of art research. Information on this service may be obtained by contacting the Getty Art History Information Program (401 Wilshire Blvd., Suite 400, Santa Monica, CA 90401). The project is a joint effort of the Getty Art History Information Program and Scuola Normale Superiore in Pisa, Italy, and will publish "SN/G Report on Data Processing Projects in Art."

Online bibliographic databases are widely used in the visual arts today. "Guidelines for Computer Literature Searching in Art Education," by Priscilla C. Geahigan and George Geahigan (*Studies in Art Education* 23 [1982]: 48-60) offers an introduction to online searching and a list of appropriate databases in art as well as the arts-related humanities and social science fields. "Using an Art Database in an Academic Library," by Paula Baxter, is one of a group of articles on database searching in the arts in *Art Documentation* (Summer 1983). Ilene R. Schechter's "Art Database Searching" (*Art Documentation* 1 [Summer 1982]: 94-95) and "Searching the Visual Arts: An Analysis of Online Information Access," by Darlene Brady and William Serban (*Online* 5 [October 1981]: 12-32) also discuss the general topic of online searching in the arts.

Important online databases in the visual arts include RILA (International Repertory of the Literature of Art), which covers all entries in the database since its inception in 1975. RILA, produced as a service of the Getty Art History Information Program, is slated to merge with RAA (Repertoire d'Art et d'Archeologie), produced by the Centre National de la Recherche Scientifique (Paris). RILA covers all aspects of Western art from late antiquity to the present. *News from RILA*, an occasional newsletter published by RILA, provides news of online coverage of the database.

A second important online source is ARTBIBLIOGRAPHIES MODERN, or ART MODERN (DIALOG file 56). This bibliographic database corresponds to the semiannual *ARTbibliographies MODERN*. It covers all aspects of nineteenth- and twentieth-century art and design, as well as major nineteenth-century themes which began in the eighteenth century. The file covers 1974 to the present, and is updated semiannually.

DIALOG Information Services, Inc., has announced the upcoming availability of THE ARCHITECTURE DATABASE as file 179. The database will initially consist of BOOKS CATALOGUE OF THE BRITISH ARCHITECTURAL LIBRARY and ARCHITECTURAL PERIODICAL INDEX. BRS Information Technologies offers as file JSAH, JOURNAL OF THE SOCIETY OF ARCHITECTURAL HISTORIANS from 1941 forward.

WILSONLINE includes ART INDEX, the online version of the print index of the same title, from 1984 to the present. The database is updated twice weekly and covers the journal literature as well as reviews and catalogs.

The Research Libraries Group (RLG) Art and Architecture Program links museums and art libraries which use RLIN. Two special databases have been developed through the program and are in RLIN: THE ON-LINE AVERY INDEX TO ARCHITECTURAL PERIODICALS and SCIPIO (SALES CATALOG INDEX PROJECT INPUT ON-LINE), which provides online access to auction catalogs.

The researcher interested in art-related topics should be sure to include other relevant databases in the online search. Databases such as PSYCHINFO and PHILOSOPHER'S INDEX should not be overlooked.

MAJOR ART ORGANIZATIONS, PUBLISHERS, AND SPECIAL COLLECTIONS

At the international level, much impetus has come from various projects aided by UNESCO. For example, since 1949, UNESCO and its national commissions have worked with art publishers throughout the world to establish a central archives service of art reproductions. In this undertaking, UNESCO has had the assistance of the International Council of Museums. Other organizations that have been active in recent years include the Artists' International Association, International Association of Art Critics, and the International Union of Architects.

Within the United States, the variety of national, regional, and state organizations is too great for more than a sampling at the national level. The American Federation of Arts (41 East 65th St., New York, NY 10021) was founded in 1909 to broaden public art appreciation, especially in those areas of the country not served by large museums, and to promote international exchanges of art. Its membership includes 500 art institutions and 3,000 individuals. The program of activities ranges from circulating exhibitions to preparation of curricula on visual education. The Federation gives editorial advice and assistance in the publication of the *American Art Directory, Sources of Films on Art,* and *Who's Who in American Art.*

The National Art Education Association (1916 Association Dr., Reston, VA 22091), an affiliate of the National Education Association, was founded in 1947 to promote study of the problems of teaching art as well as to encourage research and experimentation. Its membership includes approximately 8,000 art teachers, supervisors, and students. Regular publications include *Art Education* and *Studies in Art Education*.

Other national organizations that should be mentioned are the American Art Association, the American Association of Museums, and the College Art Association. Of special interest to librarians is the Art Libraries Society, with headquarters in Coventry, England, which publishes *Art Libraries Journal* (1976-), and its more recent American counterpart, Art Libraries Society/North America (c/o Pamela J. Parry, 3775 Bear Creek Cir., Tucson, AZ 85749) which has published the *ARLIS/NA Newsletter* since November 1972 (since 1982, *Art Documentation*), and which is active in the development of machine-readable databases. ARLIS/NA is the publisher of print materials as well, such as *Reference Tools for Fine Arts Visual Resources Collections*, edited by Christine Bunting (1984).

The Visual Resources Group of the Mid-America College Art Association, now Visual Resources Association, encourages research and promotes communication through such publications as *International Bulletin for Photographic Documentation of the Visual Arts: The Journal of the Visual Resources Association* (formerly MACAA *Newsletter*). The American Association of Architectural Bibliographers is yet another specialized organization concerned with visual arts information sources and services.

Certain publishers have been particularly noted for their fine art books. Harry N. Abrams, of New York, has issued such series as Pocket Library of Great Art, Collector's Editions, Panorama of World Art, and the Library of Great Painters. The New York Graphic Society and Frederick A. Praeger deserve mention. The famous Swiss firm of Skira was noteworthy for Great Centuries of Painting and Taste of Our Time. The British firm, Phaidon Press, has been publishing distinguished books on individual artists for over 50 years. Thames and Hudson, also of London, is noted for its World of Art series. Studio Vista and Penguin Press have produced high quality paperbacks. While not a specialist in art books, Prentice-Hall has produced a noteworthy series entitled Sources and Documents in the History of Art.

Collections in the fine arts are numerous and are found in public, academic, and special libraries. Examples in public libraries are the Art and Architecture Division of the New York Public Library and Fine Arts Library of the Westminster City Libraries (London). The Avery Architectural Library of Columbia University, the Fine Arts Library of Harvard University (which now combines holdings from the Fogg Art Museum and the Widener Library), and the Marquand Library of Princeton University (noted for its *Index of Christian Art*) are leading examples of academic libraries. Other notable art libraries in this country include the Frick Art Reference Library in New York; the Dumbarton Oaks Research Library in Washington, D.C.; the Ryerson and Burnham Libraries of the Art Institute of Chicago; the Archives of American Art in Washington, D.C., and the Henry E. Huntington Library and Art Gallery in San Marino, California. Among the notable libraries of Europe that deserve special mention are the Victoria and Albert Museum Library, London, and the libraries of the Courtauld Institute of Art and the Warburg Institute, University of London; Rijksbureau voor Kunsthistorische Documentatie, The Hague; Bibliothèque Forney, Paris; Kunstbibliothek, Berlin; Zentralinstitut für Kunstgeschichte, Munich; Akademie der Bildenden Kunst, Vienna; Kunsthistorisches Institut, and Biblioteca Berenson, Florence; Biblioteca dell'Instituto Nazionale de Archeologia e Storia dell'Arte, Rome; and Instituto Amatller de Arte Hispanico, Barcelona. Catalogs of several of these libraries have been published by G. K. Hall.

Additional information may be found in *Subject Collections*, by Lee Ash (6th edition, R. R. Bowker, 1985), *ASLIB Directory, Subject Collections in European Libraries*, by Richard Lewanski (2nd edition, R. R. Bowker, 1978), in the Freitag *ELIS* article already mentioned, and in the *Handbook* of the Center for Research Libraries.

NOTES

[1]Gerd Muehsam, *Guide to Information Sources in the Visual Arts* (Santa Barbara, Calif.: ABC-Clio, 1978), p. 12.

8 PRINCIPAL INFORMATION SOURCES IN THE VISUAL ARTS

ARTS IN GENERAL

Bibliographic Guides

212. **Art Research Methods and Resources: A Guide to Finding Art Information.** 2nd ed. Rev. and enl. Lois Swan Jones. Dubuque, Iowa, Kendall/Hunt, 1984. 332p.

A useful and informative literature guide on the various reference tools in the field, coverage includes both the broad and general reference materials and also those that are highly specialized for scholars and specialists. The earlier edition in 1979 was commended for its attention to methodology as well as sources, although the resources section was considered more successful than either the section on methodology or the one on obtaining the material. The new edition has enlarged the coverage to four sections, the first of which is intended for the novice and serves as a manual of preparation. The second section describes methodology for doing art research projects, while the third section provides an annotated listing of 1,500 tools including online databases. The fourth section covers the procedures on obtaining materials and describes research library collections. Appendices include multilanguage glossaries of art terms; indexes are provided. *Visual Arts Research: A Handbook*, by Elizabeth B. Pollard (Greenwood Press, 1986) covers information sources of both the fine and applied arts, with chapters devoted to separate categories of information.

213. **Fine Arts: A Bibliographic Guide to Basic Reference Works, Histories, and Handbooks.** 2nd ed. Donald L. Ehresmann. Littleton, Colo., Libraries Unlimited, 1979. 349p.

Although it is beginning to show its age, this is a useful source of information regarding reference literature in the arts. This edition incorporates all relevant titles from Chamberlin (see entry 215n) in a classified annotated listing of nearly 1,700 reference books. These tools represent the major body of reference literature published in the Western languages between 1830 and 1978. There are 322 items of pre-1958 vintage not included by Chamberlin, in addition to newer materials. Annotations are descriptive for the most part but evaluative comments are found in some entries. The book is divided into two sections, the first one covering reference works with major divisions by type, while the second section lists histories and handbooks arranged by geographical area and period of time. There are detailed author-title and subject indexes.

214. **Guide to Basic Information Sources in the Visual Arts.** Gerd Muehsam. Santa Barbara, Calif., ABC-Clio, 1977. 266p.

This is a collection of bibliographical essays by Muehsam, an outstanding art librarian, now deceased, designed to offer "general strategical information needed to conduct research in the visual arts." The essays follow a thematic line in identifying types of publications while providing historical background. These essays are followed by listings of materials cited and furnish over 1,000 titles, mostly in English. The work is intended primarily for students in the field and helpful information is provided regarding search strategies, forms of materials (museum publications, exhibition catalogs, etc.), and schools of art. The work is divided into four major sections covering core materials, periods of Western art, forms and techniques, and national schools. It has been commended for its lucid approach to literature searching and fact retrieval, which should continue to prove useful even as the book grows older.

215. **Guide to the Literature of Art History.** Etta Mae Arntzen. Chicago, American Library Association, 1980. 616p.

An extremely comprehensive work which covers over 4,000 reference and research items in the field. The emphasis is on the needs of advanced researchers but the coverage, which features chapters on art history, proves useful to a general audience as well. There are four main sections covering general reference sources, general primary and secondary sources, specific art forms (painting, sculpture, etc.), and serials. This work represents a complete revision of the old standard in the field by Mary Walls Chamberlin, *Guide to Art Reference Books* (American Library Association, 1959). It retains 40 percent of Chamberlin's materials, but annotations are revised and rewritten. The Chamberlin effort, long considered a landmark publication, annotates over 2,500 titles ranging from ready reference to highly specialized, topical materials. Annotations are descriptive and frequently provide critical commentary.

216. **Reference Tools for Fine Arts Visual Resources Collections.** Christine Bunting, ed. Tucson, Ariz., ARLIS/NA, 1984. 55p. (Occasional Papers, No. 4).

Developed as part of the series of Occasional Papers produced by the Art Libraries Society of North America, this small literature guide represents a cooperative effort of a number of specialists and practitioners in the various fields and subfields of the arts and architecture. Recognizing the need to provide up-to-date coverage of the vast array of materials which should prove of value to the professional, this work identifies several hundred titles of art books. There are three major sections, covering professional literature, art reference, and sources of art history, subdivided by medium. The reference works include indexes, directories, handbooks, etc. There is an author-title index.

217. **Research Guide to the History of Western Art.** W. Eugene Kleinbauer and Thomas P. Slavens. Chicago, American Library Association, 1982. 229p. (Sources of Information in the Humanities, 2).

Another in the series of literature guides edited by Slavens, a professor of library science at the University of Michigan, in which he collaborates with an authority in the field, this work is designed for library school students and librarians. It covers first the work of Kleinbauer, which consists of a series of bibliographic essays on the field of art history. This is the major segment, and presents interpretations of topical material such as "psychological approaches" and "studying the art object." The second segment is by Slavens and covers reference works. This is an annotated list of major reference tools. Although the annotations are full and informative, the entries represent standards in the field rather than newer reference books.

Bibliographies and Catalogs

218. **Art Books: A Basic Bibliography of Monographs on Artists.** Wolfgang M. Freitag. New York, Garland, 1985. 351p. (Garland Reference Library of the Humanities, v. 574).

This is a listing of 10,543 monographs on 1,870 individual artists representing all time periods and geographic locations. There is an emphasis on European and North American artists, and the work is based on the collection of the Harvard Fine Arts Library, where Freitag serves as librarian. The bibliography was produced with a grant for aiding the study of art history from the Getty Trust, and begins with a list of 150 biographical sources. The major segment of the text is an alphabetical listing by artist of monographs which include biographies, bibliographies, catalogs, and *catalogues raisonnés*. Of course, the major artists receive more entries than do the lesser-known ones. There is an author index, and the bibliography includes titles in various languages. This effort draws on the previous work by Edna Louise Lucas, *Art Books: A Basic Bibliography on the Fine Arts* (New York Graphic Society, 1968), which contains 4,000 entries, including many on individual artists.

219. **Art Books, 1876-1949: Including an International Index of Current and Ceased Serial Publications.** New York, R. R. Bowker, 1981. 780p.

Published after *Art Books, 1950-1979* (1979), this more recent work is derived from the Bowker database which produced the *American Book Publishing Record Cumulative, 1876-1949* as well as *Ulrich's* (see entry 5). The 1950-1979 effort does not include serials and was produced from the 1979-1980 database of *Books in Print*, as well as from a survey of 7,000 art museums which were asked to supply catalogs of permanent collections. The subject index is developed on the basis of LC subject headings and provides the fullest information (author, title, publication, physical description, notes, tracings, etc.). The author index and the title index provide further access. Unique to this work are a geographic guide to museums and a permanent collection catalog index. The most recent effort, *Art Books, 1980-1984* (1985), includes the index of serial publications, but deletes the directory of museum permanent collections. It appears that the identity now has been established for what will prove to be a valuable serial-type bibliography.

220. **Arts in America: A Bibliography.** Bernard Karpel, ed. Washington, D.C., Smithsonian Institution, 1979. 4v.

This much-needed and well-received comprehensive bibliography, primarily of books on the fine and decorative arts of the United States, includes sections on theater, dance, and music. The first three volumes consist of twenty-one separate bibliographic listings which provide over 20,000 separate entries. Volume 1 covers art of the native Americans, decorative arts, design, sculpture, and art of the West. Volume 2 covers painting and the graphic arts, while volume 3 provides access to the related performing arts as well as photography. This volume also covers dissertations, theses, and visual resources, while volume 4 is an index of authors and subjects. The work has been criticized for the variations in the listings due to the varying styles and forms of the contributors. Nevertheless, it represents an outstanding contribution to art research and reference and the chief bibliographic tool for American art.

221. **Card Catalog of the Manuscript Collections of the Archives of American Art.** Wilmington, Del., Scholarly Resources, 1981. 10v. Supp. 1981-1984, 1985.

Originally housed in the library of the Detroit Institute of Arts, and now part of the Smithsonian Institution in Washington, the Archives was started in 1954 in order to provide documentation of all areas and aspects of American art history. The reproduction of its master catalog now provides an excellent source of information on manuscripts in the collection. There are nearly 6,000,000 items in 5,000 different collections. All items are available on microfilm either through interlibrary loan or at the regional centers in Boston, Detroit, New York, Washington, and San Francisco; thus the work furnishes complete bibliographic control. Most items are biographical and much of the information is accessed through names of artists. There is no subject approach. Another important work from the Archives is the *Collection of Exhibition Catalogs* (G. K. Hall, 1979), which gives the catalog cards for about 15,000 exhibition catalogs identified through a survey of libraries in both the public and private sectors. Arrangement is by name of gallery or museum and under the artist's name. Material covers the nineteenth and twentieth centuries, with an emphasis on the latter.

222.   Catalogue of the Harvard University Fine Arts Library, the Fogg Art Museum. Boston, G. K. Hall, 1971-1972. 15v. First Supp., 1976, 3v.

The library of the Art Museum at Harvard University ranks as one of the top art libraries in the United States. It has served as the basis for several bibliographies in the field such as those by Freitag (see entry 218) and Lucas (see entry 218n). G. K. Hall provided an enormous resource for the art world in its photoreduction of the card catalog consisting of some 360,000 cards. This work provides access by author, subject, and added entries (all of which are interfiled) of books and auction catalogs in the Harvard collections and those of associated libraries. The catalogs are treated separately and arranged alphabetically by dealer and then by date of sale in volume 15. A supplement of newly acquired works appeared in 1976.

223.   Dictionary Catalog of the Library. Freer Gallery of Art. Boston, G. K. Hall, 1967. 6v.

Another in the G. K. Hall line of catalog reproductions, this, like the others, reproduces the cards of a notable library. The Freer Gallery has excellent depth in Oriental, Near Eastern, and nineteenth-century American art and its library resources are useful to people with a serious interest. Volumes 1-4 cover materials in the Western languages, while volumes 5-6 provide access to Oriental-language items. There are about 40,000 publications represented, including books, pamphlets, and periodicals. An important feature is the inclusion of analytics for relevant periodical articles. Each section (Eastern and Western languages) is accessed individually through its authors, subjects, and titles in a unified, alphabetical arrangement.

224.   From Museums, Galleries, and Studies: A Guide to Artists on Film and Tape. Susan P. Bessemer and Christopher Crosman, comps. Hamden, Conn., Greenwood Press, 1984. (Art Reference Collection, No. 6). 199p.

A timely and useful source of information on over 600 films, videocassettes, and audiocassettes which are currently available for loan, rental, or purchase. Educators, students, historians, and interest groups or professional organizations can use this guide to identify filmed and taped interviews with artists. At a time when oral history is playing an increasingly important role in the planning of research and resource collections, this should be a welcome tool. For the most part the work is restricted to the visual arts and includes painters, sculptors, architects, photographers, film and video artists, craftsmen, folk artists, and graphic artists. Annotations vary in length but complete bibliographic identification is provided for all entries. Another fine source, although older, is *Films on Art: A Source Book* from the Canadian Film Institute in association with Watson-Guptill (1977).

This lists over 450 films available in the United States and Canada alphabetically by title with complete bibliographic information.

225.   **Kunstgeschichte in Festschriften.** Paul Ortwin Rave. Berlin, Mann, 1962. 314p.

For a quarter of a century, this little volume has been regarded as an important asset to the study and research of art history. It is limited to the listing of essays on art history which are found in festschriften published to 1960. Essays in festschriften are sometimes quite elusive, but are still of importance to scholarly inquiry. The work begins with a list of the titles of the festschriften included, then a list of the essays contained within the titles. There are nearly 6,000 essays in all, covering a wide range of subjects within the framework of art history. The final segment provides indexes of the festschriften titles and of the authors of the essays, as well as the subjects of their writings, which include both artists and places.

226.   **Library Catalog of the Metropolitan Museum of Art.** 2nd ed. Rev. and enl. Metropolitan Museum of Art. Boston, G. K. Hall, 1980. 48v. First Supp., 1982; Second Supp., 1985.

Since the appearance in 1960 of the initial edition of this major source, it has been recognized as one of the chief bibliographic tools in the field. The new edition incorporates from the first edition all holdings still part of the collection, with the inclusion of material from the eight supplements which followed it. (The supplements are still being produced for those libraries who do not wish to invest in this new edition.) This dictionary catalog of author, subject, and title cards of the library holdings is in the style familiar to users of G. K. Hall products. Much recataloging was done to update terminology and spelling and to include new art developments. Sales catalogs are accessed by subject and by collector or auction house in the final three volumes. Two supplements have appeared since its publication.

Indexes, Abstracts, and Serial Bibliographies

*227.   Art Index. 1929- . Q. Ann. cum. New York, H. W. Wilson.

This major indexing tool in the field covers nearly 200 periodicals and museum bulletins in all fields related to the arts (archaeology, architecture, art history, city planning, crafts, graphic arts, industrial design, interior design, landscape architecture, museology, photography, and film, as well as the fine arts). Coverage is international and represents the most comprehensive source of bibliographic information on periodical literature. Listings of articles appear under both author and subject, while book reviews are listed separately under the author of the book being reviewed. Exhibitions are listed under the artist or appropriate form heading, and illustrations are listed under the article they accompany (but not individually). Illustrations without accompanying text are indexed under artist's name. Available online from October 1984 to date. The database (same name) is available through WILSONLINE and is updated twice a week. About 24,000 records per year are added; as of June 1986 there were 48,000 records.

*228.   ARTbibliographies MODERN. Vol. 4, 1973- . Semiann. Santa Barbara, Calif., ABC-Clio.

ARTbibliographies MODERN indexes and abstracts books, periodical articles, theses, and exhibition catalogs related to art and design of the nineteenth and twentieth centuries. Entries are arranged alphabetically and include artists' names and subjects. There are both an author index and an index of museums and art galleries. Online coverage is available through DIALOG with a database of the same name from 1974 to date. It is updated twice a year (the same as the print volume); about 4,000 records are added semiannually. As of May 1986 there were 80,000 records. With the demise of *LOMA: Literature of Modern Art* (see entry 230), this twice-yearly bibliography established itself as its successor and assumed the numbering system of the previous publication. (The 1969-1971 volumes of *LOMA* were considered as volumes 1-3 of the present effort.) This left the 1972 period without coverage. A competing publication, now defunct, *Art, Design, Photo* (see entry 230n) also regarded itself as the heir-apparent to *LOMA*; with the same editor, it began its coverage with 1972, thus providing uninterrupted access.

229. **Bibliographic Guide to Art and Architecture.** 1975- . Ann. Boston, G. K. Hall.

Although this work serves as an annual supplement to the *Dictionary Catalog of the Art and Architecture Division* of the New York Public Library (G. K. Hall, 1975, 30v.; Supp., 1976), it has gained recognition as a serial bibliography in its own right. Providing comprehensive coverage of the field, it reflects the broad collection development scheme of the library. It is not limited to the cataloging done for the division but also includes entries from the MARC tapes of the Library of Congress. Coverage includes materials from the fields of painting, drawing, sculpture, architecture, and the applied arts. Entries are listed under authors, titles, and subjects in a dictionary arrangement and represent a variety of formats (monographs, serials, and nonbook materials).

230. **LOMA: Literature of Modern Art, An Annual Bibliography.** 1971-1973. Ann. London, Lund Humphries.

Although this annual bibliography lasted only three years and ceased publication with its coverage of 1971, it was recognized as an important source which provided a much-needed coverage of modern art. An international listing of books, articles, catalogs, and other related materials on twentieth-century art and artists, its coverage was broad-based. Included were the fine arts, drawings, prints, ceramics, textiles, and graphic design in two parts (artists and subjects). About 5,000 documents were listed each year. With the termination of this useful tool, the editor, Alexander Davis, began another annual bibliography, *Art, Design, Photo* with a new publisher (Hertfordshire, England, Idea Books) in 1973, which continued the coverage of *LOMA* beginning with the year 1972. This put it into competition with **ARTbibliographies MODERN* (see entry 228) since it also covered the art world of the nineteenth and twentieth centuries in a broad-based and comprehensive manner. *Art, Design, Photo* was unable to survive beyond coverage of the 1976-1977 season.

231. **Original Index to Art Periodicals.** Frick Art Reference Library. Boston, G. K. Hall, 1983. 12v.

Another of the photoreproductions of the catalog cards of an important library collection by G. K. Hall, this multivolume work presents a file of information developed over a forty-five-year period from 1923 to 1969. It furnishes analytics developed for English, French, and Italian journals of the nineteenth and twentieth centuries, with detailed coverage of artists cited in the indexed articles as well as individual art objects, reproductions, exhibitions, provenance, and locations. Entries are provided for authors, artists, galleries, exhibitions, and portraits in a single, unified, alphabetical arrangement. An earlier work of similar character which is recognized for its value is *Index to Art Periodicals* by the Ryerson Library of the Art Institute of Chicago (Boston, G. K. Hall, 1962). This eleven-volume effort provides photoreproduction of the library's card file through 1960. The analytics are extremely useful since there is no duplication with *Art Index* (see entry 227). A supplement in 1975 covered the period 1961 to 1974.

232.   **Répertoire d'art et d'archéologie.** 1910- . Ann. Paris, Morance.

This is a highly regarded, classified, annotated bibliography of books, pamphlets, and periodical articles recognized for its extensive coverage of materials on an international basis. Since its inception in 1910, it has undergone several changes in sponsorship and presently appears under the auspices of the Comité Français d'Histoire de l'Art with the aid of UNESCO. Books were covered beginning in 1920, and classifications are broad, generally by period and country. There is an index of artists as well as an author index and a subject index. Oriental and primitive art are excluded, but are covered in *Bulletin signalétique 526: art et archéologie.* It covers international publications on the art of Asia, the Near East, and pre-Columbian America. This quarterly abstracting service is part of the large-scale program of the Centre National de la Recherche Scientifique. It is also available online through Questel (which has an office in Washington, D.C., as well as Paris). The database is *FRANCIS: ART ET ARCHÉOLOGIE. The complete file of about 30,000 citations dates from its beginning as a print resource in 1972. It adds about 500 records per quarter.

*233.   **RILA, Repertoire international de la litterature de l'art/International Repertory of the Literature of Art.** 1975- . Semiann. Williamstown, Mass., College Art Association of America.

An introductory or demonstration issue appeared in 1973, providing initial exposure to what has turned out to be an important and comprehensive international abstracting tool. It covers books, periodical articles, newspaper articles, festschriften, congress reports, exhibition catalogs, museum publications, and dissertations relating to postclassical European and post-Columbian American art. Therefore, it complements *Bulletin signalétique 526: art et archéologie* (see entry 232n). The abstracts are arranged alphabetically by author under topical headings representing forms such as reference works, or subjects and periods such as medieval art. Access is aided by an exhibition list and an author-subject index. *RILA* is available online through DIALOG as *Art Literature International.* Coverage is complete from 1973 to date and the database is updated semiannually, as is *RILA.* As of March 1986, there were 82,000 records with about 9,000-10,000 added each year.

234.   **Twentieth Century Artists on Art: An Index to Artists' Writings, Statements, and Interviews.** Jack Robertson. Boston, G. K. Hall, 1985. 488p.

A recent work which promises to have great value to art specialists, librarians, students, and researchers in related fields is this index to the thoughts of some 5,000 artists from sixty different countries. Art is defined broadly and includes the fine arts, photography, video, architecture, performance, and earthworks. Sources are in Western languages, with 75 percent in English. There are about 14,000 citations to documents which have appeared in nearly 500 different publications. These sources are listed separately and are accompanied by OCLC and LC card numbers. Indexing of these materials represents a unique activity which must be regarded as a plus for its intended audience.

235.   **The Worldwide Art Catalog Bulletin.** 1963/1964- . Q. Boston, American Library Edition.

An extremely useful source for the art librarian seeking information on the availability of exhibition catalogs is this publication from the leading jobber in the field. Worldwide

Art Center was created in 1962 to establish some control over these elusive documents and was supported by the major national art bodies. It represents the only central record of exhibition catalogs, which are valuable sources of information for both reference and research. Catalogs are listed for exhibitions which have been held all over the world. Each is described in detail and sold through the Center. Nearly 1,000 galleries and museums in numerous countries are represented. The quarterly issues provide indexes of titles, artists, periods, media, and subjects, with a cumulative annual index appearing in December. *SCIPIO is a database available online through RLIN (Research Libraries Information Network). It provides announcements of sales and catalogs of major American and European auction houses. Citations are given to over 13,000 sales catalogs and publications of upcoming sales as well as subsequent sales price lists. It identifies catalogs from several of the major art museums.

Dictionaries, Encyclopedias, and Handbooks

236. Artists' and Illustrators' Encyclopedia. 2nd ed. John Quick. New York, McGraw-Hill, 1977. 327p.

Originally published in 1969 as a source of information for professionals and specialists engaged in the arts on a broad scale (fine arts, photography, graphic arts, and printing), this work earned an excellent reputation for its comprehensive coverage. The new edition has been enlarged with the inclusion of 800 more entries. Entries are brief and provide identification or exposition of the materials, techniques, and procedural methods relevant to the various fields. There are many illustrations, primarily line drawings, to clarify the techniques or provide examples of the objects described. There are also many definitions, some of which pertain to terms used rarely or infrequently. Terminology is especially useful in the areas of television and motion picture graphics.

237. The Artist's Handbook of Materials and Techniques. 4th ed. Ralph Mayer. New York, Viking, 1981. 733p.

This is one of the established sources in the field which has gained an excellent reputation for depth of coverage and accuracy. A survey of reference librarians recognized this title as a vital work for both the practitioner and the librarian serving his or her needs. Originally published in 1940, the third edition appeared in 1970. The purpose of the tool has been and continues to be to provide the artist with a full and up-to-date account of both materials and procedures. The new edition continues in the style of its predecessors in providing coverage in-depth of pigments, oil painting, tempera painting, watercolor, solvents, new materials, conservation practices, etc. Included also are notes, bibliographies, and an index.

238. The Britannica Encyclopedia of American Art. Chicago, Britannica Educational Corporation; distr., New York, Simon & Schuster, 1973. 669p.

This one-volume cyclopedia devoted to American art is regarded as an excellent source of information and is written in a clear and interesting style. Art is defined in broad terms and covers painting, sculpture, architecture, furniture, photography, landscape architecture, crafts, industrial design, etc. A composite work with contributions from over thirty distinguished personalities including historians and curators, the tool succeeds in providing information which although brief, adequately describes or identifies the topics. There are some 1,100 entries for which there appear 800 illustrations; nearly half of the illustrations are in color. The omission or lack of an index has been criticized as adversely affecting the retrieval of information. There are a bibliography and a glossary as well as a guide to museums and public collections.

239. **A Dictionary of Art Terms and Techniques.** Ralph Mayer. New York, Thomas Crowell; distr., New York, State Mutual Books, 1981. 447p.

One of the standard art dictionaries in the field, this is a reprint of the 1969 publication. It provides coverage of the terminology and techniques of a broad spectrum of art activity. This compact volume contains over 3,000 entries which are considered to be authoritative and informative. The purpose is to define those terms encountered by the student or specialist in the literature of the field. There is no coverage of architecture or of Oriental art, and biographies are not included. This work is not as technical in nature as the more detailed *Artists' and Illustrators' Encyclopedia* (see entry 236), although it is not without its technical side. There are entries on schools, styles, and periods, with some illustrations provided. The emphasis is on the procedures and materials of the artist.

240. **Dictionary of 20th Century Art.** Bernard S. Myers and Shirley D. Myers, eds. New York, McGraw-Hill, 1974. 440p.

This convenient little volume provides easy access to basic facts, definitions, and identifications of modern art and its personalities. Based on the editors' earlier effort of greater magnitude, *McGraw-Hill Dictionary of Art* (see entry 243), the present volume concentrates on the period of art history from the turn-of-the-century to the present. It provides a good overview for students and laypersons of the contemporary art scene. Relevant entries from the larger dictionary were utilized, for the most part, but the emphasis on modern developments dictated the inclusion of additional new entries. There is much biographical information, and many contemporary artists are identified, together with their works. Numerous illustrations add to the general appeal of this item, while the bibliography adds to its value for the general reader.

241. **Encyclopedia of World Art.** New York, McGraw-Hill, 1959-1968; repr., 1972. 15v.

Considered to be the cornerstone of every reference collection in art, this magnificent work was published simultaneously in Italian and in English. Providing treatment of considerable length, the signed articles represent the best scholarship on an international level. Bibliographies are extensive and are regarded as a real strength. Entries are alphabetically arranged but the emphasis on monographic-length articles makes use of the index (volume 15) mandatory. Biographies of artists, although numerous, tend to be brief, with the major emphasis on the articles regarding various schools, movements, and national characteristics in which the personalities are mentioned. The scope is broad and covers the entire field of visual arts in all countries and periods. Each volume contains about 500 plates, some of which are in color. The index volume is detailed and provides access through some 20,000 entries.

242. **Iconography of Christian Art.** Gertrud Schiller. Translated by J. Seligman. Greenwich, Conn., New York Graphic Society, 1971-1972. 2v.

At the time of publication of volume 1, this was considered to be part of a set projected to be five volumes. However, volume 2, which appeared in 1972, was the last to be translated from this excellent German work. *Ikonographie der christlichen kunst* (Gütersloh, West Germany, Mohn, 1966-1980) is in the midst of volume 4, and presumably is still in progress. Volume 1 covers Christ's incarnation, childhood, baptism, temptation, transfiguration, works, and miracles, while volume 2 covers the Passion. The volumes are arranged chronologically, and in biblical sequence treat the thematic material. There is excellent, authoritative text considered to be well written and thoroughly researched. The numerous black-and-white illustrations (about 600 in each volume) serve to enhance the exposition of the pictorial themes. A thematic index in volume 2 provides access to information in both volumes.

243. **McGraw-Hill Dictionary of Art.** Bernard S. Myers and Shirley D. Myers, eds. New York, McGraw-Hill, 1969. 5v.

Over 125 contributors provided articles, some of considerable length, to this excellent reference tool. Coverage is given to the entire realm of the arts on an international basis from primitive to contemporary times. Articles are well written and interesting; many are signed and provide brief bibliographies. Included are biographies as well as expository articles on styles, periods, movements, buildings, museums, schools, and trends. Terms are defined and concepts are explained. There are extensive cross-references between entries and the volumes are fully and attractively illustrated (1,200 halftones, 400 color photographs, 200 line drawings). An important aspect is the attention given to the arts of the Far East and the Near East. A small library should consider this as a good alternative to the *Encyclopedia of World Art* (see entry 241).

244. **The Oxford Companion to Art.** Harold Osborne, ed. Oxford, Clarendon, 1970; repr., c1984, 1986. 1277p.

Another useful tool in the Oxford Companion series, this one has been reprinted several times. There are about 3,000 entries, arranged alphabetically. The major focus is on painting and sculpture, although other aspects of the visual arts such as architecture and ceramics are covered. Applied arts and handicrafts receive little attention. Articles vary in length from a brief paragraph to a number of pages on broad topical categories such as perspective. Although they are not signed, the authors' expertise is evident in the exposition given the various elements covered: national and regional schools of art, movements, concepts, styles, techniques, themes, iconography, biographies, and museums. Articles are introductory in nature and include cross-references but no bibliographies. An extensive bibliography in the appendix provides additional references.

245. **The Oxford Companion to Twentieth-Century Art.** Harold Osborne, ed. New York, Oxford University, 1981; repr. (with corrections), 1985. 656p.

One of the strong features of the earlier work, *Oxford Companion to Art* (see entry 244) is the coverage given to contemporary art movements and artists. This newer title provides even more timely information on the nature of the modern art scene. There are numerous biographies of individual artists as well as informative treatments of styles, movements, and schools. Terms are defined in a lucid fashion, in the manner of the previous works in this series. The tool is intended to serve as a handbook or guide for students and interested laypersons seeking enlightenment on the subject of modern art. Such recent aspects as computer art and body art are treated, along with the more standard elements such as dada and art deco. Living artists are covered, with their achievements summarized to the mid 1970s. Illustrations are included and a selective bibliography is appended.

246. **Phaidon Dictionary of Twentieth Century Art.** 2nd ed. Oxford, Phaidon, 1973; repr., New York, Dutton, 1977. 420p.

Long considered a useful reference tool, this work provides well-written articles on both the movements and the artists whose creative influences have emerged during this century. There are many artists who are still active as well as those whose achievements were mainly in the earlier decades. Extremely useful as a biographical source, the work includes hundreds of individuals who are relatively unknown and obscure. Architects are not covered. Coverage is international in scope and bibliographies are found in some of the entries. Articles tend to be brief but are highly informative, and the work has been commended for expert writing and editing. There are no illustrations.

247. **Praeger Encyclopedia of Art.** New York, Praeger, 1971. 5v.

Another of the excellent reference works that have been translated from a foreign language, this set was derived from *Dictionnaire universal de l'art et des artistes* (Hazan, 1967, 3v.). Approximately 400 new articles were added to the English edition, which seeks to provide a comprehensive and authoritative source for both students and laypersons who are interested in the history of world art. About 4,000 articles cover a wide range of topics including biographies, periods, styles, schools, and national art, as well as the art of civilizations. Some 1,000 survey articles of some length were contributed by an excellent and representative group of international experts. Articles are signed. This appears to be a good complementary source to *McGraw-Hill Dictionary of Art* (see entry 243), which provides more entries on art techniques but less coverage of the art of nations. Illustrations are numerous and attractive.

Directories

248. **American Art Directory.** 1898- . Bienn. New York, R. R. Bowker.

Now in its fifty-first edition (1986), this directory is acknowledged as the standard in the field. Originally entitled *American Art Annual* (vols. 1-37, 1898-1945/1948), it is now published biennially. The frequency has varied in the past, but it seems to have established its pattern both in terms of frequency and format. The directory provides information on several thousand art museums, libraries, associations, schools, and studios, with American and Canadian units receiving primary emphasis. There are three major substantive sections covering art organizations (including libraries) in the United States and Canada, art schools in the United States and Canada, and art information. The last named is a miscellaneous section covering units abroad as well as state art councils, directors and supervisors of art education in school systems, art magazines, newspapers, scholarships, and exhibitions. The fourth segment is composed of the indexes which provide access by organization, personnel, and subject.

249. **American Art Galleries: The Illustrated Guide to Their Art and Artists.** Les Krantz, ed. New York, Facts on File, 1985. 304p.

This is a comprehensive directory of nearly 1,100 art galleries of importance to art patrons, collectors, and dealers. Galleries are defined in terms of their activities, which include both selling and exhibiting, thus eliminating those museums and exhibition centers which do not provide opportunity for purchase. Arrangement is alphabetical by state, then by city, with the galleries then arranged alphabetically under the city. Galleries from all fifty states and the District of Columbia are represented. Each entry provides a history of the gallery, identification of its leading artists and their media, and enumeration of any specializations in art styles or group exhibits. Addresses, telephone numbers, key personnel, and business hours are included. There are excellent illustrations of selected art objects, some of which are in color. An important feature is an extensive artist index.

250. **Archives of American Art: A Directory of Resources.** Garnett McCoy. New York, R. R. Bowker, 1972. 163p.

Since its appearance fifteen years ago, this tool has achieved recognition as a valuable source of information regarding the papers held by the Archives. The Archives was established in 1954 in Detroit, Michigan, in order to preserve and make available personal papers. The Archives has since become a part of the Smithsonian Institution but operates with five regional centers in Detroit, New York, Boston, San Francisco, and Washington, D.C. The directory identifies 555 groups or collections of papers which are available for use in microfilm at any of the centers. A more recent contribution of great magnitude is the *Card Catalog of the Manuscript Collections of the Archives of American Art* (see entry 221).

251. **Harvard University Art Museums: A Guide to the Collections.** Kristin A. Mortimer, with William G. Klingelhofer. New York, Abbeville, 1985. 344p.

Harvard's collection is one of the most distinguished university art collections, and this catalog presents a sampling of the many items held by the three museums now designated The Harvard University Art Museums. The tool was produced in celebration of the opening of the Arthur M. Sackler Museum, which joins the William Hayes Fogg and the Busch-Reisinger museums in providing an excellent and well-balanced study of the visual arts. The guide has nearly 400 reproductions of art objects, of which 80 are in color, and represents a diversified collection scheme. The Sackler Museum contains ancient, Islamic, and Oriental art; the Fogg has Western, European, and American; while the Busch-Reisinger is limited to European with an emphasis on German art. Objects are identified by title, artist, date, medium, source, and acquisition number. Arrangement is generally by time period, medium, or country and most items are given brief description and historical coverage.

252. **IFLA Directory of Art Libraries.** Jacqueline Viaux, comp. New York, Garland, 1985. 480p. (Garland Reference Library of the Humanities, v.510).

A group effort of art librarians of the International Federation of Library Associations, this directory should prove of value to researchers and scholars as well as librarians in the field. Art libraries from all over the world with the exception of the United States and Canada are listed. The title of this work appears in four languages (English, French, Spanish, and German), which together with Russian represent the official languages of IFLA. Coverage is given to the holdings of art libraries in nearly fifty countries listed in alphabetical order. The index identifies all countries in each of the five languages and provides cross-references. Entries include telephone number, policy of access, hours, loan policies, founding date, and services. Size of holdings is given by subject and type of format. There is a subject index. Information on U.S. and Canadian libraries is found in *Directory of Art Libraries and Visual Resource Collections in North America* (Neal-Schuman, 1978), by Judith A. Hoffberg, compiled for ARLIS/NA. A supplement was published in 1979.

253. **International Directory of Arts. 1986-87.** 18th ed. Frankfurt, West Germany, Art Address Verlag; distr., Detroit, Gale, 1986. 2v.

This is the most comprehensive international directory in the art field, identifying a host of representative organizations and personalities associated with the arts. The eighteenth edition (1986-1987) is in two volumes and provides information on over 140,000 addresses and related facts, with 20,000 new listings and 25 percent corrected data in various chapters. Information is gathered through a survey of organizations and individuals throughout the world. Volume 1 covers museums and institutional galleries, universities, academies and art schools, restorers, and experts. Volume 2 identifies dealers and their galleries, publishers, book dealers, artists, and collectors. Arrangement is generally alphabetical by country, then by city. Frequency of publication has varied in the past but the pattern of biennial appearance has been established in recent years. The tool is especially useful for museums, research libraries, and specialized collections. It has been criticized for its lack of indexing.

254.   **Looking at Art: A Visitor's Guide to Museum Collections.** Adelheid M. Gealt. New York, R. R. Bowker, 1983. 609p.
     Different from most catalogs and guides to specific collections, this work provides background knowledge and insight into the nature of the types of art produced through time. It is a good information piece on the thoughts and influences which have shaped the styles and developments. The book is divided into two major sections, the first of which covers the history of collecting and the growth and practices of art museums. The second part contains a number of chapters devoted to the history of art in the Western world from ancient times to the present. There is also coverage of Asian, pre-Columbian, and tribal arts. There are lists of major museums and lists of artists which identify their media as well as dates. The volume also provides a concluding bibliography and a detailed comprehensive index.

255.   **Museums of the World.** 3rd rev. ed. Munich, West Germany, Saur; distr., Detroit, Gale, 1981. 623p.
     With publication of the first edition in 1973, this directory established a reputation for comprehensive coverage of a variety of museums throughout the world. Included among the various units devoted to the sciences, technology, history, and specialized studies are those devoted to the arts and archaeology. Arrangement is by continent, then by country and city, with the museums then listed alphabetically. Names of the museums are in the native language although the descriptions are in English. The new edition covers thousands of museums in 163 countries. Entries are brief and give address, date of founding, and enumeration of collections or strengths. There are both name and subject indexes. *The Directory of World Museums*, by Kenneth Hudson and Ann Nicholls (2nd edition, Facts on File, 1981) provides similar coverage and lists the museums under the English form of their name. A new, selective survey of collections is *Art Museums of the World*, edited by Virginia Jackson (Greenwood Press, 1987, 2v.). It covers some 200 museums, each provided with a lengthy historical essay. Directory-type information such as directors, departments, and telephone numbers is not given.

256.   **The Official Museum Directory.** 1961- . Ann. Washington, D.C., American Association of Museums.
     Since it began twenty-five years ago, this work has undergone changes both in title and in frequency, but since 1980 has appeared annually. Canadian museums were excluded in 1983. Regarded as the standard tool for the identification of Museums in the United States, it identifies over 6,000 units of various types (art, history, science, etc.). There are four major sections, beginning with an alphabetical listing by state, then city, then name of institution. A second section lists the institutions alphabetically by name, while the third section provides an alphabetical arrangement by names of directors and department heads. The final section lists institutions by type or category. Entries include name, address, founding date, key personnel, activities, hours, special collections, and general scope.

257. Slide Buyers' Guide: An International Directory of Slide Sources for Art and Architecture. 5th ed. Norine D. Cashman and Mark M. Braunstein, eds. Littleton, Colo., Libraries Unlimited, 1985. 241p.

Since its initial edition in 1972, this directory has established a solid reputation for its comprehensive coverage of sources of slides on a worldwide basis. Originally a biennial with a different publisher, the work has settled into a less frequent but more viable pattern of four to five years between editions (4th edition, 1980; 3rd edition, 1976). It remains an extremely important tool for those who work with this medium, for there is nothing else like it. Listings emphasize U.S. and Canadian sources in the first section, while the second section provides coverage of Asia, Australia, Great Britain, Europe, Ireland, and the Middle East. Commercial sources are grouped separately from museum sources for each country. The evaluative commentary is regarded as accurate. Both name and subject indexes provide access.

258. World Museum Publications: A Directory of Art and Cultural Museums, Their Publications and Audio-Visual Materials, 1982. New York, R. R. Bowker, 1982. 711p.

The first issue of what purports to be a serial directory, this work provides the most comprehensive information to date on museum publications. Developed through a survey of nearly 10,000 museums in 111 countries, it presents listings of over 30,000 publications in various formats (books, catalogs, bulletins, journals, newsletters, pamphlets, posters, and picture books). Audiovisual titles, such as films, filmstrips, slides, recordings, and videotapes, are also included. Material is presented in five different indexes: geographic guide to museums, museum publications and audiovisual materials arranged alphabetically by museum, author index, publications by title, and audiovisual materials by title. A listing of publishers and distributors completes the volume. This should prove to be a valuable resource for academic libraries and for specialized art libraries.

Biographical Sources

259. Allegemeines Lexikon der bildenden Künstler von der Antike bis zur Gegenwart. Ulrich Thieme and Flexi Becker. Leipzig, Germany, Seeman, 1907-1950; repr., 1970-1971. 37v.

This is considered the most complete and scholarly work on biographical information in the whole art field. It includes nearly 50,000 artists from all countries and all time periods. The emphasis is on painters and engravers, but architects and sculptors are also covered. Articles vary in length but generally provide good depth of coverage, with the longer ones signed by the contributors. Locations are provided for works of art, and this work is known for the bibliographies accompanying the majority of the entries. These include reference to books, catalogs, and periodical articles. Entries are arranged alphabetically by names of personalities. The work is continued by a supplementary effort by Hans Vollmer entitled *Allegemeines Lexikon der bildenden Künstler des XX Jahrhunderts* (Leipzig, East Germany, Seeman, 1953-1962, 6v.). Although there is some overlap with Thieme (which included a few living persons at time of publication), the concentration on twentieth-century artists is for the most part unique. It includes about 6,000 brief biographies with bibliographical references.

260. Artist Biographies Master Index: A Consolidated Index to More Than 275,000 Biographical Sketches of Artists Living and Dead. Barbara McNeil, ed. Detroit, Gale, 1986. 700p.

As part of the Gale Biographical Index series, this is a spinoff from the *Biography and Genealogy Master Index* (Gale, 1986). These specialized indexes are convenient and relatively economical in terms of time needed for searching; therefore, most art collections will purchase this work even though the *BGMI* may be kept in another part of the library. The index identifies references in over seventy English-language biographical dictionaries, some of which are multivolume publications covering a broad spectrum of the art world. Included are the usual painters and sculptors along with architects, photographers, cabinetmakers, fashion and graphic designers, illustrators, and ceramics and computer graphics artists. Thousands of individuals are covered, many with multiple references. Although it will not preclude the use of the other biographical sources in the library, due to its limitation to English-language source material, this work represents a good addition to any art collection.

261. **Artists of the American West: A Biographical Dictionary.** Doris Ostrander Dawdy. Athens, Ohio, Swallow, 1974-1985. 3v.

A comprehensive biographical source which covers over 4,000 artists who worked and lived in the western part of this nation. Limited to artists born before 1900, there is excellent coverage given to twentieth century art since many of the individuals achieved their greatest success during this period. Limited to painters, illustrators, and printmakers for the most part, entries are arranged alphabetically and include dates and plates of birth and death, primary area of residence, location of works, and references to additional sources of information in books and periodical literature. Biographical information is brief. There is a classified bibliography of source materials relating to all three volumes and a general index to the set in volume 3.

262. **Biographical Dictionary of Japanese Art.** Yutaka Tazawa, ed. Tokyo, Kodansha International; distr., New York, Harper & Row, 1981. 825p.

Developed as the final volume in a three-volume dictionary on Japan, this should prove to be of value to the reference collection in its focus on the art and artists of the East. Coverage is broad, as it should be in a general purpose tool intended to represent the multifaceted artistic production of the Japanese. Included are biographical sketches grouped by media and type of art (painting, printmaking, architecture, sculpture, calligraphy, graphic design, tea ceremony, gardens, ceramics, swords, metalwork, textiles, and lacquer). Heaviest emphasis is placed on figurative artists. Arrangement is alphabetical by names in English transliteration and entries are adequate (in some cases anecdotal). Appendices are varied and useful and include a glossary, maps, a bibliography, and historical charts and tables.

263. **The Classified Directory of Artists' Signatures, Symbols, and Monograms.** Enl. and rev. ed. H. H. Caplan. Detroit, Gale, 1982. 873p.

Originally appearing in 1976, this tool gained a reputation as a solid piece of work in helping to identify artists by their signatures on monograms. Several thousand artists are covered, with the first section alphabetically arranged by name and providing facsimile signatures. The second section treats monograms arranged under the first letter, while section 3 provides a listing of illegible signatures which are arranged under the first recognizable letter. The final segment presents symbols arranged by general shape (circle, star, etc.). Preceding the text is an introductory section written in five different languages, evidence of the international character of this work. In general, the new edition includes a greater number of lesser-known British artists than did the original.

264. **Contemporary Artists.** 2nd ed. Muriel Emanuel, et al., eds. New York, St. Martin's Press, 1983. 1041p.

The first edition of this work appeared in 1977 and covered over 1,300 artists world-wide. The present revision has deleted 450 of those artists while adding 150 new names. Generally, artists who died before World War II are excluded, although not all biographees are still living. Those whose works are still influential, such as Picasso and Pollack, are retained. Artists from various media in the fine and applied arts are covered if they have exhibited their work in important art galleries, have been included in museum shows, or are represented in the permanent collections of major museums. Entries include a brief biography, references to exhibitions and collections in which the artist has been represented, a bibliography by and about the artist, name of agent or dealer, and a critical signed essay. It has been recommended that libraries retain the first edition together with this revision, to provide better reference service.

265. **Creative Canada: A Biographical Dictionary of Twentieth Century Creative and Performing Artists.** Toronto, University of Toronto, 1971-1972. 2v.

A good example of a specialized biographical dictionary, this work is published in association with the McPherson Library at the University of Victoria. Each volume covers about 500 artists "who have contributed as individuals to the culture of Canada in the twentieth century" and whose contributions have been described in print. The rationale is that artists have not really achieved status if their works have not been praised in books, periodical articles, or newspapers, and the coverage is intended to be limited to significant artists. Excluded from coverage are architects and practitioners in the applied arts while musicians, dancers of various types, radio, television, and film performers as well as producers, directors, and designers join painters and sculptors in the listing. Arrangement is alphabetical by name with entries varying in length according to the amount of documentation available. A general index provides access.

266. **Dictionary of Contemporary American Artists.** 4th ed. Paul Cummings. New York, St. Martin's Press, 1982. 653p.

This biographical dictionary is recognized as a standard for identification of American artists, about three-quarters of whom are still living. The present edition adds seventy-one new artists while deleting seventeen names, for a total of 923 individual entries. Brief information is provided regarding education, teachers, teaching career, scholarships or prizes, address, dealer, exhibitions, collections, special commissions, and notes on the artist's specialty; and a bibliography of books by and about the subject is included. There are approximately 125 black-and-white illustrations scattered throughout the work. There is much more detail here than in *Who's Who in American Art* (see entry 275), although this work is much more selective in terms of number of artists covered. It covers mostly painters but includes sculptors and printmakers as well. There are an index of artists with a pronunciation guide for difficult names, and a key to museums and galleries in which the artists are represented.

267. **Dictionary of Woman Artists: An International Dictionary of Women Artists Born before 1900.** Chris Petteys, et al. Boston, G. K. Hall, 1985. 851p.

More than 21,000 female artists are covered, making this the most comprehensive source of information to date. Painters, printmakers, illustrators, and sculptors are included, while photographers, architects, craftswomen, and designers are not. Although this is one of several publications recently dedicated to the identification of women artists, it is unequalled in terms of its utility in identifying elusive or obscure names. Entries provide full name, married name, pseudonyms, birth and death dates, medium, subject or thematic matter, residence, education, exhibitions and awards, and references to source material from which the biographies were derived. Bibliographic references to additional material are also included. This work should prove to be of major value in art reference work.

268. **Dictionnaire critique et documentaire des peintres, sculpteurs, dessinateurs, et graveurs de tous les pays.** New ed. Emmanuel Bénézit. Paris, Grund, 1976. 10v.

Rated by art librarians as the second most vital source after *Art Index* (see entry 227) in a survey conducted several years ago, this multivolume biographical dictionary has retained its reputation through the years since its initial appearance in three volumes (1911-1923). The present edition is a complete revision of the 1948-1955 effort of eight volumes, although the format is the same and similar information is given. Coverage includes artists from the fifth century B.C. to the mid-twentieth century, and represents both Eastern and Western cultures. Entries vary in length from a few lines to several columns, but generally provide a list of chief works and museums where they are displayed. Reproductions of symbols and signatures, including those of anonymous artists, at the end of each key letter of the alphabet. There is a brief bibliography of sources in volume 10.

269. **Dizionario enciclopedico bolaffi dei pittori e degli incisori italiana.** Torino, Italy, G. Bolaffi, 1972-1976. 11v.

A comprehensive biographical dictionary of Italian painters and engravers, this tool has earned a reputation for its extraordinary coverage. There are over 12,000 entries representing Italian art from the eleventh to the twentieth centuries. There are numerous illustrations in black-and-white and a fair number of full-color plates. Entries include biographical descriptions, critical analyses, information regarding authenticity, market valuations, and art sales of note. This tool represents the best source of information on Italian artists, since it provides identification of relatively obscure and minor personalities as well as the more important figures. Many of the articles are signed by the contributors and good bibliographies are included.

270. **Guide to Exhibited Artists.** Santa Barbara, Calif., ABC-Clio, 1985. 5v.

Each volume of this important multivolume set covers a different medium and each can be purchased separately. The most extensive volume is the one on European painters, but the most unique and important in the sense of not being duplicated by other works are the volumes on printmakers and on craftsmen. The remaining volumes cover sculptors and North American painters. The set as a whole provides listings of 16,000 contemporary artists for which information is given on nationality, address, type of work, medium, date and place of birth, gallery representation, and recent exhibits. Information is relatively up-to-date and should be welcomed by librarians, students, and collectors, as well as critics and writers. Each volume is indexed separately.

271. **Index to Artistic Biography.** Patricia Pate Havlice. Metuchen, N.J., Scarecrow, 1973. 2v. Supp., 1981.

A valuable index to the biographies of about 70,000 artists representing all time periods and all geographic regions, this work covers sixty-four art publications. Primarily biographical dictionaries and works of collective biography, these sources appear in ten different languages and were published between 1902 and 1970. Entries in this index include artists' names, dates of birth and death, nationality, medium, and coded references to the source book with volume number. A one-volume supplement appeared in 1981 and provided references to an additional seventy titles. Together with its supplement it stands along with *Artist Biographies Master Index* (see entry 260) as the most likely source of biographical information on an international scale.

272. **Mallett's Index of Artists, Including Painters, Sculptors, Illustrators, Engravers, and Etchers of the Past and Present.** Daniel Trowbridge Mallett. New York, R. R. Bowker, 1935. Supp., 1940; repr., Detroit, Gale, 1976. 2v.

Another of the standard biographical sources along with Thieme (see entry 259) and Bénézit (see entry 268), this work covers over 25,000 artists whose works are exhibited in leading galleries or who are subjects of inquiry of modern students. Artists represent many different phases and media of the art world, and come from all countries and time periods. Since this is primarily an index, limited biographical information is provided in each entry (name, pseudonym, nationality, period of productivity, residence, and dates). There are references to twenty-two general reference works and over 1,000 specialized sources providing fuller biographical treatment. The supplement provides entries for artists of all countries and periods not covered in the main edition, with a necrology from 1935-1940. Although criticized for certain inaccuracies, it remains a likely first source for biographical information.

273. **Mantle Fielding's Dictionary of American Painters, Sculptors, and Engravers.** 2nd ed. Rev. and enl. Mantle Fielding. Glenn B. Opitz, ed. Poughkeepsie, N.Y., Apollo Book, 1986. 1081p.

There have been several reprints and revisions of this standard biographical tool since its appearance in 1926. The 1965 work was a reprint with addenda containing corrections and new material, while the 1983 effort was a complete revision which doubled the coverage from about 5,000 to over 10,000 names. The present edition provides information on nearly 13,000 American artists of all time periods. They are arranged alphabetically and the volume is by far the most attractive in terms of typeface. Material has been updated and corrections have been made. (Although Fielding had a good reputation for inclusiveness, the work has been criticized for inaccuracies in the past.) The present work provides a comprehensive source of information on both major and minor artists of the United States.

274. **Who Was Who in American Art.** Peter Hastings Falk, ed. Madison, Conn., Sound View, 1985. 707p.

This work is compiled from the original thirty volumes of *American Art Annual* (see entry 248n) between 1898 and 1933, which included biographies, and the four subsequent volumes of *Who's Who in American Art* (see entry 275n) between 1936 and 1947. It represents an excellent source of information on 25,000 deceased personalities associated in some way with American art. Included among the entries are painters, sculptors, print-makers, illustrators, photographers, cartoonists, critics, curators, educators, and craftsmen whose creative activity spanned a fifty-year period from the 1890s to the 1940s. Entries include name, profession, last known address, dates of birth and death, education, locations of works, exhibitions, awards, memberships, and references to the volume of either of the two source works in which the artist was last covered.

275. **Who's Who in American Art.** 1936/1937- . Bienn. New York, R. R. Bowker.

Originally published as part 2 of the *American Art Annual* (see entry 248n) in volumes 1-4, 1936-1947, this work has appeared irregularly in the past. The seventeenth edition (1986) represents a comprehensive biographical directory of a variety of living personalities from all spectra of the arts in the United States as well as Canada and Mexico. Media represented are painting, sculpture, graphic arts, illustration, design, and various crafts. In addition to artists, there are important collectors, critics, historians, curators, and dealers. There are over 11,270 entries, alphabetically arranged, with each entry given about 200 words. Entries include birthdate, education, publications, collections, commissions, professional affiliations, honors and awards, style and techniques, media, dealer, and mailing address. The work is indexed by geographic location and professional classification. There is a necrology section covering 1953-1986.

276. **Who's Who in Art: Biographies of Leading Men and Women in the World of Art Today.** 1927- . Bienn. London, Art Trade.
      The frequency of this comprehensive biographical directory of primarily British artists has varied widely in the past (including a hiatus of fourteen years between the third and fourth editions). It has established itself as a predictable two-year offering during this decade. The twenty-second edition (1986) provides a comprehensive listing of living artists working in a variety of media in the United Kingdom, with a few other "representative" artists included. About 3,000 artists are covered, of which 90 percent are British. Entries vary somewhat but are generally one paragraph in length. They provide birthdates, education, memberships in professional societies and organizations, list of exhibitions, and a list of collections in which the subjects are represented. Also included are present addresses and manner of signing their work.

277. **World Artists 1950-1980.** Claude Marks. New York, H. W. Wilson, 1984. 912p.
      The Wilson Company offers a series of fine biographical dictionaries, and this recent effort provides a useful source of information for any library collection. Biographies of over 300 artists who achieved some prominence in the years following World War II are included. Painters, sculptors, and graphic artists from many countries and representing numerous styles and movements are listed. These are generally the important personalities who influenced the field in some fashion. Entries provide full names, dates of birth and death, a detailed biographical-critical essay of two to five pages (identifying locations and dates of exhibitions and museums and galleries showing the subject's work). There is also a brief bibliography of books and articles about each artist. Pictures generally accompany the entries.

278. **World Encyclopedia of Naive Art.** Oto Bihalji-Merin and Nebojša Tomasević. New York, Scala/Philio Wilson; distr., New York, Harper & Row, 1984. 735p.
      Naive artists are defined by the authors as those who practice their art worldwide "but outside historical and stylistic categories." This type of classification and coverage given to those who practice in this manner makes this a unique and valuable reference tool. Opening with an expository essay on 100 years of naive art, the purpose of the work is described through an explanation and summary of the subject. There are biographical sketches for over 800 artists from nearly fifty countries, although many more are listed. There is a bias toward artists in the authors' native land, with Yugoslavian artists receiving eighty-six entries, while the United States receives fifty-nine entries. Included are a number of historical surveys of naive art in various countries, and a listing of relevant art exhibitions, museums, and galleries throughout the world.

Histories

279. **African Art: An Introduction.** Frank Willett. New York, Praeger, 1971; repr., 1981, 1985. 288p. (Praeger World of Art Series).

Still regarded as a top-notch introduction to African art, this work provides an excellent overview of the development of African art in its social and historical context. There are nearly 250 illustrations, with over 60 in color, which serve to highlight the various art forms and their distinctive characters. Willett has served as a professor of African art at Northwestern University and brings a high level of expertise and understanding to this work. He provides a useful and informative source of information on the geography, culture, and social conditions in which African art developed. He is able to provide exposition of such elements as ancient sculpture, rock drawings and paintings, masks, decoration, etc. There is a bibliography, which is still useful, and an index provides access.

280. **American Art: Painting, Sculpture, Architecture, Decorative Arts, Photography.** Milton W. Brown, et al. New York, Abrams, 1979. 616p.

An authoritative and comprehensive history of the whole spectrum of American arts, this tool is based on two earlier works, *American Art to 1900,* by Brown (Abrams, 1977) and John Jacobus's *American Art of the 20th Century* (Abrams, 1973). The content of the two titles has been combined, revised, and expanded to provide an expansive yet cohesive survey of the development of American art from the earliest times to the present day. There are over 750 illustrations (104 in color) which help provide insight into the nature of artistic expression in the eight periods covered. Coverage begins with the colonial period and is followed with sections on the Jackson years, Civil War to 1900, etc., with the final segment on the arts subsequent to 1960. There are extensive bibliographies and a detailed index.

281. **Art: A History of Painting, Sculpture, Architecture.** Rev. ed. Frederick Hartt. Englewood Cliffs, N.J., Prentice-Hall, 1985. 2v.

A comprehensive history by a distinguished expert, the first edition of this work earned the respect of both librarians and art students, with its well-written text and nearly 1,300 illustrations. In the revision, this now-standard work has been modernized, with a new emphasis on women artists as well as a change in chapter sequence. Volume 1 covers the period from prehistoric times to the late Gothic, while volume 2 embraces the period from the Renaissance to the present day. Considered by reviewers to be an indispensable item combining erudition with lucidity, events and achievements are described and schools and movements are explained. Serving as the basis for the revision are the results of the latest research in the field. Similar to the initial effort, the present work has a glossary, bibliography, and detailed index.

282. **Art and Life in America.** Rev. ed. Oliver Waterman Larkin. New York, Holt, Rinehart & Winston, 1960. 559p.

Written as a text or guide for students in the fields of American art and American civilization, this volume has become a standard in the field. First published in 1949, it represents a survey of the history of architecture, sculpture, painting, and to some degree "the minor arts" in this country. Divided into several different parts or segments, each of which represents a period of distinctive nature with respect to art, separate introductions provide expositions of important cultural and literary developments. The perceptions of "typical" Americans are quoted on the arts, and a broad perspective of creative influences is provided. Both bibliographical notes and an index of names and titles help to identify precise elements in this broad-based coverage from colonial to modern times.

283. **Art Censorship: A Chronology of Proscribed and Prescribed Art.** Jane Clapp. Metuchen, N.J., Scarecrow, 1972. 582p.

A work which retains a large measure of its value, even with the passage of time, this chronology of censorship begins with the year 3400 B.C. and ends with 1970. Censorship is broadly defined as restrictions upon art or artists imposed by state, church, individuals, or society for economic, social, political, moral, or aesthetic reasons. Thousands of such incidents are recorded, with listings arranged by century, year, month, and day. As one might (or might not) expect, more than half of the events took place during this century. The events are documented with good bibliographical references, and represent a wide spectrum (painting, sculpture, graphics, architecture, and decorative arts). There is a detailed index to names, titles, and subjects.

284. **Art of the Mediterranean World, A.D. 100 to 1400.** Hugo Buchthal. Washington, D.C., Decatur House, 1983. 207p.

Developed as a tribute to the author, a renowned art historian and teacher, the book contains a selection of his articles written over a thirty-five-year period from 1940 to 1975. As such, they provide insight and greater-than-usual depth in describing significant developments on the topic. There are four major segments: Islamic and Indian art, Sicilian manuscript illumination, Byzantine manuscript illumination, and iconography. Great care is evident in the representation of illustrations and the attractive format, as one might expect of a work of this type. The four editors (art historians and former students) have contributed commentaries or postscripts and provided additional bibliography. Although not a history in the real sense, this work has utility in its depth of coverage regarding the artistic developments in the Mediterranean world.

285. **Art through the Ages.** 8th ed. Helen Gardner. New York, Harcourt Brace Jovanovich, 1986. 1008p.

If a single work could be called a classic in the field, it must surely be this one-volume encyclopedic history of art. Originally published in 1926, this effort has served the needs of both high school and college students as well as reference librarians in their search for information on schools, movements, art forms, and developments from ancient to modern times. Planned as a college text, it has undergone constant change and revision, ever increasing its scope of coverage. There are many illustrations, and bibliographies are provided at the ends of the chapters. Gardner was a professor of art history at the school of the Art Institute of Chicago and designed the original scheme in line with her teaching responsibilities. The book's emphasis has traditionally been on European arts.

286. **The Arts of China.** 3rd ed. Michael Sullivan. Berkeley, Calif., University of California, 1984. 320p.

Developed from an earlier work (1973), this title has been recognized for its broad coverage of the development of Chinese art from its beginnings to the present. Each edition has added new insights through material recently identified through research and study. The work retains its scholarly tone and character. It is well illustrated. Background information useful to students at all levels of understanding is presented in the introductions to the various ages. Art trends are described and examples of both typical and monumental nature are given. It remains an important source of information, especially for its up-to-date coverage of art developments today. There is a bibliography as well as additional special features, with an index to facilitate access.

287.   **The Arts of Mankind.** Andre Malraux and George Salles, eds. London, Thames and Hudson, 1960- ; repr., New York Golden Press, 1961- . 18v. (In progress).

Originally planned in forty volumes, only eighteen volumes have been issued thus far. Each volume has been prepared by noted scholars and provides a detailed history of the periods covered. Most of the completed works have summarized development in the ancient or medieval periods (e.g., Archaic Greek Art). There are numerous illustrations and maps, some of which are in color. Each volume is cataloged separately by the Library of Congress although a series added entry is provided. For a list of titles in the series, consult the OCLC terminals. Largely a work of French scholarship, the series has appeared in both English and American editions and in some cases the titles have varied slightly. Progress has slowed in the recent past, with the last volume appearing in 1973.

288.   **5,000 Years of the Art of India.** Mario Bussagli and Calembus Sivaramamurti. New York, Abrams, 1971. 335p.

Heavily illustrated with about 400 color reproductions, this is an attractive work on Asian art. It should be pointed out that the quality of color has been criticized by reviewers in the past, as has been the unevenness in style of writing. Although both authors have excellent credentials in art history, Bussagli's writing is much more stylistic and eloquent, whereas sections by Sivaramamurti are stiff and pedestrian. Coverage is given to Indian art through the Mughal period, but also embraces developments in Southeast Asia, Tibet, Ceylon, and Indonesia. Although the tool can be recommended for its content, there is no bibliography or index.

289.   **The Formation of Islamic Art.** Oleg Grabar. New Haven, Conn., Yale University Press, 1973. 233p.

A revised and enlarged edition of this title has been slated for publication in September 1987. An exposition of the development of Islamic art and architecture over a 400-year period from the seventh to the eleventh centuries, this work was well received at time of publication. Designed as a text for college students, it provides an excellent perspective on the nations under Muslim control during this period of Islamic expansion in examining the social forces which fashioned the style and contributions of artists. The work is scholarly in nature and places greatest emphasis on the design and ornamentation of architectural structures. There are over 130 illustrations in black-and-white which provide further insight into the artistic elements. Each chapter has a bibliography and there is a chronology of important dates.

290.   **History of Art: A Survey of the Major Visual Arts from the Dawn of History to the Present Day.** 3rd ed. Horst Woldemar Janson. Rev. and exp. by Anthony F. Janson. New York, Prentice-Hall, 1986. 2v.

One of the standard histories in competition with Gardner's *Art through the Ages* (see entry 285), this work is now in its third edition. Since Janson's death, the work has been carried on by his son and appears in two-volume paperback format. Always regarded as a solid and comprehensive description of the development of Western art, it emphasizes painting, sculpture, and architecture. Some attention is given to Oriental and pre-Columbian periods, with coverage brought to the present day. The work contains numerous illustrations, some in color, all of which serve to provide the enlightenment needed by students. It will probably continue to be the top choice as a textbook for art history classes. The bibliography is up-to-date, and a good index is included.

291. **History of Italian Renaissance Art: Painting, Sculpture, Architecture.** 2nd ed. Frederick Hartt. New York, Prentice-Hall, 1979. 702p.

A third edition, revised and expanded, is planned for October 1987, and it is hoped that it will retain the excellent qualities of the present work. Since its appearance in 1969, this has been considered the best textbook on the Italian Renaissance period. Much of its utility lies in the integrated treatment given to painting, sculpture, and architecture in its exposition of the technical and stylistic qualities of that very creative era. There are numerous reproductions, and hundreds of individual works are described and analyzed. The illustrations enhance these analyses. Hartt has conceded a bias toward Florentine art, but has provided an excellent survey of the period from about 1250 to 1575. A bibliography is provided, along with a glossary, chronology, and index to works and subjects.

292. **History of Modern Art: Painting, Sculpture, Architecture.** 3rd ed. H. H. Arnason. Rev. and updated by Daniel Wheeler. New York, Abrams, 1986. 744p.

Another standard in the field which has received recent revision is this well-known survey of modern art covering developments in Europe and America from 1850 to the present day. The new edition represents the most timely history of what may be referred to as the current art scene, describing the origins and influences which shaped the styles and fashions in painting, sculpture, and architecture. The work is arranged chronologically and designed to appeal to college students and interested laypersons. There are hundreds of attractive illustrations, so many, in fact, that earlier editions have been criticized for a somewhat limited text. Biographical sketches of major artists are included. A bibliography is provided.

293. **The Oxford History of English Art.** T. S. R. Boase, ed. Oxford, Clarendon Press, 1949- . 6v. (In progress).

Originally designed as an eleven-volume comprehensive history of British art from its beginnings to 1940, each volume of this work has been written by a different authority, who covers a time period in his or her area of specialization. Like the other Oxford multivolume sets, it represents a grand attempt to provide in-depth coverage of a scholarly nature, complete with bibliographies. The first volume to be completed was volume 5 (1307-1461), by Joan Evans, followed in order of publication by volume 2 (871-1100), by D. T. Rice (1952); volume 3 (1100-1215), by Boase (the general editor of the series); and volume 4 (1216-1307), by Peter Brieger. Only one volume appeared in each of the next two decades: volume 7 (1553-1625), by Eric Mercer in 1962; and volume 9 (1714-1800), by Joseph Burke, which was the last volume to appear (1976). With Boase's death in 1974, the completion of the set remains uncertain; meanwhile libraries have generally kept the volumes together on the shelves.

294. **Pelican History of Art.** Nicholas Pevsner, ed. New York, Penguin, 1953- . 44v. (In progress).

Projected as a fifty-volume set, the individual titles of this work cover time periods and/or nations of the world with respect to history of art and architecture. Volumes vary considerably in scope and cover a wide spectrum of topics and trends. To date forty-four volumes have appeared, some in their second or third editions. For an up-to-date listing, see Sheehy (see entry 2). Individual titles are by authorities and are highly regarded for both depth of coverage (e.g., the volume on Italian painting from 1500-1600), and useful surveys (e.g., the volume on Japanese art and architecture). One new title has appeared in the 1980s, covering the Indian subcontinent. Each title is cataloged separately by the Library of Congress, which provides a series added entry to bring the titles together. Most librarians consider the titles to be very useful for both text and illustration.

295.   **The Sociology of Art.** Arnold Hauser. Trans. by Kenneth J. Northcott. Chicago, University of Chicago, 1982. 768p.

This broad treatment of art by a distinguished historian and art theorist has. been commended for the quality of its translation from the German-language work published in 1974. Unlike Hauser's earlier two-volume work, *The Social History of Art* (Knopf, 1951), the present title is more theoretical and analytical and less concrete in examining art on a number of different levels. Operating with the idea that all art has a sociological basis in terms of its reflection of and interaction with society, a variety of topics is covered, including artists, their public, criticism, consumerism, pop art, and folk art as well as the fine arts. There is no index, but the table of contents is detailed enough to provide access.

296.   **Storia dell'arte italiana.** Adolfo Venturi. Milano, Italy, Hoepli, 1901-1940; repr., New York, Kraus-Thomson, 1983. 11v. in 25.

This is considered one of the important and profound contributions to the history of Italian art. The original edition appeared in 1901, and since then several volumes have been added to bring it to the present total. Each volume is monographic in nature and covers an art form and/or a time period. The entire set is comprehensive in its coverage of the various art forms from the beginnings to the end of the sixteenth century. Each volume has a separate index of places and artists. There was no general index until 1975, with the publication of Jacqueline D. Sisson's *Storia dell'arte italiana: index* (Kraus-Thomson, 1975). This two-volume effort integrates the individual indexes and provides additions and corrections.

297.   **The Visual Arts: A History.** 2nd ed. Hugh Honour and John Fleming. New York, Prentice-Hall, 1986. 639p.

With its initial appearance in 1982, this work quickly developed a reputation for excellent coverage in certain areas considered weak in both Gardner (see entry 285) and Janson (see entry 290). Beginning with the earliest civilizations, this chronological survey of world art provides a descriptive narrative accompanied by illustrations, some of which are in color. It is considered to be stronger than both Gardner and Janson in its treatment of modern art, with an excellent writing style which makes vivid the concepts and developments covered. The purpose is to be exploratory rather than critical in providing an idea of the visual arts in a historical and aesthetic context. Included are a chronology, glossary, and bibliography as well as an index to provide access.

298.   **A World History of Art.** Hugh Honour and John Fleming. New York, Macmillan, 1982. 639p.

This one-volume world history was published in the same year as the authors' initial edition of *The Visual Arts: A History* (see entry 297) for another publisher. Like the other contribution, this one is well written, clear, and well organized. It provides a concise, straightforward examination of art throughout its history to the present day. Treatment of non-Western art is superior to that offered by either Gardner (see entry 285) or Janson (see entry 290), with sections on the art of Nigeria, New Zealand, China, and India given prominence, as are the representative regions of the West. Similar to *The Visual Arts* in its desire to avoid judgments or evaluative statements, its exposition is excellent and a good perspective on art is provided.

Art Reproductions

299. **Art in Time.** Patricia Pate Havlice. Metuchen, N.J., Scarecrow, 1970. 350p.

An old favorite of reference librarians, this retrospective index covers all of the pictures which appeared in the art section of *Time* magazine between 1923 and 1969. They are indexed in a single alphabet with selective rather than comprehensive subject entries and author-title entries as well. *Time* has been a good source for pictures of art objects over the years through its consistent reporting of exhibitions and current events, and the index has proved to be a useful identification tool. It may be used to supplement *Art Index* (see entry 227), which does not cover *Time*. Havlice's *Art in Life* (Scarecrow, 1959) indexed pictures of paintings and graphic arts in *Life* from 23 November 1936 through 1956. A supplement was published in 1965.

300. **Arts of the United States: A Pictorial Survey.** William Harvey Pierson and Martha Davidson, eds. New York, McGraw-Hill, 1960; repr., Athens, Ga., University of Georgia, 1975. 452p.

At the turn of the century, the University of Georgia assembled a collection of slides for the use of schools, museums, and libraries, a project funded by a grant from the Carnegie Corporation. This manual or guide for teachers, librarians, and museum personnel is divided into two parts, the first of which contains essays on the different subjects covered by the slides. The second part is a catalog of the slides arranged by subject, providing identification by number and including a description as well as a black-and-white illustration. There is an index of artists, titles, and subjects. The collection consists of some 4,000 reproductions, all of high quality, and has proved to be a useful resource for the intended audience.

301. **Contemporary Art and Artists: An Index to Reproductions.** Pamela Jeffcott Parry. Hamden, Conn., Greenwood Press, 1979. 327p.

This is a comprehensive index to pictures of art published in about sixty books and exhibition catalogs from the 1940s to the 1970s. Included are paintings, sculpture, prints, drawings, happenings, environments, earthworks, and video art. Parry is a prolific writer and contributor to art bibliography and has served as editor of *Arlis/NA Newsletter*. The only area purposely excluded from coverage here is architecture. Entries include title of work, date, medium, location, and publication in which a picture appears. Arranged under names of artists, there are both subject and title indexes. Most individuals who died prior to 1950 are not included (with the exception of those who were influential in recent years). This attractive and easy-to-use work has met with a warm reception from librarians.

302. **Illustration Index.** 2nd ed. Lucile E. Vance and Esther M. Tracey. Metuchen, N.J., Scarecrow, 1966. 527p.

This has become a standard tool for identification of pictures appearing in a number of popular periodicals as well as a selective listing of books. This second edition replaced the initial effort in 1957 and its 1961 supplement by including their content together with additional material in an expanded volume which provides coverage to July 1963. Several supplements have followed to provide continuous coverage, and have been mislabeled as editions. The "third edition" by Roger C. Greer (Scarecrow, 1973) covers the period July 1963 to December 1971, while the "fourth edition" by Marsha C. Appel (Scarecrow, 1980) embraces a five-year period, 1972-1976. The "fifth edition," also by Appel (Scarecrow, 1984), similarly covers the period 1977-1981. The pattern is to index eight to ten highly pictorial magazines (*American Heritage, National Geographic*, etc.) for illustrations of a variety of subjects such as animals, architecture, plants, Indians, furniture, personalities, etc. Thousands of entries provide references, with description of type of illustration. Arrangement is by subject.

303.   **Picture Sources 4.** 4th ed. Ernest H. Robl. New York, Special Libraries Association, 1983. 180p.

This is a frequently revised and updated directory of picture collections which has earned a place in the hearts of those who have an interest in picture research. The new edition has listings for nearly 1,200 collections, of which 200 have been added since the third edition in 1975. Information is gathered through a survey of existing facilities which house pictures, maps, art reproductions, and news photographs. Although entries in earlier editions were arranged by subject, the present effort lists all collections in one alphabetical sequence. Helping to provide access is a detailed subject index. Entries provide the usual directory-type information, including collection size and scope. An important tool for general reference, with special value for the art librarian.

304.   **Reproducing Art: The Photography, Graphic Reproduction and Printing of Works of Art.** John Lewis and Edwin Smith. New York, Praeger, 1969. 143p.

A useful and well-developed handbook on art reproduction, this work provides exposition and clarification of the various processes and elements involved. Beginning with an informative essay on the background of eighteenth-century reproduction printmaking together with an explanation of the ethics and purposes, Lewis and Smith describe the modern practices involved in the photography of various types of art. Covered here are paintings, drawings, prints, and three-dimensional objects. The view camera is recommended and its use is described in some detail. This is an attractive and desirable volume in view of the fact that coverage of such material is elusive. There is an appendix on key-line drawings but no index.

Art Sales

305.   **American Art Auction Catalogues, 1785-1942: A Union List.** Harold Lancour. New York, New York Public Library, 1944. 377p.

An old friend to those involved with the retrieval of information regarding the sale of art is this union checklist of over 7,000 catalogs of auction sales of art objects. Covering a span of 157 years, it represents material originally published in the *Bulletin of the New York Public Library*, between 1943 and 1944. This tool identifies locations of the catalogs listed in twenty-one libraries. Art objects represent a broad spectrum and include paintings, drawings, sculpture, furniture, rugs, jewelry, textiles, musical instruments, and curios. Not covered are books, maps, bookplates, stamps, and coins. There is a list of auction houses and an index of owners. A comprehensive source of information on European sales is *Répertoire des catalogues de ventes publiques intéressant l'art ou la curiosité* by Frits Lugt (The Hague, Nijhoff, 1938-1953) which in three volumes provides a chronological list of over 58,000 catalogs of art sales held between 1600 and 1900.

*306.   **Annual Art Sales Index: Oil Paintings, Drawings, Water Colours, and Sculpture.** 1968/1969- . Ann. Poughkeepsie, N.Y., Apollo Book.

The title of this work has changed several times in line with a change in scope in which two of the publisher's serials, one covering oils the other watercolors, were merged. Later, sculpture was added to the field of coverage. The text is written in both English and

French, with the summaries given in English. The index provides listings of thousands of art items sold at auction throughout the world. Details of the sale including prices given in pounds, dollars, and currency of the sale are identified, and a physical description of the art work is included. Name, nationality, and dates of artists are provided. Dates of sales are revealed as are references to illustrations in auction catalogs. *ArtQuest is an online database which contains all the information in the indexes since 1970. It is updated on a monthly basis and as of July 1986 had a file size of 700,000 records. About 65,000 entries are added each year and access is available through Pergamon Infoline.

307. **Art and Antique Auctions World-Wide, 1982/83.** 2nd ed. Janny Stuurman-Aalbers and Reinold Stuurman. New York, Facts on File, 1982. 320p.

This was the first issue of what was planned to be an annual review of art sales of nearly 200 auction houses located all over the world. Providing comprehensive coverage of the various fields of art, it includes paintings, drawings, and sculpture, as well as extensive listings of antiques and collectibles of decorative or hobbyist nature. Tiles, jewelry, classic automobiles, musical instruments, icons, rugs, and photographs are included as well as numerous other components of the collector's art. Indexed by name of the artists are paintings, drawings, and etchings only. *Art Prices Current* (London, Art Trade, 1908-1973) provided an annual record of sales at European and American auction houses over a period of sixty-five years except for a brief suspension of publication during World War I. Its focus was narrower and was limited to paintings, drawings, miniatures, engravings, and prints.

308. **Art at Auction: The Year at Sotheby's.** 1967- . Ann. London, Sotheby Publications.

Now in its 254th season, Sotheby (now Sotheby Park Bernet) is one of the major art auction houses in the world, with offices and facilities in both London and New York. For a number of years, librarians and art devotees have anxiously awaited the appearance of its annual review of the preceding season. It is generally a slick and beautiful catalog, handsomely illustrated with photographs of objects sold. The sections with color may be described as lavish in appearance. The work is arranged according to medium, country, or style, with chapters on various topics. The format has changed at different times but generally some of the prime items sold are highlighted in expository essays which sometimes embrace historical topics as well. All forms of art are sold at Sotheby; therefore, it provides an excellent record of notable sales. *Christie's Review of the Season* (Oxford, Phaidon; distr., Salem, N.H., Salem House, 1985) is also a yearly record of an international auction house which provides fine reproductions of art objects to illustrate the sale of notable items. Its coverage dates back to the 1920s.

309. **The Artist's Guide to the Art Market.** 4th ed. Betty Chamberlain. New York, Watson-Guptil, 1983. 252p.

Chamberlain was the founder and major force behind the Art Information Center in New York, which helped artists find outlets for their work, so she brings impeccable credentials to this difficult task. Originally published in 1970, the guide has earned a good reputation as a practical tool for artists seeking a place either to exhibit or to sell. Advice is given regarding the practice of exhibiting, the various galleries, pricing, selling, commissions, contracts, marketing, and groups or organizations. Exposition of galleries is especially useful with regard to their functions, routines, and elements of desirability. Attention is also given to career opportunities, taxes, theft, and the status of the self-employed artist. An index is provided.

310. **Artist's Market, 1987: Where and How to Publish Your Graphic Arts.** Susan Conner, ed. Cincinnati, Ohio, Writer's Digest Books, 1986. 568p.

Although convention has dictated monographic-type cataloging entry for this work, it has been consistent in its annual appearance over the past thirteen years. It represents an excellent handbook of the field of commercial art, providing artists and illustrators with needed information regarding sales. There are over 2,500 listings of freelance art buyers, more than 600 of whom appear here for the first time. Arranged by the type of market, there are sections on advertising, audiovisual and public relations firms, art/design studios, associations and institutions, book publishers, fashion, greeting cards, performing arts, record companies, etc. Entries provide the usual directory-type information including address, as well as descriptions of buyers' interests and contract information. There is an essay on self-promotion which has become standard in this tool.

311. **Encyclopedia of Modern Art Auction Prices.** Michèle Bérard. New York, Arco, 1971. 417p.

This work provides a useful record of the sales of modern art over an eight-year period from September 1961 to July 1969. Coverage is given to artists beginning with the Impressionists who had at least one work which sold for $2,000 or more during this period. Nearly 300 artists are covered and the information appears in one of three categories: drawings, water colors (including tempera and gouaches), and paintings. Prints are not included. Entries are alphabetical by name of artist within the categories, and include prices paid for their works at the leading auction houses. There is a biography for each artist. There is an index of sales which furnishes information on dates, locales, and principals included in the sales.

312. **Leonard's Annual Price Index of Art Auctions.** 1981- . Ann. West Newton, Mass., Auction Index.

Due to the immense size of the art market, a number of serial indexes of sales have recently appeared. *Leonard's Index of Art Auctions* was established as a quarterly publication to provide a record of original works of art sold at the major auction houses in this country. Since the season runs from September to the end of August, the annual cumulation appears in October or thereabout. Unlike many of the other guides, there are no illustrations here; instead, listings identify sales from around twenty American auction houses. Purchases are arranged by artist in alphabetical order, and listings are by price with the most expensive items first. Art work includes oils, water colors, pastels, gouache, mixed media, drawings, and sculpture. There is a good annual review of paintings sold at auction for the year, with a description of trends.

313. **World Collectors Annuary.** 1946/1949- . Ann. Delft, Netherlands, Brouwer.

Since its beginning in the years following World War II, this work has come to be recognized as an authoritative and comprehensive record of sales in the art world. It has a reputation for reporting the most important and valued items sold during the year in Europe and the United States, with the range of prices somewhere between five and seven figures for each entry. Paintings, water colors, pastels, and drawings are represented for which information is given regarding description, provenance, place and date of sale, price, and bibliographic references. To facilitate access to individual items, a cumulative index to the first twenty-four volumes was compiled and published as *World Collectors Index 1946-1972* (Voorburg, Netherlands, World Collectors, 1976). *World Collectors Index* (Voorburg, Netherlands, World Collectors, 1977-) covered the 1973-1974 season, the intent being to publish biennially.

PAINTING AND DRAWING

Bibliographies and Introductory Works

314. **American Drawing: A Guide to Information Sources.** Lamia Doumato. Detroit, Gale, 1979. 246p. (Art and Architecture Information Guide Series, 11).

The Gale series has been recognized as one of the best reference sources for bibliographic information, having achieved a high standard in coverage of the literature of the field. This work by Doumato, a former reference librarian at the Museum of Modern Art, maintains the high quality in the series. She provides an annotated bibliography of books, parts of books, exhibition catalogs, and periodical articles on American artists working from the 1890s to the present day. Several prominent illustrators are also included as subjects, although cartoonists are excluded. There is coverage of important library research collections as well. The initial effort in the series was Sidney Starr Keveaney's *American Painting* (Gale, 1974) in which he identified source materials published between 1946 and 1973.

315. **American Popular Illustration: A Reference Guide.** James J. Best. Westport, Conn., Greenwood, 1984. 171p. (American Popular Culture).

A recent work of much value to the field due to its treatment of illustration, a field not generally the subject of bibliographic coverage. With the spread of popular culture in the past few years, this has proved to be a useful tool in both public and academic library settings. The author is an instructor in the field of American illustration and designed the bibliography to reflect his course coverage. There is a brief history of the topic from 1800 to the present day which should prove enlightening for those who need to research its origins. Then follows a critical analysis of the significant titles in a number of categories: histories, illustrated works, biographies, technique, social context, etc. Appendices list periodical titles, research collections, and illustrated books. The bibliography is well done on a subject of importance to art reference librarians and their patrons.

Dictionaries, Encyclopedias, and Handbooks

316. **Cyclopedia of Painters and Painting.** John Champlin and Charles C. Perkins. New York, Scribner's, 1885-1887; repr., Port Washington, N.Y., Kennikat, 1969. 4v.

An old standard in the art reference department is this reference work from the latter part of the nineteenth century. A great deal of material is covered, with all entries organized in a single alphabet. There are biographies of painters as well as descriptive articles on famous paintings. Biographies cover the highlights of the artists' lives and provide listings of their works. A useful feature is the inclusion of museum and gallery locations of the listed works. Some bibliography is included as well. The articles on paintings describe them briefly and give some information on their history, as well as the museums involved, and provide bibliographical references. There are reproductions of monograms and signatures for many of the painters, and a few illustrations.

317. **Dictionary of Modern Painting.** 3rd ed. Rev. and enl. Carlton Lake and Robert Maillard, eds. New York, Tudor, 1964. 416p.

Since the initial English-language edition in 1955, this translation of a French publication has been highly regarded by art reference librarians in this country. It has universal appeal (it was translated into German at the same time). Basically it covers the schools, individuals, terminology, movements, techniques, and exhibitions of modern art, beginning with the Impressionists and ending with some important artists still alive in the mid-twentieth century, but who had made their reputation prior to the war. There are many reproductions, with a good percentage in color, which help to illustrate the forms and schools described. Entries contain cross-references and there is a list of authorities who have contributed to the work.

318. **Encyclopedia of Oil Painting: Materials and Techniques.** Frederick Palmer. Cincinnati, Ohio, North Light/Writers Digest Books, 1984. 288p.

This handbook is considered to be a useful reference work that succeeds in its objective to explain in lucid fashion the purposes of the implements, equipment, and materials as well as the rationale and basic concepts of painting. Palmer is both an artist and a teacher and brings much good advice to his commentary. Such elements as easels, palettes, brushes, rags, and pigments are described in terms of their utility, and color is explained in a thorough fashion. Techniques of glazing, collage, tonking, encaustic, serigraphy, and painting from photographs are covered. Generally intended for the beginner rather than the advanced art student, the work is aided by the inclusion of over 250 illustrations, most of which are in black-and-white. There is an index of painters as well as a general index.

319. **Encyclopedia of Painting: Painters and Painting of the World from Prehistoric Times to the Present Day.** 4th ed. Bernard S. Myers, ed. New York, Crown, 1979. 511p.

This is a comprehensive, one-volume effort which provides numerous illustrations which are well integrated with the textual description. With an eye toward economy and balanced coverage, Myers has produced another work which has been found to be useful in libraries. Painters, movements, and styles are covered in one alphabetical dictionary-type arrangement. The work has kept its format since the initial edition in 1955, with each revision adding some new material. This edition continues in that vein with its incorporation of new entries on contemporary artists and styles. Considered to be strong in biographical coverage, much of the total information is provided through the treatment of personalities.

320. **Encyclopedia of Themes and Subjects in Painting: Biblical, Historical, Literary, Allegorical, and Topical.** Howard Daniel. New York, Abrams, 1971. 252p.

This attractive handbook is quite distinctive and has been regarded as a useful reference source for the last decade and a half. Arranged alphabetically are the themes derived from the source elements identified in the title and used in European painting from the early Renaissance to the mid-nineteenth century. There are about 400 topics or themes, most of which are illustrated with reproductions of adequate size and quality. The largest proportion of the themes or subjects represents mythological or religious events, thus the work has value for students in the areas of religion and literature. There is a list of illustrations but the main weakness is the lack of an index.

Biographical Sources

321. **Contemporary Graphic Artists: A Biographical, Bibliographical, and Critical Guide to Current Illustrators, Animators, Cartoonists, Designers, and Other Graphic Artists.** Volume 1. Maurice Horn, ed. Detroit, Gale, 1986. 272p.

Developed on a similar plan to that for *Contemporary Authors* (see entry 784), the important serial biography by the same publisher, this is projected as a semiannual publication. The lengthy title provides a clear idea of its scope and content, and it opens with a history of the graphic arts and illustration written by the editor. Arrangement is alphabetical by name and over 100 artists are identified, most of them cartoonists. This emphasis is justifiable since biographical information on cartoonists is, at best, difficult to find. The definition of "contemporary" is broad, since several of the artists are nineteenth century figures. Biographies are brief but informative and the bibliographical references are good. There is no index for the volume.

322. **The Dictionary of British Artists, 1880-1940; An Antique Collectors' Club Research Project Listing 41,000 Artists.** Jane Johnson and A. Greutzner. Suffolk, England, Antique Collectors Club, 1976; repr., 1986. 567p.

This dictionary provides an excellent source of information on British painters following the Victorian period, since it lists every artist who exhibited in any one of forty-seven selected representative galleries during this time period. Entries are brief and provide dates of birth and death, residence, memberships and honors, places and frequency of exhibitions, and sometimes, art schools attended. The introduction consists of a descriptive essay on the groups, movements, societies, and galleries that developed during this time period. In each entry, there is an indication when one of the artist's pictures brought more than £100 at an auction during 1970-1975.

323. **Innovators of American Illustration.** Steven Heller, ed. New York, Van Nostrand Reinhold, 1986. 224p.

An interesting introductory work is provided here by a distinguished authority in the field. The editor is presently art director of the *New York Times Book Review* and has served in that capacity with several periodicals. He presents a collection of interviews conducted between 1984 and 1985 with twenty-one American illustrators. Such individuals as Maurice Sendak, Milton Glaser, and Edward Sorel are questioned about their careers from the beginning to the present. They describe their working habits, motivations, and philosophical views on the role of illustration, as well as their education, training, and the personalities who were influential in their lives. Although not necessarily part of the reference collection, this book will have value for both teachers and students.

324. **Larousse Dictionary of Painters.** New York, Larousse, 1981. 467p.

Like other reference books bearing the Larousse name, this one is well illustrated with hundreds of reproductions, many of them in color. It is a highly useful biographical dictionary of the principal figures in painting in both Europe and North America. Information is given regarding the artist's life and contributions to the world of art, in a depth adequate to provide a solid idea of his or her prominence. An important element is the inclusion of locations where the artist's works are displayed. Many nations are represented, including some which are generally not considered important for their artistic influences. This adds to the value of the dictionary.

325. **The Lives of the Painters.** John Canaday. New York, Norton, 1969; repr., 1972. 4v.

One of the standard biographical dictionaries in the field is this multivolume effort by a distinguished art historian. Volume 1 covers the late Gothic to the Renaissance, volume 2 the Baroque period, and volume 3, Neoclassicism to post-Impressionism. Coverage is given to 450 painters born before 1840. The style employed is a narrative essay linking the commentary throughout. Historical insight is provided as is a good understanding of the individual's contribution in relationship to others in the art world. The emphasis is on style and achievement rather than biographical description. Volume 4 contains reproductions both in color and black-and-white of the artists who are represented in the contents of volumes 1-3.

326.   **Nineteenth Century Painters and Painting: A Dictionary.** Geraldine Norman. Berkeley, Calif., University of California, 1977. 240p.

This work opens with a brief description of the major movements within the art world during the nineteenth century, such as Romanticism and Impressionism. This is a useful essay accompanied by color reproductions to illustrate the stylistic features. The major body of the text is given to biographies of about 700 artists of the period. Many of these articles are illustrated in black-and-white. There are also entries for schools, practices, and techniques. Entries vary in length, with some of the longer articles dedicated to less prominent individuals for whom in-depth information is generally not available. Considered a strength is the coverage given to Hungarians, Russians, and others who have escaped attention in the past.

Histories

327.   **American Painting.** Jules David Prown and Barbara Rose. New York, Rizzoli, 1979-1986. 2v.

Originally published in 1969, this history of American painting gained recognition as a detailed description of the events and happenings with excellent exposition of the work of individual artists. Volume 1 is by Prown and covers the colonial period to the armory show. Fine coverage is provided of individuals like West, Copley, Stuart, Cassatt, Sargent, and Whistler. It ends with the emergence of the Ashcan School and the Armory Show, a landmark in modern art. Volume 2 is by Rose, and continues the coverage to the present day, embracing the important as well as the faddish elements and movements which characterized contemporary art. Both volumes contain color reproductions and are handsome works. They were revised in 1979, but Rose's volume was updated more recently in 1986.

328.   **Chinese Painting: Leading Masters and Principles.** Osvald Siren. London, Lund Humphries, 1956-1958; repr., New York, Hacker, 1974. 7v.

This multivolume work has been considered a vital source of information since its appearance thirty years ago. It covers the history of Chinese painting, a complex and many-faceted subject, from the earliest times to the end of the Ch'ing dynasty in 1912. Siren's scholarship remains foremost in Chinese art and the coverage given to individuals and developments is authoritative and complete. Generally considered a necessary purchase for academic libraries, the reprint edition has been criticized for a lower quality of reproduction in the 900 black-and-white prints. The provision of the lists of works by Chinese painters is an asset to scholars and students; bibliographies are international in scope and include materials in the Chinese language.

329.   **A Concise History of Modern Painting.** 3rd ed. Enl. and updated. Sir Herbert Reed. New York, Praeger, 1974; repr., New York, Thames and Hudson, 1985. 329p.

Considered in most quarters to be a fine one-volume history of the origins and development of modern art, this work made its initial appearance in 1959. Since then it has achieved popularity and wide distribution in libraries and is regarded as a staple in the reference department. Beginning with Cezanne, it clearly traces the elements, influences, and styles of modern painting. The work has an adequate number of illustrations, although at times they have been criticized for poor quality. Errors which appeared in the first edition have been corrected, and presently it is a useful tool for those needing a lucid and informative survey work.

330.   **The Development of the Italian Schools of Painting.** Raimond van Marle. The Hague, Nijhoff, 1923-1938; repr., New York, Hacker, 1971. 19v.

An extensive and comprehensive treatment of Italian art, this survey of painting from the sixth century to the beginning of the sixteenth century has no equal in the English language. Scholarly in nature, it provides many references and includes bibliographies for each chapter. Each volume has an index of artists, iconography, and places. The work has been criticized for certain instances of misleading information and obsolete commentary. Until Venturi's *Storia dell'arte italiana* (see entry 296) is translated, however, this is the best work available for those who must use the English language. An important feature is the total of more than 5,500 illustrations, which suffer somewhat in the reprint version. The final volume is a general index to the whole set.

331.   **Painting in the Twentieth Century.** 2nd ed. Werner Haftman. New York, Praeger, 1965. 2v.

A translation from an earlier German work from the mid-1950s, this work provides a good survey of painting in the twentieth century. Volume 1 provides an analysis of the artists and their work, while volume 2 gives a pictorial survey which includes over 1,000 reproductions, some of which are in full color. Volume 1 is a profound examination of the psychological and philosophical elements associated with contemporary painting and the personalities who engaged in it. About 500 artists are covered, with short biographies, each of which is given a number of bibliographical references. Although it has been criticized for a bias toward German and Italian art, Haftman's work provides enough information on other areas to be recommended as a general source. There are both name and subject indexes in volume 1.

Reproductions and Catalogs of Collections

332.   **American Paintings in the Collection of the Metropolitan Museum of Art.** Metropolitan Museum of Art. Kathleen Luhrs, ed. New York, The Museum, 1980. 1v.

This is the first, and to date, the only volume published in a new series highlighting the American paintings in New York's Metropolitan Museum. This volume covers a limited period of time and represents the work of painters born between 1846 and 1864. This should be an indication of the potential magnitude of the projected effort, but unfortunately the track record of the Metropolitan has not been good on this topic. Fifteen years earlier in 1965, volume 1 of a projected three-volume effort was issued as *American Paintings: A Catalogue of the Collection of the Metropolitan Museum of Art*, by Albert Ten Eyck Gardner and Stuart P. Feld. It never got beyond the first volume, which covers painters born by 1815. The new work covers paintings accessioned by the Museum prior to January 1979. There are references to artists' biographies and sources of quotations. Works mentioned but not illustrated are identified by museum location or source of reproduction.

333. **American Paintings in the Museum of Fine Arts, Boston.** Boston Museum of Fine Arts. Boston, The Museum; distr., Greenwich, Conn., New York Graphic Society, 1969. 2v.

A standard item in art reference, this scholarly catalog lists all American paintings in the excellent collection held by the Museum. The first volume contains the text and provides coverage of artists alphabetically arranged. Pictures are listed in chronological order, and each entry provides description, measurement, and provenance. There are brief biographies of the artists with good bibliographical references, and references to exhibitions in which the paintings have been displayed. The catalog provides a listing of over 1,000 paintings with more than 600 reproductions, some of which are in color. Reproductions are in volume 2 and are arranged chronologically, with paintings by individual artists grouped together. The catalog was published in celebration of the Museum's centenary and is representative of the attractive published catalogs of the leading museums of the world.

334. **Catalogue of Reproductions of Paintings 1860 to 1979: With Seventeen Projects of Exhibitions.** 11th ed. United Nations Educational, Scientific and Cultural Organization. Paris, UNESCO, 1981. 275p.

First published in 1949, this is best considered a guide to high-quality reproductions of the work produced by prominent artists during the period designated. The goal of UNESCO in producing this catalog was to make these works more familiar to people all over the world by the promotion and distribution of fine reproductions. The emphasis, then, is on the acquisition of individual reproductions, and color reproductions from books and periodicals are not included unless they can be purchased separately. Arrangement is alphabetical by artist and then chronological by date of painting. The original works are identified with name of painter, dates and places of birth and death, title, date, medium, and size; reproductions are identified with process, size, UNESCO archives number, printer, publisher, and price. Full instructions for ordering are included, and small black-and-white reproductions are given for each entry. There is a companion volume on the same order covering the early period, *Catalogue of Reproductions of Paintings Prior to 1860: With Fifteen Projects for Exhibitions* (Paris, UNESCO, 1981), also in its eleventh edition.

335. **Finder's Guide to Prints and Drawings in the Smithsonian Institution.** Washington, D.C., Smithsonian Institution, 1981. 210p.

This was the first in a series of guides planned to enumerate the collections of the Smithsonian Institution in order to make these resources available or accessible to students and scholars. Individual prints and drawings in a total of forty-nine collections are indexed. Information provided is names of artists, subjects, historical period, and locations. Also covered are water colors, pastels, posters, scientific and engineering drawings, and books with original illustrations. General information regarding the collections includes availability of catalogs or directories, publications, photoduplication services, exhibition programs, loan policy, hours, and type of public access. A special feature of value is a location guide to graphic artists which identifies over 10,000 artists whose works are owned by the eight major Smithsonian art collections. The text has an index to facilitate access.

336. **Fine Art Reproductions of Old and Modern Masters: A Comprehensive Illustrated Catalog of Art through the Ages.** Greenwich, Conn., New York Graphic Society, 1980; repr., 1984. 576p.

First published in 1946, this title has become a fixture in art reference departments, where its use varies widely from one library to another. This catalog of the reproductions available for purchase from the New York Graphic Society has itself become an attractive collection of reproductions. Arranged by groupings such as old masters, twentieth-century painting, and American painting, the catalog gives a historical overview in providing color illustrations for each work. Although they are small in size, they are extremely attractive and provide a good idea of how the reproductions will look. The society has high quality prints and is considered a useful source for libraries. Included are name and date of artists; nationality; title with date and location of the original; and catalog number, size, and price of reproduction. There are indexes of artists and subjects.

337. **Index to Reproductions of American Paintings: A Guide to Pictures Occurring in More Than Eight Hundred Books.** Isabel Stevenson Monro and Kate M. Monro. New York, H. W. Wilson, 1948. 731p. First Supp., 1964, 480p.

An old standard in the field of art reference, this work will retain its value as long as its source materials (books that it indexed) remain in libraries. Especially useful for libraries through the years due to the great number of sources covered, the work indexes pictures of American paintings in 520 books and over 300 exhibition catalogs. Alphabetically arranged by name of artist, title of the work, and in some cases by subject, entries include dates of artist, dates and locations of paintings, and references to books which provide reproductions. A supplement appeared in 1964 which indexed more than 400 books and catalogs published between 1948 and 1961. A more recent update is by Smith and Moure (see entry 338). A companion work is *Index to Reproductions of European Paintings: A Guide to Pictures in More Than Three Hundred Books* (H. W. Wilson, 1956), by the same authors. It follows the same plan, except for its concentration on books with no listings from catalogs. A supplementary item is *World Painting Index*, by Havlice (see entry 339).

338. **Index to Reproductions of American Paintings Appearing in More Than 400 Books, Mostly Published since 1960.** Lyn Wall Smith and Nancy Dustin Wall Moure. Metuchen, N.J., Scarecrow, 1977. 931p.

Commended for their thoughtful selection of source material, the authors have provided a useful continuation to the Monros' index and supplementary volume (see entry 337). The arrangement is somewhat similar to the original, with artists listed alphabetically, followed by titles of paintings with references to reproductions in books. There are indications of ownership in permanent collections. Much of the source material is highly specialized in nature, making it more useful in libraries with more extensive art collections. The subject index makes access possible on a wide range of topics such as allegories, animals, architectural subjects, and Indians, as well as portraits of individuals. There is no index by title alone.

339. **World Painting Index.** Patrice Pate Havlice. Metuchen, N.J., Scarecrow, 1977. 2v. First Supp. 1973-1980, 1982, 2v.

This work was intended to supplement and update both works by Monro and Monro (see entry 337), since it covers both European and American paintings among others. The basic edition covers reproductions in nearly 1,200 books and catalogs published from 1940 to 1975. Volume 1 is alphabetically arranged by names of artists and provides references to the books which contain the reproductions. Volume 2 is a title list which refers the user back to volume 1. Criticized for a noticeable bias in favor of Western art and lack of cross-references for variant names, it is still regarded as an important reference tool. The supplement covers 617 art books and catalogs published between 1973 and 1980.

Arrangement and style are similar to the initial offering, including the feature of separate title listing of paintings by unknown artists. There is no subject approach in Havlice which approximates that by the Monros.

ARCHITECTURE

Bibliographic Guides

340. **American Architecture and Art: A Guide to Information Sources.** David M. Sokol. Detroit, Gale, 1976. 341p. (American Studies Information Guide Series, v. 2).

This is a compact and practical one-volume bibliography of books, articles, serials, and exhibition catalogs on both architecture and painting, with a section on the decorative arts as well. Annotations are provided for the entries and the arrangement is topical. Although more extensive listings are contained in other more specialized bibliographies on both architecture and painting, it is a real asset to have such comprehensive coverage in such a convenient package. There are three indexes which provide access by author, short title, and subject, with reference to entries given by number. There are sections on individuals as well as general coverage of movements and developments in the fields. Although criticized for certain omissions of titles, the tool is a useful source of information.

341. **Architecture: A Bibliographic Guide to Basic Reference Works, Histories, and Handbooks.** Donald L. Ehresmann. Littleton, Colo., Libraries Unlimited, 1984. 338p.

A companion piece to other guides by Ehresmann in the fine arts (see entry 213) and in the decorative arts (see entry 367), this is an essential tool for both collection development and reference. It provides an annotated bibliography of books which have proved to be useful and informative. Books listed are primarily in the English language but there is coverage of foreign titles in Western European languages. Emphasis is on a practical bibliography and the titles listed are generally available in American libraries. There are 1,350 entries; arrangement is by form or type such as reference books, or by chronological coverage (prehistoric) or by geographic coverage (Oriental). There are both author-title and subject indexes.

342. **Directory of International Periodicals and Newsletters on the Built Environment.** Frances C. Gretes. New York, Van Nostrand Reinhold, 1986. 175p.

Considered to be an outstanding resource item for its audience of specialists is this directory of serial literature on what is now being referred to as the built environment. The tool is divided into fourteen sections dealing with various subjects (architecture, office practice, building types, historic preservation and architectural history, interior design, fine arts, planning, landscape design, building construction and services, engineering, real estate development, etc.). The arrangement of entries is alphabetical within each topical division, and they include complete bibliographic information as well as description of the content. This is a welcome aid to the librarian who serves architects, engineers, designers, planners, and contractors, since the number of documents in these fields has increased dramatically over the past few years. Included are a listing of indexes and abstracts, title index, and a geographical index of countries where the serials are published.

343. **Pro File: The Official Directory of the American Institute of Architects.** 1978- . Irreg. Philadelphia, Archimedia.

This directory of architectural firms published under the auspices of the AIA began in 1978 and appears irregularly. Member firms are listed alphabetically by name within a geographical arrangement, in typical directory fashion. Each entry provides addresses of all offices of the firms and indication of types of practice, as well as the name of the present company. Also included are names of personnel, analyses of work distributions by gross income percentages, geographical work distributions, and awards. There are indexes of both companies and individuals. The AIA also sponsored *American Architects Directory* (R. R. Bowker, 1955-1970), which listed names and addresses of members and of other prominent architects with biographical information. Included were a geographical index and lists of fellows and award winners.

Bibliographies, Indexes, and Abstracts

344. American Architectural Books: A List of Books, Portfolios, and Pamphlets on Architecture and Related Subjects Published in America before 1895. New exp. ed. Henry Russell Hitchcock. New York, Da Capo, 1976. 150p.

The first edition of this standard bibliography appeared in 1938-1939 and was recognized as a valuable asset for those doing research on American architectural history. The 1962 edition reprinted the third edition (1946), which provided a listing of over 1,450 documents. These publications were described with notes of important editions, and locations were identified from among more than 130 libraries where copies could be found. Errors were corrected and a few titles added. The most recent edition in 1976 is largely a reprint of the 1962 edition, with a new introduction by Adolf K. Placzek, and an appendix representing a short title list in chronological order of Hitchcock's entries, originally issued as a separate publication by the AIA.

*345. Architectural Periodicals Index. 1972/1973- . Q. Ann. cum. London, Royal Institute of British Architects.

A subject index to architectural periodicals found in the British Architectural Library of the Royal Institute (RIBA), this work covers about 450 titles, the majority of which are British. Subjects are assigned through headings utilized in *Architectural Keywords*, a vocabulary control device developed by RIBA in 1982. Arrangement is classified by those subjects, with alphabetical arrangement of titles within the categories. Foreign titles are identified with indication of language and presence of English abstracts or summary. There is a name index as well as a topographical and building name index. *Comprehensive Index to Architectural Periodicals, 1956-1970* (London, World Microfilms, 1973) offers coverage of the card file of the library on twenty reels of microfilm. This represents a retrospective index of some 200 periodicals in an arrangement similar to *Architectural Periodicals Index*. The majority of these listings first appeared in the quarterly issues of *RIBA Bulletin*. *Architectural Periodicals Index* is also available on DIALOG.

*346. Avery Index to Architectural Periodicals. Columbia University. Avery Architectural Library. Boston, G. K. Hall, 1973. 15v. Supp. 1-4, 1975-1986, 7v.

One of the leading architectural collections in this country belongs to the Avery Library of Columbia University. G. K. Hall has provided an excellent service by reproducing the card file, which contains analytics of periodical articles in titles received at the library. The 1973 edition superseded the original 1963 work by absorbing all its entries and those of its supplements. Since then, supplements have appeared which continue to update the listings. The most recent appeared in four volumes in 1986, and covered the period from 1979 to 1982. It was the first supplement to be computer generated. This set and its supplements include periodical titles not only in architecture but also in decorative arts, sculpture, city planning, and archaeology. There is good coverage of writings on individual architects. With about 700 periodicals indexed, this is the most comprehensive periodical source, although it is limited to periodicals in the Western languages. The index is available online through a database by the same name, which covers the period from 1979 to date. It is available through RLIN, updated daily, and had 31,000 records in May 1986.

347. **Catalog.** 2nd ed. enl. Columbia University. Avery Architectural Library. Boston, G. K. Hall, 1968. 19v. Supp. 1-3, 1972-1977, 4v., 4v., 3v.

In addition to the extensive holdings of the Avery Library, one of the outstanding architectural collections in the country, this catalog contains all books on the subject of architecture and art held anywhere in the university in any of its libraries. Through the years, this has come to be recognized as one of the most comprehensive sources of bibliographic information in the field. A catalog first appeared in 1895 in printed form, and G. K. Hall produced the first catalog of this type in 1958, a six-volume work which was received warmly by librarians in the field. The supplements bring coverage to June 1977, and it is hoped that another update will be available soon.

348. **The Literature of British Domestic Architecture 1715-1842.** John Archer. Cambridge, Mass., MIT Press, 1985. 1078p.

A thorough and detailed bibliography of 360 titles printed in Great Britain and Ireland during the eighteenth and nineteenth centuries, this item will be of interest to bibliographers all over the world. Three major essays precede the bibliography and provide coverage of the relationship of architecture to the book trade, describe the elements of format and content, and discuss the development of architectural theory in Great Britain. The bibliography is detailed in its coverage of the early publications, and variant editions are noted, as are library locations. There are another 150 titles or so in the appendices, which together with those in the main body of the work provide excellent coverage of this elusive albeit important topic. Many of the works described are of landmark importance. The book is illustrated in black-and-white and contains an index as well as notes and references.

Dictionaries, Encyclopedias, Handbooks, Etc.

349. **Atlas of European Architecture.** Brian Sachar. New York, Van Nostrand Reinhold, 1984. 369p.

An attractive and practical handbook to the study of European architecture is this country-by-country exposition of notable buildings. Each of the twelve chapters is devoted to a specific country (arranged alphabetically), in which towns and cities are also listed alphabetically. Entries for each of the 3,500 buildings covered are chronological by date of construction, listed under the cities. The book is sure to please individuals involved with architectural studies, such as architects, students, art historians, and preservationists as well as laypersons with an active interest in architecture. Entries provide name, date, address, architect, photograph, and some notes of special features. Also listed when available is information regarding the tourist information office, architects' institute, and major museums with special collections. There are also a bibliography, index of architects and artists, and index of cities and towns.

350. **Dictionary of Architectural and Building Technology.** Henry J. Cowan and Peter R. Smith. New York, Elsevier Science Publishing, 1986. 287p.

This is an up-to-date and informative new volume on the technical terminology of modern architecture and related areas. It contains about 5,000 terms, 1,500 of which have been added since publication of an earlier work by Cowan in 1973. The emphasis is on the science of architecture and building with fine coverage provided of elements such as structures, materials, acoustics, lighting, thermal environment, building services, solar heating, etc. Definitions are brief but informative and are enhanced by over 120 illustrations, including diagrams and charts. The tool should prove highly useful to those who are active in the construction of buildings or its study (teachers, students, architects, engineers, consultants, and contractors). Another useful source is John Fleming's *The Penguin Dictionary of Architecture* (3rd edition, Penguin, 1980).

351. **Encyclopedia of American Architecture.** William Dudley Hunt. New York, McGraw-Hill, 1980. 612p.

A practical and informative reference book for the layperson is this compendium of miscellaneous facts and definitions. Written in nontechnical language, definitions and identifications are clear and appear to be adequate. There are more than 200 articles on history, building types, systems and structures, materials, preservation, etc., with about fifty on prominent architects. There is a special attempt to include women and minorities in the various articles when appropriate. The work is considered to be a useful tool for the general reader, although not as technical as the advanced student might want or need. Comprehensive coverage is provided from the pre-Columbian period to the present. The encyclopedia contains an index, uses cross-references, and provides brief bibliographies. A related source is the richly illustrated *World Atlas of Architecture* (G. K. Hall, 1984).

352. **Illustrated Dictionary of Historic Architecture.** Cyril M. Harris, ed. New York, McGraw-Hill, 1977; repr., New York, Dover Publications, 1983. 581p.

Originally published under a different title, this work is still regarded as an excellent source of information on architectural history. There are about 5,000 terms, all of which bear clear definitions and explanations. There are no biographies among the entries; the emphasis is on styles, forms, and component elements of architecture. The illustrations are excellent and some 2,100 line drawings with a few photographs help to define both the character and characteristics described in the entries. They are brought together from a variety of sources and are well integrated, providing a cohesive coverage of topics. Entries vary from a single line to a half-page and cover about 5,000 years from ancient to modern architecture. Oriental terms are accompanied by their calligraphic symbols.

353. **Sir Banister Fletcher's a History of Architecture.** 19th ed. John Musgrove, et al. Stoneham, Mass., Butterworths, 1987. 1621p.

Upon his death in 1953, Fletcher left a trust fund to the Royal Institute of British Architects and the University of London for the revision and updating of his well-illustrated history. First published in 1896, the tool set a standard in the field for its excellent coverage of architectural styles and features of various historical periods. The present edition has incorporated several important changes, most important of which is the increased coverage given Asian, African, Australian, Oceanic, and American cultures from the precolonial period to the present. The organization is roughly chronological with seven major parts or segments beginning with ancient Egypt and Greece and concluding with the twentieth century. It continues as an essential reference book for the amount of information it contains, this revision being the product of a distinguished group of contributors from various parts of the world.

Biographical Sources

354. **Macmillan Encyclopedia of Architects.** Adolf K. Placzek, ed. New York, Free Press/Macmillan, 1982. 4v.

This is an extremely useful biographical dictionary of 2,400 prominent architects from all countries and all time periods who either were born prior to 1931 or are deceased. The biographees were selected by an editorial board and approved by specialists of international stature. In addition to architects, there are engineers, bridge builders, landscape architects, and town planners as well as a few patrons and writers. Criteria imposed were the influence of individuals, the importance of their work, and their productivity. Articles generally are of essay length and may be 10,000 words long, although some figures are covered in less than 100 words. There are also a glossary of terms, an index of names, and an index of architectural works. Related titles include *Contemporary Architects*, edited by Muriel Emanuel (St. Martin's Press, 1980) and *Avery Obituary Index of Architects* (2nd edition, G. K. Hall, 1980).

355. **Master Builders: A Guide to Famous American Architects.** Diane Maddex, ed. Washington, D.C., Preservation, 1985. 203p. (Building Watchers Series).

This detailed exposition of the lives of forty American architects is a biographical dictionary of a selective nature. Although in paperback, this is a useful tool and should be purchased by reference departments for the attention it gives to major characteristics, important developments, and resulting influences of the architects' work. A portrait is provided for each individual, and even more important, illustrations of his or her major contributions are included. The arrangement of entries is chronological, beginning with William Thornton, who designed the U.S. Capitol, and ending with Venturi, Rauch, and Scott Brown. In addition to the basic text, there are short entries on another seventy architects who are identified by business firms and representative projects. There are a bibliography and an index of architects.

356. **Who's Who in Architecture from 1400 to the Present.** J. M. Richards, ed. New York, Holt, Rinehart & Winston, 1977. 368p.

Since its appearance in 1977, this work has been used consistently in reference departments, and in the minds of most librarians represents a vital source of information on 600 architects, engineers, town planners, and landscape architects. It covers the accomplishments of those who were involved in the creative conceptual development of buildings since the time of the Italian Renaissance to the present throughout the Western world. It also includes individuals from outside the West if their cultures have developed as a result of Western influences. About fifty major architects are treated in great depth with lengthy expository essays, while the remainder are treated briefly. Many articles have bibliographies, and cross-references are given. There is a classified bibliography at the end.

SCULPTURE

Bibliographic Guides

357. **American Sculpture: A Guide to Information Sources.** Janis Ekdahl. Detroit, Gale, 1977. 260p. (Art and Architecture Information Guide Series, v. 5).

This is an especially useful resource in view of the lack of bibliographic coverage on the topic of American sculpture. Compiled by a college art librarian with a knowledge of the needs of both students and specialists, the work opens with a general section of research materials which covers bibliographies, catalogs, indexes, biographical sources, encyclopedias, dictionaries, and directories. The second section treats the history and aesthetics of American culture in seven chapters, while the final section provides listings of sources for nearly 220 American sculptors. Books, parts of books, periodical articles, and exhibition catalogs are identified and described in terms of their principal features. There are author, title, and subject indexes, and a list of institutions with extensive collections of sculpture in the appendix.

Bibliographies, Indexes, and Abstracts

358. **Fifteenth Century Italian Sculpture: An Annotated Bibliography.** Sarah Blake Wilk. Boston, G. K. Hall, 1986. 401p. (A Reference Publication in Art History).

One of a series of twenty Renaissance bibliographies, most of which are in the planning stages at G. K. Hall, this work provides listings of 2,000 documents. Most entries are annotated and represent excellent bibliographic coverage of Florentine sculpture, with the inclusion of figures such as Donatello, Ghiberti, Brunelleschi, and Luca della Robbia. One section is given to modern scholarship, while others identify early sources and studies of technique and materials. There are surveys of a general nature as well as treatments of specific or specialized topics reported in monographs, and articles in several Western languages. Also included are theses and other unpublished works. Most coverage is given to works on individual sculptors. Unlike its subject matter, the tool is unattractive, with a typescript appearance, but it is a useful vehicle for both students and specialists.

359. **Sculpture Index.** Jane Clapp. Metuchen, N.J., Scarecrow, 1970-1971. 2v. in 3.

This excellent index of pictures of sculpture in 950 publications is a staple in the reference departments of art libraries. Listings are dictionary style under names of artists, titles, and subjects, which adds greatly to ease of use. Sources include art histories, collection and exhibition catalogs, and art reference books, and are generally available in public, school, college, and special libraries. Although the emphasis is on modern sculpture after 1900, all periods are represented. The sculpture of Europe and the contemporary Middle East is covered in volume 1, while volume 2 embraces the Americas, the Orient, Africa, the Pacific area, and the classical world. Locations of original sculpture are given, and there is an excellent list of both private and public collections by country and city. Entries include nationality and dates of sculptors, materials, size, museum identification numbers, and references to documents. All types of sculpture are included.

Dictionaries, Encyclopedias, and Handbooks

360. **A History of Western Sculpture.** John Pope-Hennessy. Greenwich, Conn., New York Graphic Society, 1967-1969. 4v.

These four volumes are truly monographic works in their own right and are brought together under the collective title with the aid of a consultant editor. Volume 1, *Classical Sculpture*, is by George M. A. Hanfmann; volume 2, by Roberata Salvini, is *Medieval Sculpture*. Herbert Keutner has contributed volume 3, *Sculpture: Renaissance to Rococo*, while volume 4, by Fred Licht, is entitled *Sculpture: 19th and 20th Centuries*. In all volumes, the connection between sculpture and the social, political, and economic forces is described and carefully analyzed. Historical lines are traced and developed in a manner which provides insight into the reaasons behind creative development in different eras. A good survey of sculpture is provided through the four volumes, each of which has fine illustrations, a bibliography, and an index.

361. **An Introduction to Italian Sculpture.** 3rd ed. John Pope-Hennessy. New York, Phaidon, 1985-1986. 3v.

An important work in the field which first was published in 1955, this is now in its third edition. Titles for the individual volumes have remained unchanged over the years, although succeeding editions have incorporated additional elements, modifications, and corrections when needed. Volume 1 covers Italian Gothic sculpture roughly from Pisano to Ghiberti, while volume 2 treats the Italian Renaissance from Donatello to Tullio Lombardo. Volume 3 describes the High Renaissance and Baroque. Typically, the volumes include introductory chapters on leading sculptors and trends, plates, notes on sculptors, an index of sculptors, and an index of places. Works are treated chronologically in each volume and biographies of artists are included.

362. **The Sculpture and Sculptors of the Greeks.** 4th ed. rev. Gisela Richter. New Haven, Conn., Yale University Press, 1970. 317p.

Richter died at the ripe old age of ninety, two years after publication of the fourth edition of her work, which first appeared in 1929. As curator of classical art at the Metropolitan Museum prior to her retirement, she brought expertise and authority as well as a skillful writing style to the production of this important edition. Many additions and corrections were incorporated because of new discoveries and modern perspectives. The first part of the book describes the course of events in sculpture through a chronological survey and exposition of technical considerations. Part 2 covers individual sculptors in chronological order from the archaic period through the first century B.C. This work can be used and appreciated by a wide range of readers, from those with a general interest to the serious student.

363. **Sculpture in America from the Colonial Period to the Present.** Wayne Craven. New York, Crowell, 1968. 722p.

For many years, the author's name has been familiar to those who work with the bibliography of art, and this particular effort has always been regarded as a solid contribution to the field. It provides a fine overview of the relationship between sculpture and the other arts in different art periods in this country. Individual sculptors are treated from colonial times to the present. Most commendable in the view of critics is the excellent treatment given to the sculpture and sculptors of the nineteenth century, since this period has been generally overlooked in the past. The work represents a good blend of scholarship, judgment, and professional expertise, and has been regarded as a must purchase for libraries.

Biographical Sources

364. **Contemporary American Women Sculptors.** Virginia Watson-Jones. Phoenix, Ariz., Oryx, 1986. 664p.

A timely reference tool with an emphasis on the contribution of female artists, this biographical dictionary covers over 300 American sculptors. A quick check reveals good coverage of those who have earned recognition such as Louise Nevelson, Nancy Grossman, and Lee Bontecou. The inclusion of less prominent personalities represents a real service in helping to identify our contemporary artists. Much of the information appears for the first time and was gathered through questionnaires mailed to art historians, museums, and art associations. Each entry provides brief biographical information, professional accomplishments, and a statement from each artist. There is a black-and-white reproduction of one of each artist's works.

365. **Dictionary of American Sculptors: 18th Century to the Present.** Glenn B. Opitz, ed. Poughkeepsie, N.Y., Apollo Book, 1984. 656p.

This recent work covers over 5,000 American sculptors from the eighteenth century to the present, although emphasis is on nineteenth- and twentieth-century figures. Those working in this area are aware of the difficulty in finding any detailed commentary on individual sculptors of this period; therefore, the work fills a real need for documentation of obscure and even more prominent individuals. There are many living and recently deceased biographees who submitted data directly. These entries join those for whom data were gathered from sources such as *American Art Annual* (see entry 248n). The work has been criticized for failure to include information subsequent to the 1970s, and a subsequent volume is planned which may address this oversight. Bibliographical references are provided in some cases.

366. **New Dictionary of Modern Sculpture.** Robert Maillard, ed. Trans. by Bettina Wadia. New York, Tudor, 1971. 328p.

Although it is getting older, this is still considered a useful biographical dictionary in those libraries which have need for information on modern sculpture. A translation of a French work, it first appeared in English in 1960. It is strictly biographical, with no entries for the description of art movements, countries, or topical coverage. Articles are signed with the initials of the contributors and about 600 sculptors are treated. Each entry provides brief biographical information about the sculptor; highlights accomplishments; and describes the medium, style, and characteristics of his or her work. Best known works are identified, and generally each entry is accompanied by a reproduction of one or two of them. No bibliographical references are provided.

APPLIED AND DECORATIVE ARTS

Bibliographic Guides

367. **Applied and Decorative Arts: A Bibliographic Guide to Basic Reference Works, Histories, and Handbooks.** Donald L. Ehresmann. Littleton, Colo., Libraries Unlimited, 1977. 232p.

A companion volume to the author's other publications on the fine arts (see entry 213) and architecture (see entry 341), this is a useful and needed literature guide in the broad field of the decorative arts. Basically, it is a classified and annotated bibliography of 1,240 books in the Western languages published between 1875 and 1975. It embraces the various fields associated with handicrafts, fashion, and antique collecting and provides sections on folk art, arms and armor, ceramics, clocks, watches, costume, enamels, furniture, glass, ivory, jewelry, lacquer, leather and bookbinding, medals and seals, metalwork, musical instruments, textiles, and toys and dolls. In addition, there are general sections on applied and decorative arts and on ornament. Excluded are drawing, graphic arts, and mosaic, since they are considered adjuncts to the fine arts. There are author and subject indexes.

Dictionaries, Handbooks, and Biographical Sources

368. **Dictionary of the Decorative Arts.** John Fleming and Hugh Honour. New York, Icon Editions/Harper & Row, c1977, 1986. 896p.

This is a reprint of the well-known and popular *Penguin Dictionary of Decorative Arts*, which has been recognized as a useful and comprehensive source of information. The authors are well known in the field of art history, have published extensively in the past, and furnish impeccable authority for a work of this kind. The emphasis is on furniture and accessories found in both European and American homes both past and present. There are about 4,000 entries which include definitions, expositions, and descriptions of materials, techniques, manufacturers, and individual personalities associated with the decorative arts. Bibliographies are furnished for a number of the entries which enable the user to pursue additional readings on the subject. The work is well illustrated and represents a welcome addition to the reference collection.

369. **Folk Artists Biographical Index: A Guide to over 200 Published Sources of Information on Approximately 9,000 Folk Artists.** George H. Meyer, et al., eds. Detroit, Gale, 1987. 496p.

The editor is Director of the Museum of American Folk Art, and brings his expertise to bear in creating this comprehensive index to information on over 9,000 folk artists found in over 200 biographical dictionaries and collective works. This should prove to be of substantial benefit to librarians, as biographies of folk artists tend to be elusive and difficult to locate. As one might expect, the variety of media represented in the folk arts is great and covers such activity as sculpture, furniture making, carving, weaving, pottery making, and quilting, and such products as samplers, coverlets, decoys, and canes. Individuals are listed alphabetically and entries include birth and death dates, type of work, period, and citations for source materials. The work provides excellent access through indexes of museums in which the artists' works are displayed, ethnic origin, medium, and type of work.

370. **The Oxford Companion to the Decorative Arts.** Harold Osborne, ed. New York, Oxford University Press, 1975; repr., 1985. 865p.

Basically a reprint of the earlier edition, which was well received by librarians as another useful source of information in the Oxford Companion series, this new edition provides a bibliography on the final page for the article on decorative papers. The decorative arts as a study embraces those fields and crafts not covered in the *Oxford Companion to Art* (see entry 244), and may be defined as "creations that are valued primarily for their workmanship and beauty of appearance." These include leather working, ceramics, furniture, jewelry, costume, glassmaking, landscape gardening, clock-making, enamels, lacquer, toys, lace, embroidery, etc. Entries vary in length from brief to survey-type, and articles are unsigned. The emphasis is on Western arts, with the countries of the East and Eastern Europe receiving less coverage.

Antiques and Collecting

BIBLIOGRAPHIES

371. **Antiques and Collectibles: A Bibliography of Works in English, 16th Century to 1976.** Linda Franklin Campbell. Metuchen, N.J., Scarecrow, 1978. 1091p.

This bibliography is targeted for the researcher and the serious collector as well as the librarian. It provides a comprehensive listing of books, exhibition catalogs, periodical titles, theses, and dissertations on the subject of antiques and collectibles. There are 10,783 entries covering most of the recognized fields of the serious collector, with the exception of stamps, coins, and vehicles. Library locations are given for books published prior to 1925. In the vast territory regarded as collectibles, there are many objects and types of objects which make no claim on artistic merit, such as fruit jars in the glass section, bathroom fixtures (covered in furniture), agricultural objects such as barbed wire, and physicians' tools of various kinds. There are no annotations, and the work will serve mainly as an indicator of titles available within the infinite parameter of collectors' fancies.

GENERAL GUIDES, DICTIONARIES, HANDBOOKS, ETC.

372. **Kovels' Know Your Antiques.** Rev. and updated ed. Ralph Kovel and Terry Kovel. New York, Crown, 1981. 364p.

As bearers of the name most familiar to those interested in books for the hobbyist, the Kovels have kept busy producing new and informative guides and dictionaries. This volume provides an introduction to the world of antiques through exposition of the various objects and types as well as the nature of their market. Consideration is given to such categories as pottery and porcelain, glass, bottles, furniture, lighting devices, silver, pewter, tinware, etc. Helpful hints to the novice or beginning collector are provided in boldface type, although one must be careful of putting too much stock in such brief commentaries. Illustrations are numerous and well composed, and bibliographic references are given in each chapter. As is true of the other works by the Kovels, this will prove useful in the reference department.

373. **Kovels' Know Your Collectibles.** 1st ed. Ralph Kovel and Terry Kovel. New York, Crown, 1981. 404p.

A companion volume to *Know Your Antiques* (see entry 372), this guide should be of use to people interested in the purchase or sale of those items which have not yet reached the status of antiques. Collectibles are less than 100 years old if American and less than 200 years old if European, while the older objects fall into the category of antiques. There is a wide range of material as well as a wide range of value associated with the collectible, and these considerations are handled well by the Kovels. Items chosen were considered to be those most popular and of most interest to collectors. Chapters cover furniture, American art pottery, dinnerware, porcelain, jewelry, metalwork, and glass. Clocks, toys, advertising items, etc., are also considered. There is a useful essay on collecting and selling as well as protecting your antiques. Numerous illustrations accompany the descriptions provided. Each chapter includes a bibliography.

374. **The Lyle Official Antiques Review 1987.** Anthony Curtis, comp. and ed. Glenmayne, Scotland, Lyle; distr., New York, Putnam, 1986. 672p.

Another of the annual guidebooks to the values of antiques is this publication, now in its sixteenth year. Its emphasis is on the British market and many of the valuations shown are based on the prices paid for objects at Christie's auction house in London. Pieces are arranged alphabetically within the major categories and are priced through examination of sales records at both auctions and sales the previous year. Prices are given in American dollars, thus providing the American consumer with a useful tool in determining probable costs of elegant furniture, silver, and less glamorous objects such as photographs and weather vanes. Like others of its type, this guide proves to be of real use to collectors and those who serve their needs.

375.   **Miller's International Antiques Price Guide.** American ed. Judith Miller and Martin Miller, eds. New York, Viking, 1987. 694p.

Since its appearance in 1979, the Miller publication has gained a healthy respect and earned a reputation for quality and thoroughness of coverage. This is the first edition produced especially for the U.S. market. As such, one would hope it would offer more extensive coverage of American-made antiques than is evident in the 10,000 objects covered. As was true in previous editions, each item is represented by a clear photograph and a brief but informative description. Price ranges establish this market for the more well-to-do Americans, as there are precious few items under $100.00, and a large number sell for more than $2,000. Organized in forty-nine major categories (pottery, radios, etc.), items are listed alphabetically either by type or brand name. Attractive and useful with good color illustrations, this is an excellent complement to the numerous Kovel-type catalogs, which generally emphasize the more affordable pieces.

376.   **Sotheby's International Price Guide, 1985-1986.** John L. Marion, ed. New York, Vendome; distr., New York, Rizzoli, 1985. 688p.

Another entry into the world of annual price guides is this first issue of the antique season at Sotheby's. Differing from other guides which provide valuations determined by sale and auction prices as well as asking prices from a number of outlets, this one permits examination of the actual sales of a fine auction house. This issue covers approximately 8,000 items, all of which are illustrated in black-and-white. These items were sold the year before and are listed in one of the twenty-three categories handled by Sotheby's. Since the firm does not deal in lower priced antiques, the guide will be used by those who are interested in the elegant upper register of the market. Limitations of course should be understood, since much that is regarded as interesting and desirable to Americans will not be covered.

377.   **Warman's Antiques and Their Prices.** 21st ed. Harry L. Rinker, ed. Willow Grove, Pa., Warman, 1987. 700p.

This is one of the oldest annual guides to the antique market and has proved to be a valuable resource for the American collector through the years. Like its predecessors (and likely its successors), it is divided into two major parts. The first section is devoted to American pattern glass and provides extraordinary coverage in terms of patterns included and detail. Line drawings give a good idea of the features and distinctive character of the patterns. About one-fourth of the book is devoted to this area, acknowledged as one of the best among annual guides. The remainder of the guide is devoted to the general collector, and categories are arranged alphabetically from "ABC Plates" to "Zsolnay Pottery." Prices are given for a broad range of items within each category. As always it is well illustrated with about 1,000 pictures for the 50,000 entries. Warman's continues as a meritorious purchase for those who are interested in the antique market.

SPECIALIZED GUIDES, DICTIONARIES, HANDBOOKS, ETC.

378.   **American Furniture, 1620 to the Present.** Elizabeth Bidwell Bates and Jonathan L. Fairbanks. New York, Richard Marek/Putnam, 1981. 561p.

An extraordinary reference work providing comprehensive coverage of the development of American furniture styles from the colonial period to the present day. Furniture is treated chapter-by-chapter in different periods, which are illustrated with reproductions of both paintings and photographs. About 1,400 reproductions (100 in color) show the pieces in their museum setting, and diagrams are provided of the structure of the furniture. Informative commentary helps the reader understand the place of the furniture within the social and historical context. Fairbanks is curator of American decorative arts at the Boston Museum of Fine Arts, and together with Bates brings a great deal of expertise and authority to the topic. Included also are a glossary of cabinetry terms, a bibliography, and an index.

379. **Answers to Questions about Old Jewelry: 1840 to 1950.** 2nd ed. Jeanenne Bell. Florence, Ala., Books Americana; distr., Rutland, Vt., Tuttle, 1985. 390p.

A detailed table of contents provides access to the wealth of information contained in this volume; there is no index. A growing interest in the collection of jewelry has made a guidebook of this type a necessity in most libraries. Section 1 provides the historical background and describes the different motifs and personalities associated with the creation of jewelry in 5 different periods: 1840-1860 (Victoria and Albert); 1861-1889 (Victorian); 1890-1915 (Edward and Art Nouveau); 1920-1930s (Art Deco); and 1940-1950s (Modern). Section 2 treats the materials used in making jewelry, while section 3 identifies simple tests to determine the authenticity of the composition of these materials. Section 4 provides a catalog of marks and a biographical dictionary of prominent designers and craftsmen. Valuations are given along with small black-and-white pictures of the pieces.

380. **The Antiques Directory: Furniture.** Judith Miller and Martin Miller, eds. Boston, G. K. Hall, 1985. 639p.

Another of the Miller publications (see entry 375), this work maintains the quality and informative content of the others. Furniture from all over the world is treated, and over 7,000 photographs help to illustrate the differences in style and appearance. Intended as a guidebook for those who seek profit or collect in the field, the work accommodates the needs of its intended audience in a country-by-country arrangement, subdivided by form or type (tables, chairs, etc.). As with most guidebooks, the commentary at the beginning of each section is brief and serves only to introduce the reader to the furniture of a particular country. Pictures are described in terms of styles, dates, size of objects, and periods represented. The emphasis is on British furniture. There is a useful outline chronology of developments by country from 1450 to 1920. The work contains an index but no bibliography.

381. **Collector's Dictionary of the Silver and Gold of Great Britain and North America.** 2nd ed. Michael Clayton. Ithaca, N.Y., Antique Collectors Club, 1985. 481p.

Those individuals for whom silver and gold play an important role in their collecting habits will appreciate the comprehensive nature and breadth of coverage of this fine dictionary. First published in 1971, it has come to be recognized as a standard item in reference departments for its excellent treatment of gold and silver work from the Middle Ages to the nineteenth century. Entries are generally short, ranging from one to two paragraphs in length, but they cover a wide variety of topics and include cross-references. General topics such as "American silver" are explained and defined along with specific artifacts, objects, personalities, styles, and techniques. Formerly associated with Christie's Auction House, the author brings expertise and authority to the descriptions and interpretations he provides. There is a bibliography of books and catalogs on selected topics at the end.

382. **The Collector's Encyclopedia of Heisey Glass 1925-1938.** Neila Bredehoft. Paducah, Ky., Collector Books; distr., Newark, Ohio, Heisey Collectors of America, 1986. 415p.

This encyclopedia furnishes a detailed record of the Heisey lines and the thousands of desirable items which were produced by the factory. It begins with a historical overview of the fortunes of the Heisey Company. The major segment of the text is catalog material based on information contained in Heisey catalogs of the period covered. All photographs are taken from these sales catalogs and are mostly black-and-white. Each color in the line is illustrated, however, with representative pieces from that line. Entries contain pattern numbers, names, dates, decorations, and indication of marks. Included with the purchase of the encyclopedia but also selling as a separate item is a price guide which provides price ranges for all items and lines described in the encyclopedia.

383. **Dictionary of Furniture.** Charles Boyce. New York, Facts on File, 1985. 331p.

An up-to-date, comprehensive source of information on furniture and furniture making in all countries and time periods, this work was readily accepted by librarians in the field. Furnishing brief entries, alphabetically arranged, coverage is given to numerous topics, issues, styles, personalities, and terms. These are explained in an informative and lucid manner, in enough detail to satisfy most queries. Both Western and Eastern influences and individuals are treated. The tool is especially helpful in its treatment of modern furniture and designers, since biographical information on twentieth-century furniture makers is elusive. An old standard, first published in 1938, is *The Encyclopedia of Furniture*, by Joseph Aronson (Crown, 1965). This older work can be used to supplement the coverage of the newer one, since each contains material not found in the other.

384. **Encyclopedia of Pottery and Porcelain 1800-1960.** Elisabeth Cameron. New York, Facts on File, 1986. 366p.

An important new work is this compendium of the world of pottery and porcelain operating over a period of 160 years. The approximately 9,500 alphabetically arranged entries include decorators, designers, factories, materials, styles, techniques, and basic terminology as well as individual potters. Marks are described within the context of the entries for individuals and firms although they generally are not illustrated. The emphasis is on European (especially English) and American pottery, although Japanese ceramics are not overlooked. There are 450 black-and-white reproductions, with 32 illustrations in color, providing a good indication of the nature or character of the representative forms and styles. Considered to be the best single guide available for its coverage of major personalities and elements within this important time span, the encyclopedia provides bibliographical references as well.

385. **The Macmillan Encyclopedic Dictionary of Numismatics.** Richard G. Doty. New York, Macmillan, 1982. 355p.

This work has proved to be a real asset to any library which seeks to improve its holdings in this area, for it has a value which goes beyond the normal one-year lifespan of valuation guides. As a dictionary, it defines terms important to the field in a lucid and concise manner. Coverage is univeral in terms of topics and representative coins, with all periods of time and all geographic areas represented. Between 600 and 700 illustrations are furnished to clarify the textual descriptions and further enlighten the reader. Entries are arranged alphabetically and number about 300; they provide brief definitions together with longer expositions describing history, value, and appearance. There is a good bibliography of additional source material at the end, but no index.

386.   Price and Rarity Guide to Lionel Postwar, 1945-1969. Tom McComas and James Tuohy. Wilmette, Ill., TM Productions, 1986. 102p.

An inexpensive and brief guide designed to satisfy the needs of those who collect in the area, this is representative of those works devoted to a specific type of toy. Lionel trains have been part of American childhood for many years, and represent the most popular and widely collected (although certainly not the most valuable) brand. The guide covers the final twenty-five years of the original company from its resumption of production following the war to its purchase by General Mills in 1970. As such, it is one of several guidebooks on Lionel trains written by these authors. This work covers approximately 1,300 varieties of trains; 250 color illustrations are well integrated with the text and enhance the narrative. Arrangement is topical, with chapters on type of equipment. Entries provide catalog numbers, dates of production, descriptions, and valuations.

387.   Price Guide to Antique and Classic Cameras, 1985-86. 5th ed. James M. McKeown and Joan C. McKeown, eds. Grantsburg, Wis., Centennial Photo Service, 1985. 544p.

This is the fifth edition of this guide to appear in the last twelve years and represents an excellent source of information on the specialized interest of antique cameras. One of several guides in this field, it affords a useful and convenient source of information on a subject which has received increased attention on the part of collectors. Arranged alphabetically by manufacturer and chronologically within that category, both still and motion picture cameras are treated separately. In all, about 5,000 cameras from all over the world and all periods of time are listed, making it a useful source for identification. It is illustrated with black-and-white photographs for a number of the pieces. Each entry provides valuation and brief description and is accessed through a detailed index.

388.   Scott 1987 Standard Postage Stamp Catalogue. 143rd ed. William W. Cummings, et al., eds. Sidney, Ohio, Scott Publishing; distr., New York, Harper & Row, 1986. 4v.

The 1986 catalog maintains the high level of quality and comprehensiveness of this long-time standard work in the field. It is represented in four volumes covering the various countries of the world with the United States, Great Britain, and Canada covered in volume 1, and the other countries of the world arranged alphabetically in volumes 2-4. The *Scott Catalogue*s have long been regarded as the standards of the field in every way, providing comprehensive coverage and remaining the basic source for pricing information. Many illustrations of various issues are provided, earning the guide its well-deserved reputation as the leading identification and valuation tool for philatelists. The same editor was responsible for the *Scott 1987 Specialized Catalogue of United States Stamps* (Scott Publishing, 1986), the sixty-fifth edition of what is considered to be the most useful and important reference guide to stamp issues of our country.

389.   The Sotheby's Directory of Silver, 1600-1940. Vanessa Brett. London, Sotheby's Publications; distr., New York, Harper & Row, 1986. 432p.

Although there is no shortage of reference works on silver, this survey of 2,000 elegant pieces sold at auction by Sotheby's spans a period of sixty years' auctioneering from the 1920s to the mid-1980s. It should be regarded as an important tool not only for the record it provides of prices and costs over the years, but for identifying the work of high-quality silversmiths from both Europe and the United States. Each piece is illustrated, and information is given on category, manufacture, size, and weight as well as sales. Additional information is furnished regarding the silversmith. Unfortunately, makers' marks and monograms are not included, which may be regarded as a deficiency in an otherwise useful work. The arrangement is by country and then by maker, in a sequence which is roughly chronological. An index facilitates access.

390. **Standard Catalog of World Coins.** 13th ed. Colin R. Bruce, II, ed. Iola, Wis., Krause Publications, 1987. 2v.

This is a standard in the field and provides an in-depth survey of coin issues from approximately 1,000 different governments dating from the mid-eighteenth century. It continues to be a work unmatched for its comprehensiveness, depth of coverage, and up-to-date and reliable valuations. Information regarding history, mintmarks, and quantities is provided in the format now familiar to both dealers and collectors. Countries appear in alphabetical arrangement, with the coins listed by denomination, lowest to highest. Within the denomination, issues are listed chronologically. Illustrations are in black-and-white and mintage quantities are provided. There are many helpful introductory and supplementary pages covering a variety of features such as foreign exchange and identification pointers. The fifth edition of Albert Pick's *Standard Catalog of World Paper Money* (Krause Publications, 1986) provides the same type of comprehensive coverage and contributes similar information to those who collect and deal in paper.

Crafts and Design

BIBLIOGRAPHIES, INDEXES, AND ABSTRACTS

391. **How-To: 1400 Best Books on Doing Almost Everything.** Bill Katz and Linda Sternberg Katz. New York, R. R. Bowker, 1985. 377p.

Another of the Katz publications which provides annotated bibliographies of self-help items, this volume focuses on manual, creative, and recreational arts. Coverage of subject areas is varied and each entry carries complete bibliographic identification as well as descriptive, sometimes, chatty, analyses of documents selected. Basically, it is a list of 1,400 manuals concerned with the learning or acquisition of skills or techniques. Government publications are included and publication dates generally fall between 1980 and 1984. Although it has been criticized for unevenness in the quality of books cited, this work represents an important source of information on recently published items.

392. **Index to Handicraft Books 1974-1984.** Carnegie Library. Science and Technology Department. Pittsburgh, University of Pittsburgh, 1986. 411p.

Unlike the Katz item (see entry 391), this work provides a sharp focus on handicraft projects found in books and furnishes citations to over 900 books where these projects can be found. Arrangement is alphabetical by subject of project and citations are furnished that include author, title, and page numbers. There is a listing of books at the beginning for which complete bibliographic identification is provided. More than 12,000 subject headings are employed, with many cross-references given in the entries. The work originated as a card file prepared by the library staff to supplement such works as Joyce F. Shields's *Make It: An Index to Projects and Materials* (Scarecrow, 1975). This earlier work provides an index to craft projects identified in English-language publications between 1968 and 1974.

DICTIONARIES, ENCYCLOPEDIAS, HANDBOOKS, ETC.

393. **The Arco Encyclopedia of Crafts.** H. E. Laye Andrew. New York, Arco Publishing, 1982. 432p.

As one might expect, a variety of information in what has been termed as an encyclopedia of crafts is included in this work, and coverage ranges over a wide spectrum of craftwork from the very traditional to the very new. Emphasis is on techniques employed in the crafts rather than specific projects. There are more than 120 crafts enumerated, with 850 illustrations to enhance the text. Historical information is given for a number of crafts described. There are many useful charts and diagrams included in the appendices which facilitate the successful completion of projects such as conversion charts (metric) and color charts. There are lists of suppliers, craft associations, and museums organized by countries.

394. **The Complete Stitch Encyclopedia.** Jan Eaton. Woodbury, N.Y., Barron's Educational Series, 1986. 173p.

This is a detailed and comprehensive manual to the various forms of stitchery which have been popular through the years. Identification is furnished for over 450 different stitches, arranged by type. Categories are organized according to degree of difficulty, with the simplest techniques listed first. There are numerous illustrations in full color for each stitch and detailed instructions given for successful application. The photographs are integrated with the narrative, and sequence photographs are provided for the more complicated techniques. Advice is given regarding such matters as choice of thread along with brief historical information on some of the older techniques. A related work, *The A F Encyclopedia of Textiles* (Prentice-Hall, 1980), is now in its third edition and provides a fine exposition of various fibers, designs, and processes involved in the manufacture of textiles. Brief chapters cover the various topics and include numerous illustrations.

395. **Encyclopedia of Batik Designs.** Leo O. Donahue. Philadelphia, Art Alliance; distr., East Brunswick, N.J., Associated University Presses, 1981. 630p.

Batik as a form of textile decoration employing wax resist methods emerged in the eighteenth century, having been introduced by the Dutch East India Company. It very quickly became high fashion and through the years has enjoyed a steady popularity marked by spurts of increased interest. In this volume, exposition is given not only to the creation of the batik but also to the block on *tjap* for printing on cloth. The processes are explained in detail and many photographs enhance the descriptions provided of the routines and the creation of various effects. There are a glossary of terms, a bibliography, and an index.

396. **The Encyclopedia of Crafts.** Laura Torbet, ed. New York, Scribner's, 1980. 3v.

This is a detailed and comprehensive encyclopedia which provides in-depth information on about fifty different crafts. There are approximately 12,000 entries for specific terms associated with these crafts. Designed as a basic tool for the craftsman as well as the fledgling operative, coverage is given to such varied activities as basketry, mosaics, block printing, fabric printing, jewelry, ceramics, stained glass, metalworking, batik, etc. Articles vary in length from a short paragraph to several pages. Many cross-references are provided, with indication given in boldface type within an article to a routine that has its own entry. Considered an excellent source book, the arrangement is alphabetical, and 2,500 illustrations are furnished. There is no index.

397. **Encyclopedia of Design.** New York, Hart Publishing, 1983. 399p.

Designed for the benefit of artists and craftsmen who need designs of various kinds, this title provides over 4,000 illustrations from different cultures throughout the world. The reproductions appear in the twenty-nine chapters devoted to various cultures of the world such as Assyrian, Celtic, Chinese, Coptic, etc. Most important is the fact that the pictures belong in the public domain and are freely available for reproduction without seeking permission or paying fees. Chapters vary considerably in depth of coverage and range from two to ten pages in length. Numerous designs are furnished in different media, including pottery, masks, tapestry, furniture, and stained glass. There is a bibliography of source material with precise references given.

398. **The Facts on File Dictionary of Design and Designers.** Simon Kervis. New York, Facts on File, 1984. 533p.

This dictionary has been recognized as a fine reference tool on design and has earned the respect of those who work in the field of art reference. It renders an informative treatment of personalities with biographies of designers, patrons, and historians from the mid-fifteenth century to the present and is important for its coverage of obscure individuals as well as prominent ones. Biographies are brief and provide dates, place of birth, training, and influences upon the persons as well as their achievements. The terminology of design and designing is also covered, with entries given to the various types such as ceramics, furniture, glass, interior decoration and metalwork. Generally the emphasis is on the styles and techniques of Europe and North America. Many cross-references are provided in the entries.

399. **An Illustrated Dictionary of Ceramics.** Rev. ed. George Savage and Harold Newman. New York, Thames and Hudson; distr., Boston, Little, Brown, 1985. 319p.

For those libraries that cannot afford the hardcover edition published in 1974, this paperback issue may suffice. There is a warning however, that the paperback edition should not be lent, resold, hired out, or otherwise circulated without the publisher's consent. The hardcover edition is still preferred by art departments since the paperback edition does not contain the color reproductions. Other than that there is not much difference between the editions, and the black-and-white illustrations are of good quality. The definitions are brief but informative and will provide enlightenment for those seeking to define the terminology of the field. Many cross-references are furnished. The subtitle aptly describes the scope as "Defining 3,054 Terms Relating to Wares, Materials, Processes, Styles, Patterns, and Shapes from Antiquity to the Present Day." The emphasis is on English ceramics.

400. **The Macmillan Atlas of Rugs and Carpets.** David Black, ed. New York, Macmillan, 1985. 255p.

A useful and detailed expository work on the history and development of the craft of carpet making, this atlas furnishes information on the individual countries involved in the practice. Beautiful illustrations (200 in color and 150 in black-and-white) show the various designs and techniques. The work begins with a description of the methods of weaving and carpet design and provides general guidelines for analyzing carpets. The next chapter covers the history of carpets and examines and compares developments in countries from which it is considered most desirable to obtain these products (Turkey, Persia, India, etc.). The largest portion of the work covers individual countries with maps, and detailed information is given for each style produced. Included are the braided, hooked, and embroidered rugs of this country as well as Navaho blanket weaving.

Fashion and Costume

BIBLIOGRAPHIES, INDEXES, AND ABSTRACTS

401.   **Costume Index: A Subject Index to Plates and to Illustrated Texts.** Isabel Stevenson Monro and Dorothy E. Cook. New York, H. W. Wilson, 1937. 338p. Supp., 1957, 210p.

An old standard in the field, this work indexes plates appearing in over 600 titles which provide coverage of costume. These sources were rated in terms of their priority, a useful feature at the time of publication but less important with the passage of time. Any full-page illustration has been defined as a plate, and occasionally illustrations without accompanying text are included, in cases where such reproductions are unique. No titles without illustrations are included. Coverage is broad and historical costumes from any period with the exception of biblical times are identified under geographic locations, classes of persons, or details of costume. The supplement covers nearly 350 books published between 1936 and 1956, in a manner similar to the basic edition. A continuation of coverage may be found in Jackson Kesler's *Theatrical Costume: A Guide to Information Sources* (Gale, 1979), which is a bibliography of materials dating from 1957 to the 1970s.

DICTIONARIES, ENCYCLOPEDIAS, HANDBOOKS, ETC.

402.   **American Costume, 1915-1970: A Source Book for the Stage Costumes.** Shirley Miles O'Donnol. Bloomington, Ind., Indiana University Press, 1982. 270p.

An essential work for any costumer is this exposition of American costume over a period of fifty-five years. Beginning with the period of World War I, it provides separate chapters in chronological sequence: "World War, 1915-1919"; "The Twenties (1920-1929)"; "Depression (1930-1939)"; "World War (1940-1946)"; "The 'New Look' (1947-1952)"; "Space Age (1953-1960)"; and the "Sixties (1960-1970)." The background of each period is described along with general information on dress, then specific coverage is accorded men's, women's, and children's fashions. Also included are details on grooming, hair styles, and accessories as well as colors and motifs. There are suggestions for costumers and lists of plays for the different time periods. Illustrations are provided.

403.   **Essential Terms of Fashion: A Collection of Definitions.** Charlotte Mankey Calasibetta. New York, Fairchild Publications, 1986. 244p.

This is an up-to-date dictionary which is especially useful for its inclusion of very contemporary terminology. It also provides good coverage of the traditional terms of the field, and has been commended for its historical precision. Arrangement is by broad categories of articles of clothing, accessories, or style such as boots, robes, and pleats. These are subdivided by specific types. Definitions are brief for the most part, but adequate, and cross-references are furnished. Illustrations in the form of line drawings are useful and accompany many of the entries. The terms are those used in the faashions of men, women, and children, and the work has been received well by both librarians and designers.

404.   **The Fashion Encyclopedia: An Essential Guide to Everything You Need to Know about Clothes.** Catherine Houck. New York, St. Martin's Press, 1982. 215p.

An interesting, revealing, and highly readable survey of the field of fashion, this handbook provides a great deal of information from a variety of sources. Coverage is given to style, personalities, production, care, and purchasing of a variety of material, clothing, and accessories. Arrangement is alphabetical by topic and there are many black-and-white illustrations. Among other things such topics as furs, jewelry, discount houses, mail order, and thrift shops are treated. An especially useful feature is the list of trademarks, copyright, and certification marks of the various products, firms, and processes. Although not scholarly, the tool will prove to be useful for the variety of information it provides.

405. **The Illustrated Encyclopedia of Costume and Fashion 1550-1920.** Jack Cassin-Scott. Poole, England, Blandford; distr., New York, Sterling Publishing, 1986. 160p.

This tool lives up to its descriptive title in being well illustrated, since the total of 150 color reproductions provides excellent images of over 300 costumes. Detail is clearly shown and reveals the styles worn by lords and ladies, children, military figures, peasants, and musicians. Costumes are described briefly and dates are furnished. In most cases, type of fabric is given and country of origin established. The work has been criticized for certain oversights among the illustrations provided, such as cropping of the lady's train in one plate and a portion of a skirt in another. It remains a worthwhile addition to the reference department, however, for its comprehensive coverage and attractive format.

406. **A Visual History of Costume: The Twentieth Century.** Penelope Byrde. London, Batsford, 1986. 144p.

This is the most recent of what has become a highly stylized five-volume series on costume, each volume of which is done in the exact same format with the same number of pages. An English publication from Batsford, it is sold in the United States by Drama Book Publishers. Sequentially, the series begins with coverage of the sixteenth century by Jane Ashelford (1983), followed by the seventeenth century by Valerie Cumming (1984), the eighteenth century by Aileen Ribeiro (1983), and the nineteenth century by Vanda Foster (1984). The volumes are considered extremely useful sources of information about the styles of costume, illustrated through a series of reproductions of the artwork of the time. Illustrations are chronologically arranged, appear both in color and black-and-white, and depict men and women dressed in fashions of the day. These are mostly English, and captions describe the costume features. Each volume begins with an introduction surveying the world of fashion in that century, and provides an index and a selective bibliography.

407. **Who's Who in Fashion: A Biographical Encyclopedia of the International Red Series Containing Some 6,000 Biographies.** Karl Strute and Theodor Dolken, eds. Zurich, Who's Who the International Red Series; distr., New York, UNIPUB, 1982. 3v. in 2.

This is the first edition of what purports to be a triennial directory of important personalities and institutions related to fashion from Western European countries. Also treated are the related areas of cosmetics and jewelry, and altogether about 6,000 individuals are identified and described. These people represent all phases or elements of the fields (artistic or creative, economic, and even scientific interests). They include costume designers, beauty operators, and jewelers. Entries vary in length but furnish birthdates, parents, spouses, children, home and work addresses, education, career information, current job, publications, memberships, awards, specialties, and hobbies. The appendices provide useful information such as listings of national and international organizations, schools and training institutes, museums, fairs, societies, prizes, and journals. A number of photographs of individuals are included. Volume 1 covers fashion, while volumes 2-3 cover beauty and jewelry.

Photography and Printmaking

BIBLIOGRAPHIES, INDEXES, AND ABSTRACTS

408.   **Old Master Print References: A Selected Bibliography.** Lauris Mason, et al. White Plains, N.Y., Kraus International, 1986. 279p. (Print Reference Series).

This is a selective bibliography on eminent printmakers, similar to the earlier volume in the series (see entry 409). It provides a listing of artists with birth and death dates, followed by a chronological listing of references. This particular volume covers printmakers from the fifteenth through the seventeenth centuries, with slight representation of eighteenth-century artisans. Bibliographic references range from seventeenth-century writings to 1984 publications. The book is international in coverage; foreign-language titles are translated into English. References include books, journal articles, exhibit catalogs, and book reviews. Mason has been a solid contributor to the bibliography of printmaking and serves as editor of *Print Collectors Quarterly* (KTO, 1977-) which publishes essays on eminent printmakers.

409.   **Print Reference Sources: A Select Bibliography, 18th-20th Centuries.** 2nd ed. Rev. and enl. Lauris Mason and Joan Ludman. Millwood, N.Y., KTO, 1979. 363p.

The first edition of this work appeared in 1975 and covered 1,300 printmakers listed alphabetically. Under their names were listings of both primary and secondary sources about them. It proved to be a useful tool since information on printmakers tends to be difficult to obtain. This edition was enlarged to cover an additional 500 printmakers, with a total of some 5,000 citations. The purpose of the tool remains the same, to provide a selective listing of source material on the printmakers of the eighteenth and nineteenth centuries. Sources identified represent a variety of types and forms including *catalogues raisonnés, oeuvre-catalogues*, museum and dealer publications and checklists, and essays from both book and periodical literature. Both out-of-print and currently available items are identified, a feature which will have value for a varied audience ranging from librarians to print collectors and dealers. A complementary work is *Old Master Print References* (see entry 408), which covers the period from the fifteenth through the seventeenth centuries.

DICTIONARIES, ENCYCLOPEDIAS, HANDBOOKS, ETC.

410.   **American Prints in the Library of Congress: A Catalogue of the Collection.** Karen F. Beall, comp. Baltimore, Md., Johns Hopkins University Press, 1970. 568p.

This is considered to be an outstanding reference book in the field of graphic arts, since it identifies approximately 12,000 American prints from 1,250 different artists. These works span the complete history of our country dating from the colonial period to the year of publication. The Library of Congress has one of the truly outstanding collections in this area, and the catalog provides documentation which would be difficult to find elsewhere. The arrangement is alphabetical by artist's name, under which are listed the prints in the Library's collection. Information includes date of execution, imprint, medium, and size. The analytical notes are useful. There are indexes for iconography, names, and also for print series. A seven-page bibliography is included. The work was copied and made available by University Microfilms in 1981. Another important catalog title, in four volumes, is *Library Catalog of the International Museum of Photography at George Eastman House* (G. K. Hall, 1982).

411. **Contemporary Photographers.** George Walsh, et al. New York, St. Martin's Press, 1982. 837p.

A biographical dictionary of 650 prominent photographers, either living or recently deceased, this work provides a distinctive and useful source on what is generally elusive information. Planned as a quinquennial publication, it covers photographers from all over the world including a good representation of those from communist nations. Selection was determined by an advisory board composed of distinguished authorities. Entries provide the usual biographical information as well as listings of exhibitions, group expositions, galleries, and museums that display the subjects' work, and a bibliography of books and articles by and about them. An important feature is the critical essay on the style and quality of the photographers' work as well as statements from them on the topic.

412. **Graphic Arts Encyclopedia.** 2nd ed. George A. Stevenson. New York, McGraw-Hill, 1979. 483p.

For a one-volume work of moderate size, this compendium provides comprehensive coverage of the graphic arts. Arrangement is alphabetical and entries vary in length from brief identifications to essays. Terminology, technical applications, equipment, and processes represent a variety of activities such as copy preparation, art reproduction, copying, and printing. The coverage of equipment is brought up-to-date for the time of publication, although some of the material is dated. Machinery covered includes word processors, keyboarding equipment, video display terminals, typesetters, printing presses, microfilm equipment, process cameras, and color copiers. The writing is clear and free of technical jargon and the definitions are enhanced by the inclusion of about 300 black-and-white illustrations. There are numerous tables and charts, a bibliography, and an index.

413. **International Center of Photography/Encyclopedia of Photography.** Cornell Capa, et al., eds. New York, Crown, 1984. 607p.

Designed for a more advanced and sophisticated audience, this encyclopedia contains 1,300 entries providing technical awareness, biographical coverage, and aesthetic understanding. Many cross-references appear in the entries and there are numerous illustrations to augment the exposition provided. Biographies cover prominent individuals over a 100-year period from 1840 to 1940 and are illustrated with examples of the biographees' work. Trends in the field are identified and described, and a bibliography is furnished. A work similar in content and form is *The Photographer's Bible: An Encyclopedic Reference Manual* by Bruce Pinkard (Arco Publishing, 1982). Techniques, equipment, and personalities are covered alphabetically in articles of varying length. There are numerous illustrations as well.

414. **Macmillan Biographical Encyclopedia of Photographic Artists and Innovators.** Turner Browne, ed. New York, Macmillan, 1983. 722p.

An extensive biographical dictionary of 2,000 photographers and photographic artists, this volume includes individuals both living and dead. The major photographers are covered, of course, but more important is the utility of the tool in identifying individuals who are less prominent and relatively difficult to find. About 25 percent of the personalities date from the nineteenth and early twentieth centuries, and selection for inclusion is generally based on contribution to the field. Coverage is international and those included have generally had works shown or have had publications or awards. There are nearly 150 reproductions of representative works and separate listings of museums and galleries. This is a valuable resource because of the number of individuals covered.

415.   **The Poster: A Worldwide Survey and History.** Alain Weill. Boston, G. K. Hall, 1985. 422p.

Bringing a great deal of expertise to the subject from his career as head of the Poster Collection at the Louvre's Museum of Decorative Arts, and presently a consultant on the topic, Weill provides an informative and substantial history of posters from 1469 to the 1980s. Developments are explained and landmark events described in a clear and revealing style. Personalities are identified in a separate section and a bibliography is furnished. Coverage is chronological by country and is enhanced by over 650 illustrations, with 300 in color. With the increased interest in posters today as marked by the number of sales and prices paid, this is a timely and useful tool for collectors, artisans, and students.

REPRODUCTIONS AND SALES

416.   **Gordon's Print Price Annual.** 1978- . Ann. New York, Martin Gordon.

Another of the useful indexes to sale items developed during recent years is this record of sales of prints, issued on an annual basis. Covering auction sales for the year, entries are listed alphabetically and include title, medium, size, date, references, measurements, notes and remarks, as well as margins and conditions. Naturally, auction houses and prices are enumerated. Prints are of various combinations and represent not only individual pieces, but sets, pairs, groupings, and artists' portfolios. Coverage is provided of sales from about twenty-five leading auction houses worldwide. Useful information regarding exchange rates is given along with the addresses and telephone numbers in a listing of auction houses. It covers about 30,000 entries each year.

417.   **Photographic Art Market: Auction Prices: Spring Auctions 1982 thru Fall Auctions 1985.** Robert S. Persky, ed. New York, Photographic Arts Center, 1987. 152p.

This is a highly informative guide to the sales of important photographs in the large auction houses of Butterfield's, Christie's, Phillips, and Sotheby's. This is the fourth issue in the series and incorporates all sales reported in volume 3 (1983-1984) while updating the listings to late 1985. The arrangement is alphabetical by names of photographers, under which are listed the titles of photographs. Entries include price, auction house, lot number, physical description, and date of negative or print. Prices for individual prints are listed in a chronological sequence by date of auction. The work is plain in appearance, with listings provided without benefit of illustration, but it continues as a useful resource item for collectors and dealers.

418.   **Photography Index: A Guide to Reproductions.** Pamela Jeffcott Parry, comp. Westport, Conn., Greenwood Press, 1979. 372p.

A useful index limited solely to photographs appearing in over eighty books and exhibition catalogs representing artistic, journalistic, and documentary photography, this work has met with a warm reception from both patrons and librarians. There are three major sections consisting of a chronological index to anonymous photographs, an index by photographer, and a subject and title index. Photographers are identified by dates of birth and death and nationality when known. Photographs are identified by title and date and type of photographic medium. Anonymous photographs are listed by date and by subject or title. There are many entries for people and places, making this work useful for purposes of reference.

419. **Print Index.** Pamela Jeffcott Parry and Kathe Chipman, comps. Westport, Conn., Greenwood Press, 1983. 310p. (Art Reference Collection, No. 4).

Another work from Parry which is extremely useful in the art reference area is this index to the prints of more than 2,100 graphic artists. These prints appeared in over 100 English-language publications. With the focus on the graphic arts, rather than the more customary painting and sculpture, the tool is somewhat unique. This uniqueness, of course, is its strength and serves to make it an important purchase for a reference department. Publication dates of the sources vary over a long span of time from the late nineteenth century to several published during this decade. Artists are identified with birth and death dates and nationality. There is an index of subjects and titles.

420. **The Printworld Directory: Contemporary Prints and Prices.** 1982- . Ann. Bala Cynwyd, Pa., Printworld; distr., Detroit, Gale.

Another recent entry in the field of art sales reporting is this useful directory on the world of printmaking. More than 1,200 contemporary artists are identified, biographical information is provided, and gallery affiliations are enumerated. The directory is developed through surveys of the artists, who are listed alphabetically. They find it to their advantage to provide information regarding their works which have sold out as well as those currently available. Criteria for listing the prints are their price ($100.00, at least), signature (must be signed), and number (not more than 300). Emphasis is on today's artist, and most illustrations are of works from this decade. There are indexes of the artists, and of the print publishers and workshops. The work also contains a listing of galleries specializing in original graphics.

9 ACCESSING INFORMATION IN THE PERFORMING ARTS

WORKING DEFINITION OF THE PERFORMING ARTS

The term *performing arts* has not become standardized in its usage. It is used to differentiate the arts or skills which, by their nature, require public performance as opposed to those whose beauty is appreciated through the sense of sight (the visual arts). Generally, three elements are considered necessary for consideration as a performing art: there must be the piece performed, the performer, and the audience hearing, viewing, or experiencing the performance.

MAJOR DIVISIONS OF THE FIELD

As used in this guide, the performing arts include music, dance, the theater, film (including video), radio, and television.

Music is commonly defined as the art of organizing sounds. Its principal elements are melody (single sounds in succession), harmony (sounds in combination), and rhythm (sounds in a temporal relationship). The two major divisions are vocal music and instrumental music. Vocal music includes songs, operas, oratorios, etc., while instrumental music includes solos, chamber music, and orchestral music. Musical instruments may be classified as stringed (violin, harp, guitar, etc.), woodwind (flute, bassoon, oboe, English horn), brass (trumpet, cornet, bugle, trombone), percussion (drums, chimes, bells, gongs, etc.), keyboard (piano, organ), and other (accordion, concertina, harmonica, bagpipes, etc.). The modern system of musical notation began to be used around 1700.

The librarian responsible for a music collection will need to keep in mind three major elements: 1) the music itself, which will follow somewhat the divisions outlined above; 2) the literature about music, which will divide itself rather more along the conventional lines for all disciplines, but with some special characteristics; 3) the vast array of recordings on discs, tapes, cassettes, etc., which are a part of any modern music library and which pose problems all their own in terms of organization, retrieval, and use.

The dance may be defined as movement of the body to a certain rhythm. There are three major divisions of the field: folk dancing, ballroom dancing, and theater dancing. Folk dancing, which originated in open-air activities, is characterized by great vigor and exuberance of movement. Ballroom dancing had its origin in the European courts of the Renaissance and is an indoor, participant activity. Theater dancing is a spectator activity that may be traced to religious dances in the ancient world and to performances known as "masques" in the courts of Renaissance Europe. Its most characteristic modern form is the ballet. The dance is usually (though not necessarily) accompanied by music.

Theater is the art of presenting a performance to an audience. In modern usage, the term is normally restricted to live performances of plays. A distinction is sometimes drawn between theater and drama; theater is restricted in meaning to those matters having to do with public performance, while drama includes the literary basis for performance (i.e., the texts of plays). Frequently, the texts of plays are classed with literature. Libraries with subject departments often put plays in a literature department and other works about the theater in a performing arts department. Topics closely related to theatrical performance are acting, costume, makeup, directing, and the architecture of theaters.

Films may conveniently be divided into feature-length (an hour or more) and shorts. Many feature-length films are fictional, often based on books of some popularity. Others, known as documentaries, are prepared for informational purposes. A blending of these forms may result in stories that are essentially colorful travelogues. Two other forms are animated cartoons and puppet features. Short subjects are often filmed by independent producers and sold to distributors of feature-length films to complete an entertainment package. However, they are also widely used by schools, universities, churches, clubs, businesses, etc., for informational and educational purposes. Indeed, films of this latter kind will probably constitute the bulk of those included in most library film collections. Radio depends solely upon sound for its effects. Television bears many similarities to film, but it can also include "live" coverage of events, as can radio. Music videos provide entertainment in the home in yet another format. Marilyn Kaye's "Watching the Music" (*Illinois Libraries* 68 [June 1986]: 365-69) provides a good introduction to the medium.

Coverage of these four areas is reasonably good in the major general encyclopedias. The pivotal article on music in *Encyclopaedia Britannica: Macropaedia* (15th edition, revised 1985), is entitled "Music, Art of" (v.24, pp. 491-550), and is followed by articles on more specialized aspects, such as "Music, The History of Western" and "Musical Forms and Genres." The key dance article in *Britannica* is "Dance, Art of" (v.16, pp. 986-1008), which is followed by related articles like "Dance, Western" and "Dance and Theatre, East Asian." One must not overlook the article on "Ballet" (v.1, pp. 839-41). "Theatre, Art of" (v.28, pp. 515-30) and "Theatre, The History of Western" (v.28, pp. 531-48) give the *Britannica* overview and are followed by articles like "Theatre and Stages" and "Theatrical Production." The *Britannica* puts information about film into a key article—"Motion Pictures" (v.24, pp. 379-445).

Lester Asheim's chapter on music in *The Humanities and the Library* (pp. 151-98) is still a good introduction to the organization and use of a music collection. It is supplemented and updated by "Music Libraries and Collections," by Guy A. Marco, in *Encyclopedia of Library and Information Science* (Dekker, 1976, v.18, pp. 328-493). Music in the general library is covered in "Music and

Fine Arts in the General Library," by Guy A. Marco and Wolfgang Freitag (*Library Trends* 23 [January 1975]: 3212-546). Other useful works covering music librarianship include Carol Bradley's *Reader in Music Librarianship* (Microcard Edition Books, 1973) and Malcolm Jones's *Music Librarianship* (Saur, 1979). John E. Druesedow, Jr., has written *Library Research Guide to Music* (Pierian, 1982), which offers the student clear advice on where to find music information and how to proceed with searches of the music collection. The newer *Music Librarianship: A Practical Guide*, second edition, by E. T. Bryant and G. A. Marco (Scarecrow, 1985) also covers the topic. A classic in the field of music librarianship is *Music Libraries*, by Jack Dove (Deutsch, 1965), which is a rewritten and updated version of the 1937 work of the same title by L. R. McColvin and H. Reeves.

Special topics in music librarianship have received coverage in the Music Library Association's Technical Reports series. Recent issues have covered sheet music cataloging and processing (Report no. 15, 1984), Library of Congress headings for recordings of Western and nonclassical music (Report no. 14, 1983), the MARC music format (Report no. 13, 1982), and the acquisition and cataloging of sound recordings (Report no. 11, 1980).

Cataloging and processing have received considerable attention from music librarians. Besides the special issues published by the MLA, materials of importance include *The Anglo-American Cataloguing Rules*, second edition (American Library Association, 1978), which has chapters on music and sound recordings; *Class M* (3rd edition, 1978) issued by the Library of Congress; and *Library of Congress Subject Headings*, tenth edition. The *Code internationale de catalogage de la musique*, prepared by the International Cataloging Code Commission of the International Association of Music Libraries, has appeared in parts since 1957, but all but the most highly specialized collections have continued to use *AACR2*, in keeping with collections of which they may be part.

Selection of materials is discussed in "Music" in *Selecting Materials for Libraries*, by Robert Broadus (2nd edition, H. W. Wilson, 1981, pp. 352-63). Collecting popular music is the theme of *Drexel Library Quarterly* 19 (Winter 1983), edited by Tim LaBorie.

Indexes and databases appropriate to music are the topics of Thomas J. Heck's "The Relevance of the 'Arts and Humanities' Database to Musicological Research" (*Fontes Artis Musicae* 28 [January/June 1981]: 81-87) and "Music Literature Indexes in Review" by M. A. Keller and C. A. Lawrence (*Music Library Association Notes* 36 [March 1980]: 575-600).

Education and qualifications for music librarianship are discussed in J. B. Young's "Education for Music Librarianship" (*Music Library Association Notes* 40 [March 1984]: 510-28) and in S. T. Sommer's "Qualifications of a Music Research Librarian" (*Fontes Artis Musicae* 26 [April 1979]: 95-97). A related article, "Qualifications for Conservatory Librarians," by J. Harrington, appears in the same issue of the journal (pp. 93-95).

Recordings have received substantial attention in recent years. The International Association of Music Libraries sponsored *Phonograph Record Libraries: Their Organization and Use*, edited by Henry F. J. Currall (Archon, 1970). Derek Langride dealt with collecting and classifying jazz records in *Your Jazz Collection* (Archon, 1970). The classic work is still *Preservation and Storage of Sound Recordings*, by Andrew G. Pickett and Meyer M. Lemcoe (Library of Congress, 1959), but time has rendered some parts obsolete. More recent are Jerry

McWilliams's *The Preservation and Restoration of Sound Recordings* (American Association of State and Local History, 1979) and Jay E. Daily's *Cataloging Phonorecordings: Problems and Possibilities* (Dekker, 1975).

Barbara K. Gaeddert has prepared *The Classification and Cataloging of Sound Recordings: An Annotated Bibliography* (Music Library Association, 1977), and Judith Kaufmann has written *Recordings of Non-Western Music: Subject and Entry Access* (Music Library Association, 1977). Other aids that may be useful include Julian Hodgson's *Music Titles in Translation: A Checklist of Musical Compositions* (Bingley, 1976) and D. W. Krummel's *Guide for Dating Early Published Music: A Manual of Bibliographical Practices* (Joseph Boonin, 1974). Two journals, *Fontes Artis Musicae* (International Association of Music Libraries) and *Notes* (Music Library Association, U.S.), deserve mention. The former, which is multilingual and international in scope, covers the work of the association, the proceedings of its conferences, and substantive articles on issues of interest to music librarians. *Notes* carries substantive articles and is also an excellent source of reviews of new publications, bibliographies, and articles on particular collections of interest.

The organization and use of film collections also requires some variation from conventional library practice. Books to consider include *Film Library Techniques: Principles of Administration*, by Helen P. Harrison (Hastings, 1973) and *The Film User's Handbook: A Basic Manual for Managing Library Film Services*, by George Rehrauer (R. R. Bowker, 1975). *In Focus: A Guide to Using Films*, by Linda Blackaby, Dan Georgakas, and Barbara Margolis (Cine Information, 1980) provides information on selecting, acquiring, and using films in programs. The journals *Film Library Quarterly* (unfortunately no longer published) and *Sightlines* carry articles about film, video, artists, and filmmakers, and also provide filmographies and source lists.

USE AND USERS OF
PERFORMING ARTS INFORMATION

Of all the performing arts, music has been the most studied in terms of information use and users. Malcolm Jones's *Music Librarianship* (Saur, 1979) introduces, very generally, types of music libraries and their users in "Music Libraries and Those They Serve" (pp. 13-23). More specific studies of the use of the literature of music can be found in the journal literature. The reader will want to see, for example, R. Griscom's "Periodical Use in a University Music Library: A Citation Study of Theses and Dissertations Submitted to the Indiana University School of Music from 1975-1980" (*Serials Librarian* 7 [Spring 1983]: 35-52); R. Green's "Use of Music and Its Literature over Time" (*Notes* 35 [September 1978]: 42-56); and David Baker's "Characteristics of the Literature Used by English Musicologists" (*Journal of Librarianship* 10 [July 1978]: 182-200). An earlier study of particular materials use is David L. Vaughn's "Characteristics of Literature Cited by Articles in the *Musical Quarterly* 1955-1958 and the *American Musicological Journal*" (master's thesis, University of North Carolina, 1959).

The behavior of authors and publications in computational musicology has been investigated in "Bibliometrics and Computational Musicology," by Miranda Lee Pao (*Collection Management* 3 [Spring 1979]: 97-109).

The topic of use and users of information in music is also addressed in S. M. Clegg's "User Surveys and Statistics for Music Librarians" (*Fontes Artis Musicae* 32 [January 1985]: 69-75).

COMPUTERS IN THE PERFORMING ARTS

There have been numerous instances of the use of computers in the performing arts and in the management of information for the fields of music, theater, film, and video.

Two major projects are the computer index The London Stage, chronicled by Ben Ross Schneider, Jr., in his *Travels in Computerland: Or Incompatibilities and Interfaces* (Addison-Wesley, 1974), and the National Tune Index by Gustave Rabson and Carolyn Rabson ("The National Tune Index: A System Overview," *Computers and the Humanities* 15 [January 1981]: 1ff.). Other information system applications are noted in "Information Systems and Services in the Arts and Humanities," the review by Joseph Raben and Sarah K. Burton in the *Annual Review of Information Science and Technology* (v.16, 1981) and in the earlier review in the same publication (v.7, 1972).

Music output computer programs have received much attention. Coverage of these applications is included in Leland Smith's "Editing and Printing Music by Computer" (*Journal of Music Theory* 17 [1973]: 292-309), Donald Bird's "A System for Music Printing by Computer" (*Computers and the Humanities* 8 [1974]: 161-72), David A. Gomberg's "A Computer Oriented System for Music Printing" (*Computers and the Humanities* 11 [March/April 1977]: 63-80), and the many works by Harry B. Lincoln. His book, *The Computer and Music* (Cornell University Press, 1970), although older now, still deserves mention. S. Bauer-Mengelberg addresses the very special problem of copyright in "Computer Implemented Music Analysis and the Copyright Law" (*Computers and the Humanities* 14 [June 1980]: 1-21).

Computers have been used in ear training and music instruction. The former is addressed in "OSU's GAMUT: Semi-intelligent Computer-Assisted Music Ear Training," by Ann K. Blombach, in *Sixth International Conference on Computers and the Humanities*, edited by Sarah K. Burton and Douglas D. Short (Computer Science Press, 1983, pp. 14-15). A recent article on computer-aided teaching in music is David L. Schrader's "Microcomputer-Based Teaching: Computer Assisted Instruction in Music Comes of Age" (*College Music Symposium* 22 [1981]: 27-36). The use of computers in stylistic analysis is discussed in the second edition of this guide (p. 273).

A listing of library automation projects in music has been compiled by Garrett H. Bowles in *Directory of Music Library Automation Projects* (Music Library Association Technical Reports No. 2, revised, Music Library Association, 1979). Some entries mention general music computer applications as well as those directly related to libraries.

Online access to RILM ABSTRACTS (Repertoire International de Litterature Musicale) is available through DIALOG (file 97). The database covers the international literature of music and its related fields. The file is updated irregularly, and is "generally 5 or more years late" according to the DIALOG *Database Catalog*. Keller and Lawrence and Thomas J. Heck ("Computerized Bibliographic Retrieval in Music: A State of the Art Critique," in *Sixth International*

Conference on Computers and the Humanities, pp. 249-52) discuss online databases for music.

The H. W. Wilson system for online access, WILSONLINE, includes features that allow searching for performance reviews in the Wilson database family. The use of five-letter symbols which relate to article contents allows the user of *Readers' Guide to Periodical Literature* and the other indexes to locate reviews of drama, motion pictures, operas and operettas, dance performances, videotapes, and radio and television programs.

Nonbibliographic files for the performing arts include VIDEO NEWS, VIDEO WEEK, and BILLBOARD INFORMATION NETWORK, all of which serve their industries with online data and news.

MAJOR ORGANIZATIONS, PUBLISHERS, INFORMATION CENTERS, AND SPECIAL COLLECTIONS

The number of national and international organizations in the fields of the performing arts is so great that attention can be given only to those which are most significant to the librarian. Guides to the specific fields of the performing arts will offer additional information in greater detail.

The International Association of Music Libraries has branches in most developed countries (U.S. branch: Sibley Music Library, Eastman School of Music, Rochester, NY 14604). It currently sponsors the *International Inventory of Music Sources/Repertoire International des Sources Musicales (RISM)*. Since 1954, it has published *Fontes Artis Musicae*, the journal cited earlier. The International Music Council (1 rue Miollis, Paris F750 15, France), one of the first nongovernmental agencies established under UNESCO sponsorship, studies the development of music and produces numerous publications. The International Musicological Society (Case Postale 56, CH-4001, Basel, Switzerland), founded in 1927 to promote research, has published *Acta Musicologica* since 1928.

The Music Library Association (P.O. Box 487, Canton, MA 02021) supports a wide range of activities including publication of *Music Cataloging Bulletin* and, since 1943, *Notes*. The Association for Recorded Sound Collections (P.O. Box 75082, Washington, DC 20013) was founded in 1966 and includes in its membership people in the recording and broadcasting industries, as well as librarians. It publishes *ARSC Journal* and *ARSC Bulletin*. The Music Educators' National Conference (1902 Association Dr., Reston, VA 22091) was founded in 1902 and has over 60,000 members. It publishes *Music Educators' Journal* and the quarterly *Journal of Research in Music Education*. The American Musicological Society (University of Pennsylvania, 201 S. 34th St., Philadelphia, PA 19104) publishes *Journal of the American Musicological Society* and periodic lists of master's theses and doctoral dissertations in the field. The American Guild of Organists (630 Fifth Ave., New York, NY 10020) is one of many specialized groups; it publishes *Music/AGORCCO* monthly.

By contrast with music, the number of organizations devoted to the dance is small; those that do exist seem to be largely concentrated in the areas of ballet and teaching of the dance. The Ballet Theatre Foundation (890 Broadway, New York, NY 10003) appeals to the broader public for support and publishes *American*

Ballet Theatre Newsletter. The National Association for Regional Ballet (1860 Broadway, New York, NY 10023) promotes festivals and other educational activities in the United States and Canada. The Imperial Society of Teachers of Dancing (70 Gloucester Place, London, England) has a branch in the United States (c/o Mary Phillips, 4883 Battery Ln., Bethesda, MD 20814). The Society publishes the bimonthly *Imperial Dance Letter.* The Dance Educators of America (P.O. Box 509, Oceanside, NY 11572) and the Dance Masters of America (P.O. Box 1117, Wachulla, FL 33873) both consist of dance teachers and have regional groups which supplement national activities.

The International Federation for Theatre Research (Department of French, University of Lancaster, Lancaster, England) disseminates scholarly information through *Theatre Research International.* The American Society for Theatre Research (Theatre Arts Program, University of Pennsylvania, Philadelphia, PA 19104) issues a *Newsletter* and semiannual *Theatre Survey.* The International Theatre Institute, established in 1948, has a branch in the United States (1860 Broadway, New York, NY 10023) and publishes *Theatre Notes* and *International Theatre Information.*

The American Theatre Association (1010 Wisconsin Ave., N.W., Washington, DC 20007) is concerned with all phases of educational theater. Its divisions include American Community Theatre Association, Army Theatre Arts Association, Children's Theatre Association, Secondary School Theatre Association, University and College Theatre Association, and University Resident Theatre Association. Publications include *Theatre News, Placement Service Bulletin*, its convention program, and an annual directory.

The Theatre Library Association (111 Amsterdam Ave., Rm. 513, New York, NY 10023) includes actors, booksellers, writers, and researchers in its membership; it issues *Broadside* and *Performing Arts Resources*, an annual.

The University Film Association (Department of Cinema and Photography, Southern Illinois University, Carbondale, IL 62901) publishes *UFA Digest* and *Journal.* The American Federation of Film Societies (3 Washington Square Village, New York, NY 10012) includes librarians, students, and teachers; it publishes *Film Society Bulletin* and *Film Critic.* The American Film Institute (30 East 60th St., New York, NY 10022) supports a wide range of archival, research, and production activities. Publications include *American Film* and *Guide to College Courses in Film and Television.* The Federation of Motion Picture Councils (142 N. Tucker, Memphis, TN 38104) includes state and local groups which review films; it publishes *News Reel* and *Motion Picture Ratings Preview Reports.* The Educational Film Library Association (45 John St., Ste. 301, New York, NY 10038) evaluates books and films through *EFLA Evaluations, Sightlines,* and *EFLA Bulletin.* The Film Library Information Council (Box 348 Radio City Station, New York, NY 10019) used to publish *Film Library Quarterly.*

ACT (Action for Children's Television) and the National Council for Children and Television are concerned with cultural, social, and research aspects of children's television. ACT publishes *RE:ACT* (46 Austin St., Newtonville, MA 02160) and sponsored *Exploring the Arts: Films and Video Programs for Young Viewers*, edited by Paula Rohrlick (R. R. Bowker, 1982). NCCT (20 Nassau St., Princeton, NJ 08540) publishes *Television and Children*, a quarterly.

Music publishing often occurs outside the normal trade channels. One of the best-known firms is Breitkopf and Härtel (Postbox 1707, Walkmuhlstr. 52,

Wiesbaden, West Germany), which has published serious and classical music since about 1750. C. F. Peters (U.S. office: 373 Park Ave. S., New York, NY 10016) was founded in Leipzig in 1800. The famous British firm of Novello & Co., Ltd. (Borough Green, Sevenoaks, Kent, England) was founded in 1811. A major American firm is G. Schirmer (609 Fifth Ave., New York, NY 10017), founded in 1861. In 1883, the Theodore Presser Co. (Presser Place, Bryn Mawr, PA 19010) was founded. Further information about publishers of serious and educational music may be obtained from the Music Publishers' Association of the United States (810 Seventh Ave., New York, NY 10019), while information about publishers of popular music is available from National Music Publishers' Association (205 E. 42nd St., New York, NY 10017).

The American Music Center (250 W. 54th St., Rm. 300, New York, NY 10019) was appointed official U.S. Information Center on Music in 1962 by the National Music Council. The American Composers' Alliance (170 W. 74th St., New York, NY 10023) specializes in manuscripts and published music of contemporary American composers.

The Committee on Research in Dance (Department of Dance Education, New York University, 35 W. 4th St., Rm. 675D, New York, NY 10003) serves as a clearinghouse for research information about the dance.

The International Theatre Studies Center (University of Kansas, Lawrence, KS 66044) publishes the results of its research in various professional journals and issues the following semiannual publications: *Theatre Documentation, Afro-Asian Theatre Bulletin,* and *Latin-American Theatre Review.* The Wisconsin Center for Theatre Research (University of Wisconsin, 1166 Van Hise Hall, 1220 Linden Dr., Madison, WI 53706) concentrates on the performing arts in America. The Institute of Outdoor Drama (University of North Carolina, Chapel Hill, NC 27514) provides advisory and consultation services, research, and bibliographical work.

The most outstanding music collection in the United States is in the Library of Congress, which benefits from copyright deposit. The Music Division, established in 1897, has issued numerous catalogs, several of which are listed elsewhere in this book. Another notable collection is found in the Music Division of the Research Library of the Performing Arts in Lincoln Center (part of the New York Public Library). Music from the twelfth to the eighteenth centuries is a specialty of the Isham Memorial Library of Harvard University, while primary sources in early opera scores and librettos are a special strength of the University of California Music Library in Berkeley. The Center for Research Libraries has several microform collections of research materials. In Europe, the Austrian National Library (Vienna), the Royal Library of Belgium (Brussels), the State Library of the Czech Socialist Republic (Prague), the Bibliothèque Nationale (Paris), the Deutsche Staatsbibliothek (Berlin), the British Museum (British Library) (London), the Biblioteca Nazionale Centrale (Florence), and the Vatican Library (Rome) have outstanding collections.

The Dance Collection in the Research Library of the Performing Arts (New York Public Library) includes photographs, scores, programs, prints, posters, and playbills as well as instruction manuals and other literature on the dance. The Archives of Dance, Music and Theatre (University of Florida Libraries) contains about 20,000 similar memorabilia relating to the performing arts in the twentieth century.

The Theater Arts Library (University of California at Los Angeles) has screenplays and pictures in addition to the general collection of English- and foreign-language books on the film. The Harvard Theatre Collection (Houghton Library) has rare letters, account books, diaries, drawings, promptbooks, and playbills from the United States, Britain, and Europe. Similar materials relating to British and American theater from 1875 to 1935 (especially the Chicago Little Theatre Movement 1912-1917) are found in the Department of Rare Books and Special Collections, University of Michigan. The Theatre Collection in the Research Library of the Performing Arts (New York Public Library) is one of the most notable anywhere. Bibliographic access is provided through its published catalog. The Free Library of Philadelphia has over 1,200,000 items relating to the theater, early circuses, and minstrel and vaudeville shows.

The Library of Congress has several notable film collections, including those received on copyright deposit. The Dell Publishing Company has about 3,500,000 pictures dealing with movie and television personalities.

These represent but a small sampling of the collections in the United States and Europe that contain specialized information about the performing arts.

10 PRINCIPAL INFORMATION SOURCES IN THE PERFORMING ARTS

PERFORMING ARTS IN GENERAL

Bibliographic Guides

421. American and English Popular Entertainment: A Guide to Information Sources. Don B. Wilmeth. Detroit, Gale, 1980. 465p. (Performing Arts Information Guide Series, v.7; Gale Information Guide Series, v.7).

The subject matter of this tool is defined as those amusements created and staged by professional showmen for unsophisticated audiences in order to turn a profit. There are three major segments in this useful annotated bibliography of 2,500 books, articles, and dissertations. Part I lists a number of sources on entertainments prior to the nineteenth century, and general sources on the topic. The second part covers specific types or forms of entertainment such as Wild West Shows, minstrel shows, vaudeville, burlesque, dime museums, stage music, lyceum and Chautauqua, and puppet shows. Also included in this segment are optical and mechanical entertainments prior to the introduction of cinema. Part III surveys writings on the popular theater. The emphasis is on nineteenth-century entertainment although some sources do cover twentieth-century developments. As might have been expected, there is some overlap with the author's *The American Stage to World War I: A Guide to Information Sources* (see entry 596).

422. The Literary Adviser: Selected Reference Sources in Literature, Speech, Language, Theater, and Film. Thomas P. Slavens. Phoenix, Ariz., Oryx, 1985. 196p.

The most recent guide of this type to embrace the field in such a comprehensive manner, this compact work provides an annotated listing of nearly 650 reference sources. Arrangement is by geographical division and genre headings representing the types or forms of reference tools such as dictionaries and encyclopedias, or biographies. Annotations describe purpose and coverage of the individual titles, which are primarily American and British although others are included. This should prove to be a useful source of information for those interested in the major tools of the wide group of fields categorized as the performing arts. There are a table of contents and a set of indexes providing access through author, title, and subject.

423. **Performing Arts Research: A Guide to Information Sources.** Marion K. Whalon. Detroit, Gale, 1976. 280p. (Performing Arts Information Guide Series, v.1).

This is the initial volume of the Gale series which has continued to provide useful bibliographies for specialists and students (see also entry 421). It arranges the material in seven parts or segments, identifying guides; dictionaries, encyclopedias, and handbooks; directories; play indexes and finding lists; sources for reviews of plays and motion pictures; bibliographies, indexes, and abstracts; and illustrative and audiovisual sources. Annotations are descriptive and brief but provide information adequate to determine the content and scope of the tools. Coverage embraces a variety of fields and in addition to theater and film includes dance, costume, music, visual arts, literature, and rhetoric. Although the tool is beginning to show its age and has been criticized for certain oversights in its organization and index references, it continues to serve a useful purpose. It is hoped that a new edition will appear soon.

Bibliographies and Indexes

424. **Guide to the Performing Arts** (1957-1968). Ann. New York, Scarecrow, 1960-1972.

Beginning as a supplement to *Guide to the Musical Arts* (Scarecrow, 1953-1956), this work absorbed that title and became a separate publication in 1957. It lasted for a period of twelve years, incorporating *Guide to Dance Periodicals* in 1965 (see entry 574). It indexed about fifty periodicals, primarily U.S. and Canadian, for articles, reviews, and even illustrations. Coverage was broad, spanning the whole spectrum of the performing arts (film, television, theater, dance, etc.). Entries were not annotated and were arranged under authors, titles, and subjects, although the general subject headings were frequently criticized by reviewers. Ironically, the last volume by a new team of editors received the heartiest commendations for improvements in format.

425. **Index to Characters in the Performing Arts.** Harold S. Sharp and Marjorie Z. Sharp, comps. Metuchen, N.J., Scarecrow, 1966-1973. 4v. in 6.

Since its publication, this four-volume set has been regarded as an excellent source of information for the identification of characters in the various genre of the performing arts. Volume 1 covers nonmusical plays (two volumes), volume 2 treats operas and musical productions (two volumes), volume 3 lists characters in ballets, while volume 4 covers radio and television. The established pattern was for a two-part coverage beginning with an alphabetical listing of characters for which cross-references were provided to productions, and a list of citation symbols identifying title, type of production, number of acts, author or composer, name of theater, and place and date of first performance. Thousands of characters, both fictitious and real, major and minor, are treated.

426. **Performing Arts Books, 1876-1981: Including an International Index of Current Serial Publications.** New York, R. R. Bowker, 1981. 1656p.

Another of the spinoff publications derived from the *American Book Publishing Record database, this tool provides a list of more than 50,000 books published or distributed in the United States during the specified time period. Coverage is comprehensive in terms of the subjects enumerated and represents all facets of the performing arts (music, dance, theater, television, radio, film, opera, musical theater, circus, and popular entertainment). Entries provide full bibliographic description and are classified according to Library of Congress and Dewey systems. The subject index includes 12,000 headings (Library of Congress) and is accessed with the aid of author and title indexes. There is a listing of serials with a separate subject and title index which is taken from the *Bowker Serials Bibliography database.

Biographical Sources and Directories

427. Contemporary Theatre, Film, and Television: A Biographical Guide Featuring Performers, Directors, Writers, Producers, Designers ... Monica M. O'Donnell, ed. Detroit, Gale, 1984- . 2v.

This work expands and supersedes two of the standard long-running serials, *Who's Who in the Theatre* (see entry 653) and *Who Was Who in the Theatre* (see entry 653n). It provides good biographical sketches for hundreds of currently employed personalities as well as prominent retirees from the United States and Great Britain. The subtitle (which is abbreviated in the entry above) continues with "Managers, Choreographers, Technicians, Composers, Executives, Dancers, and Critics in the United States and Great Britain." There is an emphasis on U.S. nationals. Entries provide personal data, education, debut dates, credits, awards, etc., and vary somewhat in length because of the amount of material furnished by the biographee or found in secondary sources. Subsequent volumes will cover new personalities, in a manner similar to that of *Contemporary Authors* (see entry 784), and will update entries for those covered in *Who's Who in the Theatre*, including recently deceased individuals. It appears this will be a biennial publication.

428. The Lively Arts Information Directory: A Guide to the Fields of Music, Dance, Theater, Film, Radio, and Television in the United States and Canada ... Steven R. Wasserman and Jacqueline Wasserman O'Brien, eds. Detroit, Gale, 1985. 1040p.

The magnitude of this work is expressed in the complete subtitle, which goes on to state that it covers national, international, state, and regional organizations; government grant sources; foundations; consultants; special libraries; research and information centers; educational programs; journals and periodicals; and festivals and awards. The first edition appeared in 1982; thus it apparently has adopted a triennial frequency. Indexing varies with each component, for the national and international organizations are accessed through a KWIC index while foundations are approached through subject and geographical indexes. There are over 9,000 listings, over a third more than in the initial edition, and the work is derived in part from the publisher's database of listings from the *Encyclopedia of Associations* (Gale, 1984) but with enough additional material from a variety of publications to make it a worthwhile purchase.

429. Performing Arts Biography Master Index: A Consolidated Index to over 270,000 Biographical Sketches of Persons Living and Dead. Barbara McNeil and Miranda C. Herbert, eds. Detroit, Gale, 1982. 701p. (Gale Biographical Index Series, No. 5).

Beginning as *Theatre, Film, and Television Biographies Master Index* (Gale, 1979) this new title expanded and increased coverage by more than double the number of citations to sketches in biographical dictionaries. The number of biographical dictionaries indexed was increased in similar fashion from about 40 to over 100 sources. It continues as a biennial publication, providing coverage of personalities representing a wide spectrum of the performing arts (theater, film, television, classical and popular music, dance, puppetry, magic, etc.). Entries provide dates of birth and death and references to the biographical dictionaries (including page numbers). The biographical sources are considered to be readily available in library reference collections, making this a practical reference tool.

430.   **Performing Arts Libraries and Museums of the World/Bibliothèques et musees des arts du spectacle dans le monde.** 3rd ed. Andre Veinstein and Alfred S. Goulding. Paris, Centre Nationale de la Recherche Scientifique, 1984. 1181p.

The first edition of this work appeared in 1960, the next edition seven years later. After seventeen years, the third edition was issued. This is an outstanding source of information on the collections of performing arts held in museums and libraries all over the world. Traditionally the text is written in both French and English. Entries provide information regarding size and composition of collections, regulations governing their use, and business hours of the various public and private institutions covered. Information is gathered through questionnaires, and arrangement of entries is alphabetical by country, then by city, with place names given in French. There is an index of names which includes persons, places, and institutions.

431.   **Performing Arts Resources.** 1974- . Ann. New York, Drama Book Specialists.

This is an annual publication sponsored by the Theatre Library Association, which provides in each issue articles describing the location, identity, and content of various collections of the performing arts. Earlier volumes covered such diverse units as the research collections in New York City, the motion picture section of the Library of Congress, and the Federal Theatre Project holdings at George Mason University. The work is intended for the use of serious students, scholars, and archivists in order to facilitate the search for materials on theater, film, broadcasting, and popular entertainments. More recent volumes have tended to emphasize collections on very specific topics as well as performance aspects.

MUSIC

Bibliographic Guides

432.   **Information on Music: A Handbook of Reference Sources in European Languages.** Guy A. Marco and Sharon Paugh Ferris. Littleton, Colo., Libraries Unlimited, 1975-1984. 3v.   *Ref ML113.M33 v.1, v.2*

Originally planned as an eight-volume work to supplement the coverage of reference and research materials provided by Duckles (see entry 433) and others, this important series has apparently been concluded with the publication of volume 3, *Europe*, in 1984. The set begins with volume 1, *Basic and Universal Sources* (1975), which furnishes annotated entries for over 500 tools in the field of music and related areas. Volume 2 (1977) covers the Americas and annotates over 800 reference sources relating to music in the Western hemisphere. The final volume on Europe appeared seven years after volume 2, and continued the same tradition of providing citations to numerous sources, including individual encyclopedia articles from *M.G.G.* (see entry 495) and *The New Grove* (see entry 498). Annotations are for the most part brief but informative, and there are references to additional reviews. Each volume is separately indexed, although volume 2 contains a comprehensive index for volumes 1 and 2. An appendix in volume 3 updates materials in the preceding volumes.

433.   **Music Reference and Research Materials.** Vincent H. Duckles and Michael A. Keller. New York, Schirmer Books, 1987. 608p.   *1994*

The single most important and popular guide for music students, teachers, and librarians, this new edition has been thoroughly revised and updated after twelve years.

Ref ML113.D83 1994

The basic format remains unchanged, with arrangement by category of tool such as dictionaries, encyclopedias, catalogs, histories, etc. The work provides bibliographic information and annotations for about 2,000 different reference books. Since Duckles's recent death, Keller, who succeeded him as head of the music library at the University of California at Berkeley, is largely responsible for the new edition and apparently has maintained the standard which made the title an indispensable work for students and specialists. There are indexes of persons, subjects, and titles.

434. **Research Guide to Musicology.** James W. Pruett and Thomas P. Slavens. Chicago, American Library Association, 1985. 175p. (Sources of Information in the Humanities, No. 4).

Ref ML 113 P83 1985

The fourth in a series of literature guides edited and co-authored by Slavens, a professor of library science at the University of Michigan. The first part of the two-part format is by Pruett, a musicologist, who provides a series of survey essays on various subjects relating to music scholarship, elements of musicology, and periods of music history. The surveys close with selective bibliographies listing the important sources of information on the topics described. The final section, by Slavens, is an annotated bibliography of reference tools classified by form or type, beginning with dictionaries and encyclopedias and ending with miscellaneous bibliographical tools. There are listings of periodicals and indexes by author/title and subject.

PERIODICALS

435. **Musical Periodical Literature: An Annotated Bibliography of Indexes and Bibliographies.** Joan M. Meggett. Metuchen, N.J., Scarecrow, 1978. 116p.

Originally developed for use by the author's students in a music bibliography course at the University of Southern California, this compact little volume provides information on periodicals, a topic not targeted by any other English-language guide. Therefore, even though it is beginning to show its age, its unique coverage makes this a worthwhile addition to a music collection. The music periodical literature is approached in several different ways through five sections of the guide: history of music periodicals in general, history of music periodicals in the United States, music periodical literature in general nonmusic indexes and bibliographies, music periodical literature in special nonmusic sources, and music periodical literature in music indexes and bibliographies. The sixth segment furnishes a list of music periodicals. Annotations provide good descriptions of coverage, features, and scope. An index is provided to facilitate access.

Ref ML128.P24.M43

Bibliographies and Catalogs

436. **Bibliography of Black Music.** Dominique-René De Lerma. Westport, Conn., Greenwood Press, 1981-1984. 4v. (Greenwood Encyclopedia of Black Music).

There has been a recent emphasis on bibliographic coverage of black music, and this work has earned praise from reviewers for its comprehensive nature and ambitious scope. Volume 1 provides a bibliography of reference works (catalogs, bibliographies, encyclopedias, discographies, iconographies, directories, dissertations, etc.). Especially useful is a listing of nearly 200 periodicals related to the topic. Volume 2 represents the Afro-American idiom and covers general histories, and works on spirituals, ragtime, musical theater, concert music, blues, gospel, popular, and jazz. Volume 3 covers

Ref ML128.B45.D44 v.1

geographical studies, including books, articles, dissertations, essays, etc., on the music of various geographic regions; it furnishes a section on ethnomusicology. Volume 4 covers theory and education and enumerates sources on instrumentation, performance, notation, etc. The arrangement of material over the entire set follows the organization established by *RILM* (see entry 455). Volumes 3 and 4 have indexes.

437. **Dictionary Catalog of the Music Collection.** New York Public Library. Boston, G. K. Hall, 1982- . 44v.
    One of the leading collections of both music literature and printed music is presented in this set. The first edition appeared in 1964 and was supplemented in 1973 and 1976. Like its predecessor and similar publications from G. K. Hall, this is a photographic reproduction of the catalog, which offers detailed information on books, pamphlets, essays, periodical articles, and micromaterials as well as scores and librettos. The present edition includes imprints through 1971 and represents more than 3,500,000 individual documents. Special strengths of this collection are acknowledged to be in the areas of folk songs, Americana, music periodicals, programs, and various elements of printed music such as operas, historical editions, vocal music, etc. There is also a supplement, entitled *Bibliographic Guide to Music* (see entry 446).

438. **Doctoral Dissertations in Musicology.** 7th North American ed., 2nd International ed. Cecil Adkins and Alis Dickinson, eds. Philadelphia, American Musicological Society, International Musicological Society, 1984. 545p. Supp. 1984-1985, 1986, 41p.
    This represents the seventh publication of the combined listing of American and Canadian doctoral dissertations and the second cumulative listing of international doctoral dissertations. It is a comprehensive bibliography of 6,500 dissertations from all over the world, which supersedes its predecessors due to its cumulative nature. Most dissertations are North American (nearly 35 percent) while the remainder are products of thirty countries (listed since 1972). Arrangement is by period covered and classified by topical subdivisions. There are references to abstracts in *Dissertation Abstracts* (see entry 15) and *RILM* (see entry 455). Works-in-progress are identified with asterisks and there are separate indexes for both subject and author. *Ref ML 128.M8.D62*

439. **Folk Music in America: A Reference Guide.** Terry E. Miller. New York, Garland, 1986. 424p. (Garland Reference Library of the Humanities, v.496).
    This is a selective listing of scholarly articles, books, dissertations, and even encyclopedia articles on the topic of folk music. Annotations, although brief, are informative, and emphasis is given to relatively recent writings from the past three decades. The introduction provides an understanding of what may or may not be considered folk music. Treatment is subsequently given to such elements as the music of American Indians and Eskimos; Anglo-American folk songs and ballads; and the more contemporary bluegrass, country and western, and protest music. There are sections on instruments and instrumental music such as banjo and dulcimer as well as black and ethnic folk music. This should prove to be a basic reference tool in the music collection.

440. **International Jazz Bibliography: Jazz Books from 1919 to 1968.** Carl Gregor, Duke of Mecklenburg. Strasbourg, France, P. H. Heitz, 1969. 198p. Supp. 1970, Universal ed., 1971, 109p. Supp. 1971/1972/1973, Universal ed., 1975, 246p.
    The initial volume of this work included 250 monographic discographies and 300 discographies published as appendices in books, along with books and pamphlets covering all elements of jazz during the specified time period. Types of books listed include

biographies, monographs, histories, theories, analyses, reference works of various kinds, dissertations, and theses. Over 1,500 items are identified, for which full bibliographic data are furnished. Arrangement is alphabetical by author with additional indexes providing access by names, countries, and subject. The supplements cover titles overlooked the first time and titles published subsequent to the initial effort. They are arranged by subject, then alphabetically by author, and cover additional topics such as drums and percussion and jazz background.

441. **The Literature of Jazz: A Critical Guide.** 2nd ed. Donald Kennington. Chicago, American Library Association, 1980. 236p. *Ref ML128 J3 K45 1980*

Originally published in Great Britain by the Library Association, this bibliography has earned a respected position among the useful reference works in the field of music. Essentially, it is a listing of the important books on jazz and it attempts to enumerate all the significant material in the English language published through 1979. Chapters cover the various aspects of the literature beginning with general background and following with such categories as histories, biographies, analysis, theory and criticism, reference sources, periodical literature, and organizations. There are full bibliographies at the end of each chapter. Chapters on the blues and jazz education are new to this edition. Emphasis is still on English-language materials. There are name and title indexes.

442. **Medieval Music: The Sixth Liberal Art.** Rev. ed. Andrew Hughes. Toronto, University of Toronto, 1980. 360p. (Toronto Medieval Bibliographies, No. 4).

This edition adds over 250 citations to the 2,000 or so items covered at the time of initial publication in 1974. These documents are listed separately and receive separate indexing. Classification numbers for these materials are interpolated into the main body of the text by use of cross-references. Indexing is thorough and there is exposition in the text to facilitate the search for subject classifications, which are based on twenty-nine main categories with numerous subcategories (geographical, chronological, individuals, genres, etc.). Essentially a bibliography of books and periodical articles on all aspects of medieval music, this work appeals to the relatively unsophisticated user who needs to find out about the topic. Annotations are brief and there are separate indexes of authors and subjects.

443. **Music in Harvard Libraries: A Catalogue of Early Printed Music and Books on Music in the Houghton Library and the Eda Kuhn Loeb Music Library.** David A. Wood. Cambridge, Mass., Houghton Library; distr., Cambridge, Mass., Harvard University Press, 1980; repr., Woodbridge, Conn., Research Publications, 1985. 306p.

This important bibliography contains both music literature and music in print. The material here regarded as early music was printed before 1801 and had been cataloged at Harvard by January 1967. Thus it serves as a resource tool for library use but is even more important as an identification or verification tool for the serious student and scholar of music. Songsters and sheet music for songs are excluded, as are liturgical books, hymnals, psalters, libretti, and musical manuscripts. Coverage embraces monographs, treatises, pamphlets, music periodicals, as well as a large collection of scores, part-books, etc. Arrangement is alphabetical by author, composer, publisher, or title. Full bibliographic descriptions are provided.

444. **Popular Music: A Reference Guide.** Roman Iwaschkin. New York, Garland, 1986. 658p. (Garland Reference Library of the Humanities, v.642).

Another of the Garland bibliographies, this recent contribution to the literature of popular music in all phases provides coverage of more than 5,000 items, some of which

Ref ML128.P63. I95 1986

receive annotations. There is comprehensive coverage of the vast field of popular music, with such categories as folk, country, Cajun, black, jazz, and stage and screen, as well as rap music, African pop, Grand Ole Opry, and jazz in Germany. The book includes a section on biographies, another on education and instruments, and another on the music business. Songs and recordings receive separate treatment, as do literary works, including novels and poetry. The listing of periodicals is a useful resource feature.

445. **Répertoire international des sources musicales/International Inventory of Musical Sources.** Munich, Henle, 1960- . (In progress).

This is a joint effort on the part of the International Musicological Society and the International Association of Music Libraries and is commonly referred to as *RISM*. It is a catalog of all bibliographies of music, writings about music, and textbooks on music published up to 1800, with locations where they can be found identified. Over 1,000 libraries worldwide are cooperating in this venture. The two major series are A, alphabetical, and B, systematic or classified. Series A (followed by volume number in roman numeral) includes individual editions in circulation from 1500 to 1800, are arranged alphabetically by composer or editor. Series B (followed by volume number in roman numeral) arranges the materials chronologically by category or genre such as "manuscripts of polyphonic music." Bibliographical descriptions are generally given in greater detail in the B section. This large-scale effort has earned the respect of music bibliographers everywhere. Recently, Series C has begun as a continuation of a series of directories of international libraries (see entry 528).

Indexes, Abstracts, and Serial Bibliographies

446. **Bibliographic Guide to Music.** 1975- . Ann. Boston, G. K. Hall.

A serial bibliography in its own right, this work serves as an annual supplement to the *Dictionary Catalog of the Music Collection* for the New York Public Library (see entry 437). Beginning with coverage of the year 1975, it enumerates all types of music materials (including printed music) cataloged by the library during the period under scrutiny (September through August). Additional cataloging is included through the use of MARC tapes from the Library of Congress in the areas of music literature (bibliography, history, criticism, and philosophy of music) and music instruction. The age of materials cataloged in any single year varies considerably, with both recently acquired items and older documents cataloged for the first time. Produced by computer, it serves many purposes including those of reference, acquisition, and cataloging.

447. **A General Index to Modern Musical Literature in the English Language, Including Periodicals for the Years of 1915-26.** Eric Blom. Philadelphia, Curwen, 1927; repr., New York, Da Capo, 1970. 159p.

Despite an unfavorable review in *ARBA* 1971 by Dennis North, this work continues to be pressed into service by music librarians. One must concede that it loses some value as it ages, but it is still useful for those interested in a retrospective search relating to American and British musical scholarship of the time. Entries include citations to books available primarily in Great Britain but also in the United States, and to some out-of-print publications as well. Periodical articles are also included. There is a dictionary arrangement of authors and subject entries. The subject entries are analytic in nature and provide cross-references to author entries, identify periodical issues, and furnish references to parts of books.

448. **An Index to Musical Festschriften and Similar Publications.** Walter Gerboth. New York, Norton, 1969. 188p.

This is a comprehensive listing of materials about music which heretofore have been "concealed" in collections developed to honor specialists in the field. There are about 3,000 articles culled from nearly 600 volumes representing an array of periods and topics. Based on a volume published three years earlier, the present work includes festschriften published through 1967. It also covers works from certain national groups not previously included, such as those in the Slavic languages. Material includes biocritical and bibliographical sources on music and musicians from books and journals, largely foreign and often difficult to locate. There are three major segments, beginning with a list of the festschriften, followed by a subject listing of the articles, and concluding with an index by author and specific subject.

449. **Index to Opera, Operetta and Musical Synopses in Collections and Periodicals.** Jeannette M. Drone. Metuchen, N.J., Scarecrow, 1978. 171p.

This work has retained its value in the music library for its extensive coverage of seventy-four collections as well as of four periodical series. The tool is divided into four parts and provides references to English-language synopses or plot summaries of numerous operas, operettas, and musical comedies from 1926 to the time of publication. Part 1 is a listing of collections and periodicals used, followed by an index of titles of specific musical works, with references to their source documents in the second part. The third segment lists the composers and their works, while the final section provides a bibliography of additional sources of synopses. Although subsequent editions were planned to index the periodical literature more extensively, this is the only volume published to date.

450. **Music, Books on Music, and Sound Recordings.** 1973- . Semiann. Ann. cum. Quin. cum. Washington, D.C., National Union Catalog. *Ref Z881.A1 C3282*

Now part of the National Union Catalog series, with its quinquennial cumulation, this work is a reproduction of the catalog cards supplied by the Library of Congress and seven other leading music libraries. It covers music in breadth and identifies printed music and recordings as well as books about music and musicians. The recordings are not limited to musical works, but represent the vast range of materials held (educational, literary, political, etc.). This work supersedes *Library of Congress Catalog: Music and Phonorecords* (Library of Congress, 1953-1972), which appeared semiannually but was limited to entries from LC printed cards. The present serial is an indispensable tool for music librarians for reference, cataloging, and acquisition purposes.

451. **The Music Index: The Key to Current Music Periodical Literature.** 1949- . Mo. Ann. cum. Detroit, Information Service.

This is the major indexing service for music literature and covers approximately 350 periodicals worldwide, some of which are indexed selectively. Indexing is by author and subject and the work surveys the world of music in comprehensive manner from musicology to the music industry. Obituaries, reviews of recordings, and book reviews are included. Music reviews are listed under name of composer, title, and medium. Reviews of performances are listed under name of performer. Its major problem has always been and continues to be its tardiness of appearance, with annual cumulations about six to seven years behind and monthlies delayed about six months. For this reason, sources such as *Music Article Guide* (see entry 453) serve to supplement the coverage.

Hum Ind area

452. **Music Library Association. Notes.** 1934- . Q. Canton, Mass., Music Library Association.

The leading periodical for music librarians is the official publication of the Association. From 1934 to 1942, frequency was somewhat irregular and the publication was suspended during 1939. Since 1943, it has appeared on a quarterly basis and continues to provide excellent comprehensive listings of recently published books and a section of excellent book reviews. Music scores are also identified and reviewed. There is an index to recordings which identifies reviews in other periodicals, and includes both tapes and discs. This is arranged alphabetically by name of composer and provides a list of references which are rated in accordance with the judgment given by the reviewer, similar to what is done in *Book Review Digest* (H. W. Wilson, 1905-). There are also a listing of current music publishers' catalogs and frequent reviews of new music periodicals.

453. **Music Article Guide: An Annotated Quarterly Reference Guide to Significant Signed Feature Articles in American Music Periodicals.** 1966- . Q. Philadelphia, Music Article Guide.

This index to periodical literature has been a feature of music library collections from the time of its initial publication. It has been used to supplement the coverage provided by *Music Index* (see entry 451) both in terms of its content and its relative promptness of appearance compared to *Music Index* in the past. The emphasis on American periodicals provides a unique scrutiny of 175 periodicals for important or significant articles rather than the entire contents of any one issue. There are brief annotations for the articles of importance primarily to music educators, arranged under a variety of subject headings. Each issue also provides a directory listing of American music periodicals.

454. **Popular Music Periodicals Index.** 1973-1976. Ann. Metuchen, N.J., Scarecrow.

This short-lived annual index attempted to cover the field of popular music in the manner that *Music Index* (see entry 451) covers classical music. Although there was some overlap in terms of titles indexed, this work placed a greater emphasis on personalities mentioned in the articles. About fifty-five popular music periodicals were indexed fully in any given volume, with an additional dozen periodicals selectively covered. There was little or no duplication of titles from *Readers' Guide to Periodical Literature* (H. W. Wilson, 1901-). There were both subject and author indexes, the former providing the most assistance in locating relevant items. Periodicals were generally English-language items, although content was universal. It was edited by Dean Tudor and Andrew Armitage, who also produced the short-lived *Annual Index to Popular Music Record Reviews* (Scarecrow, 1972-1977). Despite its short run, this tool is still used by librarians today.

*455. **RILM Abstracts of Music Literature.** 1967- . Q. New York, International Repertory of Music Literature.

The title is an acronym for the name in French of the sponsoring organization, and the work has been recognized as a major contribution to the field of music bibliography. It provides abstracts of articles (both in books and periodicals), books, reviews, dissertations, iconographies, catalogs, etc., in the field of music. Over 300 journals in forty-three languages are treated. Each issue is indexed by author and subject, with the fourth issue a cumulative work to the three preceding numbers in the volume. Abstracts are signed and include identification of keywords for purposes of indexing. There are nine major divisions, including reference materials, collected writings, ethnomusicology, instruments, etc. *RILM ABSTRACTS is also available online from DIALOG and as of October 1985 had a file size of 60,000 items. Online coverage was available for the period from 1971 to

1980 at that time, with updating three times per year. About 6,500 new records are added annually.

Printed Music Sources —
Bibliographies, Indexes, and Catalogs

GENERAL

456.   **American Music before 1865 in Print and on Records: A Biblio-Discography.** New York, Institute for Studies in American Music, Brooklyn College, 1976. 113p. (Institute for Studies in American Music Monographs: No. 6).

This is a useful, classified and annotated bibliography of American music originally printed prior to 1865, some of which is still available for purchase through normal channels. Additionally, there is a discography of LP's issued to the time of publication. There are several useful features including a segment on music in performing editions which lists works containing the music as it was conceived by its composers. Another segment covers music in books which includes references to music unavailable in other editions. Purchasing information is furnished along with series identification and content of anthologies. Considered to be reliable and well-constructed to provide access through an excellent index, the work remains a good choice for reference departments.

457.   **A Basic Music Library: Essential Scores and Books.** 2nd ed. Pauline Shaw Bayne and Robert Michael Fling, eds. Chicago, American Library Association, 1983. 357p.

Originally published in 1978, this work has gained an enviable reputation among music librarians for its excellent coverage of materials useful to a music collection. As such, it represents a good collection development aid as well as reference tool. Designed to provide librarians in small and medium-sized libraries with a selective list of music materials, its coverage includes lists of anthologies of scores, study scores, performing editions, vocal scores, instrumental methods, and studies as well as music literature consisting of reference books, biographies, periodicals, etc. This edition is an extensive revision of the earlier effort and furnishes a selective listing of music dealers in the appendix. The index is well constructed and provides easy access to material within.

458.   **A Bibliography of Early Secular American Music (18th Century).** Oscar Sonneck. Rev. and enl. by William Trent Upton. Washington, D.C., Library of Congress, 1945; repr., New York, Da Capo, 1964. 616p.

A standard work in the field, this bibliography provides an authoritative listing of eighteenth-century music. The emphasis is on songs by American composers, both published and unpublished. Arranged by title, bibliographical identification is provided, and composers, contents, publishing details, and library locations are given. Individual pieces and collections are identified, and there is a bibliography of secondary materials published during this period. Especially useful is the listing of first lines (accompanied by title and composer) in the appendix. Another classic work which serves as a complementary source is Richard J. Wolfe's *Secular Music in America 1801-1825* (New York Public Library, 1964, 3v.) which provides an extensive listing of nearly 10,000 titles and editions published in this century. The arrangement here is alphabetical by composer, with indexing similar to Sonneck's. Also fitting into the historical pattern is Priscilla Heard's *American Music, 1698-1800: An Annotated Bibliography* (Blakely Press, 1903-1959; repr., Peter Smith, 1941-1967, 14v.).

459.   The Book of World-Famous Music, Classical, Popular and Folk. 3rd ed. Rev. and enl. James M. Fuld. New York, Dover, 1985. 714p.

First published in 1966, this work has been a favorite of reference librarians since it first became available. Now in its third edition, it traces the development of 1,300 popular melodies back to their original sources. Included are the various types of music mentioned in the title, along with identification of original singers and interesting commentary. The new edition is essentially a reprint of previous works but with a supplementary section which contains new information and corrections to entries in the main text. Entries provide symbols as cross-references to the supplement for revisions. The work thus has the same scope and remains a listing of musical compositions both vocal and instrumental written over a period of 500 years. Arrangement of entries is by title; incipits or opening bars are provided as are opening words for the vocal compositions. Entries include identification of the earliest publication and information regarding its use and performance. Much of this information is chatty and much is important, such as biographical notes on composers, but all is interesting. *Ref ML113. F8 1985*

460.   The Catalogue of Printed Music in the British Library to 1980. Laureen Baillie and Robert Malchin, eds. New York, Saur, 1981-1986. 62v.

Although this set bears a price tag of over $10,000, it is a vast resource which provides access to about 1,000,000 entries previously found in an array of bibliographic tools (slip catalog, accession lists, Royal Music Library catalog, and a catalog of music published between 1503 and 1800). Much of the inconsistency and diversity of cataloging styles has been ameliorated through the computerization process. Of interest to those primarily interested in printed music is the fact that this tool has a much higher proportion of this material when compared to the New York Public Library's *Dictionary Catalog of the Music Collection* (see entry 437). Entries are found under composers' names or under form headings such as "Songs," in which individual titles are identified. Another recent work is *The Catalogue of Music in the Bath Reference Library to 1985*, by Jon A. Gillaspie (Saur, 1986, 4v.) which furnishes a listing of manuscripts and related items. Since Bath served as a center for the performance of music during the eighteenth and nineteenth centuries, the work provides a panorama of musical history. *Music in the Royal Society of London 1660-1806*, by Leta Miller and Albert Cohen (Information Coordinators, 1987), is a catalog of journal reports and manuscripts of this eminent scientific society on the subject of music. Acoustics, the ear and hearing, and various instruments and inventions are among the topics covered.

461.   Film Music: From Violins to Video. James L. Limbacher, ed. and comp. Metuchen, N.J., Scarecrow, 1974. 835p.

Since the area of film music has been relatively overlooked, this book has filled a need in reference work. Although it has been criticized for certain omissions and lack of clarity regarding its selection criteria, it has been used by both serious students and interested laypersons in pursuit of information on the nature of film music up to 1972. Part 1 consists of excellent notes and commentary on film music by composers such as Dimitri Tiompkin and Sir William Walton, while part 2 provides various listings. These include an alphabetical list of titles with dates, chronological list of films with composers, composers and their films, and musical scores by film title. A supplementary work by the same author is *Keeping Score: Film Music 1972-1979* (Scarecrow, 1981) which continues the listings in three major sections arranged by film titles, composers, and recorded musical scores.

462. Handbook of Early American Sheet Music 1768-1889. Harry Dichter and Elliott Shapiro. New York, Dover, 1977. 287p.

This is essentially a reprint of a work published in 1941, with some revision and modification. It was designed to provide an awareness of the more important and more interesting music of a bygone era which is still in existence today, rather than a complete history of every piece of sheet music from that time period. There are three major segments of the publication, the first of which is the most important and lists both vocal and instrumental works in a classified arrangement under headings such as "Music of the American Revolution" and "Uncle Tom's Cabin." These headings are grouped into time periods and organized chronologically. Entries include title, publisher, date, names of individuals associated with the work or for whom it was written, composer, number of pages, first line of the song, and description of cover illustrations and references to plate mark numbers. There are seventy-six reproductions of cover illustrations. The second part provides a directory of publishers, while part 3 enumerates lithographers and artists working on American sheet music prior to 1870.

463. Historical Sets, Collected Editions, and Monuments of Music: A Guide to Their Contents. 3rd ed. Anna Harriet Heyer. Chicago, American Library Association, 1980. 2v.

First published in 1957, this is a standard work in music libraries which now identifies over 1,300 sets and collections of music published in the Western world up to 1980. This is a substantial increase over the second edition, which included 900 sets, primarily due to the increased publication of scholarly editions of music over the past two decades. There is an attempt to provide comprehensive coverage of nineteenth- and twentieth-century sets, thus making this an excellent tool for scholars in locating scores. The main part is alphabetical by composer and indicates contents volume-by-volume of these sets and editions, with complete bibliographical information. Another important work is Sydney Robinson Charles's *A Handbook of Music and Music Literature in Sets and Series* (Free Press, 1972), which also covers collected works and major sets as well as monographs and periodicals in series.

464. Music-in-Print Series. 1974- . Irreg. Philadelphia, Musicdata. Supp., 1979- . Ann.

Corresponding somewhat to *Books in Print* are these much-needed listings of available music in print. Individual volumes cover different types of music, both vocal and instrumental, and are compiled from publishers' catalogs in order to provide a continuous record of music available to the performer, instructor, and student. There are six volumes to date, covering sacred choral music (2nd edition, 1985), secular choral music (1982), organ music (2nd edition, 1984), classical vocal music (1976), orchestral music (1979), and string music (2nd edition, 1980). The continuous record is maintained through an annual supplement which contains a separate section providing updates for all volumes in the series. Thousands of editions have been identified from nearly 1,000 different publishers worldwide. Entries provide title, composer, arranger, instrumentation, and publisher.

465. Music Library Association Catalog of Cards for Printed Music, 1953-1972: A Supplement to the Library of Congress Catalogs. Elizabeth H. Olmsted, ed. Totowa, N.J., Rowman and Littlefield, 1974. 2v.

The title provides an indication of the content of this work, which was four years in the making under the sponsorship of the Music Library Association, aided by numerous volunteers. What Olmsted (the music librarian at Oberlin) and her fellow workers have done is to identify 30,000 entries of music cataloging which had been submitted to the Library of Congress by cooperating libraries but for some reason had not been entered into the *National Union Catalog*. The volunteers did a good job of editing to provide at least some conformity to acceptable standards of the Library of Congress, although there is some unevenness among the entries. Most deficient is the poor quality of reproduction, with some entries virtually unreadable. Although it serves partially as a supplement to the *Library of Congress Catalog: Music and Phonorecords* (see entry 450n), this does not identify the libraries responsible for the cataloging except for New York Public and Harvard University.

VOCAL MUSIC

466. American Oratorios and Cantatas: A Catalog of Works Written in the United States from Colonial Times to 1985. Thurston J. Dox, comp. Metuchen, N.J., Scarecrow, 1986. 2v.

This is a work of major proportions and one that was needed by reference librarians since it identifies 3,450 choral pieces which span the history of our country from its beginnings to the present day. Dox is a professor of music at Hartwick College and used his expertise to construct a tool that received plaudits for both its organization and detail. There are four sections beginning with oratorios, followed by choral cantatas, ensemble cantatas, and choral theater. Entries provide publication information, locations for both published and unpublished items, performance requirements, text (source), length, and number of movements. Some annotations are given as well as commentary from composers and critics.

467. Children's Song Index: An Index to More Than 22,000 Songs in 189 Collections. Helen Grant Cushing, comp. New York, H. W. Wilson, 1936; repr., St. Clair Shores, Mich., Scholarly Press, 1977. 798p.

This is the most comprehensive index to children's songs; therefore, it retains a large measure of its value even as it grows older. More than 22,000 songs are identified from 189 collections. Similar to Sears's *Song Index* (see entry 473) in structure and composition, the main entry is under title, where full bibliographic description is provided. Cross-references are furnished from alternate titles, different titles in different collections, translated titles, original titles in certain languages, first lines, and even first lines of choruses. There are added entries under composers and authors. Unlike Sears, subject headings are also included. A more recent work is *Index to Children's Songs: A First Line and Subject Index*, by Carolyn Sue Peterson and Ann D. Fenton (H. W. Wilson, 1979). Covering 5,000 songs in nearly 300 song books likely to be found in local libraries, there is access by title, first line, and subject.

Ref ML128.S3.C45 1976

468. Choral Music Review Index, 1983-1985. Avery T. Sharp. New York, Garland, 1986. 260p. (Garland Reference Library of the Humanities, v.674).

This is a useful source of recent reviews of over 2,000 pieces of choral music in sixteen English-language journals for a three-year period. Most of the works are Christian sacred hymns, making it an especially valuable source for religion collections, choir directors, and choir members. The secular music listed is generally intended for schools, and therefore of interest to school libraries and music instructors. Arrangement of entries falls under three main categories: octavos (single compositions), collections, and extended choral works (liturgy, oratories, etc.), and is alphabetical by title. Entries include titles, composers, arrangers or editors, performers, publishers, vocal ranges, and languages, as well as commentary on accompaniment and use. Separate indexes are furnished for composer, arranger, editor, use, level of group, instrumentation, and voicing.

469.   **Index to Song Books: A Title Index to over 11,000 Copies of 6,800 Songs in 111 Books Published between 1933 and 1962.** Robert Leigh. Stockton, Calif., privately published, 1964; repr., New York, Da Capo, 1973. 237p.

This index picked up in point of time where Sears's *Song Index* (see entry 473) left off, much like the de Charms and Breed *Songs in Collections: An Index* (see entry 474). Coverage differs substantially between the two, however, since there is a greater emphasis in Leigh's work on folk, community, and popular song books published in this country. This includes songs of the twentieth century. Of course the songs themselves are from all over the world and include popular hits, children's songs, carols, hymns, and operatic arias. Only song books that provide both words and music are included, with cross-references furnished for alternate titles and famous lines. Arrangement is by title with no entries for composers or lyricists. Only 35 of the 111 books indexed are duplicated in de Charms and Breed.

470.   **Popular Music, 1920-1979: An Annotated Index of over 18,000 American Popular Songs.** 2nd ed. Nat Shapiro and Bruce Pollock, eds. Detroit, Gale, 1985. 3v.

This is a major cumulation of what was an eight-volume set which indexed the popular music of this country in five- or ten-year intervals. This comprehensive work organizes the entries alphabetically by title and describes alternate titles, country of origin for songs from other countries, lyricists, composers, dates, history, performers, and record labels. There are indexes of composers and lyricists, important performances, and awards. There is also a list of publishers. The original eight volumes are still available for those libraries that have collected them and do not wish to invest in the new work, but the new edition facilitates access and provides up-to-date publisher lists. The series continues with subsequent publications, volume 9, 1980-1984 (Gale, 1986) and volume 10, 1985 (Gale, 1986).

471.   **Popular Song Index.** Patrice P. Havlice. Metuchen, N.J., Scarecrow, 1975. 933p. First Supp., 1978. Second Supp., 1984.

This is an extensive index of 301 song books, mainly U.S., but also including several British, Canadian, and French works. The emphasis is on folk songs, as it is in Leigh's *Index to Song Books* (see entry 469), although coverage is from 1940 to 1972. It is complementary to the work by de Charms and Breed (see entry 474), beginning its coverage with 1940 imprints, and emphasizing popular music rather than classical. Main entries are under titles, with cross-references from actual first lines and first lines of choruses. There is also an index of composers and lyricists. The supplements continue the coverage, with the first supplement adding seventy-two anthologies published between 1970 and 1975; the second supplement covers another 145 song books published between 1974 and 1981.

472.   **Repertoire for the Solo Voice.** Noni Espina. Metuchen, N.J., Scarecrow, 1977. 2v.

Although this is a selective guide to solo vocal literature, its listings are extensive, with 9,726 songs and arias taken from modern editions available at time of publication. The music covers a time period of 600 years in terms of its origins. The guide is fully annotated and entries provide title, voices for performance, authorship, range, descriptive commentary on the general character, and specific features of the work, level of difficulty for accompanist, and bibliographical source. There are an index of sources with names of poets and librettists, and an index of composers. As is the case with most works of this type, there has been some criticism of omissions, particularly the work of the avant garde, and certain important operas which should have been included. Nevertheless, it has proved to be a useful resource.

473. **Song Index** ... Minnie Sears. New York, H. W. Wilson, 1926. 650p. Supp. 1934; repr., Hamden, Conn., Shoe String Press, 1966. 2v. in 1.

The complete title of the basic edition indicates that it is "an index to more than 12,000 songs in 177 song collections comprising 262 volumes." This was the original work that many of the other song indexes in this section were designed to supplement. Despite its age, it remains an important index and is still widely used in all kinds of libraries including, of course, music libraries. Sears established an excellent pattern of coverage which represented titles, first lines, and names of lyricists and composers all in one alphabet for ease of access. The bulk of the entries are under title, with added entries provided under author and composer. The supplement adds another 7,000 songs from 104 song collections published up to 1932. More recent song indexes by Leigh (see entry 469), de Charms and Breed (see entry 474), Havlice (see entry 471), and Shapiro and Pollock (see entry 470) supplement this work but do not supersede it. *Ref ML128.S5 S81*

474. **Songs in Collections: An Index.** Desiree de Charms and Paul F. Breed. Detroit, Information Service, 1966. 588p.

Designed to supplement to a degree the coverage of Sears's *Song Index* (see entry 473), this represents a good companion volume to the original edition of *Popular Song Index* (see entry 471), since they both begin their coverage with 1940 imprints. Anthologies in de Charms range from 1940 to 1957. De Charms concentrates primarily on anthologies of art songs and operatic arias, with less emphasis on traditional folk song collections. (There are just a few popular song books which are, of course, the primary focus of *Popular Song Index*.) Songs in 400 collections are indexed, with separate sections given to composed songs, anonymous and folk songs, carols, and sea chanties. There is an index to first lines and one to authors, with the collections listed at the beginning of the volume.

Ref ML128.S3.D37

475. **Vocal Chamber Music: A Performer's Guide.** Kay Dunlap and Barbara Winchester. New York, Garland, 1985. 140p. (Garland Reference Library of the Humanities, v.465).

A recent work which has proved to be of value in music libraries, this guide defines vocal chamber music as composition for one voice and one instrument (other than keyboard or guitar) up to a dozen solo voices and twelve solo instruments. Compositions for solo voices and chorus also are given when no instrumentation is needed. Works included cover 300 years, dating from 1650 to 1980, and generally are available for purchase, making this a practical listing for the music instructor. Entries provide composer, title, publisher, and scoring. There are an index to publishers or collections and one to voice type. Unfortunately, there is no index to instruments identified.

INSTRUMENTAL MUSIC

476. **ASCAP Symphonic Catalog.** 3rd ed. American Society of Composers, Authors and Publishers. New York, R. R. Bowker, 1977. 511p.

This is a catalog of 26,000 compositions of chamber music, chamber ensemble, and choral work which have been licensed by the Society for performance in this country. Arrangement of entries is by composer's name, with symphony titles listed alphabetically. Entries furnish information on instrumentation and performance time as well as author and publisher of text. Publication dates are generally provided as well. Compositions include those of both American and foreign composers as long as they have been licensed by the Society. The catalog has been commended for its clarity and has become an important resource for those interested in public performance. The rival licensing organization Broadcast Music, Inc., also has a catalog of licensed works entitled *BMI Symphonic Catalog* (BMI, 1971). It is updated by an annual supplement that began in 1978.

477. **British Broadcasting Corporation. Central Music Library. Catalogues.** London, BBC, 1965-1967. 9v.

These unnumbered catalogs were developed by the BBC in the mid-1960s and represent the vast store of material suitable for performance on the air. Four catalogs were produced, two of them emphasizing instrumental music. *Chamber Music Catalogue* (London, BBC, 1965) identified both printed and manuscript material in chamber music, the compositions for violin and keyboard, and those for cello and keyboard. Arrangement is by composer and information regarding selection, arranger, imprint, and location is given. A brief bibliography is also provided. *Piano and Organ Catalogue* ... (London, BBC, 1965, 2v.) is an extensive listing of 48,000 pieces for solo piano, duets, trios, etc., with selections included for both left and right hand only. Organ works are identified for both solo and other formats. Vocal music is represented in *Choral and Opera Catalogue* (London, BBC, 1967, 2v.) and *Song Catalogue* (London, BBC, 1966, 4v.).

478. **Building a Chamber Music Collection: A Descriptive Guide to Published Sources.** Ella Marie Forsyth. Metuchen, N.J., Scarecrow, 1979. 191p.

This is a useful selection guide to what the author considers the best available scores for a particular medium. About 300 compositions are identified and classified by type of instrument. Priority order is given to the listings within each classification, beginning with those most important to a basic collection. Selection for a work of this type must necessarily be subjective to a certain degree, and there are the usual problems with omissions and inclusions, but the work is valuable for the detailed information provided. This would include publication and performance information, level of difficulty, and references to sources of music analysis and commentary found in a separate annotated bibliography. Additional help is found in the listing for a core collection and directory of publishers. There is an index of composers as well as one for popular titles.

479. **Guide to the Pianist's Repertoire.** 2nd ed. Rev. and enl. Maurice Hinson. Bloomington, Ind., Indiana University Press, 1987. 856p.

Now after 14 years, the second edition of this useful and important title has appeared in an enlarged form. Known for its extensive coverage of composers and their works in the past, the new edition assures continued recognition in this regard. Hundreds of composers from countries all over the world are listed and their compositions enumerated. Works have been graded for each composer, and related bibliographic entries of books and periodical articles have been integrated into the main body of the work. The general bibliography includes books, articles, and dissertations, and the appendices include a useful directory of publishers. Several indexes to composers and others conclude the work.

480. **Instrumental Music Printed before 1600: A Bibliography.** Howard Mayer Brown. Harvard University Press, 1965. 559p.

This is a scholarly work which attempts to include all known publications in the field prior to 1600, beginning with the period of the 1480s, shortly after the development of the printing press. Arrangement is chronological, and under each year publications are listed alphabetically by author or publisher. The contents are described and references are provided to modern editions which contain the entries. Much of the music included has been lost or was never published, making the work of great value to music historians. Vocal music is included only if it contained instrumental parts or segments. Although the work has been criticized for omissions (the inevitable challenge to an all-encompassing bibliography), Brown has succeeded in providing a work that has been admired by those it was designed to serve.

481. **Music for the Piano: A Handbook of Concert and Teaching Material from 1580 to 1952.** James Friskin and Irwin Freundlich. New York, Dover, 1973. 434p.

Originally published in 1954 as volume 5 of the Field of Music Series edited by Ernest Hutcheson, the 1973 edition is a slightly modified and corrected but otherwise unchanged work. The period of coverage still spans a term of nearly 400 years and ends with the year 1952. Freundlich prepared a new preface, and a revised and updated biographical appendix was developed. More than 500 composers are identified on an international basis, with good coverage of modern Soviet composition even though much of it is no longer available. Entries provide indication of form, difficulty, technical requirements, and publisher. Included are some critical essays on periods or stylistic developments.

482. **The Piano in Chamber Ensemble: An Annotated Guide.** Maurice Hinson. Bloomington, Ind., Indiana University Press, 1978. 570p.

Even with a new edition of Hinson's comprehensive *Guide to the Pianist's Repertoire* (see entry 479), there will still be a call for this more specialized volume. Limited to those works in which the piano shares the performance with other instruments, its arrangement of entries makes it a useful source for any performer or instructor. First covered are works for the piano and a solo instrument in which a number of unusual instruments are identified; second are compositions for the piano and two other instruments, progressing up to the piano and seven other instruments. Entries generally provide a brief musical analysis which is valuable in furnishing insight into the nature and character of the piece. There is a list of American publishers and agents and their publications.

THEMATIC CATALOGS AND ANTHOLOGIES

Thematic catalogs are those highly specialized reference tools used by musicologists and trained music librarians to identify compositions. They provide listings of incipits (beginnings or opening bars up to twelve notes). An important contribution to music reference since their initial appearance in the eighteenth century, they are developed on a variety of subjects (single composer, form, style, historical period, or school). Only a few are given here, along with a few anthologies of musical compositions, for which the numbers are legion.

483. **Dictionary of Musical Themes.** Rev. ed. Harold A. Barlow and Sam Morganstern. New York, Crown, 1975; repr., London, Faber, 1983. 642p.

Called by Sheehy and others the "Bartlett" for musical themes, this has been a vital work which has evolved from Barlow's earlier efforts in the 1940s and subsequent years. The first few notes from 10,000 themes of instrumental music are listed (rather than the notation from the initial lines most typical of thematic catalogs). Arrangement is by composer, followed by titles. The notation index is what makes this work a useful identification source, since it arranges the themes alphabetically by notation after having transposed them to the key of C. The tune or melody of the theme can be played on a keyboard or vocalized for ready identification. An index of titles provides easy access if a title is known and one wishes to check its theme. There is a companion volume, *Dictionary of Opera and Song Themes* ... (see entry 484).

484. **Dictionary of Opera and Song Themes, Including Cantatas, Oratorios, Lieder, and Art Songs.** Rev. ed. Harold A. Barlow and Sam Morganstern. New York, Crown, 1976. 547p.

Originally published in 1950 under a different title, this is a companion work or complementary volume to *Dictionary of Musical Themes* (see entry 483). Over time it has changed only slightly except for the title. It lists notations from themes of vocal composition of all types (operas, oratorios, cantatas, art songs, and miscellaneous vocal works). Its basic approach and format are similar to *Dictionary of Musical Themes*, and the initial notes of some 8,000 themes are enumerated alphabetically by composer, then by title of work. Opera themes are identified by act and scene and words are included with the musical bars. The notation index is similar to that of the companion volume, with transposition to key of C and alphabetical arrangement of notes. There are also indexes of first lines and of songs.

485. **The Directory of Tunes and Musical Themes.** Denys Parsons. Cambridge, England, Spencer Brown, 1975. 288p.

Another useful work for identification of musical compositions is this effort by Parsons, which is considered easier to use by those with no musical background. Incipits (opening bars) are arranged with symbols indicating the direction of succeeding notes, whether descending, ascending, or repeated. While it is difficult to imagine, librarians have reported success with this relatively simple strategy. In terms of number of entries, the work compares favorably with the two volumes by Barlow and Morganstern (see entries 483 and 484), with a total of 15,000 items, representing both vocal and instrumental pieces. There are separate categories of classical themes as opposed to popular tunes. The former are covered through listing of composers, opus numbers, and titles of larger works from which the compositions were taken, while the popular works are identified by composer and date.

486. **Historical Anthology of Music.** Rev. ed. Archibald Thompson Davison and Willi Apel. Cambridge, Mass., Harvard University Press, 1977. 2v.

This is a vital anthology of early music. Volume 1 covers Oriental, Medieval, and Renaissance music to 1600, while volume 2 covers the Baroque, Rococo, and pre-Classical period from 1600 to 1800. Transcribed in modern notation and furnishing notes concerning the medium, the effort is considered to be a highly readable representation of the music of the period. Each volume contains about 200 contributions of many of the important figures of the time. Two recordings accompany the volumes and were released in 1969 and 1976. The commentary provided by the eminent authors is well developed and includes references to both readings and recordings. Paul Henry Lang's *The Symphony 1800-1900: A Norton Music Anthology* (W. W. Norton, 1969) is specialized to a form of music in the century following the Classical period. Selections from Beethoven, Berlioz, Brahms, Dvorak, etc., are some of the masterpieces included.

487. **National Anthems of the World.** 6th ed. W. L. Reed and M. S. Bristow, eds. Poole, England, Blandford Press; distr., New York, Sterling Publishing, 1985. 496p.

This is an anthology or collection of both music and words of the national anthems of various nations. A new edition generally appears every five years; this edition builds or supplements the coverage of the fifth edition (1978) by providing the anthems of newly independent countries. It also incorporates the revisions or modifications which have occurred in the anthems of established nations. Generally, both words and music are included, with the language in the original text. English translations are furnished, and both authors of texts and composers are identified. In addition, there are brief historical descriptions which include the dates that the works were officially designated as national anthems.

488.   **The Ring of Words: An Anthology of Song Texts.** Philip Lieson Miller. New York, W. W. Norton, 1973. 518p.

This is a much-expanded version of an anthology originally published in 1964. It contains hundreds of songs for which the sources are presented in both the original language and in English translation. Original poems represent a variety of European languages (German, French, Italian, Russian, Scandinavian, and Spanish). In addition to the song texts, which are translated line by line, the author furnishes biographies of each poet and commentary regarding the settings and variations from the original versions. The work on this tool has impressed both reviewers and specialists in the field. Not only is its content carefully planned and well-executed, but its organization facilitates its use.

489.   **Thematic Catalogues in Music: An Annotated Bibliography.** Barry S. Brook. New York, Pendragon Press, 1972. 347p.

Barry Brook of New York University has been one of the most respected names in music bibliography and has been one of the influential figures in the creation of *RILM Abstracts* ... (see entry 455). This work received excellent reviews and was warmly received by music librarians. Essentially, it is a bibliography of thematic catalogs, which have been the most useful and at the same time the least controlled category of reference tool. This is a listing of 1,450 such catalogs, many of which were unpublished or in process at the time of publication of Brook's work. It is without a doubt the most comprehensive source of its kind, and supersedes earlier, less-detailed efforts. It is of inestimable importance to the music librarian with its full bibliographic descriptions and references to related works. There is a good exposition on thematic catalogs at the beginning, as well as an index of subjects and authors at the end.

490.   **A Treasury of Early Music.** Carl Parrish. New York, W. W. Norton, 1958. 331p.

This is an extremely useful anthology of musical compositions from both major and minor figures in the field, covering the period of music prior to the Classical period (1750). It serves as a companion piece and complementary effort to an earlier effort by Parrish, *Masterpieces of Music before 1750* (W. W. Norton, 1951). The two works do not duplicate each other and different composers appear in each. Although many of the compositions are familiar, there are some that are relatively obscure. There is a balanced coverage of nationalities and religious faiths among the works chosen for inclusion, and all pieces are introduced by excellent notes describing the historical background. A series of four recordings related to this anthology is published by Hayden Society Records, at various times, the first issues of which appeared nearly sixty years prior to publication of the anthology. The most recent appeared in 1982.

Dictionaries, Encyclopedias, and Handbooks

GENERAL

491.   **Dictionary of Contemporary Music.** John Vinton. New York, Dutton, 1974. 834p.

Long considered an outstanding reference work, this erudite and thorough effort is the result of eight years of research and funding by a number of organizations, both private and public. It covers the world of contemporary music in-depth and furnishes articles on musical elements, compositional techniques, movements, countries, and biographies of nearly 1,000 modern composers. The biographical sketches include listings of principal works and bibliographies. Numerous terms are defined in a clear and lucid manner. This work has served as an excellent source of information on distinctive qualities of twentieth-century music in the Western tradition and has maintained high editorial standards. Concert music is treated in detail while certain popular contemporary elements such as jazz, pop music, and folk music are surveyed in a general manner.

492.   **Encyclopedia of Music in Canada.** Helmut Kallman, et al., eds. Buffalo, N.Y., University of Toronto Press, 1981. 1076p.

This is the largest, most comprehensive, and most detailed reference source on Canadian music and has received a warm reception from both reviewers and librarians. It fulfills its purpose to describe music in Canada and to help define the country's musical relations with the rest of the world. There are over 3,000 entries with more than 160 extensive survey-type articles on such topics as ethnomusicology. Biographies are provided which include living persons as well as those deceased. Music of all types is treated although the emphasis is on art music. Performing groups, institutions, organizations, manufacturers, and musical compositions are covered as well. There are many cross-references and a number of bibliographies and discographies. An interesting feature is the index of persons, places, things, etc., that did not receive a separate entry.

493.   **The Guinness Book of Music.** Robert Dearling and Celia Dearling. Enfield, England, Guinness Superlatives; distr., New York, Sterling Publishing, 1986. 237p.

This is a revised and somewhat expanded edition of the authors' earlier volume with a slightly different name. Like other works from Guinness, this is a highly readable and interesting survey designed both to appeal and to enlighten. There is a topical arrangement beginning with instruments of the orchestra, followed by non-European instruments. The typical Guinness touch is seen in the listings and approaches provided for the various topics such as groupings of composers who lived to be ninety, those who had the same last name, and those who committed suicide. Various chronologies are included such as one on vocal music and another on instrumental music. There is even a chapter on keys which lists popular works, by their respective keys. There are name and instrument indexes.

494.   **The International Cyclopedia of Music and Musicians.** 11th ed. Oscar Thompson, ed. New York, Dodd, Mead, 1985. 2609p.

This is regarded as one of the most comprehensive one-volume reference books in the field and has maintained this reputation since its initial appearance in 1939. It is a useful source of information, providing brief articles, but also some lengthier survey-type essays. It gives accurate and reliable data on a variety of topics, issues, individuals, and developments. Included are entries on music history, criticism, folk music, opera, compositions, etc. Extensive articles are signed by the contributors, many of whom are known scholars of the subject. Biographical coverage of composers is excellent and the narratives are accompanied by calendars of their lives and a listing of their works. The new edition contains an addendum of nearly 100 pages recording the developments in music from 1975 to the present. It adds significant bits of information to entries from the main text as well as entirely new entries on individuals, topics, and organizations.

495.   **Die Musik in Geschicte und Gegenwart.** Kassel, West Germany, Barenreiter, 1949-1987. 17v.

Known by all who are involved in any way with music reference, the *MGG*, edited by Friedrich Blume, is considered the most scholarly and comprehensive work of its kind. Not until publication of the *New Grove Dictionary* ... (see entry 498) was there anything even approaching it in the English language. The work is international in scope and the product of a team of experts who contributed signed articles covering individuals and compositions. Serious music is covered in depth and popular elements are treated more concisely. There are extensive bibliographical notes and numerous illustrations. A product of nineteen years of labor, the alphabetical arrangement is covered in volumes 1-14. More recently, the supplements have been issued in volumes 15-16, also covering the entire alphabet. The index volume has recently been published as volume 17.

496. The New College Encyclopedia of Music. Rev. ed. J. A. Westrup and F. L. Harrison. New York, W. W. Norton, 1981. 768p.

Basically a reprint in paperback of the 1976 edition which had been revised by Conrad Wilson, this British work was first published in this country in 1960. It has earned an excellent reputation as a useful reference which emphasizes the coverage of major contemporary figures and their work. It contains about 6,000 entries on a variety of topics including composers, musical instruments, genres, operas, performers, etc. Terms are defined in a clear and concise manner, and there are illustrations to accompany a good proportion of the entries. Short bibliographies are furnished with some of the descriptions given. Previous reviews have pointed out some notable omissions of some major American figures such as Scott Joplin and Dave Brubeck, but the work is successful in providing a useful resource for nonscholarly interests.

497. The New Grove Dictionary of American Music. H. Wiley Hitchcock and Stanley Sadie. New York, Grove's Dictionaries of Music, 1986. 4v.

This is the most recent effort to be published in the Grove's series, and like the major twenty-volume publication (see entry 498), it has earned the respect of those who must minister to information needs of both scholars and nonspecialists. With four volumes, it is by far the most comprehensive and detailed work on the subject and provides good expositions, descriptions, and identifications of both personalities and subjects in the realm of American music. Known to music librarians as "Amerigrove," it describes the whole range of American musical culture from acid rock to serious concert music and, naturally, embraces grand opera as well as country and western contributions. There are 2,500 entries, two-thirds of which are biographical. Articles vary in length from 200 to 10,000 words depending upon the importance of the subject.

498. The New Grove Dictionary of Music and Musicians. Stanley Sadie, ed. London, Macmillan; Washington, D.C., Grove's Dictionaries of Music, 1986. 20v.

If music librarians were to vote on the most important single title in the reference department, chances are this multivolume encyclopedia would be the overwhelming choice. Having had a distinguished history in terms of its recognized quality, this British work was first published at the turn of the century and has had a greater impact with each succeeding edition. The newest issue is basically a reprint with minor corrections of the monumental 1980 publication which made it the closest competitor to the *MGG* (see entry 495) in depth and comprehensiveness. Its coverage is timely and authoritative, with about 23,000 articles, 8,000 cross-references, 3,000 illustrations, and 17,000 biographies of all types of personalities associated with music. This is a masterful publication which is useful to both specialists and nonspecialists and has succeeded in providing an international perspective through purposeful elimination of its former British bias. Arrangement is alphabetical and articles are signed by their distinguished authors, with more Americans than Britons serving as contributors. Definitely an outstanding item and a must for the music library collection.

499. The New Harvard Dictionary of Music. Don Michael Randel, ed. Cambridge, Mass., Belknap/Harvard University Press, 1986. 942p. *Ref ML 100. N485 1986*

This tool earned an excellent reputation under its original editor Willi Apel with its initial publication in 1944 and the revision which followed twenty-five years later. This new edition with a new editor should retain its status as an indispensable reference tool. There are nearly 6,000 entries contributed by seventy distinguished scholars, all specifically commissioned to update, rewrite, or add material. The result is a complete overhaul which makes a notable work all the more useful. Continuing the established pattern, there are no biographies, but instead, excellent definitions and descriptions of a wide range of topics embracing all aspects of music including individual compositions. It is recommended that the earlier edition be retained since much material was deleted or revised to include more modern concepts. As in the earlier work, there are a number of good illustrations.

500. The New Oxford Companion to Music. Denis Arnold, ed. New York, Oxford University Press, 1983. 2v. *Ref ML100. 937 09 1983 v.1 v.2*

This is a thorough revision of *The Oxford Companion to Music* by Percy Scholes (10th edition, 1970). It is essentially an entirely new work. The Scholes volumes, which began in 1938, were known for their anecdotal style and inherent charm, but the new publication is far more comprehensive in coverage, and provides greater breadth and precision. There is a certain uniformity or evenness of coverage lacking in the original work, and this one, therefore, is a far better reference tool. Coverage is international, with an acknowledged emphasis on Western culture. Entries cover composers and their works, opera plots, terms, and institutions as well as theory, form, notation, etc. Contemporary music receives much better coverage than in the past. There are many illustrations to enhance the text, and the work should appeal to a varied audience. It is aimed primarily at the interested layperson. Michael Kennedy's *The Oxford Dictionary of Music* (Oxford University Press, 1985) covers personalities, compositions, instruments, and terms in brief fashion, although it should not be considered a condensed version of *The New Oxford Companion.*

CONCERT MUSIC, ETC.

501. Cyclopedic Survey of Chamber Music. 2nd ed. Walter Willson Cobbett. New York, Oxford University Press, 1963. 3v.

Cobbett died in 1937, seven years after publication of the first edition in two volumes. The first two volumes of the revision are simply reprints or reissues of the original with minor changes in the text and insertion of symbols in the margins to act as cross-references to volume 3. In general, the work is a comprehensive treatment of chamber music in all aspects, with signed articles on topics, issues, persons, instruments, and organizations. Biographies of composers include lists of their works. Colin Mason edited the revision and prepared an additional volume which furnishes a selective survey of the field from 1930 to the time of publication. There are also a bibliography, additions and corrections to the earlier volumes, and an index of composers.

502. Enciclopedia della musica. Milan, Italy, Rizzoli, 1972-1974. 6v.

Considered by most music librarians to be an outstanding source of information on all aspects of music development, this vital source provides over 15,000 signed articles on a variety of topics. Coverage includes biographies, histories, definitions, and expositions on the music and musicians of all countries and time periods. There are over 300 black-and-white illustrations and 48 color plates. To be sure, there is an emphasis on Western tradition, especially European development and contribution. Major figures are given detailed treatment with a complete catalog of their works. Those needing to identify particular pieces by Bach, Beethoven, Brahms, Chopin, Debussy, Donizetti, Handel, Haydn, Liszt, Mozart, Palestrina, Schubert, and Vivaldi need go no further than the appendices.

503. Music Titles in Translation: A Checklist of Musical Compositions. Julian Hodgson. London, Bingley; distr., Hamden, Conn., Linnet Books, 1976. 370p.

This handbook furnishes the user with a simple scheme to determine the English equivalents of titles of musical compositions in foreign languages. About 7,000 compositions are listed alphabetically in both their original language and in variant English translations. All listings are in one alphabet, enabling the user to seek an English translation of a foreign title or to determine the foreign equivalent of a translated English title. Therefore, the 7,000 titles result in 14,000 entries. In some cases, more than one English translation is found in the entry for a foreign title. The aim was to be as comprehensive as possible and it would not be easy to challenge the inclusiveness of the work. Names of composers are provided in the entries as well, although there is no index of composers.

504. Popular Titles and Subtitles of Music Compositions. 2nd ed. Freda Pastor Berkowitz. Metuchen, N.J., Scarecrow, 1975. 209p.

This has long been recognized as a useful and convenient handbook for the identification of musical compositions through their popular titles. Musical pieces are of the classical concert variety and include sonatas, symphonies, concertos, etc. They have been identified or labeled with popular titles like the *Moonlight Sonata* not usually by the composer but by others such as publishers, performers, and publicists. The labels may have remained despite the dismay of the composer, possibly because of their selling qualities. Popular titles in this work date from 1600 to the present day. Entries are arranged alphabetically by popular title and include descriptive statements of the origins of these titles. Over 500 compositions are listed both in English and in the original language. There are a bibliography and an index of composers.

OPERA

505. Annals of Opera, 1597-1940. 3rd ed. Rev. and corr. Alfred Lowenberg, comp. Totowa, N.J., Rowman and Littlefield, 1978. 1756col.

This is one of the standards in the field of music reference and has been regarded as an indispensable source of information on the identification of operas since its initial publication in 1943. The second edition (1955) separated the indexes into a second volume and was somewhat less convenient. The new work joins the basic text to the indexes in a single unit. Several thousand operas are listed in chronological order according to date of first performance. Entries provide name of composer, title of opera, author of text, place of first performance, name of theater when known, number of acts, and history of later performances. References are furnished to translations of text and revivals as well. There are four indexes to provide access: operas; composers (with dates of birth and death and titles of operas); librettists; and a general index listing other individuals, subjects, and places. This work was edited by Harold Rosenthal, who has prepared a supplementary volume, *Annals of Opera, 1940-1981* (Barnes & Noble, 1983).

Ref ML102.06.L6 1978

506. The Concise Oxford History of Opera. 2nd ed. Harold Rosenthal and John Warrack. New York, Oxford University Press, 1979. 561p.

Considered a reliable source of information since its original 1964 edition (which was corrected in 1966 and 1972), this is a comprehensive reference title on the opera. The new edition represents a complete revision and is an excellent first source for brief treatment of operas, performers, composers, and terminology. There are numerous entries for countries and cities which provide background information on the nature of their involvement with the development of opera. Particular aims may also be found among the entries along with characters, institutions, companies, and festivals. The work is international in scope with a British perspective and describes the major themes and contributions of individuals rather than an extensive listing of their credits.

507. The Limelight Book of Opera. Arthur Jacobs and Stanley Sadie. New York, Limelight Editions, 1985. 563p.

This is a revision of an earlier work with a different title and describes in-depth the features of eighty-seven major operas by forty-one composers. The operas cover a time span of 400 years; therefore, this tool would be an excellent reference guide in any library serving the needs of both specialists and nonspecialists. The operas are described through a three-part approach: a general introduction placing the opera and its composer in historical perspective, followed by a plot synopsis, and finally, a musical commentary. Although the commentaries are brief, they have been commended for their clarity and use of musical excerpts. Arrangement of operas is by composer within chronological time period groupings beginning with Purcell in the seventeenth century and ending with contemporaries Britten and Menotti. There is an additional chapter on twentieth-century composers not previously described, as well as a general bibliography.

508. The Metropolitan Opera Stories of the Great Operas. John W. Freeman. New York, W. W. Norton, 1984. 547p.

This is an excellent choice for the reference collection since it presents the description of plots of 150 operas by 75 composers presented at the Metropolitan Opera House. These not only represent the major works which are more readily found such as those by Mozart, Verdi, Wagner, and Puccini but more important, lesser known selections which are on the periphery of the Met's repertoire. For each opera, the source and language of the libretto is furnished along with information of initial performances at the Met and elsewhere, and listing of characters. Story lines are furnished by scenes and acts along with titles of the important arias. There are a picture and a brief biography for each composer. There are no cast listings, unlike an earlier work by William H. Seltsam, *Metropolitan Opera Annals: A Chronicle of Artists and Performances* (H. W. Wilson, 1947; Supp., 1957). This title provides a chronological record of the casts of the operas performed from the first season in 1883 to time of publication.

509. The New Kobbe's Complete Opera Book. Gustav Kobbe. Earl of Harewood, ed. London, New York, G. P. Putnam, 1976. 1694p.

This is an extensive revision of an old standard in the field which has been expanded to include over 300 opera plots, twice the number of *The Metropolitan Opera Stories ...* (see entry 508). First published around 1920, the work has undergone frequent revision with only one of any real substance (1954). It is considered the most complete volume providing opera synopses, since the storylines are given in great detail. Arrangement is by century, subdivided by country. Brief notes are given on composers, and musical motifs are described. Older operas are included if they are still being performed, and there is good coverage of modern opera as well. Dates of first performance and important revivals are enumerated with names of important singers. The work is especially generous in its coverage of Wagner, Verdi, and Britten.

MUSICAL THEATER AND FILM

510.   **The American Musical Theatre: A Chronicle.** Exp. ed. Gerald Bordman. New York, Oxford University Press, 1986. 787p.

This is a slight expansion of Bordman's 1978 edition, which covered the musical theater from 1866 to the 1970s. Beginning with a prologue which summarizes the development of musical theater in this country from its beginnings to 1866, the new work covers each season in detail up to the 1980s. Developments of the season are described, "hits" are identified, and musicals are enumerated by date of opening. Included are plot synopses, names of performers, important songs, and a brief analysis of the impact of the show or its relative position in the context of musical theater. Critical comments from reviewers are included. Biographies are given for various personalities (composers, playwrights, actors, etc.). An index for shows and sources identifies original sources from which the musicals were derived. Also included are a song index and an index of personal names.

511.   **Encyclopedia of the Musical Film.** Stanley Green. New York, Oxford University Press, 1981. 344p.

With the popularity of the musical film in American entertainment, it is important that libraries provide some resource tools in keeping with the interests of their patrons. Generally intended for the interested layperson as well as the film specialist, this work provides useful information on those films developed in this country and in Great Britain. Arrangement of entries is alphabetical and general information is given on a variety of personalities (actors, producers, directors, composers, etc.) with identification of their best-known works. In addition to personalities, the films, and even major songs, receive separate entries. There is an index of title changes, as well as a general bibliography and a discography. Clive Hirschhorn's *The Hollywood Musical* (Crown, 1981) is a good pictorial handbook of American musicals, from the *Jazz Singer* in 1927 to the time of publication. Included are plot synopses, cast lists, song listings, and miscellaneous information which is accessed by several good indexes.

512.   **Encyclopedia of the Musical Theatre.** Stanley Green. New York, Dodd, Mead, 1976; repr., New York, Da Capo, 1980. 488p.

Over 200 musicals are covered in this useful companion volume to *Encyclopedia of the Musical Film* (see entry 511). Musical theater is defined in a narrow sense as musical comedy, play, farce, or even opera and operetta in a commercial run. Not included are Gilbert and Sullivan, limited engagements, vaudeville, plays with only a couple of songs, or revues that are not really musical. Entries are arranged alphabetically and cover a variety of topics. Central to the publication are the entries on the musical productions in which are included plot description, cast, background material, best-known songs, dates of both London and New York openings, theaters, and number of performances. Films are identified with performers and dates. In addition, there are entries on over 600 personalities (actors, actresses, composers, lyricists, etc.). Over 1,000 major songs are also entered individually and are briefly described in terms of theme, and singers, composers, and lyricists are identified. There are a bibliography and a discography. Another useful work by Green is *The World of Musical Comedy* (4th edition, A. S. Barnes, 1980), in which the story of the American musical stage is told through a detailed examination of the careers of composers and lyricists.

513.   **The Gilbert and Sullivan Companion.** Leslie Ayre. London, Allen, 1972; repr., London, Papermac, 1987. 485p.

This work was warmly received at the time of publication and has demonstrated its value as a useful tool for librarians in their dealings with both specialists and laypersons. There is a good description of the famous partnership at the beginning, which most readers will find interesting as well as informative. The major segment of the text is an alphabetical arrangement of entries related to the Gilbert and Sullivan productions. These include major performers, plot summaries, songs, and explanations of obscure references dating from 1871 to the time of publication. Entries for the operettas themselves, in addition to providing synopses of plots, provide full song texts, although not complete libretti. This work will remain an important source as long as G and S productions are prominent stage offerings.

514.   **Songs of the Theater.** Richard Lewine and Alfred Simon. New York, H. W. Wilson, 1984. 897p.

This recent effort updates and expands two previous works by the same authors, and identifies 17,000 songs from 1,200 American musicals on stage, film, or television. Songs are both published and unpublished and span a time period from 1891 through 1983. Selection of songs or selectivity of musicals varies with the time period, with greater selectivity exercised for the early period to the 1920s. Coverage is comprehensive for the professional New York stage from the 1920s, for which songs are identified from every theater production seen on Broadway. It also includes songs of off-Broadway productions if they run at least fifteen days. There are a chronological listing and an alphabetical listing of shows, and a title listing of songs which includes composers, lyricists, and shows. There is a separate index of films and television productions.

POPULAR MUSIC (JAZZ, FOLK, ROCK, COUNTRY, ETC.)

515.   **The Complete Encyclopedia of Popular Music and Jazz, 1900-1950.** Roger D. Kinkle. New Rochelle, N.Y., Arlington House, 1974. 4v.

This is a detailed and thorough survey of a fifty-year period in popular music production. Reviewers gave it high marks and the years have demonstrated that it is a most worthwhile tool by any standard used to measure its value. The first volume is an excellent chronology of events in popular music during this time period. It identifies major musicals, for which are given casts, opening dates, number of performances, and major songs. In addition to the musical, for each year important songs are entered individually. Separate entries are also furnished for musical films which include cast and song listings. Hit recordings are also identified and are arranged by artist. Volumes 2-3 are biographical dictionaries which furnish sketches of over 2,000 personalities from pop, jazz, country and western, and blues. Discographies are included in each sketch. Volume 4 provides indexes of personal names, Broadway musicals, and popular songs, and includes appendices which contain award winners and notable recordings.

516.   **A History and Encyclopedia of Country, Western, and Gospel Music.** Linnell Gentry. Nashville, Tenn., McQuiddy, 1961; repr., St. Clair Shores, Mich., Scholarly Press, 1979. 380p.

Although this title is aging and its distribution was hampered by small publishing operations in which the author originally served as publisher, this has been a useful reference tool for the diversity of information it contains. (In the second edition of this guide, Rogers called it a vital reference work.) Part of its vitality lies in the choice of thirty-seven reprint articles which were taken from a variety of journals including *Harper's, Time, Life,* etc. These cover numerous topics on popular music and prove to be interesting and informative even today. Other sections of the work include a biographical dictionary of over 300 prominent figures, a listing of country music radio shows since 1924, and a comprehensive listing of 3,800 names. It remains a good curiosity handbook for those libraries that own it, and should be increasingly valuable as an historical record.

517. Hit Parade: An Encyclopedia of the Top Songs of the Jazz, Depression, Swing and Sing Eras. Don Tyler. New York, Quill/William Morrow, 1985. 257p.

This is an interesting and useful chronology of a variety of popular songs which will appeal to a wide audience. Although serious students and specialists will prefer the coverage given by Kinkle (see entry 515) in its detail and concern for scholarly precision, this inexpensive paperback is a desirable addition to a general reference collection. Entries are alphabetically arranged by title in chapters which are classified in chronological order. Each entry furnishes name of composer and lyricist, followed by a fairly detailed description of the song. This normally covers circumstances of its introduction, performers, revivals, etc. Introductory material preceding each chapter describes in a highly informal manner the nature of the period. Some errors have been pointed out but, in general, it is a good purchase for a general audience. There are indexes of song titles and of proper names.

518. Resource Guide to Themes in Contemporary American Song Lyrics, 1950-1985. B. Lee Cooper. Westport, Conn., Greenwood Press, 1986. 458p.

A newer tool which has proved valuable for research on song themes is this handbook covering American song production over the past thirty-five years. Categories are defined in terms of socio-economic elements of importance today, such as death, education, marriage and divorce, occupations, race relations, urban life, youth culture, etc. These categories are then subdivided into more specific themes. A most interesting sociological study is possible through the linking of these topics with music of our time, and comparisons are surely in order with other decades. Several tables show relationships of songs to various events. Both the bibliography and the discography are lengthy and useful.

519. Variety Music Cavalcade, 1620-1969: A Chronology of Vocal and Instrumental Music Popular in the U.S. 3rd ed. Julius Mattfeld. New York, Prentice-Hall, 1971. 766p.

One of the very important works in the field is this highly respected chronology of popular music. It spans a period of 350 years beginning with the Pilgrims, and provides brief descriptions of various events along with the listings of songs. The events are social, political, and literary and help to provide some idea of the context of the period in which the songs were developed. Songs are of varied type and include hymns, all types of popular secular music, sacred songs, choral compositions, and instrumental and orchestral works. Only musical elements (not social events) are indexed along with dates which lead the user to the proper year. Songs are listed alphabetically under the year of publication and are accompanied by information on composer, lyricist, publisher, and copyright date.

520. Year by Year in the Rock Era: Events and Conditions Shaping the Rock Generations That Reshaped America. Herb Hendler. Westport, Conn., Greenwood Press, 1983; repr., New York, Praeger, 1987. 350p.

This is a detailed chronology of the twenty-eight-year period from 1954 through 1981 in which rock music is placed within the context of social events in much the same manner as *Variety Music Cavalcade* (see entry 519) treats popular music. The author is a former record company executive and has provided a wealth of information by covering each year individually and listing major performers, dancers, and news of the rock music industry along with social, cultural, and political information gleaned from the news. Statistics, fashions, slang, etc., are included. In addition, there is an interesting section analyzing the rock era by category such as cost of living, *Time* "Man of the Year" winners, and top television shows. The work concludes with a detailed bibliography. Another chronology of the same period is *Rolling Stones Rock Almanac: The Chronicle of Rock and Roll* (Collier Books/Macmillan, 1983). The introduction of this work describes the history and development of rock and roll and its relationship to rhythm and blues, country and western, etc. The years 1954-1982 are described individually, first with a brief introductory essay, then by a calendar of events. This work is a good buy at about one-third the price of *Year by Year in the Rock Era*.

MUSICAL INSTRUMENTS

General technical handbooks have been emphasized. Check the specialized bibliographic guides, especially Duckles (see entry 433) for material on particular instruments.

521. **Dictionary of Pipe Organ Stops.** Stevens Irwin. 2nd ed. New York, Schirmer Books/Macmillan, 1983. 422p.

Devised as a handbook for organists and students of the instrument, this work first appeared in 1962 and was considered an important contribution to the literature of music instruction. The new version has maintained that standard while providing extensive revision and expansion. Many of the definitions have been modified and enlarged with greater attention to detail, but the most salient alteration has been the addition of twenty-five new plates and a similar number of charts as well as seven new appendices. There has been some rearrangement of material covered, which is reflected in the table of contents. The charts are generally informative and of value to both the instructor and student, with such topical matters as thirteen famous color reeds and thirteen famous octaves. Appendices provide such material as a list of Baroque stops. There are a list of questions for students and a bibliography.

522. **Musical Instruments: A Comprehensive Dictionary.** Corr. ed. Sybil Marcuse. New York, W. W. Norton, 1975. 608p.

This work was first published in 1964, and this edition is essentially a reprint with some corrections. It has become a staple in music libraries for its coverage of musical instruments from all periods from the earliest times to the present day. Although the information provided here may be found in other more general sources, this specialized dictionary is highly convenient for music patrons. Entries are furnished for hundreds of different instruments and the identifications are clear and accurate. Instruments are listed in English, with equivalent foreign terms identified. There are some illustrations, which are excellent in quality but few in number. A more recent work by the same author is *A Survey of Musical Instruments* (Harper & Row, 1975) which places the instruments in technical groupings or families such as idiophone and chordophone.

Ref ML102, I5 M37

523. **Musical Instruments of the World: An Illustrated Encyclopedia.** The Diagram Group. New York, Paddington/Two Continents, 1976; repr., Oxford, Facts on File, 1985. 320p.

The strength of this work lies in its illustrations of the musical instruments, for there are over 4,000 drawings which identify every conceivable piece of music-making equipment. The arrangement of this impressive work is by type, with sections on vibrating air instruments, self-vibrating instruments, vibrating membrane instruments, vibrating string instruments, and mechanical electronic instruments. Divisions by geographical areas, time periods, and instrumental ensembles are also given when appropriate. The Diagram Group is an organization of artists, writers, and editors which promotes understanding of essential features of construction and technique through the publication of highly illustrated works of this type. There are a small section with twenty-five to thirty biographies of important instrument makers, virtuosos, and writers; a bibliography; and a directory of museums. A name-subject index provides access.

524. **The New Grove Dictionary of Musical Instruments.** Stanley Sadie, ed. New York, Grove's Dictionaries of Music, 1984. 3v.

More than just a spinoff of the *New Grove Dictionary of Music and Musicians* (see entry 498), this specialized survey of musical instruments from all periods and geographical regions transcends the coverage given the topic in the magnificent general encyclopedia. Sadie edited both works, and for this specialized set he has revised, modified, updated, and in some cases replaced the articles as they appeared in the major work. The attempt here was to achieve complete coverage of the world of musical instruments, whereas the original set, although comprehensive, was still subject to certain limitations in this regard. Especially well-covered are non-Western and folk instruments. There has been some criticism of the quality of illustrations, but there is no argument with the depth and quality of the identification, and description of the history, structure, creation, and use of the various instruments.

Directories, Annuals, and
Current Awareness Services

525. **The American Music Handbook.** Christopher Pavlakis. New York, Free Press, 1974. 836p.

Although its value surely diminishes with increasing age and the current issues of *Musical America* (see entry 530), this standard item has remained an important tool and one that music librarians are not willing to retire. Although there are many areas and topics which are shared by *Musical America*, as in most cases where similar sources are available, coverage tends to be complementary as much as it may be redundant. All areas of musical activity in this country are given adequate coverage, and Pavlakis (a composer, teacher, and publisher) has provided over 5,000 entries. Included are service institutions and organizations, performing organizations, individual musicians and composers, instrumental ensembles with founding dates, conductors and concert masters, bands, vocal groups of all kinds, summer theaters, festivals, contests, awards, grants, schools and their degrees, fellowships, managers, and suppliers. The information appears in thirteen sections and is accessed through a name index.

*526. **Billboard.** 1894- . Wk. New York, Billboard Publications.

Considered to be to music what *Variety* (see entry 696) is to theater and film, this well-known publication appears in a newspaper/magazine format. With a weekly circulation of nearly 50,000, it represents one of the most popular offerings and provides excellent current awareness of news in the music field. The focus is on publishing, recording, and selling music, and articles cover personalities, recent contracts, shows recently given or soon to be seen, as well as new albums and tapes. The writing style is snappy and informal, and the publication does an excellent job of keeping readers abreast of developments in rock, pop, country, and folk music. Although there is a rather costly index, all materials including reviews are indexed in *Music Index* (see entry 451). *BILLBOARD INFORMATION NETWORK is an online database which includes charts appearing in the magazine. The aim is to provide market research data on records, video products, and computer software for home entertainment. It is available from the publisher, covers the most recent three weeks, and is updated daily.

527.   **Directory of Music Faculties in Colleges and Universities, U.S. and Canada.** 1967- . Bienn. Binghamton, N.Y., College Society.

Both the title and frequency of this important computer-produced tool have varied in the past. The first three editions (1967-1970) were entitled *Directory of Music Faculties in American Colleges and Universities*, and appeared on an annual basis. The fourth edition (1970-1972) initiated the change both in title, which signalled an expansion of the scope to include Canadians, and in frequency, to a biennial publication. The most recent edition is the eleventh (1986-1988), published in 1987. The tool furnishes a listing of music faculty members in colleges and universities and provides several approaches. There are an alphabetical listing by state of colleges and universities accompanied by a listing of faculty members with area of interest; a listing of faculty by area of interest; a listing of faculty members alphabetically arranged; and a listing of schools by type of degrees offered.

528.   **Directory of Music Research Libraries.** 1967- . Irreg. Kassel, West Germany; distr., New York, Barenreiter. (Repertoire international des sources musicales, Series C).

This outstanding directory furnishes the student and scholar with an international guide to the holdings and practices of music research libraries all over the world. It was developed as a companion work to *RISM* (see entry 445). Part I (1967) covers libraries in the United States and Canada that have been inventoried in series A and B (pre-1800 material). Part II (1970) covers thirteen European countries (Austria, Belgium, Switzerland, East and West Germany, Denmark, Ireland, Great Britain, Luxembourg, Norway, the Netherlands, Sweden, and Finland). It includes sources for the nineteenth century and some libraries not inventoried in *RISM*. Part III (1972) covers Spain, France, Italy, and Portugal and provides increased depth in descriptions of the collections. These early volumes were published by the University of Iowa. The German publisher, Barenreiter, took over and issued a set of the previously published parts as volumes 1-3 in 1975. Volume 4 appeared in 1979 and covered Australia, Israel, Japan, and New Zealand; it was the first volume to be issued directly under the auspices of RISM as part of its recently created series C. A change of editorial policy established the directory as dealing with the total problem of gaining access to the collections described, and information is given regarding not only library collections but also such important aspects as public holidays, names of RISM contacts, copyright information, library systems, etc. A second edition of volume 1 was issued in 1983; and most recently, volume 5, covering Czechoslovakia, Hungary, Poland, and Yugoslavia, appeared in 1985.

529.   **Music Industry Directory, 1983.** 7th ed. Chicago, Marquis Who's Who, 1983. 678p.

This is the successor to the *Musician's Guide* (Music Information Service, 1954-1980), which was published on an irregular basis six times during a twenty-six-year period. It remains to be seen whether this new tool will adopt a consistent policy in this regard, since this is the only volume thus far. A great deal of reorganization has taken place, and it appears that the always useful directory has been vastly improved. As in the previous works, identification is furnished for a host of elements in the music industry (music associations, societies, arts agencies, American Federation of Musicians union locals, foundations, competitions, festivals, schools, libraries, journals, orchestras, opera companies, critics, managers, agents, record companies, and publishers). These have been reclassified under seven major headings, and easier access is provided through a detailed table of contents as well as separate indexes for some of the sections. Omitted are summer camp programs, music teachers, piano technicians, and recipients of prizes and awards. Of course, certain oversights occur and have been pointed out, but together with *Musical America* (see entry 530) this title offers a vital service.

530. **Musical America: International Directory of the Performing Arts.** 1969- . Ann. New York, ABC Leisure Magazines.

Originally appearing as a special directory issue of *High Fidelity* magazine and bearing separate pagination, this work is now an independent and essential reference tool. During its formative period, it was published under the auspices of *Billboard* magazine (see entry 526), but it now appears under the masthead of ABC Leisure, which has continued to publish *High Fidelity*. The directory furnishes names and addresses by state, then city of solo performers, orchestras, performing arts series, dance companies, opera companies, choral groups, festivals, music schools, contests, foundations and awards, music publishers, service and professional music organizations, artist managers, music periodicals, and music critics. Coverage is international, with the inclusion of a foreign listing of companies and organizations. The tool also serves as a yearbook, with a section of articles covering the events in music and dance for the previous year.

531. **Songwriter's Market.** 1979- . Ann. Cincinnati, Writer's Digest Books.

The 1987 edition of this popular guide to the market place continues in the same manner as its previous issues and of other titles in the Writer's Digest Series. There is an introductory narrative on the profession of songwriting, followed by extensive listings of commercial firms involved in the sale and purchasing of songs. There has been an increased interest in songwriting the past few years, and as a result this tool has been receiving more use than it has in the past. Emphasis is on the American music industry although there are listings for international firms based in other countries of the world. Music publishers, record companies, and record producers are all included. Appendices provide information on a host of topics such as contracts, record-keeping and even rip-offs. Also, a glossary and detailed index are furnished.

532. **Symphony Orchestras of the United States.** Robert R. Craven, ed. Westport, Conn., Greenwood Press, 1986. 521p.

This is a useful directory which contains a great deal of information on American orchestras not readily available elsewhere. Descriptions are brief, generally running about three pages, but are well written and describe adequately the significant characteristics of each unit. Selection of orchestras was based on membership of the American Symphony Orchestra League (ASOL), where they were designated as major and regional orchestral units, and metropolitan orchestras with the highest budgets. In addition, an orchestra was included from each state that was not represented in the previous categories, for a total of 126 orchestras. Coverage includes descriptions of the history, organization, budget, and activities as well as discography, chronology of music directors, bibliography, and an address and contact person for each orchestra. There are a general bibliography, a chronology of orchestra founding dates, and a detailed index to the contents.

Histories

GENERAL

533.   A History of Western Music. 3rd ed. Donald Jay Grout, with Claude V. Palisca. New York, W. W. Norton, 1981. 818p.

Now in its third edition, this highly acclaimed historical survey of Western music was originally published in 1960. It has been considered an outstanding textbook for music history classes and represents one of the fine contributions of the W. W. Norton Company. The third edition remains largely unchanged in textual narrative from the previously revised edition in 1973, but has expanded its extensive bibliographical coverage to include more recent works. The work reads well today just as it has done for nearly thirty years in earlier editions. There are a glossary, bibliography, and a chronology of musical developments as well as a number of illustrations. Title, subject, and name indexes are furnished. An earlier work from Norton is Paul Henry Lang's *Music in Western Civilization* (W. W. Norton, 1941), which treats musical development within a social, political, and cultural context.

Ref ML160.G87 1988

534.   Music History from the Late Roman through the Gothic Periods, 313-1425: A Documented Chronology. Blanche Gangwere. Westport, Conn., Greenwood Press, 1986. 247p.

This is an outline or chronology of musical history covering early musical developments over a period of over 1,100 years. Greenwood has planned a series of these which eventually will cover the entire history of music in Western civilization. This work identifies important elements with respect to contributions and theoretical influences, and covers terms, notations, and musical instruments. References to sources provide exposition and interpretation and furnish examples of the technique, form, or style under scrutiny. Many of these references are to encyclopedia articles as well as separate monographs. Information is given regarding geographical regions; maps are included. This should become one of the most frequently used tools for answering historical inquiries.

535.   Music since 1900. 4th ed. Nicholas Slonimsky. New York, Scribner's, 1971. 1595p.

First published in 1938, this has been one of the standard historical sources providing an overview of musical developments in the twentieth century. The author has been the editor of *Baker's Biographical Dictionary* (see entry 546) through several editions and is considered one of the experts in the field. Primarily, the work is a chronology of stylistic trends from 1900 to 1969 (with the fourth edition) and includes letters and other primary source material as well. The author's commentary on the various aspects is cogent and well developed, and indexes are clear and effective. At the age of ninety-two, Slonimsky has prepared a *Supplement to Music since 1900* (Scribner's, 1986) which covers in detail the period 1970 to 1985 on a day-to-day basis. It is an excellent chronicle of recent developments, made all the more impressive in that the venerable author has reviewed errors and inaccurate assessments made in the basic work.

536.   New Oxford History of Music. London, Oxford University Press, 1954- . Projected 10v. (In progress).

Ref ML160, N44 v.1 -v. 10

Carrying the name of Oxford University, this multivolume history of music has earned an excellent reputation for detailed coverage and scholarly bearing. Its overall effectiveness has been marred somewhat by a lack of promptness in its completion as a set, but individual volumes, all by scholars of distinction, have proved to be valuable tools. At long last it seems to be drawing to a conclusion, and awaits only the addition of volume 9 and of a final index volume. In its entirety it represents a comprehensive and detailed survey of music from the earliest times to the present. The set contains volume 1, *Ancient and Oriental Music*, by Egon Wellesz (1957); volume 2, *Early Medieval Music up to 1300*, by Dom Anselm Hughes and Gerald Abraham (1954); volume 3, *Ars Nova and the Renaissance, c.1300-1540*, by Dom Anselm Hughes and Gerald Abraham (1960); volume 4, *The Age of Humanism, 1540-1630*, by Gerald Abraham (1968); volume 5, *Opera and Church Music, 1630-1750*, by Nigel Fortune and Anthony Lewis (1975, 1985); volume 6, *Concert Music, 1630-1750*, by Gerald Abraham (1986); volume 7, *The Age of Enlightenment, 1745-1790*, by Egon Wellesz and Frederick W. Sternfeld (1973); volume 8, *The Age of Beethoven, 1790-1830*, by Gerald Abraham (1983); and volume 10, *Modern Age, 1890-1960*, by Martin Cooper (1974).

537. **The Norton History of Music Series.** New York, W. W. Norton, 1940- . (In progress).

Norton Publishing has long been associated with quality histories in the field of music. Most of that recognition may be attributable to this group of individual monographs, which are recognized as the Norton History of Music series. These independent works (none has a volume number) all cover different time periods, and were done by scholars and specialists on each topic. When taken collectively, they do, indeed, constitute a history of music from the earliest times to the present, although there are notable gaps in the coverage. The emphasis in these works is on the style, characteristics, and development of musical thought rather than an account of happenings or descriptions of a biographical nature. The titles, listed chronologically by period of coverage, are *The Rise of Music in the Ancient World: East and West*, by Curt Sachs (1943); *Music in the Middle Ages*, by Gustav Reese (1940); *Music in the Renaissance* (1959), also by Reese; *Music in the Baroque Era: From Monteverdi to Bach*, by Manfred F. Bukofzer (1947); *Music in the Romantic Era*, by Alfred Einstein (1947); *Music in Our Time: Trends in Music since the Romantic Era*, by Adolfo Salazar (1946); and William W. Austin's *Music in the Twentieth Century: From Debussy to Stravinsky* (1966).

538. **Source Readings in Music History.** Oliver William Strunk, ed. New York, W. W. Norton, 1965. 5v.

This was considered a landmark publication at the time it first appeared in one volume in 1950 as an anthology of nearly 100 writings on the subject of music. These documents represented the thoughts of various cultures and geographic regions in all periods of time from the ancients to the Romantics. This work expands the earlier version and treats the periods in separate volumes. Volume 1 covers antiquity and the Middle Ages; volume 2, the Renaissance, volume 3, the Baroque, volume 4, the Classical era, and volume 5, the Romantic period. Writings of both composers and theorists as well as philosophers and scientists and numerous others are represented, and provide a rich array of opinions and pronouncements. All foreign documents have been translated into English.

SPECIALIZED BY TOPIC OR COUNTRY

539.   **History of Musical Instruments.** Curt Sachs. New York, W. W. Norton, 1940; repr., 1968. 505p.

This is another of the scholarly histories from Norton which has achieved the status of a classic work. One of the first monographic histories on the topic in the English language, it is divided into four parts. The origins and development of instruments are described in an interesting and informative manner. The first part considers the earliest times, reflecting on the primitive and prehistoric era; second, a study of antiquity focuses largely on the instruments of the Greeks and Romans. The Middle Ages are covered next, then finally the modern Western world. There are an excellent bibliography for additional readings and an index to provide access.

540.   **Our American Music: A Comprehensive History from 1620 to the Present.** 4th ed. John Tasker Howard. New York, Crowell, 1965. 944p.

This has been a standard work in the field since its initial appearance as *Our American Music: 300 Years of It* in 1931. It has undergone revisions in 1939 and in 1946. With the fourth the title was changed, indicating an expanded coverage up to the time of publication. The work is a comprehensive history of the developments, personalities, and occurrences in American music, and in this regard it furnishes a needed service. Over the years, the tool has been praised for its breadth but criticized for its superficial nature, since Howard felt it was his task to be a chronicler rather than a critic. What commentary is given is of a speculative nature and has not changed much from previous editions, but the coverage of recent music is worth the purchase price. There are photographs and a bibliography much enlarged from that of the earlier editions.

541.   **A Short History of Opera.** 2nd ed. Donald Jay Grout. New York, Columbia University Press, 1965. 852p.

At long last, after twenty-two years, the third edition of this vital work is imminent, and is slated for October 1987. Originally published in 1947, the second edition appeared in 1965 with the purpose of updating the material by bringing the historical coverage to 1960. Bibliographies were updated, and additional illustrative material was included. The opera is treated in a comprehensive manner, beginning with the lyric theater of the Greeks. Arrangement is chronological, with attention given to musical styles. Descriptions are scholarly and the intended audience (specialists and students) have derived much value from both the articles and the excellent bibliography. It is assumed that the third edition will be modified in much the same manner, while retaining those qualities that have earned the title a position of respect.

Biographical Sources

BIBLIOGRAPHIES AND INDEXES

542.   **Black Music Biography: An Annotated Bibliography.** Samuel A. Floyd, Jr., and Marsha J. Reisser. White Plains, N.Y., Kraus International, 1987. 302p.

From the same writers who created *Black Music in the United States: An Annotated Bibliography* for the same publisher in 1981, this is a major work in the documentation of black musicians of all types and styles of performance. Coverage is given to a relatively small but important segment of eighty-seven composers and performers over a hundred-year period beginning with the 1850s. Nearly 150 monographic works have been identified and described in detail. Performers range in nature from Michael Jackson to Leontyne Price, and there is an excellent detailed introduction providing a summary of the literature. An earlier work which documents the contributions of female musicians is *Women in Music: A Biobibliography*, by Don L. Hixon and Don Hennessee (Scarecrow, 1975). It presents an alphabetical list of women musicians who are identified briefly; coded references refer to any of the appropriate forty-eight sources from which the entries were derived.

543. **Index to Biographies of Contemporary Composers.** Storm Bull. Metuchen, N.J., Scarecrow, 1964-1974. 2v.

The first volume of this work appeared in 1964 and identified biographical material on nearly 6,000 composers from sixty-nine sources. The second volume, published ten years later, serves to update material on 4,000 of the previously covered personalities and adds another 4,000 individuals to their ranks. Entries in both volumes are arranged alphabetically, and brief identification is given along with citations to listed sources. A listing of 108 biographical sources is used for the second volume, thus providing an index to biographies of about 10,000 figures in 177 different works. These individuals are contemporary in that they were born during this century, were still living at time of publication, or had died after 1949. This work is recognized as a useful source for quick identification of modern personalities.

544. **Literature of Rock, II, 1979-1983: With Additional Material for 1954-1978.** Frank Hoffman and B. Lee Cooper. Metuchen, N.J., Scarecrow, 1986. 2v.

This work is a continuation of an earlier volume by Hoffman from the same publisher, *The Literature of Rock, 1954-1978* (1981), covering a twenty-five year period prior to this one. The present work adds to the material covered in the earlier issue and at the same time extends the coverage a few more years. Together, both works furnish a selective annotated bibliography of books and periodical articles arranged in subject categories reflecting a chronological sequence. Such periods as doo wop, rhythm and blues, soul, etc., are included. Most entries are for individuals, although some subjects are given. Source material includes fanzines, trade magazines, books, undergrounds, etc. Each volume has a detailed index and a useful discography.

545. **Opera and Concert Singers: An Annotated International Bibliography of Books and Pamphlets.** Andrew Farkas. New York, Garland, 1985. 363p. (Garland Reference Library of the Humanities, v.466).

This is a comprehensive bibliography of 1,500 biographies and autobiographies in twenty-nine different languages. Also included are 300 monographs covering more than one subject, which are listed in a separate section. Annotations are excellent, providing useful information and written in a sprightly style. There is a warning from the author that most libraries do not possess more than half the books listed; therefore, this should serve as a purchasing guide to strengthen the collection. A list of unpublished manuscripts is given at the end. All in all, this is an impressive and complete contribution. Another bibliography published in the same year is *Concert and Opera Singers: A Bibliography of Biographical Materials*, compiled by Robert H. Cowden (Greenwood Press, 1985). Although personalities are duplicated to a great extent in the two works, the latter includes entries from reference books and periodicals. It has only a small number of annotations.

DICTIONARIES AND ENCYCLOPEDIAS

Concert Music and Opera

Ref ML105.B16 1992

546. Baker's Biographical Dictionary of Musicians. 7th ed. Nicolas Slonimsky. New York, Schirmer Books/Macmillan, 1984. 2577p.

Now in its seventh edition, this standard work has been an indispensable item in reference departments since its initial appearance in 1900. It has established a reputation for comprehensiveness which the new edition maintains, covering 13,000 personalities, both living and dead, from all geographic areas and periods of time. It has been criticized in the past for relative weakness in coverage of living performers, and the new edition furnishes an additional 1,000 biographical sketches, many of which represent contemporary popular crooners, rock singers, etc. The tool furnishes information on a variety of people associated with music, and in addition to composers and performers, there are conductors, scholars, educators, librarians, etc. Most entries have been revised and updated. Biographies vary in length from a few lines to several pages and include bibliographies and lists of composers' works. These unfortunately have not been updated from the sixth edition.

547. Contemporary American Composers: A Biographical Dictionary. 2nd ed. Ruth E. Anderson. Boston, G. K. Hall, 1982. 528p.

First published in 1976, this work has been revised to omit certain categories of individuals, such as those who have written only one or two compositions and those who did not respond to the questionnaires. Still, the number of entries has increased and presently the tool identifies over 4,000 composers of concert music. These people were born after 1869 and are American citizens or have resided in this country for an extensive period of time. Entries furnish dates of birth and death, education and training, professional and academic appointments, awards and commissions, and mailing address. Due to the reliance on the questionnaire, some caution should be exercised in reporting the information as accurate, but all things considered, the tool is valuable for its breadth of coverage. A more recent work is *A Dictionary of American Composers*, by Neil Butterworth (Garland, 1984) which provides depth but sacrifices breadth. It covers 558 composers of serious music from the eighteenth century to the present in detailed fashion.

548. A Dictionary of Pianists. Wilson Lyle. New York, Schirmer Books/Macmillan, 1984. 343p.

One of the rare biographical sources devoted to the artists of the piano, this tool provides information on 4,000 classical pianists from the eighteenth century to the present day. Listings are arranged alphabetically and the entries are straightforward except for the inclusion of occasional editorial comments which may seem anomalous within the context of the work. Coverage excludes those individuals whose performance can be categorized as jazz, ragtime, blues, and pops (but interestingly enough embraces an entry on Liberace). There appears to be a slight bias toward inclusion of figures of British or European extractions but, in general, the tool should prove of value to music librarians and their patrons. Another biographical dictionary on instrumentalists of a special type is *Great Masters of the Violin: From Corelli and Vivaldi to Stern, Zuckerman, and Perlman*, by Boris Schwarz (Simon & Schuster, 1983). This is a highly useful survey of the lives and times of violinists from the sixteenth century to the present day. It is written in an anecdotal and informed style and draws upon a wealth of information derived from a variety of sources including the author's personal knowledge.

549. Greene's Biographical Encyclopedia. David Mason Greene. Garden City, N.Y., Doubleday, 1985. 1348p.

A recent biographical tool, this work covers over 2,400 prominent composers representing all nations and time periods. Greene is known for his irreverence in the columns he has done as a contributing editor to *Musical Heritage Review* (Paganiniana Publications, 1977-) and these biographical sketches are presented in an interesting, informal, and entertaining manner sure to appeal to the intended audience of nonspecialists. Entries are rich in detail and include information on personal traits and habits as well as the more conventional standard material. They give personal data, analysis of the major works, and a listing of their availability as recordings. Arrangement is chronological to facailitate comparisons within schools or periods. A narrower time span is covered in Jerome Roche and Elizabeth Roche's *A Dictionary of Early Music from the Troubadours to Monteverdi* (Oxford University Press, 1981). This work provides brief but well-written sketches of 700 early composers whose works appear on recordings, in published editions, or in textbooks, or who are the subject of current scholarship.

550. International Encyclopedia of Women Composers. Aaron I. Cohen. New York, R. R. Bowker, 1981. 597p.

With the recent emphasis on documentation of the contributions of minority groups to both culture and progress in society, the decades of the 1970s and the 1980s brought a new interest in the work of both blacks and women. This is a highly useful encyclopedia which provides descriptions of the lives and accomplishments of female composers of all ages and parts of the world. Over 5,000 entries provide biographical sketches, listings of contributions, publications by the composer, and a bibliography of works about her. Separate sections furnish photographs of a number of the individuals. Appendices include a listing of sources from which the biographies were derived and a bibliography of additional reading. Indexes give access by country and century, profession, instrument, musical form, etc. A discography is also supplied.

551. Musicians since 1900: Performers in Concert and Opera. David Ewen, comp. and ed. New York, H. W. Wilson, 1978. 974p.

Ewen's contributions to music reference are numerous, and this is another of his well-designed and highly informative biographical tools. Designed to supersede his earlier effort, *Living Musicians* (H. W. Wilson, 1947) and its 1957 supplement, this work expands on those tools by including deceased performers as well. Criteria for inclusion suggest that the biographees have left a permanent impression upon the musical culture of the twentieth century. The lives of nearly 450 of the most distinguished performers and conductors from both the concert hall and the opera stage are described in detail, accompanied by a photograph and a few references for additional reading. The emphasis is on contributions during the twentieth century, so a number of individuals born during the nineteenth century are also covered. Ewen's *Composers since 1900: A Biographical and Critical Guide* (H. W. Wilson, 1969), is a standard reference tool for biographies of 230 important twentieth-century composers. The first supplement (1981) updates information in the original entries and adds forty-seven biographies of composers who have come into prominence since 1969.

552. Who's Who in American Music. 2nd ed. Compiled and edited by Jaques Cattell Press. New York, R. R. Bowker, 1985. 1200p.

This work was published two years after the appearance of the first edition, and it apparently has taken on the character of a biennial publication, even though it is treated as a monograph by the Library of Congress. It is a typical Cattell publication, giving great attention to details, and covers 8,000 individuals associated primarily with semiclassical (but including some classical) music in America. Musicians, critics, publishers, and editors are among the various groups represented in the listing. The arrangement of entries is alphabetical, and they furnish addresses, personal data and information on major accomplishments and writings. *Who's Who in American Music: Classical* (2nd edition, R. R. Bowker, 1985) is structured along the same lines. It covers 9,000 personalities who are currently active and influential contributors to serious music in this country. A British publication less limited in scope is *International Who's Who in Music and Musicians' Directory* (10th edition, Cambridge, England, International Who's Who in Music, 1985). This provides biographical sketches of over 10,000 musicians all over the world. They are primarily associated with the fields of classical and semiclassical music.

553. **Who's Who in Opera: An International Biographical Directory of Singers, Conductors, Directors, Designers, and Administrators ...** Maria F. Rich, ed. New York, Arno, 1976. 684p.

There are over 2,300 entries covering individuals of various segments of the opera world, as identified in the title, in this book. Information was garnered through a questionnaire sent to members of 144 opera companies and festivals in thirty-three countries. Entries generally provide type of voice (for singers) or profession (for others), nationality, date of birth, spouse, spouse's occupation, and number of children, education and training, debut, awards, major companies, roles, world premiere, indication of activity in recording and teaching, agent, and residence. Criteria for inclusion for singers were that they had at least five major roles in the five years prior to the publication date, and similar restrictions were applied to individuals from other fields covered. Included is a useful section profiling 101 opera companies in terms of budget, personnel, and performance.

Popular Music (Jazz, Folk, Rock, Country, Etc.)

554. **American Musicians: Fifty-Six Portraits in Jazz.** Whitney Balliett. New York, Oxford University Press, 1986. 415p.

Described by the author as a "highly personal encyclopedia," this collective biography represents a compilation of Balliett's numerous contributions to *The New Yorker* over a twenty-five-year period beginning with the early 1960s. The book begins with biographies of two writers: jazz historian Hugues Panassié and discographer Charles Delaunay. It then treats jazz musicians in chronological sequence. The names are well known to most people who have even a passing acquaintance with jazz: "King" Oliver, Sidney Bechet, Duke Ellington, Coleman Hawkins, etc. The author has used his personal interviews with the subjects or their associates as well as standard biographies and various accounts to produce cogent and well-developed narratives as well as biographical highlights. Numerous quotations provide real insight into each subject's nature.

555. **Blues Who's Who: A Biographical Dictionary of Blues Singers.** Sheldon Harris. New Rochelle, N.Y., Arlington House, 1979; repr., New York, Da Capo, 1981. 775p.

Considered to be the most substantial and complete source of biographical information on blues singers, this work lists the personalities by their real names. As a result, there are many cross-references from variations and stage names to the proper entries. Hundreds of personalities are covered and (although Mahalia Jackson and Billie Holliday have been omitted) coverage is excellent among those local singers, both urban and rural, who achieved some measure of national or international recognition. Howlin' Wolf, Muddy Waters, and B. B. King are listed, of course, among many others. Entries include a biographical sketch, birthdate and place, marriages, children, instruments, songs composed, influences, and critical comments concerning their work. A detailed list of professional concert appearances, television and radio shows, films, etc., is provided. *Great Guitarists*, by Rich Kienzle (Facts on File, 1985) offers lengthy biographical essays on the lives of sixty guitarists, including blues performers as well as jazz and rock people. Suggestions about good recordings for further listening are given.

556. **The Encyclopedia of Folk, Country, & Western Music.** 2nd ed. Irwin Stambler and Grelum Landon. New York, St. Martin's Press, 1984. 902p.

Generally regarded as one of the leading biographical dictionaries, this edition of the encyclopedia updates and extends the number of entries in the previous edition from 500 to over 600 names. Many of the popular and known performers are present from the contemporary scene, data being derived from responses to questionnaires supplied by them or by their estates, if deceased. In a number of cases, documents and other literature provided the source material. The biographies are lengthy and detailed for the most part, although the material does not seem to go beyond 1980. An excellent section includes music awards from a variety of organizations, and there is a useful and comprehensive bibliography. *Artists of American Folk Music: The Legends of Traditional Folk Music ...*, edited by Phil Hood (William Morrow, 1986) is a highly selective biographical encyclopedia which may be considered supplementary to this entry. It covers only thirty-one different groups or solo performers, but it does so in-depth. Articles run from three to six pages in length. The selection includes such individuals as the Kingston Trio, Peter, Paul, and Mary, Bob Dylan, Woody Guthrie, Pete Seeger, and Leadbelly, who are considered leaders in the troubadour tradition.

557. **The Harmony Illustrated Encyclopedia of Rock.** 5th ed. Mike Clifford. New York, Harmony/Crown, 1986. 272p.

This work of British authorship appears frequently (4th edition, 1983) and is considered by many to be the best biographical source on rock music. It has been a consistent favorite among devotees of the genre. It covers approximately 1,000 performers with some emphasis on British stars, thus overlooking some reasonably important American contributors. As is true of any work of this type, there are some errors and oversights, but the quality of writing is excellent and the content is well presented in an entertaining fashion with many illustrations. Norm N. Nite's *Rock On: The Illustrated Encyclopedia of Rock n' Roll. Volume 2: The Years of Change 1964-1978* (Harper & Row, 1984) is an update of an earlier work published in 1979 and provides revisions and enlargements of the biographies of over 1,000 artists. It gives good accounts of their careers and includes good discographies. *Lillian Roxon's Rock Encyclopedia*, edited by Ed Naha (Grosset & Dunlap, 1978) is a tried and true source of information always considered to be authoritative, now spiced up by Naha's flippant style. An old favorite is another work by Irwin Stambler, *Encyclopedia of Pop, Rock, and Soul* (St. Martin's Press, 1975). This biographical dictionary of performers, producers, and others important on the rock scene also defines terms and styles. Considered one of the best of its kind at the time it was published, it is now beginning to show its age.

558. **Kingsbury's Who's Who in Country & Western Music.** Kenn Kingsbury, ed. Culver City, Calif., Black Stallion Country Press, 1981. 304p.

A useful biographical dictionary of country music personalities, this comprehensive source provides a brief but informative biographical portrait of 716 individuals. These personalities are not limited to performers but include country music industry people such as publishers and record company executives. Biographies are brief and highly stylized in length and coverage, but do an adequate job in identifying and describing individuals. Pictures are included as well. Recording artists, studio musicians, disc jockeys, composers, agents, etc., are listed, although the emphasis is, of course, on the performers. There are excellent listings of 2,000 radio stations, record companies, publishers, talent agencies, and award winners. *The Illustrated Encyclopedia of Country Music*, by Fred Dellar and others (Harmony Books/Crown, 1977) is a biographical dictionary written in a light fashion and covers approximately 450 performers in adequate detail. It is a chatty, well-illustrated, enjoyable tool.

559.   **Who's Who in Rock Music.** William York. New York, Scribner's, 1982. 413p.

This serves as an excellent source for identification of rock musicians of every type and represents a vast array of musical talents who had performed in recording sessions. There are over 12,000 alphabetically arranged entries for solo performers, groups, and studio musicians. Information is up-to-date and represents a doubling in size of the number of entries from the previous edition in 1978. Entries for individuals include name, instrument, birth and death dates, group association and dates, sessions played, and discography. Entries for groups furnish similar information and name changes of the group through the years. It is considered an indispensable source for its comprehensive coverage. *The Rock Who's Who: A Biographical Dictionary and Critical Discography*, by Brock Helander (Schirmer Books/Macmillan, 1982) furnishes the rock fan with an excellent biographical source on the lives of 300 individuals including disc jockeys, music industry people, songwriters, and performers. Inclusion is selective and implies a significant contribution to the development of contemporary popular music. Possibly of most importance are the excellent detailed discographies following each biographical sketch.

560.   **Who's Who of Jazz: Storyville to Swing Street.** 4th ed. John Chilton. New York, Da Capo, 1985. 375p.

This is an excellent and up-to-date listing of over 1,000 jazz personalities born before 1920 and raised in the United States. Biographies vary in length with the prominence of the individual and range from a brief paragraph to two full pages. Emphasis is placed on the person's career and musical development rather than his or her personal life. A section with photographs and a list of jazz periodicals arranged by country of publication are included.

Leonard Feather provided an excellent series of biographical dictionaries keyed to different decades. *The Encyclopedia of Jazz* (Horizon, 1960) was a revised edition of an earlier work and furnished biographies and illustrations of more than 2,000 performers of that time, with a guide to their recordings. *The Encyclopedia of Jazz in the Sixties* (Horizon, 1966) updated its predecessor; and Feather and Ira Gitler collaborated on *The Encyclopedia of Jazz in the Seventies* (Horizon, 1976). This volume extends the coverage of the series from 1966 to 1975 and adds lists of jazz films and recordings.

Recordings

Discographies or lists of recordings are of prime importance to both specialists and afficionados and compose a prolific segment of the reference literature. They are done on a variety of topics representing musical forms, schools, types, and individual composers and performers. Generally, they are arranged by name of performer when they are not the subject of the discography. Only a few are given here.

561. **American Premium Record Guide, 1915-65: 78's, 45's, and LP's Identification and Values.** 3rd ed. L. R. Docks. Florence, Ala., Books Americana; distr., Rutland, Vt., Charles E. Tuttle, 1986. 378p.

This is an especially useful discography and guide to the recordings of popular music over a fifty-year period. It covers a variety of record types, as enumerated in the title, but is limited to the disc format. The recordings are divided into four major styles: jazz/big band, blues, country and western, and rhythm and blues. The jazz/big band section receives the most coverage, closely followed by rhythm and blues, which includes rock and roll. Entries are listed by name of performer and provide valuations as well as identification, making this an extremely valuable and comprehensive source for record collectors. The tool includes a glossary of terms and valuable hints for collecting and understanding the market.

562. **Bibliography of Discographies.** 1977- . New York, R. R. Bowker. (In progress).

This valuable listing of discographies has been planned in five volumes, each of which is dedicated to a different category or type of music. Volume 1, *Classical Music, 1925-1975*, by Michael H. Gray and Gerald D. Gibson, was issued in 1977 and listed over 3,000 discographies of serious concert music under the name of the composers or performers or subject of the efforts. Entries provide name of compiler and imprint of book or periodical title, whichever is the source, but do not indicate the quality or comprehensiveness of the discography. Coverage embraces works in all European languages. Volume 2, *Jazz*, by Daniel Allen, appeared in 1981 and identified more than 3,500 discographies of jazz, blues, ragtime, gospel, and rhythm and blues published between 1935 and 1980. Although there are a few variations, the general format and arrangement parallels those of the first volume. Volume 3, *Popular Music*, by Gray, was published in 1983 and covers rock music; motion picture and stage show music; country, old time, and bluegrass music; and finally, the pop music of balladeers and orchestral themes up to 1982. Yet to come is volume 4, to deal with ethnic and folk music, and volume 5, general discographies. *The Journal of the Association for Recorded Sound Collections* has been supplementing the volumes through its column "Bibliography of Discographies."

563. **The Cash Box/Black Contemporary Singles Charts, 1960-1984.** George Albert and Frank Hoffman. Metuchen, N.J., Scarecrow, 1986. 704p.

Formerly called rhythm and blues, black contemporary music appeals to an ever-growing audience of white Americans. *Cash Box* magazine has treated the music in a variety of ways over the past twenty-five years. Its listings were fragmented and scattered in different sections and under different categories. This work follows a format established by these authors in previous publications on pop and country music, and makes the weekly chart information of twenty-five years of listings easy to find and convenient to use. Arrangement is alphabetical by performers, with a list of recorded songs alphabetically organized under their names. Entries provide name of song, date of entry onto the chart, record label and number, weekly position, and total weeks on the chart. Another alphabetical listing of song titles includes cross-references to the performers. Additional interesting information is given in the appendices. A recent discography on an individual is *Count Basie: A Bio-Discography*, by Chris Sheridan (Greenwood Press, 1986). It provides detailed listings of Basie's recordings from 1929 to 1984. These, of course, cover a wide spectrum of musical types and forms, and number about 1,000 sessions.

564. International Discography of Women Composers. Aaron I. Cohen, comp. Westport, Conn., Greenwood Press, 1984. 254p.

The increased interest in the contributions of females to society and culture has led to the production of several reference sources in the field of music, and Cohen has been a leader in this regard (see entry 550). This discography furnishes listings of the recorded music of 468 women composers of concert music. It is hoped that with efforts like this, there will be an increased awareness, not only of the quantity but of the quality of much of this work, so that it is more frequently performed. The entries are arranged alphabetically by name of composer, under which the recordings are listed along with performers, instruments, record label and number, and dates and nationality of composer. There is a directory of record companies, and there are lists of composers by country of origin and by instrument and form. Treatment of composers is comprehensive, dating from the twelfth century to the present day. There is an index of titles to provide access.

565. Jazz Records 1897-1942: Fifth Revised and Enlarged Edition. Brian Rust. Chigwell, Essex, Storyville Publications, 1982. 2v.

Considered the standard source for both music librarians and devotees, the fifth edition of this title is an update, correction, and extension of earlier versions. It lists over 30,000 jazz recordings by American and British artists in standard format, arranged by name of performer. Entries include personnel, instruments, and listing of recording sessions. Information is given about the matrix number, label, and catalog issue number (78s only), with indication of vocals. A song index covers over 16,000 titles and an artist index includes over 10,000 band leaders, musicians, singers, and arrangers. There are numerous cross-references to clarify obscure pseudonyms. Since publication of *The Complete Entertainment Discography from the Mid-1890's to 1942* by Rust and Allen G. Debus in 1973, and *The American Dance Band Discography, 1917-1942* by Rust in 1976, the jazz discography now more closely restricts the entries to jazz and blues recordings. A major foreign contribution that supplements this work is *Jazz Records, 1942-1965 —1942-1969: A Discography*, by Jorge Grunnet Jepsen (Holte, Denmark, K. E. Knudsen, 1963-1970). This is a detailed compilation of jazz records in eight volumes. It is much respected for its comprehensiveness.

566. Popular & Rock Price Guide for 45's: The Little Record with the Big Hole. 3rd ed. Jerry Osborne. Phoenix, Ariz., O'Sullivan Woodside; distr., Aurora, Ill., Caroline House, 1981. 168p.

This compact little work from a small publishing house continues to be regarded as an excellent source of information for both music librarians and collectors. The new edition has eliminated all 78s, treated in a superficial way in the preceding issue, which bore a different title (*Popular and Rock Records Price Guide 1948-1978*, 2nd edition, 1978). The more recent volume continues coverage of the thirty years prior to publication but lists about 50,000 45s, a substantial increase over the previous edition. Arrangement is alphabetical by artist and entries furnish title, label, number, and current price (dependent upon condition). The emphasis is on those records deemed to be collectible rather than on a comprehensive discography in the field, and reissues are noted only if they have value to collectors. Quite different is Felix Aeppli's *Heart of Stone: The Definitive Rolling Stones Discography, 1962-1983* (Pierian, 1985) which aims to list in chronological order all musical recordings of the group "that found their way onto record or film." There are over 4,000 entries including bootlegs and unverified recordings. The information provided is standard (recording dates, songs, format, location, producers, composers, release date, etc.).

567. Popular Music: An Annotated Guide to Recordings. Dean Tudor. Littleton, Colo., Libraries Unlimited, 1983. 647p.

This represents an update and revision of the separate buying guides by Dean Tudor and Nancy Tudor issued in 1979: *Black Music; Grass Roots Music; Jazz;* and *Contemporary Popular Music.* These appeared as a four-part set entitled American Popular Music on Elpee, and each generally provided a listing of between 1,000 and 2,000 recordings published on long-playing discs and tapes. The volumes began with a common introductory essay on popular music and concluded with directory listings and useful bibliographies. Priorities in purchasing were identified. The new edition continues in the same tradition but consolidates the four volumes into one and provides updates in all areas. The criteria remain the same and reflect largely the record's impact, influence, and prominence. This appears to be a successful effort, albeit not without some losses. It represents a sensible approach to collection development through the provision of a more convenient packaging of information.

568. Schwann Compact Disc Catalog. 1985- . Mo. New York, ABC Consumer Magazines.

The *Schwann* catalogs have been popular guides to available recordings since the initial appearance of the basic guide in 1949, *Schwann Long Playing Record Catalog.* Since that time, the work has undergone several name changes and changes of scope, but always has been highly regarded as a comprehensive source of purchasing information on thousands of sound recordings, both disc and tape, available from hundreds of record distributors and publishers. Classical, popular, rock, jazz, country, opera, ballet, and electronic music recordings are all included. Compact discs were originally covered on a quarterly basis in addition to the monthly catalog featuring LPs. With the growing emphasis in the industry on CDs, however, the *Schwann Catalog* has included greater coverage of them. Since July 1986, it has provided listings of new releases of CD, LP, and cassette recordings on a monthly basis, but is cumulative only for the CDs rather than the LPs. *Super Schwann* (New York, ABC Consumer Magazines) is issued on a quarterly basis and lists all recordings available in all formats and categories.

569. The World's Encyclopedia of Recorded Music. Francis F. Clough and G. J. Cuming. London, Sidgwick and Jackson; distr., New York, London Gramophone Corporation, 1952; repr., Westwood, Conn., Greenwood Press, 1970. 890p. (includes First Supp.). Second Supp. (1951-1952), 1953, 262p. Third Supp. (1953-1955), 1957, 564p.

This encyclopedia has long been considered a prime source of information on music recordings, as witnessed by its numerous reprintings over the years. Originally based on an older work, it provides a comprehensive listing of all electrically recorded music of permanent interest (concert music) up to the time of publication. It is not limited to recordings that are available but includes identification of those items that have been discontinued as well. A work of great magnitude, the main text and supplements cover the period up to 1955. They embrace music and recordings from all countries of the world. There is detailed bibliographic information on each entry, which may include identification of certain parts, although there are no annotations. It has been highly commended from the time of its initial appearance for its thoroughness, comprehensiveness, and convenience of use.

DANCE

Bibliographies, Catalogs, and Indexes

570.   **Ballet in England: A Bibliography and Survey, c. 1700-June 1966.** Sheila Felicitée Forrester. London, Library Association, 1968. 224p. (Library Association Bibliographies, No. 9).

This bibliography of resource items has been an important reference tool since its appearance nearly twenty years ago. It covers ballet over a period of 266 years, ending just prior to year of publication. It is a classified and annotated listing which identifies 664 documents on a wide range of topics and issues pertinent to the study of English ballet. The appendices include a guide for further study and a list of exhibitions. An analytical index of names, titles, and subjects provides good access to bibliographic information. An older bibliography not restricted to writings on the ballet is Cyril William Beaumont's *A Bibliography of Dancing* (London, Dancing Times, 1929; repr., New York, Blom, 1963). This is an annotated bibliography of 422 entries, arranged alphabetically by author, and compiled from the holdings of the British Library. Access is furnished through a detailed subject index.

571.   **A Bibliography of Dancing: A List of Books and Articles on the Dance and Related Subjects.** Paul David Magriel. New York, H. W. Wilson, 1936; repr., New York, Blom, 1966. 229p. Supp. 1936-1940, 1941.

This comprehensive bibliography on all aspects of the dance has been a standard work and is still considered an important tool in spite of its age. It covers dance and related areas of music, decoration, costume, masques, mime, and pantomime, and furnishes over 4,300 items which include documents relating to folk dance and ballet. Many rare and uncommon books are identified and their locations are given in the Library of Congress, Harvard, Boston Public Library, and New York Public Library. Periodical literature is also included, some of which is relatively obscure; thus the work has been and continues to be an important resource for scholarship. The arrangement of entries is classified by subject with some, but not many, annotations. There is an author and subject index.

572.   **A Bibliography of the Dance Collection of Doris Nyles and Serge Leslie.** Serge Leslie and Doris Nyles. Annotated by Serge Leslie. Edited by Cyril Beaumont. London, C. W. Beaumont, 1966-1981; repr., London, Dance Books, 1981. 4v.

From the time of its original appearance in the 1960s, this small-scale publication of the holdings of a private collection has been regarded as a valuable bibliography. It covers 2,000 items related to the dance. The most recent reprint of this work continues in the earlier tradition of restrictive printing, since it also is a limited edition of only 525 copies. Regardless of the relatively few copies available through the years, the work has been considered a real asset in identifying useful source materials. The emphasis is on the ballet, but folk dancing and social dancing are included as well. The arrangement is alphabetical by author, with volume 1 covering A-K and volume 2, L-Z. Each volume has an index which provides subject access. Volumes 3-4 were published by Dance Books and cover mainly twentieth-century publications.

573.   **Dictionary Catalog of the Dance Collection ...** New York Public Library. Boston, G. K. Hall, 1974. 10v. Ann. Supp., 1976- .

The complete title of this work goes on to describe it as "a List of Authors, Titles, and Subjects of Multi-media Materials in the Dance Collection of the Performing Arts Research Center of the New York Public Library." As it has done for other important specialized collections, G. K. Hall has produced a listing of catalog cards based on the cataloging done prior to October 1973. The catalog includes some 300,000 entries for nearly 10,000 items, as well as relevant materials in other parts and divisions of NYPL. Included are books, periodicals, playbills, letters, pamphlets, manuscripts, films, scrapbooks, tapes, and dance scores. Some of the entries have detailed descriptions of contents. The work is considered to be an especially strong collection on folk dance and religious and ritualistic dance. *The Bibliographic Guide to Dance* has continued the coverage as an annual supplement listing material cataloged during the preceding year.

574. **Guide to Dance Periodicals.** 1931-1962. Frequency varies. Gainesville, Fla., University of Florida.

This was one of the few specialized indexes in the field of dance, and was a respected publication for over thirty years. It was then incorporated into the *Guide to the Performing Arts* (see entry 424) as one of the important additions to that more comprehensive publication. Over a span of thirty years, the specialized index varied in frequency, beginning with a series of four quinquennial editions, 1931/1935-1946/1950. Subsequently, its appearance was biennial from 1951/1952 to the final issue in 1961/1962. Although criticized for lack of promptness, it was an excellent index of nineteen periodicals by subject and author, compiled by S. Yancey Belknap. There was a separate index of illustrations.

Dictionaries, Encyclopedias, and Handbooks

DANCE IN GENERAL

575. **The Book of the Dance.** Agnes De Mille. New York, Golden Press, 1963. 252p.

This is one of the important tools in the field and has been regarded as a real asset to the library collection by both librarians and their patrons. It is a first-rate reference work providing historical background, encyclopedic exposition, and excellent biographies. De Mille has been praised for her style and writing ability in creating a work of high quality and versatile character. It is divided into three major sections: ritual and social dance, theater and ballet, and choreography. Various topics, issues, personalities, and subjects are treated in an interesting and informative manner. All periods of time and many countries are considered, and many definitions are provided. Biographies of performers are brief, but informative, and the illustrations are excellent.

576. **The Dance Encyclopedia.** Rev. and enl. ed. Anatole Chujoy and Phyllis Winifred Manchester, comps. New York, Simon & Schuster, 1967. 992p.

Originally published in 1949, this title has earned the respect and admiration of both specialists and dance buffs. The revised edition just about doubled the original size, and it furnishes about 5,000 entries covering all phases of the dance. Ballet is emphasized, and there are more features, topics, and personalities relating to this form than is true of the others. The various dance forms are given the most extensive treatment, with longer survey articles written by specialists. Many of the articles are signed. Included in the same alphabetical arrangement are brief biographies of personalities, types of dances, definitions of terms, etc. Individual ballets are covered, and entries furnish synopses, choreographers, designers, composers, original casts, and performance dates. This work is considered especially strong in coverage of American ballet.

577. **Dictionary of the Dance.** W. G. Raffé, comp. New York, A. S. Barnes; distr., London, T. Yoseloff, 1964; repr., 1975. 583p.

Always considered a comprehensive source of information on dance and dancing, this continues to be one of the important reference tools. All countries and time periods are included, and coverage is excellent for specific dances and dance types. There are over

5,000 entries alphabetically arranged. Information covers development and origin as well as form and technique. It is especially strong on folk and ethnic dances; coverage is aided by a geographical index which arranges the dances by country. No biographies are included, but the work is heavily illustrated with a variety of pictures. There is a comprehensive bibliography of items from the fifteenth century to the present, and a subject index facilitates access.

578. **The Encyclopedia of Dance and Ballet.** Mary Clarke and David Vaughan, eds. London, Pitman; distr., New York, G. P. Putnam, 1977. 376p.

The emphasis of this work is on contemporary dance styles as well as classical ballet. Since it is ten years younger than *The Dance Encyclopedia* (see entry 576), it is able to provide more recent information. The focus of the work is on dance, which has been raised to a theatrical level in any of the media of the twentieth century. Entries cover a variety of topics including individual dancers, companies, choreographers, individual ballets, and different dance types. There are over 2,000 entries prepared by specialists from various countries, and more than 200 illustrations. Major developments are identified with an emphasis on recent changes. There are a glossary of technical terms and a general bibliography.

579. **Theatre in the East: A Survey of Asian Dance and Drama.** Faubion Bowers. New York, Nelson, 1956; repr., Salem, N.H., Ayer, 1980. 374p.

This is an extensive survey of the dances of fourteen different countries or regions, each of which is treated in an individual chapter. Illustrations are abundant and some are taken from the work of *Life* magazine photographers. Hailed as a great asset to both specialists and laypersons who wish to study or travel to the Orient, the work provides historical overviews and excellent descriptions of folk, traditional, and modern dances in India, Ceylon (Sri Lanka), Burma, Thailand, Cambodia, Laos, Malaysia, Indonesia, Philippines, China, Vietnam, Hong Kong, Okinawa, and Japan. The author and his wife visited these areas, and have produced an impressive and attractive guide.

BALLET

580. **Ballet Guide: Background Listings, Credits and Descriptions of More Than Five Hundred of the World's Major Ballets.** Walter Terry. New York, Dodd, Mead, 1976; repr., 1982. 388p.

Based somewhat on an earlier work by the author, this handbook provides brief synopses and identifications of 500 important ballets. In addition to synopses, the tool furnishes historical information, dates of first performance, choreographers, composers, scenery and costume designers, ballet company, principal dancers in first performances, and major recreations of roles. The synopses themselves are well done and informative, and the additional background information is highly useful. The arrangement of entries is alphabetical by the title of the ballet, and the work is well illustrated. It covers ballet on an international level. A glossary of terms and a good index are included.

581. **Complete Book of Ballets: A Guide to the Principal Ballets of the Nineteenth and Twentieth Centuries.** Rev. ed. Cyril William Beaumont. London, G. P. Putnam, 1951; repr., 1956. 1106p.

This has been considered a vital reference work since its initial appearance in 1938. It provides comprehensive coverage of nearly 200 important ballets over a period of 150 years. Entries are arranged chronologically under the names of the choreographers, and furnish excellent descriptions of the stories. Also included is information about authors of the themes or sources, costume and scenery designers, composers, as well as a listing of the original casts. A useful feature is excerpts from the reviews of the first performances. Those ballets which debuted in London, Paris, or St. Petersburg were given preference for inclusion, and both classic works and contemporary contributions are covered. Supplements to the original work appeared in 1945, 1954, and 1955. A more recent guide written with a similar purpose is *The Ballet Goer's Guide*, by Mary Clarke and Clement Crisp (Random House, 1981). It applies a British perspective to the coverage of nearly 150 of today's most frequently performed ballets. Included is information on choreography, plot, and historical background, and it contains numerous illustrations, some of which are in color. Descriptions are lively and cogent, and the work is important to ballet enthusiasts.

582.   **Complete Stories of the Great Ballets**. Rev. and enl. ed. George Balanchine. New York, Doubleday, 1977. 838p.

   This is a leading handbook of ballet synopses because of its detailed and comprehensive coverage. Originally published in 1954 with a revision in 1968, none of its three editions have had the same title. The latest edition covers over 400 ballets, either of classic stature and of lasting importance, or significant and written in the past twenty-five years. The main part consists of stories and reviews by Balanchine, followed by sections on history, chronology and careers; an essay on how to enjoy the ballet; and notes on dancers, dancing, and choreography. There are an illustrated glossary, an annotated section on ballet records, and a general bibliography. A detailed analytical index facilitates access.

583.   **The Concise Oxford Dictionary of Ballet**. 2nd ed. Horst Koegler. New York, Oxford University Press, 1982. 459p.

   Since its first appearance in English in 1977, this tool (based on an earlier German work) has come to be regarded as a first-rate reference book providing brief and informative descriptions, identifications, and definitions. The new edition does not supersede the older work inasmuch as many entries from the original effort have been deleted to create a more compact and more convenient volume. New subjects and topics of interest have been added, making this easily the most up-to-date ballet dictionary. Many of the entries furnish bibliographical references for further reading on the topic, and various personalities are covered. Possibly more coverage could have been given to the younger and recently successful individuals, since the emphasis on established stars duplicates much of what is available elsewhere. Coverage is comprehensive and the whole spectrum of ballet is considered, with treatment given to modern and ethnic dance.

584.   **A Dictionary of Ballet**. 3rd ed. George Buckley Wilson. London, Cassell, 1974. 539p.

   This highly useful dictionary furnishes about 2,500 entries on a variety of topics and issues pertinent to the study of ballet. Originally published as a Penguin imprint in 1957, it was revised in 1961. The most recent edition represents a substantial revision and update of terms and topics. Included in the coverage are such aspects as history; choreography; individual ballets; stage design; ballet companies; and biographies of leading dancers, composers, and choreographers. Ballet is treated in a broad sense since there is coverage of modern dance as well as Spanish and Indian dances. The emphasis is on classical ballet, however, and definitions and identifications relate primarily to ballet in Great Britain, France, West Germany, and the United States.

585.   **A Dictionary of Ballet Terms**. 3rd rev. ed. Leo Kersley and Janet Sinclair. London, A & C Black, 1977; repr., New York, Da Capo, 1981. 112p.

   This work has taken a turn toward the more technical side since its initial publication in 1952. At that time, it was meant for popular consumption, but more recently the definitions have appealed to a more sophisticated audience. It remains a compact little volume with several hundred entries; some of the definitions are lengthy and detailed. It brings together related terms, sometimes in its liberal use of cross-references, other times in treating several terms under a single subject heading. There are many line drawings which serve to illustrate a number of the techniques defined. Another useful tool is Gail Grant's *Technical Manual and Dictionary of Classical Ballet*, now in its third edition (Dover, 1982). Unlike the Kersley and Sinclair work, this one provides pronunciations as well as definitions of dance terms. It also furnishes line drawings of main positions.

586.   **A Dictionary of Modern Ballet.** Francis Gordon and Robert Maillard, eds. New York, Tudor, 1959. 360p.

Originally published in French in 1957, the English translation of this work has met with a warm reception from librarians and reviewers. Emphasis is on the ballet in the leading European countries and in the United States, and the purpose of the tool is to provide comprehensive coverage which includes history, repertoire, and personalities. This is done in one alphabetical arrangement which serves to identify ballets, organizations, companies, dancers, composers, and choreographers. Definitions of terms are not furnished. It has served well as a supplementary source to *The Dance Encyclopedia* (see entry 576) but is impressive in its own right for its illustrations, which are numerous and of high quality. There are nearly 700 entries providing good coverage of the field, although some notable omissions of personalities have been pointed out by reviewers.

587.   **The Guinness Guide to Ballet.** Oleg Kerensky. Enfield, England, Guinness Superlatives; distr., New York, Sterling Publishing, 1981. 224p.

Kerensky is a noted authority and writer on the subject of ballet and has succeeded in developing an interesting and comprehensive guide. The emphasis is on British and American ballet, although coverage is of international proportions. Brief treatment is given to a broad spectrum of aspects and considerations such as history, language, training of dancers, career, stars, music, costume and decoration, choreographers, etc. There are good, colorful illustrations, and a well-developed index provides access. An older work which has been a familiar reference tool in past years is *The International Book of Ballet*, by Peter Brinson and Clement Crisp (Stein and Day, 1971). The emphasis is on the ballets of thirty-eight major choreographers, under whose names are listed 115 different ballets grouped by period and type. This work covers a time period from the seventeenth century to the time of publication. A work must still be performed to have been included. There is a bias toward British choreographers among the contemporary contributors.

Directories, Annuals, and
Current Awareness Services

588.   **Dance Resources in Canadian Libraries.** Clifford Collier and Pierre Guilmette. Ottawa, National Library of Canada, 1982. various paging. (Research Collections in Canadian Libraries: Special Studies, No. 8).

This is an extensive survey of research and educational materials and centers available in Canada for the study of dance. It is bilingual (French/English), and provides a good state-of-the-art assessment, while serving as a tool for collection development for new and existing collections. There are five sections or parts, the first one dealing with the methodology used in the collection of data, followed by a historical overview in part 2. Part 3 furnishes a statistical summary identifying size of monograph and serial collections and presence of nonbook collections in Canadian libraries arranged by province, while the final section considers observations and suggestions for the future. Appendices identify serials available in Canada, reference works related to dance, and a directory of colleges and other postsecondary institutions which offer diplomas or degrees. There is a list of collections by province with numerical information on holdings and an index.

589. **Dance World.** 1966-1979. Ann. New York, Crown.

The fourteen volumes that were issued in this annual survey of the New York dance season before it ceased publication are still regarded as a vital collective resource in reference work. It was similar to *Theatre World* (see entry 635) in the use of illustration, arrangement, and format. Each volume provided an excellent pictorial overview, including much useful information on the season just completed (June 1 to May 31). Although the focus was on the New York stage, there was some coverage of other companies and productions, with a section on regional U.S. companies. Also included were lists of personnel of various companies, repertoires, opening and closing dates, cast lists for dance events, festivals, and biographies of choreographers and key performers. Both dance scenes and individuals were highlighted in the high-quality photographs.

590. **Dancemagazine.** 1927- . Mo. New York, Dance Magazine.

This is the most popular and widely known dance periodical in the country, with a circulation of about 65,000. It began life as the *American Dancer* in 1927 and was absorbed into *Dancemagazine* in 1942. Today it is an excellent current awareness tool providing coverage of dance activities throughout the world. An important monthly calendar is impressive in its comprehensiveness and attention to detail. Another important feature for reference work is the directory of dance schools. Articles cover all aspects of the subject, including information on performers, tours, costumes, dance companies, etc. Excellent photographs contribute to the informational qualities of this periodical. *National Square Dance Directory* (National Square Dance Directory, 1979-) has varied in frequency from annual to biennial, but has consistently provided a listing of square dancing clubs arranged by state, then alphabetically by city. Entries include title, type of club, level of dancing, persons in charge, location of dance, and addresses and telephone numbers. Coverage is not limited to the United States, but includes various groups around the world on several continents. It includes square dancing, round dancing, clogging, and contra clubs.

Histories

591. **Dance.** Jack Anderson. New York, Newsweek Books, 1979. 160p.

This is the first trade paperback edition based on the hardbound issue in 1974. Jack Anderson, a long-time dance critic and writer, prepared a history of dance as part of a series covering areas of the arts and humanities (music, theater, painting, architecture, etc.). His cogent, well-designed work traces the development of dance from the ritualistic stages to today's intricate choreography of modern and classical styles. This is an excellent introduction to dance with many illustrations, some of which are in color. Coverage runs from the latter part of the sixteenth century to the mid-1970s, with an excellent selection of both artists and techniques. The major performers are given biographical coverage; a useful chronology identifies dance events along with historical phenomena.

592. **The Dance in America.** Rev. ed. Walter Terry. New York, Harper & Row, 1971; repr., New York, Da Capo, 1981. 272p.

This work has been judged to be of exceptional importance. The complete history of the American contribution is chronicled, along with illustrations and excellent descriptions of the work of people like Isadora Duncan, Ted Shawn, and Martha Graham. A recognized expert in the field who served as the dance critic of the *New York Herald*

Tribune, the author has published widely. Beginning with the earliest developments in this country, he furnishes excellent descriptions of European and Oriental influences and surveys all periods to the present day. There are biographies of leading performers, and coverage is given to ethnic dancers, black dance, and the regional ballet movement. It continues to be a much-used and highly popular work.

593. **World History of the Dance.** Curt Sachs. New York, W. W. Norton, 1937; repr., 1973. 224p.

This has been an important contribution from the Norton Company ever since it was translated in 1937 from a German work completed in 1933. It is a successful attempt to categorize and describe the development of dance through an interpretation of its forms, themes, and steps from antiquity to the present day. Emphasis is on sociological conditions attached to dance origins and the significance of religion, war, fertility, or social dance within the time frames presented. Another useful tool is Selma Jeanne Cohen's *Dance as a Theatre Art* (Dodd, Mead, 1974; repr., London, Dance Books, 1977) which provides a selection of important writings on dance. Introductions have been prepared for each of the documents, the selection of which represents exemplary planning.

Biographical Sources

594. **Biographical Dictionary of Dance.** Barbara Naomi Cohen-Stratyner. New York, Schirmer Books/Macmillan, 1982. 970p. (A Dance Horizons Book).

Nearly 3,000 figures are described in this most comprehensive of biographical dictionaries. Included are individuals representing all aspects of dance and performance such as performers, choreographers, composers, impresarios, designers, theorists, and teachers. They span a period of 400 years in both Europe and America. Entries are alphabetical and furnish personal and career information including education, training, development, and accomplishments, with special attention given to roles and choreographical productions. All forms of dance are covered in various theatrical styles (opera, ballet, striptease, Broadway musical, etc.) and even include television variety performances. Obviously, the greatest value of a comprehensive work of this type is to shed light on some of the obscure and little-known personalities for whom information is difficult to locate.

595. **The Complete Guide to Modern Dance.** Don McDonough. Garden City, N.Y., Doubleday, 1976. 534p.

The emphasis of this work is on the choreographers, and over 100 are covered in detail on a variety of levels. Material is arranged in a chronological sequence of five periods, beginning with the forerunners of modern dance and culminating with contemporary contributions. Choreographers are arranged alphabetically within the time frames. Entries furnish a biographical sketch, accompanied by descriptions of one or more of the major works along with a chronology of all the person's works. The appendix contains a general chronology of significant dates and events in the development of modern dance. There is also a bibliography with additional readings, and a general index provides access.

THEATER AND DRAMA

Bibliographic Guides

596. **The American Stage to World War I: A Guide to Information Sources.** Don B. Wilmeth. Detroit, Gale, 1978. 269p. (Performing Arts Information Guide Series; v. 4).

This annotated literature guide furnishes "balanced" rather than thorough coverage of the American theater as a purveyor of entertainment, as well as a business and producer of drama. There are sections on general works of reference, history (both general and local), actors and acting, other personalities associated with the American theater, scenery and lighting, foreign-language theater in this country, and popular theater. Primarily a listing of secondary and tertiary sources, the work will not measurably aid the scholar, but will provide the fledgling or undergraduate with a good starting point. There are listings of guides to theater collections, both current and suspended periodicals, and author, title, and subject indexes.

597. **A Guide to Reference and Bibliography for Theatre Research.** 2nd ed. rev. and exp. Claudia Jean Bailey. Columbus, Ohio, Publications Committee, Ohio State University, 1983. 149p.

An annotated guide to a broad range of materials available to students and researchers in the field, this tool is divided into two major sections. The first part represents general reference, standard tools, national bibliography, library catalogs, indexes of periodicals and newspapers, and lists of dissertations. The second section covers theater and drama and furnishes more specialized materials. Emphasis is on British and American theater. Arrangement in both sections is classified with entries by author, geographical location, or chronological sequence. Over 650 titles are included, with publication dates up to mid-1979. There is an author-title index.

598. **The Puppeteer's Library Guide: The Bibliographic Index to the Literature of the World's Puppet Theatre.** Frances J. Crothers. Metuchen, N.J., Scarecrow, 1971-1983. 2v.

Originally projected as a six-volume set, twelve years passed between publication of the first two volumes. Volume 1 treats the historical background of puppetry and identifies all types of materials available on the subject. The collections of nearly forty libraries served as the basis or source of the titles. There are a historical overview of world puppetry, a listing of bibliographies on the subject, a history of puppets, and a description of the Punch and Judy drama throughout the world. Most important is the listing by country of published materials. Organizations, periodicals, and guides are enumerated. Volume 2 treats the puppet as an educator and focuses on twentieth-century English-language materials. Again, coverage of materials is comprehensive and includes articles, serials, monographs, chapters in books, theses, and dissertations. Some entries are annotated.

PERIODICALS

599. **American Theatrical Periodicals, 1789-1967: A Bibliographical Guide.** Carl Joseph Stratman. Durham, N.C., Duke University Press, 1970. 133p.

This guide lists nearly 700 titles of serials of all kinds from dailies to annuals, and includes directories published over a period of more than 175 years. These represent the publications of 122 cities in thirty-one states. Locations are given in nearly 140 libraries in the United States and Canada, and include even the British Library. Arranged chronologically by year of initial issue, then alphabetically by title, the entries list original title, editor, place of publication, publisher with address, frequency, notes on missing issues, dates of first and last issue, changes in title, etc. Includes index of titles and names. This is a companion work to *A Bibliography of British Dramatic Periodicals, 1720-1960* (see entry 600).

600. A Bibliography of British Dramatic Periodicals, 1720-1960. Carl Joseph Stratman. New York, New York Public Library, 1962. 58p.

The author was a distinguished bibliographer in the field of theater and drama. His untimely death in 1972 ended a period of extensive productivity in providing researchers, specialists, and students with useful listings in both English and American theater studies. This work serves as a companion to the more recent *American Theatrical Periodicals, 1789-1967* (see entry 599). It furnishes 674 titles of British periodicals over a span of 240 years. It is a compact volume which arranges the entries chronologically, giving locations of complete files in both American and British libraries. A variety of periodicals is covered, and for those libraries that have the bibliography, it remains a useful resource item.

Bibliographies, Catalogs, and Indexes

601. Bibliography of Medieval Drama. 2nd ed., rev. and enl. Carl J. Stratman. New York, Ungar, 1972. 2v.

This is one of Stratman's most important works, updating the initial edition published in 1954. It is arranged in ten sections (primarily geographical) which cover general studies, festschriften, liturgical, Latin drama, English drama, Byzantine drama, French drama, German drama, Italian drama, Low Countries drama, and Spanish drama. Many plays are identified in manuscripts, published texts, and various editions. Works about them from a variety of sources, books, articles, and dissertations are also listed. Devised primarily to aid the student of English drama, it should be considered only supplementary to any specialized bibliographies on any of the countries covered. There are over 9,000 entries, with library locations given for manuscripts and book material. Entries provide author, title, imprint, pagination, etc., with asterisks marking the most important works. A general index provides access.

602. Catalog of the Theatre and Drama Collections. New York Public Library. The Research Libraries. Boston, G. K. Hall, 1967-1976. 51v. Supp. to Part I, *Drama Collection*, 1973. 548p. Supp. to Part II, *Theatre Collection*, 1973. 2v. Ann. Supp., 1976- .

Another of the important contributions to reference and research by G. K. Hall is this massive reproduction of the card catalog of this outstanding collection of theater and drama materials established in 1931. Publication of this catalog has been in several parts, related to different components of the collection. Parts I and II were published in 1967. Part I, *Drama Collection: Author Listing* (6v.) and *Listing by Cultural Origin* (6v.), consists of 120,000 entries for plays published separately or in anthologies and even periodicals. Part II, *Theatre Collection: Books on the Theatre*, has over 120,000 entries from over 23,500 volumes relating to all aspects of the theater (history, biography, acting, etc.). A 548-page supplement to part I and a two-volume supplement to part II were published in 1973. Part III, *Non-Book Collection*, was published in thirty volumes in 1975 and represents over 740,000 cards on such items as programs, photographs, portraits, press clippings, etc. Coverage for parts I and II has been continued by an annual supplement, *Bibliographic Guide to Theatre Arts*, appearing since 1976. This lists materials newly cataloged by the New York Public Library with additional entries furnished from the Library of Congress MARC tapes.

603. Cumulated Dramatic Index, 1909-1949. A Cumulation of the F. W. Faxon Company's Dramatic Index ... Boston, G. K. Hall, 1965. 2v.

A most useful identification and verification tool is this cumulation of the forty-one volumes of *Dramatic Index*, which was issued separately and also as part two of the *Annual Magazine Subject Index* during those years. These annual indexes were themselves cumulations of a quarterly listing of *Dramatic Index* published in *Bulletin of Bibliography* on a continuous basis. The work contains references to articles about drama, theater, actors, actresses, synopses, reviews, and play texts. Articles are entered under subjects, texts of plays under title with cross-references from author, and costume portraits under actor and character. The appendices consist of several useful listings: author list of books about the theater, author list of play texts, and title list of play texts. It is a great convenience to have the forty-one years cumulated in a single work.

604. **International Bibliography of Theatre.** 1985- . Ann. New York, Theatre Research Data Center, Brooklyn College, City University of New York; distr., New York, Publishing Center for Cultural Resources.

This is a recently conceived, comprehensive annual bibliography of theater on an international basis. The year 1982 was covered initially in the 1985 publication, with 1983 coverage being issued in 1986. Regardless of the delay, this should prove to be a valuable source of information for students and specialists in locating information about all essential components and personalities related to theater. Aided by the computer, this work identifies periodical coverage in various languages (Catalan, English, French, German, Italian, Polish, Russian, the Scandinavian languages, and Spanish). Books published in Austria, Canada, England, France, East and West Germany, Italy, Poland, the U.S.S.R., Spain, and the United States are treated. Entries are classified by subject, and the subject index comprises the greatest part of the work.

605. **Theatre and Allied Arts: A Guide to Books Dealing with the History, Criticism, and Technic of the Drama and Theatre and Related Arts and Crafts.** Blanche M. Baker. New York, H. W. Wilson, 1952; repr., New York, Blom, 1967. 536p.

Still considered a vital work is this classified, annotated bibliography of some 6,000 books primarily in English with an American emphasis. These were published between 1885 and 1945, and at time of publication represented essentially a practical bibliography of readily available items. Although time has changed the nature of its use somewhat, and the materials are not so readily available as they once were, the work continues to be pressed into service as an identification and verification tool. It is divided into three parts: drama, theater, and actors; stagecraft and allied arts; and miscellaneous reference material. Each section is further divided by subject or geographic region. Entries provide author, title, imprint, pagination, and indication of illustrations. There are author and subject indexes.

BIBLIOGRAPHIES AND INDEXES OF PLAYS

606. **The Federal Theatre Project: A Catalog Calendar of Productions.** George Mason University. Fenwick Library. Westport, Conn., Greenwood Press, 1986. 349p. (Bibliographies and Indexes in the Performing Arts, No. 3).

Much has been written in recent years about the Federal Theatre Project, a product of the New Deal through the WPA. It was the only federally funded theater in this country and operated between 1935 and 1939, employing many professionals and helping young people to shape their careers. Hopes for a permanent national theater, unfortunately, were shattered by mounting criticism regarding its moral and political character. The materials from FTP were housed in the archives of George Mason University's Fenwick Library on indefinite loan from the Library of Congress and remained there for ten years between 1974 and 1984. This catalog calendar identifies nearly 2,800 individual productions, arranged alphabetically by title and including date and location of performance, theater, name of director or choreographer, etc. Materials in the collection are identified and indexed and include costume and set designs, playscripts, music, photographs, programs, etc.

607. **Index of Plays 1800-1926.** Ina Ten Eyck Firkins. New York, H. W. Wilson, 1927. 307p. Supp. 1927-1934, 1935. 140p.

An early commitment of the Wilson Company was the indexing of plays, and Firkins was one of the pioneers in this area. Her basic work is a comprehensive index of nearly 8,000 English-language plays by over 2,200 authors over a period of 126 years. The plays are identified with the name of anthology or other source provided. The first part is the author index, in which complete bibliographic information is provided for each entry and additional description is given of the number of acts and type (comedy or tragedy, etc.). The second part is a title and subject index with references to the author list. Firkins produced a supplement eight years later which identifies over 3,000 plays by over 1,300 authors. A more recent index is Gordon Samples's *The Drama Scholars' Index to Plays and Filmscripts: A Guide to Plays and Filmscripts in Selected Anthologies, Series, and Periodicals* (Scarecrow, 1974-1980). This work provides a balanced selection of plays from all periods and various parts of the world. It is useful primarily because many of the sources of plays have not been indexed elsewhere.

608. **Index to Full Length Plays, 1895 to 1925.** Ruth Gibbons Thomson. Boston, F. W. Faxon, 1956. 307p. Supp. 1926 to 1944, 1946.

This is another of the landmark indexes necessary to identify authors and titles in the field. An earlier effort by Thomson spanned the period 1926-1944 (F. W. Faxon, 1946). Ten years later, she produced this more extensive volume which preceded it in coverage, establishing the first publication as a supplement. Both titles overlap to some extent the coverage given by Firkins (see entry 607). Thomson's focus in both volumes is on full-length plays and the work provides a title index which includes author, translator, number of acts, number of characters, subject, and scene. There are author and subject indexes with references to the title index for full information. A bibliography identifies publishers and dates at the end. Norma Olin Ireland's *Index to Full Length Plays, 1944 to 1964* (F. W. Faxon, 1964) continues the coverage with another twenty years of indexing. There is a dictionary index of authors, subjects, and titles. Both anthologies and separate play texts are included.

609. **An Index to One-Act Plays.** Hannah Logasa and Winifred Ver Nooy. Boston, F. W. Faxon, 1924. 327p. (Useful Reference Series, No. 3). Supp. 1-5, 1933-1964, 5v.

Logasa was one of the pioneers of this century in indexing. Her early effort concentrated on one-act plays. Children's plays and adult plays are both included, as are both anthologies and separate publications. The basic volume covers plays published from 1900 to 1924. These are limited to English-language dramas but do include translations from foreign works. Each supplement continues the coverage, adding another eight to nine years of indexing up to 1964. The third supplement (1941-1948) adds radio plays, while the fourth and fifth supplements (1948-1964) include television plays as well. Access is provided by title, author, and subject indexes in each volume.

610.   **Index to Plays in Periodicals.** Rev. and exp. ed. Dean H. Keller. Metuchen, N.J., Scarecrow, 1979. 824p.

  This has been an important reference tool since it first appeared in 1971. The expanded edition is cumulative since it includes the nearly 7,500 entries from the first edition and its 1973 supplement along with 2,145 new citations. Thus, nearly 10,000 plays appearing in nearly 270 periodicals through 1976 are enumerated. There are two major sections. The first is an author listing which identifies the author's name and dates, title, brief description, number of acts, and volume and date of periodical. The second is a listing by title which provides references to the author entries. All types of plays in various languages are covered, and cross-references are given for joint authors, translators, etc. The work continues to serve as a valuable identification tool along with other indexes in the collection.

611.   **Ottemiller's Index to Plays in Collections: An Author and Title Index to Plays Appearing in Collections Published between 1900 and Early 1975.** 6th ed. Rev. and enl. by John M. Connor and Billie M. Connor. John Henry Ottemiller. Metuchen, N.J., Scarecrow, 1976. 523p.

  An old favorite among reference librarians is this index to plays appearing in anthologies. Since its initial appearance in 1943, the work has gained a position of prominence for those who must identify dramatic titles or authors. The present edition furnishes over 10,000 citations to nearly 3,700 plays by nearly 2,000 authors. More than 1,200 collections published either in England or the United States are identified. Plays are universal in nature, ranging from ancient to modern; excluded from coverage are collections of children's plays, amateur plays, one-act plays, holiday and anniversary plays, and radio and television plays. If plays of this type appear in an anthology which is indexed, then they are included in the listing. All plays are in the English language, and foreign translations are covered. Main entries are listed by author and the work concludes with a title index.

612.   **Play Index.** 1949/1952- . New York, H. W. Wilson.

  This continuing publication from the Wilson Company is the chief reason why some of the other indexes have ceased publication (see entries 608 and 609). Coverage at this point is from 1949 to 1982, and has been handled in six volumes which vary in frequency from four to eight years. Presently, it appears that a quinquennial pattern of appearance has taken root, with the last volume covering the period 1978-1982. Editorship has changed hands and the last volume was handled by Juliette Yaakov. The work itself is comprehensive and includes all types of plays from all types of sources, one-act plays, full-length plays, children's plays, either separately published or parts of collections. All are English-language items, but translations are included as are publishers from all over the world. Generally about 4,000 plays are covered in each volume, although there was a slight decline in the number in the latest volume. The main listing is a dictionary index of authors, titles, and subjects followed by a list of collections indexed. A cast analysis is provided which lists plays under gender of cast and number of characters. Finally, there is a directory of publishers. Heavily used in the past is Marietta Chicorel's *Chicorel Theater Index to Plays* (Chicorel, 1970-1976). The play index segments of this index series were issued in volumes 1, 2, 3, 8, 9, and 25, published between 1970 and 1976. They utilize over 3,000 anthologies and 150 periodicals to produce over 58,000 entries. Plays of all types, times, and countries are included. Volume 21 treats drama literature and identifies books and articles on all aspects of drama. Volumes 7, 7A, and 7B represent indexes to the spoken arts and cover recordings of play readings. A more recent work is Herbert H. Hoffman's *Recorded Plays:*

Indexes to Dramatists, Plays and Actors (American Library Association, 1985). This source may be of use to scholars and theater buffs in identifying various types of recorded plays (LPs primarily, but also cassettes, video, film, and other discs).

Dictionaries, Encyclopedias, and Handbooks

GENERAL

613. The Crown Guide to the World's Great Plays: From Ancient Greece to Modern Times. Rev., updated ed. Joseph T. Shipley. New York, Crown, 1984. 866p.

Since its initial edition in 1956, this has been regarded as an excellent source of information regarding what the editorship has deemed to be "great" plays. Coverage remains excellent for the total of 750 entries, many of which are newer types of drama such as the products of the "angry young men" and theater of the absurd pieces. Some older plays have been added when their impact has been noticed in the last few years. Of course, many entries previously listed were dropped; thus one might retain the earlier edition. One-act plays are included here as well as the Greek plays that have continued to be performed. For each entry is given story line, play history and production, excerpts from reviews, and notes on cast members. One may quibble with Shipley's definition of "great," which includes popular plays with lengthy runs, but one must agree that it is an indispensable source for those interested in theater and drama.

614. Drury's Guide to Best Plays. 3rd ed. James M. Salem. Metuchen, N.J., Scarecrow, 1978. 421p.

This standard work by F. W. Drury was first published in 1953, with the latest previous revision in 1969. It has established itself along with Shipley (see entry 613) as the best handbooks of their kind. The third edition by Salem continues in the excellent tradition of the earlier issues and furnishes approximately 1,600 play listings ranging from the Greek and Roman classics to recent Broadway hits. Only plays that appear in English (whether translated or not) are identified and no musical plays are included. This is a useful reference work for those planning or producing plays as well as those who purchase them for library collections. Entries provide author, title, date of first production or publication, publisher or anthology, royalty fee, synopsis, and identification of number of acts, sets, and actors. Indexes by cast, subject, and title with lists of award-winning plays and recommendations are included. The fourth edition of this work, again by Salem, is scheduled for appearance in mid-1987.

615. Enciclopedia dello spettacolo. Rome, Maschere, 1954-1962. 9v. Supp. 1955-1965, Rome, Unione Editoriale, 1966, 1292col.

The most comprehensive work in the field, there is nothing comparable to it in the English language. A heavily illustrated encyclopedia of the "spectacle," which includes a wide range of entertainments (theater, opera, ballet, motion pictures, vaudeville, the circus, etc.). Good, in-depth information (unfortunately, in Italian) is given about all aspects, including performers, authors, composers, directors, designers, types of entertainment, dramatic themes, historical and technical subjects, organizations and companies, and place names. Contributions are from an international roster of authorities, and coverage ranges from antiquity to the present day. The ten-year supplement supersedes an earlier supplement on the cinema done in 1963. (The illustrations are retained.) The newer supplement is primarily a biographical dictionary of contemporary personalities not covered in the main set. A later addition (1968) is an index of titles of works mentioned in the main set and in the supplement.

616. The Encyclopedia of World Theater: With 420 Illustrations and an Index of Play Titles. New York, Scribner's, 1977. 320p.

Martin Esslin, noted theater critic and author, has prepared an amplified and expanded version of a German reference work published in 1969. The present volume presents an excellent overview and furnishes brief entries for various personalities (actors, actresses, playwrights, directors, designers) and various facets of the theater. The 400 illustrations are of scenes, theaters, and individuals and add an excellent visual dimension to the useful narrative. Coverage is better for Continental Europe than is true of most works of this type. Most issues and phenomena are treated in a more catholic manner, although many German-oriented entries were deleted in favor of those of more importance to the English-speaking world. There are about 2,000 entries, many of which contain bibliographical references. An index to play titles (mentioned in the articles) and illustration credits provide additional access.

617. An International Directory of Theatre Language. Joel Trapido, et al. Westport, Conn., Greenwood Press, 1985. 1032p.

Considered by reviewers to be an excellent choice because of its scope and depth of coverage, this is the most recent dictionary of theater terminology. Coverage is broad, with approximately 15,000 terms described, two-thirds of which come from the English language. The remainder represent terms derived from sixty foreign languages. Selection of foreign terms was limited to those that have been used in English-language theater publications in a romanized form. The terminology spans theater history from ancient times to the present day. Entries identify language, literal meaning, and definition. Some entries include additional description with references to supporting documents. Cross-references are numerous, and an extensive bibliography concludes the effort.

618. McGraw-Hill Encyclopedia of World Drama: An International Reference Work. 2nd ed. Stanley Hochman, ed.-in-chief. New York, McGraw-Hill, 1984. 5v.

This is a most welcome revision and expansion of the 1972 edition, which was received in a lukewarm manner. The revised edition provides more complete coverage of national and ethnic theater traditions and of theater in specific countries, while retaining the pleasant and useful illustrated format. As in the earlier edition, the emphasis is on dramatists, with individuals receiving the majority of the entries. Entries for major personalities include biographies, critiques of their work, synopses of selected plays, and a bibliography of editions which includes references to plays in anthologies or collections. Biographical and critical references are given as well. Bibliographies for most entries are useful and up-to-date. Articles on theater companies and title entries for anonymous plays are provided. Articles are signed for the most part. Volume 5 furnishes a general index to facilitate access.

619. The Oxford Companion to the Theatre. 4th ed. Phyllis Hartnoll, ed. New York, Oxford University Press, 1983. 934p.

An old standard in the reference department since the initial edition in 1951, this work in its present edition was forced to cut back its coverage to maintain a suitable price level. The final product is a most worthwhile tool although it does not supersede the third edition entirely. All peripheral entries (ballet, opera, vaudeville) have been deleted and the survey articles on theater in individual countries have been shortened considerably. The cuts have been most drastic (50-80 percent) in stage management and production articles (lighting, scenery, make-up, etc.). The new work does an excellent job in its focus on the "legitimate theater." Scholarship is up-to-date and coverage is given to a variety of new topics such as "Chicano Theatre." Improved treatment of U.S. and British regional theater is evident, with larger numbers of contemporary personalities and developments included. It remains an indispensable tool.

620. **The Reader's Encyclopedia of World Drama.** John Gassner and Edward Quinn, eds. New York, Crowell, 1969. 1029p.

The focus of this work is on drama as literature and not on the performance aspects, therefore coverage is given to the written works, authorship, and literary characteristics. A number of survey articles examine the development of drama in individual countries from time of origin to contemporary styles and forms with brief bibliographies provided. Significant playwrights are treated in separate entries giving biographies, critical evaluations, and listings of important works. Plays are included among the entries and receive brief synopses and some critical comments. All articles are signed, and there is an appendix of basic documents in dramatic theory. No indexes.

621. **Theatre Language: A Dictionary of Terms in English of the Drama and Stage from Medieval to Modern Times.** Robert Hamilton Ball. New York, Theatre Arts, 1961. 428p.

This tool was warmly received at the time of its publication and is still regarded as the standard work in the field. It covers over 3,500 terms and phrases representing three major categories: technical terms; standard nontechnical terms; and slang, jargon, or cant. The focus is on English-language terminology but foreign words are included if they have been adopted into the English language. Coverage is especially strong of technical terms, but terms peculiar to grand opera or ballet are omitted. A good complementary work is Wilfred Granville's *Theater Dictionary: British and American Terms in the Drama, Opera, and Ballet* (Philosophical Library, 1952; repr., Greenwood Press, 1970). Although criticized by American reviewers for being too heavily concentrated in British terminology, its definitions are excellent and include examples of usage and word history.

622. **Variety Presents: The Complete Book of Major U.S. Show Business Awards.** Mike Kaplan, ed. New York, Garland, 1985. 564p. (Garland Reference Library of the Humanities, v.572).

The focus of this handbook is on awards, and treatment is given to Oscars, Emmys, Grammys, Tonys, and Pulitzer Prizes for plays. All winners and runners-up are listed for each prize from the beginning, with coverage given to the end of the year 1983. The work is well illustrated with pictures of award winners and presenters and furnishes titles and casts. No evaluative commentary is given but the tool furnishes many facts on movies, plays, and television, which are accessed by a detailed index. *Variety International Showbusiness Reference* (Garland, 1983) is a more comprehensive (and expensive) Kaplan effort which compiles a great deal of information on show business. It furnishes biographies of over 6,000 personalities; award listings; film, television, and stage credits; festivals; long-running plays; necrology, etc.

SPECIALIZED BY TIME PERIOD OR GEOGRAPHIC REGION

623. **Crowell's Handbook of Classical Drama.** Richmond Y. Hathorn. New York, Crowell, 1967. 350p.

A useful handbook of Greek and Roman drama, this work continues to be frequently used in reference departments. The arrangement of entries is alphabetical and coverage includes biographies of dramatists, summaries of myths and legends, identification of gods and heroes, and definitions of historical and dramatic terms. Place names are identified and described, and an especially useful feature is the inclusion of many characters from the plays. Plays still in existence are identified with date of composition or first performance, and entries include brief synopses and some evaluative commentary. Primarily intended for students and interested laypersons, but specialists will find it useful for some of the author's interpretations of controversial subjects.

624. **Crowell's Handbook of Contemporary Drama.** Michael Anderson, et al. New York, Crowell, 1971. 505p.

Developed as a guide to the trends and issues in drama in Europe and the Americas since World War II, the emphasis of this work is on written drama rather than theater. Therefore, an active playwright like Neil Simon receives only a brief entry while other more literary (but far less popular) talents receive more coverage. Included here are outstanding dramatic works in addition to the biographical accounts, along with theater companies and national developments in specific countries. Some terms are defined as well. Entries on individual plays are detailed with much opinion being expressed by the contributors. Especially important is the coverage given to avant garde dramatists and their work. No index is provided.

625. **Dictionary of the Black Theatre: Broadway, Off-Broadway, and Selected Harlem Theatre.** Allen Woll. Westport, Conn., Greenwood Press, 1983. 359p.

There are two major sections in this useful work describing theatrical contributions related to the black experience. Part 1 enumerates the shows themselves and describes some 300 plays, revues, and musicals "by, about, with, for and related to blacks" from *A Trip to Coontown* in 1898 to *Dreamgirls* in 1981. Entries furnish information on playhouse, opening date, number of performances, writing and production credits, cast, songs, content, and critical reception (accompanied by excerpts from the press). The second section considers personalities and organizations and provides career information and stage credits for individuals and groups. Cross-references are supplied between the two sections. Less comprehensive in total coverage is Doris E. Abramson's *Negro Playwrights in the American Theatre, 1925-1959* (Columbia University Press, 1969), although more in-depth analysis is given to the twenty plays (and playwrights) selected. Biographical coverage and critical appraisals are included.

626. **The Encyclopedia of the American Theatre 1900-1975.** Edwin Bronner. San Diego, Calif., A. S. Barnes, 1980. 659p.

Not an encyclopedia in the true sense, this is a highly useful handbook providing information on nonmusical plays by American or Anglo-American authors which were performed either on or off-Broadway during the first three quarters of this century. Arrangement is alphabetical by title and entries provide date of opening, theater, number of performances, and brief synopses or "capsule reviews." Authors are sometimes listed within the body of comments, with quotations from contemporary reviews as well as critical comments from Bronner. Cast members, producers, directors, and revivals are also noted, as are some set and costume designers. There are six appendices: notable premieres of the century, debut roles, debut plays, 100 longest running productions, statistical records by season, and the listing of four major awards (Pulitzer Prize, *New York Times* Critics, Obie, and Tony). Although some omissions have been pointed out, the work is highly useful to basic research.

627. **The Encyclopedia of the New York Stage, 1920-1930.** Samuel L. Leiter and Holly Hill, eds. Westport, Conn., Greenwood Press, 1985. 2v.

This is the first issue of a planned series covering all plays, musical and nonmusical, revues, and revivals staged either on or off-Broadway in the decade between 16 June 1920 and 15 June 1930. Included are the productions of ethnic and foreign-language groups as well as important "amateur" companies like the Provincetown Players. Entries provide information on author, director, producer, opening, length of run, plot, reviews, and in some cases, interesting anecdotes about the staging, performance, or writing. There are a number of useful appendices including a chronology, subject listing, locales, foreign-language productions, ethnic groups, awards, sources of plays (novels), institutional theaters, foreign companies and stars, critics cited, seasonal statistics, and theaters. Indexes by proper name and title and a bibliography are furnished.

628. **Modern World Drama: An Encyclopedia.** Myron Matlaw. New York, Dutton, 1972. 960p.

This encyclopedia is useful for its comprehensive coverage of modern drama. Entries, arranged alphabetically, provide summaries of the modern drama of individual countries, biographies of playwrights who lived in the twentieth century, names of plays (some of which are given full plot outlines as well as information on publication and first production), and definitions of technical terms for recent theater movements. No performers, producers, or directors are given separate entries, and it appears that European playwrights receive more detailed coverage than do Americans. Limitations apparently reside in the rather arbitrary manner of selecting the entries, since they reflect the author's "own tastes and attitudes." A character index and a general index provide access.

629. **The Oxford Companion to American Theatre.** Gerald Bordman. New York, Oxford University Press, 1984. 734p.

This is the first edition of this specialized version of the Oxford Companion series, and it provides a comprehensive source of information on the American theater. Especially strong is the biographical coverage of performers, playwrights, composers, librettists, choreographers, producers, managers, directors, and designers as well as orchestrators, photographers, publicists, critics, scholars, and even architects. Represented in addition to the legitimate stage are various forms of live theater, such as minstrel shows and vaudeville. Excellent coverage is given also to individual plays, musicals, and revues, a feature not included in *Oxford Companion to the Theatre* (see entry 619). Entries include production date, plot summary, and commentary. Organizations, companies, unions, clubs, societies, periodicals, and newspapers are included, making this an extremely welcome resource for the specialist and the layperson alike.

Directories, Annuals, and
Current Awareness Services

For current awareness tools on play productions, there are computerized databases linked to specific cities, providing information on entertainment events. See *Data Base Directory* (see entry 6) and *Directory of Online Databases* (see entry 7) for cities and their computerized systems.

630. **American Theatrical Arts: A Guide to Manuscripts and Special Collections in the United States and Canada.** William C. Young. Chicago, American Library Association, 1972. 166p.

This is a highly useful directory of 138 institutions with collections of primary source material on the theatrical arts (legitimate theater, vaudeville, burlesque, motion pictures, television, dance, opera, and circus). Included in these collections are manuscripts, playbills, theater history, promptbooks, posters, letters, diaries, logbooks, brochures, scrapbooks, photographs, recordings, contracts, etc. Much of the material has not been cataloged and is not entered in any national listings, making the tool an extremely valuable aid to inquiry and research. The materials are linked to various types of theatrical personalities including actors, directors, authors, designers, choreographers, composers, critics, dancers, etc. Arrangement is alphabetical by state, then by institution, and entries indicate quantity of items and furnish brief descriptions. Access is by name and subject indexes. Louis A. Rachow's *Theatre and Performing Arts Collections* (Haworth, 1981) surveys six or seven of the important special collections in articles written by the curators or heads of the collections. Included are the Billy Rose Theatre Collection at New York Public Library and the Library of Congress.

631. **Best Plays of 1894/1899- and Yearbook of the Drama in America.** 1920- . Ann. New York, Dodd, Mead.

This annual review of play production is an excellent vehicle for keeping abreast of developments in the world of theater. Although the title has varied in the past, as did the frequency in the early years, it is now simply referred to as the Best Plays series, although old-timers may still call it the "Burns Mantle" after a former editor. Mantle has provided retrospective coverage of the early years with three volumes: *1894/1899* (1955), *1899/1909* (1944), and *1909/1919* (1933). These volumes identify plays and furnish lists of plays produced with date, theater, and cast. The annual began in 1920 and has maintained its regularity. It furnishes digests and evaluations of selected plays; title lists of plays produced in New York including author, number of performances, theater, cast, and outline of plot; a list of plays produced outside of New York; a list of Shakespeare festivals; statistics; actor lists with dates of birth; and a list of prizes and awards. There are indexes of authors, plays, casts, producers, etc. Otis L. Guernsey's *Directory of the American Theater, 1894-1971* (Dodd, Mead, 1971) is a convenient index to the series by author, title, and composer for a period spanning seventy-seven years.

632. **The New York Theatrical Sourcebook.** 1984- . Ann. Association of Theatrical Artists and Craftspeople. New York, Broadway Press.

This is a highly useful directory of sources and services in the New York City area for those involved with the entertainment industry. The largest segment is "Products and Services," which furnishes a classified listing of nearly 2,500 different businesses organized under such categories as "Books, Fake." Props, stage designs, costumes, special effects, puppets, and other paraphernalia are acquired through the listings which furnish address, telephone number, hours of operation, and sometimes, descriptive notes. Cross-references are given between entries. There is an alphabetical listing of these companies with references to the "Products" section. The appendices are useful and provide additional listings including design collections, unions, concert halls, etc. Especially noteworthy is a listing of services available during odd hours. *The Stage Managers Directory*, edited by Cathy Blaser and David Rodger (Broadway Press) is a periodic source of information. The 1987 edition (published in 1986) covers over 260 stage managers, especially those in the New York area. It serves as a guide for employers and a communication tool for stage managers. It includes resumes detailing their background and experience. Listings are paid for by those who are covered.

633. Regional Theatre Directory: A National Guide to Employment in Regional Theatres. 1985- . Ann. Dorset, Vt., Dorset Theatre Festival and Colony House/Theatre Directories.

This recently created paperback guide to the employment opportunities in regional theater contains union addresses and Equity contracts, organizations, audition lists, references to useful publications, theater listings with information regarding contracts and hiring practices, as well as estimated salaries. Applications, apprenticeships, internships, etc. are given by geographical region. The 1986 issue contains an evaluation of the computerized casting services in New York City and a narrative on the folly of a scattergun approach to job hunting. Also available from the same publisher is *Summer Theatre Directory* which began as an annual in 1984, and is organized along the same lines. Both tools are designed as placement aids for actors seeking employment, and both are recommended for purchase by libraries with an interest in theater. Indexing is excellent in both titles.

634. Theatre Companies of the World. Colby H. Kullman and William C. Young, eds. Westport, Conn., Greenwood Press, 1986. 2v.

This is a comprehensive directory of theater companies around the world. The definition proposed in the text for theater companies suggests permanent acting groups under contract for a specific period each year who perform a season of plays that includes nonmusical productions. There is some hedging on the criteria, however, in order to accommodate the practices in various regions which may be disposed to handle repertory theater in their own way. Thus, part-time companies without contracts are included as well as those who engage in mime, puppetry, dance, etc. Entries provide name, address, significance, history, names of playwrights associated with a company, philosophy of production, facilities, and future plans. Plans are to produce a separate listing for the United States; therefore, representation from this country is limited.

635. Theatre World. 1944/1945- . Ann. New York, Theatre World.

This important survey of the year in theater has undergone several name changes, but began life with its present title. From 1950 to 1965 it was called *Daniel Blum's Theatre World* in honor of its editor, and for a time it was called *John Willis' Theatre World* in tribute to the subsequent editor. Regardless of the title, it has remained an excellent pictorial and factual record of theater productions in the United States. Its emphasis is on Broadway but coverage is given to off-Broadway, regional theater, and touring companies. It provides opening and closing dates, cast lists, producers, directors, authors, composers, song titles, theaters, designers, agents, technicians, etc. Biographies of cast members are given in a brief, stylized format, and many pictures are included of scenes and personalities involved. There is an extensive index which expedites access to the information in legitimate plays, solo performances, and musicals. Some of this information (without illustrations) may be found in *Best Plays* (see entry 631).

Histories

GENERAL

636. **History of the Theatre.** 4th ed. Oscar G. Brockett. Boston, Allyn and Bacon, 1982. 768p.

From the time of its initial publication in 1968, this work was regarded as one of the best one-volume general histories of the theater. The new edition continues this tradition and provides an excellent overview of the theater from the primitives to the contemporary stage. Scholarship and attention to detail are apparent in this carefully researched and well-documented survey of theatrical practices all over the world. The emphasis is on European theater, as it has been in the past, and American theater as an outgrowth of those influences. Excellent coverage is given to the Greek, Roman, and Renaissance theaters. Such elements as performance practices, architecture, and theatrical conditions are covered. There is a selective bibliography, and an index provides access. The fifth edition of this fine work is scheduled for publication in mid-1987.

637. **A History of World Theatre.** Margot Berthold. Trans. by Edith Simmons. New York, Ungar, 1972. 733p.

A highly successful and scholarly effort by a German professor, this work provides a European perspective which is useful to American scholars and students. Although it treats the American scene all too briefly in sections on Broadway and experimental theater, there are other tools which fill this need. Important here is the worldly view provided in a history of the theater from the time of ancient ceremonies and ritualistic practices to the trends and developments of the twentieth century. The author, a professor of theater history and methodology at the University of Munich, furnishes insight into the topic derived from awareness of historical, anthropological, and aesthetic influences. The book remains a useful tool for laypersons as well as those with professional interest.

638. **Plays, Players, and Playwrights: An Illustrated History of the Theatre.** Rev. ed. Marion Geisinger. New York, Hart, 1975. 800p.

The author has been part of the world of theater as both an actress and an avid student for a number of years, and has provided this revision of a work completed only four years earlier. The newer edition, like the initial effort, is a heavily illustrated history of the theater with 400 photographs and over 80 drawings. It is comprehensive in its coverage, beginning with ancient Greece and Rome and ending with a separately indexed chapter, "Theatre of the 70's." Included in the chronological study are biographical pieces on various personalities and play summaries. Thirteen chapters focus on different time periods and countries. American legitimate theater is well covered, as is American musical theater. The illustrations make this an excellent complementary tool, and it can be used as a text at the high school or college level.

639. **The Theatre: Three Thousand Years of Drama, Acting and Stagecraft.** Rev. and reset illustrated ed. Sheldon Cheney. New York, McKay, 1972. 710p.

An old standard in the field, this work first appeared in 1929 and gained a reputation as the major historical source dealing with the whole realm of theater history. Its emphasis is on acting and stagecraft. Since that time, of course, other works such as Brockett's

History of the Theatre (see entry 636) have appeared which share the burden and divide the audience. It remains a useful vehicle, however, for its interesting, spirited style meant to entertain as well as enlighten. The new edition adds some sixty illustrations and about fifty pages of new text, primarily on the modern theater. There is a new bibliography by Arthur Hopper.

SPECIALIZED BY TIME PERIOD OR GEOGRAPHIC REGION

640. **American Theatre Companies 1749-1887.** Weldon B. Durham. Westport, Conn., Greenwood Press, 1986. 598p.

The first of a projected three-volume series on resident acting companies in this country, this work covers a most interesting and creative period, 1749-1887. Included are P. T. Barnum's American Museum Stock Company and the Thalia Theatre Company, a prominent and successful German-language theater in New York City. Coverage begins with the first important English-speaking company in the colonies and continues through the beginning of the last company organized and managed in the style of the English playhouse. A total of eighty-one theater groups is treated. Entries provide dates and locations of operations, manager, description of artistic and business practices, performers, designers, technicians, etc. An analytical description of the group's repertory and a bibliography of published and archival resources for further study are included. The excellent factual analysis makes this an important tool.

641. **Annals of the New York Stage.** George Clinton Densmore Odell. New York, Columbia University Press, 1927-1949. 15v.

This massive set chronicles the period from 1699 to 1894 and remains the legacy of a single individual who persevered in the effort for over twenty years. Unfortunately, Odell was to fall short of his goal of reaching the year 1900, but his scholarship, care, and attention to detail have enabled thousands of scholars, researchers, students, and critics to draw upon a wealth of well-organized information. Each volume proceeds in chronological sequence, covering a period of years (volume 1, to 1798; volume 2, 1798 to 1821, etc.). Included in the record are the actors, plays, theaters, critical commentary, and historical background of the period. Plays are identified along with cast listings and comments from contemporary critics and reviewers. Many portraits of now obscure performers are included, for which access has been facilitated through the publication of *Index to the Portraits in Odell's Annals of the New York Stage* (American Society for Theatre Research, 1963).

642. **Calendar of English Renaissance Drama, 1558-1642.** Yoshiko Kawachi. New York, Garland, 1986. 351p. (Garland Reference Library of the Humanities, v.661).

This is an important new work for those interested in the study of English drama. It furnishes a detailed chronology on a day-to-day basis of the Elizabethan period and carries it to the time of Cromwell, when the theaters were closed. Compiled from a variety of primary and secondary source material, the calendar identifies all types of staged entertainments, including masques, regardless of whether they were performed by professionals or amateurs. Included in the entry are dates, name of company, place, title of play, type (tragedy or comedy), author, and source of play text. There are indexes to plays, playwrights, and dramatic companies to facilitate access to the contents of this useful tool.

643. Documents of American Theater History: Famous American Playhouses. William C. Young. Chicago, American Library Association, 1973. 2v.

The author is linked to the field of theater through his acting, writing, and teaching, and planned this work as a multivolume effort documenting the history of the American theater. He has covered famous playhouses in this two-volume segment, with volume 1 covering the period 1716-1899 and volume 2 covering the years 1900-1971. A variety of interesting materials has been collected and excerpts are provided from newspapers, periodicals, letters, diaries, journals, autobiographies, reviews, magazines, playbills, publicity materials, and architectural descriptions. Some 200 buildings of historical, architectural, or socio-cultural prominence are included. Sections on New York theaters, regional theaters, etc., are arranged within chronological periods. Three indexes provide access by name, geographical location, and personal name.

644. The London Stage, 1660-1800: A Calendar of Plays, Entertainments and After-pieces ... Carbondale, Ill., Southern Illinois University Press, 1960-1968. 5 pts. in 11v.

Proceeding in chronological sequence in the manner of Odell's *Annals of the New York Stage* (see entry 641) is this record of play production in London covering a period of 140 years. The work furnishes a treasury of information to the scholar and serious inquirer as expressed in its complete subtitle, which continues "Together with Casts, Box-receipts and Contemporary Comment, Compiled from the Playbills, Newspapers, and Theatrical Diaries of the Time." Much detail is gleaned from the materials presented and one is able to determine not only the types of plays appealing to Londoners during this time period but the reception given them by the critics. Each volume is preceded by an introduction which provides monographic treatment of the conditions of the theater and its activity. Ben Ross Schneider's *Index to the London Stage, 1660-1800* (Southern Illinois University, 1979) is a computer-produced index to all names and titles appearing in the set.

645. The London Stage, 1890-1899: A Calendar of Plays and Players. J. P. Wearing. Metuchen, N.J., Scarecrow, 1976. 2v.

Clearly following *The London Stage, 1660-1800* (see entry 644), the compiler has furnished a listing of the plays and players on the London stage during the last decade of the nineteenth century. Derived from a variety of sources, the format is established for the entries as a series of playbills. Arrangement is chronological by date of opening and by theater when there was more than one play opening on the same night. Entries furnish title, author, genre, theater, length of run and number of performances, cast, production staff, and references to reviews of opening night performances. A detailed general index facilitates access. Wearing's second effort covering the decade 1900-1909 was published in two volumes in 1981, followed by another examining the period 1910-1919, also in two volumes, in 1982.

646. The Medieval Stage. Edmund Kerchever Chambers. London, Oxford University Press, 1903, repr., 1978. 2v.

An old standard in the field, this work is still considered the most comprehensive and authoritative history of the period. The medieval stage is considered from the fall of the Roman Empire to the Tudor period. The work is divided into four major sections. Part 1, "Minstrelsy," and part 2, "Folk Drama," are covered in volume 1. Part 3, "Religious Drama," and part 4, "Interludes (Tudor)," are covered in volume 2. Bibliographies are provided, and appendices contain original documents. A subject index facilitates access. Another major effort by Chambers is *The Elizabethan Stage* (London, Clarendon Press, 1923; repr. with corrections, 1974). This is a four-volume work which is also a standard in the field, though parts of it, such as the section on the Elizabethan playhouse, have been updated in other histories. The variety of topics includes the Court and control of the stage, companies and playhouses, staging at Court and in the theaters, and various plays and authors. Appendices contain original documents, and a general index is provided.

647. **20th Century Theatre.** Glenn Meredith Loney. New York, Facts on File, 1983. 2v.

An attractive and easy to use chronological record of theatrical developments in the United States and Great Britain, this work has proved to be a popular choice for librarians and their patrons. The arrangement is year-by-year from 1900 to 1979, classified by topics such as American premieres, British premieres, revivals and repertories, births/deaths/ debuts, and theaters/productions. Within each topic, the activities are listed chronologically from 1 January to 31 December. Many production photographs are used. A chronology of this type will work as a date finder, personality identifier, and event locator when the indexes are sufficient to provide access. It appears that this is true in this case with a general index of names, production tables, and miscellaneous subjects (awards, companies, schools, etc.).

Biographical Sources

648. **A Biographical Dictionary of Actors, Actresses, Musicians, Dancers, Managers, and Other Stage Personnel in London, 1660-1800.** Philip H. Highfill, et al. Carbondale, Ill., Southern Illinois University Press, 1973- . (In progress).

Originally projected as a sixteen-volume biographical dictionary to serve somewhat as a companion piece to *The London Stage, 1660-1800* (see entry 644), this enormous effort reached its tenth volume in 1984. Since it is only up to Nash, it is likely that the original sixteen-volume projection will be increased before it is finished. Brief biographical sketches are furnished for all persons who were members of theatrical companies, occasional performers, patentees or servants of the patent theaters, opera houses, amphitheaters, pleasure gardens, theatrical taverns, music rooms, fair booths, and other places of public entertainment. The tool is remarkable and extremely valuable for its coverage of the unheralded as well as the famous and is a treasure house of information in this regard. The information is derived from a variety of sources, and there are many fine portraits and illustrations. Entries vary from brief identifications to lengthy descriptions of several pages.

649. **British Dramatists since World War II.** Stanley Weintraub, ed. Detroit, Gale, 1982. 2v. (Dictionary of Literary Biography, v.13).

This is a detailed description and analysis of sixty-nine of the most significant or potentially most significant playwrights in modern British play production. Such individuals as Tom Stoppard, Samuel Beckett, Harold Pinter, and Christopher Fry are treated in-depth in articles that include production lists, books published, biographical sketches, critical commentary, production photographs, programs, playscript drafts, and bibliographic references. Appendices provide a collection of essays on a variety of topics, such as Britain's postwar theater, theater companies, and stage censorship. There is a general bibliography for further reading. This tool is an extremely useful resource for both students and specialists seeking further information about important dramatists.

650. **Contemporary Dramatists.** 3rd ed. James Vinson, ed.; D. L. Kirkpatrick, associate ed. New York, St. Martin's Press, 1982. 1104p. (Contemporary Writers of the English Language).

Continuing in the tradition and style of the earlier editions, which received considerable praise from critics, is the third edition which, like the others, covers in excellent detail the lives and works of some 300 playwrights, primarily British and American. There are forty new entries in this work and about 100 of the previous essays have been revised or rewritten with information updating the contributions and activities of the dramatists. More than just a biographical dictionary, this tool continues to provide excellent evaluative commentary as well as a full bibliography of each dramatist's published works. There are references to critical studies, and manuscript collections are identified. In addition, there are separate sections for screen writers, television writers, radio writers, and musical librettists, limited to listings of their works. An appendix provides an additional listing of playwrights who have died since the 1950s. A title index is included.

651. The Great Stage Stars: Distinguished Theatrical Careers of the Past and Present. Sheridan Morley. New York, Facts on File, 1986. 425p.

One of the more attractive biographical dictionaries to come out in recent years, this work covers a period of 400 years, with an emphasis on those who performed in London rather than New York. Of those personalities who are living (definitely in the minority) few could be said to be young, and many are vintage. The author is the son of Robert Morley and has been a critic and an author of biographies of theatrical personalities. His descriptions are excellent and his use of comments taken from reviews blends in well with the quotes from the performers themselves. Approximately 200 personalities are covered and there are about fifty photographs which help the reader to an informative and enjoyable experience.

652. Notable Names in the American Theatre. Clifton, N.J., James T. White, 1976. 1250p.

Actually the second edition of Walter Rigdon's *Biographical Encyclopedia and Who's Who of the American Theater* (Heinemann, 1966), this work is considered an excellent reference source by librarians and their patrons. It is divided into nine sections. The first lists New York productions between 1900 and 1974. Then follows "premieres in America," which furnishes title, author, premiere date, and length of run. Similar information is provided for "premieres of American plays abroad." Following that is a segment on "theater group biographies," then one on New York theater buildings, and then a listing of awards. "Biographical bibliography" furnishes references to books about theater personalities, while the necrology is a comprehensive listing of deceased individuals from the colonial period to the present. Of course, the major focus is the "notable names" segment, which consists of detailed biographies of living Americans and others who have made an important contribution to the American theater. All types of individuals are included: performers, playwrights, designers, producers, etc. William C. Young's *Famous Actors and Actresses on the American Stage* (R. R. Bowker, 1975) is a companion work to the author's volumes on theaters (see entry 643) and provides brief biographies and critical evaluations of 225 actors and actresses. Portraits are included as are references to the sources of the critiques.

653. Who's Who in the Theatre: A Biographical Record of the Contemporary Stage. 17th ed. Detroit, Gale, 1981. 2v.

This is the final edition of the long-standing series (begun in 1912) originally published by Pitman of London. The Gale Company has chosen to expand the scope with a new serial publication, *Contemporary Theatre, Film, and Television* (see entry 427). *Who's Who* was limited to theater personalities, the original emphasis being on those who were associated with the London stage. In recent years, there has been greater coverage of Americans, especially in this edition. About 2,400 people from all areas of theater are included: performers, dramatists, composers, critics, managers, historians, etc. Although the emphasis is on living individuals, a necrology is included. Volume 2, the playbills volume, includes playbills from both London and New York. *Who Was Who in the Theatre, 1912-1976: A Biographical Dictionary of Actors, Actresses, Playwrights, and Producers of the English-Speaking Theatre* (Gale, 1978) is an omnibus volume, and again, most likely the final offering in this series, which has also given way to the new publication. This composite volume covers over 4,000 deceased individuals who had been covered in *Who's Who in the Theatre* between 1912 and 1972. Entries were consigned to *Who Was Who* either through death or inactivity over a ten-year period.

Reviews and Criticism

654. **American Drama Criticism: Interpretations, 1890-1977.** 2nd ed. Floyd Eugene Eddleman, comp. Hamden, Conn., Shoe String Press, 1979. 488p. Supp. I, 1984, 255p.

This work supersedes the first edition by Palmer and Dyson (1967) and its two supplements (1970, 1976). It provides a listing of interpretations of American plays published over a period of nearly ninety years. These interpretations (critiques, reviews, etc.) appeared in 200 books and monographs and in over 400 periodicals. The arrangement of entries is by playwright and then by title. Only the works of dramatists who are or were citizens of the United States are included, except for a few Canadians and Caribbean writers whose works are performed here. The date of first production is noted and musical plays are included. There are indexes of critics and of adapted authors and works. The supplement, also by Eddleman, furnishes a listing of 1,300 interpretations published between 1978 and 1982.

655. **Broadway in the West End: An Index of Reviews of American Theatre in London, 1950-1975.** William T. Stanley. Westport, Conn., Greenwood Press, 1978. 206p.

As a member of the faculty of library science at the University of Southern California, Stanley produced a useful work on an interesting theme. Listed here are reviews of Broadway plays as they appeared on the pages of sixteen London newspapers and *Punch* over a twenty-five-year period. Entries are arranged by name of author or adapter of the stage play, and furnish name of theater, dates of the run, number of performances, and references to reviews. There are three sections, the first of which is the bibliography. Following that is a chronology of important dates, and finally there is a title list of shows which serves as an index. The appendices contain several listings, such as the twenty-five longest running American productions in London, the twenty-five longest running American musicals in London, and seating capacities of theaters.

656. **Drama Criticism.** Arthur Coleman and Gary R. Tyler. Denver, Colo., Alan Swallow, 1966-1971. 2v.

Another of the checklists of interpretations from Alan Swallow which have become well-known in reference collections of literature is this two-volume effort. The interpretations are all in English and appeared in books or periodicals, but the plays are from different countries of origin. Volume 1 provides listings of interpretations or critiques of American or English plays. These critiques were published between 1940 and 1964. Volume 2 (published five years later) covers classical and continental plays for which the interpretations were published between 1950 and 1968. Arrangement of entries is alphabetical by dramatist, then by title of play. Over 1,000 periodicals have been examined and there is a useful bibliography of books containing criticism.

657. Dramatic Criticism Index: A Bibliography of Commentaries on Playwrights from Ibsen to the Avant-Garde. Paul F. Breed and Florence M. Sniderman, comps. and eds. Detroit, Gale, 1972. 1022p.

Another checklist of criticism or interpretations, all of which are in the English language, this work identifies 12,000 entries derived from 630 books and 200 periodicals. Most of the plays and playwrights are modern and represent various countries. Entries are arranged alphabetically by playwright; plays are listed alphabetically under playwright. References vary in terms of the length of the critiques, which may range from one or two pages to monographic proportions, as in a chapter of a book. Reviews of play performances are included only if literary criticism is lacking. The work is indexed by play title and by critic. There is a listing of books which were indexed.

658. European Drama Criticism, 1900-1975. 2nd ed. Helen H. Palmer. Hamden, Conn., Shoe String Press, 1977. 653p.

This is a companion effort or complementary work to Eddleman's *American Drama Criticism* (see entry 654) and represents a useful and convenient source book for critical writings on European plays. This checklist covers a period of seventy-five years and furnishes references to critiques in various languages (although the emphasis is on English materials). This work cumulates the entries from an earlier edition and supplements and adds material. The plays and the dramatists are universal in nature from every time period of play production from Aeschylus to Yeats. Playwrights included represent major figures with recognized impact, although as is inevitable for a work of this type, major omissions have been noted. There is a listing of books and journals indexed.

659. Major Modern Dramatists. Rita Stein, et al., comps. and eds. New York, Ungar, 1984-1986. 2v. (Library of Literary Criticism).

This set is part of the well-known Library of Literary Criticism series, which seeks to provide a collection of excerpts of literary criticism on various literary efforts. In the past, its focus has been on the literary products of a language or a country rather than on a literary genre. Thus, this series departs from its tradition by having established this set on dramatists. Volume 1, issued in 1984, covers American, British, Irish, German, Austrian, and Swiss dramatists, while volume 2 (1986) extends European coverage to French, Belgian, Russian, Polish, Spanish, Italian, Norwegian, Swedish, Czech, and Hungarian playwrights. The format and purpose of the set are similar to those of previous efforts in providing an overview of the critical reception given to a dramatist from the beginning of his or her career up to the present time through excerpts from reviews, articles, and books. This is a selective effort limited to those playwrights who have established an international reputation beginning with Ibsen and late nineteenth-century realism up to the present.

660. The New York Times Theatre Reviews, 1870/1919- . Bienn. New York, New York Times, 1971- .

The first segment to be published of this chronological collection of reviews covers the years 1920-1970 and appeared in ten volumes in 1971, with the final volume given to indexes and appendices. This has been continued on a biennial basis beginning with the years 1971/1972. The segment covering the early years, 1870-1919, was published in five volumes in 1976. Thus we are able to consult a review as it appeared in the *New York Times* for a period of over 100 years. Reviews are arranged chronologically and there are excellent appendices of awards and prizes and of productions and runs by season. The work is indexed by titles, production companies, names of performers, and names of others associated with the staging of the play. Reviews are detailed and have earned a reputation for quality and perceptiveness. *New York Theatre Critics Reviews* (New York Theatre Critics Reviews, 1940-) is a useful weekly publication which furnishes copies of reviews as they appeared in a variety of New York newspapers as well as periodicals and even on network television. A useful tool in comparing reviews from different critics.

661. **Selected Theatre Criticism.** Anthony Slide, ed. Metuchen, N.J., Scarecrow, 1985-1986. 3v.

The complete set of three volumes covers the first half of the twentieth century in providing a collection of original reviews to productions of the New York stage. Reviews are reproduced in their entirety from an array of periodicals: *Century Magazine, The Critic, The Forum, The Green Book Magazine, Life, The New York Clipper, The New York Dramatic Mirror, The Red Book Magazine*, and *Variety* (see entry 696). Volume 1 covers the period 1900-1919, volume 2, 1920-1930, and volume 3, 1931-1950. All types of shows are included: dramas, revues, comedies, and musicals, over 500 in all. Arrangement in each volume is alphabetical by title, and production information is given along with the reviews. James M. Salem's *A Guide to Critical Reviews* (Scarecrow, 1984-) appears in several parts, each dealing with a different entertainment form. Citations to critical reviews are furnished rather than the reviews themselves. Part 1 covers the American drama 1909-1982, and was last issued in 1984. It is a continuing publication. (See entry 709 for more information.)

Play Production

662. **Producing Theatre: A Comprehensive Legal and Business Guide.** Donald C. Farber. New York, Drama Book Specialists, 1981. 382p.

Farber, an attorney, has combined and updated the contents of his two earlier works published in the 1960s to provide what has been described as a comprehensive and comprehensible guide to the legal documents and procedures involved in play production. It is geared to the business of producing plays anywhere, be it on Broadway, resident theater, stock, etc., and covers all possible and probable aspects. Information on contractual agreements is presented in precise and understandable fashion, furnishing samples of actual contracts. Considered to be the most authoritative legal and business guide in the realm of theater, the work contains 14 chapters which trace a commercial production from its acquisition as a property to details of a long run and tours and even sale of motion picture rights. A general index provides access. A reprint of this work is scheduled to appear in mid-1987 from Limelight Books (New York) and will be issued as the first Limelight edition.

663. **The Small Theatre Handbook: A Guide to Management and Production.** Joann Green. Harvard, Mass., Harvard Common; distr., Port Washington, N.Y., Independent Publishers Group, 1981. 163p.

The small theater is defined as having an annual budget of under $100,000; this work is a manual of management practice for these theaters. The author has served as the artistic director of the Cambridge Ensemble Theatre and therefore is well equipped to handle the discussion of problems and to provide practical directions. The work is considered most useful in regard to organization and administration, furnishing many examples: budgeting, fund raising, etc. Information on production, such as choosing the play, directors, actors, etc., is somewhat sketchy. In general, the tool should be helpful to people associated with the business end of play production in colleges, neighborhood theaters, repertories, etc. Another work written in this vein is *The Complete Play Production Handbook*, by Carl Allensworth, et al. (Harper & Row, 1982). This is more focused on the production end in its goal of assisting schools, colleges, and little theaters in mounting a creditable production.

664.   **Stage Makeup.** 7th ed. Richard Corson. Englewood Cliffs, N.J., Prentice-Hall, 1986. 389p.

This specialized handbook is a standard in the field and is revised frequently (6th edition, 1981). It is used by instructors, makeup artists, and actors who are responsible for their own makeup. There are many illustrations to help the user understand the narrative on techniques of applications with considerations of skin tone, facial anatomy, and lighting. Application of grease-paint, beards, wigs, artificial limbs, and appurtenances is described in-depth. The new edition updates information on hair styles and fashions and is a must for the theater collection. Another specialized work, this one dealing with another aspect of stage preparation, is Francis Reid's *The Stage Lighting Handbook*, now in its second edition (Theatre Arts Books, 1982). Geared to the needs of amateurs, this tool describes the purposes, equipment, rigging, etc., and enumerates the basic steps in lighting design.

665.   **Stagecraft: The Complete Guide to Theatrical Practice.** Trevor R. Griffiths, ed. Oxford, Phaidon, 1982; distr., New York, Drama Book, 1984. 192p.

This British work furnishes a practical handbook to all basic aspects of nonprofessional play production. Its ten chapters cover such considerations as directing, stage management, acting, set design, light design, costumes, makeup, and even the conduct of a workshop. Chapters are contributed by authorities in these topical areas, and the work is heavily illustrated both in color and black-and-white. Although the British terminology may seem awkward at first, the material furnished is useful and in keeping with the overall purpose, which is to achieve the best possible production with the fewest pitfalls. A glossary is provided, and a general index aids access. *Theatre Design and Technology* (U.S. Institute for Theatre Technology, 1978-) is a quarterly journal for professional technicians and production people. It provides several articles in each issue on stage design, scenery, props, etc., for members of the organization.

FILM, RADIO, TELEVISION, AND VIDEO

Bibliographic Guides and Introductory Works

666.   **Film: A Reference Guide.** Robert A. Armour. Westport, Conn., Greenwood Press, 1980. 251p.

This is a useful and well-developed reference guide for the person who is about to undertake a serious study of some aspect of film. It has earned praise from reviewers both for its convenience and its content. Written in essay form, the work is divided into various chapters, all of which cover a topic of interest and importance. These include history of film, film production, film criticism by genre, major actors, directors, etc. There is a chapter on reference works and periodicals in the field which should prove of value. Each chapter contains a bibliography. A chronology of American film and a description of film research collections are included in the appendices. Fay C. Schreibman's *Broadcast Television: A Research Guide* (American Film Institute, 1983) is a small but useful guide in an area not generally covered by such tools.

667. Film Theory and Criticism: Introductory Readings. 3rd ed. Gerald Mast and Marshall Cohen, comps. New York, Oxford University Press, 1985. 852p.

The essential character of this work has remained the same through the years, and it has earned an excellent reputation for the selection of articles and essays by theorists of various traditions and backgrounds. Much of the material is repeated from the second edition (1979), but all voices seem to be heard, with a strong representation of the new breed of critic who has been schooled in the nature of the film art rather than literary criticism. The categories or sections of the work represent those topics deemed to be basic to the study of film theory, with groupings of an expository nature relating to film and reality, the medium, audience, etc. The essays generally run from twenty to thirty pages, but vary in length.

668. Guidebook to Film: An Eleven-in-One Reference. Ronald Gottesman and Harry M. Geduld. New York, Holt, Rinehart and Winston, 1972. 230p.

An old standard which is still considered an important contribution, this work continues to receive heavy use by film librarians and their patrons. It is an excellent starting point for a variety of searches, and provides an array of useful information. Not only does it provide annotated listings of books and periodicals, theses, and dissertations, but it also lists museums and archives, film schools, equipment and supplies, film organizations and services, festivals and contests, and awards. There is a glossary of terms as well, which will be useful to the amateur filmmaker. A more recent work is *Moving Pictures: An Annotated Guide to Selected Film Literature, with Suggestions for the Study of Film,* by Eileen Sheahan (A. S. Barnes, 1979). It furnishes good annotations for film reference books grouped by type, such as encyclopedias, bibliographies, indexes, etc. Designed for college students, it is especially useful for that audience.

PERIODICALS

669. Union List of Film Periodicals: Holdings of Selected American Collections. Anna Brady. Westport, Conn., Greenwood Press, 1984. 316p.

To facilitate research in the field, this finding list covers the periodical holdings of thirty-five American libraries with important film collections. Periodical titles are from nearly sixty countries and include a broad range of emphases in the field, such as film as art, industry and entertainment, and sociological and psychological perspectives. Over 1,600 titles are listed and country of publication, language, ISSN, publication dates, and title changes are given. Numbers of volumes the various libraries hold are enumerated. There is an index of title changes which includes those titles having undergone at least three changes, and a geographical index lists the titles under country of publication.

Bibliographies and Catalogs

670. A Bibliography of Theses and Dissertations on the Subject of Film: 1916-1979. Raymond Fielding. Houston, Tex., University Film Association, School of Communication, University of Houston, 1979. 72p.

For those needing access to formal research at both the master's and doctoral levels, this compact work furnishes a compilation of these efforts over a period of sixty-three years. Over 1,400 theses and dissertations are identified which cover all aspects of film study. They are made accessible through a subject index. Index headings are broad, such as violence in film; studies of individual writers, directors, performers, etc., can be accessed through the subject heading "Critical Biographical Studies of Particular Writers." This work is the third product of the University Film Association, and provides the user with a convenient package that saves much time when compared to the use of *Dissertation Abstracts* (see entry 15). John M. Kittross has produced *A Bibliography of Theses and Dissertations in Broadcasting 1920-1973* (Broadcast Education Association, 1978) which identifies 4,300 efforts completed at American universities.

671. **The Film Index: A Bibliography.** Writers Program of the Work Projects Administration of the City of New York. Volume 1, New York, H. W. Wilson, 1941. Volume 2, New York, Kraus International, 1985. Volume 3, New York, Kraus International, 1985.

This three-part annotated bibliography has had a long and interesting history since the first volume appeared in 1941. It was not to be completed until forty-four years later, because of cutbacks in the budget of the WPA in 1939. The Wilson Company published the first volume, *The Film as Art*, with the Museum of Modern Art. This is an extensive, annotated bibliography of books and articles on the history, technique, and types of motion pictures based primarily on the collections of the Museum of Modern Art and the New York Public Library. The remaining cards for the other two volumes have been held in the archives of the Museum; Kraus has finally arranged for their publication. Volume 2, *The Film as Industry*, covers English-language materials excluding newspapers based on the holdings of the New York Public Library, with additional listings derived from periodical indexes. Entries are classified under major subject headings in alphabetical order. Volume 3, *The Film in Society*, identifies books and articles under such topics as education, censorship, moral and religious aspects, etc. All annotations are original from their period of preparation and the complete set is an important contribution to film research.

672. **Filmed Books and Plays: A List of Books and Plays from Which Films Have Been Made, 1928-1983.** A. G. S. Enser. Lexington, Mass., Lexington Books/D. C. Heath, 1985. 705p.

Enser, a British librarian, has revised his work once again. It now cumulates the two previous issues (1928-1974 and 1975-1981) and adds an additional two years of coverage. Basically, it is a list of English-language films which were based on books and plays. Thus, it provides a unique approach to both film buffs and serious students for identifying such works over a fifty-five-year period. Never claiming to be a completely exhaustive listing, the bibliography is accessed through excellent indexes. Entries in the title index give the name of the distributing company and year of registration, as well as author, publisher, and book title. The author index list works by the author which have been made into films and includes publisher, as well as film distributor. There is a "change of original title" index which lists original book titles that differ from their motion pictures. An update is due to appear in late 1987 (Aldershot, Hampshire, England, Gower) which will bring the coverage through 1986.

673. **The Macmillan Film Bibliography: A Critical Guide to the Literature of the Motion Picture.** George Rehrauer. New York, Macmillan, 1982. 2v.

A long-time contributor to the reference literature of film study, the author is a professor at Rutgers University and has used his expertise to produce his most extensive work. This two-volume set covers in a profound and analytical manner the contributions of nearly 6,800 books on the topic. Although there are a few items which are not annotated, most of the entries provide excellent descriptions of the content, and an assessment of value. Some of these annotations are quite lengthy and have been praised for their wit and sometimes caustic commentary. Arrangement is alphabetical by title in volume 1, while volume 2 provides indexes by subjects, authors, and scripts.

674. Motion Picture Performers: A Bibliography of Magazine and Periodical Articles, 1900-1969. Mel Schuster. Metuchen, N.J., Scarecrow, 1971. 702p. Supp. 1970-1974, 1976.

This is a standard work in the field and has been considered a vital resource in locating articles on obscure figures. Well-known personalities, of course, receive many more entries, reflecting the greater coverage given them in periodicals over the years. Arrangement is alphabetical by names of performers and coverage is limited to English-language publications, most of which are American. Under each name the articles appear in chronological order. No reviews are indexed but the work identifies material about the lives of movie stars, most of whom are associated with the sound era. Schuster's companion work, *Motion Picture Directors: A Bibliography of Magazine and Periodical Articles, 1900-1972* (Scarecrow, 1973), lists similar biographical and career-oriented articles for approximately 2,300 directors, filmmakers, and animators.

675. Motion Pictures: A Catalog of Books, Periodicals, Screenplays, Television Scripts and Production Stills. University of California, Los Angeles. Library. Boston, G. K. Hall, 1976. 775p.

This is an expansion of the 1972 edition of the same work. It lists cards in the catalog of a major collection at the university. Rich in both primary and secondary sources, the catalog is divided into five major sections, the first of which is an author listing of books, journals, personal papers, archival records, and certain memorabilia. Part 2 is a listing of published screenplays arranged by title of film, while part 3 is a listing of 6,000 unpublished screenplays. Part 4 lists television scripts and identifies about 3,000 works by title of the film and of the script. The final segment identifies not only production stills but posters, pressbooks, programs, etc. Although there are inconsistencies in the format of cards and other minor flaws, the work is needed by film researchers.

676. Radio and Television: A Selected, Annotated Bibliography. William E. McCavitt, comp. Metuchen, N.J., Scarecrow, 1978. 229p. *Supp. One: 1977-1981*, 1982, 155p.

The basic edition furnishes 1,100 annotated entries representing selections from the literature of broadcasting over a period of fifty years from 1926 to 1976. There is a classified arrangement of twenty-one broad subject headings, including such topical matter as history, regulation, organization, broadcasting, audience, etc. These categories are generally subdivided further. The work has been criticized in the past for lack of sufficient access because of the fragmentation and scatter of entries on similar subjects, and the general categories are awkward as subject headings for some of the entries. There is an author index which provides access by name when known. The supplement has added six new subject headings (news, advertising, corporate video, home video, etc.) but still contains no detailed subject index. The work is recommended for those with a serious interest.

Filmographies and Catalogs

Film listings are extremely valuable to both reference and research in film work. Catalogs of important collections and numerous filmographies based on genres or an individual's work are available. Additional items to verify or identify motion pictures are found in the section "Dictionaries, Encyclopedias, and Handbooks," while the "Review" section contains evaluative tools.

677. **An Actor Guide to the Talkies: A Comprehensive Listing of 8,000 Feature-Length Films from January 1948, until December, 1964.** Richard Bertrand Dimmitt. Metuchen, N.J., Scarecrow, 1967-1968. 2v.
This is one of the most popular of reference books in the field and provides an excellent means of identifying both actors and film titles. The extensive coverage is of seventeen years and the book is convenient to use and easy to access. Volume 1 is a listing of films alphabetically arranged by title, and provides a cast list for each entry. Volume 2 is a name index to thousands of actors mentioned in the cast lists with references to their coverage in volume 1. This work has been continued by Andrew Aros's *An Actor Guide to the Talkies, 1965 through 1974* (Scarecrow, 1977), which lists nearly 3,500 additional films and their casts. Films in both editions are American and foreign and were released in this country during the time period under consideration.

678. **The American Film Institute Catalog of Motion Pictures Produced in the United States.** New York, R. R. Bowker, 1971- . (In progress).
Planned to be completed in nineteen volumes, this work, if and when completed, will be the most extensive listing of films ever compiled. Based in the Library of Congress and funded by grants from both public and private sources, it is to be developed in several series or parts. Part A will cover films 1893 to 1910; parts F1 through F6 will describe feature films from 1911 through 1970, parts S1 through S6 will cover short films from 1911 through 1970; and parts N1 through N6 will identify newsreels from 1908 through 1970. Presently, only two units have been published in the F series: F2, covering feature films 1921-1930 (2v.), and F6, 1961-1970 (2v.). The first volume of each unit lists films alphabetically by title and furnishes complete information on physical description, production credits, cast credits, and content (genre, source, summary). There are indexes of credits and of subjects. *The Film Catalog: A List of Holdings in the Museum of Modern Art*, by Jon Gartenberg, et al. (G. K. Hall, 1985) was published in honor of the fiftieth anniversary of MOMA's film department. The catalog describes some 5,500 titles acquired between 1935 and 1980, ranging from fiction and documentary to television commercials.

679. **National Union Catalog. Audiovisual Materials.** 1983- . Q. Washington, D.C., Library of Congress.
This microfiche catalog is the latest entry in a line of resource tools to the cataloging of the national library which began with the *Library of Congress Catalog: Motion Pictures and Filmstrips*. This was issued quarterly and in quinquennial editions between 1953 and 1973. Its identity was established at that time as part of the *National Union Catalog* as well, and it attempted to cover all educational motion pictures and filmstrips released in this country. From 1972-1978, it was known by the title *Films and Other Materials for Projection*, and added sets of slides and other transparencies to its field of coverage. From 1979-1982, it was the *Library of Congress. Audiovisual Materials*, and included video recordings and kits. Presently bearing the masthead of NUC and appearing in microfiche

format, its purpose and organization remain much the same. Succeeding issues in a volume cumulate those before it in furnishing indexes by name, subject, title, and series.

680.   **Title Guide to the Talkies: A Comprehensive Listing of 16,000 Feature-Length Films from October, 1927, until December, 1963.** Richard Bertrand Dimmitt. Metuchen, N.J., Scarecrow, 1965. 2v.

Another popular and well-used work is this comprehensive library of films over a period of thirty-six years. Its purpose, unlike that of *An Actor Guide to the Talkies* (see entry 677), is to identify the sources of films, whether they were novels, stories, plays, or even poems. It has also served as an extremely valuable resource in identifying screen-writers. Motion pictures are listed alphabetically and indication is given of the original work and authorship. This work, like *An Actor Guide to the Talkies*, has been updated by Andrew Aros's *A Title Guide to the Talkies, 1964 through 1974* (Scarecrow, 1977). Aros has indexed over 3,400 more films with a greater proportion of foreign films. He also includes more novelizations (novels created from films and published at the time of the films' release). There is an author index, and it is possible to determine from these works what motion pictures have been based on the author's work. Another ten years was added by Aros's *A Title Guide to the Talkies, 1975 through 1984* (Scarecrow, 1986) which continues the pattern of coverage.

681.   **Western Movies: A TV and Video Guide to 4200 Genre Films.** Michael R. Pitts. Jefferson, N.C., McFarland, 1986. 623p.

This is an example of a recent comprehensive filmography and guide to feature films of what continues to be one of the most popular genres. The western is considered this country's most original contribution to filmmaking. Films ranging from forty minutes and up, made for either television or screen, are included here with the intention of providing a guide to what is available in video format. A wide range of film is covered with *western* broadly defined, for not only are the classics such as *Stagecoach* included but also the musicals. Even the two-hour pilot of the *McCloud* television series is found here. Also included are a bibliography, directory of video dealers, and trivia lists. Entries furnish title variations, cast, director, running time, etc., as well as plot and a brief critique, and are arranged alphabetically by title. An index of names provides further access.

Indexes, Abstracts, and Serial Bibliographies

682.   **The Critical Index: A Bibliography of Articles on Film in English, 1946-1973 ...** John C. Gerlach and Lana Gerlach. New York, Teachers College Press, 1974. 726p.

One of the very useful indexes through the years, the Gerlachs have indexed articles from twenty-two English-language journals over a period of nearly thirty years. Covered are directors, producers, actors, critics, and writers, in a names section alphabetically arranged. A section on topics is classified under a hierarchy explained in the front of the work. Such topics as history, aesthetics, techniques of filmmaking, the relationship of film to society, and various film genres are employed. Annotations are provided in cases where the titles are not descriptive of the contents. Approximately 5,000 articles are enumerated, with access provided through author and title indexes. Appendices include lists of archives, bibliographies, periodicals, etc. This complements the coverage of *Film Literature Index* (see entry 683).

683. **Film Literature Index: A Quarterly Author-Subject Periodical Index to the International Literature of Film.** 1973- . Q. Ann. cum. Albany, N.Y., Filmdex, Inc.

This work complements the coverage of *The Critical Index* (see entry 682), which limits itself to U.S., British, and Canadian journals. This quarterly publication indexes material from some 300 periodicals which are scanned for pertinent articles. Recently, it has included television periodicals as well. Since its first issue in 1973, it has developed an excellent reputation not only for its coverage of a vast number of journals which include foreign offerings, but also for its organization and ease of use. Developed originally as a pilot offering at SUNY-Albany, with a grant from the New York State Council on the Arts, the work has continued without interruption and occupies a prominent position among such tools.

684. **International Index to Film Periodicals.** 1972- . Ann. New York, R. R. Bowker.

An excellent example of a cooperative indexing project of international proportions is this effort sponsored by the International Federation of Film Archives (FIAF). It provides a convenient package of index entries cumulated over the year at various archives in Europe and North America and contributed by them to this effort. These entries originally appeared on catalog cards which were distributed to subscribers of the service from FIAF. About sixty to eighty film periodicals are selected from the index based on their representation of their country's thinking and articles of lasting quality. There are separate sections of reviews, biographies, and studies of individual films. The counterpart to this work in the field of television is *International Index to Television Periodicals: An Annotated Guide* (London, International Federation of Film Archives, Bienn., 1979/1980-), which provides cumulations of entries indexed on cards by a service. It covers important articles from nearly 100 periodicals worldwide. There are separate indexes for general subjects, individual programs, and biography, as well as an author index.

685. **The New Film Index: A Bibliography of Magazine Articles in English, 1930-1970.** Richard Dyer McCann and Edward S. Perry. New York, E. P. Dutton, 1975. 522p.

An index which is important for the period of time it covers, this work was intended to fill a gap subsequent to the coverage provided by *The Film Index* (see entry 671). It fits nicely in the time period between that work and *Film Literature Index* (see entry 683) and indexes about 12,000 articles arranged in over 275 different subject categories. Annotations are brief but informative. Coverage is given largely to those articles which treat film as art or entertainment (volume 1, *Film Index*) rather than in an instructional or technical manner. The work does not index reviews of individual films or books. Another title which may be used is Linda Batty's *Retrospective Index to Film Periodicals, 1930-1971* (R. R. Bowker, 1975), which indexes fourteen periodicals. Although its title is somewhat of a misnomer since only one of the fourteen periodicals began in the 1930s, it does provide a convenient source of identification for periodical articles without having to search the general indexes.

Dictionaries, Encyclopedias, and Handbooks

686. **The Complete Directory to Prime Time Network TV Shows, 1946-Present.** 3rd ed. Tim Brooks and Earle Marsh. New York, Ballantine Books, 1985. 1123p.

Defining prime time in broad terms as the time period from 6:00 P.M. to sign-off, this now-familiar work furnishes the librarian and patron with an excellent source of information on television network series. First published in 1979, it has been updated twice and follows a pattern of about three years between issues. In addition to network series, it includes the top shows in syndication. Entries are arranged by title of the program and include dates of showing, broadcast history, cast, story line, and memorable episodes. The present work covers series through 1984 and is indexed by names. There are several interesting and useful appendices. Another work which overlaps in coverage is Vincent Terrace's *The Complete Encyclopedia of Television Programs, 1947-1979* (A. S. Barnes, 1979). Much of the same information is provided for series television, but the two titles can be used together to assure that coverage is as complete as possible.

687. **Filmmaker's Dictionary.** Ralph S. Singleton. Beverly Hills, Calif., Lone Eagle, 1986. 188p.

This concise and compact volume is filled with the terminology of filmmaking practice. It is written in simple language but provides a useful service in helping the user to become familiar with both technical terms and slang expressions employed by professionals in the field. More than 1,500 terms, representing every aspect of the art, are defined. There are abundant cross-references from the entries to other related definitions, making this a most convenient and practical dictionary. Most interesting are the almost anecdotal bits of background information attached to many of the definitions. The work will be used for browsing as well as ready-reference work. Another useful dictionary of film terminology is Frank E. Beaver's *Dictionary of Film Terms* (McGraw-Hill, 1983), which achieves a good balance between the technical and the popular.

688. **A Guide to World Cinema: Covering 7,200 Films of 1950-84 ...** Elkan Allan, ed. London, Whittet Books; distr., Detroit, Gale, 1985. 682p.

Rather than a guide which implies a certain selectivity or evaluative nature, this is a listing of the thousands of motion pictures shown at the British Film Institute over a thirty-four-year period. With such a huge quantity, naturally a wide variety of films is listed, ranging from the classic to the absurd. This is in part what gives this work strength as a valuable identification tool for all libraries supporting film research and inquiry. The work provides for each film what are referred to in the subtitle as "capsule reviews"—brief but informative commentaries taken from the original program notes. Most entries also include a very small production still. The comprehensive coverage and relative depth of information provided make this a notable purchase for the collection, even though it has been criticized for its small print size.

689. **Halliwell's Film Guide.** 5th ed. Leslie Halliwell. New York, Scribner's, 1986. 1124p.

The name Halliwell is a familiar one to librarians and patrons of the entertainment arts for the useful and convenient series of guides which he has produced over the years. The fifth edition of this work appeared just two years after the fourth edition and adds 400 new entries covering the 1983-1984 period, as well as indication of video availability for 1,000 of the entries. An additional 1,500 entries are included for films of the 1930s, and there appear to be more critical quotes from the time of the film release. The arrangement of entries is alphabetical by title. The tool remains an excellent source for identification and description of films of interest to both the specialist and the film buff. Another of the author's important handbooks is *Halliwell's Filmgoer's Companion*, now in its eighth edition (Scribner's, 1984). It has been regarded as an excellent source for the general moviegoer and covers a broad range of topics. It provides definitions, identifications, and descriptions of personalities, individual film titles, and terminology, all in one alphabetical sequence. *Halliwell's Television Companion*, now in its second edition (London, Granada, 1982) provides similar coverage for television films, series, and personalities.

690. **The New York Times Encyclopedia of Film.** Gene Brown and Harry M. Geduld, eds. New York, Times Books, 1984. 13v.

Similar to the *New York Times Film Reviews* (see entry 713) in format, this monumental collection of articles from the *New York Times* is arranged chronologically from 1896 to 1979. Included are all types of writings pertaining to motion pictures: news items, features, interviews, reports, and promotional pieces. As one might expect, reviews are studiously avoided, allowing the *New York Times Film Reviews* to retain its uniqueness in that area. Many illustrations are included, although the work has been criticized for the poor quality of the reproductions. Many subjects are covered, with a good proportion of the articles on personalities (producers, commentators, critics, and news correspondents, as well as performers). There is an index volume which is alphabetically arranged, providing access to the desired subject.

691. **Radio Soundtracks: A Reference Guide.** 2nd ed. Michael R. Pitts. Metuchen, N.J., Scarecrow, 1986. 337p.

The purpose of this revised edition of an earlier work is to identify programs from the golden age of radio (1920s to 1960s) which are available on tapes and records. It is divided into five parts, the largest of which lists over 1,000 programs available on tape. Entries are arranged by name of program, and include network, length, stars, and brief commentary. Part 2 covers radio specials on tape, while part 3 identifies those available on long-playing records. Part 4 is "Performers' Radio Appearances on Long Playing Records" and part 5 describes compilation record albums composed of radio material. Over 2,700 entries are furnished in all, and the work should be extremely useful both for identification of the historical factual material and for information regarding the recording.

692. **Radio's Golden Years: Encyclopedia of Radio Programs, 1930-1960.** Vincent Terrace. San Diego, Calif., A. S. Barnes; distr., London, Tantivy, 1981. 308p.

An absorbing compendium of information on the great years of radio programming, this work identifies 1,500 network and syndicated entertainment programs. The arrangement is alphabetical by title of the program; entries include storyline, cast lists, announcer and music credits, sponsors, program openings, network and syndication information, length, and dates. A variety of entertainment programs is described (adventure, comedy, crime, drama, game shows, musicals, mystery, science fiction, and westerns). There are a number of good illustrations. A name index provides access. Another useful tool which will overlap to some degree is John Dunning's *Tune in Yesterday: The Ultimate Encyclopedia of Old-Time Radio, 1925-1976* (Prentice-Hall, 1976). Its arrangement is similar, but Dunning offers more background information, with biographical facts about performers. *Primetime Radio Classics is a database available online through The Source and CompuServe. It provides information on episodes of classic radio programs from the 1930s to the 1950s in a variety of categories. Cassettes may be ordered.

Directories, Annuals, and
Current Awareness Services

693. **Feature Films: A Directory of Feature Films on 16mm and Videotape Available for Rental, Sale and Lease.** 8th ed. James L. Limbacher, comp. and ed. New York, R. R. Bowker, 1985. 734p.

Settled into what appears to be a biennial pattern of appearance, this directory has undergone a change of title to eliminate 8mm films from its coverage. This edition carries over 22,000 entries for items which are available from leading distributors. They are arranged alphabetically by title and include releasing company, year of release, running time, special information, and distributor's name. A feature film is defined as any film over one 16mm reel long or forty-eight minutes' running time. Most distributors are U.S. but there are some Canadian firms listed as well. Included are a directors' index, foreign-language index, and a directory of names with addresses. *The Video Source Book* (National Video Clearinghouse, 1979-) is an annual publication that identifies over 40,000 prerecorded video program titles available on videotape and videodisc. It is arranged by title, and a subject category index is furnished to provide access to materials of interest to home, business, or institutions.

694. International Motion Picture Almanac. 1929- . Ann. New York, Quigley.

This has been a leading publication and a universal purchase for film libraries throughout its long history. It is a treasure house of miscellaneous information and statistical data. Included is a who's who providing brief biographical sketches of numerous film personalities. There are also sections on pictures, corporations, theater circuits, buying and booking, equipment and suppliers, services, talent and literary agencies, organizations, advertising codes, world market, press, nontheatrical motion pictures, censorship, etc. It also gives information on the industry in Great Britain and Ireland. *International Television Almanac* (Quigley, 1956-) is also published on an annual basis. Statistical reporting and information on people and developments make it a useful tool for television study. It identifies television stations, shows, networks, personnel, and feature releases, and provides information on the industry in Great Britain and Ireland as well. *Screen World* (Crown, 1949-) has been appearing annually since it was started by David Blum. Since 1966, it has been edited by John Willis and has continued as a highly regarded resource for its survey of film releases in the previous year. Major films are identified with the cast list and production credits. The volume is profusely illustrated with film scenes. There are no plot summaries, but it does have a useful biographical section. Recently, the publisher has reprinted the first twenty volumes of this notable serial.

695. Television & Cable Fact Book. 1982- . Ann. Washington, D.C., Television Digest.

This has proved to be a most useful reference tool for those needing up-to-date information on the television and cable industries. It appears in two separate publications. The *Stations* volume covers technical facilities, ownership, personnel, rate, and audience data for all television stations in the United States. Entries are arranged by state, then alphabetically by city, with separate treatment for Canadian and international stations. The *Cable and Services* volumes provide similar coverage of those aspects related to cable industries. *The Home Video & Cable Report* (Knowledge Industry Publications, 1982-) is an even more up-to-date tool, providing a weekly service. It is the most current print tool for information on the home video and cable industries. *Television Digest* is a weekly report of technical, financial and marketing developments in the industry. It is available online from NewsNet and contains material from 1982 to the present.

696. Variety. 1905- . Wk. New York, Variety, Inc.

The leading current awareness journal and official newspaper of show business, for which it is analogous to *Billboard* (see entry 526) in the music field. There are sections on movies, radio and television, music, records, and vaudeville, providing information of a varied nature on recent developments, trends, personalities, etc. Theater is covered in detail, with reviews of various shows, information on casting, gate receipts, etc. It is well-known for its reviews of top records of the week. Excellent coverage is given to the business aspects of this wide range of performing arts. *Art Murphy's Boxoffice Register* (Art Murphy's Boxoffice Register, 1982-) has established itself as an annual publication. It provides financial reporting from *Variety* for film distributors for the box office year. Films are identified and income given; arrangement is alphabetical by title. *HOLLYWOOD HOTLINE is a computerized database available through CompuServe and NewsNet. It provides news of the entertainment industry including films, music, and home entertainment. It covers programming, contracts, movie summaries, soap operas, record albums, etc., from 1983 to the present. It is updated daily. Available online through the publisher, Baseline Inc., is another computerized database providing an array of useful files: *BASELINE, which contains biographies of creative, technical, and administrative personnel for various segments of the entertainment industry (film, television, theater); listings of over 35,000 films released in the United States for both theaters and television, theater productions, and television series for the past twelve years; current production information on over 1,400 films and television series; citations to articles in major entertainment trade journals including *Variety*; demographics on audiences attending opening nights; daily information on the Hollywood entertainment community; and synopses and evaluations of literary properties available for purchase, calendar, stocks, and travel.

697. **The Video Register and Teleconferencing Resources Directory 1987.** 9th ed. Martha Csenge, et al., eds. White Plains, N.Y., Knowledge Industry Publications, 1986.
      The ninth edition of this annual directory provides a listing of manufacturers, tele-conferencing suppliers and service units, dealers, consultants, cable access centers, program distributors, trade association workshops, publications, etc. Since two directories were joined together as one publication, it provides information on a variety of sources as well as some marginal elements to both video and teleconferencing. Both sections begin with introductory material describing the contents. Each has an index to facilitate access. Much of what is covered is difficult to find elsewhere, especially information on tele-conferencing equipment and suppliers.

Histories

698. **The American Film Industry: A Historical Directory.** Anthony Slide. Westport, Conn., Greenwood Press, 1986. 431p.
      Slide and his team of eight research associates have put together a new and detailed dictionary of the historical development of the film industry in this country. There are about 600 entries, all well written and informative. Such aspects as producing and releasing companies, technological innovations, film series, genres, organizations, and technical terms are treated. Entries vary in length from just a few lines to a few pages depending upon the importance of the subject. There is a general index of persons, subjects, organizations, etc., and numerous cross-references are included. This work is especially useful for the relative depth of the entries, which provide a great deal of detail. Benjamin Hampton's *A History of the Movies* (Friede, 1931; repr., Arno, 1970) is a true history of the American film industry and is a classic work regarded as a major contribution even today.

699. **American History, American Television: Interpreting the Video Past.** John E. O'Connor, ed. New York, Ungar, 1983. 420p. (Ungar Film Library).

This is a collection of fourteen essays of a historical and critical nature regarding the role of television in American history and culture. The essays cover a variety of subjects ranging from Milton Berle to the 1980 political campaign. Each article treats programming and production issues and industry and public response. News, documentaries, and entertainment programming are all covered in this fashion. There is a good annotated bibliography with accompanying commentary. The work will be helpful to students of television, history, and communications in general. Those studying sociology and anthropology will also benefit by the exposition provided. In addition to the bibliography, there is a useful guide to archival and manuscript sources.

700. **A History of Narrative Film.** David A. Cook. New York, W. W. Norton, 1981. 721p.

This is an important work focused on the development of narrative film. It should be of use to a variety of patrons from serious students to laypersons. It is presented in scholarly fashion, well documented throughout, and provides good illustrations of major scenes from some of the films described. Detailed information is found on individual filmmakers, and their movies are examined in a critical manner. National cinemas and many films are covered. Film elements are analyzed, and in some cases public reaction and influence on the field are gauged. The layperson will be especially interested in the quantity of production stills taken from a variety of motion pictures over the years. There are a good bibliography and a glossary as well. Both public libraries and academic libraries will be well served by this tool.

701. **Producers Releasing Corporation: A Comprehensive Filmography and History.** Wheeler Dixon, ed. Jefferson, N.C., McFarland, 1986. 166p.

This is a delightful and thoroughly interesting historical overview of the life of a typical "B" movie production company located in Hollywood's "Poverty Row." These small operations would turn out movies in less than one week using unheralded actors and minimal sets. Budgets for the entire production generally did not exceed $20,000, and although the films were shoddy in every way, they do represent an important segment of the history of the American film industry. This work records the story of PRC through a brief narrative and a good chronology. A survey is given of the westerns produced by the studio; biographical sketches are furnished for personnel. Filmographies are included for the leading directors, as well as a checklist of films from the company. A detailed index helps to provide access.

Biographical Sources

702. **A Biographical Dictionary of Film.** 2nd ed. rev. David Thomson. New York, Morrow, 1981. 682p.

The first edition of this work was published in 1981 and was praised by reviewers for its literate and witty, albeit opinionated, coverage of actors and directors. Librarians found it to be a vital source, one which was refreshingly entertaining but at the same time cogent and effective as a critical tool. Thomson is a Briton whose "obsessive work provides a sharp expression of personal taste, jokes, and digressions, insults, and eulogies." The new edition updates material for the entries in the earlier work and adds about forty-five new personalities, mainly Americans who have had a strong impact in recent years (Robert DeNiro, Goldie Hawn, Steven Spielberg, Al Pacino, etc.). It retains its charm and continues to be a top-rated biographical dictionary.

703.   **Film Directors: A Complete Guide.** 1983- . Michael Singer, comp. and ed. Ann. Beverly Hills, Calif., Lone Eagle.

The fifth edition (1987) of this annual biographical directory has been enlarged and now covers over 1,800 living directors from all over the world. Arrangement of entries is alphabetical by name and each entry furnishes basic information of interest to those who wish to identify or further examine the work of an individual filmmaker. Included are birthdate, birthplace, agent's name, address, and phone number as well as a chronological listing of films (including television works) with year of release, country of origin, and distributor. The value of this work lies in the comprehensive coverage of contemporary figures that one might not find elsewhere. *Biographical Dictionary of Film* (see entry 702) or George Sadoul's *Dictionary of Film Makers* (Berkeley, University of California Press, 1972) should be used for greater biographical detail. The latter is a translation of a French work and is a selective biographical dictionary of 10,000 producers, directors, scenarists, photographers and others associated with filmmaking, but not actors or actresses. Entries are brief but informative and commentary is subjective. More limited in scope but also important is Larry Langman's *A Guide to American Film Directors: The Sound Era, 1929-1979* (Scarecrow, 1981) in two volumes.

704.   **The Illustrated Who's Who of the Cinema.** Ann Lloyd and Graham Fuller, eds. New York, Macmillan, 1983. 480p.

A total of 2,500 biographies covering people from all areas of the cinematic world is furnished, along with some 1,500 illustrations. Actors, actresses, producers, directors, scene designers, costumers, art directors, composers, screenwriters, cinematographers, etc., are all represented along with critics and censors. Generally conceded to be a record of the personalities of what might be called "mainstream cinema," there is excellent coverage of people from the 1920s to the 1940s, with less elaboration given to personalities of the 1950s and 1960s. Biographies are brief and include a short filmography which identifies the person's first and last motion picture and a representative number in between. An updated edition of this work will be published in late 1987 by the authors as *The Illustrated Who's Who in Cinema* (Portland House). A quite different work is *The Illustrated Encyclopedia of Movie Character Actors*, by David Quinlan (Harmony Books/Crown, 1985), which provides more detail and interesting and perceptive descriptions of 850 British and American character actors. The glib and witty characterizations make this work a pleasure to read.

705.   **The International Dictionary of Films and Filmmakers.** Christopher Lyon and Susan Doll, eds. Chicago, St. James, 1984- . 3v. (In progress).

To date three of the projected four volumes have been completed, two of which are biographical dictionaries. Volume 1 (1984) provides information on 600 of the world's most frequently studied films. Volume 2 (1984) covers over 450 directors and filmmakers of international renown. The arrangement is alphabetical by name and entries provide brief biographies; filmographies; selective bibliographies of books and articles, both by and about the personality; and an informative critical evaluation of the individual's work. Volume 3 (1986) covers actors and actresses of international stature and provides similar coverage to that accorded the directors in volume 1. Yet to come is volume 4, which will cover the contributions of writers and production artists. As one might expect, there is some variation in the quality of the critical essays, as well as the fullness of the biographical entries, but in general the tool is useful for its depth and detail.

✓706.   **Who Was Who on Screen.** 3rd ed. Evelyn Mack Truitt. New York, R. R. Bowker, 1983. 571p.

Since its initial appearance in 1974, this retrospective biographical dictionary has been a popular purchase for reference collections serving the needs of both film buffs and specialists. With each edition, it has enlarged its coverage, and the present work covers no fewer than 13,000 individuals who died between 1905 and 1981. Where needed, entries from the previous editions have been revised. The arrangement of entries is alphabetical. They furnish brief biographical identification along with a complete listing of film credits with dates. The latter contribution especially establishes this tool as a basic reference work. Both shorts and features are identified. Inclusion is not limited to actors alone but extends to prominent personalities who have had cameo appearances such as Picasso, Hitchcock, and Maugham.

707.   **Who's Who in Television and Cable.** Steven H. Scheuer, ed. New York, Facts on File, 1983. 579p.

This is a biographical dictionary of 2,000 living television and cable personalities, most of them leading executives of the three major commercial networks, public television, and cable services. Also included are performers, executives of major local stations, agents, and others. The emphasis is definitely not on the performers, for notable omissions are people like Mary Tyler Moore, Carl Reiner, and Harvey Korman. Entries are alphabetically arranged and highly structured, providing occupational category, business address, date and place of birth, education, career highlights, achievements and awards, and a personal fact or two such as city of residence and names of family members. There are numerous photographs, and access is provided through an index by job title or position. Also included is a corporation index which groups entries under networks or cable systems.

Reviews

*708.   **CINEMAN MOVIE REVIEWS.** (database) Cineman Syndicate, Inc.

A computerized database available online through Dow Jones, The Source, and several other vendors, this service is updated on a weekly basis. There are over 4,000 reviews written by critic Jay A. Brown. Reviews include a summary of nearly 100 words, a list of principal actors, and an evaluation rating ranging from "great" to "poor." There is a coming attractions column on a biweekly basis. Included are new releases, current movies, coming attractions, historical reviews (1926-present) and top box office films. Brown's reviews appear on an annual basis in *Rating the Movies: For Home Video, TV, and Cable* (Beekman House; distr., Crown). *MOVIE REVIEWETTES is another database available online from CompuServe. It furnishes reviews which include plot summaries and ratings, written by Eliot Stein. These generally appear prior to or concurrently with the films' release in theaters.

709.   **Guide to Critical Reviews, Part IV: The Screenplay, Supplement One: 1963-1980.** James M. Salem. Metuchen, N.J., Scarecrow, 1982. 698p.

Since the initial volume of the first edition of this work over twenty years ago, the basic four volumes of this bibliography of critical reviews have appeared at different times and in different editions with various supplements. Part I of the main volume is now in its third edition (1984) and covers American drama from 1909 to 1982. Part II (2nd edition, 1976) covers the musical from 1909 to 1974. Part III (2nd edition, 1979) treats foreign drama from 1909 to 1974. This supplement is to part IV which has not been revised since the first edition in two volumes in 1971. The first edition was entitled *The Screenplay from The Jazz Singer to Dr. Strangelove* and covered a period of about thirty-five years. This supplement continues the coverage of that work by adding another seventeen years of reviews. The reviews are generally from well-known periodicals such as *Film Quarterly, Life, Newsweek, Rolling Stone, The New Yorker,* etc. and the reviews should not be difficult to find. The volumes, including this one on the screenplay, continue to be a popular, useful purchase for the reference department.

710. **Magill's Cinema Annual.** 1982- . Ann. Englewood Cliffs, N.J., Salem.

This is a handy and extremely useful guide to a select number of films of the previous year. Beginning with coverage of the year 1981, it has served as a supplement to the extensive multivolume *Magill's Survey of Cinema* (see entry 711). The reviews are lengthy and well constructed and cover on the average eighty films released in the United States. Entries include production credits, direction, screenplay, cinematography, editing, art direction, music, MPAA rating, running time, and principal characters. Foreign films are included if they were released in this country during the time period. There is also a section of additional films which treats briefly the same number of films that appear in the "Selected Films" category. In addition, there are an obituary section and a listing of popular awards. There are a number of indexes providing excellent access including subject, title, performer, screenwriter, etc.

711. **Magill's Survey of Cinema: Foreign Language Films.** Frank N. Magill, ed. Englewood Cliffs, N.J., Salem, 1985. 8v.

This is the latest edition in the extensive multivolume sets which are parts of a series bearing the Magill name. This set covers 700 foreign films arranged alphabetically by the title used in the United States. The reviews themselves are new and the result of a fresh viewing of the films by about 180 contributors. The reviews are preceded by identifications which include origin, release date, U.S. release date, producers, directors, screenplay, photographer, editor, art, costume, sound and music direction, and running time. Cast lists are given also. The original set in the series appeared in 1980 as *Magill's Survey of Cinema: English Language Films, First Series.* This was a four-volume set, followed in the next year by a six-volume set, the *Second Series.* The third issue was *Magill's Survey of Cinema: Silent Films,* a three-volume set published in 1982. It covered silent motion pictures from 1902 to 1936. In all cases, the essays are well written and range from 1,000-2,500 words in length, including plot summaries and critical commentaries. *Magill's Cinema Annual* (see entry 710) serves as an update each year.

712. **The Motion Picture Guide, 1927-1984.** Jay Robert Nash and Ralph Ross Stanley. Chicago, Cinebooks, 1985-1987. 12v.

This ten-volume set and two index volumes (vols. xi, xii) form one of the most comprehensive and detailed of all reference tools for the identification and description of films. There are 25,000 entries on English-language motion pictures as well as notable foreign films, with a separate volume devoted to silent films. Volumes are arranged sequentially in alphabetical order, and entries are arranged by title. Ratings are provided from zero to five stars and included are year of release, running time, production/releasing company, and color status. Cast lists are given, and most important, good analytical reviews are provided. The reviews are interesting, with their sometimes incisive and sometimes anecdotal commentary. Interesting background information regarding the performers or the making of the films is also included. The two-volume index, published in 1987, provides access to alternate titles, series, and awards. The entire series evidently will be continued by means of an annual guide which started in 1986.

713. **New York Times Film Reviews, 1913-1968.** New York, New York Times, and New York, Arno, 1970. 6v. Bienn. Supp., 1969/1970- .

This monumental work is one of the best sources of available reviews for motion pictures. The original six-volume set covers a period of fifty-five years. For the early years of silent pictures through several great periods of Hollywood genre films ending with the late 1960s, the reviews are chronologically arranged by date of appearance in the newspaper and are reproduced in the first five volumes of this work. Altogether 17,000 films are covered in excellent fashion; the newspaper's critics have had a reputation for thoroughness and perceptivity. Volume 6, the index volume, contains appendices of overlooked reviews, New York Critic's Circle Awards, Academy Awards, and many illustrations. The index is detailed and is divided into separate sections for titles, people, and corporations. The series is kept up-to-date with biennial cumulations beginning with the period 1969-1970, generally published a year or two following the period of coverage (1981-1982, supplement published in 1984). *The New York Times Directory of the Film* (Arno, 1971) is a reprinting of the personal name and corporate index sections from the index volume of the main set. It is useful for its references to the date and page of the newspaper.

714. **Variety Film Reviews, 1907-1980.** New York, Garland, 1983-1985. 16v.

Using the idea developed for the production of the *New York Times Film Reviews* (see entry 713), this is another multivolume collection of reviews from a single source. In this case, the film reviews are taken from *Variety* (see entry 696) and cover a period of seventy-three years in fifteen volumes. Volume 16 serves as an index of titles. The reviews are furnished in chronological sequence in order of their appearance in the magazine. Since feature-length films and shorts were not distinguished from each other until 1927, both types are included up to that time. After June 1927 only feature-length films are included. Similar to the *New York Times Directory of the Film* (see entry 713n) is Max Joseph Alvarez's *Index to Motion Pictures Reviewed by Variety, 1907-1980* (Scarecrow, 1982). It furnishes a separately published title index to the reviews and includes short subjects and re-releases.

11 ACCESSING INFORMATION IN LANGUAGE AND LITERATURE

WORKING DEFINITIONS OF LANGUAGE AND LITERATURE

Language and literature are treated together in this guide because they are interdependent and because one of the primary ways of organizing literature is by the language of the literary work under consideration.

The common definitions of *language* and *literature* suggest that language has to do with spoken and written words and the systems for their use, and that literature comprises the writings that capture ideas. Some dictionary definitions of literature also posit that it has the characteristics of "lasting value" or "permanent interest." Literature, like philosophy, relates in a sense to all fields: hence we speak of the "literature of science," the "literature of the arts," and "social science literature," when we discuss the writings of a particular discipline or field of study.

Because of the possible confusion over definitions, it may be best to define literature by the forms, or genres, that it takes. Lester Asheim's chapter on literature in *The Humanities and the Library* (pp. 199-267) suggests such a working definition and provides capsule descriptions, with examples, of the literary forms which are of interest to the student or librarian.

The issue of value in literature is an important one. While the issue is of interest in all the fields of the humanities, the fact that criticism of one work frequently becomes part of the body of literature itself is nowhere more evident than in the field of literary scholarship. The critical literature is subject, then, to subsequent criticism as well.

An additional source which will help clarify problems in defining and characterizing language is Edward Sapir's classic *Language: An Introduction to the Study of Speech* (Harcourt, 1921; repr., 1955). The chapters on defining language are reprinted in Donald W. Lee's *English Language Reader: Introduction, Essays and Exercises* (Dodd, 1964), a text for the university student.

MAJOR DIVISIONS OF THE FIELD

Both of the two basic approaches to the division of literature — by language and by form — are usually taken into account in customary divisions of the field. Division of literature on the basis of the language in which it is written may require some refinements and modifications. For example, the volume of literature written in English is so large that further subdivision is desirable. In this case, the term "English literature" is restricted to the literary output of the United Kingdom that appears in English, or even to the literature of England alone. Separate provision is customarily made for American literature, Australian literature, etc. At the other extreme, some of the world's smallest literatures may be grouped together under a parent language.

The two basic forms of literature are prose and poetry. Prose is normally divided into novels, short stories, and essays. Poetry is normally treated as a unit, but it may be further subdivided by type (lyric poems, epic poems, etc.). The drama, as a literary record of what is to be performed on stage, has an independent life of its own and is also considered to be one of the major literary forms. Modern drama is ordinarily in prose, but it may also be in verse or may consist of both poetry and verse.

Another approach to the organization of literature is by historical periods or literary movements, often in combination with the basic schemes described above.

In addition to the general coverage and that of individual languages and literatures available through the *Encyclopedia Americana* and *Encyclopaedia Britannica: Macropaedia*, the student is referred to the introductory and historical sections of chapter 12, "Principal Information Sources in Language and Literature." Many pertinent comments on reference work will be found in the chapter "Literature" in Asheim's *The Humanities and the Library*.

USE AND USERS OF INFORMATION IN LANGUAGE AND LITERATURE

Scholars in the field of literature have been subject to user studies in greater numbers than almost any other field in the humanities. That literary scholars and writers in the area of criticism cite sources in their works makes it possible for the bibliometrician to carry out citation studies of various sources.

Among the many studies of use and users in literature are Edwin S. Gleaves's *Characteristics of the Research Materials Used by Scholars Who Write in Journals in the Field of American Literature* (ACRL Microcard, 130, for ACRL, 1961); John Cullars's "Characteristics of the Monographic Literature of British and American Literary Studies" (*College and Research Libraries* 46 [November 1985]: 511-22); R. Heinzkill's "Characteristics of References in Selected Scholarly English Literary Journals" (*Library Quarterly* 50 [July 1980]: 352-65); M. Stern's "Characteristics of the Literature of Literary Scholarship" (*College and Research Libraries* 44 [July 1983]: 199-209); John Budd's "A Citation Study of American Literature: Implications for Collection Management" (*Collection Management* 8 [Summer 1986]: 49-62); and John Budd's "Characteristics of Written Scholarship in American Literature: A Citation Study" (*Library and Information Science Research* 8 [April 1986]: 189-211).

Other aspects of citations have been investigated by Carolyn Frost, in "The Use of Citations in Literary Research: A Preliminary Classification of Citation Functions" (*Library Quarterly* 49 [October 1979]: 399-414). Virginia Doland looks at use from another perspective in "Portrait of the Critic as Journal Reader: A Study of Readership Patterns among Literary Scholars," in *Challenges to an Information Society* (Knowledge Industry Publications for ASIS, 1984, pp. 222-26).

Finally, languages and literature are addressed in Yolanda Beh's "Library and Information Resources and Services for Users in Language and Literature," in *The Library in the Information Revolution* (6th edition, Congress of Southeast Asian Librarians, 1983, pp. 500-29).

COMPUTERS IN LANGUAGE AND LITERATURE

The number of computer applications in the fields of language and literature is too great to mention many here. Indeed, Kathleen Turner and others have shown that in the journal *Computers and the Humanities* the greatest proportion of articles have dealt with dictionaries, indexes, and concordances and computer applications in their development.[1] For our purposes, though, there exist sources which cover applications in literary analysis, concordancing and dictionary development, textual criticism, machine translation, morphological and syntactic analysis, and instructional processes. Susan Hockey's *A Guide to Computer Applications in the Humanities* (Johns Hopkins University Press, 1980) is almost wholly devoted to literary and language applications. More than a dozen papers, some of which address the topic of writing and composition, are found in *Sixth International Conference on Computers and the Humanities*, edited by Sarah K. Burton and Douglas D. Short (Computer Science Press, 1983). Several language applications are covered in *Data Bases in the Humanities and Social Sciences*, edited by Robert F. Allen (Paradigm, 1983). Finally, *ARIST* (*Annual Review of Information Science and Technology*) reviews in volume 7 (1972) and volume 16 (1981) cover language and literature applications.

Among online offerings in language and literature, MLA BIBLIOGRAPHY (file 71 in DIALOG) and LANGUAGE AND LANGUAGE BEHAVIOR ABSTRACTS (LLBA), file 36 in DIALOG, are the primary ones.

MAJOR ORGANIZATIONS, INFORMATION CENTERS, AND SPECIAL COLLECTIONS

Languages

The oldest, largest, and best-known of the organizations that promote the study and teaching of languages in this country is the Modern Language Association of America (10 Astor Place, New York, NY 10003). Founded in 1883, it has more than 24,000 members, primarily college and university teachers, and it conducts an immense range of programs and activities. Publications include *MLA Newsletter* (quarterly); *PMLA* (quarterly); *Job Information List—English* (quarterly); *Job Information List—Foreign Languages* (quarterly); *Directory* (annual); and *MLA International Bibliography* (annual).

The American Council on the Teaching of Foreign Languages (579 Broadway, Hastings-on-Hudson, NY 10706) was founded by MLA in 1966, but now exists as a separate entity. Its publications include *Foreign Language Annals* (6/yr.) and *Series on Foreign Language Education* (annual).

The International Federation of Modern Language Teachers (Seestr. 247, CH-8038 Zurich, Switzerland) is made up of multilingual and unilingual associations. It corresponds at the international level to the National Federation of Modern Language Teachers Associations (Gannon University, Erie, PA 16541), a federation of national, regional, and state associations in this country that publishes *Modern Language Journal* (6/yr.).

The International Association of Learning Lab Directors (Ellis Hall, Ohio University, Athens, OH 45701) conducts workshops and seeks to improve the liaison between manufacturers and users of language lab equipment.

The American Association of Language Specialists (Suite 9, 1000 Connecticut Ave., N.W., Washington, DC 20036) is a small group of interpreters, editors, and translators.

Literature

The International Comparative Literature Association (Comparative Literature Program, Ballentine Hall #402, Indiana University, Bloomingdale, IN 47405) promotes the worldwide study of comparative literature.

The American Comparative Literature Association (University of Michigan, Ann Arbor, MI 48109) promotes the study and teaching of comparative literature in American universities, publishes a newsletter, cosponsors *Yearbook of Comparative and General Literature*, and assists in the publication of two quarterly journals: *Comparative Literature* and *Comparative Literature Studies*.

The Coordinating Council of Literary Magazines (666 Broadway, 11th Floor, New York, NY 10012) assists "little magazines" in a variety of ways.

Regional interests are served by such groups as the Society for the Study of Southern Literature and the Western Literature Association.

Various library, literary, and children's literary associations serve a host of special clienteles with interests in aspects of books, literature, and publications.

Information Centers in Language and Literature

The identification of information centers as distinct from professional organizations, on the one hand, and from special collections, on the other, is not a clearcut and simple matter. Many (but by no means all) professional organizations conduct programs of research and information dissemination. Many libraries holding special collections do the same. Nevertheless, mention should be made here of a few noteworthy examples.

The first is the Folger Shakespeare Library (201 East Capitol St., Washington, DC 20003), which has an active research and publication program in British civilization of the Tudor and Stuart periods and theatrical history as these relate to Shakespeare.

The Center for Hellenic Studies (3100 Whitehaven St., Washington, DC 20003) is an international center associated with Harvard University. It conducts research in such areas as classical Greek literature, philosophy, and history.

The Center for Textual Studies (323 Main Library, Ohio State University, Columbus, OH 43210) conducts research on definitive texts of nineteenth- and twentieth-century authors, including the publication of definitive editions of Hawthorne and Emerson.

Special Collections in Language and Literature

The number of special collections in language and literature is so vast that mentioning names beyond the obvious giants like the Library of Congress, the British Library, the Bibliothèque Nationale, the New York Public Library, and Harvard University could easily run to several pages. Once again, the works of Young, Ash, and Lewanski are very useful. Searching under fairly specific headings, including the names of individual authors, will often be most fruitful. The *Handbook* of the Center for Research Libraries also devotes considerable space to special collections in European and American literature.

NOTES

[1]Kathleen Turner and Matthew Marino, "Beyond Word Crunching," in *Sixth International Conference on Computers and the Humanities* (Rockville, Md.: Computer Science Press, 1983), 717-24.

12 PRINCIPAL INFORMATION SOURCES IN LANGUAGE AND LITERATURE

LANGUAGE AND LINGUISTICS

Bibliographies

715. Bibliography and Index of Mainland Southeast Asian Languages and Linguistics. Franklin E. Huffman. New Haven, Conn., Yale University Press, 1986. 640p.

A comprehensive listing which, in all probability, will become a standard in the field, this bibliography divides languages into five major categories: Austroasiatic, Tibeto-Burman, Tai-Kadgi, Miao-Yao, and Mainland Austronesian. About 10,000 titles on Southeast Asian languages, published up to 1985, are identified and represent all forms of published materials as well as informal papers including conference presentations. Arrangement of entries is alphabetical by author, with cross-references furnished from multiple authors and variant names. Materials written in various languages of the world are identified and English translations are provided for entries in other than the common European language systems. An informative introduction describes the language classifications employed, and a detailed index provides ready access.

716. A Bibliography of Contemporary Linguistic Research. Gerald Gazdar, et al., comps. New York, Garland, 1978. 425p. (Garland Reference Library of the Humanities, v.119).

This is a useful and practical listing of scholarly reports and studies drawn from professional journals, conference proceedings, specialized anthologies, and litho-printed books. The listing is extensive, numbering about 5,000 entries beginning with the year 1970. It is convenient and handy for specialists who are interested in determining current or recent issues in terms of possible research topics. Monographs, book reviews, and material written prior to 1970, have not been included. Topical emphases of the entries reflect the major concerns of researchers (syntactic, semantic, philological, and pragmatic theories of linguistics). Items included are mainly, but not limited to, English, and there are indexes by language and subject. Harold Byron Allen's second edition of *Linguistics and English Linguistics* (AHM, 1977) provides a guide for college students to nearly 3,000 items on linguistics and related studies dated to 1975.

717. Bibliography of Semiotics, 1975-1985. Achim Eschbach and Victoria Eschbach-Szabo, with Gabi Willenberg, comps. Philadelphia, John Benjamins, 1986. 2 pts. (Library

& Information Sources in Linguistics, v.16; Amsterdam Studies in the Theory and History of Linguistics Science, Series V).

This is the most recent contribution to this important series under the direction of E. F. Koerner, which has included bibliographies on various aspects of linguistics. Semiotics embraces the study of signs and signaling systems and is interpreted by some to include such areas as pragmatics, semantics, and syntactics.

Nearly 11,000 entries are furnished for the ten-year period covered. Books, monographs, dissertations, articles, conference proceedings, festschriften, and reviews are all included. The coverage is international and several countries and languages are represented. (The U.S.S.R. is a notable omission because of the unavailability of bibliographies identifying materials on this subject.) Part 1 consists of an alphabetical list of nearly 700 periodicals that publish in this field, followed by the first half of the bibliographical entries; part 2 provides the second half of the bibliographical listings as well as indexes of reviews, subjects, and names.

718. **World Dictionaries in Print 1983: A Guide to General and Subject Dictionaries in World Languages.** New York, R. R. Bowker, 1983. 579p.

Another of the Bowker spinoffs from the publisher's magnificent computerized database, this work supplies identification and purchasing information for over 13,500 titles of dictionaries of all types. Half the entries represent foreign-language titles, and all items are arranged under four major groupings of indexes. The subject index collects entries alphabetically by compiler under several thousand LC subject headings. The title index lists all entries alphabetically. In both indexes, one is able to find such information as editor, compiler, translator, title, subtitle, imprint, collation, grade range, LC number, ISBN, and price in currency of the publishing country. An author-editor-compiler index supplies title and publisher. The language index groups only the titles under 238 language headings. There is a key to publishers and distributors which gives up-to-date addresses, and the foreword provides useful information about ordering from publishers abroad.

Indexes, Abstracts, and
Serial Bibliographies

719. **Bibliographie linguistique des annees.** 1939/1947- . Ann. Comité International Permanent de Linguistes. Utrecht, Spectrum.

With its initial publication covering an eight-year period in two volumes, this service achieved worldwide recognition as a massive work of documentation. It provides coverage of linguistics on an international level and identifies books, reviews, and articles from such diverse countries as South Africa, Belgium (Flemish publications), Czechoslovakia, Finland, France, Italy, the Netherlands, Norway, Poland, Spain, and Switzerland in volume 1. Coverage in volume 2 furnishes listings from Austria, Belgium (French publications), Denmark, England, Greece, India, Ireland, Portugal, the Soviet Union, Sweden, Turkey, and the United States. There is an author index to both volumes. The work continues as an annual publication and is highly regarded for its comprehensive coverage of periodical articles. There is no subject index, but the detailed table of contents facilitates access.

*720. **Bulletin signalétique 524: Sciences du langage.** 1947- . Q. Paris, Centre National de la Recherche Scientifique.

Part of the massive international documentation service undertaken by the Centre National (see entries 46 and 99), this work appears on a quarterly basis and provides listings of periodical articles in the field. It began as an abstract journal, with linguistics covered in *Bulletin signalétique: Philosophie, sciences humaines* from 1947 to 1960; from 1961 to 1966, linguistics was treated in *Bulletin signalétique, Sec. 21: Sociologie, sciences du langage*, and from 1967 to 1968 in *Bulletin signalétique 24: Sciences du langage*. The present title was adopted after 1968, at which time it ceased providing abstracts and became a bibliography only. At present, it covers the biology and pathology of language, psycholinguistics, sociolinguistics, ethnolinguistics, historical linguistics, descriptive studies, semiotics, and communications. There is a classified arrangement with author and subject indexes. It is available online from Questel as *FRANCIS: SCIENCES DU LANGAGE, providing coverage from 1972 to date. As of the latter part of 1986, it contains over 54,000 citations, adding about 1,000 records per quarter.

*721. **Linguistics and Language Behavior Abstracts: LLBA.** 1967- . Q. San Diego, Calif., Sociological Abstracts.

Formerly *LLBA: Language and Language Behavior Abstracts*, edited at the University of Michigan Center for Research, this abstract journal changed its title in 1985. It continues to cover an array of disciplines related to language and linguistics and treats a variety of journals, books, and monographs from communications and education as well as linguistics. Included are titles in acoustics, anthropology, comparative literature, ethnology, information science, medicine, psychiatry, psychology, and philosophy. Abstracts are grouped in broad divisions such as linguistics and philosophy and are subdivided by more specific topics. Over 1,000 journals are surveyed for articles of potential relevance and represent a number of languages and countries. There is an author index. It is available online through BRS and DIALOG, with a file size of 80,000 records as of early 1987. The file coverage is from 1973 to date and adds about 8,000 records per year.

722. **Modern Language Review.** 1905- . Q. London, Modern Humanities Research Association.

This is one of the most respected review journals in the humanities and provides reviews of studies of medieval and modern languages and literatures. Known for its lengthy, detailed, and thoughtful book reviews, it is a top priority in those libraries emphasizing or supporting communications and language studies. As in many review journals in the humanities, there is a certain amount of delay following publication of the items prior to their review in the journal. *Modern Language Quarterly* is an American contribution published through the University of Washington since 1940. Several studies of literary works and literary forms appear in each issue and represent Western European and American scholarship. The publication features comparative reviews on topics and issues in the field.

723. **Year's Work in Modern Language Studies.** 1929/1930- . Ann. London, Oxford University Press.

The war years witnessed an extended suspension of publication for this useful reviewing source; therefore, volume 11 covers the period 1940 to 1949, in which year it resumed its annual frequency. Language and literature are treated in a variety of settings and time periods: medieval Latin, Romance languages, Germanic languages, and Slavonic languages. The focus is on developments from the medieval period to the present day. General linguistics was added to the field of coverage nearly fifteen years ago and has become an important element. *Studies in Philology* from the University of North Carolina is a quarterly journal which began in 1906. It furnishes textual and historical research in classical and modern languages and literature. It is of use primarily to the scholar and specialist.

Linguistics Dictionaries and Handbooks

724. **A Dictionary of Linguistics and Phonetics.** 2nd ed. David Crystal. New York, Basil Blackwell, 1985. 339p.

The author, a prominent British linguist and editor of the journal, *Linguistics Abstracts* (Oxford, Basil Blackwell, 1985-), has provided an updated and expanded edition of his previous work issued in 1980. After only a few years, his earlier effort had achieved a prominent position among those dictionaries designed for both students and researchers in the field. The new work has over 2,100 terms used as main entry items, with over 100 of them new and reflecting recent directions and theories in linguistics. There are over 100 new secondary terms (included within the entries for other terms). Many of the definitions have been reworked or expanded. Entries may include descriptions, examples, diagrams, and references to additional reading. Apparently, the new edition continues the tradition of high quality established by the first one.

725. **Encyclopedic Dictionary of Semiotics.** Thomas A. Sebeok, ed. New York, de Gruyter, 1986. 3v.

Sebeok, a professor of linguistics at Indiana University, has performed an excellent service in coordinating the efforts of numerous individuals who served on the editorial board and the panel of contributors in producing this significant work. There are 426 signed entries from 236 contributors from all over the world, including information of three types: historical background and present usage of terms with some recommendations to standardize current conventions, biographies of deceased prominent personalities in semiotics, and appraisal of the impact of semiotics on inquiry in other fields. Articles vary in length from those of a monographic nature (over twenty pages on semantics) to explanations of one paragraph. It is generally agreed that semiotics has been well served through publication of this scholarly effort.

726. **The Linguistic Atlas of England.** Harold Orton, et al., eds. London, Croom Helm; Atlantic Highlands, N.J., Humanities Press, 1978. 1v. (various paging).

An important segment of reference literature is the linguistic atlas, which through maps and some narrative describes the linguistic composition of an area or country. In most cases, these are multivolume sets appearing at different intervals which together give a complete picture of the geographic area involved. Therefore, one of the remarkable virtues of this work is its one-volume coverage of a small but highly complex country in terms of its linguistic elements. There are nearly 250 phonological maps, 65 lexical maps, 83 morphological maps, and 9 syntactic maps, each showing the distribution of their topical phenomena in England. Important to the novice is the useful introduction describing the manner of reading and interpreting the maps. This work has become a popular item for college classes.

727. **Longman Dictionary of Applied Linguistics.** Jack Richards, et al. New York, Longman, 1985. 323p.

The authors have established a reputation as experts in the field of applied linguistics with their work in the area of language teaching as well as other aspects. This is what appears to be the first dictionary to specialize in applied linguistics; it furnishes over 1,500 entries of terms used in the practice. Definitions are lucid and contain related terms within the body of a single entry. British and American pronunciations are given in most cases, and there are many cross-references between entries. Focused primarily on the applied linguistics of language teaching, rather than language planning or lexicology, or translation, the work provides a good overview of the field and includes many of the terms from theoretical linguistics as well. Useful for both the college student and the language teacher.

728. **A Pocket Guide to Literature and Language Terms.** Benjamin W. Griffith. Woodbury, N.Y., Barron's Educational Series, 1986. 154p.

Although one may wonder at the purchase of a paperback pocket-sized work for the reference department, it is felt that the inexpensive price of this item ($2.95) warrants its consideration. Designed for the college student who must operate in both linguistics and literature courses, this compact little volume does an admirable job and could be used in any library serving the needs of college and high school students. The first part of this convenient and easily handled work deals with literature terminology, while the second part is focused on grammar and composition. This latter segment also provides assistance in developing bibliographic entries. There is an index to both parts, and in general, although it is compact, the work is a worthwhile purchase.

729. **The World's Major Languages.** Bernard Comrie, ed. New York, Oxford University Press, 1987. 1025p.

This is an important and reliable handbook providing extensive information on particular languages and families of languages. The editor is a respected contributor and noted specialist in the area of Slavic languages and has written the introduction as well as two of the fifty chapters, each of which is devoted to a particular language or family. It is apparent that each chapter receives careful and thorough treatment by one of the forty scholars responsible for its development. Historical, sociological, and linguistic elements are covered, and detailed treatment is given to such aspects as graphic systems, morphology, word formation, and syntactic patterns. For inflected languages, charts indicate declension and conjugation classes. Most chapters have bibliographical notes and references. A general index provides access.

English-Language Dictionaries

UNABRIDGED

730. **Funk & Wagnalls New Standard Dictionary of the English Language.** Isaac K. Funk, et al. New York, Funk & Wagnalls, 1964. 2816p.

The 1964 edition is the latest in a long line of reprints, remediations, and added-on supplementary issues. In character and personality, it is still a 1913 work, which at the time represented a complete revision of the first edition published in 1893. The style is, of course, that of a prescriptive dictionary in the manner of the traditional attempt to prescribe the nature of the language in terms of propriety or correctness. Usage labels are employed to show the status of a given term, and examples of usage are taken from the "great" writers of the past, even drawing from classical literature. Known for its excellent coverage in geography and biography, names and places are included alphabetically within the main text, rather than placed into separate glossaries.

731. The Oxford English Dictionary. James A. H. Murray, et al., eds. New York, Clarendon/Oxford University Press, 1933. 13v. Supp. 1-3, 1972-1982.

The original descriptive dictionary which portrayed the language as it was rather than prescribing what it should be, *OED* is unexcelled as a scholarly and comprehensive historical dictionary. Nearly 2,000,000 quotations illustrate changes in meaning over time for some 415,000 words from their beginnings in the recorded literature. Murray served as editor from 1878 until his death in 1915 when William A. Craigie assumed his responsibilities. A ten-volume set appeared in 1928, entitled the *New English Dictionary on Historical Principles* (*NED*) (Oxford, Clarendon Press), followed by a supplementary volume in 1933. At this time, the set was reissued in thirteen volumes under its present name, with some corrections of typographical errors. It remains an indispensable tool, the best of its kind in the English language, quoting more than 5,000 authors from the twelfth century onwards. Three of four projected supplementary volumes have been published which, when completed, will furnish an additional 60,000 newer words. In addition, a compact edition of *OED* is now available, *The Compact Edition of the Oxford English Dictionary: Complete Text Reproduced Micrographically. Volume III: A Supplement to the Oxford English Dictionary, Volumes 1-IV,* edited by R. W. Burchfield (Clarendon/Oxford University Press, 1987, 1412p.).

732. The Random House Dictionary of the English Language. Jess Stein, ed.-in-chief. New York, Random House, 1981. 2059p.

Originally published in 1966, this is the newest of the unabridged dictionaries (although it has been described as lying somewhere between an unabridged and a desk dictionary in size). The work contains about 260,000 terms and represents some elements of the new breed of dictionary. Although not as revolutionary in some respects as *Webster's Third* (see entry 734), it is more daring in its decision to appeal to a popular rather than scholarly audience. (Editors compose usage examples rather than cite the literature.) It is of the descriptive type, but employs usage labels more frequently, and is therefore more prescriptive than *Webster's Third*. It avoids obscenities. It is considered up-to-date in its definitions and furnishes personal and place names within the body of the main text in the style of the older *Funk & Wagnalls* (see entry 730). There are some useful listings of foreign words (German, French, Spanish, and Italian) as well as an atlas and gazetteer segment.

733. Webster's New International Dictionary of the English Language. 2nd ed. William Allan Neilson, ed.-in-chief. Springfield, Mass., Merriam, 1961 (1934). 3194p.

Descended from a line of distinguished dictionaries from the Merriam Company beginning in 1828, this edition was an important contribution to the prestige and respect accruing to the Webster name. The first edition of the *New International* appeared in 1909, and this work represented a complete revision in 1934. Subsequent printings and reissues showed slight modifications such as a new words section added to the front in 1939. This work remained available for several years following the publication of the third edition in 1961 (see entry 734). Basically, it remains an excellent dictionary based on the rationale of providing a prescriptive tool for maintaining the integrity of the language. Many usage labels are furnished and examples of usage are quoted from the fine literature of the past. Approximately 600,000 words are included, many of which are obsolete or archaic. Word meanings are in historical sequence, earliest to most recent (a Merriam characteristic), and there are a separate gazetteer and a biographical dictionary. This main volume is retained in libraries along with the newer edition.

734. Webster's Third New International Dictionary of the English Language. Phillip Babcock Gove, ed.-in-chief. Springfield, Mass., Merriam, 1961; repr., 1969. 2662p.

It is difficult to imagine the controversy caused by the publication of this work, which placed the prestige and authority of the Merriam Company on the side of the new linguists as opposed to the traditional grammarians. No longer was this a prescriptive tool, but rather one that described the language as it was, using only a few usage labels. Many words regarded as vulgar, colloquial, or incorrect were not qualified as such. About 100,000 new terms were added, including the raw and racy language of the streets. About 250,000 of the older terms were deleted, furnishing a total of 450,000 words. Quotations include those from the popular literature and are taken from modern authors rather than classic writers. The biographical dictionary and gazetteer sections have been dropped, and about all that remains the same from the second edition (see entry 733) is the historical sequence of definitions given. This is the preferred dictionary of the American people and is found in every library.

DESK OR COLLEGE

Desk dictionaries are generally understood to be those which stand on the desk and can be found in the possession of secretaries, college students, professors, businesspersons, etc. They are the most common purchase for adults.

735. The American Heritage Dictionary. 2nd college ed. William Morris, ed. Boston, Houghton Mifflin, 1982; repr., 1985. 1568p.

The college edition of the *American Heritage Dictionary of the English Language* (itself a desk dictionary published in 1969) came out in 1976 and was a reprint in smaller size. Over 200,000 definitions are given, ranging from the language of Shakespeare to that of present day idiomatic expression. The dictionary had quite an impact in its attempt to provide guidance to proper usage not only with labeling of words, but also with usage notes regarding controversial terms. Etymologies are not as extensive as those in the 1969 edition. There are separate biographical and geographical segments, although certain proper nouns appear in the main text. The work has been attacked by groups who do not appreciate its coverage of some controversial terms and expressions. It remains an excellent choice as a dictionary that attempts to retain propriety, but is not reluctant to portray the language as it is.

736. The Concise Oxford Dictionary of Current English. 7th ed. J. B. Sykes, ed. New York, Oxford University Press, 1982; repr., 1984. 1264p.

This is referred to as a small desk dictionary; it has 40,000 entry words. The sixth edition of this work, published in 1976, was an extensive revision and was based in large part on the supplements to the *O.E.D.* (see entry 731); thus many older terms were discarded in favor of those in current usage. It also provided more extensive treatment of words from outside the British Isles. This new edition follows that pattern and is not as great a revision as its predecessor, but still draws upon the files of the supplements to the *O.E.D.* It continues to be like the *O.E.D.*, a descriptive rather than a prescriptive dictionary, and it records the language as it exists among English-speaking peoples. Alternative forms of the entry words appear in parentheses. Definitions are arranged according to frequency of use rather than historical sequence.

737. **International English Usage.** Loreto Todd and Ian Hancock. New York, New York University Press; distr., New York, Columbia University Press, 1987. 520p.

This is a highly useful dictionary-style handbook which covers English usage in all parts of the world where English is either the first language or an important second language. Interesting and informative comparisons are made about various practices and pronunciations of different nations and regions. There is an attempt to establish coverage which is balanced between descriptive and prescriptive approaches, with distinctions made between logical regional characteristics and actual errors. Generally the style of writing is lucid, although some passages can be understood only by a specialist. This is a scholarly work, but it can be used successfully by the interested layperson. Access is facilitated by a good index and numerous cross-references.

738. **Webster's Ninth New Collegiate Dictionary.** Springfield, Mass., Merriam-Webster, 1983; repr., 1987. 1564p.

Comparable in size to the *American Heritage* (see entry 735), with 200,000 definitions for 160,000 entry terms, this has long been regarded as the top choice among college students and academicians. This edition replaces one done ten years earlier, and like the others is based on the entries for *Webster's Third* (see entry 734). Emphasis is on the standard language, with slang and colloquialisms included. There are 11,000 new words and meanings and a total of over 600 illustrations. Entries are now dated, thus providing a better coverage of word history. Also included are a handbook of style with a guide to punctuation, capitalization, etc., and a special section listing foreign words and phrases that occur frequently in English. Unlike *Webster's Third*, there is a separate section for biographical and geographical names in the appendices, along with listings of colleges and universities. It continues as an excellent example of an abridged dictionary. *12,000 Words: A Supplement to Webster's Third New International Dictionary* (Merriam-Webster, 1986) includes many current terms (e.g., *hot tub, humongous,* and *zonked*).

USAGE, SLANG, AND IDIOMS

739. **Dictionary of American Regional English.** Frederic G. Cassidy, ed. Cambridge, Mass., Harvard University Press, 1985- . (In progress).

Volume 1, A-C, is the initial effort of what promises to be a massive undertaking in providing a comprehensive multivolume dictionary of folk expressions, unused meanings of common terms, regional colloquialisms, and words belonging to ethnic or social groups in the United States. Entries include parts of speech, variant spellings, geographical roots, usage labels, cross-references, and definitions. Etymologies are sometimes covered. A series of computer-generated maps shows geographical distribution of the word and gives some idea of the density of the population affected. The initial volume contains an important essay on language changes in American folk speech, guide to pronunciation, and an explanation of the maps. As this set develops, it should become the standard work on the subject.

740. **The Dictionary of Cliches.** James Rogers. New York, Facts on File, 1985. 305p.

An interesting and useful work identifying over 2,000 commonalities of language usage, this volume embraces idioms, proverbs, and quotations. Not surprisingly, Shakespeare and the Bible are two of the leading sources for the cliches, a language species much despised and denigrated by linguists. Nevertheless, they are important features of language study, and this dictionary provides useful information on meanings and definition, as well as etymologies. Entries are covered in-depth, with enough information to provide insight and enlightenment (even though some of the etymologies are speculative in nature). Entries are arranged alphabetically and there is a detailed index of cross-references at the end of the book. The work is thorough and should be of use to a variety of library patrons.

741. **A Dictionary of Slang and Unconventional English: Colloquialisms and Catch-phrases** ... 8th ed. Eric Partridge. New York, Macmillan, 1984. 1400p.

The standard in the field, the Partridge work is the original slang dictionary from the time of its initial appearance in 1937. Previous editions have reprinted the original and added supplements (addenda) to the back. Now, at last, there is an integrated work which brings together in one alphabetical arrangement the original and subsequent supplements as well as additional new words and corrections. (Cockney is no longer included as a label and such words have been deleted since it is now accepted as mainstream English.) Partridge had collected most of this material (5,000 of the 6,000 entries) prior to his death in 1979. The new editor, Paul Beale, has initialed those entries which he contributed to the volume. The new work maintains the tradition of the old and will continue as the major work of its kind. *New Dictionary of American Slang*, by Robert L. Chapman (Harper & Row, 1986) is the most recent entry in this field, focusing on American slang. Hundreds of new terms from the past twenty years are included.

742. **Harper Dictionary of Contemporary Usage.** 2nd ed. William Morris and Mary Morris. New York, Harper & Row, 1985. 641p.

The new edition of this dictionary follows the original by ten years, in which time the title has gained recognition as the most comprehensive and up-to-date dictionary of American word usage. A prescriptive work by virtue of its nature and purpose, it features a lively style and an interesting commentary on some of the difficult elements of American usage. Experts on the panel were asked to vote and comment. An important consideration is the easy-to-read format, with large print and generous leading. More important is the tool's recency, for which there is no equal among the works of this type. Such terms as *hot pants* and *house husband* are described as well as more traditional words from the past. This is definitely a needed reference work for most American libraries.

743. **Oxford Dictionary of Current Idiomatic English.** A. P. Cowie, et al., comps. New York, Oxford University Press, 1975-1983. 2v.

Volume 1 of this work, covering verbs with prepositions and particles, was published in 1975; volume 2, dealing with phrases, clauses, and sentence idioms, appeared eight years later in 1983. The intention of the set is to furnish a coverage sufficiently broad enough to answer various practical questions and inquiries regarding the use of idioms. Both volumes taken together cover some 40,000 idioms. Idiomatic statements are defined clearly, and examples of usage from contemporary literature and speech are furnished. Foreigners learning English will be aided by some of the warnings given to avoid wrong usage or construction. As is sometimes true of Oxford works, there is a British emphasis or slant.

ETYMOLOGY, SYNONYMS, ETC.

744. **The Concise Oxford Dictionary of English Etymology.** T. F. Hoad, ed. New York, Clarendon/Oxford University Press, 1986. 552p.

Another of the Oxford dictionaries, this, like the others, is a work of high quality. Its parent work, C. T. Onions's *The Oxford Dictionary of English Etymology* (Oxford, Clarendon Press, 1966) was the first comprehensive etymological dictionary of the English language since 1910, and established an excellent reputation for scholarship and breadth of coverage. The new concise edition was begun by an assistant editor to Onions, G. W. S. Friedrichsen, and finally completed by Hoad. In truth, it shows little change from the style or content of the original, although abridgement is noticeable within the entries. Many abbreviations are employed which require referral to a list. Entries furnish dates and origins of various senses of meaning, all arranged in chronological order for each term. Brief definitions are given, but the dictionary should not be used for that purpose. Not appearing here, unfortunately, is the interesting and helpful introduction summarizing the history of the English language, which was an important element in the original edition. A useful supplementary work is Adrian Room's *A Dictionary of True Etymologies* (Routledge & Kegan Paul, 1986), which provides correct origins of nearly 1,200 words about whose origins popular misconceptions exist.

745. **Dictionary of Collective Nouns and Group Terms ...** 2nd ed. Ivan G. Sparkes, ed. Detroit, Gale, 1985. 283p.

The second edition of a work originally published in 1975, this is a historical dictionary on collective nouns, group terms, and phrases. Over 1,800 of these terms are listed, with examples of their use and changes of meaning. The work is divided into two parts, the first of which provides a definition with examples of use within the meaning or sense given. The second part provides an index which lists items about which a collective term has been furnished. There is a great curiosity value to a work of this kind and the dictionary will not only inform, but entertain as well. Most of the words tend to be obsolete, rare, or obscure (e.g., a *kindle* of cats).

746. **Roget's Thesaurus of English Words and Phrases.** New ed. Susan M. Lloyd. London, Longman, 1982. 1247p.

A true standard in the field, this thesaurus was originally produced by Peter Mark Roget in 1852. Since that time, it has become representative of the category of synonyms dictionaries, its contribution being the classification scheme developed originally by Roget and expanded by others who served as editors. Knowledge is divided into approximately 1,000 classes or topical divisions under several main headings, such as abstract relations, space, matter, intellect, etc. Words are placed under the topics which they represent or express. Other synonym dictionaries pale in comparison since they simply arrange words alphabetically and provide one-word definitions or alternatives. The thesaurus treats word relationships within an idea framework.

Foreign-Language and Bilingual Dictionaries

747. **The American Heritage Larousse Spanish Dictionary: Spanish/English, English/Spanish.** Boston, Houghton Mifflin, 1986. 572p.

Continuing in the tradition of high-quality lexicographic work associated with the American Heritage name is this recent bilingual dictionary. The Larousse publishing family has joined with Houghton Mifflin in producing a unique work providing excellent coverage of Latin American Spanish as well as European usage. For this reason it should prove especially useful to those in both the Southeastern and Southwestern regions of the United States. The work compares favorably in scope and depth to other dictionaries of its type, with good coverage given to idioms and to scientific and technical terms. Among the special features is a verb table at the beginning of the volume, to which are keyed the entries for all the irregular verbs. This is especially useful for students trying to conjugate verbs.

748. **The Cambridge Italian Dictionary.** Barbara Reynolds, gen. ed. New York, Cambridge University Press, 1962-1981. 2v.

A span of nineteen years passed from the appearance of the first volume to publication of volume 2 of this work. With its completion, the librarian and the patron have been given an excellent translation tool. Volume 1 is Italian-English, and volume 2, English-Italian, the rationale behind the dictionary being the development of a word book useful to English-speaking individuals. With this lexicographic theory in mind, it is understandable that the work provides no explanations of English grammar and includes no guides to English pronunciation; unfortunately, Italian coverage is also lacking in that regard, and remains the primary deficiency of an otherwise rich and useful source of words of all time periods and types.

749. **Deutsches Wörterbuch.** Jakob Ludwig Karl Grimm and Wilhelm Grimm. Leipzig, Hirzel, 1854-1960. 16v.

This is the great German dictionary which was finally completed more than 100 years after it was started. It was the first dictionary to promote the idea of a compilation based on historical principles, and was the creation of Jakob Grimm, the great German philologist, who with his brother, Wilhelm, began the arduous process. The brothers Grimm today are probably better remembered by most Americans for their collection of fairy tales, done very early in their careers, but it is the dictionary which has served as their greatest legacy. It influenced the development of the *O.E.D.* (see entry 731) and others of its type. It was the purpose of this work to give an exhaustive account of the words of New High German, the literary language, from the end of the fifteenth century onwards. Etymologies and senses are illustrated by literary quotations. Since 1965, there has been an ongoing effort to develop a revised and expanded edition incorporating the results of new research. A more practical purchase for most American libraries would be *Cassell's German and English Dictionary*, compiled by H. C. Sasse, et al. (Collier Books/Macmillan, 1966, repr., 1986). A small inexpensive paperback, it provides a concise but useful dictionary for the traveler or student in the initial stages of learning the language.

750. **Greek Dictionary: Greek-English and English-Greek.** Paul Nathanail, comp. Boston, Routledge & Kegan Paul, 1985. 556p.

Regarded as a useful and more than adequate dictionary, this relatively inexpensive paperback edition packs a great deal of information into a small package. Related items are brought together while maintaining an alphabetical order. The vocabulary is considered to be well chosen and balanced, although there is a tendency to favor the demotic form. Although it is designed for English-speaking users, there is no guide to English pronunciation. Some hints in this direction for the Greek language would have been helpful even though Greek orthography is rather regular. *The Oxford Turkish-English Dictionary*, by A. D. Alderson and Fahir Iz, is now in its third edition (Clarendon Press/Oxford University Press, 1984) and is considered the best existing tool for translation of contemporary Turkish texts. Many technical terms are included, and the complicated Turkish morphology and idiom are handled well.

751. **Harrap's New Standard French and English Dictionary.** Completely rev. and enl. ed. J. E. Mansion, ed. London, Harrap; distr., New York, Scribner's, 1971-1980. 4v.

This has long been one of the leading dictionaries of its kind, and this four-volume edition is the most recent issue of a work that had its beginning in the 1930s. Since then, it has undergone several name changes and modifications. The present edition is a thorough revision designed to provide a work which was reasonable in terms of size, and of wide scope. Emphasis has been placed on modern, technical, scientific, and industrial elements as well as the modern language, complete with colloquialisms and idioms. These are labeled for propriety and indicate slang, vulgarism, etc. The work has been criticized for the inclusion of dated material from past editions but at the same time has been praised for the inclusion of modern technical terminology.

752. **New Revised Velázquez Spanish and English Dictionary.** Mariano Velázquez de la Cadena, et al. Rev. by Ida Navarro Hinojosa, et al. Piscataway, N.J., New Century Publishers, 1985. 788p.

Considered one of the best dictionaries of its kind, this new edition replaces the one published in 1974. The tool is comprehensive, with over 150,000 entries for which information is given on pronunciation as well as translation. About 700 new entries have been added, providing up-to-date coverage which includes regional variations for Latin America and Spain. Always considered strong in technical terminology, obsolete terms, and esoteric language, the dictionary has a comprehensive nature which exceeds most works of this type. Revisions for terms requiring changes from the last edition as well as new entries are included in the middle of the volume between the two sections of the work. In the appendices are brief grammars of Castilian and English, geographical terms, proper names, abbreviations, and other valuable listings.

753. **Oxford Latin Dictionary.** P. G. W. Glare, ed. New York, Clarendon Press/Oxford University Press, 1982; repr., 1983. 2126p.

Another scholarly work in the Oxford line-up of dictionary and word source books developed through scholarly pursuits and careful attention to detail, this dictionary appeared in eight fascicles over a period of fourteen years from 1967 to 1981. A milestone was reached with the publication of the complete edition in one volume. The work has replaced an older and outdated standard in the field from Harper & Row as well as a more recent work which falls short in comprehensiveness and detail. There is a rich selection of entry words from the Latin literature; quotations illustrate in historical fashion the various senses or meanings which the words have assumed through time. A thorough, precise, and valuable item for reference work.

754. **The Oxford Russian-English Dictionary.** 2nd ed. Marcus Wheeler. New York, Clarendon Press, 1984. 930p.

This is one of two dictionaries from Oxford which appeared in 1984. Together they provide a complete approach to the study of the Russian language. This work contains 70,000 entries derived from various dictionaries judged to be useful and of value. The work includes colloquialisms, idioms, and technical terms as well as general standard terminology. Explanations are given, as are translations, and useful appendices of official abbreviations and geographical names are furnished. The companion work is *The Oxford English-Russian Dictionary*, edited by P. S. Falla (1984), which contains about 90,000 terms, phrases, and vocabulary items. Originally compiled for the benefit of Russian users, it has developed beyond that point with the expansion of the English words. The dictionaries are complementary, and now both are designed primarily for the English-language user.

Should be purchased in all libraries needing to provide services to specialists as well as students.

Histories and Directories

755.   The American Language: An Inquiry into the Development of English in the United States. 4th ed., corr., enl. and rewritten. Henry Louis Mencken. New York, Knopf, 1936; repr., 1960. 796p. Supp. 1-2, 1945-1948. 2v.

This monumental work is the most well-known and respected history of the American language. It was completed by H. L. Mencken, the famous journalist for the *Baltimore Sun* over fifty years ago. There is nothing to rival it either in breadth or depth of treatment of the English language in America. The work provides historical treatment of the development of the English language in the United States in eleven chapters covering a variety of topics. Included are such topical divisions as the two streams of English, the beginning and growth of the American language, pronunciation and spelling, common speech, proper names, slang, etc. The work contains an appendix which includes a segment on non-English dialects and a general index to provide access. The supplements are developed along the same lines as the basic work, with the first volume adding to chapters 1-6 and the second volume enhancing chapters 7-11.

756.   A History of the English Language. 3rd ed. Albert Croll Baugh and Thomas Cable. Englewood Cliffs, N.J., Prentice-Hall, 1978. 438p.

The initial edition of this work was published in 1935, and since that time it has become the leading reference history as well as textbook for courses covering the historical development of the English language from its beginnings to the present. It includes a segment on the development of the language in this country, but for greater detail on that topic one should consult Mencken's *The American Language* (see entry 755). Treatment is given to the evolution of the language within the context of the political, social, and intellectual history of England. This is considered the best one-volume survey history on the topic. Bibliographies are up-to-date and are linked to the recent scholarship in the field.

757.   World Guide to Terminological Activities, Organizations Terminology Banks, Committees. 2nd completely rev. and enl. ed. Magdalena Krommer-Benz. Munich, Verlag Dokumentation; distr., New York, K. G. Saur, 1985. 158p.

For those interested in the development or maintenance of standards within the various disciplines and fields of study, this work will be of assistance in identifying organizations and activities on an international scale. It is felt that the lack of uniform terminology and inconsistency in language use in some fields or disciplines of study hamper the effectiveness of research and ultimate progress within the field. This is especially true of the newer areas of inquiry. Listed here are over 200 agencies and institutions and their committees concerned with terminology. All disciplines of study and all major languages are included, with an emphasis on Western European units. The arrangement is by UDC according to subject interest. There are indexes of names, subject matter, and acronyms.

explicators- reviews of poems, short stories

descriptive bibliographies — physical description of

LITERATURE
work

General Works

BIBLIOGRAPHIC GUIDES AND INTRODUCTORY WORKS

758. **The Art of Literary Research.** 3rd ed. Richard D. Altick. Rev. by John J. Fenstermaker. New York, W. W. Norton, 1981. 318p.

Since its initial appearance in 1964, this has been regarded as one of the most useful, best constructed, and most interesting of all introductory guides in the field of literature. The third edition carries on the good work of the earlier editions and provides excellent narrative and provocative exposition of the principles and practices involved in literary research. Fenstermaker's revision retains the original character of Altick's contribution, but furnishes a needed modification with respect to modern practice and theory. Advice is given regarding bibliographic procedures, note taking, and library practices, and insight is provided into writing as an art and practice which requires high standards and commitment. The title continues as a top choice for reference departments.

759. **A Guide to Serial Bibliographies for Modern Literatures.** William A. Wortman. New York, Modern Language Association of America, 1982. 124p.

This is a compact but important annotated listing of serial bibliographies in the area of modern literature. Nearly 1,000 titles are identified, primarily English-language works, but also including foreign-language products. It is useful for its currency, with listings up to 1975, and is highly regarded for its comprehensive coverage of all modern literatures. Various types of bibliographies are enumerated (comprehensive, classified, author, and subject) as well as indexing and abstracting services. Entries furnish information regarding general coverage, bibliographic description, and publishing characteristics. This work is intended primarily for students but is of importance to librarians, teachers, professors, and others interested in the control of the literature.

760. **Key Sources in Comparative and World Literature: An Annotated Guide to Reference Materials.** George A. Thompson, with the assistance of Margaret M. Thompson. New York, Ungar, 1982. 383p.

Over 1,200 reference tools are identified and described in this work, including handbooks, encyclopedias, biographical dictionaries, terminologies, guides, etc. An array of bibliographical tools, bibliographies, indexes, and research reviews is covered, both in sections dealing with general and comparative literatures and in those dealing with national and period literatures. Classical, Romance, French, Italian, Hispanic, German, Oriental, and other European types are included, as well as literature in English. As is inevitable in a work of this sort, certain literatures are given short shrift (Oriental, Latin American, African, etc.) but the work is to be commended for its attempt at comprehensive coverage. The arrangement of entries is classified within chapters and access is provided through three indexes: editor and compiler, title, and subject.

761. **Literary Research Guide: An Evaluative, Annotated Bibliography of Important Reference Books and Periodicals on English, Irish, Scottish, Welsh, Commonwealth ...** 2nd ed., 2nd rev. printing. Margaret C. Patterson. New York, Modern Language Association of America, 1984. 559p.

The subtitle goes on to include "American, Afro-American, American Indian, Continental, Classical, and World Literatures, and Sixty Literature-Related Subject Areas." Nineteen categories of literature-related reference tools, beginning with general guides and proceeding to the various national groups and types, are described. Entries provide bibliographic information (author, edition, imprint, number of pages, series title, paperback availability, LC and Dewey numbers, and presence of a bibliography). There is a useful introduction on library classification systems. Access is facilitated through a general index of authors, titles, and subjects. The overriding concern of the author is to provide an awareness of the content of the best reference books available and their use in scholarly research.

Periodicals

762. **The International Directory of Little Magazines and Small Presses.** 1973/1974- . Paradise, Calif., Dust Books.

This annual guide and directory replaces the *Directory of Little Magazines* (1965-1972) and continues its volume numbering. Therefore, its initial volume under this title was volume 9. It continues to provide information of a directory nature for little magazines (address, telephone number, scope, editor, subscription price, average length, and circulation figures), but also includes comments by the editors on the policies and types of material published. Lists of recent contributors are furnished as well. Small presses are covered in much the same fashion, with editor, address, scope, average price for books, production methods, and size of press runs. Editors' comments on the nature of the press are also given. Access is aided through subject and geographic indexes which should prove useful to those seeking publishing outlets.

763. **MLA Directory of Periodicals: A Guide to Journals and Series in Languages and Literatures.** 1979- . Bienn. New York, Modern Language Association of America.

A companion volume to the important *MLA International Bibliography* (see entry 769), this directory provides information on more than 3,000 journals and series which have been indexed in that work. The projection has been for a biennial publication, although this may vary. It is without a rival in terms of providing up-to-date information on currently available titles of serial nature in the field. Arrangement is alphabetical by title of journal or series, with each entry furnished a sequence number which is referred to in the indexes. Four indexes provide excellent access: editorial personnel; language other than English, French, German, Italian, and Spanish; sponsoring organizations; and subject. Another useful tool is Margaret C. Patterson's *Author Newsletters and Journals ...* (Gale, 1979), which identifies and annotates over 1,100 titles devoted to the collection and distribution of criticism, bibliographies, biographical information, etc., on the lives and works of single authors.

BIBLIOGRAPHIES

764. **Articles on Twentieth Century Literature: An Annotated Bibliography, 1954 to 1970.** David E. Pownall. New York, Kraus-Thomson, 1973-1980. 7v.

Completed after seven years' labor, this seven-volume bibliography represents an expanded cumulation of sixteen years of listings from the "Current Bibliography" section of *Twentieth Century Literature*, a quarterly journal published by IHC in Los Angeles.

Additional bibliographies and reference periodical sources are also included. Limited to journal articles only, nearly 400 journals were surveyed for relevant articles in the course of this effort. The arrangement is by name of author (used as subject). Entries are numbered and all are cross-indexed in volume 7. The work excludes all book reviews, review articles, popular journalism, and basic articles on teaching literature. Coverage is comprehensive, the intent being to survey all authors who actually lived into and published works in the twentieth century. More than 20,000 articles are identified, with those on European authors being especially useful. The journal continued its regular coverage of "Current Bibliography" until 1979, then sporadically until 1981.

765. **Bibliography of Comparative Literature.** Fernand Baldensperger and Werner P. Friedrich. Chapel Hill, N.C., University of North Carolina Press, 1950; repr., New York, Russell & Russell, 1960. 701p. (University of North Carolina Studies in Comparative Literature, No. 1).

For many years, this has been considered the most extensive and authoritative bibliography of books, periodical articles, and even some dissertations covering comparative literature from ancient to modern times. Entries are classed into one of four books or sections: books 1 and 3 represent themes, motifs, genres, and international literary relations, while books 2 and 4 deal with specific national literatures arranged according to country or author exerting influence. Comprehensive in respect to its vast scope covering the world literature, the work is highly selective in the entries chosen for inclusion. Access is provided by means of a detailed table of contents since no index is furnished. Coverage was continued for a time by *Yearbook of Comparative and General Literature* (see entry 771).

766. **Psychocriticism: An Annotated Bibliography.** Joseph Natoli and Frederick L. Rusch. Westport, Conn., Greenwood Press, 1984. 267p.

This is a collection of annotated references to essays by writers who have applied psychological principles in their interpretation of literature. There are over 1,400 entries, representing essays published subsequent to 1969. These are organized by literary period, beginning with ancient and classical literature and ending with the twentieth century. There is an opening chapter which identifies essays of a general nature on psychology and literature. Following that are separate chapters given to the different periods. They begin with references to the period as a whole, then give citations to works on individual writers. Each entry is annotated with a brief description of the essay's content. Both an author index and a subject index are provided to facilitate access to the appropriate entry.

INDEXES, ABSTRACTS, AND SERIAL BIBLIOGRAPHIES

767. **Chicorel Index Series.** New York, Chicorel Library Publishing, 1970-1978. 27v.

This is a series of computer-produced indexes to a wide range of materials found in anthologies, periodicals, and audiovisual materials. Although the coverage varied widely in terms of disciplines and topics, its original emphasis was on literature and the performing arts. During the 1970s, when these indexes were being produced, they achieved acclaim not only for their breadth of coverage, but also for the excellent indexing they provided, enabling users of various levels to quickly find what they were seeking. Several volumes were given to both poetry and fiction as well as drama (see entry 612n). Most relevant to the study of literature were volume 4, poetry on discs, tapes, and cassettes; volume 5, A-C poetry in collections; volume 6, A-C index to poetry; volumes 12-12A, index to short stories in anthologies and collections; volumes 20-20A, index to poetry and poets, and volumes 23-23B, index to literary criticism. These volumes are still consulted in reference departments today.

768. **MLA Abstracts of Articles in Scholarly Journals.** 1970-1975. Ann. New York, Modern Language Association of America.

A useful abstracting service designed to complement the *MLA International Bibliography* (see entry 769), this work features a classified arrangement which paralleled the organization of its companion work. It was to be used in conjunction with the *Bibliography* since it did not have cross-references, an author index, or a detailed subject index. Its function was to provide abstracts of some of the articles from a small percentage of the journals covered in the *Bibliography*. Only journal articles were so treated, even though monographs and festschriften are also included in the *Bibliography*. Abstracts were arranged by broad subject or language groupings, with further subdivision by time period and author. Although this work ceased publication after five years, it should not be overlooked in a literature search covering the period of time within its scope.

*769. **MLA International Bibliography.** 1921- . Ann. New York, Modern Language Association of America.

This is the monumental bibliography known and respected by language and literature students both in this country and abroad. A standard work in the field, it has changed title and scope since its inception in 1921, when it was limited to writings by Americans on the literature of various countries, and known as *American Bibliography*. Since 1956, it has been a more expansive source of bibliographic information and was named *Annual Bibliography* from 1956 to 1962. Since 1963, it has had its present title and includes writers from a variety of other languages, although primarily American and European. Books, articles, monographs, and festschriften are all included. Presently, it appears in five volumes, with volume 1 given to the English-speaking nations; volume 2 to European, Asian, African, and South American literatures; volume 3 to linguistics; volume 4 to general literature; and volume 5 to folklore. The volumes may be purchased separately or in several combinations with author and subject index. The file is available online through DIALOG from 1968 to about 1985, with 100,000 records added each year, 60,000 of which are retrospective materials. A recent issue is *MLA International Bibliography of Books and Articles on the Modern Languages and Literatures, 1983. Volume I-V: Classified Listings with Author Index* and *MLA International Bibliography of Books and Articles on the Modern Languages and Literatures, 1983. Volume I-V: Subject Index.*

770. **The Romantic Movement: A Selective and Critical Bibliography.** 1979- . Ann. New York, Garland. (Garland Reference Library of the Humanities).

This annual bibliography from Garland is a continuation of a bibliography by the same title which appeared in *ELH*, a quarterly journal of English literary history, from 1936 to 1948; then in *Philological Quarterly*, 1949-1963; and finally in *English Language Notes*, from 1964 to 1978. The present work continues the plan and follows the rationale of the earlier publication in its desire to cover a movement rather than a time period. Time periods of Romanticism vary with different languages (the English section being stabilized between 1789 and 1837). Other languages covered are French, German, and Spanish, as well as Italian, which has recently been added. *The Romantic Movement Bibliography, 1936-1970 ...* (Pierian, 1973) is a compilation in seven volumes with indexes to the contents of the first thirty-four years of the bibliographic listings. It was edited by A. C. Elkins, Jr., and L. J. Forstner.

771.   **Yearbook of Comparative and General Literature.** 1952- . Ann. Bloomington, Ind., Indiana University Press.

This is considered an extremely useful source of information, furnishing articles, news items, biographical sketches, and announcements pertinent to the study of comparative literature. Most important was the inclusion of the "Annual Bibliography" which was developed to serve as a supplement to Baldensperger's *Bibliography of Comparative Literature* (see entry 765). Unfortunately, this section was discontinued after volume 19, which covered the 1969 period. Following that, a list of English translations from other languages appeared on an annual basis through 1980 (volume 29) and represented the only bibliographic contribution of the *Yearbook*. Since then, the emphasis has moved away from bibliographic work to current awareness. The *Yearbook* remains a collaborative effort among several professional associations, including the American Comparative Literature Association and the Comparative Literature Section of the MLA.

DICTIONARIES, ENCYCLOPEDIAS, AND HANDBOOKS

772.   **Columbia Dictionary of Modern European Literature.** 2nd ed., fully rev. and enl. Jean Albert Bédé and William B. Edgerton, gen. eds. New York, Columbia University Press, 1980. 895p.

Published initially in 1947, this was recognized as one of the best one-volume works on the subject of comparative literature of the modern period. The new edition maintains the high standard of scholarship, with excellent biographical sketches, critical evaluations, and survey articles on the various national literatures. *Modern* is defined as beginning with the period "toward the end of the 19th century when Europe was swept by a wave of new revolutionary movements, largely inspired by the French symbolists and known by different names ... symbolism, decadence, and modernism." More than 1,850 biographical sketches are given for individual authors, each of which is furnished with bibliographic references. There are excellent survey articles on the various national literatures, and all articles are signed. Over 500 scholars have contributed to this comprehensive study. Many of the articles from the earlier edition have been revised and some have been deleted.

773.   **Encyclopedia of World Literature in the 20th Century.** Rev. ed. Leonard S. Klein, gen. ed. New York, Ungar, 1981-1984. 4v.

Based originally on a German work published in 1960-1961, the first English-language edition of this work appeared in three volumes between 1967 and 1971. The new edition represents a thorough revision of the earlier work; approximately 70 percent of the material is new. A strong push toward evenness of entries and a uniformity of style as well as a truly international coverage have produced an extraordinary work. There are excellent survey articles on national literatures, including Third World countries, but the emphasis is on biographical/critical articles. Critical excerpts and bibliographies are supplied for each person covered, and the variety of international authors treated is truly impressive. The new edition maintains the tradition and reputation established by the earlier work.

774.   **A Glossary of Literary Terms.** 4th ed. M. H. Abrams. New York, Holt, Rinehart & Winston, 1981. 220p.

The present edition of an established handbook recognized as an outstanding tool since its initial publication in 1957, this edition represents a thorough revision and updating of the material. Additional illustrations have been included and a greater number of references to literary and critical material have been furnished. Rather than a list of entries with definitions, the work is more of a handbook, providing a series of essays bringing together related terms in the body of a textual narrative. There is an alphabetical index at the end to facilitate access to the desired term and related passages. The work is clearly written, comprehensive in coverage, and well developed stylistically and substantively, and is a valuable addition to the reference collection. The fifth edition of this work is scheduled for publication in September 1987.

775.   **A Handbook to Literature.** 5th ed. Hugh C. Holman and William Harmon. New York, Macmillan, 1986. 647p.

For over fifty years students and teachers have relied on this title, originally referred to by the name of its author, W. F. Thrall. The new edition follows the established pattern, providing definitions of 1,500 words and phrases important to the study of English and American literature. Entries are arranged alphabetically and vary in length from the briefest of identifications (one line or so) to several pages for the survey articles on movements. Cross-references are furnished between entries. The new edition contains 100 new terms and many others show evidence of revision or modification. The well-known and useful feature, the chronological "Outline to Literary History," is still present. Included also are the listings of Nobel and Pulitzer prizes. A new feature is the inclusion of references for many of the entries, indicating from what source the definition or exposition was drawn. This work will continue to be a top choice among librarians and their patrons.

776.   **Masterplots: 2,010 Plot Stories and Essay Reviews from the World's Fine Literature.** Rev. ed. including the four series and further critical evaluations. Frank N. Magill, ed. Englewood Cliffs, N.J., Salem, 1976. 12v.

Begun in the late 1940s and early 1950s, this work unfolded in four series over a period of nearly twenty years, covering various forms of literature (fiction, poetry, essays), at which time it was known as *Masterpieces of World Literature in Digest Form*. Since that time, there have been many spinoffs and variations from Salem Press capitalizing on the popularity and prestige of this work, which was the most highly acclaimed source of plot summaries in the field. It brings together in one multivolume set 1,300 detailed and well-constructed plot summaries included in those first four series, which characteristically provided identification of form, author, period, type of plot, locale, date of first publication, principal characters, themes, and a brief critique. Included in this set are approximately 700 new essay-reviews, which are in-depth, evaluative analyses that have been added to the original coverage. These essay-reviews now characterize the products of Salem Press. *Masterplots Annual Volume* appeared from 1954 to 1976, also edited by Magill. It furnished about 100 essay-reviews of outstanding books published in this country. It was succeeded by *Magill's Literary Annual* beginning in 1977, and to date supplies essay-reviews of some 200 new books each year from those appearing in the United States. Another important cumulation from Salem Press is *Survey of Contemporary Literature* (rev. edition, 1977) in twelve volumes, furnishing updated reprints of 2,300 essay-reviews from the complete run of *Masterplots Annuals* between 1954 and 1976. It also includes material from the *Survey of Contemporary Literature* supplement. (See also entries 907 and 908.)

777.   **The New Guide to Modern World Literature.** Martin Seymour-Smith. New York, Peter Bedrick Books; distr., New York, Harper & Row, 1985. 1379p.

An expansion and updating of the author's earlier work, *Funk & Wagnalls Guide to Modern World Literature* (1973), this new work has been extensively revised and modified, with much additional coverage given to a variety of topics. For some reviewers, this title represents a storehouse of "provocative argument, wit, passion, humor, personal asides, philosophical speculation, and even wisdom" while others resent its "breathtakingly opinionated" manner. Of Jean Paul Sartre it states: "He is a sort of philosopher (but in the French, not the British sense: professional British philosophers shudder at his name and think of bedrooms, spit and semen)." Auden was "flash," while Windham Lewis was a "giant of letters," etc. The work is divided into thirty-three chapters devoted to the literature of a nation or an ethnic group, in which twentieth-century themes are described and the various literary forms analyzed. This guide should be made available for library patrons, who ought also to be forewarned of its extraordinary nature.

778.   The Originals: An A-Z of Fiction's Real-Life Characters. William Amos. Boston, Little, Brown, 1985. 614p.

An innovative theme or focus for this work is the identification of real-life personalities who served as models for fictional characters. Almost 3,000 individuals are identified in this fashion and represent characters from novels, plays, essays, and poetry. A span of 400 years is covered, from the time of Shakespeare to date, with many nationalities included. The arrangement is alphabetical by fictional character, and entries furnish title, publication date, author, and the name of the real person who served as the model or partial model for the character. The length of entries varies considerably, and longer articles may describe the life and times of either or both the real and fictional characters. Photographs of some of the real people are given as well. A more traditional tool for identification of characters is Magill's *Masterplots Cyclopedia of Literary Characters* (Salem, 1963; repr., 1977). Over 16,000 characters from 1,300 novels, dramas, and epics of world literature are enumerated. Arrangement is alphabetical by the title of the work and information is given on author, time of action, and date of first publication or presentation. Characters are described in order of significance. An index by characters facilitates access.

779.   The Oxford Companion to Children's Literature. Humphrey Carpenter and Mari Prichard. New York, Oxford University Press, 1984; repr. with corr., 1985. 584p.

The authors are a husband and wife team working in much the same manner as Iona Opie and Peter Opie did in developing their *Oxford Dictionary of Nursery Rhymes* (see entry 942). This work covers children's literature on a broad scale and in a comprehensive manner, covering literature in all languages and countries where information could be found. There are approximately 2,000 entries in all, of which 900 are biographical sketches. Summaries are given for hundreds of children's titles and various topics, most of which are timely and of importance, such as "television and children." Articles vary in length in proportion to the importance of the topic, with lengthy descriptions given to Lewis Carroll and to *Alice in Wonderland*. The work will be used frequently by those writers whose interests parallel the topical coverage.

780.   Princeton Encyclopedia of Poetry and Poetics. Enl. ed. Alex Preminger, ed. Princeton, N.J., Princeton University Press, 1974. 992p.

This work is a reissue, with an added supplementary section, of the author's highly regarded *Encyclopedia of Poetry and Poetics*, published in 1965. There are about 1,000 individual entries of varying length (from 20 to 20,000 words) depending upon the importance or scope of the topic. Designed with the general reader as well as the student and scholar in mind, the work has enjoyed a great deal of popularity among all elements of its targeted audience. History, theory, technique, and criticism of poetry are covered, ranging from the earliest times to the present. A successful blend of scholarship and lucidity has earned this publication a reputation as a standard work. The poetry of various nationalities and ethnic groups is covered in useful survey articles. The supplementary section, new to this edition, furnishes an eighty-three-page coverage of new developments and topics not previously covered. Another standard in the field of general poetry is Babette Deutsch's *Poetry Handbook: A Dictionary of Terms*, now in its fourth edition (Funk and Wagnalls, 1974). It continues to be a useful handbook for the poet and the general reader or student. It employs a dictionary arrangement and defines techniques and components of the poetic art through examples of poetry.

781.   **The Reader's Encyclopedia.** 2nd ed. William Rose Benét. New York, Crowell, 1965. 1118p.

First published in 1948, this convenient and valuable handbook has been a standard in the field ever since. The work furnishes brief articles on a variety of topics and personalities (scientists and philosophers, as well as creative writers). The coverage is international and all periods of time are treated, an impressive attempt at comprehensiveness for a one-volume work. Entries cover authors, titles, characters from literature, literary terms, allusions, and movements. Important historical figures and topics are identified, as are terms from the sciences, fine arts, philosophy, etc. Entries for titles furnish plot summaries, and those for literary characters give full identification. Musical compositions and art works are also included. World literature received a boost in this edition, with increased coverage of the Orient, the Soviet Union, Latin America, and the Near East.

782.   **Thesaurus of Book Digests: Digests of the World's Permanent Writings from the Ancient Classics to Current Literature.** Hiram Haydn and Edmund Fuller. New York, Crown, 1949; repr., New York, Bonanza Books, 1968. 831p.

Another old favorite is this collection of digests or plot summaries of what the authors refer to as the world's permanent literature. The digests are very brief and highly stylized in the form of "thumb-nail sketches," giving just a skeletal picture of the work. The arrangement is alphabetical by title. The literary works covered represent a wide range of contributions, from the classics to the important modern writings. This handbook may also be used to identify characters, since they are indexed separately from the authors. A supplementary effort by Irving Weiss and Anne de la Vergne Weiss is *Thesaurus of Book Digests, 1950-1980* (Crown, 1981). About 1,700 fiction and nonfiction books published over a thirty-year period are included, as well as some earlier works of this century not covered by Haydn and Fuller. Plots, themes, or summaries are furnished. For lengthier treatments, one should consult other handbooks and critical works.

BIOGRAPHICAL AND CRITICAL SOURCES

783.   **Author Biographies Master Index: A Consolidated Index to More Than 658,000 Biographical Sketches.** 2nd ed. Barbara McNeil and Miranda C. Herbert, eds. Detroit, Gale, 1984-1987. 3v.

This biographical index updates and expands the first edition published in 1958, and now contains nearly 660,000 citations to biographical sketches in the first two volumes as compared to 413,000 in the earlier work. It represents a massive job, indexing some 400 separate directories and biographical dictionaries from cover to cover. All time periods and most areas of the world are included, producing a universal index covering all genres as well as children's authors and illustrators. Typical coverage includes name, birth and death dates, and coded references, and is strongest on British and American authors of modern times. The work retains listings from the first edition but updates the entries with references to new editions of biographical works. Cross-references are lacking; therefore, a single author may appear in more than one place because of variant forms. The first supplement appeared in 1987, and is identified as volume 3. McNeil's *Twentieth Century Author Biographies Master Index: A Consolidated Index to More Than 170,000 Biographical Sketches* (Gale, 1984) is a new undertaking derived from the above work. It is limited to living authors and those who have died during this century. It appears in paperback and is reasonably priced. Another useful index is Patricia Pate Havlice's *Index to Literary Biography* (Scarecrow, 1975) which indexes biographical sketches of nearly 70,000 authors who appeared in fifty volumes of collective biography and literary dictionaries. The first supplement appeared in 1983, identifying 53,000 authors covered in fifty-seven literary dictionaries and biographical sources. Nationality and principal genre are given along with dates and coded references.

784. **Contemporary Authors: A Biobibliographical Guide to Current Writers in Fiction, General Non-Fiction, Poetry, Journalism, Drama, Motion Pictures, Television, and Other Fields.** Detroit, Gale, 1962- . (In progress).

The initial series in Gale's massive attempt to keep abreast of biographical coverage of authors in various fields, this work furnishes good biographical sketches of authors from many countries. Personal information, career highlights, previous works as well as those in progress, and sometimes bibliographical references are included in the entries. The work continues (volume 118 was published in 1986), generally favoring American writers and excluding scientific and technical writers. The *New Revision Series* includes entries from the original series which need revision; only those entries requiring significant changes are modified. Beginning in 1981, this revision has reached about twenty volumes, and is the favored method of updating the series at present. It replaces the *First Revision Series*, an ill-fated attempt to update whole volumes of the original series begun in 1975 and discontinued after four years and forty-four volumes. Also defunct is the *Permanent Series*, which was established in 1975 to furnish biographies of deceased personalities and retired individuals removed from the current series. This was discontinued after two volumes. These complicated, expensive, and time-consuming attempts to provide continuous biographical coverage mark Gale as a true leader in biographical publishing. The most recent contribution is the *Contemporary Authors Autobiography Series*, begun in 1984 with volume 1, which contains twenty to thirty autobiographical essays by important creative writers. The plan is to include nonfiction writers in subsequent volumes.

785. **Contemporary Literary Criticism: Excerpts from Criticism of the Works of Today's Novelists, Poets, Playwrights, Short Story Writers, Scriptwriters, and Other Creative Writers.** Detroit, Gale, 1973- . (In progress).

Close to forty volumes have appeared in this series since its inception in 1973. Presently, it provides selected excerpts from criticism of the work of fewer than 100 authors per volume, and is limited to those who are still living or who have been deceased for twenty-five years or less. There is a heavy emphasis on English-language writers, although others are included if their work is fairly well known in the United States. Almost any authors who have been critiqued are eligible for inclusion; therefore, there is a good mix of individuals represented. Each author receives about five excerpts taken from books, articles, and reviews. Citations to the source documents are furnished.

786. **Contemporary Literary Criticism: Yearbook 1984- ....** 1985- . Ann. Sharon K. Hall, ed. Detroit, Gale.

A recent addition to the *CLC* line, the subtitle reads, "The Year in Fiction, Poetry, Drama, and World Literature and the Year's New Authors." The *Yearbook* began in 1985 with coverage of 1984, and was identified as volume 34 of the *Contemporary Literary Criticism* series (see entry 785). *Yearbook 1985*, published in 1986, is volume 39 in the series. Like other issues in the series, the yearbooks furnish the cumulative index to all author entries in the series and the cumulative index to critics. Sections of the yearbook include the year in review, new authors, prize winners, obituaries, literary biography, and literary criticism. There are several essays on the various genres covered during the year and highlights of important activities and developments of notable authors. Critical essays of new writers represent an important contribution to reference work.

787. **Critical Survey of Short Fiction.** Frank N. Magill. Englewood Cliffs, N.J., Salem, 1981. 7v.

Although British and American writers are emphasized heavily in this work, non-English-language authors are also covered, receiving about 25 percent of the coverage in the text. The first two volumes furnish more than fifty essays on the history, characteristics, and nature of the short story, some of which contain bibliographies. Volumes 3-6 provide over 260 articles on major writers and cover the influence, characteristics, and analysis of each individual's work along with biographical information and citations to additional works. These essay-reviews combine both analysis and plot summaries of the short stories, and are characteristic of Magill's efforts at present, unlike *Masterplots* (see entry 776), which was primarily concerned with the plot. Volume 7 contains nearly 400 one-page sketches of "current" authors, written by the authors themselves.

788. **European Writers.** George Stade, ed.-in-chief. New York, Scribner's, 1983- . 7v. (In progress).

Presently, there are seven volumes of a projected thirteen-volume set designed to provide lengthy articles on the lives and achievements of European writers, as well as plot descriptions of their works. The essays run about 15,000 words and are written by qualified young scholars, professors emeriti, as well as critics, poets, and novelists. The first two volumes cover the Middle Ages and the Renaissance, while volumes 3 and 4 cover the Age of Reason and the Enlightenment. Volumes 5-7 deal with the Romantic century. There are thirty-six articles, twenty-five of which are on individual writers in volumes 1-2; and twenty-seven essays on twenty-nine writers in volumes 3-4. Volumes 5-7 consist of seventy essays. Volumes 8-9 are projected for publication in 1988. Essays are arranged chronologically and are considered to be clearly written. There is a good overview of the periods covered in volume 1 by the late editor, William T. H. Jackson of Columbia University. An index to the whole set is planned following completion of the volumes describing the twentieth century.

789. **International Authors and Writers Who's Who.** 10th ed. Ernest Kay, ed. Cambridge, England, International Biographical Centre; distr., Detroit, Gale, 1986. 879p.

An unusual feature of this serial effort seems to be an apparent decline or decrease in the number of authors covered with each successive edition. The eighth edition carried 14,000 writers, the ninth edition provides 9,600 entries, while the present work has been reduced to the coverage of about 8,000 writers, even though journalists and magazine editors are listed for the first time. There is a heavy emphasis on English and American writers. Entries generally provide place and date of birth, profession, education, major publications, and address, although there is some variation in completeness of information supplied. Pseudonyms appear not to be well covered despite the publisher's claims in this regard, and no cross-references are given.

790.   **Literary Criticism Index.** Alan R. Weiner and Spencer Means. Metuchen, N.J., Scarecrow, 1984. 685p.

This index was designed to fill a need for access to the vast number of bibliographies and checklists of criticism that have multiplied in recent decades. It provides references to these bibliographies rather than to any critical studies directly. The work covers eighty-six guides or bibliographies of criticism, and is arranged by author of the creative works. One would look up an author and be referred to a checklist of bibliographies which contains references to critical studies of his or her work. Under the author's name are listed general works followed by entries for criticism of individual works. This represents a useful tool for those who are in need of such information.

791.   **Literature Criticism from 1400 to 1800: Excerpts from Criticism of the Works of Fifteenth, Sixteenth, Seventeenth, and Eighteenth Century Novelists, Poets, Playwrights** ... Dennis Poupard, ed. Mark W. Scott, assoc. ed. Detroit, Gale, 1984- . (In progress).

A new series from Gale, this one serves as a complement to the three others covering the nineteenth and twentieth centuries (see entries 785, 793, and 797). Each volume of this series will cover between fifteen and twenty individuals from all over the world. Volume 1 appeared in 1984 and was followed by volume 2 in 1985. Such writers as Henry Fielding, Aphra Behn, and Jonathan Swift are treated in terms of the critical response given to their work. Entries are arranged alphabetically within each volume and critical comments are furnished, beginning with contemporary writings and proceeding to modern day views. It is useful to see the trend in critical acceptance or rejection and the relationship to time periods. Citations are given to the sources and there is a bibliography of additional references for each author. A cumulative index includes all entries from any of the four titles in this series.

792.   **Magill's Bibliography of Literary Criticism: Selected Sources for the Study of More Than 2,500 Outstanding Works of Western Literature.** Frank N. Magill, ed. Englewood Cliffs, N.J., Salem, 1979. 4v.

Culled from the world's great literature are the titles of 2,500 important and influential works either in English or in English translation which are the focus of the effort to identify critical and interpretive material. With a large staff, Magill was able to uncover over 36,000 citations to such material, examining the efforts of 613 major writers. Many of these source items have never appeared in a checklist or bibliography, the emphasis being on critiques in the English language, hopefully published during the past twenty years. These studies appeared as books, parts of books, and periodical articles, and deal with literature of all types from all countries. The arrangement is by author, then individual work. Studies are then listed alphabetically by author. The number of studies generally runs between twelve and twenty-five for each work covered.

793.   **Nineteenth Century Literature Criticism: Excerpts from Criticism of the Works of Novelists, Poets, Playwrights, Short Story Writers** ... Detroit, Gale, 1981- . (In progress).

Following the same plan as Gale's three other series, which complement the coverage given here (see entries 785, 791, and 797), this work treats those authors who died during the nineteenth century. All types of creative writers are included from Europe, Great Britain, and the United States. Short excerpts of critical studies are furnished for each entry. Each volume covers the works of about twenty-five different writers, and there are

more than ten volumes available in the series. Entries furnish a brief biographical introduction, bibliography of works published, excerpts from the critics, and a suggested
reading list for further inquiry. The excerpts are substantial, as they are in the other series,
and adequately convey the sense of the critique. Excerpts are arranged chronologically,
beginning with contemporary criticism and proceeding to modern thinking.

794.   **Postmodern Fiction: A Bio-bibliographical Guide.** Larry McCaffery, ed. Westport,
Conn., Greenwood Press, 1986. 604p.

Postmodernism, according to the author, is generally meant to embrace those writers
who have established their careers since the 1960s. This places the guide in a unique
position in terms of relative recency of individuals and their works. Most checklists and
bibliographies have a much greater time span, and in truth pay little attention to the "post-
moderns." A variety of writers is included, ranging from genre specialists such as science
fiction writer Roger Zelazny, commercially successful writers such as Günter Grass, and
Latin American contributors like Gabriel Garcia Marquez, to a number of critics and
contributors to popular magazines. Part 1 provides fifteen general articles analyzing the
modes of postmodern fiction and criticism, while part 2 furnishes over 100 biocritical
descriptions on individual writers. Also included is a bibliography of additional readings
on postmodern criticism.

795.   **Survey of Modern Fantasy Literature.** Frank N. Magill, ed. Englewood Cliffs, N.J.,
Salem, 1983. 5v.

Responding to the obvious need for a work of this type for the genre of fantasy
fiction, Salem Press has marshalled its considerable expertise and resources to provide an
important and popular product. Fantasy literature includes both high and low fantasy,
fairy tales, folklore, and horror dating from Victorian times to the present. Included here
are 500 representative works of European and American authors for which are furnished
essay-reviews of approximately 1,000 to 3,000 words, depending upon the work's
significance. Entries include brief author information, date of book publication, type of
work, time period, locale, brief description of essay-review, plot, and bibliography. An
earlier product of the publisher was Magill's *Survey of Science Fiction Literature* (1979),
also in five volumes. It follows the same pattern and guidelines in analyzing in-depth 500
world famous science fiction novels.

796.   **Twentieth Century Authors: A Biographical Dictionary of Modern Literature ...**
Stanley Jasspon Kunitz and Howard Haycraft. New York, H. W. Wilson, 1942; repr.,
1985. 1577p. Supp., 1955, 1123p.

This is the original "old favorite" for identifying modern authors, a product of the
Wilson Company, who commissioned Kunitz to develop a line of biographical dictionaries.
They were all highly stylized, bearing a portrait and providing bibliographies of the
author's work, as well as a brief biography highlighting the career. This particular tool
concerned writers of all nations whose books are familiar to English-language readers. A
supplement appeared in 1955 by Kunitz and Vineta Colby, with whom he later collaborated
in producing *European Authors 1000-1900* (H. W. Wilson, 1967). This was done in the
same general manner. A complementary work, *World Authors 1950-1970*, edited by John
Wakeman, appeared in 1975. This neither duplicated nor updated the main work but
provided biographical sketches of nearly 1,000 additional authors of literary importance or
unusual popularity. Continuing in this vein were additional publications: *World Authors,
1970-1975*, edited by Wakeman (1980), and *World Authors 1975-1980*, edited by Vineta
Colby (1985). Each of the five-year volumes furnishes sketches of over 300 authors. A

useful tool is *Index to the Wilson Authors Series* (rev. ed., H. W. Wilson, 1986), which furnishes quick access to entries in all the volumes mentioned above.

797. **Twentieth Century Literary Criticism: Excerpts from Criticism of the Works of Novelists, Poets, Playwrights, Short-story Writers ...** Dennis Poupard, ed. Detroit, Gale, 1978- . (In progress).

The subtitle goes on to indicate that the authors treated had lived (and died) between 1900 and 1960. This complements the coverage of *Contemporary Authors* (see entry 784), for which the major focus is on living authors, and fits nicely with the two other Gale series dealing with the nineteenth century (see entry 793) and earlier centuries (see entry 791). Each author entry provides a portrait, an in-depth bibliography, a bibliography of principal work, and most important, a selection of excerpts of literary criticism arranged chronologically from the time of publication of the work to the most recent efforts. About forty authors are covered in each volume of this continuing publication, and coverage of each varies in length from ten to over thirty pages.

WRITERS' GUIDES AND DIRECTORIES

798. **Fiction Writer's Market.** 1981- . Jean M. Fredette, ed. Ann. Cincinnati, Ohio, Writers Digest Books.

One of a line of annual guides for creative writers from the publisher, this work targets the needs of novelists and short story writers. Over 1,500 markets are identified, a good percentage of them newly added to each annual edition. Identified in each case are the subject interests, needs, method of payment, terms of the agreement, as well as suggestions or tips to facilitate the process. There is a category index to the different periodicals and publishers to provide access by subject or scope, as well as indexes by publisher and title. The work contains short articles for other sources of a how-to-do-it nature. *Writer's Yearbook: Your Guide to Getting Published This Year*, is an annual, enlarged version of *Writer's Digest* magazine, with a number of feature articles and lists of publishing events for the preceding year. Features include a listing of the 100 best magazine publishers from a writer's point of view and a survey of today's book publishers.

799. **Literary Market Place.** 1940- . Ann. New York, R. R. Bowker.

Subtitled "The Business Directory of American Book Publishing," *LMP* is the most well known and frequently used directory of its type on the market. It provides up-to-date listings of organizations, periodicals, and publishing houses and identifies officers and key personnel, all of whom are involved in the placing, promotion, and marketing of literary property. A variety of topical headings is used, including book publishing, book clubs, associations, book trade events, conferences and contests, agents, etc. The volume embraces radio, television, and motion picture interests as well. A useful alphabetical listing of names identified in the directory with address and telephone number, as well as references to pages in the directory, is provided.

800. **The Poet's Marketplace.** Joseph J. Kelly. Philadelphia, Running Press, 1984. 174p.

One of the few guides focusing on the needs of the poet, the intention of this work is to help serious poets find the right outlets and derive appropriate rewards for their labor. Chapters cover such useful and important aspects as submission of manuscripts and keeping abreast of the market. Other considerations include listings of magazines that publish poetry, chapbook publishers, book publishers, and alternative markets. Also covered are contests, awards, grants, and associations. Directories and guides to self-publishing are listed in the appendix, an especially useful feature in view of trends in that direction. One might be advised to read the first chapter, which provides helpful guidelines on how to use the directory in order to exploit it to the fullest. A related title is the *1987 Poets Market: Where to Publish Your Poetry*, by Judson Jerome (Writers Digest Books, 1987).

801. **The Writer's Handbook.** 1936- . Ann. Boston, The Writer.

The fiftieth issue of this standard work in the field, like earlier volumes, provides a number of essays and articles covering the art, craft, technique, and business of writing for publication, with contributions from significant (popular) authors such as Isaac Asimov, Stephen King, and Evan Hunter. Both the writing scene in general as well as more specialized phases or areas are treated. Covered are various forms of writing: fiction, nonfiction, poetry, drama and television, and juvenile and young adult areas. Business practices are also described. Possibly the most important feature is the market guide, which covers a number of potential outlets for publication, including magazine articles with various subject emphases; fiction outlets; poetry; college, literary, and little magazines; humor; juvenile; etc. Prizes, organizations, and agents are also identified. A similar tool, although not an annual, is *Writer's Encyclopedia*, edited by Kirk Polking and others (Writers Digest Books, 1983). This provides definitions and identifications of terms, business practices, and organizations, and furnishes advice for writers. The emphasis is on print publishing, but radio and television are also covered, as are advertising, songwriting, etc. Most useful is the appendix segment, with sixty-three entries furnishing samples of writing projects and identifying pay rates.

802. **Writer's Resource Guide.** Bernadine Clark, ed. Cincinnati, Ohio, Writers Digest Books, 1983. 473p.

Unlike the host of tools developed to aid the writer in the marketing of his or her craft, this one functions as a manual of execution. The question of researching topics is covered in several chapters and involves such considerations as the library as a research tool, government information sources, researching fiction, finding experts, and conducting interviews. Toward this end, there are a number of articles consisting of interviews with knowledgeable authors and writers. A large segment of the work is divided into research areas or topics such as philosophy and religion. It furnishes bibliographic information to further reading, and lists and describes organizations and clubs in terms of their services and practices. There are separate title and subject indexes.

QUOTATIONS AND PROVERBS

803. **Familiar Quotations: A Collection of Passages, Phrases, and Proverbs Traced Back to Their Sources in Ancient and Modern Literature.** 15th and 125th anniversary ed., rev. and enl. John Bartlett. Ed. by Emily Morrison Beck. Boston, Little, Brown, 1980. 1540p.

This is the standard work of its kind; most searches for quotations or imperfectly remembered lines of poetry begin with Bartlett. The first edition of this landmark title appeared in 1855, and it has been a fixture in libraries ever since. New editions are issued on the average every seven to ten years, and each one generally adds contemporary authors to the coverage. The fifteenth edition retains the chronological arrangement of authors quoted and appears in larger size, permitting more quotations per page. Over 400 authors have been added (both contemporary and historical), and both the "Anonymous" and

"Bible" segments have been enlarged. Ancient Asian writings have been increased in number. There is an author index, but most important for this tool (and others like it) is the detailed index by keywords.

804. **The Home Book of Quotations, Classical and Modern.** 10th ed. rev. Burton Egbert Stevenson. New York, Dodd, Mead, 1967; repr., New York, Greenwich House; distr., New York, Crown, 1984. 2816p.

Another of the well-known standards in the field of quotation handbooks is the work of Stevenson, who published a series of "Home Books," all of which were warmly received by reference librarians. This particular tool was the mainstay of the Stevenson line and was first issued in 1934. It was frequently revised, each new issue adding new entries, until 1967. The tenth edition contains more than 50,000 quotations, all of which are arranged alphabetically by subjects, which are then subdivided by smaller and more specific headings. Access is provided through an author index, which includes full name, identifying phrase, dates of birth and death, and references to all quotations listed. Most important, of course, is the keyword index which provides access to the quotations.

805. **The Oxford Dictionary of English Proverbs.** 3rd ed. Rev. by F. P. Wilson. Oxford, Clarendon Press, 1970. 930p.

It is difficult to imagine many libraries which provide services in language and literature which do not have this important title. It is generally a first choice when searching for proverbs in the English language, the emphasis, of course, being on the language as employed by Britons. The first edition appeared in 1935 and contained about 10,000 proverbs; since then the coverage has increased somewhat and there have been slight changes in arrangement. The present edition contains more proverbs than supplied by the second edition, but also includes material from the first edition which had been deleted from the second. Each proverb is dated, with references to its use in the literature from its beginning and subsequent changes of meaning identified. Many of the proverbs come from M. P. Tilley's *Dictionary of the Proverbs in England in the Sixteenth and Seventeenth Centuries* ... (University of Michigan Press, 1950).

806. **The Oxford Dictionary of Quotations.** 3rd ed. Oxford, Oxford University Press, 1979; repr., 1985. 907p.

First published in 1941, this has been an important reference tool over the years. Proverbs and nursery rhymes are excluded since they are covered in other Oxford publications (see entries 805 and 942). The work provides a comprehensive listing of quotations, all of which are arranged alphabetically. Sources of the quotations are authors of every description, both English-language and foreign, as well as the Bible and Prayer Book. Also included are quotes from anonymous authors. Indexing is excellent, although not as detailed as in the second edition. Approximately 70,000 entries are contained in the index, for which there is an indication of the author's name along with a page reference. Retained from earlier editions is a separate Greek index.

807. **Writers on Writing.** Jon Winokur. Philadelphia, Running Press, 1986. 160p.

A compact little collection of quotations of writers on the art and practice of writing, this work will be of most interest to students and teachers. More than 1,500 quotations are classified under broad topics such as plagiarism. The claim is that the work results from twenty years of compulsive collecting in this area, and it does provide a pleasurable and interesting experience. Another of the recent books in this vein is *The Writer's Quotation Book: A Literary Companion*, edited by James Charlton (Pushcart Press; distr., W. W.

Norton, 1985). First appearing in 1980, the present edition represents an expansion to over 400 quotations. These cover all aspects of literary production: writing, publishing, editing, etc. Unfortunately for reference service, its use is limited since there is no index. The second edition of this work is scheduled to appear in 1987.

Literature in English

BIBLIOGRAPHIC GUIDES

808. American Prose and Criticism, 1820-1900: A Guide to Information Sources. Comp. by Elinor Hughes Partridge. Detroit, Gale, 1983. 575p.

This is a useful bibliography and research guide designed to identify sources of information in books on nineteenth-century American nonfiction. It complements an earlier work by Peter A. Brier from the same publisher, which covers the first half of the twentieth century, *American Prose and Criticism, 1900-1950*, completed in 1981. Both works are developed on the same lines and together are designed to help students and specialists identify significant primary and secondary works of and about their respective periods. Representative writings of various types are included, such as history, travel, narrative, diaries, science, and politics, as well as works by individual authors known primarily for belles lettres. The first section covers general secondary works (bibliographies, periodicals, historical and literary studies), the second section is arranged by genre and lists both primary and secondary sources, while the third section treats individual authors. There is an author/title index.

809. Guide to American Literature. Valmai Kirkham Fenster. Littleton, Colo., Libraries Unlimited, 1983. 243p.

Developed as a guide for both graduate and undergraduate students, this work provides annotated listings of sources considered to be important or essential to the study of American literature. It is divided into two major parts or segments, with part 1 given to general guides and reference sources. Covered are such forms as bibliographic guides; indexes; literary surveys; criticism; political, social, and intellectual history; language; anthologies and series; and other relevant reference tools. Part 2 comprises the major portion of the work and furnishes source materials for the study of 100 important writers. John Dos Passos, W. E. B. Du Bois, and Lillian Hellman are just a few of the names included. Primary sources are listed first, by date of publication, followed by secondary sources classified by type (biography, criticism, bibliography, reference work). Author, title, and subject indexes are included.

810. A Guide to English and American Literature. 3rd ed. Frederick W. Bateson and Harrison T. Meserole. London and New York, Longman, 1970; repr., 1976. 334p.

Originally entitled *A Guide to English Literature*, the two previous editions from the same publisher (1965-1967) established this work as one of the useful bibliographic guides designed for both the graduate and undergraduate student in developing an awareness of existing sources of study. Major editions and important commentaries are identified for those who are to pursue literary topics in a serious manner. The work begins with a general introductory section which is then followed by chapters on literary periods. Included are such studies as medieval, Renaissance, Augustan, Romantic, and modern English literature. American literature is given separate treatment, and there is a chapter on literary scholarship. A general index provides access.

811. **A Research Guide for Undergraduate Students: English and American Literature.** Nancy L. Baker. New York, Modern Language Association of America, 1985. 61p.

This compact little volume has gained rapid popularity among undergraduate students as a useful bibliographic guide since its initial publication in 1982. The new work was issued with the idea of acquainting students with all aspects of library use, including computer technology. Only two chapters have been revised, but the changes are significant, introducing the student to the potential of online search services in solving bibliographic problems. This is true of the chapter on the card catalog, where the user is introduced to online catalogs. Also in the chapter on locating periodical literature, the online systems DIALOG and BRS are described and endorsed. It is obvious that the message is an important one and should be considered not only by students but by their teachers at every level.

812. **Selective Bibliography for the Study of English and American Literature.** 6th ed. Richard Daniel Altick and Andrew Wright. New York, Macmillan, 1979. 180p.

Although not as enjoyable as Altick's *The Art of Literary Research* (see entry 758), this work is a practical and concise guide to English and American literature, intended primarily for the graduate student. Undergraduates have also found it to be highly useful inasmuch as it is limited to works of high quality. It has become a standard in the field since its initial edition in 1960, and represents the first choice of most college teachers. Inclusion of an entry generally indicates excellence except in cases where there are no other works on the topic. In such instances, evaluative annotations are furnished to "qualify" its inclusion. There are over 630 items, each of which is numbered. The arrangement is classified, and included are a glossary of terms and a name-title-subject index. An older work still regarded as useful is *A Reference Guide to English, American, and Canadian Literature* ..., by Inglis F. Bell and Jennifer Gallup (Vancouver, University of British Columbia, 1971). This is planned for undergraduates and is divided into two parts: a classified annotated bibliography of standard research tools, and bibliographies of individual authors. The index is by author, not by title.

BIBLIOGRAPHIES AND CATALOGS

813. **American Diaries: An Annotated Bibliography of Published American Diaries and Journals.** Comp. by Laura Arksey, et al. Detroit, Gale, 1983- . (In progress).

This first volume of a projected two-volume set identifies diaries written between 1492 and 1844. Volume 2 will cover the years 1845 to 1980. The first volume is partially based on an earlier work by William Matthews entitled *American Diaries: An Annotated Bibliography of American Diaries Written prior to the Year 1861* (University of California Press, 1945), although the new work has been expanded somewhat, with 2,500 entries as compared to 2,400 in Matthews. Bibliographic information is given in greater detail for the entries retained from the earlier version, although Matthews's annotations have been used. Some of these have been clarified or modified when necessary. The new work includes diaries excluded by Matthews in cases where the authors were out of the country in a foreign mission or living in a U.S. territory. Alaskan, Hawaiian, and Spanish-American material has been newly added. Volume 2, projected for 1985 completion but still forthcoming, is to cover another 2,500 diaries.

814. **American Literary Magazines: The Eighteenth and Nineteenth Centuries.** Edward E. Chielens, ed. Westport, Conn., Greenwood Press, 1986. 503p. (Historical Guides to the World's Periodicals and Newspapers).

This is the first volume of a two-volume set covering the history of literary magazines in this country. Volume 1 covers the period 1774 to 1900 and describes ninety-three of the most important titles of the time. Included for each entry is an extensive history of its publishing and editorial policy. The work is scholarly in nature, providing documentation through notes. Also furnished is a bibliography of additional sources for further reading. Reprint editions are identified, as are existing runs of the periodicals and availability of indexes. Title changes are recorded, and volume and issue data are given along with frequency and names of key figures. Also provided is an opening essay on periodical publishing during this period. The appendices contain listings of literary magazines and a chronology.

815. **American Literary Manuscripts: A Checklist of Holdings in Academic, Historical, and Public Libraries, Museums, and Authors' Homes in the United States.** 2nd ed. Albert J. Robbins, et al., comps. and eds. Athens, Ga., University of Georgia Press, 1977. 387p.

Since the publication of the first edition in 1960, this has been recognized as a valuable tool for scholarship. Few of the participating libraries and institutions are able to publish their own catalogs. As was the case with the earlier issue, the second edition involved a large-scale effort sponsored in part by the American Literature Section of the Modern Language Association. The manuscript holdings (creative works, diaries, letters, documents, and memorabilia) of 2,800 American writers are listed, an increase of over 400 from the first edition. The number of libraries has increased more than two-fold from 273 in the first edition to 600 in the present edition. The file of data was started by Robbins at Indiana University, where it is maintained.

816. **American Literature.** Harvard University Library. Cambridge, Mass., Harvard University Library, 1970. 2v. (Widener Library Shelflist, v.26-27).

Another of the publications of the extensive shelflist of Widener Library at Harvard University, this two-volume set identifies 50,000 books and periodicals in the American literature categories of the catalog. Included are literary histories, anthologies, and works by and about individual authors. Also covered are the categories of British and American fiction, which are organized alphabetically and include another 8,000 items. Also important is the material found in *English Literature*, published in four volumes in 1971 (Widener Library Shelflist, v.35-38). This contains 112,000 books, pamphlets, and periodicals listed in the English literature classifications of the shelflist. These computer-produced shelflists furnish a copy of the classification schedule, a chronological listing, and an author-title listing.

817. **American Women Writers: Bibliographical Essays.** Maurice Duke, et al., eds. Westport, Conn., Greenwood Press, 1983. 434p.

This work is considered an important contribution to the body of reference literature developed on female authors in recent years. Much systematic effort is still needed, and publications like this help to develop the continuing body of critical inquiry. The essays cover twenty-four female writers, following the pattern established by James Woodress twelve years earlier in *Eight American Authors: A Review of Research and Criticism* (W. W. Norton, 1971), which itself was a revised edition of a work published fifteen years before that. In all these efforts, the essays describe and analyze a wide range of secondary works on the authors. Bibliographies, editions, manuscripts and letters, biography, and critical studies are covered. Authors covered in both works range from the colonial period to the present.

818.   **The Annotated Bibliography of Canada's Major Authors.** Robert Lecker and Jack David. Toronto, ECW Press; distr., Boston, G. K. Hall, 1979- . (In progress).

Projected as an eight-volume work, this series is steadily moving toward completion, with the publication of volume 6 in 1985. The series is to be divided evenly, with four volumes given to prose writers and four volumes to poets. Both primary and secondary sources are identified for about six writers in each volume. No biographical information is given. Two sections contain works by the author and are divided between complete publications and contributions to publications. References are given to manuscript collections and audiovisual materials while, reprints and individual titles within a work are identified. The other two sections contain works about the authors (articles, books, theses, interviews, audiovisuals, honors, book reviews, etc.). This is a highly useful series bringing together a body of material on significant Canadian writers.

819.   **Articles on American Literature, 1900-1950.** Lewis Gaston Leary. Durham, N.C., Duke University Press, 1954. 437p.

Leary first published a bibliography of this sort in 1947; it covered the period 1920-1945. This work supersedes that publication in its coverage of the first half of the twentieth century. The tool is derived from the bibliographies published in two literary journals: *American Literature* (on a quarterly basis since 1929), and *PMLA* (on an annual basis since 1922). Coverage back to 1900 has been accomplished through examination of a number of periodicals and other bibliographies. The work has been continued by Leary's *Articles on American Literature, 1950-1967* (1970) which, although operating on the same general plan, gives greater coverage to articles appearing in foreign journals. Following that was *Articles on American Literature, 1968-1975* (1979), which in addition to providing supplemental coverage to the earlier works, includes additions and corrections to those volumes. *Articles on American and British Literature: An Index to Selected Periodicals, 1950-1977*, compiled by Larry B. Corse and Sandra Corse (Swallow/Ohio University Press, 1981) is intended for undergraduates in small college libraries. It indexes forty-eight common literary periodicals, and entries are arranged by nationality, then period, then subject.

820.   **Articles on Women Writers: A Bibliography.** Narda Lacey Schwartz. Santa Barbara, Calif., ABC-Clio, 1977. 236p.

Nine years after this bibliography of articles and dissertations on women writers was published, it has become volume 1 of a set, the second volume of which is entitled *Articles on Women Writers, Volume 2, 1976-1984* (ABC-Clio, 1986). In both cases, coverage is limited to women writing in the English language, but from a number of countries of the Commonwealth, United States, etc. Volume 1 treats 600 personalities who were subjects of at least one scholarly or popular article published between 1960 and 1975. Volume 2 encompasses more writers, over 1,000, which reflects both an increased interest and also a broadened search strategy on the part of the author. Schwartz has included feminist abstracting services as well as traditional indexes, giving another dimension and added perspective of women's writing. Sources are varied and range from literary journals to the common and popular periodicals. A most useful reference tool for literature study.

821.   **Bibliographies of Studies in Victorian Literature for the Thirteen Years 1932-1944.** William D. Templeman, ed. Urbana, Ill., University of Illinois Press, 1945. 450p.

The first in a series of retrospective bibliographic compilations of listings originally published in certain literary periodicals, this work and its continuations have become familiar reference tools. The Templeman effort provides a reprint of the bibliographies published in the May issue of *Modern Philology* from 1933 to 1945. Arrangement of the bibliographies is year-by-year, and the work includes an author index of individuals mentioned in section IV of each year. Austin Wright's *Bibliography of Studies in Victorian Literature for the Ten Years 1945-1954* (University of Illinois Press, 1956) continues the effort for the next ten years, with reprints of the annual "Victorian Bibliographies" section from *Modern Philology*. Robert C. Slack's *Bibliography of Studies in Victorian Literature for the Ten Years 1955-1964* (University of Illinois Press, 1967) divides the coverage between two journals. From 1955 to 1956 "Victorian Bibliographies" appeared in *Modern Philology*, and it was then incorporated in the journal *Victorian Studies* (1957-). The last cumulation to appear was Ronald E. Freeman's *Bibliography of Studies in Victorian Literature for the Ten Years 1965-74* (AMS, 1981), which reprints the bibliographies from *Victorian Studies*. The work is continued on an annual basis in *Victorian Studies* (see entry 836n).

822. **Bibliography of American Literature.** Nathaniel Jacob Blanck. New Haven, Conn., Yale University Press, 1955- . (In progress).

Projected for eight volumes, this monumental but highly selective series moved toward completion with the publication of volume 7 in 1983, ten years after the appearance of volume 6. Progress has been slow and has required grants from both private and public agencies to sustain this effort, which complements the work of the early American bibliographers Charles Evans and Joseph Sabin. When completed, about 300 American writers from the Federal period to moderns who died before 1930 will have been covered in-depth in alphabetical arrangement. (Volume 1, *Henry Adams to Donn Byrne* through volume 7, *James Kirke Paulding to Frank Stockton*.) About forty writers are covered in each volume in systematic fashion, including first editions; reprints containing textual or other changes; and a selected listing of biographical, bibliographical, and critical works. Only authors of literary interest are included and all listings are organized chronologically under their classifications. Excluded from coverage are periodical and newspaper publications, later editions, translations, and volumes with isolated correspondence.

823. **Bibliography of Bibliographies in American Literature.** Charles H. Nilon. New York, R. R. Bowker, 1970. 483p.

An older but still useful tool identifying resources for the study of American literature, this work furnishes identifications of more than 6,400 bibliographies. Bibliographies of various types are listed, including separate publications, periodical articles, and parts of books. As a professor of English at the University of Colorado, Nilon brought a great deal of expertise to the project and developed a work that has some excellent features, most important of which is a thorough and detailed index of names and titles. The work is divided into four major sections: bibliography, authors, genre, and special subjects (almanacs, humor, the Negro, etc.). Comprehensive in nature, the listings cover a period of 400 years.

824. **Canadian Writers and Their Works.** Toronto, ECW; distr., Dover, N.H., Longwood Publishing Group, 1983- . 6v. (In progress).

Intended as a twenty-volume set, this large undertaking is devoted to Canadian fiction and poetry of the nineteenth and twentieth centuries. The work is to be divided equally, with ten volumes on poetry and ten on fiction. Each volume furnishes an introduction and then covers in detail the work of five authors. The format for these essays written by various experts in the field provides for a brief biography, discussion of the tradition in which the author has worked, an analysis of major works, and a selective bibliography of primary and secondary sources. To date, six volumes have been published, which means the projected completion date of 1987 in all likelihood will not be met. This is a worthwhile effort, however, and merits the time spent on it. It is a most helpful vehicle for teachers, undergraduates, and interested laypersons.

825. **Index to British Literary Bibliography.** Trevor Howard-Hill. New York, Oxford University Press, 1969- . 5v. (In progress).

This is an important and highly specialized bibliography projected in six volumes, five of which have been completed. It is focused on works which cover the bibliographical tradition in England. Volume 1, *Bibliography of British Literary Bibliographies*, covers books, parts of books, and periodical articles written in English and published in the English-speaking world after 1890. The subject of these works is the bibliographical and textual examination of British titles (manuscripts, books, printing, etc., of works published in England or written by British subjects abroad). Volume 2 provides identification and analysis of bibliographies of the work of Shakespeare. Volume 3 is not yet completed but will deal with the period prior to 1890. Volumes 4-5 consider British literary and textual criticism, and list writings and authors from 1890 to 1969. They describe bibliographical aspects of works printed in Britain from 1475 to the present day. Volume 6 is a combined index to volumes 1-2 and volumes 4-5. Upon completion of volume 3, a new cumulative index will be issued.

826. **Literary Writings in America: A Bibliography.** Millwood, N.Y., K.T.O. Press, 1977. 8v.

A project of great magnitude conducted under the auspices of the W.P.A. from 1938 to 1942, this work was an attempt to document the creative writings of hundreds of individuals in order to establish control of materials which up to that time had been elusive. This set evolved from the work of that time and provides photographic reproductions of some 250,000 entries of works by over 1,000 American writers for the period 1850-1940. Arrangement is alphabetical by author and listings are organized under certain form headings: bibliography, collected works, separate works, periodical publications, biography, criticism, and reviews. The extraordinary coverage of relatively obscure figures makes this an important work to scholarship. Sources of the entries vary and include over 2,000 volumes of magazines, over 500 volumes of literary history, and over 100 bibliographies.

827. **Literatura Chicana: Creative and Critical Writings through 1984.** Roberto G. Trujillo and Andres Rodriguez, comps. Oakland, Calif., Floricanto Press/Hispanex, 1985. 95p.

This slender volume was completed in response to a need to help document the writings of an important American minority group which up to now has not received much attention in the area of bibliographic control. Limited to material found in books, the work is divided into various forms and genres, with headings such as poetry, novels, short fiction, theater, literary criticism, *literatura chicanesca*, oral tradition, anthologies, literary periodicals, unpublished dissertations, bibliographies, autobiographical works, and video and sound recordings. The compilers are librarians at Stanford University and have used their bibliographic skills well in identifying nearly 800 items. Each entry furnishes the author's name, the title of the work, imprint, and pagination. There is a useful introductory essay by Luis Leal on bibliographies in the field. Indexes are by author and title.

828. The New Cambridge Bibliography of English Literature. Cambridge, England, Cambridge University Press, 1969-1977. 5v.

The earlier edition of this work, *Cambridge Bibliography of English Literature* (1940, 4v.; Supp., 1957) was edited by F. W. Bateson. It established a standard for excellent and authoritative coverage of a large number of sources relating to the periods and authors of Great Britain, beginning with Old English and Latin literature of the British Isles. The volumes are arranged chronologically for the years 600-1900, with volume 4 being an index volume. The new edition continues in the same tradition and is recognized as an indispensable reference and research tool in English literature. The pattern of coverage is similar to the original publication, covering hundreds of major and minor figures with both primary and secondary sources. Each period is covered in terms of important sources of all types. The new edition provides coverage to the mid-twentieth century, since volume 5 covers the period 1900-1950. Period studies are not limited to creative literary efforts, but include sections on travel, sport, education, etc. In most cases, this work has superseded the earlier edition although the latter may be retained for certain background chapters not included in the new edition.

829. Selected Black American, African, and Caribbean Authors: A Bio-Bibliography. James A. Page and Jae Min Roh, comps. Littleton, Colo., Libraries Unlimited, 1985. 388p.

This convenient and useful volume identifies the work of nearly 650 writers of African descent, the primary focus being on the Afro-American literature of the United States. Included also are some representative figures of the mother continent and also some from the Caribbean. To be included an author must have had at least one book published, and must have been covered in collective works or handbooks. Poets must have had more than one book of poems published; playwrights at least one play published or performed; and essayists must have produced a body of work in the arts, biography, criticism, history, etc. The arrangement of entries is alphabetical by author and each entry furnishes dates, places of birth and death, family, education, address, career information, list of works, comments on career, and a list of sources.

830. The Shorter New Cambridge Bibliography of English Literature. George Watson, ed. New York, Cambridge University Press, 1981. 1622p.

Intended for smaller libraries and for home and office use, this work is an excellent abridgement of *The New Cambridge Bibliography of English Literature* (see entry 828). Following the plan of the original, as is usually the case with the "shorter" editions, this work provides coverage from 600 to 1950, but eliminates the background material and a number of minor authors that have made the lengthier tool an important work for scholars. The primary section or the major corpus of an author's works have been retained, although the secondary section consisting of books and articles on the author has been reduced considerably. The coverage of periods retains the bibliographies, literary histories, anthologies, and critical surveys.

831. A Short-Title Catalogue of Books Printed in England, Scotland, and Ireland, and of English Books Printed Abroad 1475-1640. Alfred William Pollard and G. R. Redgrave. London, Bibliographical Society, 1926; repr., Oxford, Oxford University Press, 1946. 609p.

One of the most important and certainly most well known reference sources in English literature is this standard bibliography known as *STC*. Its coverage is comprehensive and the work identifies over 26,500 editions covering a period of time rich in English history and creative thought. The arrangement is alphabetical by author and other main entries. The entries provide author's name, brief title, size, printer, date, reference to Stationers' registers entry for the item, and symbols for libraries possessing copies of the work. A serious attempt was made to locate all known copies of rare materials, and there is a representative listing of libraries for more common materials. Included among the libraries are fifteen in this country. A complementary work is William Warner Bishops's *A Checklist of American Copies of Short-Title Catalogue Books* (2nd edition, University of Michigan Press, 1950; repr., Greenwood Press, 1968). This work identifies *STC* items held in over 110 libraries in this country.

832.   **Short-Title Catalogue of Books Printed in England, Scotland, Ireland, Wales, and British America and of English Books Printed in Other Countries, 1641-1700.** Donald Goddard Wing. New York, Columbia University Press, 1945-1951. 3v.

Developed as a complementary work to *STC* (see entry 831), this work continues the coverage for another sixty years. Over 200 libraries are identified for their holdings of English works published during this period. Common books are limited to five locations in the United Kingdom and five in the United States, with an attempt made to disperse the listings geographically in order to facilitate access for scholars and specialists. Wing devised his own location symbols identifying the various libraries involved. Recently, there has been an attempt to revise and enlarge the coverage provided by Wing in terms of number of locations and depth of bibliographic information provided. This work (2nd edition, rev. and enl., Index Committee of the Modern Language Association of America, 1972-) began with the publication of volume 1, *A1-E2926*, in 1972. Ten years later, volume 2 appeared, covering entries *E2927-01000*. Over 300 libraries have been identified thus far.

INDEXES, ABSTRACTS, AND SERIAL BIBLIOGRAPHIES

833.   **Abstracts of English Studies.** 1958- . Q. Calgary, Alta., University of Calgary.

This is an important abstract journal which provides abstracts of articles appearing in journals from various countries on the subject of literature in the English language. American, Commonwealth, and English literatures are covered. English philology is also within its scope. The journal has had an interesting and varied existence, beginning life as the monthly official publication of the National Council of Teachers of English. From 1962 to 1980, it was a monthly except for July and August (10/yr.). Beginning in June 1980, it was taken over by the University of Calgary, and in April 1981 it became a quarterly. Abstracts are taken from hundreds of different journals and represent an excellent selection of contemporary thought.

834.   **American Literary Scholarship.** 1963- . Ann. Durham, N.C., Duke University Press.

This is one of the important review journals in the field and has earned an excellent reputation since its appearance over twenty years ago. It consists of a series of bibliographic essays furnishing an analysis of published research on the various aspects of American literature. Each issue of this annual publication provides chapters on individual authors or joint authors; also covered separately is the period of American literature up to 1800. Fiction and poetry as well as drama and folklore are some of the literary genres which receive treatment in a manner similar to that used in *The Year's Work in English Studies* (see entry 846). Each volume or issue carries its own index.

835. **Annual Bibliography of English Language and Literature.** 1920- . Modern Humanities Research Association. Ann. Cambridge, England, Cambridge University Press.

This is one of the important annual bibliographies in the field, and the most significant title which is targeted to English language and literature. It furnishes a variety of publications on English and American literature and identifies books, pamphlets, and periodical articles. Also included are reviews of books which have been listed. The work is divided into two major sections, language and literature. Arrangement of entries in the language section is by subject, while the entries in the literature segment are organized in chronological sequence, an arrangement which has been criticized by reviewers in the past. The work provides indexes of both authors and subjects to facilitate access.

836. **Annual Bibliography of Victorian Studies.** 1976- . Ann. Edmonton, Alta., LITIR Database.

The Victorian period is defined as the time period from about 1830 to the beginning of World War I in 1914. This annual bibliography contains English-language materials of various kinds: books, periodical articles, and reviews relating to that interesting period. It is not limited to literary subjects but attempts to treat the period in its entirety. The work is composed of seven major segments or categories, beginning with general and reference works and including fine arts, philosophy and religion, history, social sciences, and science and technology. Most important is the section on language and literature, which includes subsections on individual authors. Reviews are cited after the work itself. Several indexes provide access: subject, author, title, and reviewer. A cumulation for the years 1976-1980 appeared in 1982. *Victorian Studies* (Indiana University Press, 1957-), a quarterly journal, has published an annual bibliography of books and periodical articles since its first year. "Victorian Bibliography" serves as a continuation of the list originally published in *Modern Philology* and was a project of a Committee on Victorian Literature of the Modern Language Association of America. Periodic cumulations of these bibliographies have been published (see entry 821).

837. **Comprehensive Index to English-Language Little Magazines, 1890-1970.** Series One. Millwood, N.Y., Kraus-Thomson, 1976. 8v.

This multivolume set has proved to be of value to students and specialists in their efforts to identify and locate material of consequence to literary and other studies which was produced in this type of periodical. A "little" magazine appeals to a particular audience, generally of a specialist nature, and therefore has little circulation (and advertising). Many of these titles have come and gone through the years; therefore, this type of index has real value in identifying worthwhile but relatively obscure articles. This work covers 100 English-language publications, 59 of which are partially or totally American. The intention was to index complete runs of defunct titles and current periodicals through 1970. Indexing is by personal name ("works by" and "works about"), with subject entries for biographies or critical works on an individual.

838. **Essay and General Literature Index, 1900-1933: An Index to about 40,000 Essays and Articles in 2144 Volumes of Collections of Essays and Miscellaneous Works.** Ed. by Minnie Earl Sears and Marian Shaw. New York, H. W. Wilson, 1934. 1952p. Supp., 1934- .

Although other areas of the humanities are covered in this standard work, it is literature that receives the greatest emphasis. Originally, the work succeeded the *ALA Index ... to General Literature* (2nd edition, American Library Association, 1901-1914), which indexed books of essays, travel, sociological matters, etc., up to 1900. A supplement covered the publications of the first decade of the twentieth century. *EGLI* indexes essays in books published since 1900, the original volume covering the first thirty-three years. *EGLI* is kept up-to-date on a semiannual basis, with cumulations annually, and quinquennially since 1955-1959. Prior to that it furnished seven-year cumulations. To date, the series has permanent cumulations covering 1934-1984, indexed from over 14,000 collections and anthologies. One may find essays on authors, forms, movements, genres, and individual titles of creative works. *Essay and General Literature Index Works Indexed 1900-1969* (H. W. Wilson, 1972) is a cumulative index to the 10,000 essays which have been covered during that period. It is arranged by main entry and title.

839. **Index of English Literary Manuscripts.** P. J. Croft, et al., eds. London, Mansell; distr., New York, H. W. Wilson, 1980- . (In progress).

This work, designed for scholars and specialists in the field, describes the existing manuscripts of literary works by a select group of Irish and British authors who wrote during the period 1450-1900 (following the invention of printing). The choice of authors is based partially on their inclusion in George Watson's *Concise Cambridge Bibliography of English Literature* (2nd edition, Cambridge University Press, 1965) but is not limited to that listing. Some 400 libraries, depositories, and archives in a variety of geographic locales were approached regarding their holdings. These units were located not only in England, but in North America, the Soviet Union, continental Europe, Australia, New Zealand, and South Africa. Private collectors are included as well. Presently the following volumes are available: volume 1 in two parts, 1450-1625, volume 3, 1700-1800, part 1; and volume 4, 1800-1900, part 1. Yet to come are volume 2, 1625-1700; the concluding parts of volumes 3-4; and volume 5, which will contain indexes of titles, first lines, names, and repositories. Authors are listed alphabetically within the volume. The manuscripts are described in detail in terms of ownership over the years. Present locations are given.

840. **Index to Little Magazines.** Denver, Colo., Alan Swallow, 1949-1970. Irreg.

During its time, this was the leading serial index to articles and contributions appearing in those literary and artistic magazines which have small readership and circulation. Many of them are of high quality and reach a specialized audience. Great value accrues to the indexes since titles and their contents are obscure and difficult to retrieve. Many major writers begin their career writing for little magazines, with their specialized audiences. Each volume treats anywhere from thirty to fifty titles which have been indexed for that year. Most of the periodicals are literary but there are also some from the arts. The intent of the publishers was to emphasize titles which could have permanent value in terms of the quality of writings they include. Throughout its brief existence, there was variation in all phases of publication regarding this index (frequency, publisher, and title). It ceased to appear after the 1966/1967 volume, which was published in 1970.

841. **Interviews and Conversations with 20th-Century Authors Writing in English: An Index.** Stan A. Vrana. Metuchen, N.J., Scarecrow, 1982- . (In progress).

Series II of this work appeared in 1986 and augmented the coverage of the earlier volume by adding more personalities. In both efforts, the arrangement is alphabetical by name of the author. Interviews are then listed chronologically. These interviews, published between 1900 and 1980, are taken from a variety of sources (newspapers and periodicals, both general and literary, from the United States and foreign countries). Also included, much to Vrana's credit, are African and Asian titles as well as those from the Western nations. Monographic sources are also covered, but are listed separately. About 3,600 interviews are identified in the first volume, 4,500 in the second volume, providing an extraordinary and convenient access tool for this important material. A supplementary volume is planned for the period 1981-1985.

842. **Shakespeare Survey: An Annual Survey of Shakespearian Study and Production.** 1948- . Ann. Cambridge, England, Cambridge University Press.

This is a highly useful and highly successful annual review of studies in a specialized but prominent area of literary research. In the past, it has been under the combined sponsorship of several scholarly and cultural organizations: the University of Birmingham, University of Manchester, Royal Shakespeare Theatre, and the Shakespearian Birthplace Trust. Volumes are given to specific themes which provide a focus for the articles of that year directed toward a particular element or feature of Shakespearian study. The scope is international and articles are furnished by scholars from a number of countries and regions. Most important in terms of bibliography is the regular feature "The Year's Contribution to Shakespearian Study," which is a critical survey of research and publication in the field.

843. **Speech Index: An Index to 259 Collections of World Famous Orations and Speeches for Various Occasions.** 4th ed., rev. and enl. Roberta Briggs Sutton. New York, Scarecrow, 1966. 947p. Supp. 1966-1980, 1982, 466p.

Originally published in 1935, this useful source provides indexing of significant speeches culled from a variety of sources and settings. Included are political speeches, historical speeches, scientific speeches, awards and acceptance speeches, etc. The index is limited to speeches which were printed in books and monographs, since speeches appearing in periodicals can be found through other indexes. The fourth edition combines the material from the three previous editions and adds new material and some older items previously not included. About 200 collections of speeches are indexed by author, subject, and type of speech in a dictionary arrangement. Charity Mitchell's *Speech Index: An Index to Collections of World Famous Orations and Speeches for Various Occasions*; fourth edition supplement, 1966-1980 (Scarecrow, 1982) indexes over 130 books of speeches in the same manner as the earlier volume. It cumulates the 1966/1970 and the 1971/1975 supplements to the fourth edition, and adds material from books published from 1975 to 1980.

844. **Wellesley Index to Victorian Periodicals, 1824-1900.** Walter E. Houghton, ed. Toronto, University of Toronto Press, 1966- . 3v. (In progress).

Thus far three volumes of this useful index planned as a multivolume set have appeared, the last one published in 1979. The work is intended to provide students and specialists of Victorian studies with an improved access to relevant materials. Providing subject, book review, and author indexing, it is especially valuable for citations to contemporary criticism of Victorian writers. When the set is completed, it will be a more detailed index than any existing at this time and will include certain journals not picked up by the other sources. Volume 1 covers the indexing of eight major journals; volume 2 treats twelve titles; and volume 3 covers another fifteen, including *Westminster Review*. The volumes are divided into two major sections, with part A furnishing tables of contents for each issue of the titles and part B providing bibliographies of the contributors arranged by author.

845. **The Year's Scholarship in Science Fiction, Fantasy, and Horror Literature.** 1980- . Ann. Kent, Ohio, Kent State University Press.

Beginning in 1983 (covering the year 1980), this new work provides annual coverage of the scholarship published on these genres. Commentary, criticism, and interpretation are included in the works identified and annotated. Annotations are descriptive and indicate the nature of the work, with the narratives running between 50 and 100 words per item. Coverage is comprehensive and includes a wide range of materials: books, periodical articles, dissertations, scholarly reprints, and audiovisual materials. Book reviews are excluded. The materials are divided into ten sections, including important coverage of individual author studies. This work effectively continues two earlier cumulations (1972-1975 and 1976-1979) of annual bibliographies appearing in *Extrapolation*.

846. **The Year's Work in English Studies.** 1919/1920- . Ann. English Association. London, Murray.

This is one of the leading review journals in the field and covers a wide range of studies of English literature. Similar to the *Annual Bibliography* (see entry 835) in the fields it covers, it has the additional feature of evaluating the importance or nature of the items indexed. The studies are drawn from both books and periodical articles published in Great Britain, the United States, and various countries of Continental Europe. Language is also treated as a subject and, since 1954, American literature studies are also included. The arrangement of entries is chronological by period covered, and the work is indexed by author and subject.

DICTIONARIES, ENCYCLOPEDIAS, AND HANDBOOKS

847. **The Arthurian Encyclopedia.** Norris J. Lacy, et al., eds. New York, Garland, 1986. 649p. (Garland Reference Library of the Humanities, v.585).

A comprehensive reference work focused on the world of King Arthur, this is not limited to literary coverage but includes the treatment of Arthur in the arts, history, chronicles, archaeology, film, etc. The time period for Arthurian themes is of course limitless, and works represent all countries and eras. The tool is handy and easy to use, covering both specific subjects and general categories such as "Arthur in the Visual Arts." The arrangement of articles is classified by categories, with a list of entries provided at the beginning of each category. Major characters and themes as well as individual works and authors are treated. Articles are signed by contributors and there are black-and-white illustrations. The title should prove to be of value to both students and specialists.

848. **The Cambridge Guide to English Literature.** Michael Stapleton. Cambridge, England, Cambridge University Press, 1983. 992p.

This work is similar to the *Oxford Companion to English Literature* (see entry 855) in structure, although it has a greater scope, covering English writing in a number of countries including the United States. This handbook covers the various components associated with English literature over the past 1,000 years or more. The focus is entirely on literature (somewhat unlike the *Oxford*). It would appear that only 2 of the 3,100 alphabetically arranged articles were not written by Stapleton, a respected editor and writer. These were lengthy survey articles, "The English Language," by M. H. Strang, and "The Bible in English," by C. H. Sisson. Entries cover authors, titles, characters, and literary terms, and are arranged alphabetically. There are many cross-references between entries. Historical or mythological descriptions are excluded for the most part.

849. The Cambridge Handbook of American Literature. Jack Salzman, ed. New York, Cambridge University Press, 1986. 286p.

A rather slender and inexpensive work compared to most handbooks of this kind, the handbook can best be likened to *The Concise Oxford Companion to American Literature* (see entry 851). Coverage of this work includes movements, periodicals, plot summaries, biographical sketches of writers, and important bibliographical details. Entries are brief but informative and are arranged alphabetically. Personal opinions are avoided in the critical commentary, in favor of the presentation of historical attitudes toward individual authors. Chronologies of American history and of American literature are placed side-by-side. Also included is a selective bibliography of important critical works published in the past 50 years.

850. Companion to Scottish Literature. Trevor Royle. Detroit, Gale, 1983. 322p.

A specialized handbook to the whole realm of Scottish literature, this has been judged to take up the study where *The Oxford Companion to English Literature* (see entry 855) leaves off. Entries are alphabetically arranged and include biographical sketches of various personalities (poets, novelists, dramatists, and critics) who have written either in English or Gaelic and have made solid contributions to the literary tradition. There are more than 1,200 entries of varying length depending upon the importance of the topic or the breadth of the issue. Historical events are included along with personalities and literary movements, and bibliographies are included in the lengthy articles. Most important is the coverage of minor figures who may be difficult to find in the standard sources.

851. The Concise Oxford Companion to American Literature. James D. Hart. New York, Oxford University Press, 1986. 497p.

This is an abridged version of the fifth edition of *The Oxford Companion to American Literature* (see entry 853) selling for about half the price. (Similarly, it has been judged to provide about half the information of the older and larger work.) There are approximately 2,000 entries covering biographies of authors, definitions of literary terms, movements, awards, societies, organizations, and summaries of significant works. The focus is on American literature but certain references to other literatures are given if they have relevance to the study of American literature. The emphasis appears to be on more recent authors, with the more specialized writers omitted in this version. A number of cross-references are furnished between entries. Coverage of women writers has been increased, in keeping with modern trends.

852. A Dictionary of Modern Critical Terms. rev. ed. Roger Fowler, ed. New York, Routledge & Kegan Paul/Methuen, 1987. 262p.

This is an important and unique work in the depth of coverage it gives to terms associated with literary criticism. Fowler has produced a handbook that is sharply focused on literary criticism and treats in essay-length articles the history and significance of such terms as well as their relationship to modern criticism. Such topics as poststructuralism, feminist criticism, and Marxist criticism are covered. Originally published in 1973, this edition of this work has added new essays and updated the old ones. For comprehensive coverage (with brief definitions) of literary terms, genres, authors, etc., it is recommended that the user consult other works listed in this section.

853. The Oxford Companion to American Literature. 5th ed. James D. Hart. New York, Oxford University Press, 1983. 896p.

This is a highly standardized work in the field and has been a highly regarded publication since the appearance of the first edition in 1941. The fifth edition was a long time coming, since publication of the fourth edition took place in 1965. The revision is a thorough one and involves a number of modifications. Nearly 250 authors have been added since the fourth edition, along with 115 new entries summarizing books. Many entries have been deleted, especially those on peripheral topics (although many still remain). Of course, many entries have been revised. As always, the work includes biographies of American authors with lists of their major writings and brief analyses of style and subject matter, descriptions of significant individual works in various genres, definitions, identifications of awards, societies, etc., and descriptions of various issues and topics relating to social, political, scientific, etc., subjects. This continues to be a leading source of information.

854. **Oxford Companion to Canadian Literature.** William Toye, ed. New York, Oxford University Press, 1984. 843p.

Another useful work in the *Oxford Companion* series, this handbook succeeds Noah Story's *The Oxford Companion to Canadian History and Literature* (1967) and its supplement (1973). It updates and expands the coverage, with about 750 entries ranging from short biographical sketches to survey articles on such topics as children's literature, mystery and crime, etc. Titles of individual works and various genres are treated in an attempt to provide an encyclopedic overview of Canadian literary and cultural developments. French Canadian literature is included. Some entries provide references to additional reading while many have cross-references to others in the text. Coverage appears to be especially strong for the period following World War II.

855. **The Oxford Companion to English Literature.** 5th ed. Margaret Drabble, ed. New York, Oxford University Press, 1985. 1155p.

The editor is a novelist who has conducted an extensive revision of the fourth edition (1967) with the idea of providing an up-to-date work. This is the original model and oldest title in the now-extensive *Oxford Companion* series, having appeared initially in 1932. It is a true standard in the field and has become a fixture in library reference collections, with a reputation for brevity, accuracy, and comprehensiveness. The new edition furnishes biographical sketches of approximately 3,000 authors born before 1939, with special emphasis on twentieth-century writers. Allusions have been deleted, but movements and individual works are covered in detail. Biographies of earlier authors have also been expanded in the amount of detail provided. This work will remain a staple for years to come.

856. **The Oxford Companion to the Literature of Wales.** Meic Stephens, comp. and ed. New York, Oxford University Press, 1986. 682p.

A new offering in the *Oxford Companion* series, this work continues in that tradition of most useful and worthwhile tools. Covering a period from the sixth century to the present, the editor (literature director of the Welsh Arts Council) has compiled nearly 3,000 entries. They are alphabetically arranged and emphasize writers in the Welsh language, but also include those who write or have written in English or Latin as well as foreign writers who have published works set in Wales. In addition to writers, entries cover historical figures, events, movements, critics, genres, motifs, characters, and titles of major works and periodicals. Related areas generally examined in the *Oxford Companions* are given as well (customs, folklore, institutions, etc.). Useful features are a pronunciation guide and a chronology of Welsh history.

857. **The Oxford Illustrated Literary Guide to the United States.** Eugene Ehrlich and Gorton Carruth. New York, Oxford University Press, 1982. 464p.

An interesting and useful source of information for those travelers with special interests in literary sites and locales, this work provides links or associations between authors and their towns and cities. (Naturalists are given somewhat short shrift since mountains, rivers, and forests are not emphasized in this manner.) The arrangement of entries is by state, then by city or town, then alphabetically by author as subject. Brief commentary is included on the sites and the literary figures associated with it. There are many illustrations and quotations, and a detailed author-as-subject index provides access. *The Oxford Illustrated Literary Guide to Great Britain and Ireland*, by Dorothy Eagle (2nd edition, Oxford, Oxford University Press, 1981) furnishes a list of place names giving locations and literary associations and an index of authors with which one can trace a writer's career through different locales. Cross-references are given for fictitious names of real places.

BIOGRAPHICAL AND CRITICAL SOURCES

858. **American Women Writers: A Critical Reference Guide from Colonial Times to the Present.** Lina Mainiero and Langdon Lynne Faust, eds. New York, Ungar, 1979-1982. 4v.

This important work describes the lives and contributions of American women who made literature their career as well as those who wrote seriously about their work in a variety of professions (history, psychology, theology, etc.). The intention was to include all writers of established literary reputation; a representative segment of popular writers, nontraditional writers of diaries and letters, and children's authors is presented. Each entry furnishes a biographical sketch, summary of her career, and an examination of her works, as well as bibliographical references. The biography is critical and furnishes an assessment of the writer's contribution. A recognized deficiency is in coverage of black and lesbian writers, which the editors see as being alleviated with much of the biocritical material being published today. A two-volume abridged version of this work from the same publisher appeared in 1983.

859. **American Writers: A Collection of Literary Biographies.** Leonard Unger, ed.-in-chief. New York, Scribner's, 1974-1981. 4v. Supp. I-II, 4v.

This entire collection including supplements provides a series of critical studies designed to cover in depth the life and work of 156 notable poets, novelists, short story writers, playwrights, critics, historians, and philosophers from the seventeenth century to the present day. The emphasis is on the style, genre, and literary contribution of the individuals and their place within the literary tradition or milieu. The original four-volume set contains the material in a series of pamphlets published by the University of Minnesota; the essays on ninety-seven individuals have been updated bibliographically, re-edited, and newly indexed. The essays are excellent in terms of documentation. The supplementary volumes continue the original plan and add fifty-nine personalities designed to fill in gaps and to continue the coverage of major figures into the twentieth century. Now, Allen Ginsburg, E. B. White, Sylvia Plath, etc., join Henry Adams, T. S. Eliot, Ralph Waldo Emerson, etc., from the original set.

860. **American Writers before 1800: A Biographical and Critical Dictionary.** James A. Levernier and Douglas R. Wilmes, eds. Westport, Conn., Greenwood Press, 1983. 3v.

Nearly 800 entries furnish biocritical sketches by 250 scholars who have contributed their talents in developing a useful source of information. Names of prominent individuals were selected by the editors from anthologies, histories, and bibliographies. Unlike many works of this kind, the length of the entries is not correlated with the importance of the individuals, and minor figures are treated as fully as are major ones. This is an important consideration for librarians who are asked to search out information on authors who are difficult to locate. Each entry provides a biographical sketch including comments on factors which influenced the writer's development, a critical appraisal of writings, and a list of selected reading about the writer. The tool is a worthwhile purchase which will be used frequently.

861. **British Writers.** Ian Scott Kilvert, ed. New York, Scribner's, 1979-1984. 8v.

Modeled after *American Writers* (see entry 859), for which it was designed as a companion set, this in-depth collection also originated as a series of separate pamphlets first published by the British Council in 1950. It represents a collection of essays, all of which are signed by distinguished contributors, providing a detailed exposition of the life and work of significant authors. Articles range from 10,000 to 15,000 words and are placed into volumes which are arranged in chronological sequence (volume 1, *William Langland to the English Bible*, to volume 7, *Sean O'Casey to Poets of World War II*). As in the case of *American Writers*, the essays describe the writer's life and period, and provide a critical assessment of his or her works. The essays have been updated bibliographically and the content re-edited. The work is useful to a variety of patrons as well as librarians themselves.

862. **Contemporary Literary Critics.** 2nd ed. Elmer Borklund. Detroit, Gale, 1982. 600p.

About 125 British and American critics of modern times are covered in this work, 9 of whom have been added since the earlier edition in 1977. Entries for those previously covered have been updated and revised. Entries furnish brief biographical summaries, bibliographies of major writings by and about the individual, and essays of the critical stance of each one. These are from two to six pages long and include quotations, some rather lengthy, of the subject's writings. The work represents an attempt to determine the objectives of each critic, the assumptions he or she makes, and his or her accomplishments. As is true of a number of Gale publications, the critical interpretations include personal judgment on the part of the author, who is willing to point out shortcomings in style or thought.

863. **Critical Dictionary of English Literature and British and American Authors, Living and Deceased, from the Earliest Accounts to the Latter Half of the Nineteenth Century ...** Samuel Austin Allibone. Philadelphia, Lippincott, 1858. 3v. Supp., 1891, 2v. (Reprinted, Detroit, Gale, 1965. 5v.).

A standard in the field recognized by scholars of the English-speaking world as an important tool, this old favorite has been criticized through the years on a number of counts, most important of which lies in the realm of accuracy. The most useful feature is the comprehensiveness of the listing, with 46,000 authors covered in the original three volumes. Another 37,000 are added in the supplement, providing a rich source for purposes of identification and verification. Inaccuracies stem from its reliance on Robert Watt's *Bibliotheca Britannica: Or a General Index to British and Foreign Literature* (Edinburgh, Constable, 1824) for which it serves as a supplement or extension. Watt also provides biographical information of authors along with a listing of their books.

864. The Critical Temper: A Survey of Modern Criticism on English and American Literature from the Beginnings to the Twentieth Century. Martin Tucker, gen. ed. New York, Ungar, 1969-1979. 4v.

This work serves as a supplement to Moulton's *Library of Literary Criticism* (see entry 869) in its provision of extracts from twentieth-century criticism of authors who wrote prior to that time. The set is arranged in chronological order from the Old English period to the beginning of the twentieth century. The first three volumes were published in 1969 and carried excerpts from literary critics from the beginning of the twentieth century up to the 1960s. Volume 1 covered literature from Old English to Shakespeare; volume 2 covered Milton to Romantic literature, and volume 3 focused on Victorian and American literature. Volume 4 appeared ten years later as a supplement to the entire set, furnishing excerpts written in the past ten years and bringing the critical coverage to the 1970s. In all volumes, critical studies from both books and periodicals are used.

865. Dictionary of Literary Biography. Matthew J. Bruccoli, et al., eds. Detroit, Gale, 1978- . (In progress).

A series of consequence, this work was started in 1978 with the purpose of providing information reflecting the changes since the publication of the *Dictionary of American Biography* (Scribner's, 1928-1937; repr., 1943. 21v.). Volumes of this work have appeared and continue to appear with surprising regularity. The intention was to cover all writers who made a significant contribution to the literature of the United States, Canada, and England, although in 1987 the focus shifted toward modern European literature (see entry 972n). All titles in the series cover a different subject and have different editors, and focus on either a specific period of literary history or a literary movement, beginning with volume 1, *The American Renaissance in New England*, by Joel Myerson (1978). Presently, there are over fifty volumes, with no less than seven volumes awaiting publication in 1987. The volumes follow a standard format, with major biocritical essays on the important figures (which include career chronology, publications list, and a bibliography of works by and about the subject). Lesser figures are described in terms of life, work, and reputation. *The Dictionary of Literary Biography Yearbook* (Gale, 1980-) updates and supplements entries which appeared in any of the volumes. *The Dictionary of Literary Biography Documentary Series: An Illustrated Chronicle* (Gale, 1982-) appears less frequently but is designed to provide a useful selection of documents including galley pages, manuscript pages, proofs, photographs, etc., linked to a particular literary movement, period, or genre in each volume.

866. The Essential Shakespeare: An Annotated Bibliography of Major Modern Studies. Larry S. Champion. Boston, G. K. Hall, 1986. 463p. (A Reference Publication in Literature).

An especially useful tool for a student in identifying relevant and important critical studies is this annotated bibliography of 1,500 entries. The coverage is limited to modern criticism since it provides references to those published only in the twentieth century, from 1900 to 1984. Major sections or categories represented are general works, poems and sonnets, English history plays, comedies, and tragedies. Included in the general works section are bibliographies, editions, studies of sources, film studies, etc.; each of the specialized sections also contains an opening subsection on general studies. Annotations are detailed and furnish scope notes and dominant themes from each work. Although some oversights have been noted by reviewers, this promises to be an excellent purchase for the library.

867. **Great Writers of the English Language.** James Vinson, ed. London, Macmillan, 1979. 3v.

This is a collection of biocritical essays of a selection of important writers from the Anglo-Saxon period to the present day. Each volume contributes biographies of individuals associated with a different genre: volume 1 covers poets; volume 2, novelists and prose writers; and volume 3, dramatists. About 500 personalities are treated in each volume, the pattern being to begin with a brief biographical sketch. This is followed by a list of publications which appears to be quite detailed and full. There is also a list of bibliographies and of critical studies. Most important is the signed critical essay on each writer's works, which appears to be representative of British literary judgment. (Half of the contributors are from outside the United States.) Coverage of writers is broad-based and includes Commonwealth, American, and even African and Caribbean writers.

868. **Index to Black American Writers in Collective Biographies.** Dorothy W. Campbell. Littleton, Colo., Libraries Unlimited, 1983. 162p.

This is an alphabetical listing of 1,900 black writers whose biographical sketches have appeared in nearly 270 biographical dictionaries and other reference tools, including audiovisual collections and some children's works. These biographical sources were published over a span of nearly 150 years, from 1837 to 1982. Each writer has at least one listing or reference, and each source has at least two individuals from the list. Entries are alphabetically arranged and include dates, field of interest, and variant names as well as reference to a biographical source. *Black American Writers: Bibliographical Essays*, edited by Thomas Inge and others (St. Martin's Press, 1978), is a two-volume source of information of important biographical and critical writings on significant black American authors. It also identifies manuscript and special collections for further study. The essays cover individuals, groups, or a specific genre.

869. **Library of Literary Criticism of English and American Authors.** Charles Wells Moulton. Buffalo, Moulton, 1901-1905; repr., Gloucester, Mass., Peter Smith, 1959. 8v.

Serving as both an anthology of critical comment and an index to critical studies, this work has been a library standard since its publication date. It set the pattern for a number of works to follow in subsequent years by furnishing a compilation of extracts of quoted material representing critical commentary. The period covered is 680-1904, beginning with *Beowulf* and critical commentary excerpted from the Venerable Bede. Each author is given brief biographical coverage, followed by selected quotations of criticisms. These are classified and grouped as personal or individual works. Extracts can be quite lengthy, and adequately convey the sense of the critique. Martin Tucker's *Library of Literary Criticism of English and American Authors through the Beginning of the Twentieth Century* (Ungar, 1966; repr., 1975) is a four-volume update as well as an abridgment of the Moulton effort. New material has been added, with eleven new authors; other authors were dropped. Excerpts were drawn from critical essays published to 1964.

870. **Modern American Literature.** 4th enl. ed. Dorothy Nyren Curley, et al. New York, Ungar, 1969-1985. 5v. (A Library of Literary Criticism).

Established as a complementary work to Moulton's *Library of Literary Criticism* (see entry 869), this tool appeared for the first time in 1960. The fourth edition was issued in 1969 as a three-volume set which updated and enlarged the previous edition (1964). About 115 authors had been added in this compilation of excerpts of critical essays on American authors who became prominent after the turn of the century. The essays were originally published in both scholarly and popular books and journals. Citations are given to their locations. Volume 3 furnishes an index of critics. Subsequently, the first supplement appeared as volume 4 in 1976 and brought the criticism up-to-date on about half the authors in the original three volumes, and added 49 more. The second supplement recently appeared as volume 5 (edited by Paul Schlueter and June Schlueter) in 1985 and updates criticism of 143 authors previously treated, and adds 31 more to the coverage. There is an earnest attempt to include coverage of contemporary female and black writers.

871. **Modern British Literature.** Ruth Zabriskie Temple and Martin Tucker. New York, Ungar, 1966-1985. 5v. (A Library of Literary Criticism).

Similar to Curley's *Modern American Literature* (see entry 870) in structure and frequency, this title serves as a companion to that work and also supplements the Moulton effort (see entry 869). Excerpts of critical commentaries are arranged in chronological order, as is customary for these works. This arrangement is useful for the student or specialist who wishes to gauge the reception given the writings of an author over the years. The tool was published as a three-volume set in 1966 to cover the critical reception of the work of twentieth-century British authors. Each volume covered different writers, and volume 3 furnishes a cross-reference index and an index of critics. The first supplement (edited by Martin Tucker and Rita Stein) appeared as volume 4, updating the earlier criticism on about one-third of the writers and adding forty-nine more. The second supplement appeared as volume 5 in 1985 and was edited by Denis Lane and Rita Stein. It contains eleven new writers, eleven writers who had not been updated in the previous supplement, and new or updated bibliographies for all entries.

872. **The Writer's Directory.** 1971/1973- . Bienn. Chicago, St. James.

Now in its seventh edition (1986-1988), this work lists over 16,000 living writers who have had at least one book published in the English language. Providing brief biographical sketches of the who's who variety, the entries give pseudonyms, citizenship, birth years, writing summaries, appointments, bibliographies, and addresses. Writers represent varied genres and include fiction, nonfiction, poetry, and drama. Coverage is geographically comprehensive, with all areas where English is spoken or written represented (United States, England, Australia, Canada, South Africa, etc.). A most useful feature is the "yellow pages" in which writers are classified and listed under different writing categories. *Who's Who in Canadian Literature*, by Gordon Ripley and Anne Mercer (Toronto, Reference Press, 1983/1984-) is a more specialized biennial directory and furnishes about 900 sketches of living Canadian poets, novelists, playwrights, critics, editors, and short story writers. A third edition for 1987/1988 is scheduled to appear late in 1987.

HISTORIES

873. **Annals of American Literature 1602-1983.** Richard M. Ludwig and Clifford A. Nault, Jr., eds. New York, Oxford University Press, 1986. 342p.

Modeled after *Annals of English Literature* (see entry 874), this is a chronology of facts and dates focused on literary productivity. Listings are generally of books published in this country, but include some European titles considered important to an understanding of the pre-colonial and colonial period and published during that time. Listings are year-by-year with four genres identified (fiction, nonfiction, drama, and poetry). Authors are listed alphabetically each year in entries which include their birthdates, titles of their works, and genres. Parallel columns identify certain historical and literary events. Identified are the founding of newspapers, births and deaths of authors, and foreign literary works. Although there are a number of omissions in this selective work, it should prove to be of value for quick identifications.

874. **Annals of English Literature, 1475-1950: The Principal Publications of Each Year Together with an Alphabetical Index of Authors and Their Works.** 2nd ed. Oxford, Clarendon Press, 1961. 380p.

Originally published in 1935 and covering the period up to 1925, this work has been a fixture in reference departments interested in providing services in the area of English literature. Recognized as an important chronology, it has served as a model for other works in its organization and format (see entry 873). Arrangement is year-by-year with listings of authors given under each year. Important titles of their works are furnished. Complete listings are given major authors, and principal works of minor authors are given. Side columns give dates of birth and death of literary figures, founding of newspapers and important periodicals, as well as foreign events having a bearing on English literary contributions. Another useful chronology is Samuel J. Rogal's *A Chronological Outline of British Literature* (Greenwood Press, 1980), which furnishes comprehensive coverage of literary events in England, Scotland, Ireland, and Wales. It is similar in style and format to Rogal's *A Chronological Outline of American Literature* (see entry 878).

875. **British Literary Magazines.** Alvin Sullivan, ed. Westport, Conn., Greenwood Press, 1983-1986. 4v. (Historical Guides to the World's Periodicals and Newspapers).

An impressive tool covering several hundred important British periodicals by historical period is this four-volume guide. Volume 1 covers the period of Johnson and the Augustan age from 1698 to 1788; volume 2 covers the Romantic period from 1789 to 1836; volume 3 surveys the Victorian and Edwardian years from 1837 to 1913; and volume 4 brings the coverage to the present from 1914 to 1984. Entries are arranged alphabetically and each periodical is described in terms of its editorial history and general content. Significant contributors and regular features are listed. A useful bibliography of additional sources is given, and American and British library locations are enumerated. Each volume has an index of topics, titles, names, etc. Although not a history itself, this directory should prove to be an invaluable resource for the literary historian.

876. **Cambridge History of American Literature.** William Peterfield Trent, et al., eds. New York, Putnam's, 1917-1921; 4v.; repr., New York, Macmillan, 1972. 3v. in 1.

This is the original history of American literature, which although dated to some extent, is still highly respected and frequently used. Especially good is its coverage of the early period in volumes 1-2, for which it is acknowledged to be most thorough and comprehensive. Volumes 3-4 treat the later national literature and, of course, need updating. Detailed coverage is provided literary forms and important writers, but the work also describes in adequate fashion a host of less common considerations. Included are accounts of early travelers, explorers, colonial newspapers, literary annuals, and gift books. Coverage of children's literature, the English language in America, non-English writings, etc., make this a worthwhile tool, even today. Chapters are written by specialists and the bibliographies are full, although somewhat out-of-date. The Macmillan reprint omits the bibliographies.

877. **Cambridge History of English Literature.** A. W. Ward and A. R. Waller, eds. Cambridge, England, Cambridge University Press, 1907-1923; repr., 1976. 15v.

Considered for many years the most important general history of English literature, this massive work remains a model of scholarship and distinguished narrative. Individual scholars and specialists have prepared each of the chapters. The work begins with the earliest times and proceeds in chronological fashion volume-by-volume to the end of the nineteenth century. This century is given detailed coverage in three volumes, 12-14. The final volume provides an index to the whole set. Bibliographies are given in each volume and are generally extensive; although old, they are still useful. Designed originally for graduate students, the work has been reprinted several times, sometimes without the bibliographies. These cheaper reprints limit the reference value considerably in a literature department.

878. **A Chronological Outline of American Literature.** Samuel J. Rogal. Westport, Conn., Greenwood Press, 1987. 446p.

Similar in format and style to a previous work by the author, *A Chronological Outline of British Literature* (see entry 874n), this chronology begins with the year 1507 and covers important events in American literature through 1986. The usual types of literary events are highlighted, such as births and deaths of literary figures; notable occurrences; and publications of various types, including fiction, poetry, drama, essays, etc. Both important and not-so-important American writers are treated, with the criteria for inclusion being their significance or representativeness. Although there are many omissions, the comprehensiveness of this chronology is commendable. A work of this type is useful to scholars, specialists, educators, and the general public as well. There are an introductory essay, a bibliography, and an index of authors and events. The lack of a title index might be considered an oversight.

879. **The Concise Cambridge History of English Literature.** 3rd ed. George Sampson. Rev. by R. C. Churchill. New York, Cambridge University Press, 1972; repr., 1979. 976p.

This is a reprint with corrections of the 1970 edition, which at that time represented a thorough revision of the work. The first edition of this work appeared in 1941 and was followed by a second edition in 1960. Churchill's revision was undertaken with respect to work of contemporary scholars and modern scholarship. Chapters were added on the literature of the United States from the colonial period to Henry James, and the mid-twentieth-century literature of the Commonwealth and other former colonies. The work has remained a useful and popular tool for its blend of the traditional literature of the early and middle periods with that of the modern era.

880. **A Concise Chronology of English Literature.** P. J. Smallwood, comp. Totowa, N.J., Barnes & Noble, 1985. 220p.

Another useful chronology which attempts to place literary contributions within the context of historical events is this recent work. Coverage begins with the period of Chaucer in 1375 and ends with the year 1975. This makes it a useful tool for those libraries that have been operating with the *Annals of English Literature* (see entry 874) and its more limited time span (1475-1950). Two schemes are provided, one a listing of important events in English literature, the other giving important historical events that occurred at the same time. Certain European writers such as Boccaccio, Erasmus, and Machiavelli are included because of their significance in the development of English literature. The usual number of omissions or questionable inclusions applies. An index of authors' names provides access.

881. **A History of American Magazines.** Frank Luther Mott. Cambridge, Mass., Harvard University Press, 1930-1968. 5v.

An important and highly respected study of the history of American periodicals, this title is divided into four major chronological categories. Volume 1 covers the period 1741-1854, volume 2, 1850-1865, volume 3, 1865-1885, and volume 4, 1885-1905. Mott had served as dean of the University of Missouri School of Journalism and had originally projected a six-volume work. Completion of the earlier volumes had earned him a Pulitzer Prize for his detailed and scholarly coverage of a wide variety of magazines, from *Better Homes and Gardens* to the *Yale Review*. Many of the titles are literary magazines of varied stature. In each of the first four chapters, a good comprehensive history is given as well as sketches of the individual titles. Mott died in 1964; thus the twenty-one sketches he had completed for the next volume were published along with the index as volume 5. Many bibliographical notes are furnished in the set, and a chronological list of the magazines appears in volumes 1-3.

882. **A Literary History of England.** 2nd ed. Albert Croll Baugh. New York, Appleton-Century-Crofts, 1967. 4v.

This is a highly regarded and important reference history in four volumes covering the same time period as the much more detailed *Cambridge History of English Literature* (see entry 877). The style of writing is well developed and consistent from volume to volume, each of which is done by an American specialist on the topic. Volume 1 covers the Middle Ages in two parts, the Old English period to 1100 and the Middle English period 1100-1500. Volume 2 treats the Renaissance (1500-1660), and volume 3, the Restoration and eighteenth century (1660-1789). Volume 4 carries the coverage through 1939. The work is especially useful for its excellent documentation, with numerous bibliographical footnotes in the text. At the end of the new edition is a bibliographical supplement giving additional references to books and periodical articles.

883. **Literary History of the United States.** 4th ed. rev. Robert E. Spiller, et al., eds. New York, Macmillan, 1974. 2v.

This was first published in 1948 and represented the first literary history of a comprehensive nature since publication of the *Cambridge History of American Literature* (see entry 876) in 1921. It has continued to be a useful and popular work through the years. Volume 1 furnishes well-developed historical narratives covering colonial times to the present in a series of chapters written by various experts. Volume 2 contains bibliographical essays designed to provide additional resource material in support of the text. It is divided into four major sections, consisting of a guide to resources, literature and culture, movements and influences, and finally, individual authors. Nearly 250 individual authors are treated here with listings of their various contributions. Each of the four parts furnishes useful critical commentary on editions, biographies, etc.

884. **Oxford History of English Literature.** Frank Percy Wilson and Bonamy Dobrée. Oxford, Clarendon Press, 1945- . (In progress).

Similar to the *New Oxford History of Music* (see entry 536) in being a long-range project (which seems destined to elude completion) is this multivolume history of English literature. Recognized as an important source for its detailed and authoritative coverage, it is hoped that the work will eventually reach fruition as a useful alternative to the much older *Cambridge History of English Literature* (see entry 877). Each volume or part of a volume is written by a specialist in the field, and each furnishes extensive bibliographies. Still in process are both parts of volume 1, ranging from before the Norman Conquest through Middle English literature, and volume 11, the mid-nineteenth century, as well as a possible second part of volume 4 (part 1, "English Drama, 1485-1585"). Most libraries follow the lead of the Library of Congress in cataloging the volumes separately and linking them together with a series added entry in the catalog.

885. **St. James Reference Guide to English Literature.** James Vinson and D. L. Kirkpatrick, eds. Chicago, St. James, 1985. 8v.

This relatively new work provides a varied information package including over 1,200 biographical sketches, useful bibliographies of a comprehensive nature, and well-conceived critical essays. Especially noteworthy are the lengthy period and genre histories. The arrangement is by historical period, with volume 1 covering the beginnings and the Renaissance; volume 2, the Restoration and the eighteenth century; volume 3, the Romantic and Victorian years; and volume 4, the novel to 1900. Volumes 5-7 cover twentieth-century poetry, fiction, and drama respectively, while volume 8 treats Commonwealth literature. Over 400 scholars from various areas of the English-speaking world have contributed to the work. Considering the comprehensive coverage afforded by this tool and its potential in answering a host of questions, it should be regarded as an important purchase for the reference department.

FICTION

Bibliographic Guides

886. **Afro-American Fiction, 1853-1976: A Guide to Information Sources.** Edward Margolies and David Bakish. Detroit, Gale, 1979. 161p. (American Literature, English Literature, and World Literatures in English Information Guide Series, v.25).

Although this work is not without deficiencies in terms of omissions and inaccuracies, it still is important because of its comprehensive nature, incorporating several features not otherwise found in a single tool. First is a checklist of novels, a comprehensive listing of nearly 730 works dating from William Wells Brown's *Clotel* (1853) through publications in the year 1976. Second is a listing of anthologies of short stories, followed by an annotated list of bibliographies and critical studies of fifteen major writers. Finally, there is an annotated list of bibliographies and general studies on black fiction and authors. All fictional works are listed chronologically in the appendix. Although there is little material that is not duplicated in other tools, it is convenient to have these features included in one work. There are indexes by author, title, and subject to provide access.

887. **American Fiction to 1900: A Guide to Information Sources.** David K. Kirby. Detroit, Gale, 1975. 296p. (American Literature, English Literature, and World Literatures in English Information Guide Series, v.4).

Another of the Gale guides, this one identifies and describes various reference tools, bibliographies, biographies, and critical studies covering American fiction of the eighteenth and nineteenth centuries. There are two major sections of this work, the first covering general aids. Over eighty items are listed here under the categories handbooks, bibliographic works, periodicals, and general critical studies. The second section consists of about 1,350 items classified under about forty writers. Each writer is furnished a list of principal works, published letters, bibliographies, and journals. There is an annotated listing of biocritical studies published in books and journals. A companion effort from the same publisher is James Leslie Woodress's *American Fiction 1900-1950: A Guide to Information Sources* (1974). This consists of bibliographical essays on forty-four writers selected on the basis of critical esteem accorded them since 1950.

888. **Dickinson's American Historical Fiction.** 5th ed. Virginia Brokaw Gerhardstein. Metuchen, N.J., Scarecrow, 1986. 352p.

First published in 1958, this standard work has now been updated to include work published to 1984. It is a useful tool for reading guidance, providing a classified listing of over 3,000 novels published primarily between 1917 and 1984. For historical novels, time, place, social/historical phenomena, etc., are identified. The arrangement of entries is by chronological period, beginning with colonial times and ending with the mid-1970s (the turbulent years). Annotations are furnished but are not evaluative, and describe briefly the setting and plot in order to give historical perspective. Included is a subject index as well as an author/title index. Another useful source, although not as current, is Leonard Bartram Irwin's *A Guide to Historical Fiction for the Use of Schools, Libraries, and the General Reader* (10th edition, Washington, D.C., Heldref Publications, 1976). This first appeared in 1930, written by Hanna Logasa, and still represents a standard source of favorably reviewed historical novels classified by geography and time period.

889. **Science Fiction, Fantasy, and Weird Fiction Magazines.** Marshall B. Tymn and Mike Ashley, eds. Westport, Conn., Greenwood Press, 1985. 970p. (Historical Guides to the World's Periodicals and Newspapers).

Regarded as an excellent source of information on magazines of this type, this work provides comprehensive coverage of English-language periodicals dating from 1882 to the present. It is divided into several sections, the first of which furnishes listings of magazines published in the United States, Great Britain, Canada, and Australia, which are devoted wholly or in part to genre literature. Entries provide a brief history of origin and development; bibliography and sources of indexing; reprinting, etc., publication data; and numerous cross-references. Other sections give English-language anthologies, information on significant fanzines and academic journals, and annotations of an additional 178 titles from twenty-three foreign countries. Appendices furnish an index to cover artists and a chronology of magazine origins. Another important tool, *Anatomy of Wonder: A Critical Guide to Science Fiction* (R. R. Bowker, 1987), edited by Neil Barron, is now in its third edition. It identifies over 1,650 novels and short story collections. There are additional chapters on foreign-language contributions, film and television, and illustration as well as the major coverage of the primary literature, magazines, etc. Entries have been modified to include recent sequels, etc.

890. **Victorian Fiction: A Guide to Research.** Lionel Stevenson, et al. Cambridge, Mass., Harvard University Press, 1964; repr., New York, Modern Language Association of America, 1980. 440p.

As one of several bibliographic guides to Victorian literary genres from Harvard University, this work continues the established pattern, providing coverage of principal writers of the time. This work on fiction devotes separate chapters to each of the principal novelists and identifies and evaluates research studies and critical works published through 1962. A companion work and supplementary publication is *Victorian Fiction: A Second Guide to Research*, edited by George H. Ford (Modern Language Association of America, 1978). This title identifies publications between 1963 and 1974 on the work of seventeen Victorian authors. Included is a useful compilation of general materials by Richard Altick which suggests that there are 40,000 pieces of fiction in the body of Victorian literature.

Bibliographies and Indexes

891. The Afro-American Short Story: A Comprehensive Annotated Index with Selected Commentaries. Preston M. Yancy, comp. Westport, Conn., Greenwood Press, 1986. 171p. (Bibliographies and Indexes in Afro-American and African Studies, No. 10).

This is a timely and important contribution identifying over 800 short stories written in a thirty-two-year period between 1950 and 1982. These years are especially significant to the black experience in terms of its manifestation in the literature following desegregation and the 1954 Supreme Court decision. Over 300 authors are represented in this tool, which is divided into several parts. The first part is a year-by-year chronological listing with titles arranged alphabetically under each year. This is followed by a list of anthologies and collections, then by a section of commentaries on selected stories classified by type. There is an author index which also provides references to biographical sketches in five biographical encyclopedias. Helen Ruth Houston's *The Afro-American Novel: A Descriptive Bibliography of Primary and Secondary Material* (Whitston, 1977) still holds a prominent position in reference departments with its listing of the works of fifty-six black Americans published since 1964. Critical studies and reviews are identified.

892. American Fiction, 1774-1850: A Contribution toward a Bibliography. 2nd rev. ed. Lyle Henry Wright. San Marino, Calif., Huntington Library, 1969. 411p.

This has become a standard reference tool since publication of the first edition in 1939. Since that time, it has been revised on two occasions, with over 700 titles added to the second revised edition. A total of 3,500 entries includes novels, romances, short stories, fictitious biographies and travel, allegories, etc. Copies of these works are located in twenty-two libraries. All works are by American authors, and entries are alphabetical by author. Entries furnish title imprints, pagination, and occasional notes. Juvenile fiction is excluded. The work has been continued by Wright's *American Fiction, 1851-1875* (Huntington Library, 1965) and *American Fiction, 1876-1900* (Huntington Library, 1966). The former enumerates over 2,800 titles in nineteen locations, while the latter identifies copies of the first U.S. editions of 6,175 items in fifteen libraries.

893. Black American Fiction: A Bibliography. Carol Fairbanks and Eugene A. Engeldinger. Metuchen, N.J., Scarecrow, 1978. 351p.

This is a good example of an extraordinarily comprehensive bibliography on a specialized grouping of writers within the field of Anglo-American fiction. Fairbanks brought her expertise as a college English instructor to join with Engeldinger, a reference librarian, in producing a work that continues to hold a respected position in library reference work. The bulk of the work is a listing of 600 black authors and their works classified by type (novel, short fiction). Included are citations to book reviews, biographies, and criticism. Variant editions of the fictional works are identified when known. Citations are to a variety of materials such as newspapers, monographs, journals, dissertations, and conference proceedings published through 1976. There is a useful, twenty-five page bibliography of general criticism.

894. Crime Fiction, 1749-1980: A Comprehensive Bibliography. Allen J. Hubin. New York, Garland, 1984. 712p. (Garland Reference Library of the Humanities, v.371).

Based on an earlier work by the same author, this edition adds another five years of coverage and identifies a total of 60,000 titles. About 6,000 of the titles have been published since the first edition came out, and another 2,600 are earlier titles which were overlooked in the previous work. All types of crime stories are included: mystery, detective, suspense, thriller, gothic, police, and spy. The major segment of the work is an author index followed by titles arranged alphabetically, with cross-references to variant titles and pseudonyms. Access is facilitated by indexes by title, setting (geographical), series, and series character. Another recent work is Albert J. Menendez's *The Subject Is Murder* (1986) from the same publisher. This tool identifies over 3,800 titles published between the 1930s and 1985 by subjects or major thematic elements (medicine, politics, etc.) covered in separate chapters.

895. **English Fiction, 1900-1950.** Thomas Jackson Rice. Detroit, Gale, 1979-1983. 2v. (American Literature, English Literature, and World Literatures in English, v.21).

A total of about forty influential British writers are treated in-depth in this two-volume work. Volume 1, published in 1979, provides a general bibliography and covers individual authors alphabetically from Aldington to Huxley. Volume 2 covers individual authors from Joyce to Woolf. Each entry furnishes an annotated list of all fictional works by the author and includes a representative selection of other writings. There is also a bibliography of secondary sources identifying journals, biographies, critical studies in books and articles, bibliographies, and studies of individual works. The cutoff date for volume 2 is 1980. Part of the same series is S. K. Heninger's *English Prose, Prose Fiction and Criticism to 1660* (Gale, 1975), which lists about 800 primary and secondary works by type, including fiction. Jerry C. Beasley's *English Fiction, 1660-1800: A Guide to Information Sources* (Gale, 1978) continues the sequence of coverage.

896. **Fiction Catalog.** 11th ed. Juliette Yaakov, ed. New York, H. W. Wilson, 1986. 951p. (Standard Catalog Series).

As part of the well-known and highly respected standard catalog series, this work has had a long tradition; its first edition appeared in 1908. Presently, new editions are issued quinquennially with annual updates. Considered a companion work to the *Public Library Catalog* (nonfiction), this tool furnishes a selective annotated listing of several thousand English-language titles of prose fiction. Plot summaries are given in adequate detail, and arrangement and format are highly stylized. The largest proportion of the volume consists of individual entries for specific titles. Arrangement is by author, then title; excerpts from reviews are included. There is a title-subject index providing ready access by topical matter, the subject approach being one of the strong features of this work.

897. **Fiction, 1876-1983: A Bibliography of United States Editions.** New York, R. R. Bowker, 1983. 2v.

Another of the Bowker spinoffs from *Books in Print* and *American Book Publishing Record*, this is a comprehensive listing of fictional works published in the United States over a period of more than 100 years. Included are novels, novellas, short stories, anthologies, and collections. There are over 170,000 entries, generally found to be reliable (although not error-free) as is true of other works in the Bowker line. Entries emulate those in *Books in Print* and may give author, editor, title, date, price, publisher, LC number, and ISBN. Volume 1 contains a classified author index listing authors by country and period as well as a main author index. Volume 2 furnishes a title index. Full publication information is found in entries in both indexes.

898. **A Mirror for the Nation: An Annotated Bibliography of American Social Fiction, 1901-1950.** Archibald Hanna. New York, Garland, 1985. 472p. (Garland Reference Library of the Humanities, v.595).

This is a useful work identifying some 4,000 titles of American fiction written during the first half of this century and showing their connection to social history. The emphasis is on novels, but also included are short story collections, plays, and narrative poems. Entries are arranged alphabetically by author, followed by indexes of subject, title, and illustrator. Subjects such as labor and capital, marriage and family life, etc., are used, but place names predominate. Principal subject matter is described in brief annotations, and geographical setting is indicated. Excluded for the most part are the genres of western and detective stories as well as juvenile literature.

899. Nineteenth Century Fiction: A Bibliographical Catalogue Based on the Collection Formed by Robert Lee Wolff. Robert Lee Wolff, comp. New York, Garland, 1981-1986. 5v. (Garland Reference Library of the Humanities).

With the publication of the fifth volume, this set stands as the most complete bibliography of nineteenth-century English fiction available. Based on the important collection of Victorian fiction belonging to the late Robert Lee Wolff, the work identifies nearly 8,000 titles. These represent the intention of the collector to acquire any English novel published during the reign of Queen Victoria as well as any other novel published by that author even though it might fall outside the range of 1827-1901. Volumes 1-4 consist of entries for the major segment of the collection, novels by known authors. Volume 5 covers anonymous works listed by title, and pseudonymous works by pseudonyms. Volume 5 includes the title index to the entire set, as well as an index to all illustrators mentioned in the notes.

900. Science Fiction and Fantasy Series and Sequels: A Bibliography, Volume 1: Books. Tim Cottrill, et al. New York, Garland, 1986. 398p. (Garland Reference Library of the Humanities, v.611).

Another of the Garland bibliographies which emphasizes series publications of a genre (see entry 903) is this listing of 6,300 book titles in some 1,200 series. Since this work is identified as volume 1 and restricted to books, it is reasonable to assume that forthcoming volumes will cover series carried in periodicals. Like the western, science fiction and fantasy are well accommodated in the series format and much important work has appeared in this manner. Arrangement is by author, with entries furnishing series title, publisher, and publication date. Although some omissions are evident, the work is highly useful to those with an interest in the topic. There are good title and sequence indexes.

901. Science Fiction Book Review Index, 1923-1973. H. W. Hall. Detroit, Gale, 1975. 438p.

This is the lead volume and most comprehensive publication in what appears to be a series cumulated on a quinquennial basis. The initial volume covers a 50-year period and identifies reviews appearing in selected science fiction magazines. Arrangement is alphabetical by authors of the works. A directory of magazines indexed is furnished, and a title index provides access. The work has been continued by Hall's *Science Fiction Book Review Index, 1974-1979* (Detroit, Gale, 1981), and most recently *Science Fiction and Fantasy Book Review Index, 1980-1984* ... by Hall and Geraldine L. Hutchins (Detroit, Gale, 1986). The recent work identifies more than 13,800 reviews published in over 70 magazines. An important addition is a section, "Science Fiction and Fantasy Research Index," which provides about 16,000 author and subject access points to books, articles, and essays of history or criticism.

902. Short Story Index: An Index to 60,000 Stories in 4,320 Collections. Dorothy Elizabeth Cook and Isabel Stevenson Monro. New York, H. W. Wilson, 1953. 1553p. Supp. 1950-1954, 1955-1958, 1959-1963, 1964-1968, 1969-1973, 1974-1978, 1979-1983.

A valuable and highly regarded standard tool is this work which appeared originally in 1953. As its title indicates, the initial volume indexes 60,000 English-language stories published up to 1949 in several thousand collections. Indexing is by author, title, and subject in typical Wilson dictionary arrangement. Since that time, the work has continued through periodic supplements which are now on a quinquennial basis and identify several thousand stories in recently published collections. The most recent volume (1979-1983) was compiled by Juliette Yaakov and indexes 16,633 stories in 904 collections and 67 periodicals. Inclusion of periodicals began with the 1974-1978 supplement. A list of collections indexed and a directory of periodicals appear in the back.

903. **Western Series and Sequels: A Reference Guide.** Bernard A. Drew, et al. New York, Garland, 1986. 173p. (Garland Bibliographies on Series and Sequels; Garland Reference Library of the Humanities, v.625).

As part of the extensive Garland line of bibliographies, this is a useful tool for identifying those westerns which appeared in series. This particular form of the genre has been common for decades, and this tool furnishes 375 entries with dates up to the year of publication (1986). Series works imply use of the same lead character in different books, each of which has an episode which is complete in itself. The coverage embraces those works set in Canada, the French and Indian Wars, and the Civil War, as well as the American West. Both juvenile and adult series are treated. There is a brief introductory history of the genre, and a title index provides access.

Dictionaries, Encyclopedias, and Handbooks

904. **Critical Terms for Science Fiction and Fantasy: A Glossary and Guide to Scholarship.** Gary K. Wolfe. Westport, Conn., Greenwood Press, 1986. 162p.

As the first literary glossary devoted to the area of fantastic literature, this tool has found a receptive audience among librarians and their patrons. Beginning with a twenty-six-page introductory essay on fantastic literature and literary discourse, the work then provides a list of nearly 500 terms, alphabetically arranged, complete with definitions and in some cases, expositions and commentaries. Some terms are given multiple definitions— those of the author and those of other experts in the field. Certain broad concepts are defined with short essays. There are references given to authors and critics whose works are listed in a section on works consulted. Both specialists and laypersons will find this tool to be helpful and rewarding. There is an index of primary authors.

905. **Encyclopedia of Science Fiction and Fantasy.** Donald H. Tuck, comp. Chicago, Advent, 1974-1982. 3v.

More of a biobibliography than a true encyclopedic source, this work has finally been completed in three volumes. Volume 1, *Who's Who and Works, A-L,* consists of an alphabetical listing of authors, anthologists, editors, artists, etc., with biographical sketches where available. Listings of their works in the science fiction and fantasy area are furnished through 1968 and include all known editions and foreign translations. Tables of contents are given for anthologies and collections. Volume 2 covers the same territory for *M-Z* and also provides an alphabetical listing by title. Volume 3 covers a variety of topics: magazines in the field, paperbacks, pseudonyms (cross-references by pseudonym and real name), series, and general areas of interest such as publishers, films, etc. The plan is for publication of supplements on a quinquennial basis, with the next volume to cover 1969-1975. This should become a familiar purchase for reference departments.

906. **Genreflecting: A Guide to Reading Interests in Genre Fiction**. 2nd ed. Betty Rosenberg. Littleton, Colo., Libraries Unlimited, 1986. 298p.

Although the primary purpose of this item is to serve as a text for library school classes in book selection and collection management, it also furnishes the librarian with an interesting and useful handbook of miscellaneous information and bibliography of currently available works by authors in the different genres. Using the rationale that no child or adult need apologize for his or her choice of reading matter, Rosenberg surveys the popular genres (western, thriller, romance, science fiction, fantasy, and horror). There is an introductory chapter on genre literature, with succeeding descriptions of publishers, readers, and the place of such literature in libraries. Included in the coverage of each genre are listings of significant and popular authors, as well as anthologies, bibliographies, biographies, history, criticism, periodicals, awards, etc.

907. **Masterplots: Revised Category Edition, American Fiction Series**. Frank N. Magill, ed. Englewood Cliffs, N.J., Salem, 1985. 3v.

Nearly 350 novels and collections of short stories have been taken from the original *Masterplots* (see entry 776) and reprinted here in a work limited to coverage of American fiction. Thus, we have another spinoff of the monumental work originally begun in 1949. The new series is entitled the "Revised Category Edition." Coverage is uniform as we have become accustomed to in the *Masterplots* design: type of work, author and dates, type of plot, time setting, date of publication, and principal characters, a brief critical essay, and an excellent summary of the plot. There has been slight modification and updating but basically this is a remake of the older work in a convenient package. Following the same pattern and rationale and published at the same time is Magill's *Masterplots: Revised Category Edition, British Fiction Series* (Salem, 1985). Nearly 400 works of British fiction are reprinted in this three-volume set.

908. **Masterplots II: American Fiction Series**. Frank N. Magill, ed. Englewood Cliffs, N.J., Salem, 1986. 4v.

Signalling the birth of yet another publication in the *Masterplots* line-up from Salem Press is this four-volume edition focused on American fiction not previously treated in the *Masterplots* series (see entry 776). Nearly 400 modern works from the twentieth century are examined. Coverage is not limited to North America, but includes Latin America as well. Of the 198 authors whose works are treated, thirty-four, or seventeen percent, are Latin American. Thus, Gabriel Garcia Marquez and Carlos Fuentes appear, as do Algren, Bellow, Faulkner, Vonnegut, etc. This makes it a more valuable resource since exposition of Latin American literature is not easily found. Entries differ somewhat from the traditional *Masterplots*, for along with the plot summary, there is far more coverage given narrative devices, characterization, and thematic elements, and an interpretive summary is included. *Masterplots II: British and Commonwealth Fiction Series* (1987) is in the same mold and covers works of modern fiction from England, Ireland, Canada, India, Nigeria, etc. *Masterplots II: Short Story Series*, also by Magill (Salem, 1986) is a six-volume set describing over 700 short stories from all over the world. Titles are arranged alphabetically and coverage is given to story, theme, and style as well as setting, major characters, dates, authorship, etc.

Biographical and Critical Sources

909. American Short-Fiction Criticism and Scholarship, 1959-1977: A Checklist. Joe Weixlmann. Chicago, Swallow, 1982. 625p.

This work was initially developed as an update for the American portion of Jarvis A. Thurston's *Short-Fiction Criticism: A Checklist of Interpretation since 1925 of Stories and Novelettes (American, British, Continental) 1800-1958* (Swallow, 1960). It has exceeded the original work in comprehensiveness since it not only provides references to critical and scholarly works on short fiction, but also includes citations to bibliographical publications, biographical studies, and interviews. There are around 10,000 entries to essays in 5,000 books and 325 serials. Individual authors are entered alphabetically by name, under which specific titles are listed. About 500 authors are treated. *The American Novel: A Checklist of Twentieth Century Criticism*, by Donna Lorine Gerstenberger and George Hendrick (Swallow, 1961-1970) is the standard checklist in the field, with volume 1 identifying criticism published up to 1959. Volume 2 cites critical studies from 1960 to 1968. The arrangement is alphabetical by novelist. Citations to critical studies appear under individual novels. A second section gives general studies by century.

910. Beacham's Popular Fiction in America. Walton Beacham and Suzanne Niemeyer, eds. Washington, D.C., Beacham Publishing, 1986. 4v.

Similar in design and purpose to the Magill efforts, this work focuses on what is termed popular fiction. The criteria for inclusion of an author is that he or she be of the "best-selling" variety and that his or her works reflect social concerns. About 200 contemporary novelists of varied type are treated. These are primarily American, although some British writers are included. Most are living or recently deceased, and most are actively publishing, although this is not true of all. Contributors are primarily college professors. The entries follow a set pattern, covering publishing history as well as the critical reception of each writer. Individual titles are analyzed in terms of social concerns, themes, techniques, literary precedents, etc. Although constrained by the required brevity of the individual articles, the work should prove useful to a variety of patrons. A second series is promised in 1987.

911. Contemporary Authors: Bibliographical Series. V. 1 American Novelists. James J. Martine, ed. Detroit, Gale, 1986- . (In progress).

This new series from Gale is designed to furnish a selective guide to the best critical studies done on major writers. Each volume is to cover ten personalities representing a particular nationality and genre. These will complement the biographical sketches given in *Contemporary Authors* (see entry 784), and will focus primarily on English and American authors. Indexes to critics and writers will cumulate in each succeeding volume. Volume 1 covers ten well-known individuals: James Baldwin, John Barth, Saul Bellow, John Cheever, Joseph Heller, Norman Mailer, Bernard Malamud, Carson McCullers, John Updike, and Eudora Welty. Entries furnish a bibliography of works by the author, a bibliography of works about the author which include bibliographies, biographies, interviews, and critical studies. There is also a detailed bibliographic essay comparing and evaluating the critical studies. Volume 2 covers American poets (see entry 931).

912. Contemporary Novelists. 4th ed. D. L. Kirkpatrick, ed. New York, St. Martin's Press, 1986. 1003p. (Contemporary Writers of the English Language).

First published in 1972, this work has established itself as an important resource on the lives and contributions of current English-language novelists. Inclusion is determined by a panel of advisers, and about 20 percent of the entries on 600 authors are new. A number of entries from the third edition have been dropped, which probably indicates that the criteria are popularity and critical recognition, although this is not stated. Newcomers include Alice Walker and Raymond Carver although, regrettably, not Wole Soyinka, winner of the 1986 Nobel Prize for literature. The arrangement is alphabetical by author, and entries provide a brief biographical sketch, a bibliography of published works, and a signed critical essay on the author's work. Responses from the novelists are encouraged. The work shows evidence of updating of previous entries and continues to maintain a high standard.

913. **Critical Survey of Long Fiction: English Language Series.** Frank N. Magill, ed. Englewood Cliffs, N.J., Salem, 1983. 8v.

Another of the Magill offerings from Salem Press, this work furnishes critical reviews of over 270 writers of novels and novella. Volumes 1-7 contain long biographical sketches of a wide range of writers from Samuel Richardson to John Irving. Included are critical assessments of each writer's contributions and an exposition of themes. Different literary forms are identified and brief bibliographies are supplied. Volume 8 furnishes the index as well as background essays on various aspects of the novel and a lengthy discourse on the novella. Magill's *Critical Survey of Short Fiction* (see entry 787) is the counterpart to this work in seven volumes.

914. **The English Novel, 1578-1956: A Checklist of Twentieth Century Criticisms.** Inglis Freeman Bell and Donald Baird. Denver, Alan Swallow, 1959; repr., Hamden, Conn., Shoe String Press, 1974. 169p.

The English novel has been covered well in a series of publications providing citations to critical studies published in the twentieth century. The first of these checklists was this work, giving a selective listing of critical studies on long fiction written over a period of 400 years which appeared in books and periodicals between 1900 and 1957. The arrangement of entries is alphabetical by name of author, followed by specific titles of his or her works. This tool is supplemented by *English Novel Explication: Criticisms to 1972*, by Helen H. Palmer and Anne Jane Dyson (Shoe String Press, 1973), which lists criticisms from 1958 to 1972. This supplementary work was followed by its own *Supplement I*, by Peter L. Abernethy, et al. (Shoe String Press, 1976), which covered the years 1972 to 1974. *Supplement II*, compiled by Christian J. W. Kloessel and Jeffrey R. Smitten (Shoe String Press, 1981), extended coverage to 1979. The most recent volume is *Supplement III*, also by Kloessel (Shoe String Press, 1986), and covers the period from 1980 to 1985. Another useful checklist, *The English Novel: Twentieth Century Criticism* (Swallow, 1976-1982) appeared in two volumes. Volume 1 identifies critical writings on the works of about forty-five novelists from Defoe to Hardy, while volume 2 covers eighty writers of the twentieth century.

915. **Supernatural Fiction Writers: Fantasy and Horror.** E. F. Bleiler, ed. New York, Scribner's, 1985. 2v.

Nearly 150 authors have been selected as major entries in this biographical dictionary of important contributors to the genre. Among those high-ranking individuals are Poe,

Bradbury, Tolkien, Zelazny, and Henry James. Since selection is so limited at this level, one might expect many omissions, and the tool has been criticized for slighting women writers in particular. Entries furnish well-developed, informative biographical essays which analyze notable works, make comparisons with other authors, and evaluate the influence and status of the writers. Bibliographies are included as well. The arrangement of entries is classified by time period and geographical region, but a detailed index provides ready access. There is some overlap with Bleiler's *Science Fiction Writers: Critical Studies of the Major Authors from the Early Nineteenth Century to the Present Day* (Scribner's, 1982). This latter work covers seventy-five writers classified by period, and accessed by an index of names and titles.

916. **Twentieth Century Short Story Explication: Interpretations 1900-1975 of Short Fiction since 1800.** 3rd ed. Warren S. Walker. Hamden, Conn., Shoe String Press, 1977. 880p. Supp. 1-3, 1980-1987.
    Originally published in 1961, the Walker effort is recognized as a standard in the field. The third edition cites interpretations since the turn of the century in books, monographs, and periodicals of short fiction published since 1800. For this series, a short story is a work not exceeding 150 average-sized pages. (Explications describe or explain the meaning of the story and include observations on theme, symbols, or structure.) The arrangement is by author, then story title. About 850 authors are covered by interpretations published through 1975. *Supplement I* was issued in 1980 and includes an additional 186 authors from 1976 through 1978. *Supplement II* was published in 1984 and covers the period 1979 through 1981 and includes an additional 246 authors. Of the 957 writers, nearly 470 appear for the first time.

POETRY

Bibliographic Guides

917. **English Poetry, 1660-1800: A Guide to Information Sources.** Donald C. Mell. Detroit, Gale, 1982. 501p.
    Recently the Gale Company has developed a series of guides in the area of English poetry; individual titles cover different chronological periods. This work covers poetry of the period 1660-1800 and furnishes annotated entries of critical research of the twentieth century through 1979. It is divided into two parts, the first of which furnishes a bibliography of general reference sources (histories, guidebooks, etc.), collections of poetry, and criticism. Also included are bibliographies, checklists, and background studies in related areas. The second part treats thirty-one poets, with listings of standard editions, collected works, bibliographies, and critical studies. *English Romantic Poetry, 1800-1835: A Guide to Information Sources*, by Donald H. Reiman (Gale, 1979) identifies important studies relating to the work of five major poets (Wordsworth, Byron, Keats, Shelley, and Coleridge) and twelve secondary poets. Emily Ann Anderson's *English Poetry, 1900-1950: A Guide to Information Sources* (Gale, 1982) covers the modern period, with detailed coverage of sources of information on the work of twenty-one influential poets.

918. **Middle Scots Poets: A Reference Guide to James I of Scotland, Robert Henryson, William Dunbar, and Gavin Douglas.** Walter Scheps and J. Anna Looney. Boston, G. K. Hall, 1986. 292p. (A Reference Guide to Literature).

King James I, along with Henryson, Dunbar, and Douglas, constitute what has been termed a group of "Scottish Chaucericans" who until the twentieth century had been dismissed as minor figures. More recently, however, their stature has grown and their "Scottishness" has been treated more seriously rather than as a curiosity. This work identifies a variety of materials on each individual who is given separate treatment in the guide. All items are annotated. There is a fifth section in the work which lists general works that deal with the four poets collectively or provide background material. Each of the five sections has a separate index. The criticism covers a span of 450 years from 1521 through 1978, making this a useful tool for the serious inquirer.

Bibliographies and Indexes

919. **American Poetry Index: An Author and Title Index to Poetry by Americans in Single-Author Collections.** 1981/1982- . Ann. Great Neck, N.Y., Granger Book.

First issued in 1983 (for the year 1981-1982), this annual index has grown in popularity as a most useful identification tool for collections of poetry by a single poet. Each volume contains approximately 10,000 poems published in some 200 collections during the year covered. There is generally a wide range in terms of representative figures, since collections of obscure poets are almost as likely to be published as those by more familiar personalities. Arrangement of entries is alphabetical by authors and titles in a single dictionary sequence. There are a list of collections indexed and a directory of publishers with the list of collections keyed to reference numbers provided in the entries.

920. **Annual Index to Poetry in Periodicals.** 1984- . Ann. Great Neck, N.Y., Poetry Index Press.

Another annual index from Granger begun in recent years (see entries 919 and 924), this work targets poetry which was published in periodicals during the year covered. First issued in 1985 (covering the year 1984), each volume identifies around 8,000 poems which have appeared in newspapers, magazines, and journals. Similar to Granger's major work, *Granger's Index to Poetry* (see entry 922), the arrangement of entries is alphabetical by poet, title, and first line in one alphabetical sequence. There is a list of periodicals indexed which shows a wide range of works both well known and relatively obscure. The Granger Company has also begun retrospective indexing in this area. *Index to Poetry in Periodicals: American Poetic Renaissance, 1915-1919 ...* (1981), *Index to Poetry in Periodicals, 1920-1924 ...* (1983), and *Index to Poetry in Periodicals, 1925-1929 ...* (1984) index poems appearing in magazines and newspapers offering a wide range in terms of quality and popularity. Included are the products of top-notch poets as well as unknown versifiers who have written for both children and adults. Over 300 periodicals are indexed in each volume by name of poet, furnishing about 9,000 poems by over 2,000 poets per issue.

921. **The Bibliography of Contemporary American Poetry, 1945-1985: An Annotated Checklist.** William McPheron. Westport, Conn., Meckler Publishing, 1986. 72p.

This slender little volume provides a wealth of information on published collections of poetry which include the work of American poets of our time. Coverage actually goes back to the early 1940s. The first section of this annotated bibliography lists multiauthor sources arranged alphabetically by compiler, editor, or title. Only those anthologies that furnish a significant coverage of individual poets and of small presses that have published much of their work are included. The second section furnishes a list of 122 single-author studies of leading contemporary poets, arranged alphabetically by name of poet. There is a useful introduction describing key anthologies and problems in bibliographic control. *Contemporary American Poetry: A Checklist*, by Lloyd Davis and Robert Irwin (Scarecrow, 1975) identifies 3,300 single-author collections of poetry published between 1950 and 1973. This work is continued by Davis's *Contemporary American Poetry: A Checklist, Second Series, 1973-1983*, which lists 5,000 collections published during that ten-year period. Arrangement is by name of poet, and again coverage is limited to single-author works.

922. **Granger's Index to Poetry.** 8th ed., completely rev. and enl. William F. Bernhardt, ed. New York, Columbia University Press, 1986. 2014p.

Since 1904, this has been the preeminent work in the field, indexing poems in anthologies by title, first line, author, and subject. The pattern of coverage and scope changed with the seventh edition (1982), no longer providing a cumulative coverage of preceding issues. Instead, the seventh edition indexes nearly 250 anthologies published between 1970 and 1981, thereupon supplementing the coverage of the sixth edition published in 1973. The eighth edition returns to the cumulative format, indexing anthologies published throughout the twentieth century up to 30 June 1985. Over 400 titles are indexed, eighty-two of which are either new or indexed for the first time in this work. One should always retain earlier editions of *Granger*, since a number of titles are deleted as a matter of routine with each new issue. *Chicorel Index Series* (see entry 767) devoted several volumes of its twenty-seven volumes to poetry. These index poetry in collections and anthologies, enumerate titles on discs, tapes, and cassettes, and identify published works in the field. (See Sheehy, entry 2, for listing of titles in the series.)

923. **Index to Black Poetry.** Dorothy H. Chapman. Boston, G. K. Hall, 1974. 541p.

This work received numerous accolades when it was published as a landmark or first-of-its-kind index, and was included among "Reference Books of 1975" (*Library Journal*, 15 April 1976). It remains an immensely useful access tool for poems focused on the black experience regardless of the racial origin of the poet, as well as works by black poets. Thus, black poetry is defined in broad terms, and about 5,000 poems from 1,000 authors are listed. They span a period of time dating from the efforts of Lucy Terry, the earliest known black eighteenth-century slave poet, to the 1970s. There are three sections in the tool: a title and first line index, an author index, and a subject index. A total of ninety-four single-author works and thirty-three anthologies is covered, thus furnishing the means of identifying numerous obscure poets and poetry. Chapman's *Index to Poetry by Black American Women* (Greenwood Press, 1986) is another important access tool to a specialized type of poetry not easily located in standard sources.

924. **Poetry Index Annual: A Title, Author, and Subject Index to Poetry in Anthologies.** 1982- . Ann. Great Neck, N.Y., Granger Book.

Rounding out Granger's coverage of poetry on an annual basis is this index to poetry appearing in anthologies. The purpose of this work is to index all anthologies published in a single year (including new editions of older works). This supplements the more selective coverage of *Granger's Index to Poetry* (see entry 922) and complements the coverage of Granger's indexes to poems in single-author collections (see entry 919) and to poems in periodical literature (see entry 920). Indexing is by author, title, and subject, with all entries in a single alphabetical arrangement. About fifty anthologies are indexed per issue, providing access to several thousand poems. This should prove to be a useful resource for librarians and their patrons.

Anthologies

925. The New Oxford Book of American Verse. Richard Ellmann, ed. New York, Oxford University Press, 1976. 1076p.

This is the standard anthology in the field and has been recognized as such since its first appearance in 1927. Both the 1927 and 1950 editions were compiled by Bliss Carman and F. O. Matthiessen and earned the respect of teachers and librarians for their excellent representation of both classic and modern poets. This edition continues in that tradition, listing the poets chronologically beginning with seventeenth-century poet Anne Bradstreet and ending with Imamu Amiri Baraka (Leroi Jones), born in 1934. Inclusion is highly selective, and about seventy-five poets are treated. The intention is to include poems of intrinsic merit while at the same time representing the principal directions of modern poetry. The poems, like the poets who created them, appear in chronological sequence. There is an index of authors, titles, and first lines.

926. The New Oxford Book of Australian Verse. Les A. Murray. New York, Oxford University Press, 1986. 399p.

One of the "new" anthologies in the Oxford line which made its appearance during the 1980s is this collection of poems chosen by Les Murray, an important contemporary poet. His anthology is carefully developed and representative of the various elements within Australian poetry over a span of time beginning with the colonial period and running to the present day. Criteria for inclusion reflect his determination of the amount of "poetry" found in a poem as well as its liveliness and readability. Standard poems are not always included and have given way to "untypical" poems of high quality and expressive nature. Included are some works of aboriginal origin, which have not been included in standard anthologies. This is a most useful source for its unorthodox means of selection, which results in the inclusion of much obscure poetry.

927. The New Oxford Book of English Verse, 1250-1950. Helene Louise Gardner. New York, Oxford University Press, 1972. 974p.

The *Oxford Book of English Verse* is the oldest anthology in the Oxford line, first appearing in 1900 under the guidance of Sir Arthur Quiller-Couch. He was also responsible for the second edition in 1939. The first edition covered poetry up to 1900, the second edition to 1918. The present work is not a revision but a new anthology, and furnishes comprehensive coverage up to 1950. It contains nearly 900 poems. Whereas earlier editions had emphasized lyric verse, the new work represents the total range of English nondramatic poetry. American poets Ezra Pound and T. S. Eliot are also included. There are brief notes and references located at the back of the book, and access is furnished by indexes of authors and first lines. There are a number of Oxford anthologies of a specialized nature devoted to a particular period or century of English poetry which complement this general tool.

928. The Oxford Book of Irish Verse. Thomas Kinsella, ed. New York, Oxford University Press, 1986. 413p.

This recent Oxford anthology of Irish poetry takes on a new challenge in covering the period from the beginnings to the fourteenth century. It thus represents a complementary work to the earlier edition, which covered the seventeenth to the twentieth centuries. Kinsella is a master poet in his own right and has not only selected the works, but translated them faithfully, always keeping in mind the musical quality of the ancient verse. The work furnishes a well-balanced collection of Irish art, with representation of various elements of high quality as well as popular culture. The work of Swift, Goldsmith, Sheridan, Yeats, Synge, etc., blends with the numerous folk poems, songs, prayers, etc., from lesser known but equally expressive poets.

Biographical and Critical Sources

929. **American and British Poetry: A Guide to the Criticism, 1925-1978.** Harriet Semmes Alexander. Athens, Ohio, Swallow, 1984. 486p.

Another of the Swallow checklists of literary criticism, this one provides references to critical studies appearing in books and periodicals between 1925 and 1978. A wide range of poets and poetry is treated, beginning with Spenser and ending with Dickey. References are to critical studies of the entire poem rather than certain parts of the poem, unless the poem is not covered more completely by other studies or the criticism is noteworthy in some way. The arrangement is alphabetical by poet, then by title of poem. This work is similar to *Poetry Explication* (see entry 933) but includes poems up to 1,000 lines in length, whereas Kuntz limits his coverage to poems not exceeding 500 lines. Although there is overlap between the two, this work indexes titles not included in Kuntz and also treats a greater number of obscure poets.

930. **American Poets 1880-1945.** Third Series. Peter Quartermain, ed. Detroit, Gale, 1987. 2v. (Dictionary of Literary Biography, v.54).

This work is the third and final segment of a series which itself is part of the extensive *Dictionary of Literary Biography* (see entry 865). The first series appeared in 1986, the second series followed later that same year, and this, the third series, was published in two volumes in 1987. All volumes are in the same format, in keeping with the pattern of the parent series. In each volume, about forty-five American poets are listed alphabetically by name followed by dates of birth and death, then by name of the author of the entry. There is a bibliography of the poet's publications followed by a detailed biocritical essay of the poet's life and work. Concluding the entry is a bibliography of writings on the poet and library locations where manuscripts and letters may be found. One of the attractive features is the inclusion of photographs, copies of title pages, and manuscripts.

931. **Contemporary Authors Bibliographical Series. Volume 2: American Poets.** Ronald Baughman, ed. Detroit, Gale, 1986. 387p.

This tool was designed as a companion series to the monumental Gale effort *Contemporary Authors* (see entry 784). The first volume covered American novelists (see entry 911) and set the pattern for the series, each volume of which covers about ten major writers in a particular genre and nationality. In this work, eleven important poets of the post-World War II era are treated, including James Dickey, Randall Jarrell, Robert Lowell, and Anne Sexton. They are covered in separate chapters, each of which is written by a specialist, in a pattern which provides bibliographic coverage of major works, followed by listing of works about the author and his or her work. Finally, there is a bibliographic essay analyzing the contribution of the critical studies. There are two indexes which are cumulative to volumes 1 and 2, an index of authors and an index of critics.

932. **Contemporary Poets.** 4th ed. James Vinson and D. L. Kirkpatrick, eds. New York, St. Martin's Press, 1985. 1071p.

Information on about 1,000 poets is furnished in this new edition of a standard reference tool. About 800 of the poets are currently writing in the English language while a smaller, more select group has died since 1950. Individuals are selected for inclusion by an international board, and the fourth edition contains seventy new entries. The pattern of coverage for each entry represents four major segments, beginning with a biographical sketch. Also included are a full bibliography of the poet's various publications including poetry, criticism, biography, etc., and an excellent signed critical essay on the poet's work. There is also opportunity for the poets to provide their own comments on their work. A title index provides access to poems described in the main body of the work.

933. **Poetry Explication: A Checklist of Interpretation since 1925 of British and American Poems Past and Present.** 3rd ed. Joseph Marshall Kuntz and Nancy C. Martinez. Boston, G. K. Hall, 1980. 570p.

Originally published in 1950, and revised in 1962, the third edition occupies a position of respect among reference librarians who must conduct searches for critical interpretations of poetry. The 1980 edition incorporates the checklists of the earlier works and has added references to explications published up to 1977. The explications have been published in selected composite works and literary periodicals. An explication is defined by the authors as an examination of a literary work for knowledge of each part, for the relationship of these parts to each other, and for their relations to the whole. Similar to Alexander's *American and British Poetry* (see entry 929) in scope and purpose, Kuntz's work is limited to those explications which consider poems of 500 lines or less. Alexander treats poetry up to 1,000 lines in length.

CHILDREN'S LITERATURE

Bibliographies and Indexes

934. **Children's Book Review Index, Master Cumulation, 1965-1984 ...** Gary C. Arbert and Barbara Beach, eds. Detroit, Gale, 1985. 5v.

Children's Book Review Index has been an annual publication since 1975, and is a separate listing of those materials in *Book Review Index* which are identified as children's books. The subtitle of the cumulation goes on to say "a Cumulated Index to More Than 200,000 Reviews of Approximately 55,000 Titles." The work represents a treasure house of information for those doing retrospective selection for purposes of collection development. It is also of importance to those in reference who are seeking to identify, verify, and locate critical reviews of children's materials for their patrons. The reviews cited have appeared in over 370 periodicals, for which references are provided. Listings are by author, then title.

935. **Discoveries: Fiction for Elementary School Readers.** Washington, D.C., National Library Service for the Blind and Physically Handicapped, 1986. 93p.

With the recent emphasis on services to the physically disabled comes a series of brief paperback bibliographies identifying books for youngsters which are available on disc, cassette, or in Braille form from libraries. Actually, this work is a catalog of materials furnished by the National Library Service for the Blind and Physically Handicapped. This volume is intended for children from kindergarten through grade 6. *Discoveries: Fiction for Intermediate School Years* (1986) furnishes listings for grades 4 through 7. *Discoveries: Fiction for Young Teens* (1986) covers grades 4 through 9 and senior high school. The arrangement in all volumes is by topic, such as historical fiction or family life, then by format (disc, cassette, Braille, etc.). There are author-title indexes for each format. All volumes are available free of charge from the publisher.

936. **Fiction, Folklore, Fantasy & Poetry for Children, 1876-1985.** New York, R. R. Bowker, 1986. 2v.

Another of the comprehensive bibliographies produced from the Bowker database, this massive work identifies authors, titles, and illustrators of children's literature over a period of 110 years. Introductory sections on children's books and a history of the R. R. Bowker company are furnished in volume 1. Author and illustrator indexes follow. Volume 2 contains the title index as well as a section on book awards. Entries furnish author/illustrator dates and pseudonyms as well as title and imprint. The awards section seems to be less successful and has been criticized by reviewers. Newbery and Caldecott award winners are listed with date of publication rather than date of award. The first award winners in each of these categories have been omitted, and there are some misspellings. Despite these faults, the work must be considered a valuable tool.

937. **Index to Children's Poetry: A Title, Subject, Author, and First Line Index to Poetry in Collections for Children and Youth.** John Edmond Brewton and Sara Westbrook Brewton. New York, H. W. Wilson, 1942. 965p. First Supp., 1954, 405p. Second Supp., 1965, 453p.

The original volume of what is now a continuous series, this work indexed 130 collections of poetry for young people published up to the late 1930s. Title, subject, author, and first lines are indexed in a manner similar to that of *Granger's Index* (see entry 922). Over 15,000 poems by 2,500 poets are classified under a variety of subjects. The first supplement to this work appeared in 1954 and indexed over sixty-five collections published between 1938 and 1951. The second supplement was published eleven years later and covered eighty-five collections published between 1949 and 1963. *Index to Poetry for Children and Young People, 1964-1969*, by Brewton and G. Meredith Blackburn (H. W. Wilson, 1972) began the series of six-year supplements which placed increased emphasis on books at the seventh to twelfth grade levels. This was followed by *Index to Poetry for Children and Young People, 1970-1975*, by Brewton and others (H. W. Wilson, 1978). The same title and authorship continued, with the most recent supplement covering the period 1976-1981 (H. W. Wilson, 1984).

938. **Newbery and Caldecott Medalists and Honor Book Winners: Bibliographies and Resource Material through 1977.** Jim Roginski, comp. Littleton, Colo., Libraries Unlimited, 1982. 339p.

Somewhat of a cross between a bibliography and a handbook is this interesting compilation of material on the Newbery and Caldecott medalists and Honor Book winners. A good introduction describes the medals. This is followed by the main listing of awards, alphabetically arranged with dates provided. Listed for each illustrator and author are their award-winning books and other works. Also included are indications of media formats developed from their works, library collections, exhibitions, and additional readings. The time span covered is from the beginning of their careers to 1977. Appearing annually since 1940 is *Notable Children's Books*, an annual publication of the Notable Children's Books Committee of the Children's Services Division of the American Library Association. The committee selections of notable books (both fiction and nonfiction appealing to a wide range of age levels) are sold for a dollar or so. Retrospective lists are available as well: *Notable Children's Books 1940-1970* (American Library Association, 1977) has been supplemented by *Notable Children's Books 1971-1975* (no longer listed in *Books in Print*) and most recently *Notable Children's Books, 1976-1980* (American Library Association, 1984).

Dictionaries, Encyclopedias, and Handbooks

Although it is not exclusively concerned with literature in the English language, one should not overlook *The Oxford Companion to Children's Literature* (see entry 779).

939. **The Black American in Books for Children: Readings in Racism.** 2nd ed. Donnarae MacCann and Gloria Woodard, eds. Metuchen, N.J., Scarecrow, 1985. 298p.

This is a valuable collection of essays for librarians and teachers who work with young people, written by specialists in children's literature, sociology, education, and history. Intellectual freedom is described in many of the essays, all targeted to the presentation of the black experience in literature for children. Titles are described and analyzed (*Sounder, Dr. Dolittle*, etc.) and trends are explained. Illustrations are covered and picture books are treated as well. Originally published in 1972, the new edition provides information in helping to establish an informed perspective on the portrayal of the black experience. This work is extremely useful as a resource item for courses in book selection and acquisitions.

940. **Children's Literature Awards and Winners: A Directory of Prizes, Authors, and Illustrators.** Dolores Blythe Jones. Detroit, Neal-Schuman/Gale, 1983. 495p. Supp., 1984, 136p.

Arrangement of this work is in three parts, with part 1 being an alphabetical list of 144 awards presented to works of children's literature by organizations in the United States and abroad. Entries include name of award, address, founder, history, criteria, purpose, time of presentation, and full citations to all award winners and runners-up, in chronological sequence. The second part furnishes an alphabetical arrangement of authors and illustrators, with indication of their books and the awards they won. Finally, there is a bibliography of source materials on children's literary awards. Another useful tool is *Children's Books: Awards & Prizes, Including Prizes and Awards for Young Adult Books* (Children's Book Council, 1986). This tool groups the entries (awards) in four categories: U.S. awards selected by adults, U.S. awards selected by youngsters, British Commonwealth awards, and international awards. Entries describe the awards briefly and furnish lists of winners in chronological order. There is an award classification section which provides "subject" access, as well as a title index and a person index.

941. **Dictionary of American Children's Fiction, 1859-1959: Books of Recognized Merit.** Alethea K. Helbig and Agnes Regan Perkins. Westport, Conn., Greenwood Press, 1985. 666p.

This is an interesting and useful tool which provides information on award-winning books of children's fiction covering a period of 100 years. Entries are listed alphabetically by title with related entries for authors and for significant characters. Settings are also included in the index when important. Title entries furnish basic bibliographic data as well as an informative synopsis of the work and references to specific awards received. Cross-references are also provided. Most valuable is a detailed subject approach in the index which identifies numerous specific subjects or topics relevant to the listed works. The index also provides access by age of protagonist, time period, ethnic customs, etc.

942. **Oxford Dictionary of Nursery Rhymes.** Iona Opie and Peter Opie, eds. Oxford, Clarendon Press, 1951; repr., 1984. 467p.

Working together, this husband and wife team produced the most comprehensive and authoritative work ever developed on the English nursery rhyme. A useful introduction begins the work, after which about 550 nursery rhymes are featured. All of them are in current use or have been used in the recent past. The arrangement is alphabetical by the most significant word; when nonsense language is employed, the entry is listed under the opening phrase. (This strategy has worked well and most rhymes are easily located.) Along with numerous illustrations from the early published works, the earliest recorded version of the rhymes and the familiar or standard phrasing are included. Two indexes are given, the first of notable individuals associated with the nursery rhyme. There is also an index of first lines of both standard and original versions.

Biographical and Critical Sources

943. **American Writers for Children since 1960: Fiction.** Glenn E. Estes, ed. Detroit, Gale, 1986. 488p. (Dictionary of Literary Biography, v.52).
       This is one of the recent publications in the *Dictionary of Literary Biography* series (see entry 865). Like other volumes in the series, this one covers individuals determined to be influential in their genre. Nearly forty-five authors of children's fiction who have been productive since 1960 are included, thus providing useful information on some of the new realistic writers. The coverage is of high quality, with well-developed entries providing good biocritical essays and furnishing career chronologies, publications lists, and bibliographies of works by and about the subject. Individuals represent the entire realm of children's fiction popular during this time, in the areas of realism, historical fiction, fantasy, etc. Included are Judy Blume, Robert Cormier, Paul Zendel, Katherine Paterson, etc.

944. **Children's Literature Review.** 1976- . Irreg. Detroit, Gale.
       Another of the Gale efforts, this work has built a following, although the frequency of publication has been sporadic. Volumes 9-11 were issued during 1985-1986, which marked a period of increased activity. Each volume contains excerpts from criticism and reviews published in books and periodicals on the writings of a dozen or so children's authors in the spirit of *Book Review Digest* (H. W. Wilson, 1905-). Each author is treated in a separate section of the work, the entry beginning with a description of the writer's literary background and style along with a photograph. In some cases, there is an author's commentary permitting the author to reflect on his or her own work. A general commentary by a reviewer is followed by the extracts of reviews of individual titles. There are a cumulative title index for the various volumes, an author index, and an author index by nationality, since the work is international in scope.

945. **The Junior Book of Authors.** 2nd ed. rev. Stanley Jasspon Kunitz and Howard Haycraft. New York, H. W. Wilson, 1951. 309p.
       The second edition of this work by Kunitz and Haycraft furnishes biographical sketches of nearly 270 writers and illustrators, 160 of which are repeated with revisions from the first edition in 1934. Of the 108 names deleted, most are of classic stature and are covered in other Wilson publications (see entry 796). This work marked the beginning of another series, since it was supplemented by Muriel Fuller's *More Junior Authors* (H. W. Wilson, 1963) which provided 268 biographical sketches of authors and illustrators. *Third Book of Junior Authors & Illustrators*, edited by Doris De Montreville and Donna Hill (H. W. Wilson, 1972) continues the coverage with over 200 biographical sketches, as does the *Fourth Book of Junior Authors & Illustrators*, edited by De Montreville and Elizabeth D. Crawford (H. W. Wilson, 1978). The most recent addition to the series is Sally Holmes

Holtze's *Fifth Book of Junior Authors & Illustrators* (H. W. Wilson, 1983) which treats nearly 240 individuals who "have come to prominence since 1978." It would appear that this series will continue on a quinquennial basis.

946. **Something about the Author: Facts and Figures about Authors and Illustrators of Books for Young People.** Anne Commire, ed. Detroit, Gale, 1971- . (In progress).

Since 1971, this has been a prolific series, with more than forty volumes to date. Each of the volumes provides illustrated biographies of between 100 and 150 juvenile and young adult illustrators and authors. Both well-known and less popular individuals are treated, making this an excellent source of reference information. Primarily written for the youngster to read, the articles are lucid, well developed stylistically, and contain complete name and pseudonyms, date of birth, career information including awards, titles of works, publication dates, and indication of genre. Numerous illustrations are reproduced from the works. Descriptions are noncritical, similar to the series from the Wilson Company (see entry 945). There are a two-part cumulative index in each volume, an illustrations index identifying volumes where art work is furnished, and the author index. Obituaries are included. *Children's Authors and Illustrators: An Index to Biographical Dictionaries*, edited by Joyce Nakamura (Gale, 1987), is now in its fourth edition. It identifies biographies of 25,000 individuals appearing in 450 sources.

947. **Twentieth-Century Children's Writers.** 2nd ed. D. L. Kirkpatrick, ed. New York, St. Martin's Press, 1983. 1024p.

First published in 1978, this work is now recognized as a useful source of information on modern children's writers of fiction, drama, and poetry. The second edition covers over 700 individuals (an increase of 100 over the first issue). Authors are selected for inclusion by an international advisory board; arranged alphabetically; and furnished with a short biography, a bibliography of published writings, and an informative critical essay about one page in length. The essay treats their works and their significance. Locations of manuscripts are provided and references to critical studies are given. Writers in the main text have published primarily in the twentieth century, while an appendix contains sections on nearly forty figures of the nineteenth century and a list of over sixty foreign-language writers of prominence. There is a title index to provide access.

Literature in Other Languages

GENERAL WORKS

948. **Critical Survey of Long Fiction: Foreign Language Series.** Frank N. Magill, ed. Englewood Cliffs, N.J., Salem, 1984. 5v.

Another of the Magill *Critical Surveys* from Salem Press (see entries 787, 913, and 949), this work follows the pattern which has been set by the others. Volumes 1-4 cover 182 writers judged to be important contributors to the development of long fiction (novels or novel-like prose) in languages other than English. Entries for each writer furnish a list of principal long fiction, description of the writer's contribution to other literary forms, assessment of his or her major achievements, a short biographical sketch, analysis of his or her major works of long fiction, a selective list of writings other than in the long fiction genre, and a brief bibliography of biographical and critical sources about the writer. There is a useful set of essays on the history of the novel in various areas of the world in volume 5. An author-title index provides access.

949. **Critical Survey of Poetry: Foreign Language Series.** Frank N. Magill. Englewood Cliffs, N.J., Salem, 1984. 5v.

Similar in format and style to other Magill works in this series (see entries 787, 913, and 948), this work covers all major poetry of the world not in English. Nearly 200 poets are covered in the first four volumes. Each one is covered in signed articles divided into several sections: principal poems and collections, other literary forms, achievements, biography, analysis, major publications other than poetry, and a brief bibliography. Over 100 contributors are involved with the project, and the coverage is somewhat uneven in quality. The idea is to provide introductory information, and most of the articles run less than ten pages in length. Volume 5 provides twenty-seven essays on regional or national poetry, some of which are segmented into time periods. Also included is an essay describing the oral tradition, and another covers linguistics.

950. **Hoffman's Index to Poetry: European and Latin American Poetry in Anthologies.** Herbert H. Hoffman. Metuchen, N.J., Scarecrow, 1985. 672p.

A recent work which should prove useful to students and teachers is this index, which in a unique fashion excludes the poetic output in the English language. The work covers about 14,000 important poems in about 100 anthologies published since the mid-1930s. Nearly 1,800 poets are represented, with poems written in a number of languages: French, German, Spanish, Italian, Portuguese, Polish, Russian, and Ukrainian. Selection of anthologies was in part based on their availability in the English-speaking world, which adds considerably to this tool's practical value. The main section is arranged by name of poet, alphabetically, with poems listed alphabetically by title. First lines are also given. A title listing and a first line listing are grouped by languages.

951. **Women Writers in Translation: An Annotated Bibliography, 1945-1982.** Margery Resnick and Isabelle de Courtivron. New York, Garland, 1984. 272p. (Garland Reference Library of the Humanities, v.288).

The idea for this tool grew out of a meeting of the Modern Language Association, where foreign-language teachers had discussed the difficulty of locating good translations of works by women writers. The compilers are professors at M.I.T. who coordinated this project requiring the expertise of more than fifty contributors, and specialists in Portuguese, French, German, Italian, Japanese, Russian, and Spanish. The relatively slender product reflects a disappointing situation of international proportions, which permits work of women writers to go out-of-print in a relatively short time. The annotations vary in quality, as is true of most compilations, but on the whole they are informative regarding theme, genre, and literary significance. This should be a valuable tool for both teachers and librarians.

GREEK AND LATIN

952. **Ancient Writers: Greece and Rome.** T. James Luce, ed.-in-chief. New York, Scribner's, 1982. 2v.

This is a highly useful biocritical tool because of its depth of coverage of principals. The work consists of forty-seven essays by specialists from the United States, the United Kingdom, Canada, and Israel. The articles range in length from ten to more than fifty pages, and are devoted primarily to individual authors, and in some cases to groups such as Greek lyric poets. The pattern of coverage represents a brief biographical sketch, followed by an extensive critical interpretation of the writer's works. There are a bibliography of currently available editions in the original language as well as major contemporary translations, and a list of selected critical studies primarily in English. This tool is an important purchase for academic and secondary school libraries. *Greek and Roman Writers: A Checklist of Criticism*, by Thomas Gwinup and Fidelia Dickinson (2nd edition, Scarecrow, 1982) is a useful checklist of English-language criticism of the work of seventy classical authors. Critical studies are identified in both books and periodicals. It employs the normal checklist arrangement, with authors listed alphabetically, and with listings of general criticism followed by criticism of individual works.

953. Classical Studies: Classification Schedules, Classified Listing by Call Number, Chronological Listing, Author and Title Listing. Harvard University Library. Cambridge, Mass., Harvard University Press, 1979. 215p. (Widener Library Shelflist, v.57).

Another of the Harvard Library publications of the Widener shelflist, volume 57 identifies nearly 7,000 entries from the Widener classification that provide "much of what is usually thought of as classical Greek and Roman studies." Included in these schedules are works centered on the history and theory of classical scholarship and history of classical literature, although works about individual authors are excluded. Arts and sciences, rhetoric, prosody, mythology, and religion are included. This work complements other more extensive published segments of the catalog shelflist, such as *Ancient Greek Literature* ... (v.58, 1979) and *Latin Literature* ... (v.59, 1979). An important annual bibliography is *L'année philologique: bibliographique critique et analytique de l'antiquité gréco-latine* ... which lists publications in a classified arrangement. English-language studies are reported by a branch established at Chapel Hill, North Carolina, with notes written in English.

954. The Oxford Companion to Classical Literature. Paul Harvey. Oxford, Clarendon Press, 1937; repr., New York, Oxford University Press, 1984. 468p.

This is the latest reprint of a true classic, and is regarded as one of the most important tools in the field. It is a treasure house of information on a variety of topics and subjects relevant not only to literature but to the study of classical antiquity. Entries are furnished not only for classical writers, literary forms and subjects, and individual works, but also for historical events and figures, institutions, and religious observations. The rationale is that knowledge of these elements is necessary in understanding the plots and themes of classical literature. Therefore, much information is given on politics, economics, religion, art, and cultural history. *Oxford Classical Dictionary*, edited by N. G. L. Hammond and H. H. Scullard (2nd edition, Oxford, Clarendon Press, 1970) is a useful resource, although not focused on literature per se. It is a scholarly dictionary covering biography, mythology, religion, science, geography, etc., as well as literature. It includes good survey articles on topics such as music, and bibliographies accompany the articles.

ROMANCE LANGUAGES

French

955. The Concise Oxford Dictionary of French Literature. Joyce M. H. Reid. New York, Oxford University Press, 1976. 669p.

This is a successful condensation of *The Oxford Companion to French Literature*, by Paul Harvey (see entry 957n). Abridgement was achieved through compression in terms of style, format, and type size rather than elimination of articles.

Several new articles have been added where needed and older ones have been updated and in some cases expanded. Articles on French-Canadian literature have been deleted in view of their treatment in *The Oxford Companion to Canadian Literature* (see entry 854). Like others in the Companion series, this volume is highly informative, providing information on both major and minor writers, genres, plots, and literary movements. Contemporary figures and modern trends are adequately treated.

956. A Critical Bibliography of French Literature. Syracuse, N.Y., Syracuse University Press, 1947- . (In progress).

Considered a work of major importance, this bibliography was originally edited by D. C. Cabeen and in most cases is still referred to as "Cabeen." Presently five volumes and various supplements, revisions, and parts have been published. Each of the volumes is done by specialists in the field and covers a different time period. Volume 1, on the medieval period, was published originally in 1947 and enlarged in 1952. Volume 2 covers the sixteenth century, with the first edition appearing in 1956 and the revised edition in 1985. Volume 3 treats the seventeenth century (1961); and 3A, a supplement, was issued in 1983. Volume 4 covers the eighteenth century (1951), with a supplement in 1968. Volume 6 covers the twentieth century in different parts devoted to various genres (1980). As of now, volume 5, covering the nineteenth century, has not yet been published. The series represents a selective, evaluative, and annotated bibliography of books, dissertations, and periodical articles with references to reviews. As is necessary in a work of this type, each volume is separately indexed.

957. Dictionary of Modern French Literature: From the Age of Reason through Realism. Sandra W. Dolbow. Westport, Conn., Greenwood Press, 1986. 365p.

This is a detailed and thorough dictionary of French literature specialized in its coverage of the eighteenth and nineteenth centuries from 1715 to 1880. It identifies and describes all major writers and many minor figures of the period. Included among the number of writers are philosophers, historians, novelists, dramatists, and poets. Also covered are literary movements and individual works. Biographical entries furnish sketches of some length and render information adequate for identification and understanding. Similarly, good synopses and descriptions of significance are rendered for individual works. Bibliographies are included for most entries, identifying English-language sources published between 1980 and 1985. A second volume or complementary work is to continue the coverage of post-modernism from 1880 to the present. Continuing as a useful source although getting older is *The Oxford Companion to French Literature*, by Sir Paul Harvey and Janet F. Heseltine (Oxford, Clarendon Press, 1959; repr. with corrections, 1961). This is a broader-based and more comprehensive tool covering French literature from medieval times to the late 1930s. Entries furnish information on individuals, titles, places, and institutions. There are general survey articles on movements and phases of French literary development.

958. Research and Reference Guide to French Studies. 2nd ed. Charles B. Osburn. Metuchen, N.J., Scarecrow, 1981. 532p.

The first edition of this work received much acclaim when it was published in 1968, and was followed by a useful supplement in 1972. The second edition represents a complete revision of the earlier one, with 6,000 entries of importance to the study of French language and literature. The earlier edition was more comprehensive and was intended to cover the whole range of French studies. A variety of reference books is covered in the present work: concordances, dictionaries, iconographies, filmographies, encyclopedias, etc., primarily in English, French, and German. The coverage of bibliographies is excellent, and critical surveys are identified. This effort was intended as a link between the earlier edition and the machine-readable database of the *MLA International Bibliography* (see entry 769). *A Bibliographical Guide to the Romance Languages and Literatures*, by Thomas Rossman Palfrey and others (8th edition, Chandler, 1971) is a comprehensive and well-respected guide to the Romance literatures (French, Italian, Portuguese, Spanish, etc.). First published in 1939, it has been the first choice of students and specialists in identifying important studies and literary contributions.

Italian

959. **Dictionary of Italian Literature.** Peter Bondanella and Julia Conway Bondanella, co-eds. Westport, Conn., Greenwood Press, 1979. 621p.

A useful dictionary and guide to Italian literature which contains over 350 entries alphabetically arranged covering authors, genres, periods, movements, and related general topics. Most entries are on authors and provide informative sketches of their lives and achievements. Both major and minor writers are covered from the twelfth century to the present. Many of the articles are signed by the contributors. Bibliographies are furnished which include English translations of important primary texts and critical studies in books and articles in various languages. Although a few errors have been detected by reviewers, they appear to be slight, indicating a carefully prepared work. There is a useful chronology in the appendix enumerating events in Italian literature, world literature, philosophy, etc.

Spanish

960. **Bibliografiá de la literatura hispánica.** Jose Simón Diáz. Madrid, Consejo Superior de Investigaciones Cientificas, Inst. "Miguel de Cervantes" de Filologia Hispánica, 1950- . (In progress).

Beginning in 1950, this comprehensive bibliography covers all Hispanic literatures and identifies studies and critical works in books, articles, theses, and lectures. In some cases, reviews of books are identified, and library locations are given. The last volume to be reported as issued was volume 13 in 1984. Volume 2 identifies over 2,000 general bibliographies, bio-bibliographies, and indexes in the field. Volume 3 provides coverage of specific time periods for Castillian literature, the Middle Ages from the eleventh to the fifteenth centuries. Volume 4 continues the time coverage and begins the alphabetical coverage of authors from A-Augustin. Volumes 5-13 continue the alphabetical coverage up to Llusas (volume 13). Four volumes of a new edition have appeared since 1960, correcting and augmenting the earlier work. In addition, volume 1 of the third edition was published in 1983.

961. **Latin American Literary Authors: An Annotated Guide to Bibliographies.** David Zubatsky. Metuchen, N.J., Scarecrow, 1986. 332p.

This recent work is considered to be the most thorough and complete bibliography of bibliographies on Latin American authors of all types of literature. Novelists, dramatists, poets, essayists, literary critics, etc., from all regions of Spanish-speaking America are included. A variety of sources is represented, including books, magazines, journals, dissertations, and festschriften. All major writers seem to be represented as well as scores of lesser known figures. Although there are some omissions, the work is commendable both for its inclusiveness and for its attention to detail. Entries are annotated and appear in two major parts, the first of which provides an alphabetical listing by author. Part 2 gives additional bio-bibliographical sources, arranged by country or region.

962.   **Latin American Literature in the 20th Century: A Guide.** New York, Ungar, 1986. 278p.

Based on the four-volume *Encyclopedia of World Literature* (see entry 773), this one-volume work provides a compact but useful survey of literature written in Spanish and Portuguese from twenty countries of South and North America. Each country is treated separately and there is an introductory essay on literary trends and developments. This is followed by biographical sketches of a number of writers, discussion of their works, and a bibliography. There is a summary of each writer's accomplishments. The coverage in all cases has been praised for its high quality and clarity, especially important in examining some of the more complex and difficult works. This tool should become one of the mainstays on the topic in most libraries providing reference services to students and interested laypersons. David William Foster's *Handbook of Latin American Literature* (Garland, 1987) describes the national literatures of twenty-one Latin American countries, in alphabetical order. Thematic aspects, major literary figures, and literary traditions are treated.

963.   **The Oxford Companion to Spanish Literature.** Philip Ward, ed. Oxford, Clarendon Press, 1978. 629p.

Another useful resource in the Oxford line-up, this tool follows the pattern of the Companions to other literatures by providing an alphabetical approach to articles on a variety of individuals, works, and topics. Of the personalities covered, most are authors, but also included are critics, historians, philosophers, etc. Plot summaries are given for important books, and good identifications are furnished for journals, libraries, publishers' series, literary movements, groups, and forms. All elements of Spanish literature are included: Basque, Catalan, and Galician as well as Castillian, but Portuguese is excluded. The literature of many countries is covered, representing most nations of Central and South America as well as Mexico. Although no general bibliography is given, there are references to additional reading materials in many of the entries.

964.   **A Sourcebook for Hispanic Literature and Language: A Selected Annotated Guide to Spanish, Spanish-American, and Chicano Bibliography** ... Donald W. Bleznick. Metuchen, N.J., Scarecrow, 1983. 304p.

First published in 1974, the new edition of this guide for both students and scholars furnishes over 1,400 entries in a classified arrangement. Individual chapters cover style guides, bibliographies and dictionaries, translations, scholarly periodicals, and publishers. Although criticized for certain deficiencies (annotations too general in some cases, incomplete bibliographic data in some entries, misspellings, etc.) this has been acknowledged to be a useful introductory work. Author and title indexes are furnished to aid access. Another work, also in its second edition, is *Argentine Literature: A Research Guide* (Garland, 1982), compiled by David William Foster. It has two major sections: general references with thirty chapters, and the authors segment with nearly seventy-five writers. Each of the writers is given extensive bibliographic coverage (in some cases over 1,000 citations to studies in books, articles, and theses). Foster has also written *Mexican Literature: A Bibliography of Secondary Sources* (Scarecrow, 1981). This is a useful bibliography of articles, monographs, dissertations, criticism, and review articles, the emphasis being on fifty writers of the nineteenth and twentieth centuries. With access to many catalogs and bibliographic tools in his position as Professor of Spanish at Arizona State University, Foster has produced an excellent verification and identification tool.

965. **Women Writers of Spain: An Annotated Bio-Bibliographical Guide.** Carolyn L. Galerstein, ed. Westport, Conn., Greenwood Press, 1986. 389p. (Bibliographies and Indexes in Women's Studies, No. 2).

A recent collaborative effort of eighty contributors is this bio-bibliographical dictionary documenting the contributions of female writers in Spanish, Basque, Galician, and Catalan. In attempting to develop a useful tool for research, it was decided not to include those writers for whom no material could be found other than what has already been identified in a comprehensive standard bibliography by Manuel Serrano y Sanz, *Apuntes para una biblioteca de escritoras españolas desde al año 1401 al 1833* (Madrid, Establecimiento ..., 1903; repr., Madrid, Atlas, 1975). Each author is given a biographical sketch with an annotated listing of her belles lettres contributions in book format. Several listings appear in the appendices: authors by birthdate, authors in Catalan, authors in Galician, and translated titles. A title index supplies access. Scheduled for publication in 1987 is *Women Writers of Spanish America: An Annotated Biobibliographical Guide*, edited by Diane E. Marting (Greenwood Press). This promises to furnish similar coverage (much needed) of the Spanish writings of female writers from the American continents.

GERMANIC LANGUAGES

966. **Grundriss zur Geschicte der deutschen Dichtung aus den Quellen.** 2 ganz neubearb. Aufl. Karl Goedecke. Dresden, Germany, 1884-1966. 15v.

This is acknowledged to be the most complete bibliography of German literature, a necessary purchase for large reference libraries and those operating in a university environment. Obviously, it is not the type of tool which will be found in a small library setting. Bibliographical and critical comments are included regarding authors and their works, as well as extensive listings of various editions, treatises, histories, biographical and critical works, sources, etc. Each volume is separately indexed, and an alphabetical index of authors covered in all fifteen volumes was published in 1975. There is a third edition of volume 4 dealing primarily with the work of Goethe, published in five parts over a period of more than fifty years (1906-1960). A convenient and informative guide is Michael S. Batts's *The Bibliography of German Literature: An Historical and Critical Survey* (Bern, Switzerland, P. Lang, 1978). This work provides a brief overview of bibliographical tools available, with a critical review of current sources.

967. **Introduction to Library Research in German Studies: Language, Literature, and Civilization.** Larry L. Richardson. Boulder, Colo., Westview Press, 1984. 227p. (Westview Guides to Library Research).

A useful resource tool for students because of its detailed coverage of the use of libraries and bibliographic searching techniques, this has become a popular guide to the field. It embraces not only the literature but related studies of history, art, philosophy, politics, religion, and film. About 250 reference sources are identified and described in a helpful manner. Designed for the student who is studying German literature, it provides many helpful definitions of the types of tools listed, such as usage dictionaries. Works of literary criticism are included, as are major periodicals in the field. Supplementary reference works, guides to research papers, and computerized databases are also covered. There is a glossary, and a comprehensive index covers authors, titles, and subjects.

German Literature: An Annotated Reference Guide, by Uwe K. Faulhaber and Penrith B. Goff (Garland, 1979) is an older but more extensive annotated bibliography of over 2,000 reference tools, works of literary criticism, and periodicals important to the study of German literature. There is a checklist of pertinent works in related fields (art, music, etc.), which is not annotated.

968.   **The Oxford Companion to German Literature.** 2nd ed. Henry Garland and Mary Garland, eds. New York, Oxford University Press, 1986. 1020p.

The new edition of this work is a considerable update of the earlier work, which was published in 1976 and covered the field through the early 1970s. Employing the general format of the previous work (and, indeed, the pattern used in the entire Oxford Companion series), entries are alphabetically arranged and treat a variety of relevant topics. The book's coverage spans the entire history of German literature from its beginnings to the present in a well-balanced manner, describing events, writers, plot summaries, genres, literary movements, characters, historical figures, artists, philosophers, periodicals, etc. Major contemporary writers are included from both Germanies. Furnished in this array of entries is the information needed for background understanding and interpretation of German literature. A new direction and scope for the *Dictionary of Literary Biography* (see entry 865) began with the fifty-sixth volume of the series, *German Fiction Writers, 1914-1945*, edited by James Hardin (Gale, 1987). Formerly restricted to coverage of British and American authors, with this volume the series embraces modern European writers. Included are German and Swiss authors whose first important work appeared during the time period specified. Thirty-three individuals, from the obscure to the renowned, are covered. As usual, biographical essays provide basic bibliographies for each author.

SLAVONIC LANGUAGES

Russian

969.   **Handbook of Russian Literature.** Victor Terras, ed. New Haven, Conn., Yale University Press, 1985. 558p.

This work has received a great deal of praise from reviewers, who are impressed with the amount of information, precision of language, comprehensiveness of coverage, and the interesting and enjoyable style. Over 100 contributors have furnished one or two major articles and a number of minor ones within their area of expertise. There are over 1,000 entries, predominantly articles on individual writers. Also covered are literary terms and movements, historical events and figures, periodicals, societies, genres and other topics relevant to the study of Russian literature. There is an emphasis on pre-revolutionary subjects, a period which has been slighted by recent sources. Bibliographies accompany most articles and emphasize English-language publications.

ARABIC LANGUAGES

970.   **Modern Arabic Literature.** Roger Allen, comp. and ed. New York, Ungar, 1987. 370p.

This new work appears to be an excellent source of information on the seventy-one authors chosen for their importance and influence on post-neoclassical Arabic literature.

The emphasis is on twentieth-century writers, with a disproportionate number from Lebanon and Egypt, the reason probably being the traditionally greater emphasis on Arabic education at the university level in these two countries. There is a highly informative introductory essay furnishing a lucid summary of the highlights and important developments in Arabic literature, with special emphasis on the twentieth century. Authors are arranged alphabetically, and each one is treated with a selection of critical analyses from a selected group of sources both Arabic and English in origin. (Arabic works are in English translation.) Specific works are analyzed, including collections and anthologies of poems and stories.

ORIENTAL LANGUAGES

971. **Asian Literature in English: A Guide to Information Sources.** George Lincoln Anderson. Detroit, Gale, 1981. 336p. (American Literature, English Literature, and World Literatures in English, v.31).

This is a useful guide to translations into English and to critical studies and histories of the literature written in English. There are nearly 2,225 entries in the annotated bibliography, representing translations from a number of Asian countries (China, Japan, Korea, Burma, Cambodia, Indonesia, Laos, Malaysia, Singapore, Thailand, Vietnam, Mongolia, Tibet, and the Turkic regions of central Asia). Each literature section includes general bibliographies, anthologies, reference works, literary histories, literary forms, individual authors, and critical studies. Indian literature is excluded because it is treated in another volume in this series, *Indian Literature in English, 1827-1979: A Guide to Information Sources*, by Amritjit Singh (Gale, 1981). This is a bibliography of creative writing in English and includes works which have been translated from Indian languages by their authors.

972. **Guide to Japanese Prose.** 2nd ed. Alfred H. Marks and Barry D. Bort. Boston, G. K. Hall, 1984. 186p.

Another of the G. K. Hall bibliographies, this work was published initially in 1975 and was acknowledged as a useful source of information focusing on a subject which has not received a great deal of attention from Western writers. The second edition, similar to the earlier issue, identifies literary prose which is available in English translation. A good essay opens the work by examining the historical and literary context. There are two major sections of the work: pre-Meiji literature, which covers the beginnings to 1867, and Meiji literature (1868 to the present). Also issued by G. K. Hall is Richard J. Lynn's *Guide to Chinese Poetry and Drama* (Rev. ed., 1984). First published in 1973, this has proven to be a valuable critical guide to works in English translation for students and interested laypersons.

973. **The Princeton Companion to Classical Japanese Literature.** Earl Miner, et al. Princeton, N.J., Princeton University Press, 1985. 570p.

The classical era designated in the title represents the time prior to the Meiji Restoration of 1867-1968, a lengthy and productive term. Within this time span, there are a number of distinctive literary periods which are introduced with a brief history at the beginning. Many charts, maps, pictures, figures, etc., help to supplement the narrative. Several chronologies are given, as are descriptions of social groups. There are segments on arts, clothing, housing, etc. A section of major importance to reference work covers important authors and their work, with some biographies achieving essay length. Literary allusions are covered well in the glossary of literary terms. *The Indiana Companion to Traditional Chinese Literature*, edited by William H. Nienhauser, Jr., and others (Indiana University Press, 1986) is divided into two major sections. The first provides a series of ten essays on Buddhist and Taoist literatures and various genres. Part 2 contains over 500 entries on writers, individual works, genres, styles, etc. Each entry is accompanied by a bibliography.

AUTHOR AND TITLE INDEX
TO SOURCES CHAPTERS

Each item (book, serial, or database) that has been given separate entry has also been given an item number. These numbers run consecutively from the beginning of the first sources chapter (chapter 2) through the final sources chapter (chapter 12). The index refers to item numbers, not to page numbers. All sources mentioned in the annotation but not given separate entries are also indexed here. The entry number in each such case is followed by the designation "n".

The following guidelines were used in alphabetizing index entries. Articles which occur at the beginning of titles have been omitted in the index. Lengthy titles have been shortened in most cases where this could be done without ambiguity. Entries have been arranged in accordance with the "word by word" or "nothing before something" method of filing. Names beginning with "Mc" or "Mac" are treated as spelled. Acronyms and initialisms such as UNESCO or LLBA are treated as single words. Numbers (including dates) when part of the title are arranged as though written in word form except when they are part of a sequence or series. In such cases, the titles in the sequence are listed in order of numerical significance from lowest to highest. Finally, all sources available online are marked with an asterisk.

SUBJECT INDEX

The purpose of this index is to provide access to more or less broad topics that have received more than simple mention in the text. Consequently, only those organizations associated with more than one discipline are listed here. More specialized organizations will be found in the "Accessing Information" chapter for each discipline, as will bibliographic citations to works about the topics included here. Reference is to page number.